European Marketing Data and Statistics

European
Marketing Data
and Statistics

2011

46th edition

Euromonitor International Ltd, 60-61 Britton Street, London EC1M 5UX

European Marketing Data and Statistics 2011

First published 1964
Forty-sixth edition
ISBN 978-1-84264-537-6
Published by:

Western and Southern Europe
Euromonitor International Ltd - Head Office
60-61 Britton Street, London, EC1M 5UX, United Kingdom
Tel: +44 (0) 20 7251 8024
Fax: +44 (0) 20 7608 3149
email: info@euromonitor.com

North America
Euromonitor International Inc
224 South Michigan Avenue
Suite 1500, Chicago, IL 60604, USA
Tel: + 1 312 922 1115
Fax: +1 312 922 1157
email: insight@euromonitorintl.com

Latin America
Euromonitor International
Avenida Apoquindo 4501, Oficina 1102, Las Condes
Santiago C.P. 7580125, Chile
Tel: +56 (2) 915-7200
Fax: +56 (2) 915-7201

Asia Pacific
Euromonitor International (Asia) Pte Ltd
3 Lim Teck Kim Road
#08-01 Singapore Technologies Building, Singapore 088934
Tel: +65 6429 0590
Fax: +65 6324 1855
email: info@euromonitor.com.sg

China
Euromonitor International (Shanghai) Co, Ltd
Level 21 Unit 06, Tian An Center
No. 338 Nanjing Road (West), Shanghai 200003, China
Tel: +86 21 6372 6288
Fax: +86 21 6372 6289
email: info@euromonitor.com.cn

Middle East and North Africa
Euromonitor International
Dubai Silicon Oasis (HQ), F- Wing Office 606-607
PO Box 54709, Dubai, U.A.E.
Tel: +971 4 372 4363
Fax: +971 4 372 4370
email: info-mena@euromonitor.com

Central and South Africa
Euromonitor International
The Forum, Unit GS04, 6473 Northbank Lane, Century City
Cape Town, 7441, Republic of South Africa
Tel: +27 21 552 0037
Fax: +27 21 552 7071
email: info-africa@euromonitor.com

Australasia
Euromonitor International (Australia) Pty Ltd
Suite 26, Level 32, 1 Market Street, Sydney NSW 2000
Tel: +61 2 9275 8869
Fax: +61 2 9275 8793
email: info@euromonitor.com

Central and Eastern Europe
Euromonitor International
Jogailos Street 4, Vilnius, LT-01116, Lithuania
Tel: +370 5 243 1577
Fax: +370 5 243 1599
email: info@euromonitor.lt

Website
http://www.euromonitor.com

Disclaimer
This edition of European Marketing Data and Statistics has been prepared with painstaking care but the editors cannot accept responsibility for any errors which may have occurred during its compilation. We would welcome comments and feedback about the contents to assist in the compilation of subsequent editions.

Printed in the United Kingdom

Summary of contents

Table of contents

Foreword and Guide

Foreword

European Marketing Data and Statistics 2011 is a compendium of statistical information on the countries of Western and Eastern Europe. Published annually, it provides a wealth of detailed and up-to-date statistical information relevant to pan-European market planning. The information is regularly updated and held on an international database of market information comprising 23 subject areas.

Published annually since the late 1960s, **European Marketing Data and Statistics**, or EMDAS, is now in its 46th edition. All data sections have been thoroughly revised for this new edition.

The data are presented in table form and a number of extrapolated tables have been included. The data coverage includes a considerable number of long-term time-series (dating back to 1980 as available) which permit the analysis of socio-economic trends over a longer time span as a basis for forecasting. The inclusion of figures from the most recent complete year (in this edition 2009) for key parameters ensures that up-to-date information is available for analysis.

In addition to reporting on major European countries, the country coverage also includes smaller European countries and principalities. Although the availability of statistical information on these countries is limited and they are minor markets, it assists in building up a more comprehensive picture of the total European market and will be of interest to academic users.

Readers requiring detailed guidance on sources of information used in the compilation of the data are referred to the World Directory of Business Information Sources (Euromonitor International, 2010) for more comprehensive listings.

A companion volume of marketing data, International Marketing Data and Statistics (IMDAS) is also available. Country coverage in IMDAS 2011 provides a comprehensive worldwide context, and data are provided in the same format for ease of comparison with the European figures presented here. The data included in both volumes are also accessible as part of the Global Marketing Information Database (GMID) on the web.

User comments are welcomed concerning the databases in **European Marketing Data and Statistics**. Also, whilst the editors have made every effort to ensure accuracy Euromonitor International cannot accept responsibility for any errors which may have occurred.

Guide to Using the Handbook

Scope of the Handbook

European Marketing Data and Statistics (EMDAS) is a statistical yearbook of business and marketing information, featuring over 500 pages of up-to-date and detailed marketing statistics on 23 principal subject areas. These statistics are stored on a database of international marketing information and are regularly updated by Euromonitor International's research team.

The sections of EMDAS cover a wide variety of marketing topics, ranging from socio-economic trends and background information through to key consumer marketing parameters. Data covering international trade, transport, industrial output and agricultural resources are included, as well as sections on service industries such as tourism and retailing.

In EMDAS 2011, each statistical tabulation presents pan-European comparative information, either in the form of time-series from 1980 to 2009 or with single-year data for the latest year available. All the countries are listed down the left-hand column, presented in two geographical entities (Western and Eastern Europe). Where appropriate, regional subtotals are included.

Where data is in value form, units have been generally left in national currencies. However the spreadsheets on which the data is stored facilitate calculations in US dollars. These are calculated only for the latest year available (usually 2009) as fluctuations in exchange rates and contrasts in rates of inflation render year-on-year conversions meaningless.

In addition, calculations have been made where deemed appropriate to show growth rates over a defined period, and per capita data. These permit easy cross-comparisons between countries, regions and markets.

Using EMDAS 2011 is easy. Whatever topic is of interest, you simply look up the tables (using the contents) and the table will show the relevant data for all countries. The heading shows the relevant section, title summary and title of the table, and unit. A guide to the sources used in the compilation of the data appears at the foot of the table, along with any relevant notes.

The aim of EMDAS is to locate in one handbook the essential statistical information relevant to European market planning. The handbook will save the busy marketeer or researcher hours of time trawling through statistics from many sources and provides a wealth of hard-to-get information drawn from the many reports and studies compiled by Euromonitor International over the last 2-3 years - many based on trade interviews and original extrapolations. Business users and librarians will find the handbook especially useful.

Subject Coverage

EMDAS 2011 is presented in 23 separate sections or "databases" which have all been specially compiled by Euromonitor International. The subjects have been selected as those most appropriate for strategic planning and European market analysis, covering both background marketing parameters and detailed consumer market information. The 23 databases are outlined below.

1 Advertising

This section includes a range of data on advertising expenditure trends, organised into seven tables.

2 Agricultural Resources and Output
This section presents key data on land use and output of various agricultural and forestry products. There are 11 tables on the database, mostly including figures for 2009.

3 Automotives and Transport
This 25-table database covers the circulation, manufacture and sales of cars, commercial vehicles and two-wheelers, including tables on automotive fuel prices; it also covers major movements in terms of the road, rail, air and shipping transport sectors.

4 Banking and Finance
This section features tabulations mainly showing data from 1980-2009 and covering bank assets, liabilities, claims and interest rates, as well as information on credit card holders and accepting outlets.

5 Consumer Expenditure
The presentation of this section comprises total consumer spending, a consolidated breakdown by product sector, and a series of tables analysing each major consumer sector. New 2009 data have been included and all the data are presented in 20-year trends with growth rates and 2009 dollar comparisons.

6 Consumer Market Sizes
Per capita consumption and retail market sizes are included in 17 tables for 2009. The information is drawn from Euromonitor International's market information database, which forms the basis for the publication Consumer Europe (26th edition, Euromonitor International, 2010).

7 Consumer Prices and Costs
Trends in consumer prices and selected European living costs are included in 14 tables of data.

8 Economic Indicators
This database features tables of key economic data, again with the emphasis on time-series data. All the main economic indicators are covered, including GDP, GNP, inflation, money supply, public and private consumption, government finance and exchange rates.

9 Education
A range of educational statistics are included in this seven-table section, from pre-primary through to higher and university education.

10 Energy Resources and Output
This section consists of 18 tables on energy supply and demand. Coverage extends to household energy consumption with several tables containing data for more than 20 years.

11 Environmental Data
This section includes tables covering various environmental factors. Coverage includes pollution, recycling, waste generation, protected areas and threatened species.

12 External Trade
This section includes 11 tables which give a cohesive and structured trade overview covering total imports and exports and external trade breakdowns by origin, destination and commodity.

13 Health
This database comprises seven tables covering major health indicators (including a table on obese population).

14 Home Ownership
This section includes comparative data on housing stock and new dwellings completed, as well as numbers of households by tenure and type of dwelling.

15 Household Profiles
This section comprises 12 tables of comparative statistics on households. Data on average number of occupants per household are included, as well as possession of household durables.

16 Income and Deductions
This section includes six tables covering gross and disposable income parameters, as well as savings.

17 Industry
This section provides key industrial indices for a 30-year period and includes output tables covering major industrial materials.

18 IT and Telecommunications

This section features information on a number of communications and information technology topics including Internet statistics and data on mobile telephony.

19 Labour

This database covers the key employment indicators including numbers employed, unemployed and hours of work. The structure of the economically active population by age group and sex is included for latest years available, along with a breakdown of the total workforce into industry sectors.

20 Media and Leisure

This section includes eight tables covering available data on cinema, newspapers, and TV households including cable TV, satellite TV, and digital satellite pay-TV.

21 Population

This database features statistical compilations covering population trends, vital statistics, urbanisation, demographic analysis by age and sex, and population forecasts. Much of the data included are from 1980 to the latest year, forming a basis for forecasting and projections.

22 Retailing

This section has drawn on Euromonitor International's extensive European retail research in recent years, with tables covering retail sales and channels and breakdowns for different retail sectors.

23 Travel and Tourism

This database consists of 12 tabulations covering tourism values and movements, tourist accommodation and its usage, reflecting holidaying habits across Europe.

Data Coverage

Each of the statistical compilations is presented in one of four data periods:

(1) A 30-year trend table from 1980-2009, with data for each country drawn from the same consistent source. Some intermediary years have been excluded for reasons of space.

(2) A different period trend, eg 1990-2009 (20-year trend) or a recent period.

(3) Latest year available, with the years differing between countries. These are used where the information is drawn from occasional studies, eg a census, or where statistical offices vary in the speed of publishing statistics.

(4) A single year, eg 2009, where space does not permit trends or where an interactive range of information is provided (eg imports by origin, usage of GDP, etc).

The statistics in this volume are as available during the compilation period (June-October 2010). Figures for 2009 (in some cases provisional or estimated) have been included where possible. Various one-off surveys cover earlier years only.

Country Coverage

This edition of EMDAS includes a total of 44 countries in both Western and Eastern Europe. These are grouped into two geographic entities, as follows:

Western Europe

Austria	Belgium
Cyprus	Denmark
Finland	France
Germany	Gibraltar
Greece	Iceland
Ireland	Italy
Liechtenstein	Luxembourg
Malta	Monaco
Netherlands	Norway
Portugal	Spain
Sweden	Switzerland
Turkey	United Kingdom

Eastern Europe

Albania	Belarus
Bosnia-Herzegovina	Bulgaria
Croatia	Czech Republic
Estonia	Georgia
Hungary	Latvia

Lithuania	Macedonia
Moldova	Poland
Romania	Russia
Serbia and Montenegro	Slovakia
Slovenia	Ukraine

Country Note

Data for Germany prior to 1991 refer to the former East and West Germany, for the Czech Republic data prior to 1993 refer to the former Czechoslovakia, and for Serbia and Montenegro data prior to 1992 refer to the former Yugoslavia.

Sources

European Marketing Data and Statistics is based on an extensive and on-going programme of research into European markets and industries. A Europe-wide network of market analysts and researchers work to pull together available data on socio-economic patterns, market conditions and trends, living standards and background information relevant to business, export and market planning.

The principal sources used in the compilation of EMDAS are as follows:

— International and European organisations, such as the United Nations, OECD, and the International Monetary Fund.

— National statistical offices and central banks in each country.

— Pan-European and national trade and industry associations.

— Industry study groups and unofficial research publishers.

— Euromonitor International's own research publications, including one-off reports and statistical compilations.

— Original research specially commissioned for the handbook, including consumer research, trade interviews and retail surveys.

A guide to the main sources used in the compilation of each table is included at the foot of each table. For reasons of space the main sources are only briefly cited; in some cases, many different reports and publications are used in the preparation of just one table. For example, we may have extracted data from publications by the national statistical offices for all the countries covered in order to compile one table. In other cases, statistical compilations are from secondary sources, which have in turn used many different sources.

A brief guide to the main sources used in each of the databases follows.

1 Advertising

Drawn from data published by the World Association of Newspapers and various other media study groups, advertising associations and agents in various countries.

2 Agricultural Resources and Output

Mainly based on the publications and databases of the Food and Agricultural Organisation of the United Nations (FAO).

3 Automotives and Transport

Automotives data are drawn from national statistics, and the publications of various motor trades organisations. Transport statistics are based on national statistics and on various UN publications; the International Civil Aviation Organisation; the International Road Federation and Lloyd's Register of Shipping.

4 Banking and Finance

The major source of comparative financial data is the IMF's International Financial Statistics.

5 Consumer Expenditure

Drawn from the OECD and the national accounts of each country (generally published by the national statistical offices). Euromonitor International estimates have been used to reach levels of consolidation.

6 Consumer Market Sizes

Drawn from Euromonitor International's consumer market database; primary sources include trade associations and interviews with industry leaders in all countries.

7 Consumer Prices and Costs

Mainly from national statistics, the International Monetary Fund and the OECD; living costs from the International Labour Organisation.

8 Economic Indicators

The principal international sources are the OECD and the International Monetary Fund (IMF). National statistical offices (yearbooks, national accounts) and economic bulletins by leading banks are also used.

9 Education

The key international source is UNESCO with data from national statistical offices incorporated as available.

10 Energy Resources and Output

This compilation draws mainly on data from BP, the UN and the OECD/IEA, national statistics and various industry publications.

11 Environmental Data

Drawn largely from the OECD, United Nations, and the World Resources Institute, as well as national statistics.

12 External Trade

The IMF, UN and OECD track external trade flows in some detail. National statistical yearbooks are also utilised.

13 Health

Compiled from various publications from national statistical offices, OECD and UN publications and incorporating Euromonitor International estimates and calculations.

14 Home Ownership

Data are compiled from national statistical offices of each country.

15 Household Profiles

Compiled from various publications from national statistical offices, and from Eurostat and UN publications, and incorporating Euromonitor International estimates and calculations.

16 Income and Deductions

Data from national statistical offices of each country. Specific sources include Household Budget Surveys and National Accounts. Euromonitor International estimates have been used.

17 Industry

Mainly drawn from UN and OECD publications, and from national statistics. Various industry sectors are covered by associations as stated.

18 IT and Telecommunications

Mainly based on national statistics and UN data, particularly the publications of the International Telecommunications Union (ITU), and incorporating some data from the World Bank.

19 Labour

In addition to national statistics, the primary international source is the International Labour Organisation, which publishes both a statistical yearbook and quarterly bulletins.

20 Media and Leisure

Mainly drawn from the UN, UNESCO, the Council of Europe and national statistical offices.

21 Population

Drawn mainly from the statistical yearbooks of the national statistical offices supplemented with population data and forecasts from the UN, Eurostat and the Council of Europe.

22 Retailing

Drawn from a wide number of Euromonitor International's own surveys and market reports on European retailing, including Retail Trade International (Euromonitor International 2010), and also original research. Primary sources include retail trade censuses (various countries) by national statistical offices, retail trade associations, major retailers etc.

23 Travel and Tourism

A compilation sourced from the World Tourism Organisation and Euromonitor International's own research.

List of Abbreviations

BLEU	Belgo-Luxembourg Economic Union
EFMA	European Financial Management and Marketing Association
EFTA	European Free Trade Association
EU	European Union
FAO	Food and Agriculture Organisation of the United Nations
FT	Financial Times
IAA	International Advertising Association
IATA	International Air Transport Association
IBRD	International Bank for Reconstruction and Development (World Bank)
ICAO	International Civil Aviation Organisation
IEA	International Energy Authority
ILO	International Labour Organisation
IMF	International Monetary Fund
IMMA	International Motorcycle Manufacturers' Association
IRF	International Road Federation
ITU	International Telecommunication Union (a UN agency)
OECD	Organisation for Economic Co-operation and Development
SMMT	Society of Motor Manufacturers and Traders
UN	United Nations
UN ECE	United Nations Economic Commission for Europe
UNESCO	United Nations Educational, Scientific and Cultural Organisation
WHO	World Health Organisation
WTO	World Tourism Organisation
EAP	Economically active population
GDP	Gross domestic product
GNP	Gross national product
LPG	Liquefied petroleum gases
NGL	Natural gas liquids
SITC	Standard International Trade Classification
'000	thousand
gWh	gigawatt-hours
ha	hectare
hl	hectolitre
kg	kilogramme
km	kilometre
km2	square kilometre
kWh	kilowatt-hours
m2	square metre
m3	cubic metre
mn	million
MTOE	million tonnes of oil equivalent
MW	megawatts
R/P	reserves/production
TJ	terajoules
0	denotes less than 0.5 where no fraction given

Advertising

Advertising Statistics
Table 1.1

Advertising Expenditure by Medium 2009
US$ million

	Television	Radio	Print	Cinema	Outdoor	Online	Total
Western Europe							
Austria	896.3	258.5	2,169.2	19.5	252.9	139.0	3,735.2
Belgium	1,767.4	549.5	1,720.3	38.8	368.1	276.8	4,720.9
Cyprus	555.5	15.2	71.5				642.2
Denmark	463.1	59.4	1,217.1	12.1	86.9	594.5	2,433.0
Finland	391.6	71.5	1,269.7	4.7	64.6	125.0	1,927.1
France	5,745.2	1,255.7	5,833.8	161.5	2,038.2	1,630.9	16,665.3
Germany	5,543.1	853.2	13,772.3	129.2	1,031.1	1,060.6	22,389.6
Gibraltar							
Greece	852.9	77.7	1,898.6	20.8	485.4		3,335.4
Iceland	36.0		88.6	0.2	3.1		127.9
Ireland	505.6	200.9	1,434.5	13.5	249.4	35.1	2,439.0
Italy	6,643.7	936.6	3,665.8	69.5	444.7	541.9	12,302.1
Liechtenstein							
Luxembourg	15.0	29.2	135.1	1.7	5.5	11.6	198.1
Malta							
Monaco							
Netherlands	1,295.6	394.8	3,193.0	7.0	223.8	315.5	5,429.6
Norway	1,204.0	225.4	2,066.0	39.0	168.4	898.4	4,601.3
Portugal	778.5	69.1	301.5	6.9	177.0	40.1	1,373.1
Spain	4,196.6	896.3	2,690.3	27.8	693.4	854.6	9,359.0
Sweden	578.4	85.7	1,392.1	12.6	129.8	755.4	2,953.9
Switzerland	1,066.7	124.9	2,041.7	43.1	417.7	66.1	3,760.2
Turkey	859.0	54.0	529.2	16.7	139.5	186.5	1,784.9
United Kingdom	4,858.0	662.8	7,680.7	333.7	1,169.7	5,300.9	20,005.7
Eastern Europe							
Albania							
Belarus							
Bosnia-Herzegovina	412.3	8.3	29.0		16.7	1.1	467.4
Bulgaria	618.5	19.9	149.3		148.6	37.0	973.2
Croatia	767.8		320.4		56.4	16.1	1,160.7
Czech Republic	1,420.7	155.1	1,071.2	7.2	230.7	276.4	3,161.3
Estonia	43.4	13.8	73.2		13.8	20.3	164.4
Georgia	84.0	8.3	5.9		5.9		104.2
Hungary	1,786.3	226.7	567.6	2.6	194.1	110.9	2,888.1
Latvia	81.4	22.1	77.2	1.4	19.1	19.5	220.7
Lithuania	562.2	15.1	124.5	0.3	23.5	22.2	747.7
Macedonia							
Moldova	32.0	3.7	4.2	0.4	9.6	0.4	50.3
Montenegro							
Poland	1,418.8	170.1	535.1	26.9	256.6	294.5	2,702.0
Romania	474.2	38.5	105.6	3.7	59.0	18.5	699.5
Russia	4,968.3	425.0	1,845.0	72.4	1,357.0	340.0	9,007.8
Serbia	1,109.8	17.8	179.8		32.6	11.8	1,351.7
Slovakia	1,881.4	91.8	309.3	1.2	86.6	72.2	2,442.5
Slovenia	319.6	32.0	165.4	0.6	36.1	43.1	596.7
Ukraine	383.1	46.0	200.3	16.9	182.8	22.7	851.7

Source: *Euromonitor International from World Association of Newspapers/Jupiter Research*

Advertising Statistics

Table 1.2

TV Adspend 1985-2009

Million units of national currency

	1985	1990	1995	2000	2004	2005	2006	2007	2008	2009	US$ million 2009
Western Europe											
Austria	152	240	270	479	497	508	545	597	637	645	896.3
Belgium	150	234	393	782	1,004	982	1,071	1,161	1,230	1,272	1,767.4
Cyprus	2	3	16	134	222	254	291	331	373	400	555.5
Denmark	240	612	1,510	1,823	2,125	2,254	2,471	2,520	2,546	2,483	463.1
Finland	75	127	161	213	227	231	243	262	275	282	391.6
France	1,773	1,958	2,111	3,046	3,998	4,028	4,209	4,306	4,112	4,134	5,745.2
Germany	814	1,642	3,420	4,709	3,860	3,930	4,114	4,156	4,133	3,989	5,543.1
Gibraltar											
Greece	53	200	837	676	684	693	705	855	769	614	852.9
Iceland				2,823	3,187	3,414	3,789	4,061	4,552	4,447	36.0
Ireland	33	51	112	200	236	287	326	374	385	364	505.6
Italy	2,360	2,864	2,595	4,134	4,647	4,808	4,736	4,757	4,767	4,781	6,643.7
Liechtenstein											
Luxembourg	3	4	6	8	11	11	11	11	11	11	15.0
Malta											
Monaco											
Netherlands	142	271	483	783	757	779	810	863	906	932	1,295.6
Norway	9	137	2,333	4,630	5,196	5,696	5,923	6,440	7,213	7,573	1,204.0
Portugal	45	100	216	519	504	517	512	533	546	560	778.5
Spain	1,833	1,696	1,323	2,311	2,675	2,951	3,181	3,467	3,162	3,020	4,196.6
Sweden	25	324	2,373	3,959	3,749	4,143	4,546	4,695	4,605	4,427	578.4
Switzerland	88	220	339	520	737	810	889	1,054	1,117	1,159	1,066.7
Turkey	0	1	12	285	957	1,140	1,442	1,760	1,660	1,336	859.0
United Kingdom	1,088	1,548	2,267	3,327	3,392	3,455	3,282	3,380	3,211	3,115	4,858.0
Eastern Europe											
Albania											
Belarus											
Bosnia-Herzegovina					147	196	267	293	415	581	412.3
Bulgaria	2	2	2	108	325	413	477	617	790	870	618.5
Croatia					2,046	2,810	3,218	3,612	3,828	4,057	767.8
Czech Republic	876	1,382	3,772	14,516	18,153	21,350	23,681	24,374	26,288	27,085	1,420.7
Estonia	3	22	65	155	254	310	363	479	489	489	43.4
Georgia					55	63	87	110	125	140	84.0
Hungary	557	3,719	18,826	129,605	286,106	331,203	347,080	342,070	366,106	361,437	1,786.3
Latvia	2	1	5	10	17	22	27	33	37	41	81.4
Lithuania		2	16	74	606	606	777	1,145	1,317	1,396	562.2
Macedonia											
Moldova						50	77	104	254	356	32.0
Montenegro											
Poland	32	150	808	4,452	6,861	2,603	3,010	3,528	4,044	4,428	1,418.8
Romania			8	165	428	554	749	956	1,315	1,446	474.2
Russia			938	7,595	48,994	65,900	85,900	112,500	142,400	157,800	4,968.3
Serbia					27,443	36,954	41,253	62,700	69,000	75,000	1,109.8
Slovakia			58	136	444	583	739	947	1,152	1,354	1,881.4
Slovenia	3	9	29	144	191	193	195	243	261	230	319.6
Ukraine					903	1,223	1,827	2,439	2,843	2,985	383.1

Source: *Euromonitor International from World Association of Newspapers*

Advertising Statistics   **Table 1.3**

Radio Adspend 1985-2009
Million units of national currency

	1985	1990	1995	2000	2004	2005	2006	2007	2008	2009	US$ million 2009
Western Europe											
Austria	94	126	136	158	171	172	170	170	181	186	258.5
Belgium	21	48	100	186	253	290	327	376	379	395	549.5
Cyprus	2	2	6	8	8	8	9	10	10	11	15.2
Denmark	34	81	165	213	211	280	283	311	327	318	59.4
Finland	55	43	28	38	48	47	47	47	50	51	71.5
France	304	422	579	715	971	986	1,001	951	921	904	1,255.7
Germany	295	425	608	733	619	664	680	692	659	614	853.2
Gibraltar											
Greece	5	20	70	71	91	94	96	115	81	56	77.7
Iceland											
Ireland	13	20	33	55	91	106	124	140	144	145	200.9
Italy	238	217	201	454	529	534	576	622	648	674	936.6
Liechtenstein											
Luxembourg	5	7	9	12	20	20	21	22	22	21	29.2
Malta											
Monaco											
Netherlands	16	45	111	235	250	253	262	274	282	284	394.8
Norway	177	177	403	604	941	1,141	1,124	1,205	1,326	1,418	225.4
Portugal	96	43	25	62	57	56	52	51	51	50	69.1
Spain	2,139	899	346	502	540	610	637	678	655	645	896.3
Sweden		3	234	592	491	515	606	642	677	656	85.7
Switzerland	38	59	100	139	129	135	136	137	136	136	124.9
Turkey	0	0	2	47	75	80	101	111	105	84	54.0
United Kingdom	26	78	230	455	463	443	458	466	438	425	662.8
Eastern Europe											
Albania											
Belarus											
Bosnia-Herzegovina					8	10	6	10	12	12	8.3
Bulgaria	1	1	3	6	20	25	22	22	26	28	19.9
Croatia											
Czech Republic	262	413	635	1,050	2,157	2,398	2,640	2,815	2,899	2,957	155.1
Estonia		2	22	76	87	90	105	134	147	155	13.8
Georgia					6	6	7	8	10	14	8.3
Hungary	140	774	4,187	12,042	26,514	26,819	33,764	39,485	47,279	45,874	226.7
Latvia			1	5	6	7	9	10	11	11	22.1
Lithuania			4	10	20	20	24	35	37	37	15.1
Macedonia											
Moldova						19	28	34	33	42	3.7
Montenegro											
Poland	6	22	123	544	1,043	435	482	499	532	531	170.1
Romania			1	10	40	59	80	85	101	117	38.5
Russia			151	1,266	5,764	8,500	9,500	15,700	15,700	13,500	425.0
Serbia						236	456	695	1,000	1,200	17.8
Slovakia			9	14	37	45	49	54	58	66	91.8
Slovenia	9	10	13	21	9	18	19	20	22	23	32.0
Ukraine					77	103	141	212	293	359	46.0

Source: *Euromonitor International from World Association of Newspapers*

| Advertising Statistics | | | | | | | | | | Table 1.4 |

Print Adspend 1985-2009

Million units of national currency

	1985	1990	1995	2000	2004	2005	2006	2007	2008	2009	US$ million 2009
Western Europe											
Austria	180	403	671	1,134	1,186	1,255	1,320	1,446	1,530	1,561	2,169.2
Belgium	319	399	479	652	813	872	1,163	1,202	1,220	1,238	1,720.3
Cyprus	2	3	6	26	32	35	39	44	48	51	71.5
Denmark	5,481	4,967	5,478	5,965	5,667	6,180	6,767	6,800	6,876	6,524	1,217.1
Finland	447	583	556	828	817	837	859	900	912	914	1,269.7
France	3,629	2,695	3,274	4,587	4,381	4,430	4,506	4,396	4,247	4,198	5,833.8
Germany	8,756	9,920	12,037	13,476	10,573	10,550	10,836	10,951	10,553	9,911	13,772.3
Gibraltar											
Greece	87	148	292	823	1,013	1,139	1,243	1,379	1,432	1,366	1,898.6
Iceland				5,395	7,621	8,298	9,284	9,978	11,205	10,955	88.6
Ireland	99	108	175	446	927	926	1,102	1,123	1,153	1,032	1,434.5
Italy	3,108	2,069	1,792	2,976	2,711	2,783	2,882	2,909	2,731	2,638	3,665.8
Liechtenstein											
Luxembourg	27	34	46	57	89	92	95	102	102	97	135.1
Malta											
Monaco											
Netherlands	1,313	1,475	1,793	2,721	2,211	2,212	2,273	2,338	2,329	2,298	3,193.0
Norway	2,777	2,777	4,757	7,105	9,962	11,104	11,922	13,067	13,374	12,995	2,066.0
Portugal	221	150	134	280	217	218	215	217	218	217	301.5
Spain	4,302	2,940	1,677	2,427	2,248	2,341	2,485	2,016	2,146	1,936	2,690.3
Sweden	9,040	8,788	9,751	11,952	10,008	10,556	11,263	11,616	11,334	10,655	1,392.1
Switzerland	2,653	2,600	2,569	3,033	1,901	1,952	2,136	2,287	2,270	2,218	2,041.7
Turkey	0	0	13	272	682	890	1,020	1,113	1,080	823	529.2
United Kingdom	2,595	3,163	4,103	5,987	5,957	5,778	5,547	5,470	5,098	4,925	7,680.7
Eastern Europe											
Albania											
Belarus											
Bosnia-Herzegovina					22	22	27	31	35	41	29.0
Bulgaria		1	1	54	108	138	159	171	189	210	149.3
Croatia					930	1,031	1,315	1,501	1,607	1,693	320.4
Czech Republic	199	973	3,698	11,309	15,535	16,855	19,151	19,334	20,005	20,423	1,071.2
Estonia	2	17	180	400	556	638	737	908	830	824	73.2
Georgia								6	8	10	5.9
Hungary	2,169	6,626	21,732	64,682	98,050	106,208	110,735	113,436	118,961	114,847	567.6
Latvia	1	1	8	13	22	25	30	37	38	39	77.2
Lithuania		2	22	87	211	210	222	283	300	309	124.5
Macedonia											
Moldova						23	33	42	37	46	4.2
Montenegro											
Poland	19	80	428	2,247	3,646	1,543	1,593	1,653	1,682	1,670	535.1
Romania			2	67	202	198	231	253	297	322	105.6
Russia			1,364	9,564	34,584	39,300	44,600	51,900	59,000	58,600	1,845.0
Serbia					2,807	3,584	4,988	9,346	11,200	12,150	179.8
Slovakia			21	41	97	112	123	161	194	223	309.3
Slovenia	16	23	36	70	97	107	124	144	123	119	165.4
Ukraine					443	676	924	1,252	1,404	1,561	200.3

Source: *Euromonitor International from World Association of Newspapers*

Advertising Statistics

Table 1.5

Cinema Adspend 1985-2009

Million units of national currency

	1985	1990	1995	2000	2004	2005	2006	2007	2008	2009	US$ million 2009
Western Europe											
Austria	3	4	6	11	10	14	15	15	14	14	19.5
Belgium	10	10	17	25	25	29	30	26	28	28	38.8
Cyprus											
Denmark	4	23	57	46	51	57	55	59	68	65	12.1
Finland	2	1	1	2	2	2	1	2	3	3	4.7
France	67	58	46	81	103	120	126	138	117	116	161.5
Germany	65	102	160	175	147	132	117	106	100	93	129.2
Gibraltar											
Greece	2	2	2	13	14	15	16	17	16	15	20.8
Iceland				100	27	25	26	27	29	28	0.2
Ireland	1	1	4	6	10	9	10	11	11	10	13.5
Italy	12	16	17	50	76	76	70	59	51	50	69.5
Liechtenstein											
Luxembourg			1	1	1	1	1	1	1	1	1.7
Malta											
Monaco											
Netherlands	9	9	11	13	6	7	5	5	5	5	7.0
Norway	60	60	73	124	147	162	173	214	235	245	39.0
Portugal				6	7	7	6	6	6	5	6.9
Spain	91	57	29	55	41	43	41	38	24	20	27.8
Sweden	68	70	81	78	59	68	74	91	93	96	12.6
Switzerland	47	30	34	45	50	50	50	47	47	47	43.1
Turkey	0	0	1	8	23	28	33	36	43	26	16.7
United Kingdom	20	32	59	109	162	158	158	207	214	214	333.7
Eastern Europe											
Albania											
Belarus											
Bosnia-Herzegovina											
Bulgaria											
Croatia											
Czech Republic					167	154	199	192	130	138	7.2
Estonia											
Georgia											
Hungary	1	11	122	1,076	1,265	1,323	1,280	948	957	521	2.6
Latvia					0	0	1	1	1	1	1.4
Lithuania					0	0	1	1	1	1	0.3
Macedonia											
Moldova						1	1	2	4	5	0.4
Montenegro											
Poland	1	2	3	27	128	53	64	72	78	84	26.9
Romania			0	0	6	7	8	8	10	11	3.7
Russia				84	432	1,100	1,600	2,400	2,600	2,300	72.4
Serbia											
Slovakia			0	0	0	1	1	1	1	1	1.2
Slovenia						1	1	2	1	0	0.6
Ukraine					16	26	37	46	96	131	16.9

Source: *Euromonitor International from World Association of Newspapers*

Advertising Statistics

Table 1.6

Outdoor Adspend 1985-2009

Million units of national currency

	1985	1990	1995	2000	2004	2005	2006	2007	2008	2009	US$ million 2009
Western Europe											
Austria	29	54	79	112	139	157	170	171	180	182	252.9
Belgium	183	138	129	162	205	215	227	239	252	265	368.1
Cyprus											
Denmark			153	338	359	370	405	437	459	466	86.9
Finland	14	21	24	35	33	37	36	42	45	46	64.6
France	1,036	1,009	1,060	1,383	1,414	1,411	1,414	1,428	1,455	1,467	2,038.2
Germany	288	377	540	746	720	769	787	820	788	742	1,031.1
Gibraltar											
Greece	4	13	67	240	248	265	306	330	350	349	485.4
Iceland				279	288	305	330	352	394	384	3.1
Ireland	4	13	20	70	106	117	134	183	190	179	249.4
Italy	596	296	171	318	312	315	312	318	319	320	444.7
Liechtenstein											
Luxembourg					3	4	4	4	4	4	5.5
Malta											
Monaco											
Netherlands	71	72	84	139	139	151	165	165	166	161	223.8
Norway	176	176	258	263	658	759	894	979	1,028	1,059	168.4
Portugal	38	35	48	99	117	114	114	120	125	127	177.0
Spain	876	400	160	308	442	494	529	568	539	499	693.4
Sweden	343	446	573	848	925	1,000	1,065	1,037	1,055	993	129.8
Switzerland	427	386	446	592	392	402	423	437	446	454	417.7
Turkey	0	0	2	57	95	110	160	235	255	217	139.5
United Kingdom	124	191	349	592	721	762	792	828	765	750	1,169.7
Eastern Europe											
Albania											
Belarus											
Bosnia-Herzegovina					29	20	18	16	18	24	16.7
Bulgaria			17		24	49	78	158	182	209	148.6
Croatia					234	272	311	275	286	298	56.4
Czech Republic				1,190	1,938	1,943	2,502	2,748	4,266	4,398	230.7
Estonia			14	31	66	67	84	123	141	155	13.8
Georgia					3	3	6	9	9	10	5.9
Hungary	1	85	3,307	16,680	28,327	31,797	38,484	39,320	42,308	39,271	194.1
Latvia			1	2	3	4	7	8	9	10	19.1
Lithuania	1	1	5	17	32	40	46	50	55	58	23.5
Macedonia											
Moldova						26	33	41	85	106	9.6
Montenegro											
Poland	3	15	101	685	678	474	523	626	743	801	256.6
Romania			4	35	67	81	102	119	156	180	59.0
Russia			447	4,641	20,462	25,700	32,100	40,400	44,400	43,100	1,357.0
Serbia						864	1,118	1,550	1,950	2,200	32.6
Slovakia			3	9	15	23	30	40	52	62	86.6
Slovenia	0	1	3	11	15	24	30	32	29	26	36.1
Ukraine					470	599	731	1,015	1,273	1,424	182.8

Source: *Euromonitor International from World Association of Newspapers*

Table 1.7

Online Adspend 1999-2009
Million units of national currency

	1999	2000	2001	2002	2004	2005	2006	2007	2008	2009	US$ million 2009
Western Europe											
Austria			10	22	22	28	37	65	85	100.0	139.0
Belgium	7	13	11	11	32	44	72	128	166	199.2	276.8
Cyprus											
Denmark			310	418	582	742	1,794	2,422	2,785	3,187.1	594.5
Finland	6	11	15	15	23	36	47	61	79	90.0	125.0
France	79	144	115	99	179	382	542	740	1,007	1,173.7	1,630.9
Germany	77	153	185	227	271	332	495	689	754	763.2	1,060.6
Gibraltar											
Greece			2	5							
Iceland			8								
Ireland		2	3	4	9	16	26	22	23	25.2	35.1
Italy	29	139	107	99	107	138	197	284	331	390.0	541.9
Liechtenstein											
Luxembourg					5	7	8	8	9	8.3	11.6
Malta											
Monaco											
Netherlands	21	38	34	32	66	97	137	190	217	227.1	315.5
Norway		300	235	250	455	2,119	3,119	4,234	5,130	5,651.0	898.4
Portugal	4	5	5	5	4	5	7	13	21	28.9	40.1
Spain	15	53	52	72	94	162	310	482	558	615.0	854.6
Sweden	497	1,037	895	1,139	1,325	1,974	2,996	4,040	5,329	5,781.3	755.4
Switzerland	12	25	19	20	29	36	52	52	62	71.8	66.1
Turkey			1	2	8	18	30	180	250	290.0	186.5
United Kingdom	43	132	141	162	700	1,162	1,714	2,391	2,911	3,399.0	5,300.9
Eastern Europe											
Albania											
Belarus											
Bosnia-Herzegovina							1	1	1	1.6	1.1
Bulgaria					3	5	10	17	30	52.0	37.0
Croatia						9	12	43	68	85.0	16.1
Czech Republic	55	100	200	240	664	830	2,028	3,408	4,495	5,270.0	276.4
Estonia	4	13	19	20	29	40	66	149	191	228.0	20.3
Georgia											
Hungary					2,460	5,637	9,610	12,673	19,516	22,440.5	110.9
Latvia		0	0	1	1	2	3	6	9	9.8	19.5
Lithuania	0	1	0	1	5	5	10	35	46	55.1	22.2
Macedonia											
Moldova								1	4	4.6	0.4
Montenegro											
Poland			24	33	87	148	215	593	743	919.0	294.5
Romania						5	8	16	24	40	56.4	18.5
Russia	25	84	175	345	865	1,700	2,700	5,800	8,400	10,800.0	340.0
Serbia						41	93	280	466	800.0	11.8
Slovakia			2	3	8	13	15	23	31	51.9	72.2
Slovenia					3	4	7	11	20	31.0	43.1
Ukraine				5	11	13	31	56	106	176.8	22.7

Source: *Euromonitor International from World Association of Newspapers / Jupiter research*

Section Two

Agricultural Resources and Output

Agricultural Statistics

Table 2.1

Agricultural Output Indices 1985-2009

1999-2001 = 100

	1985	1990	1995	2000	2004	2005	2006	2007	2008	2009
Western Europe										
Austria	86.0	89.0	93.0	97.0	96.0	94.0	92.0	95.0	95.5	95.4
Belgium	80.0	85.0	97.0	104.0	100.0	96.0	47.0	48.0	48.0	49.0
Cyprus	85.0	91.0	99.0	101.0	107.0	97.0	94.0	91.0	88.3	84.2
Denmark	92.0	100.0	99.0	99.0	101.0	102.0	102.0	102.0	102.5	102.9
Finland	108.0	113.0	99.0	102.0	101.0	106.0	103.0	102.0	102.3	102.7
France	95.0	96.0	95.0	101.0	101.0	97.0	94.0	93.0	92.8	90.9
Germany	100.0	102.0	90.0	99.0	100.0	96.0	93.0	95.0	95.9	94.9
Gibraltar										
Greece	89.0	81.0	98.0	100.0	94.0	96.0	85.0	82.0	81.0	78.2
Iceland	114.0	97.0	94.0	101.0	105.0	104.0	104.0	104.0	104.0	103.8
Ireland	90.0	94.0	94.0	99.0	97.0	95.0	94.0	92.0	91.0	89.6
Italy	96.0	91.0	95.0	99.0	101.0	99.0	95.0	94.0	94.9	93.5
Liechtenstein	105.0	109.0	100.0	100.0	100.0	100.0	100.0	96.0	95.0	93.9
Luxembourg				111.0	94.0	89.0	53.0	56.0	50.4	44.1
Malta	63.0	68.0	87.0	98.0	97.0	90.0	98.0	95.0	94.7	94.3
Monaco			64.4	57.3	59.7	60.3	60.9	61.5	62.1	62.7
Netherlands	96.0	102.0	103.0	100.0	95.0	92.0	91.0	92.0	92.6	92.0
Norway	106.0	112.0	102.0	98.0	101.0	98.0	97.0	98.0	98.3	97.6
Portugal	81.0	101.0	99.0	100.0	103.0	96.0	100.0	96.0	96.7	95.3
Spain	77.0	88.0	73.0	102.0	107.0	94.0	101.0	99.0	96.5	94.2
Sweden	110.0	110.0	96.0	101.0	102.0	100.0	98.0	99.0	99.0	98.3
Switzerland	103.0	104.0	101.0	102.0	101.0	100.0	99.0	102.0	103.3	103.9
Turkey	75.0	88.0	91.0	104.0	104.0	110.0	110.0	101.0	100.6	99.9
United Kingdom	103.0	105.0	106.0	102.0	98.0	98.0	96.0	92.0	90.8	89.1
Eastern Europe										
Albania	81.0	86.0	99.0	100.0	112.0	111.0	117.0	113.0	114.4	115.0
Belarus		105.0	97.0	121.0	127.0	135.0	139.0	148.9	156.8
Bosnia-Herzegovina			93.0	91.0	120.0	119.0	127.0	126.0	135.5	139.8
Bulgaria	150.0	153.0	117.0	97.0	95.0	77.0	90.0	73.0	72.9	69.0
Croatia			95.0	91.0	91.0	88.0	94.0	99.0	102.6	105.8
Czech Republic			100.0	97.0	106.0	96.0	95.0	96.0	99.0	97.4
Estonia			128.0	97.0	107.0	116.0	115.0	127.0	132.1	135.2
Georgia			114.0	91.0	97.0	109.0	69.0	81.0	78.2	76.2
Hungary	125.0	123.0	91.0	93.0	119.0	103.0	101.0	97.0	101.6	97.9
Latvia			129.0	98.0	111.0	126.0	116.0	128.0	133.7	140.5
Lithuania			106.0	109.0	120.0	124.0	113.0	128.0	131.3	134.7
Macedonia			90.0	103.0	104.0	105.0	104.0	109.0	113.5	116.1
Moldova			144.0	104.0	113.0	115.0	112.0	87.0	83.2	77.5
Montenegro										
Poland	114.0	120.0	97.0	98.0	110.0	104.0	102.0	103.0	103.6	102.2
Romania	125.0	106.0	110.0	89.0	126.0	105.0	107.0	91.0	88.8	81.7
Russia			99.0	99.0	112.0	115.0	118.0	123.0	128.3	132.7
Serbia										
Slovakia			109.0	92.0	110.0	109.0	89.0	82.0	79.7	73.7
Slovenia			95.0	99.0	106.0	102.0	100.0	103.0	103.0	102.4
Ukraine			123.0	100.0	111.0	118.0	116.0	108.0	110.7	110.7

Source: *UN Food and Agriculture Organisation, FAOSTAT*

Table 2.2

Food Output Indices 1985-2009

1999-2001 = 100

	1985	1990	1995	2000	2004	2005	2006	2007	2008	2009
Western Europe										
Austria	86.0	89.0	93.0	97.0	96.0	94.0	92.0	95.0	95.5	95.4
Belgium	80.0	85.0	97.0	104.0	100.0	96.0	47.0	48.0	48.0	49.0
Cyprus	85.0	91.0	99.0	101.0	107.0	97.0	94.0	91.0	88.3	84.2
Denmark	92.0	100.0	99.0	99.0	101.0	102.0	102.0	102.0	102.5	102.9
Finland	108.0	113.0	99.0	102.0	101.0	106.0	103.0	102.0	102.3	102.7
France	95.0	96.0	95.0	101.0	101.0	97.0	94.0	93.0	92.8	90.9
Germany	100.0	102.0	90.0	99.0	100.0	96.0	93.0	96.0	97.2	96.5
Gibraltar		90.7	107.4	96.4	93.6	93.1	92.9	92.7	92.5	92.3
Greece	94.0	84.0	98.0	100.0	94.0	96.0	89.0	87.0	87.1	85.6
Iceland	114.0	97.0	94.0	100.0	106.0	105.0	106.0	106.0	106.3	106.3
Ireland	90.0	94.0	94.0	99.0	97.0	95.0	94.0	92.0	91.0	89.6
Italy	95.0	90.0	95.0	99.0	101.0	99.0	95.0	94.0	94.9	93.5
Liechtenstein	105.0	109.0	100.0	100.0	100.0	100.0	100.0	96.0	95.0	93.9
Luxembourg				111.0	94.0	89.0	53.0	56.0	50.4	44.1
Malta	63.0	68.0	87.0	98.0	97.0	90.0	98.0	95.0	94.7	94.3
Monaco		95.6	79.7	95.1	104.2	105.9	107.1	108.6	109.9	111.3
Netherlands	96.0	102.0	103.0	100.0	95.0	92.0	91.0	92.0	92.6	92.0
Norway	106.0	112.0	102.0	98.0	101.0	98.0	97.0	98.0	98.3	97.6
Portugal	81.0	101.0	99.0	100.0	103.0	96.0	100.0	96.0	96.7	95.3
Spain	77.0	88.0	73.0	103.0	107.0	94.0	102.0	99.0	96.3	94.0
Sweden	110.0	110.0	96.0	101.0	102.0	100.0	98.0	100.0	100.3	99.9
Switzerland	103.0	104.0	101.0	102.0	101.0	100.0	99.0	103.0	104.6	105.5
Turkey	75.0	88.0	90.0	104.0	104.0	111.0	111.0	101.0	100.7	100.0
United Kingdom	104.0	105.0	106.0	102.0	98.0	98.0	96.0	93.0	92.0	90.6
Eastern Europe										
Albania	74.0	82.0	99.0	100.0	113.0	112.0	119.0	115.0	116.6	117.6
Belarus			105.0	97.0	121.0	126.0	135.0	139.0	148.9	156.8
Bosnia-Herzegovina			94.0	91.0	120.0	119.0	127.0	126.0	135.5	139.8
Bulgaria	143.0	151.0	120.0	98.0	93.0	75.0	89.0	72.0	72.5	69.0
Croatia			95.0	91.0	91.0	88.0	94.0	98.0	101.6	104.6
Czech Republic			100.0	97.0	106.0	96.0	95.0	96.0	99.0	97.4
Estonia			128.0	97.0	107.0	116.0	115.0	127.0	132.1	139.4
Georgia			114.0	92.0	98.0	111.0	72.0	85.0	82.6	81.2
Hungary	124.0	123.0	91.0	93.0	119.0	103.0	101.0	98.0	102.9	99.5
Latvia			129.0	98.0	111.0	126.0	117.0	128.0	133.6	140.4
Lithuania			105.0	109.0	120.0	124.0	113.0	129.0	132.6	136.4
Macedonia			92.0	105.0	105.0	105.0	105.0	111.0	116.2	119.2
Moldova			145.0	103.0	116.0	119.0	115.0	89.0	85.0	79.1
Montenegro										
Poland	112.0	119.0	97.0	98.0	110.0	104.0	102.0	103.0	103.6	102.2
Romania	124.0	105.0	110.0	89.0	127.0	106.0	108.0	91.0	88.9	81.6
Russia			99.0	99.0	112.0	115.0	118.0	123.0	128.6	133.1
Serbia										
Slovakia			108.0	92.0	111.0	110.0	89.0	82.0	79.7	73.6
Slovenia			95.0	99.0	106.0	102.0	100.0	103.0	103.0	102.4
Ukraine			122.0	100.0	111.0	118.0	116.0	108.0	110.7	110.7

Source: UN Food and Agriculture Organisation, FAOSTAT

Agricultural Statistics

Table 2.3

Land Use and Irrigation 2009

'000 hectares

	Total Area	Land Area	Arable Land	Permanent Crops	Permanent Pasture	Irrigated Land	Irrigated as % of Land Area
Western Europe							
Austria	8,387	8,245	1,380	69	1,774	125	1.52
Belgium	3,053	3,028	840	23	493	20	0.66
Cyprus	925	924	114	40	1	46	4.98
Denmark	4,309	4,243	2,316	7	335	430	10.13
Finland	33,842	30,409	2,270	8	37	74	0.24
France	54,919	54,766	18,408	1,065	9,839	2,739	5.00
Germany	35,705	34,877	11,864	196	4,840	485	1.39
Gibraltar	1	1					
Greece	13,196	12,890	2,508	1,132	4,600	1,689	13.10
Iceland	10,300	10,025	7		2,274		
Ireland	7,028	6,889	983	3	3,297		
Italy	30,134	29,414	6,755	2,520	4,039	3,972	13.50
Liechtenstein	16	16	4		1		
Luxembourg	259	259	61	2	70	4	1.54
Malta	32	32	8	1		3	10.00
Monaco	0	0					
Netherlands	4,153	3,376	1,143	35	696	404	11.97
Norway	32,380	30,428	847	5	179	117	0.38
Portugal	9,212	9,150	912	551	1,893	580	6.34
Spain	50,537	49,898	12,538	4,820	11,020	3,840	7.70
Sweden	45,029	41,033	2,628	5	464	176	0.43
Switzerland	4,128	4,000	408	23	1,130	25	0.63
Turkey	78,356	76,963	20,857	3,002	14,617	5,215	6.78
United Kingdom	24,361	24,193	6,248	45	11,776	125	0.52
Eastern Europe							
Albania	2,875	2,740	585	119	421	368	13.43
Belarus	20,760	20,748	5,529	121	3,299	131	0.63
Bosnia-Herzegovina	5,121	5,120	1,019	94	1,025	3	0.06
Bulgaria	11,100	10,861	2,983	186	1,831	380	3.50
Croatia	5,659	5,391	844	85	50	17	0.32
Czech Republic	7,887	7,725	3,021	240	982	47	0.61
Estonia	4,523	4,239	630	6	202	4	0.09
Georgia	6,970	6,949	459	120	1,940	433	6.23
Hungary	9,303	8,961	4,588	194	985	121	1.35
Latvia	6,459	6,225	1,274	9	654	1	0.01
Lithuania	6,530	6,268	1,908	23	754	4	0.06
Macedonia	2,571	2,543	417	31	501	55	2.16
Moldova	3,385	3,288	1,807	306	341	228	6.94
Montenegro	1,381	1,345	245	16	322	2	0.16
Poland	31,268	30,425	12,520	429	3,191	128	0.42
Romania	23,839	22,989	8,340	464	4,370	3,150	13.70
Russia	1,709,824	1,637,774	121,317	1,787	92,125	4,360	0.27
Serbia	8,836	8,836	3,276	300	1,944	75	0.85
Slovakia	4,903	4,810	1,368	24	536	178	3.70
Slovenia	2,027	2,014	177	24	319	10	0.50
Ukraine	60,355	57,933	32,412	897	7,911	2,167	3.74

Source: *UN Food and Agriculture Organisation, FAOSTAT*

Agricultural Statistics

Table 2.4

Livestock 2009

'000 head

	Asses	Cattle	Goats	Horses	Pigs	Sheep
Western Europe						
Austria		1,972.2	51.6	88.1	3,124.9	301.2
Belgium	0.0	2,563.2	26.8	36.6	6,243.1	162.7
Cyprus	5.2	55.5	351.3	0.7	482.0	257.7
Denmark		1,567.1		53.7	14,016.2	156.5
Finland		902.6	6.4	69.1	1,458.6	124.9
France	17.8	19,144.2	1,262.1	417.9	14,783.8	8,044.4
Germany		12,304.8	188.0	554.7	27,247.4	2,482.8
Gibraltar						
Greece	48.6	635.3	5,464.2	26.8	906.1	8,834.7
Iceland		72.3	0.6	79.5	43.5	458.0
Ireland	5.1	6,647.5	7.3	92.0	1,532.4	5,262.1
Italy	25.0	6,085.0	967.2	305.9	9,396.7	8,409.3
Liechtenstein		6.0	0.3		3.0	3.0
Luxembourg		194.2	3.0	4.5	90.5	8.5
Malta	0.8	19.3	6.0	1.1	74.6	11.6
Monaco						
Netherlands		3,706.9	419.2	130.3	11,848.6	1,403.9
Norway		870.6	71.9	35.1	835.7	2,221.2
Portugal	123.9	1,415.4	535.8	20.3	2,273.9	3,542.8
Spain	142.1	6,630.2	2,887.4	253.6	26,965.1	21,962.6
Sweden		1,538.8		93.9	1,654.5	527.8
Switzerland	5.2	1,570.0	80.4	59.6	1,573.9	457.4
Turkey	323.3	11,260.0	6,388.7	198.6	1.2	25,465.3
United Kingdom		10,173.0	97.6	392.3	4,857.1	32,566.6
Eastern Europe						
Albania	77.2	564.0	841.3	42.5	158.0	1,856.3
Belarus	9.0	4,000.5	72.1	139.9	3,678.0	50.9
Bosnia-Herzegovina		472.3	67.3	22.3	503.3	1,051.6
Bulgaria	123.4	624.6	495.1	116.7	1,036.7	1,682.8
Croatia	4.0	485.8	121.9	10.3	1,489.3	669.1
Czech Republic		1,407.1	16.8	25.7	2,487.1	183.4
Estonia		241.6	3.5	5.1	344.6	75.3
Georgia	10.0	1,032.1	96.2	42.0	324.9	758.9
Hungary	3.5	687.0	66.7	57.3	4,135.9	1,356.9
Latvia		378.8	15.1	13.1	412.9	43.6
Lithuania		858.1	19.8	58.8	1,144.9	44.8
Macedonia		251.2	132.0	57.1	284.5	808.8
Moldova	2.0	281.6	109.6	64.8	566.7	853.7
Montenegro		113.8		5.8	13.8	248.9
Poland		5,732.8	147.5	335.9	18,151.6	345.1
Romania	29.2	2,945.0	784.1	788.3	7,052.9	7,749.7
Russia	18.5	19,725.0	2,201.0	1,278.0	16,565.0	19,897.6
Serbia		1,080.7	145.0	17.0	3,940.3	1,610.7
Slovakia		479.2	37.5	8.2	1,099.9	340.0
Slovenia		449.3	30.7	21.3	614.7	136.5
Ukraine	12.1	5,610.9	620.3	500.1	8,345.9	994.7

Source: UN Food and Agriculture Organisation, FAOSTAT

Agricultural Statistics

Table 2.5

Selected Crop Production 2009

'000 tonnes

	Apples	Bananas	Grapes	Hops	Potatoes	Rapeseed	Sugar Beet	Tomatoes
Western Europe								
Austria	451.0		424.1	0.4	755.6	187.6	2,993.7	46.8
Belgium	347.2		0.5	0.4	2,810.5	31.0	5,115.5	212.7
Cyprus	9.9	7.1	31.0		125.4			31.9
Denmark	31.3				1,730.7	689.0	1,991.5	19.3
Finland					666.7	67.7	423.0	41.3
France	1,874.3		5,288.9	1.5	6,869.9	4,775.5	31,557.2	651.8
Germany	1,060.7		1,422.0	41.0	11,291.7	5,185.9	22,514.0	66.0
Gibraltar								
Greece	255.6	4.0	900.0		856.8	7.9	829.6	1,313.8
Iceland					12.1			1.8
Ireland	14.5			0.0	360.6	25.9	403.0	12.2
Italy	2,194.2	0.4	7,539.9		1,558.5	39.5	3,559.3	5,732.9
Liechtenstein			0.2					
Luxembourg	5.0		16.4		22.4	17.0		0.1
Malta	0.9		3.4		18.8			16.9
Monaco								
Netherlands	372.8		0.1		6,966.9	10.0	5,147.7	751.1
Norway	14.0				419.0	9.0		15.0
Portugal	234.2	34.8	687.6	0.1	563.7		128.4	1,140.9
Spain	707.1	354.0	6,052.6	0.9	2,489.7	26.2	3,808.5	4,011.3
Sweden	20.3				824.7	266.2	1,948.2	16.8
Switzerland	248.6		139.1	0.0	384.7	58.8	1,669.2	31.3
Turkey	2,409.4	215.6	3,941.3		4,266.1	97.8	15,330.8	11,039.3
United Kingdom	249.4		0.9	1.3	6,005.1	1,994.5	6,909.0	74.1
Eastern Europe								
Albania	23.5	0.2	157.8	1.1	164.0		40.6	165.4
Belarus	242.4				8,919.4	594.9	4,573.6	313.3
Bosnia-Herzegovina	51.7		24.1		414.6	1.8	0.0	41.7
Bulgaria	20.3		396.0	0.4	346.3	266.1	13.5	70.5
Croatia	76.1		186.7		250.2	67.7	1,131.2	26.6
Czech Republic	137.3		109.1	6.4	695.8	1,115.5	3,044.6	29.1
Estonia	4.5				99.6	117.3		8.0
Georgia	88.2		151.0		69.4			69.5
Hungary	539.3		561.3		658.4	719.8	470.7	213.2
Latvia	27.4				677.3	207.3	174.9	0.0
Lithuania	77.2				662.4	358.9	315.1	1.3
Macedonia	135.4		227.2		192.5	0.5	11.2	123.5
Moldova	241.7		671.0		238.6	115.8	894.3	67.5
Montenegro	5.7		34.9		103.1			21.8
Poland	2,217.6			3.5	10,490.2	2,242.5	8,453.8	721.1
Romania	422.5		1,178.1	0.3	3,621.9	789.8	819.6	850.9
Russia	1,730.7		261.7	0.3	27,006.3	827.1	32,936.3	2,074.9
Serbia			417.0	0.1	805.5	69.0	2,109.2	159.9
Slovakia	35.8		50.8	0.3	237.2	459.5	638.2	55.2
Slovenia	95.3		100.7	2.2	86.9	12.3	265.3	5.5
Ukraine	690.0		406.2	1.0	19,570.6	3,412.0	14,656.1	1,572.9

Source: UN Food and Agriculture Organisation, FAOSTAT

Agricultural Statistics

Table 2.6

Dairy Products and Egg Production 2009

'000 tonnes

	Butter and Ghee	Cheese	Fresh Cows' Milk	Hens' Eggs
Western Europe				
Austria	35.1	192.7	3,216.7	97.2
Belgium	121.1	54.0	2,732.0	172.2
Cyprus		5.6	152.8	10.1
Denmark	33.3	342.8	4,748.2	81.7
Finland	54.0	94.0	2,294.8	58.7
France	411.0	1,809.2	24,503.1	853.2
Germany	443.2	2,007.2	28,717.1	786.1
Gibraltar				
Greece	4.1	236.5	806.1	96.6
Iceland	1.9	7.2	130.8	2.9
Ireland	117.4	190.6	5,386.8	33.1
Italy	125.0	1,159.1	11,421.0	702.7
Liechtenstein			11.5	
Luxembourg	0.3		278.5	1.3
Malta		0.2	39.5	7.6
Monaco				
Netherlands	100.0	669.3	11,336.3	634.0
Norway	14.0	81.2	1,602.3	53.4
Portugal	30.9	73.8	1,966.5	124.6
Spain	58.9	110.2	6,374.2	703.3
Sweden	36.0	110.5	3,050.1	94.2
Switzerland	47.5	201.2	4,140.4	39.3
Turkey	146.6	152.1	11,525.3	845.4
United Kingdom	130.0	391.0	13,530.4	606.3
Eastern Europe				
Albania	0.8	14.2	906.6	27.3
Belarus	104.1	149.8	6,307.8	187.0
Bosnia-Herzegovina	0.4	11.1	754.7	27.6
Bulgaria	2.3	78.0	1,127.6	93.8
Croatia	2.4	21.9	843.9	46.8
Czech Republic	52.2	132.1	2,813.1	100.7
Estonia	7.6	17.9	698.1	8.5
Georgia	0.6	0.0	616.7	24.7
Hungary	5.8	87.1	1,797.2	154.9
Latvia	6.3	22.9	839.4	42.4
Lithuania	12.0	77.5	1,969.3	56.4
Macedonia	8.8	7.5	334.8	17.5
Moldova	4.6	6.8	502.0	28.9
Montenegro			168.6	3.7
Poland	198.0	595.1	12,499.4	587.1
Romania	8.0	61.0	5,855.6	339.6
Russia	284.2	549.3	32,302.3	2,145.2
Serbia	1.5	18.3	1,586.3	58.8
Slovakia	9.0	69.0	1,044.6	73.1
Slovenia	5.5	17.7	670.9	23.1
Ukraine	76.9	256.5	11,137.6	884.8

Source: UN Food and Agriculture Organisation, FAOSTAT

Agricultural Statistics

Table 2.7

Meat Production 2009

'000 tonnes

	Beef and Veal	Goat Meat	Horse Meat	Mutton and Lamb	Pig Meat	Poultry	Total (including others)
Western Europe							
Austria	228.6	0.6	0.2	7.5	517.1	104.8	855.7
Belgium	268.8	0.0	2.9	3.3	1,057.3	442.7	1,771.2
Cyprus	4.3	3.8		3.5	60.3	29.4	102.0
Denmark	125.8		0.7	1.8	1,683.3	175.2	1,984.9
Finland	82.4		0.2	0.8	222.0	108.9	412.0
France	1,486.8	7.2	4.2	87.6	1,970.2	1,595.1	5,306.7
Germany	1,213.1	0.5	2.5	22.2	5,223.9	1,335.5	7,939.2
Gibraltar							
Greece	66.6	54.8	2.7	89.8	104.4	103.2	432.8
Iceland	3.6		1.0	8.6	6.2	8.1	29.8
Ireland	538.0		1.5	55.9	201.3	93.8	891.1
Italy	1,061.2	2.2	23.5	56.8	1,610.9	1,176.9	4,144.6
Liechtenstein							
Luxembourg	16.6		0.3	0.0	9.6	0.1	26.4
Malta	1.5	0.0	0.1	0.1	8.5	5.4	17.3
Monaco							
Netherlands	373.2	0.7	0.5	13.4	1,325.2	788.8	2,502.2
Norway	85.0	0.3	0.4	23.3	118.8	73.8	305.9
Portugal	106.6	0.8	0.2	25.8	398.8	247.5	784.3
Spain	662.7	8.6	5.2	142.9	3,595.2	1,204.0	5,663.2
Sweden	134.9		0.8	4.7	265.3	110.7	531.9
Switzerland	135.5	0.5	0.7	5.1	232.2	67.7	442.5
Turkey	410.2	46.0	2.0	271.8		1,157.5	1,855.7
United Kingdom	922.0		3.1	329.7	748.5	1,383.0	3,380.7
Eastern Europe							
Albania	51.0	7.7		14.5	12.9	14.2	99.2
Belarus	269.9		2.3	1.1	382.4	219.1	870.4
Bosnia-Herzegovina	26.4			1.7	9.4	35.4	71.7
Bulgaria	17.5	5.0	0.0	16.6	71.1	119.9	228.6
Croatia	36.1	0.2	3.0	2.6	66.8	51.8	161.7
Czech Republic	79.2	0.1	0.1	2.0	317.6	200.5	639.9
Estonia	15.4	0.0		0.5	47.7	11.0	73.5
Georgia	18.6	0.3	0.4	1.7	11.0	5.3	36.5
Hungary	33.4	0.3	0.0	0.8	444.5	364.9	845.0
Latvia	22.6		0.1	0.7	41.8	24.9	89.9
Lithuania	48.4	0.3	0.0	0.6	69.1	73.7	189.1
Macedonia	6.9			6.4	8.7	3.4	25.4
Moldova	10.4		0.0	2.1	35.0	29.7	78.1
Montenegro	2.9			0.7	2.2		5.7
Poland	373.7		10.3	1.4	1,767.5	1,002.2	3,189.8
Romania	146.5	4.3	8.6	43.3	421.7	323.7	971.4
Russia	1,782.6	19.2	44.4	163.6	2,162.7	2,249.1	6,465.7
Serbia	106.8			23.1	265.5	92.2	462.7
Slovakia	18.5	0.3	0.0	1.0	91.0	73.3	190.9
Slovenia	34.1	0.4	0.3	1.7	50.6	62.2	147.9
Ukraine	471.9	8.9	11.1	8.4	578.3	894.7	1,993.4

Source: *UN Food and Agriculture Organisation, FAOSTAT*

Table 2.8

Cereal Production 2009

'000 tonnes

	Barley	Maize	Millet	Oats	Rice	Rye	Sorghum	Wheat	Total (including others)
Western Europe									
Austria	857.6	2,179.6	8.8	101.9		250.1		1,739.8	5,900.8
Belgium	448.1	767.4		30.5		1.8		1,806.8	3,210.0
Cyprus	40.0			0.7				9.1	52.9
Denmark	1.3			323.4		160.4		5,089.8	9,032.5
Finland	2,211.0			1,244.5		64.3		870.2	4,285.8
France	10,908.7	16,464.2	40.3	461.9	86.0	119.5	206.4	37,573.0	72,091.1
Germany	11,724.2	5,333.3		741.6		4,220.5		26,335.6	51,479.8
Gibraltar									
Greece	304.7	2,448.3		184.9	226.0	74.1	0.1	1,792.9	5,307.8
Iceland									
Ireland	1,234.0			188.4		0.4		975.2	2,533.0
Italy	1,239.3	9,179.0		341.2	1,376.2	11.9	238.5	8,984.6	21,691.6
Liechtenstein									
Luxembourg	50.6	2.3		5.8		9.9		100.6	200.8
Malta	1.5							10.5	10.9
Monaco									
Netherlands	291.3	252.0		6.5		6.6		1,439.3	2,021.1
Norway	534.0			318.6		53.1		463.1	1,363.2
Portugal	80.2	756.2		108.4	162.2	22.3		138.1	1,444.3
Spain	9,379.0	3,506.1	0.6	1,240.1	615.7	328.2	20.0	6,861.7	26,189.3
Sweden	1,549.3			842.3		191.4		2,134.9	5,402.3
Switzerland	191.8	170.2		8.3		13.8		560.1	1,009.4
Turkey	5,295.0	4,296.4	6.9	190.3	805.7	239.4	0.2	18,334.5	26,921.9
United Kingdom	5,620.2			803.4		27.6		16,625.5	25,276.5
Eastern Europe									
Albania	3.5	233.4		21.6		3.3		264.3	521.5
Belarus	2,249.4	573.3		604.5		1,640.9		2,095.6	9,298.0
Bosnia-Herzegovina	78.5	966.9		40.7		12.1		220.8	1,322.5
Bulgaria	674.7	1,295.9	4.9	55.4	45.9	16.1	3.8	4,697.9	7,407.8
Croatia	290.8	2,595.3	0.2	88.4		3.8	0.5	875.8	3,936.5
Czech Republic	2,094.5	905.5	1.8	157.3		234.7		4,650.3	8,621.9
Estonia	346.3			75.5		81.6		355.8	898.9
Georgia	43.2	267.4		1.6		0.0		61.0	317.3
Hungary	1,253.0	8,933.9	9.1	188.5	14.3	121.5	15.5	5,747.5	17,192.9
Latvia	327.6			144.8		228.7		1,029.1	1,803.1
Lithuania	929.8	40.2		144.7		244.8		1,811.1	3,607.0
Macedonia	126.5	120.1	0.0	5.7	17.3	10.6	0.1	285.2	602.5
Moldova	247.0	1,474.1	0.6	3.1		1.3	0.0	1,326.2	3,252.5
Montenegro	1.4	6.0		0.1		0.2		1.7	9.2
Poland	3,598.0	1,813.8	10.2	1,243.7		3,610.7		8,813.9	26,106.7
Romania	959.7	7,002.6	3.1	383.4	62.8	28.8	29.9	6,876.1	15,986.3
Russia	20,927.4	7,734.3	788.3	6,219.9	783.2	4,965.9	95.2	65,221.1	115,430.8
Serbia	306.5	5,849.0	0.2	97.1		13.3	6.3	2,164.9	8,934.2
Slovakia	764.6	1,317.2	2.0	34.1		92.9	0.4	1,886.3	4,320.9
Slovenia	80.3	309.5	0.3	4.4		1.6		133.0	584.4
Ukraine	7,574.7	12,465.9	203.6	991.0	101.4	1,177.5	310.2	26,721.6	57,007.1

Source: UN Food and Agriculture Organisation, FAOSTAT

Agricultural Statistics   **Table 2.9**

Forestry and Paper Product Production 2009

as stated

	Fuelwood and Charcoal ('000 cu m)	Household and Sanitary Paper ('000 tonnes)	Paper and Paperboard ('000 tonnes)	Printing and Writing Paper ('000 tonnes)	Roundwood ('000 cu m)	Sawnwood and Sleepers ('000 cu m)	Wood Pulp ('000 tonnes)
Western Europe							
Austria	6,062	115	5,171	2,660	26,122	11,417	2,034
Belgium	711	101	1,870	1,119	4,989	1,637	499
Cyprus	2				27	14	
Denmark	1,155		423	156	2,901	342	65
Finland	5,275	221	14,721	9,437	59,964	12,122	13,869
France	33,221	769	10,231	2,998	75,560	10,549	2,088
Germany	11,933	1,485	24,742	8,941	99,107	26,805	3,307
Gibraltar							
Greece	628	51	403	17	1,858	75	5
Iceland							
Ireland	45		45		2,800	1,004	
Italy	4,704	1,488	10,210	3,327	7,711	1,801	580
Liechtenstein	4				22		
Luxembourg	30				315	134	
Malta							
Monaco							
Netherlands	290	104	3,243	910	996	267	120
Norway	3,201	16	1,813	875	11,628	2,510	2,058
Portugal	600	75	1,694	1,027	10,796	989	2,146
Spain	1,990	797	7,581	1,951	13,525	3,089	2,107
Sweden	5,900	323	12,264	3,643	86,005	19,773	12,976
Switzerland	1,459	59	1,417	455	6,114	1,548	370
Turkey	4,413	146	1,643	217	18,823	6,832	65
United Kingdom	728	892	5,284	1,083	9,565	3,315	216
Eastern Europe							
Albania	221		3	5	296	97	
Belarus	1,384	8	285	6	8,837	2,271	70
Bosnia-Herzegovina	1,351	36	118		3,654	1,389	20
Bulgaria	2,347	27	469	3	5,525	717	135
Croatia	654	1	497	296	4,476	794	93
Czech Republic	1,891	25	985	178	21,240	6,342	812
Estonia	1,322		72	0	5,737	1,555	256
Georgia	459				653	106	
Hungary	2,925	43	550	68	5,541	265	5
Latvia	1,084		77	1	11,721	3,231	2
Lithuania	1,417	12	135	5	5,696	1,331	0
Macedonia	515		27		696	11	
Moldova	94				188	31	
Montenegro	265				457	42	
Poland	3,536	290	3,249	888	39,061	3,129	1,071
Romania	4,864	88	667	13	15,509	4,025	148
Russia	43,179	178	7,809	616	229,721	24,484	7,013
Serbia	1,410	32	273		3,191	703	20
Slovakia	548	143	969	608	9,833	3,198	727
Slovenia	797	67	887	327	3,135	712	80
Ukraine	10,625	130	1,038	36	18,779	2,627	27

Source: *UN Food and Agriculture Organisation, FAOSTAT*

Agricultural Statistics

Table 2.10

Organic Farming Land Use 1985-2009

Hectares

	1985	1990	1995	2000	2004	2005	2006	2007	2008	2009
Western Europe										
Austria			335,865	271,950	344,916	360,972	361,487	372,026	382,949	388,476
Belgium	500	1,300	3,385	20,263	23,728	22,996	29,308	32,628	35,721	38,537
Cyprus				52	960	1,698	1,979	2,322	2,483	2,795
Denmark	4,500	11,581	40,884	165,258	154,921	145,636	138,079	145,393	150,104	152,983
Finland	1,000	6,726	44,695	147,423	162,024	147,587	144,558	148,760	150,374	151,961
France	45,000	72,000	118,393	371,000	534,037	560,838	552,824	557,133	580,956	585,194
Germany	24,940	90,021	309,487	546,023	767,891	807,406	825,539	865,336	907,786	936,751
Gibraltar										
Greece		150	2,401	24,800	246,488	288,255	302,256	278,397	317,824	319,895
Iceland			717	3,400	4,910	4,684	5,512	6,229	6,970	7,343
Ireland	1,000	3,800	12,634	32,355	30,670	35,266	39,947	41,122	44,751	47,679
Italy	5,000	13,218	204,494	1,040,377	954,361	1,067,102	1,148,162	1,150,253	1,002,414	1,043,990
Liechtenstein			410	690	984	1,040	1,027	1,048	1,053	1,057
Luxembourg	350	600	571	1,030	3,158	3,243	3,630	3,380	3,535	3,604
Malta					13	14	20	30	46	54
Monaco										
Netherlands	2,450	7,469	12,909	27,820	48,152	48,765	48,424	47,019	50,434	51,561
Norway	90	1,578	5,768	20,523	41,035	43,033	44,624	48,863	52,248	55,163
Portugal	50	1,000	10,719	50,002	206,524	233,458	269,374	233,475	229,717	229,936
Spain	2,140	3,650	24,079	380,838	733,182	807,569	926,390	988,323	1,129,844	1,220,221
Sweden	1,500	28,500	83,490	171,682	219,423	200,010	225,385	248,104	336,439	360,486
Switzerland			31,815	95,000	121,387	117,117	125,596	116,641	117,286	118,048
Turkey		1,037	10,000	21,000	108,597	93,133	100,275	124,263	109,387	112,952
United Kingdom	6,000	31,000	48,448	527,323	657,736	619,852	604,571	660,200	737,631	757,805
Eastern Europe										
Albania					804	987	1,170	77	280	483
Belarus										
Bosnia-Herzegovina					310	363	416	691	721	775
Bulgaria				500	12,284	14,320	4,692	13,646	16,663	18,326
Croatia			120	120	3,357	3,184	6,204	7,647	9,993	11,225
Czech Republic		3,480	14,127	165,699	260,120	254,982	281,535	312,890	341,632	370,586
Estonia				9,872	46,016	59,862	72,886	79,530	87,346	93,180
Georgia			100	100	100	130	247	251	268	279
Hungary				47,221	128,690	123,569	122,765	122,270	122,816	123,167
Latvia			1,147	20,000	57,333	118,612	135,558	173,463	161,625	179,051
Lithuania			582	4,709	41,869	69,430	96,718	120,418	122,200	137,694
Macedonia						249	509	1,333	3,380	3,922
Moldova						11,075	11,405	11,695	11,930	12,240
Montenegro								25,051	1,876	1,810
Poland		550	6,855	22,000	82,730	167,740	228,009	285,878	313,944	331,013
Romania				20,500	75,000	87,916	107,582	131,401	140,132	151,876
Russia			20,000	5,276	31,003	40,000	3,192	6,123	46,962	50,024
Serbia								920	4,494	5,068
Slovakia		15,140	18,813	48,120	73,335	92,191	121,461	117,906	140,755	153,613
Slovenia			200	5,200	23,032	23,499	26,831	29,322	29,838	32,750
Ukraine					240,000	241,980	260,034	249,872	269,984	273,930

Source: *Euromonitor International from Organic Centre Wales, University of Wales*

Agricultural Statistics   **Table 2.11**

Organic Farms 1985-2009

Number

	1985	1990	1995	2000	2004	2005	2006	2007	2008	2009
Western Europe										
Austria	420	1,539	18,542	19,031	19,826	20,310	20,162	19,997	19,961	19,945
Belgium	50	160	193	628	712	693	783	821	901	965
Cyprus				15	103	305	305	305	305	305
Denmark	130	523	1,050	3,466	3,166	2,892	2,794	2,835	2,753	2,725
Finland	60	671	2,793	5,225	4,887	4,296	3,966	4,406	3,991	4,046
France	2,500	2,700	3,538	9,283	11,059	11,402	11,640	11,978	13,298	13,586
Germany	1,610	3,438	6,642	12,732	16,603	17,020	17,557	18,703	19,813	20,655
Gibraltar										
Greece		25	568	5,270	8,269	14,614	23,900	23,769	24,057	24,635
Iceland			12	30	25	23	27	36	35	42
Ireland	8	150	378	1,014	897	978	1,104	1,134	1,220	1,298
Italy	600	1,500	10,630	51,120	36,639	44,733	45,115	45,231	44,371	44,620
Liechtenstein			22	33	42	35	41	39	37	39
Luxembourg	10	10	19	51	66	72	72	81	85	90
Malta					20	6	10	12	14	17
Monaco										
Netherlands	215	399	561	1,391	1,469	1,377	1,448	1,374	1,402	1,431
Norway	15	263	728	1,823	2,484	2,496	2,583	2,611	2,702	2,760
Portugal	1	50	349	763	1,302	1,577	1,696	1,949	1,949	2,135
Spain	264	350	1,042	13,424	16,013	15,693	17,214	18,226	21,291	22,558
Sweden	150	1,588	2,473	3,329	3,374	2,951	2,380	3,028	3,686	3,825
Switzerland	322	803	2,121	5,852	6,373	6,420	6,563	6,199	6,111	6,097
Turkey		313	2,000	10,000	12,806	14,401	14,256	16,364	15,406	16,388
United Kingdom	300	700	828	3,563	4,151	4,285	4,485	5,506	5,383	5,694
Eastern Europe										
Albania					57	75	93	100	50	57
Belarus										
Bosnia-Herzegovina					122	74	26	304	317	342
Bulgaria				50	351	351	218	240	254	269
Croatia			18	18	200	269	368	483	632	739
Czech Republic		30	176	563	836	829	963	1,318	1,946	2,191
Estonia				231	810	1,013	1,173	1,220	1,259	1,283
Georgia			5	5	5	38	47	49	53	59
Hungary				471	1,583	1,553	1,553	1,242	1,614	1,659
Latvia			90	225	1,525	2,873	4,095	4,108	4,203	4,321
Lithuania				230	1,170	1,811	2,284	2,855	2,797	3,019
Macedonia					50	50	101	127	99	118
Moldova						121	121	121	122	122
Montenegro								13	25	26
Poland		49	236	1,419	3,760	7,183	9,187	11,887	14,888	17,240
Romania				650	1,200	2,920	3,033	2,238	2,775	2,834
Russia			15	19	15	40	8	14	19	23
Serbia								35	224	413
Slovakia		36	34	100	148	196	279	280	350	392
Slovenia			40	620	1,568	1,718	1,953	2,000	2,067	2,208
Ukraine					70	72	80	92	118	128

Source: *Euromonitor International from Organic Centre Wales, University of Wales*

Automotives and Transport

Automotives and Transport Statistics

Table 3.1

Commercial Vehicles in Use 1980-2009

'000

	1980	1985	1990	1995	1996	1997	1998	1999	2000	2001
Western Europe										
Austria	208.2	237.3	295.0	347.8	353.4	362.9	374.4	386.0	395.9	402.2
Belgium	354.5	340.2	423.6	487.3	501.0	517.6	542.7	571.7	593.3	614.8
Cyprus	25.2	45.0	76.6	103.9	106.8	108.5	112.0	114.0	117.6	120.9
Denmark	259.2	267.4	300.8	342.3	348.6	354.7	366.6	382.3	393.7	401.5
Finland	166.9	200.5	294.2	280.4	286.5	294.2	307.9	320.7	327.8	335.2
France	2,570.5	3,980.0	4,910.0	5,195.0	5,255.0	5,380.0	5,500.0	5,610.0	5,753.0	5,897.0
Germany			1,989.4	3,061.9	3,121.6	3,174.1	3,279.5	3,370.0	3,533.9	3,592.1
Gibraltar	0.7	1.0	2.5	1.1	1.6	1.7	1.8	2.0	2.3	2.5
Greece	418.7	565.0	776.7	847.5	850.0	893.1	902.2	974.0	1,055.0	1,112.9
Iceland	9.0	12.7	14.5	16.1	16.6	17.5	18.1	19.4	21.1	21.7
Ireland	70.2	101.0	152.2	155.2	161.4	174.3	188.2	208.6	226.4	243.4
Italy	1,428.8	1,910.1	2,494.5	2,863.4	3,112.4	3,291.2	3,336.7	3,413.8	3,581.5	3,755.6
Liechtenstein	1.2	1.5	2.0	2.3	2.5	2.6	2.8	2.9	2.5	2.6
Luxembourg	15.5	14.0	18.1	27.1	28.0	28.3	29.7	30.8	31.4	33.3
Malta	14.2	17.5	21.2	50.9	55.7	42.8	45.3	44.9	44.3	44.7
Monaco				2.7	2.7	2.6	2.7	2.7	2.9	2.9
Netherlands	376.0	428.0	560.0	658.0	681.0	695.0	739.0	807.0	883.0	950.0
Norway	164.5	249.7	329.5	382.0	392.1	412.2	427.0	440.1	451.0	462.2
Portugal	264.0	356.0	568.0	824.0	867.0	923.0	997.0	1,066.0	1,157.0	1,211.0
Spain	1,380.9	1,570.9	2,378.7	3,071.6	3,200.3	3,360.1	3,561.6	3,788.7	3,977.9	4,161.1
Sweden	194.4	231.4	324.1	322.3	326.5	336.1	352.9	369.2	388.6	409.9
Switzerland	169.4	200.5	283.4	299.3	300.7	302.7	306.4	313.6	318.8	326.6
Turkey	428.2	553.1	709.9	982.4	1,053.7	1,182.4	1,317.0	1,405.8	1,543.1	1,588.4
United Kingdom	1,912.8	1,650.0	2,861.0	3,208.7	3,248.8	3,316.5	3,395.3	3,395.3	3,463.5	3,418.0
Eastern Europe										
Albania				48.4	41.7	45.8	50.3	53.7	67.6	79.6
Belarus			70.8	96.5	101.0	107.6	111.6	116.0	118.9	119.9
Bosnia-Herzegovina								75.2	77.5	82.1
Bulgaria			240.2	257.1	261.0	265.7	271.0	279.0	283.0	289.0
Croatia			52.4	77.4	99.5	114.5	120.6	123.4	127.2	134.3
Czech Republic			162.7	222.7	246.0	267.4	280.2	287.2	293.9	314.8
Estonia	57.5	66.4	75.6	72.6	78.0	83.1	86.9	87.2	88.2	86.0
Georgia										51.5
Hungary	190.0	216.0	272.5	324.6	334.4	342.6	355.4	363.4	384.3	398.3
Latvia			71.7	85.2	90.2	95.3	96.5	101.8	108.6	111.0
Lithuania			98.2	118.5	104.8	108.6	114.6	112.2	114.2	116.0
Macedonia			20.6	15.1	19.7	25.9	33.5	40.7	45.9	48.7
Moldova			83.4	67.4	68.6	71.4	82.6	76.7	68.5	69.4
Montenegro										
Poland	1,373.4	1,722.0	2,329.0	2,651.0	2,744.0	2,816.0	2,937.1	1,676.6	1,865.4	1,958.4
Romania			287.0	385.1	416.3	430.1	446.1	458.4	467.9	478.8
Russia										
Serbia										
Slovakia				160.2	154.2	159.7	166.1	168.8	169.6	170.2
Slovenia			49.1	60.9	65.6	66.3	72.3	77.7	59.2	61.2
Ukraine			59.7	175.7	180.0	197.6	222.1	289.7	349.9	430.8

Source: *European Automobile Manufacturers' Association (ACEA) / International Road Federation (IRF)*
Notes: *There may be wide variations from year to year in SMMT estimates and in other figures due to interpretation of definitions*

Automotives and Transport Statistics

Commercial Vehicles in Use 1980-2009 *(continued)*
'000

	2002	2003	2004	2005	2006	2007	2008	2009	Number in use /'000 persons 2009
Western Europe									
Austria	386.4	396.9	405.0	410.3	417.1	423.8	426.3	426.6	50.9
Belgium	627.8	644.6	668.4	691.4	706.3	715.7	723.3	724.0	67.3
Cyprus	120.8	122.9	121.0	121.6	118.9	119.5	120.8	121.7	139.7
Denmark	411.2	422.4	482.4	479.4	518.7	534.8	543.5	545.4	99.0
Finland	341.8	348.9	376.8	370.8	383.5	396.4	399.7	400.3	75.2
France	5,984.0	6,068.0	6,139.0	6,198.0	6,261.0	6,303.9	6,340.5	6,356.4	101.8
Germany	3,567.5	3,541.2	3,539.7	3,133.2	3,172.0	3,231.9	3,254.5	3,275.2	39.9
Gibraltar	1.4	2.0	2.6	2.1	2.3	2.3	2.4	2.4	80.7
Greece	1,136.4	1,158.2	1,185.9	1,213.3	1,246.8	1,283.0	1,299.2	1,305.2	116.0
Iceland	22.0	22.9	24.8	27.4	30.0	33.0	34.0	34.3	106.2
Ireland	258.7	278.7	296.7	316.1	349.9	359.4	367.7	369.8	83.1
Italy	3,976.0	4,166.0	4,250.9	4,274.1	4,579.6	4,765.9	4,834.5	4,855.1	80.8
Liechtenstein	2.7	2.6	2.6	2.6	2.5	2.5	2.5	2.5	69.9
Luxembourg	35.1	35.9	35.6	36.1	36.1	36.1	36.2	36.3	74.7
Malta	45.0	45.4	45.7	45.5	46.7	47.8	48.5	48.6	119.0
Monaco	3.0	3.1	3.2	3.2	3.3	3.4	3.4	3.4	104.5
Netherlands	996.0	1,039.0	1,069.0	1,070.0	1,063.0	1,069.4	1,072.7	1,073.4	65.4
Norway	464.8	470.3	480.1	493.9	514.5	521.9	528.9	534.2	111.3
Portugal	1,253.0	1,275.1	1,305.7	1,323.3	1,335.0	1,355.0	1,361.6	1,371.9	128.6
Spain	4,315.8	4,419.4	4,660.4	4,907.9	5,146.4	5,388.8	5,510.1	5,550.2	121.9
Sweden	423.0	435.3	453.3	474.6	493.4	503.1	511.4	512.4	55.7
Switzerland	332.5	336.0	343.0	352.9	360.5	372.2	377.0	377.4	49.9
Turkey	1,636.2	1,747.4	2,379.0	2,653.9	2,938.6	3,181.4	3,270.5	3,303.7	46.2
United Kingdom	3,501.3	3,694.2	3,819.4	3,943.2	4,144.7	4,294.8	4,358.2	4,375.4	71.0
Eastern Europe									
Albania	82.0	85.2	79.8	82.8	83.6	84.0	84.6	84.8	26.9
Belarus	122.5	131.9	134.6	141.6	147.7	150.1	152.2	151.5	15.7
Bosnia-Herzegovina	88.2	94.5	98.2	106.3	109.0	110.9	113.1	113.1	29.4
Bulgaria	293.0	297.7	303.2	307.2	312.3	314.8	317.1	318.0	42.3
Croatia	143.5	153.1	159.7	157.5	164.1	170.8	172.3	173.7	39.2
Czech Republic	344.8	360.7	391.4	435.2	488.6	517.0	545.0	545.5	52.1
Estonia	85.5	88.8	91.0	91.4	92.8	93.9	94.4	94.8	71.3
Georgia	45.5	42.9	68.6	68.6	71.8	74.4	74.0	73.8	16.8
Hungary	414.0	424.7	427.9	445.1	463.1	468.2	473.6	477.0	47.6
Latvia	113.9	115.6	118.3	123.8	131.7	140.2	143.9	144.4	64.1
Lithuania	121.4	126.5	130.5	137.8	142.5	147.7	150.0	150.5	44.9
Macedonia	50.1	50.1	50.1	50.2	50.2	50.3	50.3	50.3	24.7
Moldova	70.5	70.6	68.5	71.7	74.5	75.1	76.0	76.0	21.1
Montenegro	5.1	7.2	9.8	10.8	11.2	11.5	12.1	12.3	19.5
Poland	2,518.5	2,518.5	2,632.2	2,494.3	2,476.0	2,609.0	2,601.3	2,589.7	67.9
Romania	487.9	505.0	525.6	532.6	614.3	692.7	714.9	720.7	33.6
Russia		3,200.0	5,536.0	5,642.3	5,642.3	5,695.5	5,713.2	5,737.6	40.4
Serbia	127.6	181.6	246.4	272.2	281.6	289.5	303.8	306.7	41.6
Slovakia	168.7	166.8	162.7	183.3	198.1	208.6	223.8	225.5	41.8
Slovenia	63.1	65.1	68.7	72.1	75.9	83.8	86.4	86.4	42.7
Ukraine	500.0	703.0	985.7	1,050.0	1,108.6	1,163.5	1,187.2	1,189.7	25.9

Source: *European Automobile Manufacturers' Association (ACEA) / International Road Federation (IRF)*
Notes: *There may be wide variations from year to year in SMMT estimates and in other figures due to interpretation of definitions*

Automotives and Transport Statistics

Table 3.2

Passenger Cars in Use 1980-2009

'000

	1980	1985	1990	1995	1996	1997	1998	1999	2000	2001
Western Europe										
Austria	2,247.0	2,530.8	2,991.3	3,593.6	3,690.7	3,782.5	3,887.2	4,009.6	4,097.1	4,182.0
Belgium	3,158.7	3,278.8	3,833.3	4,239.1	4,307.7	4,373.1	4,458.0	4,547.2	4,628.9	4,684.5
Cyprus	92.0	120.0	178.6	219.7	226.8	235.0	249.2	257.0	267.6	280.1
Denmark	1,389.5	1,500.9	1,590.6	1,684.8	1,744.3	1,787.8	1,821.7	1,846.9	1,842.9	1,875.3
Finland	1,225.9	1,546.1	1,938.9	1,900.9	1,942.8	1,948.1	2,021.1	2,082.6	2,120.7	2,146.2
France	19,150.0	21,090.0	23,550.0	25,100.0	25,500.0	26,090.0	26,810.0	27,480.0	28,060.0	28,700.0
Germany			30,695.1	40,499.4	41,045.2	41,326.9	41,716.7	42,423.3	43,772.3	44,383.3
Gibraltar	6.5	10.6	19.8	18.4	19.0	19.3	20.0	22.5	25.8	27.4
Greece	879.8	1,188.0	1,735.5	2,204.8	2,339.4	2,500.1	2,675.7	2,910.0	3,150.0	3,423.7
Iceland	80.0	100.0	119.7	119.2	124.9	132.5	140.4	151.4	158.9	160.6
Ireland	734.4	709.5	796.4	990.4	1,057.4	1,134.4	1,196.9	1,269.2	1,319.3	1,384.7
Italy	17,686.2	22,494.6	27,416.0	30,301.4	30,624.3	31,106.8	31,370.8	32,038.3	32,583.8	33,239.0
Liechtenstein	12.6	14.8	16.9	18.8	19.3	19.9	20.5	21.2	21.8	22.6
Luxembourg	147.4	152.0	183.4	229.0	231.7	236.8	244.1	253.4	257.8	268.2
Malta	66.2	75.0	104.7	147.6	157.1	169.8	175.0	183.4	189.1	196.9
Monaco				20.7	20.9	20.8	21.4	22.6	22.9	23.0
Netherlands	4,515.0	4,901.0	5,196.0	5,633.0	5,740.0	5,810.0	5,931.0	6,120.0	6,343.0	6,539.0
Norway	1,233.6	1,514.0	1,613.0	1,684.7	1,661.2	1,758.0	1,786.4	1,813.6	1,851.9	1,872.9
Portugal	941.0	1,185.0	1,630.0	2,611.0	2,809.0	3,021.0	3,239.0	3,469.0	3,593.0	3,746.0
Spain	7,556.5	9,273.7	11,995.6	14,212.3	14,753.8	15,297.4	16,050.1	16,847.4	17,449.2	18,150.9
Sweden	2,883.0	3,151.2	3,601.0	3,630.8	3,654.9	3,701.2	3,790.7	3,890.2	3,998.6	4,018.5
Switzerland	2,246.8	2,617.2	2,985.4	3,229.2	3,268.1	3,323.4	3,383.3	3,467.3	3,545.2	3,629.7
Turkey	742.3	983.4	1,649.9	3,058.5	3,274.2	3,570.1	3,838.3	4,072.3	4,422.2	4,534.8
United Kingdom	15,437.7	19,458.2	21,989.0	24,428.6	25,547.6	26,318.3	27,010.4	27,010.4	27,959.7	28,640.3
Eastern Europe										
Albania			5.3	58.7	67.3	76.8	90.8	92.3	114.5	133.5
Belarus			604.5	939.6	1,035.8	1,132.8	1,279.2	1,351.0	1,385.9	1,432.2
Bosnia-Herzegovina			450.3					272.6	289.2	308.6
Bulgaria	500.0	600.0	1,276.8	1,647.6	1,645.0	1,648.0	1,703.0	1,756.2	1,809.4	1,914.0
Croatia			795.4	710.9	835.7	932.3	1,000.1	1,063.5	1,124.8	1,195.5
Czech Republic			2,520.4	3,043.3	3,192.5	3,391.5	3,493.0	3,439.7	3,438.9	3,529.8
Estonia	126.5	177.0	240.9	383.4	406.6	427.7	450.9	458.7	463.9	407.3
Georgia			485.0	360.6	323.6	265.6	260.4	247.9	247.9	248.0
Hungary	925.0	1,435.9	1,856.7	2,044.9	2,100.9	2,166.0	2,218.0	2,255.5	2,364.7	2,482.8
Latvia				331.8	379.9	431.8	482.7	525.6	556.8	586.2
Lithuania			493.0	718.5	785.1	882.1	980.9	1,089.3	1,172.4	1,133.5
Macedonia			230.8	285.9	274.7	283.2	288.9	290.0	299.0	304.0
Moldova			209.0	165.9	177.3	206.0	214.7	224.4	231.0	248.8
Montenegro										
Poland	2,269.9	3,450.0	5,261.0	7,517.0	8,054.0	8,533.0	9,033.9	9,282.8	9,991.3	10,503.1
Romania			1,292.3	2,197.5	2,326.1	2,447.1	2,594.6	2,703.1	2,777.6	2,881.2
Russia			8,986.3	14,195.3	15,815.0	17,631.6	17,758.5	17,296.8	17,050.0	19,120.1
Serbia										
Slovakia			860.0	1,015.8	1,058.4	1,135.9	1,196.1	1,236.4	1,247.0	1,290.8
Slovenia			578.3	698.2	727.6	764.8	797.9	829.7	866.1	881.5
Ukraine			3,272.0	4,468.7	4,736.0	4,801.9	4,877.8	5,210.8	5,372.0	5,463.0

Source: European Automobile Manufacturers' Association (ACEA) / International Road Federation (IRF)
Notes: There may be wide variations from year to year in SMMT estimates and in other figures due to interpretation of definitions

Automotives and Transport Statistics

Passenger Cars in Use 1980-2009 *(continued)*
'000

	2002	2003	2004	2005	2006	2007	2008	2009	Number in use /'000 persons 2009
Western Europe									
Austria	3,987.1	4,054.3	4,109.1	4,156.7	4,205.0	4,245.6	4,265.0	4,274.6	509.9
Belgium	4,724.9	4,772.6	4,818.6	4,861.4	4,929.3	5,006.3	5,028.7	5,041.1	468.9
Cyprus	287.6	302.5	335.6	355.1	372.9	389.6	397.0	400.4	459.7
Denmark	1,890.0	1,894.2	1,914.4	1,961.2	2,013.9	2,058.9	2,079.0	2,089.5	379.1
Finland	2,180.0	2,259.4	2,331.2	2,414.5	2,489.3	2,553.6	2,582.5	2,590.6	486.5
France	29,160.0	29,560.0	29,900.0	30,100.0	30,400.0	30,700.0	30,827.5	30,951.3	495.6
Germany	44,657.3	45,022.9	45,375.5	46,090.3	46,569.7	41,183.6	41,321.2	41,162.2	502.0
Gibraltar	12.9	12.8	13.9	14.6	14.7	15.0	15.2	15.1	516.7
Greece	3,477.1	3,696.9	3,960.2	4,204.5	4,446.5	4,821.4	4,918.6	4,928.9	438.0
Iceland	161.7	166.9	175.4	187.4	197.3	207.5	211.1	212.7	659.0
Ireland	1,447.9	1,507.1	1,582.8	1,662.2	1,778.9	1,882.9	1,915.0	1,927.8	433.2
Italy	33,706.2	34,310.4	33,973.1	34,667.5	35,297.3	35,680.1	35,892.5	36,099.6	601.1
Liechtenstein	23.3	23.5	23.9	24.4	24.3	24.5	24.8	24.9	696.6
Luxembourg	282.4	287.2	293.4	299.8	304.5	314.3	318.9	322.1	662.6
Malta	201.9	208.8	211.4	212.6	218.2	223.7	227.9	228.2	558.3
Monaco	22.6	22.7	22.9	23.0	23.1	23.2	23.4	23.4	710.3
Netherlands	6,710.0	6,855.0	7,151.0	7,299.0	7,413.0	7,597.0	7,644.8	7,645.9	465.9
Norway	1,899.7	1,933.6	1,977.9	2,028.8	2,084.8	2,153.7	2,183.0	2,208.3	460.1
Portugal	3,885.0	3,966.0	4,100.0	4,200.0	4,290.0	4,379.0	4,414.3	4,419.1	414.2
Spain	18,732.6	18,688.3	19,541.9	20,250.4	21,052.6	21,760.2	22,113.1	22,307.5	490.1
Sweden	4,042.8	4,075.4	4,113.4	4,153.7	4,202.5	4,258.5	4,282.6	4,297.0	467.0
Switzerland	3,701.0	3,753.9	3,811.4	3,861.4	3,900.0	3,955.8	3,979.9	3,989.6	527.7
Turkey	4,600.1	4,700.3	5,400.4	5,772.7	6,141.0	6,472.2	6,591.2	6,668.1	93.2
United Kingdom	28,484.0	29,007.8	29,378.2	29,747.5	29,880.0	30,177.9	30,318.3	30,483.7	494.8
Eastern Europe									
Albania	148.5	174.8	190.0	209.6	228.6	247.6	255.3	255.9	81.1
Belarus	1,515.9	1,620.1	1,671.3	1,737.1	1,814.8	1,844.1	1,868.0	1,861.7	192.5
Bosnia-Herzegovina	321.7	335.0	348.0	357.2	361.9	366.7	369.4	369.5	96.1
Bulgaria	1,951.0	1,990.0	2,041.0	2,063.6	2,072.4	2,109.9	2,127.8	2,144.8	285.2
Croatia	1,244.3	1,293.4	1,337.5	1,384.7	1,435.8	1,491.1	1,511.6	1,523.0	343.9
Czech Republic	3,647.1	3,706.0	3,815.5	3,958.7	4,108.6	4,280.1	4,366.7	4,369.2	417.4
Estonia	400.7	434.0	471.2	493.8	554.0	523.8	517.7	515.2	387.2
Georgia	252.0	255.2	255.2	269.7	273.9	278.3	277.1	276.9	63.1
Hungary	2,629.5	2,777.2	2,828.4	2,888.7	2,953.7	3,012.2	3,036.7	3,055.1	304.9
Latvia	619.1	648.9	686.1	742.4	822.0	908.5	945.1	948.1	420.7
Lithuania	1,180.9	1,256.9	1,315.9	1,455.3	1,529.8	1,597.6	1,635.1	1,637.6	489.1
Macedonia	308.0	300.0	312.5	299.8	303.5	305.6	303.3	303.0	148.4
Moldova	260.8	257.1	270.6	279.8	287.6	291.7	294.5	295.3	81.9
Montenegro									
Poland	11,243.8	11,243.8	11,975.2	12,339.4	13,384.2	14,588.7	14,937.2	15,049.6	394.6
Romania	2,973.4	3,087.6	3,225.4	3,363.8	3,225.4	3,518.4	3,557.5	3,579.3	167.0
Russia	21,152.0	23,383.0	24,208.0	25,569.7	25,569.7	27,092.5	27,413.0	27,557.1	194.2
Serbia	1,359.2	1,381.7	1,404.2	1,497.4	1,511.8	1,539.6	1,584.8	1,598.2	216.9
Slovakia	1,326.9	1,356.0	1,388.2	1,303.7	1,333.7	1,433.9	1,450.1	1,463.6	271.3
Slovenia	894.5	910.4	933.9	960.2	980.3	1,014.1	1,027.5	1,029.2	508.8
Ukraine	5,529.0	5,585.0	5,603.8	5,800.0	5,986.0	6,071.0	6,133.3	6,139.7	133.6

Source: *European Automobile Manufacturers' Association (ACEA) / International Road Federation (IRF)*
Notes: *There may be wide variations from year to year in SMMT estimates and in other figures due to interpretation of definitions*

Automotives and Transport Statistics

Table 3.3

Two-Wheelers in Use 1980-2009

'000

	1980	1985	1990	1995	1996	1997	1998	1999	2000	2001
Western Europe										
Austria	574.1	648.4	548.0	546.4	560.2	575.7	600.6	622.9	628.0	641.4
Belgium	445.7	466.1	481.8	548.5	559.0	571.6	588.1	607.9	626.9	639.8
Cyprus		40.0	51.0	50.4	46.9	45.2	44.3	44.8	43.3	42.0
Denmark				50.0	58.0	73.9	93.9	112.1	126.9	138.3
Finland			169.0	159.0	162.3	166.1	172.5	182.4	192.6	205.4
France				2,289.0	2,278.0	2,298.0	2,321.0	2,373.0	2,410.0	2,440.0
Germany			2,362.0	3,995.0	4,137.0	4,351.0	4,673.0	4,920.1	5,062.8	5,135.0
Gibraltar		1.6	2.8	6.6	6.6	5.9	5.9	6.9	8.5	9.6
Greece		162.3	256.6	475.7	517.9	571.0	633.8	710.8	781.4	853.4
Iceland		0.9	1.5	1.9	2.0	2.0	1.9	2.1	2.3	2.2
Ireland		26.0	22.7	23.5	23.3	24.4	24.4	26.7	30.6	32.9
Italy				7,905.8	8,344.7	8,655.6	8,812.4	9,367.9	9,773.1	9,979.9
Liechtenstein	0.6	1.3	1.3	1.7	1.9	2.0	2.2	2.4	2.6	2.8
Luxembourg		24.7	25.4	28.5	28.9	29.7	30.6	31.8	32.8	33.6
Malta				8.0	9.9	11.1	11.0	11.7	12.2	12.6
Monaco		4.0	4.7	5.3	5.4	5.6	6.0	6.3	6.6	6.8
Netherlands		728.0	612.0	848.0	878.0	898.0	931.0	964.0	970.8	964.8
Norway		186.6	203.5	197.8	200.5	216.8	228.5	239.6	249.9	261.9
Portugal	1,069.1	1,091.2	968.6	838.5	782.2	792.8	749.0	735.0	734.0	709.0
Spain		2,015.5	3,073.6	3,402.0	3,446.5	3,500.3	3,593.1	3,672.1	3,648.2	3,596.0
Sweden				258.9	271.0	280.0	287.5	300.0	317.3	340.6
Switzerland	808.8	862.1	763.9	721.6	716.5	727.8	733.9	744.4	732.6	751.4
Turkey	137.9	289.1	531.9	819.9	854.2	905.1	940.9	975.7	1,011.3	1,031.2
United Kingdom	1,457.0	1,148.0	879.8	900.2	921.1	955.8	1,015.5	1,041.1	1,157.7	1,212.0
Eastern Europe										
Albania			8.6	6.9	5.5	3.6	4.1	3.2	3.8	3.4
Belarus			404.1	504.2	533.9	553.5	558.3	533.7	523.6	536.0
Bosnia-Herzegovina										
Bulgaria			481.7	519.3	521.7	525.0	515.7	519.2	522.4	526.0
Croatia						42.2	50.5	58.1	65.3	73.8
Czech Republic			926.3	915.2	918.2	929.6	927.1	799.6	748.1	755.5
Estonia			2.7	3.3	4.7	5.3	6.1	6.7	6.7	6.8
Georgia			29.7	27.9	12.2	7.4	7.6	4.0	4.6	4.0
Hungary			92.3	85.3	85.6	86.6	87.0	87.6	91.2	93.1
Latvia				15.7	18.4	19.3	19.4	20.1	20.7	21.4
Lithuania				19.4	20.9	20.3	22.3	22.1	21.7	25.2
Macedonia			1.9	1.6	1.8	2.0	2.2	2.4	2.6	2.8
Moldova			196.4	144.7	109.8	93.8	77.7	61.6	45.5	29.5
Montenegro										
Poland		1,546.5	1,356.6	929.3	886.0	843.8	819.2	804.5	803.0	802.8
Romania		238.0	249.3	262.2	255.0	250.5	245.7	242.5	239.2	237.9
Russia						7,809.3	7,165.9	6,328.6	7,735.0	7,718.4
Serbia									13.7	13.5
Slovakia			286.3	229.1	223.7	222.8	240.6	181.7	181.1	180.2
Slovenia			50.4	45.9	46.6	47.3	48.0	48.7	49.4	50.1
Ukraine			3,253.4	3,102.6	3,000.5	2,794.8	2,609.2	2,372.0	2,251.5	1,960.3

Source: *Euromonitor International from SMMT/national statistics*
Notes: *Two-wheelers consist of motorcycles and mopeds*

Automotives and Transport Statistics

Two-Wheelers in Use 1980-2009 *(continued)*
'000

	2002	2003	2004	2005	2006	2007	2008	2009	Number in use /'000 persons 2009
Western Europe									
Austria	596.8	606.9	612.2	627.7	645.0	668.0	674.2	676.1	80.6
Belgium	651.2	665.4	670.0	672.0	678.9	683.4	685.8	687.9	64.0
Cyprus	40.3	41.5	41.4	40.4	40.4	41.2	41.6	42.0	48.2
Denmark	146.4	151.3	155.7	162.1	171.9	184.3	187.5	188.5	34.2
Finland	222.7	244.4	270.6	299.6	325.3	352.2	361.3	362.6	68.1
France	2,441.0	2,448.0	2,462.0	2,480.0	2,493.0	2,508.0	2,513.1	2,519.4	40.3
Germany	5,256.9	5,306.0	5,462.5	5,462.5	5,540.7	5,579.8	5,592.9	5,595.0	68.2
Gibraltar	5.7	5.6	6.2	6.6	7.1	7.2	7.4	7.3	250.6
Greece	910.6	969.9	1,042.6	1,124.2	1,205.8	1,298.7	1,327.1	1,330.6	118.3
Iceland	2.6	2.7	3.1	4.2	5.7	8.1	8.6	8.7	27.1
Ireland	33.1	35.1	35.8	36.5	37.1	37.5	37.6	37.8	8.5
Italy	10,149.5	10,295.4	10,224.6	10,263.4	10,311.5	10,354.9	10,369.4	10,403.1	173.2
Liechtenstein	2.9	3.0	3.0	3.1	3.2	3.3	3.3	3.4	93.6
Luxembourg	34.7	36.0	36.9	37.7	38.3	38.8	39.0	39.2	80.5
Malta	13.1	13.4	12.6	11.9	11.1	10.4	9.7	9.5	23.2
Monaco	6.9	7.0	7.2	7.3	7.5	7.6	7.7	7.7	234.4
Netherlands	1,002.5	1,015.6	1,038.9	1,112.9	1,220.0	1,310.5	1,340.7	1,341.6	81.8
Norway	277.0	292.3	302.9	313.3	318.1	323.8	326.1	330.1	68.8
Portugal	604.0	633.0	611.0	593.0	573.0	554.0	547.7	543.1	50.9
Spain	3,561.5	3,657.1	3,854.1	4,066.3	4,176.3	4,211.2	4,250.9	4,290.4	94.3
Sweden	370.8	397.1	433.7	471.9	509.4	547.2	559.8	561.9	61.1
Switzerland	745.1	762.9	770.6	770.3	783.5	789.9	792.1	794.4	105.1
Turkey	1,046.9	1,073.4	1,218.7	1,441.1	1,822.8	2,003.5	2,090.7	2,116.2	29.6
United Kingdom	1,256.4	1,314.0	1,338.3	1,367.1	1,393.7	1,421.4	1,430.7	1,439.2	23.4
Eastern Europe									
Albania	3.4	3.9	4.9	7.2	11.6	13.9	14.9	14.9	4.7
Belarus	525.0	506.4	454.6	444.5	427.9	414.5	399.5	398.4	41.2
Bosnia-Herzegovina									
Bulgaria	530.3	535.7	541.9	546.2	550.1	554.0	555.4	558.7	74.3
Croatia	85.3	99.2	113.0	127.9	143.5	153.7	158.2	159.4	36.0
Czech Republic	760.2	751.6	756.6	794.0	822.7	855.8	866.8	867.7	82.9
Estonia	7.3	8.1	9.1	10.2	12.6	14.8	15.4	15.4	11.5
Georgia	2.8	3.3	5.2	5.5	5.7	5.9	5.9	5.9	1.3
Hungary	97.6	103.5	114.0	122.7	130.2	135.9	138.3	139.0	13.9
Latvia	22.2	22.9	29.9	32.5	36.9	39.0	40.0	40.1	17.8
Lithuania	27.5	28.8	29.0	30.5	32.5	40.8	40.0	40.1	12.0
Macedonia	3.0	3.2	3.4	3.6	3.8	4.0	4.2	4.2	2.0
Moldova	13.4	14.4	15.7	16.9	18.2	19.5	19.9	19.9	5.5
Montenegro									
Poland	824.1	845.5	835.8	753.6	784.0	825.0	823.8	821.8	21.5
Romania	238.5	235.9	234.7	228.0	215.8	209.7	206.9	206.1	9.6
Russia	7,841.2	8,177.4	8,275.7	8,399.5	8,523.6	8,600.5	8,636.6	8,690.6	61.2
Serbia	13.4	13.3	14.8	16.0	20.4	22.7	25.4	25.5	3.5
Slovakia	179.5	178.5	180.1	182.5	183.1	185.5	186.1	186.7	34.6
Slovenia	50.6	42.4	40.2	48.7	53.2	57.5	59.4	59.6	29.5
Ukraine	1,744.4	1,369.0	1,145.4	982.6	885.9	821.1	785.0	779.6	17.0

Source: *Euromonitor International from SMMT/national statistics*
Notes: *Two-wheelers consist of motorcycles and mopeds*

Automotives and Transport Statistics

Table 3.4

Commercial Vehicle Production 1980-2009

'000

	1980	1985	1990	1995	1996	1997	1998	1999	2000	2001
Western Europe										
Austria	8.5	11.2	11.0	9.2	8.7	10.2	11.9	15.7	25.0	24.3
Belgium	47.0	48.7	90.0	103.6	89.9	96.3	114.0	98.9	121.1	128.6
Cyprus										
Denmark										
Finland	1.1	0.8	0.9	0.4	0.4	0.4	0.4	0.4	0.4	0.4
France	439.9	383.7	474.2	423.8	303.1	312.4	351.1	395.7	468.6	446.9
Germany	357.6	279.2	315.9	307.1	303.3	344.9	378.7	378.2	394.7	390.5
Gibraltar										
Greece			1.4	0.4	0.3	0.2	0.2	0.1	0.1	0.1
Iceland										
Ireland	2.6									
Italy	165.1	183.8	246.2	244.9	227.4	253.6	290.4	290.8	316.0	307.9
Liechtenstein										
Luxembourg										
Malta										
Monaco										
Netherlands	32.1	14.3	17.3	17.6	18.5	20.4	27.5	25.1	30.5	49.7
Norway										
Portugal	58.4	26.5	77.5	85.7	80.5	81.4	76.2	65.3	68.2	62.4
Spain	152.8	187.5	374.0	375.0	470.6	551.8	609.7	643.7	666.5	638.7
Sweden	63.1	60.3	74.4	102.5	95.4	104.0	114.5	108.6	35.7	38.1
Switzerland	1.2									
Turkey	19.4	37.3	62.8	49.0	69.0	101.6	104.6	75.8	133.5	95.3
United Kingdom	389.2	266.0	270.3	233.0	238.3	223.8	214.9	173.6	172.4	192.9
Eastern Europe										
Albania										
Belarus			43.0	13.0	10.5	13.0	12.7	13.6	14.6	16.8
Bosnia-Herzegovina										
Bulgaria			8.9	0.5	0.2	0.2	0.2	0.2	0.2	0.2
Croatia			129.0	31.0	35.7	38.7	41.7			
Czech Republic					37.6	52.0	44.3	29.3	29.8	9.5
Estonia										
Georgia										
Hungary	15.2	14.0	8.1	1.2	1.7	2.0	1.2	2.6	3.4	3.9
Latvia			17.1	4.3	1.2	1.1	1.0			
Lithuania										
Macedonia			14.6	1.8						
Moldova										
Montenegro										
Poland	116.0	57.1	42.8	10.6	72.5	62.1	68.7	73.3	42.6	11.9
Romania	49.1	19.8	17.6	21.2	24.5	20.5	23.0	18.6	14.0	12.0
Russia			716.9	214.9	188.5	209.7	204.5	236.4	244.6	229.0
Serbia										
Slovakia			0.9	0.2	0.2	0.2	0.8	0.3	0.4	359.0
Slovenia										
Ukraine		45.2	40.3	8.7	5.2	5.1	7.3	4.3	2.5	6.8

Source: European Automobile Manufacturers' Association (ACEA)

Automotives and Transport Statistics

Commercial Vehicle Production 1980-2009 *(continued)*
'000

	2002	2003	2004	2005	2006	2007	2008	2009
Western Europe								
Austria	19.9	21.0	21.5	22.7	26.9	28.1	25.4	15.1
Belgium	120.3	112.7	43.2	33.2	36.1	44.7	44.4	10.7
Cyprus								
Denmark								
Finland	0.4	0.4	0.5	0.4	0.4	0.3	0.4	0.1
France	309.1	399.7	438.6	436.0	446.0	465.0	423.0	252.0
Germany	346.1	361.2	377.9	407.5	421.1	504.3	513.7	275.3
Gibraltar								
Greece	0.1	0.1	0.1	0.1	0.1	0.1	0.1	0.1
Iceland								
Ireland								
Italy	301.3	295.2	308.4	312.8	319.1	373.5	364.6	192.5
Liechtenstein								
Luxembourg								
Malta								
Monaco								
Netherlands	48.9	52.2	59.9	65.6	72.1	76.7	73.3	31.3
Norway								
Portugal	68.3	73.8	75.9	81.5	83.8	42.2	42.9	23.0
Spain	588.3	630.5	609.7	654.3	698.8	693.9	598.6	249.3
Sweden	38.2	42.6	49.9	49.9	44.6	49.2	56.1	40.0
Switzerland								
Turkey	142.4	239.2	376.3	425.4	442.1	464.5	474.3	433.5
United Kingdom	193.1	188.9	209.3	206.8	206.3	215.7	202.9	107.8
Eastern Europe								
Albania								
Belarus	16.9	18.4	21.7	23.0	25.3	26.4	27.0	24.0
Bosnia-Herzegovina								
Bulgaria	0.2	0.2	0.2	0.2	0.2	0.2	0.2	0.2
Croatia								
Czech Republic	7.2	6.9	6.9	8.0	8.2	12.6	12.5	7.7
Estonia								
Georgia								
Hungary	3.3	3.8	4.1	3.5	3.2	4.0	3.7	2.1
Latvia								
Lithuania								
Macedonia								
Moldova								
Montenegro								
Poland	23.6	15.2	78.0	85.4	82.3	89.6	104.5	60.9
Romania	14.2	19.5	23.2	20.6	11.9	7.6	14.3	9.4
Russia	239.7	268.4	276.0	283.1	330.4	371.5	382.1	339.4
Serbia								
Slovakia	276.0	187.0	0.0	0.0	0.0	0.0	0.0	0.0
Slovenia		7.6	15.0	39.6	35.3	24.2	17.6	8.6
Ukraine	3.4	4.9	7.8	19.0	20.4	22.5	25.0	22.0

Source: *European Automobile Manufacturers' Association (ACEA)*

Automotives and Transport Statistics

Table 3.5

Passenger Car Production 1980-2009

'000

	1980	1985	1990	1995	1996	1997	1998	1999	2000	2001
Western Europe										
Austria	7.5	7.1	12.7	59.2	97.4	97.8	91.3	123.6	116.0	131.1
Belgium	281.7	248.5	311.8	385.9	367.5	355.8	950.5	917.5	912.2	1,058.7
Cyprus										
Denmark										
Finland	21.5	38.7	30.2	34.6	28.5	33.7	31.5	34.0	38.3	41.9
France	2,938.6	2,632.4	3,294.8	3,050.9	2,087.5	2,258.8	2,603.0	2,784.5	2,879.8	3,181.6
Germany	3,520.9	4,166.7	4,660.7	4,360.2	4,539.6	4,678.0	5,348.1	5,309.5	5,131.9	5,301.2
Gibraltar										
Greece			12.6	3.2	3.2	3.1	3.0	3.0	2.9	2.9
Iceland										
Ireland	44.6									
Italy	1,445.2	1,389.2	1,874.7	1,422.4	1,318.0	1,573.9	1,402.4	1,410.5	1,422.3	1,271.8
Liechtenstein										
Luxembourg										
Malta										
Monaco										
Netherlands	80.8	108.1	121.3	100.4	145.2	197.2	243.0	262.2	215.1	189.3
Norway										
Portugal	45.5	61.0	60.2	73.2	152.6	189.1	187.7	187.0	178.5	177.4
Spain	1,028.8	1,230.1	1,679.3	1,958.8	1,941.7	2,010.3	2,216.4	2,208.7	2,366.4	2,211.2
Sweden	235.3	400.7	335.9	387.7	367.8	375.7	368.3	385.0	279.0	251.0
Switzerland										
Turkey	31.5	60.4	167.6	233.4	207.8	242.8	239.9	222.0	297.5	175.3
United Kingdom	923.7	1,048.0	1,295.6	1,532.1	1,686.1	1,711.9	1,760.7	1,799.0	1,641.5	1,492.4
Eastern Europe										
Albania										
Belarus										
Bosnia-Herzegovina										
Bulgaria		15.0	14.6	1.1	1.4	1.8	2.1	1.9	1.8	1.9
Croatia					0.3	0.6	0.8			
Czech Republic	—			213.0	270.2	361.5	368.5	348.5	428.2	456.9
Estonia										
Georgia										
Hungary				36.5	51.8	63.5	65.8	68.0	77.3	140.4
Latvia										
Lithuania										
Macedonia										
Moldova										
Montenegro										
Poland	364.5	283.0	266.4	391.9	433.6	520.2	640.0	572.9	532.0	336.0
Romania	79.3	114.4	99.9	71.0	97.9	109.2	103.9	88.3	64.2	56.8
Russia	1,166.0	1,165.0	1,103.0	893.6	874.2	985.1	860.7	955.5	969.2	1,021.7
Serbia										9.3
Slovakia				22.3	24.4	26.4	125.1	126.5	181.3	181.6
Slovenia			74.7	63.5	72.3	74.8	111.5	118.1	122.9	116.1
Ukraine		167.5	103.4	58.7	46.9	32.0	25.7	17.8	11.7	25.0

Source: *European Automobile Manufacturers' Association (ACEA)*

Automotives and Transport Statistics

Passenger Car Production 1980-2009 *(continued)*
'000

	2002	2003	2004	2005	2006	2007	2008	2009
Western Europe								
Austria	132.8	118.7	227.2	230.5	248.1	200.0	125.4	47.2
Belgium	936.9	791.7	852.4	895.1	881.9	789.7	680.1	390.4
Cyprus								
Denmark								
Finland	41.1	19.2	10.1	21.2	32.4	24.0	18.0	11.0
France	3,292.8	3,220.3	3,227.4	3,113.0	2,723.2	2,550.9	2,145.0	1,559.4
Germany	5,123.2	5,145.4	5,192.1	5,350.2	5,398.5	5,709.1	5,526.9	4,587.3
Gibraltar								
Greece	2.8	2.6	2.4	2.3	2.2	2.1	2.1	1.8
Iceland								
Ireland								
Italy	1,125.8	1,026.5	833.6	725.5	892.5	910.9	659.2	590.7
Liechtenstein								
Luxembourg								
Malta								
Monaco								
Netherlands	182.4	163.1	187.6	115.1	87.3	61.9	59.2	55.6
Norway								
Portugal	182.6	165.6	150.8	137.6	143.5	134.0	132.2	96.4
Spain	2,266.9	2,399.4	2,402.5	2,098.2	2,078.6	2,195.8	1,943.0	1,601.1
Sweden	238.0	280.4	290.4	288.7	288.6	316.9	252.3	102.7
Switzerland								
Turkey	204.2	294.1	447.2	453.7	545.7	634.9	655.7	599.3
United Kingdom	1,629.9	1,657.6	1,647.2	1,596.3	1,442.1	1,534.6	1,446.6	850.6
Eastern Europe								
Albania								
Belarus								
Bosnia-Herzegovina								
Bulgaria	2.0	2.1	2.2	2.3	2.3	2.3	2.4	2.0
Croatia								
Czech Republic	441.3	436.3	443.1	596.8	848.8	925.1	933.3	895.0
Estonia								
Georgia								
Hungary	138.2	122.3	118.6	148.5	187.6	288.0	342.4	180.4
Latvia								
Lithuania								
Macedonia								
Moldova								
Montenegro								
Poland	287.5	306.8	523.0	540.0	632.3	695.0	840.0	761.0
Romania	65.3	75.7	99.0	174.5	201.7	234.1	231.1	251.6
Russia	980.1	1,010.4	1,110.1	1,068.1	1,177.9	1,288.7	1,308.5	1,150.6
Serbia	12.8	16.2	16.5	15.7	11.0	9.3	6.9	3.9
Slovakia	225.4	281.2	223.5	218.3	295.4	571.1	575.8	496.9
Slovenia	126.7	110.6	116.6	138.4	115.0	174.2	180.2	186.9
Ukraine	50.4	103.0	179.1	196.7	274.9	380.1	413.6	360.7

Source: *European Automobile Manufacturers' Association (ACEA)*

Automotives and Transport Statistics   **Table 3.6**

Two-Wheeler Production 1985-2009
'000

	1985	1990	1995	2000	2004	2005	2006	2007	2008	2009
Western Europe										
Austria	160.8	20.9	13.2	29.2	56.7	60.0	69.0	73.4	75.3	35.9
Belgium	58.3	61.3	8.2	6.4	4.9	4.6	4.4	4.2	3.9	2.4
Cyprus										
Denmark										
Finland	14.8	5.2	0.3	0.2	0.1	0.1	0.1	0.2	0.2	0.1
France			394.6	451.4	255.7	259.2	232.4	258.3	258.6	215.5
Germany	85.8	55.3	44.6	112.6	102.8	101.0	106.3	111.6	112.6	95.0
Gibraltar										
Greece										
Iceland										
Ireland										
Italy	808.3	894.9	1,101.1	1,048.2	685.5	695.0	708.6	720.1	723.9	738.5
Liechtenstein										
Luxembourg										
Malta										
Monaco										
Netherlands				9.3	8.0	8.0	8.0	8.0	8.0	8.7
Norway										
Portugal					0.0	0.1	0.1	0.1	0.1	0.1
Spain	173.5	384.6	279.9	284.8	230.9	249.5	253.7	265.1	268.9	234.7
Sweden		1.3	0.1	0.1	0.3	0.4	0.5	0.6	0.7	0.4
Switzerland	11.7	0.8								
Turkey				217.2	229.5	236.7	243.7	245.3	247.0	223.5
United Kingdom	2.0	1.9	11.2	25.6	26.2	34.6	42.1	50.0	52.7	34.0
Eastern Europe										
Albania										
Belarus				36.6	38.7	38.9	39.2	39.5	39.6	34.8
Bosnia-Herzegovina										
Bulgaria										
Croatia										
Czech Republic				3.9	1.8	1.6	1.0	0.9	0.8	0.6
Estonia										
Georgia										
Hungary				0.3	0.2	0.2	0.2	0.2	0.2	0.1
Latvia										
Lithuania				0.0	0.0	0.0	0.0	0.0	0.0	0.0
Macedonia										
Moldova										
Montenegro										
Poland				0.0	0.0	0.0	0.0	0.0	0.0	0.0
Romania	2.0	4.1	0.1	0.2	0.3	0.3	0.3	0.3	0.3	0.3
Russia	818.0			32.8	25.3	25.1	24.9	24.7	24.5	21.5
Serbia										
Slovakia			17.2							
Slovenia		57.5	56.2	59.9	60.8	59.5	58.2	56.9	56.0	39.9
Ukraine				0.2	0.2	0.2	0.2	0.2	0.2	0.2

Source: *Euromonitor International from SMMT/national statistics*

Automotives and Transport Statistics

Table 3.7

Automotive Diesel Price 1980-2009

Units of national currency per 10 litres (inc. tax)

	1980	1985	1990	1995	1996	1997	1998	1999	2000	2001
Western Europe										
Austria	6.21	7.81	5.98	6.25	6.67	6.88	6.31	6.36	7.78	7.48
Belgium	3.46	4.51	5.28	6.07	6.53	6.68	6.21	6.40	8.10	7.81
Cyprus										
Denmark	20.00	28.14	22.79	43.82	48.03	51.83	51.58	56.15	70.91	69.49
Finland	3.29	4.70	5.19	5.91	6.30	6.39	6.38	6.82	8.50	8.19
France		5.82	4.94	5.87	6.53	6.76	6.43	6.88	8.45	7.99
Germany			4.89	5.73	6.22	6.34	5.82	6.38	8.01	8.22
Gibraltar										
Greece	0.43	1.04	1.94	4.10	4.61	4.76	4.44	5.03	6.65	6.34
Iceland										
Ireland	3.20	7.06	6.95	6.79	7.36	7.36	7.05	7.00	8.42	8.20
Italy	2.33	4.16	6.39	6.93	7.39	7.43	7.10	7.62	8.92	8.69
Liechtenstein										
Luxembourg	3.01	4.97	3.11	4.96	5.36	5.53	5.11	5.43	6.89	6.56
Malta										
Monaco										
Netherlands	4.38	5.70	4.74	7.02	7.67	6.82	6.53	6.97	8.45	8.20
Norway	18.42	23.50	27.46	67.58	75.60	78.11	78.13	83.17	98.98	86.45
Portugal	0.82	3.29	4.96	5.22	5.60	5.74	5.64	5.49	6.54	6.69
Spain	3.51	4.51	4.81	4.93	5.43	5.60	5.30	5.65	6.95	6.93
Sweden	14.65	30.73	49.22	63.46	65.89	66.75	63.02	66.52	84.46	86.48
Switzerland	12.72	14.18	11.23	11.94	12.36	12.88	12.12	12.35	14.36	14.00
Turkey				0.19	0.40	0.79	1.19	2.37	4.35	7.33
United Kingdom	2.78	3.65	3.98	5.43	5.77	6.25	6.55	7.25	8.13	7.79
Eastern Europe										
Albania										
Belarus										
Bosnia-Herzegovina										
Bulgaria										
Croatia										
Czech Republic		55.00	98.00	156.50	166.60	187.60	180.30	189.80	247.00	241.10
Estonia										
Georgia										
Hungary	65.50	93.00	300.00	834.10	1,073.60	1,277.00	1,387.60	1,663.00	2,150.80	2,086.31
Latvia										
Lithuania										
Macedonia										
Moldova										
Montenegro										
Poland				10.01	11.90	13.98	14.61	18.35	25.55	25.52
Romania				0.42	0.59	2.25	3.19	5.32	8.48	13.22
Russia							23.21	34.98	57.83	74.11
Serbia										
Slovakia			4.29	4.54	5.11	6.73	6.54	6.12	7.47	7.07
Slovenia										
Ukraine										

Source: *Institute of Petroleum, OECD Energy Prices and Taxes/Euromonitor International*

Automotives and Transport Statistics

Automotive Diesel Price 1980-2009 *(continued)*
Units of national currency per 10 litres (inc. tax)

	2002	2003	2004	2005	2006	2007	2008	2009	US$ per litre 2009
Western Europe									
Austria	7.19	7.27	8.09	9.48	10.09	10.35	12.38	9.73	1.35
Belgium	7.26	7.56	8.81	10.40	10.79	10.94	12.52	10.21	1.42
Cyprus			7.22	8.24	8.84	9.00	10.85	8.34	1.16
Denmark	67.93	67.85	68.21	76.62	81.80	82.58	95.05	78.22	1.46
Finland	7.84	8.08	8.48	9.69	10.22	10.18	12.64	9.92	1.38
France	7.71	7.93	8.83	10.23	10.79	10.92	12.70	10.02	1.39
Germany	8.40	8.87	9.38	10.68	11.17	11.68	13.33	10.90	1.51
Gibraltar									
Greece	6.22	6.37	7.40	8.79	9.54	9.84	12.06	9.61	1.34
Iceland									
Ireland	7.74	8.04	8.82	10.36	10.95	10.80	12.72	10.19	1.42
Italy	8.56	8.77	9.38	11.08	11.65	11.62	13.42	10.81	1.50
Liechtenstein									
Luxembourg	6.32	6.38	6.90	8.43	9.17	9.35	11.64	8.45	1.17
Malta			7.17	8.78	9.83	9.48	11.19	9.61	1.34
Monaco									
Netherlands	7.90	7.95	8.89	10.23	10.87	10.98	12.87	9.96	1.38
Norway	81.98	83.88	86.80	98.30	106.48	103.46	122.75	107.20	1.70
Portugal	6.45	7.10	7.87	9.37	10.61	10.81	12.62	10.03	1.39
Spain	6.89	6.94	7.55	8.93	9.47	9.57	11.30	9.10	1.26
Sweden	83.38	81.14	85.47	103.53	111.33	109.60	133.87	115.34	1.51
Switzerland	13.35	13.58	14.46	16.38	17.40	17.68	20.25	15.97	1.47
Turkey	10.96	13.94	15.39	19.56	22.24	23.02	28.73	25.94	1.67
United Kingdom	7.55	7.79	8.19	9.09	9.52	9.69	11.75	10.39	1.62
Eastern Europe									
Albania									
Belarus									
Bosnia-Herzegovina									
Bulgaria							21.19	16.32	1.16
Croatia									
Czech Republic	217.30	218.95	248.68	278.73	289.58	287.15	317.50	262.22	1.38
Estonia			107.97	130.93	135.82	135.66	179.24	141.73	1.26
Georgia									
Hungary	2,013.35	2,098.85	2,185.63	2,500.93	2,709.10	2,630.44	3,081.01	2,690.80	1.33
Latvia		4.50	5.60	6.03	6.08	6.30	7.68	6.48	1.28
Lithuania			24.60	28.44	30.65	30.30	37.70	30.68	1.24
Macedonia									
Moldova									
Montenegro									
Poland	25.80	28.36	31.69	36.82	38.18	37.66	42.19	36.42	1.17
Romania	15.90	18.87	24.67	30.32	32.85	31.53	40.30	35.90	1.18
Russia	90.62	107.13	123.64	140.16	167.83	172.54	226.59	187.70	0.59
Serbia									
Slovakia	6.59	7.21	8.44	9.76	10.68	12.54	13.82	11.07	1.54
Slovenia					9.62	9.73	11.28	10.09	1.40
Ukraine									

Source: *Institute of Petroleum, OECD Energy Prices and Taxes/Euromonitor International*

Automotives and Transport Statistics

Table 3.8

Leaded/Lead Replacement Petrol Price 1980-2009

Units of national currency per 10 litres (inc. tax)

	1980	1985	1990	1995	1996	1997	1998	1999	2000	2001
Western Europe										
Austria	6.30	8.65	7.12	8.57	8.52	8.56	8.06	8.14	8.30	8.50
Belgium	5.73	8.38	7.18	8.41	9.24	9.94	9.44	9.68	11.02	10.75
Cyprus										
Denmark	45.30	61.35	62.82	60.89						
Finland	4.85	6.50	8.57							
France	5.15	8.52	7.71	8.94	9.45	9.80	9.58	10.01	11.67	11.22
Germany	5.96	7.37	6.25	8.65	9.00	9.32	9.75	10.05	10.43	10.82
Gibraltar										
Greece	1.02	2.01	3.37	5.99	6.44	6.69	6.49	6.69	8.11	7.89
Iceland										
Ireland	4.06	8.43	8.18	7.69	8.16	8.48	8.77	8.91	10.37	10.95
Italy	3.62	6.82	7.61	9.46	9.74	9.91	9.61	10.30	11.27	10.91
Liechtenstein										
Luxembourg	4.42	6.76	5.38	6.95	7.23	7.56	7.16	7.33	7.52	7.73
Malta										
Monaco										
Netherlands	6.51	8.77	7.76	9.35	9.71	9.51	9.20	9.57	10.03	9.89
Norway	37.15	51.28	65.44	87.74	90.58	93.32	96.85	96.85	111.76	101.95
Portugal	2.17	5.44	6.82	7.77	8.07	8.38	8.38	8.38	8.61	8.99
Spain	3.25	5.59	4.97	6.78	7.06	7.24	7.02	7.37	8.75	8.64
Sweden	29.47	46.63	64.66	78.88	81.89	85.79	84.28	87.11	98.13	99.18
Switzerland	11.60	12.60	10.80	12.30	12.57	13.22	12.60	12.93	13.09	13.23
Turkey				0.29	0.56	1.17	1.95	3.65	5.82	9.93
United Kingdom	3.29	4.31	4.86	5.97	6.16	6.72	7.11	7.72	8.49	7.97
Eastern Europe										
Albania										
Belarus										
Bosnia-Herzegovina										
Bulgaria										
Croatia	45.00									
Czech Republic	65.00	80.00	123.80	200.80	209.10	225.80	227.60	239.80	296.30	301.00
Estonia										
Georgia										
Hungary	110.00	200.00	500.00	1,010.00						
Latvia										
Lithuania										
Macedonia										
Moldova										
Montenegro										
Poland			2.78	12.25	14.45	16.94	18.53	23.34	31.48	43.20
Romania				0.59	0.87	2.76	4.17	8.15	11.41	15.22
Russia										
Serbia										
Slovakia			4.50	4.90	5.20	5.80	5.40	5.80	7.80	7.30
Slovenia										
Ukraine	806.20									

Source: *Institute of Petroleum, OECD Energy Prices and Taxes/Euromonitor International*

Automotives and Transport Statistics

Leaded/Lead Replacement Petrol Price 1980-2009 *(continued)*
Units of national currency per 10 litres (inc. tax)

	2002	2003	2004	2005	2006	2007	2008	2009	US$ per litre 2009
Western Europe									
Austria	8.71	8.76	9.07	9.93	10.44	10.12	10.92	8.61	1.20
Belgium	10.48	10.14	9.99	11.00	11.78	11.88	13.60	10.56	1.47
Cyprus									
Denmark									
Finland									
France	10.95	10.97	11.43	12.69	13.57	13.76	14.66	12.49	1.74
Germany	11.45	11.83	12.38	13.20	13.81	14.07	14.72	12.44	1.73
Gibraltar									
Greece	7.84	7.89	8.69	9.44	10.36	10.76	11.83	10.72	1.49
Iceland									
Ireland	11.75	12.60	13.42	13.97	14.40	13.97	15.33	11.78	1.64
Italy	11.53	11.67	12.07	12.98	13.55	13.20	14.02	11.67	1.62
Liechtenstein									
Luxembourg	7.88	8.15	8.39	9.34	10.00	10.12	10.64	9.24	1.28
Malta			9.41	9.91	11.63	10.95	11.92	11.37	1.58
Monaco									
Netherlands	9.69	10.02	11.03	13.30	14.96	15.53	16.28	13.90	1.93
Norway	95.70	99.83	106.70	114.02	120.01	122.50	130.48	124.43	1.98
Portugal	9.55	9.97	10.92	12.05	13.80	13.91	14.68	13.13	1.82
Spain	8.71	8.86	9.39	10.39	11.13	10.90	11.67	9.74	1.35
Sweden	106.45	112.23	119.18	126.30	129.50	127.20	138.03	122.19	1.60
Switzerland	13.37	13.48	13.65	14.46	15.44	15.50	16.43	12.46	1.15
Turkey	14.79	18.10	19.66	25.20	27.45	28.49	31.79	31.07	2.00
United Kingdom	7.70	7.99	8.45	9.10	9.40	9.38	10.66	8.99	1.40
Eastern Europe									
Albania									
Belarus									
Bosnia-Herzegovina									
Bulgaria									
Croatia									
Czech Republic	307.84	312.26	317.31	338.72	343.38	333.06	346.67	274.18	1.44
Estonia									
Georgia									
Hungary									
Latvia			4.85	5.81	6.36	6.48	7.30	6.61	1.31
Lithuania									
Macedonia									
Moldova									
Montenegro									
Poland	45.00	48.00	52.00	55.55	55.41	58.60	59.82	52.58	1.68
Romania	20.70	25.15	28.36	32.70	34.50	37.08	41.61	28.03	0.92
Russia									
Serbia									
Slovakia	7.00	7.60	8.80	9.68	10.62	12.62	12.85	10.15	1.41
Slovenia									
Ukraine									

Source: *Institute of Petroleum, OECD Energy Prices and Taxes/Euromonitor International*

Automotives and Transport Statistics

Table 3.9

Premium Unleaded Petrol Price 1980-2009

Units of national currency per 10 litres (inc. tax)

	1980	1985	1990	1995	1996	1997	1998	1999	2000	2001
Western Europe										
Austria			6.84	8.21	8.31	8.61	8.12	8.14	9.42	9.04
Belgium			6.74	7.78	8.72	9.42	9.02	9.16	11.08	10.81
Cyprus				5.50	5.50	5.75	5.77	6.05	6.46	6.65
Denmark				60.58	64.48	66.64	64.28	72.10	83.59	82.06
Finland	6.60	6.68	6.48	8.38	9.39	9.41	9.49	10.16	11.58	11.31
France			7.53	8.62	9.16	9.51	9.28	9.63	11.12	10.58
Germany			5.77	7.93	8.27	8.54	8.14	8.74	10.15	10.24
Gibraltar										
Greece			3.18	5.59	6.00	6.26	6.05	6.22	7.69	7.54
Iceland										
Ireland			7.70	7.10	7.40	7.70	7.50	7.50	8.90	8.89
Italy			7.62	8.89	9.24	9.44	9.10	9.60	10.81	10.53
Liechtenstein										
Luxembourg			5.14	6.15	6.43	6.73	6.34	6.92	8.28	7.95
Malta										
Monaco										
Netherlands		8.49	7.43	8.85	9.26	9.88	9.84	10.30	12.08	12.02
Norway			59.44	81.08	84.05	87.93	87.22	92.37	105.66	95.85
Portugal			6.53	7.82	8.12	8.43	8.43	8.38	9.02	9.52
Spain				6.42	6.67	6.99	6.65	7.00	8.19	8.07
Sweden			64.70	75.04	78.48	82.15	80.53	83.35	95.12	94.50
Switzerland			10.20	11.83	12.00	12.51	11.93	12.29	14.48	14.14
Turkey			0.02	0.29	0.56	1.16	1.92	3.63	5.83	9.92
United Kingdom			4.20	5.86	6.37	7.13	7.78	8.29	8.73	8.28
Eastern Europe										
Albania										
Belarus										
Bosnia-Herzegovina										
Bulgaria										
Croatia	43.00									
Czech Republic			124.00	192.90	204.20	220.10	219.00	231.20	287.10	273.30
Estonia										
Georgia										
Hungary				971.30	1,197.90	1,421.90	1,548.00	1,855.40	2,324.10	2,252.50
Latvia										
Lithuania										
Macedonia										
Moldova										
Montenegro										
Poland				11.75	13.95	16.60	18.36	23.30	31.37	31.52
Romania				0.59	0.87	2.66	4.05	8.14	11.21	15.17
Russia						21.53	24.23	50.70	73.93	62.50
Serbia										
Slovakia			5.42	5.01	5.36	5.81	5.53	6.14	7.89	7.32
Slovenia										
Ukraine										

Source: *Institute of Petroleum, OECD Energy Prices and Taxes/Euromonitor International*

Automotives and Transport Statistics

Premium Unleaded Petrol Price 1980-2009 *(continued)*
Units of national currency per 10 litres (inc. tax)

	2002	2003	2004	2005	2006	2007	2008	2009	US$ per litre 2009
Western Europe									
Austria	8.74	8.80	9.50	10.30	10.91	11.21	12.09	10.45	1.45
Belgium	10.53	10.20	11.40	12.80	13.53	13.84	14.56	13.16	1.83
Cyprus	6.95	6.07	7.86	8.47	9.19	9.46	10.26	8.80	1.22
Denmark	83.82	82.15	83.94	90.29	95.84	97.43	102.65	95.31	1.78
Finland	11.00	10.90	11.40	12.10	12.88	12.98	14.23	12.84	1.78
France	10.37	10.20	10.60	11.60	12.37	12.73	13.56	12.07	1.68
Germany	10.48	10.92	11.40	12.20	12.89	13.41	14.03	12.95	1.80
Gibraltar									
Greece	7.35	7.40	8.12	8.82	9.68	10.13	11.10	10.04	1.39
Iceland									
Ireland	8.55	8.71	9.50	10.50	11.17	11.16	12.25	11.00	1.53
Italy	10.48	10.59	11.30	12.20	12.86	12.98	13.79	12.32	1.71
Liechtenstein									
Luxembourg	7.73	7.78	9.00	10.20	10.82	11.22	12.35	10.35	1.44
Malta			8.71	9.46	11.05	10.40	11.32	11.22	1.56
Monaco									
Netherlands	12.10	11.59	12.53	13.52	14.15	14.59	15.37	13.43	1.87
Norway	92.70	93.73	99.85	108.16	114.57	116.83	125.28	118.80	1.89
Portugal	9.20	9.65	10.33	11.47	13.10	13.22	13.88	12.35	1.72
Spain	8.14	8.17	8.70	9.50	10.21	10.35	11.08	10.02	1.39
Sweden	96.83	94.03	99.64	109.55	114.55	116.10	125.98	121.96	1.59
Switzerland	13.55	13.12	14.01	15.27	16.43	16.84	17.85	15.07	1.39
Turkey	14.76	18.04	19.59	25.35	27.77	28.79	32.09	31.22	2.01
United Kingdom	7.98	7.60	8.02	8.67	9.12	9.43	10.71	9.93	1.55
Eastern Europe									
Albania									
Belarus									
Bosnia-Herzegovina									
Bulgaria							19.82	17.20	1.22
Croatia									
Czech Republic	245.89	248.05	266.80	284.80	295.99	295.04	303.33	272.61	1.43
Estonia			113.20	124.60	135.46	137.46	163.02	143.98	1.28
Georgia									
Hungary	2,228.60	2,327.90	2,396.20	2,601.00	2,771.57	2,761.57	2,925.78	2,844.90	1.41
Latvia			4.74	5.70	6.11	6.38	7.19	6.75	1.34
Lithuania			26.90	28.60	31.12	31.06	35.51	35.22	1.42
Macedonia									
Moldova									
Montenegro									
Poland	31.92	33.53	37.36	39.91	39.81	42.10	42.98	41.22	1.32
Romania	20.22	24.29	27.20	32.40	33.48	32.95	37.23	36.56	1.20
Russia	70.06	87.71	121.03	152.84	177.22	189.57	223.32	203.50	0.64
Serbia									
Slovakia	7.04	7.57	8.78	9.66	10.61	12.62	12.86	11.18	1.55
Slovenia			8.91	9.52	9.95	10.30	10.68	10.49	1.46
Ukraine									

Source: *Institute of Petroleum, OECD Energy Prices and Taxes/Euromonitor International*

Table 3.10

Commercial Vehicle New Registrations 1980-2009

'000

	1980	1985	1990	1995	1996	1997	1998	1999	2000	2001
Western Europe										
Austria	21.8	22.3	30.9	29.2	29.9	31.5	34.6	35.6	38.0	34.0
Belgium	32.5	31.9	49.5	45.8	48.2	57.1	63.4	72.7	68.7	73.1
Cyprus		5.4	10.6	9.2	9.5	6.1	7.2	6.5	6.2	7.8
Denmark	19.4	38.5	23.3	30.7	32.1	35.5	35.1	38.0	37.0	36.2
Finland	17.9	18.7	32.2	10.6	13.1	16.5	19.5	19.9	18.7	18.1
France	323.3	342.2	447.0	357.8	378.0	355.2	398.6	433.5	477.2	496.3
Germany	175.5	134.6	203.4	260.5	249.2	263.9	295.9	324.9	314.8	296.6
Gibraltar		0.1	0.3	0.2	0.3	0.2	0.2	0.2	0.3	0.2
Greece		19.0	44.6	11.6	13.4	15.8	17.7	23.8	25.0	22.8
Iceland		0.8	2.0	0.8	0.9	1.2	1.4	1.7	2.0	1.2
Ireland	12.2	16.2	28.4	16.4	19.3	23.1	31.4	30.1	33.6	30.6
Italy	122.3	100.7	159.5	148.1	152.9	157.6	180.0	196.3	226.4	220.2
Liechtenstein					0.2	0.2	0.2	0.2	0.2	0.2
Luxembourg		3.4	6.1	2.9	2.7	2.9	3.6	4.4	4.7	5.2
Malta		0.6	1.4			4.2	2.7	2.3	2.0	1.8
Monaco										
Netherlands	48.0	63.1	69.0	65.1	84.1	96.4	114.8	116.7	114.4	101.5
Norway	15.1	42.5	23.0	38.0	36.8	37.1	36.3	33.0	35.7	37.5
Portugal	47.0	23.1	75.8	63.0	77.2	108.8	126.2	134.8	161.0	112.9
Spain	104.5	122.0	267.7	191.4	209.6	252.2	288.8	344.7	336.8	325.6
Sweden	19.7	22.9	33.1	14.8	21.2	25.8	31.6	35.2	39.3	36.1
Switzerland	22.4	20.5	28.9	20.1	20.5	21.6	23.7	25.6	29.1	31.2
Turkey			62.1	54.7	76.2	133.9	138.1	141.2	144.3	60.7
United Kingdom	272.0	286.7	293.5	249.9	256.9	274.2	294.5	288.1	298.0	313.4
Eastern Europe										
Albania										
Belarus			12.9	5.3	6.3	7.2	8.1	7.7	8.1	7.9
Bosnia-Herzegovina										
Bulgaria			14.6	10.7	9.7	4.2	9.4	6.4	4.2	2.3
Croatia			3.0	17.0	15.3	16.9	8.4	6.4	7.2	10.4
Czech Republic						46.1	66.9	29.4	33.9	23.5
Estonia			1.3	0.7	1.1	2.2	2.2	1.5	1.8	2.2
Georgia										
Hungary		27.0	23.4	31.2	26.4	23.2	28.3	31.2	32.7	29.8
Latvia				4.1	3.9	6.4	6.6	7.5	6.0	4.3
Lithuania										1.5
Macedonia			1.8	0.9						
Moldova								4.2	4.7	5.0
Montenegro										
Poland		39.0	65.2	56.3	64.2	55.2	51.1	50.8	41.3	29.4
Romania			9.0	37.9	21.4	20.9	27.1	21.3	17.9	19.4
Russia						505.0	365.5	294.2	262.7	265.3
Serbia										
Slovakia										
Slovenia			2.9	6.2	6.0	5.8	6.0	6.9	5.1	5.7
Ukraine										

Source: *European Automobile Manufacturers' Association (ACEA) / International Road Federation (IRF)*

Automotives and Transport Statistics

Commercial Vehicle New Registrations 1980-2009 *(continued)*
'000

	2002	2003	2004	2005	2006	2007	2008	2009
Western Europe								
Austria	31.3	35.6	40.9	39.0	38.8	41.5	42.3	30.4
Belgium	60.2	62.2	70.0	74.9	72.1	78.7	78.0	60.4
Cyprus	9.5	9.2	3.8	5.1	6.1	6.5	6.8	6.6
Denmark	36.2	36.7	50.0	62.4	69.5	63.5	41.0	18.7
Finland	19.4	18.8	22.1	20.0	20.9	22.2	21.3	12.4
France	460.9	431.4	459.9	480.1	498.4	519.5	523.4	404.6
Germany	270.6	264.7	283.4	272.8	304.4	334.1	335.0	239.5
Gibraltar	0.2	0.3	1.2	0.6	0.3	0.6	0.4	0.4
Greece	20.3	20.7	27.2	25.5	26.4	27.0	25.1	15.7
Iceland	0.9	1.4	2.0	2.8	3.1	3.4	1.6	0.3
Ireland	28.4	30.5	31.2	38.4	43.6	49.8	34.1	10.5
Italy	320.2	242.3	255.1	251.4	272.0	293.0	269.6	199.0
Liechtenstein	0.2	0.2	0.2	0.2	0.2	0.2	0.2	0.2
Luxembourg	5.0	4.8	3.9	4.6	4.7	5.3	6.0	4.1
Malta	0.4	0.6	0.4	0.7	0.6	0.9	1.1	1.1
Monaco								
Netherlands	95.5	91.0	109.4	80.8	84.7	97.3	104.2	64.1
Norway	28.5	31.3	38.4	42.7	49.2	53.0	42.6	27.9
Portugal	84.7	73.4	76.6	75.1	70.5	74.8	61.7	42.0
Spain	305.9	250.2	275.3	329.2	351.1	324.5	201.4	115.6
Sweden	35.7	36.0	39.5	44.6	48.3	51.9	47.5	33.3
Switzerland	26.6	23.7	25.3	25.6	28.9	30.7	32.8	28.6
Turkey	80.3	164.6	285.2	310.2	313.7	274.0	270.3	259.1
United Kingdom	322.3	363.7	389.9	386.0	389.5	400.7	357.2	223.6
Eastern Europe								
Albania								
Belarus	7.9	7.3	7.2	7.5	7.5	7.6	7.7	7.8
Bosnia-Herzegovina								
Bulgaria	4.3	4.9	6.5	9.0	10.0	11.8	12.8	3.7
Croatia	13.3	9.1	8.2	9.1	10.3	11.2	12.7	13.6
Czech Republic	21.7	25.7	35.5	48.5	60.7	74.6	71.8	25.3
Estonia	2.5	6.3	6.2	7.9	8.2	6.6	4.1	1.2
Georgia								
Hungary	35.1	31.1	30.1	26.5	21.6	21.9	21.6	10.1
Latvia	3.2	2.0	2.5	3.0	4.9	6.7	4.0	0.7
Lithuania	1.7	2.8	4.1	5.5	6.7	9.2	6.7	1.3
Macedonia								
Moldova	4.3		12.5					
Montenegro								
Poland	20.2	40.1	50.0	36.2	41.0	78.0	80.9	51.2
Romania	23.2	28.5	35.8	40.9	40.8	45.0	45.7	16.4
Russia	247.3	273.0	281.0	286.3	331.1	374.1	384.4	378.4
Serbia								
Slovakia	8.2	12.7	13.3	18.1	24.4	29.4	32.3	17.1
Slovenia	6.0	6.4	7.7	8.0	10.4	10.7	11.4	5.9
Ukraine								

Source: *European Automobile Manufacturers' Association (ACEA) / International Road Federation (IRF)*

Automotives and Transport Statistics

Table 3.11

Diesel Car New Registrations 1985-2009
'000

	1985	1990	1995	2000	2004	2005	2006	2007	2008	2009	Diesel car registrations as % of all passenger car registrations 2009
Western Europe											
Austria	32.2	66.3	119.1	182.8	220.3	199.9	191.8	175.9	160.4	161.1	50.8
Belgium	95.0	155.4	168.0	290.3	339.3	348.6	392.3	404.1	423.4	380.8	81.2
Cyprus							1.1				
Denmark	10.4	3.6	3.9	14.9	29.2	34.9	40.2	61.2	68.9	59.7	56.1
Finland	14.4	7.2	5.5	26.3	22.1	25.1	29.5	35.6	69.2	57.4	64.3
France	264.8	762.1	897.7	1,046.5	1,392.9	1,429.0	1,427.7	1,525.7	1,584.9	1,770.4	80.3
Germany	530.7	337.6	483.5	1,026.0	1,437.3	1,425.6	1,535.9	1,504.8	1,362.7	1,705.2	44.0
Gibraltar											
Greece				2.0	8.4	4.0	5.9	8.1	9.6	9.3	4.3
Iceland	0.4		0.5	2.3	1.6	3.6	4.3	4.8	3.0	0.7	36.8
Ireland	8.6	12.2	13.1	23.4	29.5	38.0	49.0	50.5	50.8	20.7	36.2
Italy	438.7	171.0	178.8	805.2	1,318.2	1,300.8	1,350.9	1,391.2	1,096.0	1,003.4	47.1
Liechtenstein							0.6	0.7			
Luxembourg	3.5	6.4	8.0	21.1	35.0	36.6	39.3	39.6	40.3	30.1	76.8
Malta											
Monaco											
Netherlands	71.3	54.8	61.8	134.4	118.8	123.9	130.0	143.1	125.5	93.3	24.2
Norway	1.7	2.2	5.5	8.8	32.5	43.1	52.8	96.1	80.1	80.3	84.3
Portugal	2.3	10.3	21.3	62.4	111.7	127.8	126.4	139.9	146.0	111.8	70.1
Spain	125.2	136.2	274.2	735.4	1,068.9	1,036.8	1,022.3	1,144.9	804.7	668.2	72.7
Sweden	5.7	1.4	4.7	18.2	21.1	26.6	55.8	106.5	91.9	94.5	45.4
Switzerland	9.3	9.0	10.7	29.0	69.3	72.2	80.1	91.7	93.2	88.6	33.7
Turkey											
United Kingdom	66.2	128.6	405.1	313.2	835.3	897.9	898.5	967.0	929.5	898.5	46.2
Eastern Europe											
Albania											
Belarus											
Bosnia-Herzegovina											
Bulgaria											
Croatia											
Czech Republic						35.3	34.9	34.6	34.9	35.4	22.4
Estonia											
Georgia											
Hungary											
Latvia			4.2	22.0	32.7	34.7	35.7	36.3	34.3	7.4	200.0
Lithuania											
Macedonia											
Moldova											
Montenegro											
Poland							86.3				
Romania						61.2	103.2				
Russia											
Serbia											
Slovakia											
Slovenia											
Ukraine											

Source: *European Automobile Manufacturers' Association (ACEA) / International Road Federation (IRF)*

Automotives and Transport Statistics

Table 3.12

Passenger Cars New Registrations 1985-2009
'000

	1985	1990	1995	2000	2004	2005	2006	2007	2008	2009
Western Europe										
Austria	242.7	288.6	279.6	309.4	311.3	307.9	308.5	298.2	293.7	316.9
Belgium	378.2	473.5	358.9	515.2	484.8	480.1	526.1	524.8	535.9	468.8
Cyprus	12.2	19.5	13.1	19.9	43.8	38.7	37.2	36.1	35.4	34.3
Denmark	157.5	80.9	135.7	113.6	122.5	148.6	156.7	162.7	150.0	106.4
Finland	139.0	139.1	79.9	134.8	142.6	148.2	145.7	125.6	139.6	89.3
France	1,766.3	2,309.1	1,930.5	2,133.9	2,013.7	2,067.8	2,000.5	2,064.5	2,050.3	2,205.6
Germany	2,379.3	3,040.8	3,314.1	3,378.3	3,266.8	3,342.1	3,468.0	3,148.2	3,090.0	3,875.0
Gibraltar	2.0	2.1	1.7	1.7	1.4	1.2	1.3	1.3	1.3	1.4
Greece	109.4	132.5	125.4	290.2	289.8	269.7	267.7	279.8	267.2	217.3
Iceland	5.7	6.8	6.4	13.6	12.0	18.1	17.2	15.9	9.0	1.9
Ireland	60.4	81.2	86.9	225.3	149.6	166.3	173.3	186.5	151.6	57.2
Italy	1,745.9	2,348.2	1,720.0	2,412.0	2,272.4	2,244.4	2,329.9	2,493.1	2,160.1	2,129.7
Liechtenstein			1.7	1.8	1.8	1.9	1.9	2.0	2.0	2.1
Luxembourg	26.9	34.6	28.0	41.9	48.2	48.5	50.8	51.3	52.4	39.2
Malta	4.1	8.9		11.3	6.2	6.6	6.7	7.0	7.3	7.0
Monaco										
Netherlands	495.7	502.7	446.4	597.6	483.9	465.2	484.0	505.5	500.0	385.2
Norway	159.1	61.9	90.5	97.4	115.6	109.9	109.2	129.2	110.6	95.2
Portugal	104.2	212.7	229.9	257.8	197.6	206.5	194.7	201.8	213.4	159.4
Spain	575.1	1,007.0	870.5	1,381.4	1,616.2	1,649.3	1,634.6	1,614.8	1,161.2	919.3
Sweden	263.0	229.9	169.8	354.6	311.5	311.8	313.8	306.8	254.0	208.1
Switzerland	265.5	323.0	268.0	314.5	267.5	257.5	267.5	284.7	287.5	263.1
Turkey	63.9	267.8	196.9	256.9	451.3	406.8	396.5	353.5	320.9	310.7
United Kingdom	1,832.0	2,008.9	1,945.4	2,221.6	2,567.3	2,439.7	2,344.9	2,404.0	2,131.8	1,943.1
Eastern Europe										
Albania										
Belarus		45.3	82.4	65.2	86.8	84.8	83.8	83.1	81.6	82.1
Bosnia-Herzegovina										
Bulgaria	48.0	33.4	74.4	63.5	54.0	26.0	36.7	43.5	45.1	27.0
Croatia		66.2	67.6	92.4	69.6	70.5	78.8	86.2	99.0	106.1
Czech Republic				148.7	133.0	127.4	124.0	132.5	143.7	158.2
Estonia			3.1	10.2	16.5	19.6	21.3	30.9	24.3	8.2
Georgia										
Hungary	101.3	83.9	127.8	149.1	255.8	239.7	203.1	171.7	155.9	76.9
Latvia			49.3	35.7	11.3	16.7	25.6	32.5	19.2	3.7
Lithuania					9.4	10.7	14.6	21.0	21.5	6.7
Macedonia		13.8	9.0							
Moldova				12.1	32.3					
Montenegro										
Poland	259.9	358.1	311.1	478.7	318.1	235.5	238.8	292.4	320.0	321.6
Romania		82.0	87.1	66.3	145.1	215.5	256.4	312.5	285.5	112.1
Russia				821.3	1,453.3	1,578.1	2,080.9	2,570.8	2,694.9	2,735.1
Serbia										
Slovakia					57.4	56.9	59.1	59.7	70.0	77.5
Slovenia		69.3	63.5	63.5	78.8	79.4	81.5	65.5	68.5	54.7
Ukraine										

Source: *European Automobile Manufacturers' Association (ACEA) / International Road Federation (IRF)*

Automotives and Transport Statistics

Table 3.13

Two-Wheelers New Registrations 1985-2009

'000

	1985	1990	1995	2000	2004	2005	2006	2007	2008	2009
Western Europe										
Austria	49.2	20.1	29.4	45.1	39.0	45.0	47.0	53.0	51.0	58.4
Belgium	47.1	54.5	42.1	58.5	59.2	61.4	63.6	70.7	69.1	62.3
Cyprus	4.3	8.3	5.7	5.4	4.7	4.5	4.7	5.5	5.5	5.4
Denmark	2.6	1.7	2.3	13.1	7.8	10.7	12.3	14.3	13.8	10.5
Finland			95.4	11.6	25.6	30.1	36.8	42.3	41.6	28.6
France			302.4	371.8	349.8	351.5	371.8	381.6	385.2	416.6
Germany	214.7	171.2	342.7	361.3	254.8	266.0	275.7	286.2	285.9	383.7
Gibraltar	0.2	0.6	0.7	1.1	0.7	0.8	0.9	1.0	1.2	1.3
Greece	14.6	41.5	40.7	73.7	78.6	89.4	91.7	110.2	109.4	96.2
Iceland		0.1	0.1	0.2	0.4	0.4	0.5	0.5	0.5	0.1
Ireland	4.1	3.1	2.3	6.9	3.8	3.2	3.2	3.5	3.7	1.5
Italy			655.3	836.5	553.9	548.8	554.8	557.3	557.7	571.2
Liechtenstein			0.1	0.2	0.2	0.3	0.3	0.3	0.3	0.3
Luxembourg	0.5		1.3	1.7	1.9	2.0	2.2	2.3	2.4	1.9
Malta				0.5	0.4	0.3	0.4	0.5	0.5	0.5
Monaco			1.1							
Netherlands	47.7	74.4	77.0	86.6	56.7	57.7	63.6	67.0	68.1	53.5
Norway	23.6	8.8	10.1	17.3	18.9	19.2	19.5	19.8	20.1	17.5
Portugal	1.4	7.3	54.1	32.7	11.6	11.2	13.4	14.3	13.9	10.1
Spain			189.9	320.7	241.3	321.2	390.8	465.6	466.1	443.6
Sweden	11.3	7.6	10.1	28.4	53.7	40.7	42.0	46.4	45.6	42.1
Switzerland	34.2	31.1	27.1	50.8	47.9	45.2	45.7	47.9	46.6	41.5
Turkey		65.2	35.7	35.7	145.3	222.4	234.3	240.3	236.4	228.9
United Kingdom	123.6	94.4	68.9	170.1	133.9	132.8	133.1	133.5	128.2	120.1
Eastern Europe										
Albania			13.9							
Belarus		5.3	9.9	5.1	3.3	3.3	3.1	3.1	3.0	3.3
Bosnia-Herzegovina										
Bulgaria	16.0	6.0	2.8	3.5	4.0	4.1	4.3	4.4	3.4	1.5
Croatia		9.5	8.6	9.0	16.0	14.3	14.2	15.7	18.0	19.3
Czech Republic				3.9	14.1	15.6	14.5	14.1	13.7	13.5
Estonia		0.3	0.2	0.2	1.1	1.5	2.5	3.7	3.1	1.1
Georgia										
Hungary				1.3	16.2	12.5	10.7	9.4	8.6	4.3
Latvia				0.5	1.0	1.1	1.2	1.2	1.3	0.3
Lithuania				0.4	1.0	1.6	1.7	1.8	2.0	0.5
Macedonia		0.2	0.1							
Moldova										
Montenegro										
Poland	50.0	31.4	5.3	7.2	10.8	11.7	11.0	12.3	12.0	10.7
Romania		5.0	2.0	0.1	0.1	0.1	0.2	0.2	0.2	0.1
Russia				5,745.3	3,274.0	2,994.4	2,628.8	2,335.2	2,005.5	1,974.4
Serbia										
Slovakia				1.1	4.0	4.8	5.7	6.2	6.7	7.4
Slovenia		0.8	0.7	1.2	7.4	9.5	9.8	10.7	11.0	9.9
Ukraine		2.0	2.1	0.5						

Source: *Euromonitor International from SMMT/national statistics*

Automotives and Transport Statistics

Table 3.14

Airline Freight 1980-2009

Million tonne-kilometres

	1980	1985	1990	1995	1996	1997	1998	1999	2000	2001
Western Europe										
Austria	21.7	35.3	62.2	147.7	192.1	236.3	265.5	340.8	422.4	373.8
Belgium	436.1	574.7	700.9	546.6	590.9	677.6	473.0	535.4	1,041.7	870.8
Cyprus	24.4	24.3	30.1	38.8	35.4	35.7	38.2	40.7	46.0	42.9
Denmark	159.7	154.5	147.7	144.7	169.6	213.0	199.0	196.1	215.8	201.2
Finland				224.9	248.2	312.6	306.6	303.5	300.5	190.0
France	2,287.2	3,258.5	4,300.5	4,567.9	4,811.3	5,081.9	4,554.6	4,726.6	5,428.0	5,029.6
Germany	1,974.5	2,920.3	4,781.9	6,006.0	6,136.6	6,309.8	6,212.4	6,598.8	7,281.4	7,205.7
Gibraltar										
Greece	58.1	67.5	88.0	115.3	118.7	129.1	112.6	103.4	149.8	116.7
Iceland		58.6	67.8	95.7	104.0	109.3	106.1	108.9	104.8	105.7
Ireland	93.9	98.7	111.1	95.7	102.1	122.1	129.6	138.0	174.5	165.7
Italy	484.0	692.6	1,091.1	1,334.6	1,459.1	1,443.3	1,475.9	1,614.6	1,773.2	1,555.7
Liechtenstein										
Luxembourg						2,260.2	2,245.5	2,506.1	3,523.3	3,768.4
Malta	3.5	2.5	3.5	8.5	9.7	9.0	11.2	10.5	15.7	15.1
Monaco										
Netherlands	1,109.7	1,769.7	2,434.6	3,852.4	3,926.0	3,970.8	3,755.0	3,967.6	4,521.2	4,303.4
Norway	168.8	160.5	152.7	148.1	169.6	216.7	203.4	200.6	224.6	207.2
Portugal	124.8	127.8	163.1	206.9	210.9	248.5	247.5	225.1	242.9	227.8
Spain	470.7	601.4	851.9	675.4	759.8	742.4	766.9	815.9	923.2	924.4
Sweden	252.7	245.5	232.4	209.3	249.6	293.6	294.2	291.0	308.9	283.1
Switzerland	427.9	670.1	875.5	1,562.1	1,511.3	1,829.7	1,963.4	1,877.3	2,033.8	1,698.9
Turkey			73.3	177.3	207.3	255.4	246.6	312.9	393.6	358.4
United Kingdom	2,664.3	3,519.4	4,711.9	7,214.1	7,618.1	6,450.6	4,663.5	4,925.2	5,340.1	4,650.4
Eastern Europe										
Albania										
Belarus						2.6	3.5	1.8	1.9	1.7
Bosnia-Herzegovina									0.6	0.6
Bulgaria				24.4	23.9	31.6	30.4	12.4	6.7	2.7
Croatia				1.8	2.3	2.0	2.0	2.0	3.4	3.6
Czech Republic				26.8	22.2	23.1	24.7	26.2	35.0	29.1
Estonia				0.7	1.6	5.5	3.2	4.1	2.1	3.1
Georgia					1.8	1.1	2.0	2.9	2.5	2.5
Hungary	8.5	9.3	6.3	19.2	29.3	34.9	37.0	39.9	55.1	35.8
Latvia				0.7	1.1	1.1	0.9	0.4	1.5	0.9
Lithuania				1.7	1.8	2.8	2.6	1.8	2.0	2.1
Macedonia					0.7	0.8	1.0	1.5	1.6	0.7
Moldova									0.9	0.3
Montenegro										
Poland	20.8	10.5	57.0	68.9	70.0	92.0	91.8	80.3	82.9	74.2
Romania	7.4	7.0	9.0	18.9	15.7	13.4	12.1	11.3	13.4	11.0
Russia				1,604.0	899.2	833.7	736.5	592.7	1,082.1	943.2
Serbia										4.2
Slovakia				0.1	0.2	0.2	0.2	0.2	0.5	0.7
Slovenia				4.1	3.6	3.6	3.4	3.7	3.9	4.1
Ukraine				24.7	16.5	11.8	27.4	13.2	13.0	12.9

Source: *Euromonitor International from International Civil Aviation Authority/national statistics*

Automotives and Transport Statistics

Airline Freight 1980-2009 *(continued)*

Million tonne-kilometres

	2002	2003	2004	2005	2006	2007	2008	2009
Western Europe								
Austria	424.1	467.2	539.8	580.3	621.6	483.9	448.7	357.4
Belgium	655.6	604.6	717.1	710.0	745.2	987.3	839.0	817.6
Cyprus	44.1	47.7	52.5	52.1	51.3	52.6	50.7	44.9
Denmark	199.4	184.6	189.0	14.8	11.3	9.7	7.9	4.2
Finland	237.2	276.2	343.3	371.4	425.0	507.6	562.5	477.8
France	5,229.8	5,262.2	5,776.7	5,995.9	6,296.0	6,555.9	6,136.7	4,903.8
Germany	7,391.9	7,503.8	8,288.2	7,949.5	8,520.3	8,798.6	8,442.2	6,693.1
Gibraltar								
Greece	91.8	70.4	67.3	74.3	82.2	81.4	85.4	54.0
Iceland	96.7	79.8	122.3	125.9	143.3	86.2	100.3	90.7
Ireland	122.3	127.5	130.2	113.5	130.5	125.3	134.6	128.7
Italy	1,440.2	1,413.6	1,438.1	1,411.1	1,458.1	1,588.9	1,422.3	1,400.3
Liechtenstein								
Luxembourg	4,157.7	4,347.9	4,670.3	5,149.8	5,270.4	5,512.4	5,852.7	5,561.5
Malta	13.2	13.3	12.5	11.9	12.4	12.7	13.0	12.8
Monaco								
Netherlands	4,388.4	4,526.8	4,978.6	5,089.1	5,122.7	5,169.6	5,061.3	4,284.0
Norway	205.1	195.1	197.9	195.2	171.4	174.5	177.7	96.5
Portugal	212.7	224.2	262.2	261.2	320.8	351.6	375.8	381.9
Spain	856.2	918.8	1,092.6	1,078.0	1,158.3	1,267.5	1,196.9	922.5
Sweden	283.9	271.1	276.8	274.7	240.5	221.8	228.9	109.6
Switzerland	1,088.9	1,305.2	1,152.2	1,161.5	1,085.8	1,172.6	1,198.7	999.0
Turkey	396.8	390.0	383.3	394.5	474.9	466.1	502.0	485.6
United Kingdom	4,997.1	5,214.0	5,779.2	6,088.7	6,314.6	6,266.0	6,397.8	5,726.0
Eastern Europe								
Albania								
Belarus	1.4	1.3	1.3	1.3	1.4	1.4	1.4	1.4
Bosnia-Herzegovina	0.6	0.6						
Bulgaria	0.1	1.0	3.5	4.1	4.2	3.7	2.8	2.0
Croatia	3.4	3.2	2.9	2.9	2.7	2.9	3.0	2.6
Czech Republic	31.5	40.5	45.2	44.2	45.1	38.4	32.0	27.4
Estonia	1.8	2.0	1.8	1.8	1.5	1.4	1.3	1.4
Georgia	5.2	5.4	2.9	2.9	2.9	3.1	3.3	3.2
Hungary	28.7	33.1	28.1	25.5	28.1	30.8	21.6	20.8
Latvia	1.2	0.9	1.5	3.0	14.4	15.3	18.8	18.7
Lithuania	2.0	1.8	1.9	2.1	2.1	1.9	0.9	0.9
Macedonia	0.2	0.2	0.1	0.1	0.1	0.1	0.1	0.1
Moldova	0.4	0.8	0.9	0.9	1.2	1.2	1.1	0.8
Montenegro			0.1	0.1	0.2	0.2	0.2	0.2
Poland	73.5	78.5	86.3	82.2	92.1	95.4	90.6	60.6
Romania	10.1	7.8	5.6	5.9	5.8	6.5	7.4	4.3
Russia	1,089.9	1,167.3	1,482.7	1,597.3	1,986.8	2,297.1	1,783.9	1,411.0
Serbia	4.8	4.7	6.5	4.9	4.2	4.0	3.6	2.1
Slovakia	0.9	0.9	0.7	0.5	11.5	34.1	0.2	0.2
Slovenia	4.5	3.6	3.2	2.6	2.3	3.7	1.9	1.6
Ukraine	12.8	20.4	27.2	42.6	47.7	20.0	70.4	51.7

Source: *Euromonitor International from International Civil Aviation Authority/national statistics*

Automotives and Transport Statistics

Table 3.15

Airline Passengers 1980-2009

Million passenger-kilometres

	1980	1985	1990	1995	1996	1997	1998	1999	2000	2001
Western Europe										
Austria	1,953.8	2,500.6	4,172.4	6,858.1	8,791.0	10,066.0	13,908.0	15,324.0	14,232.4	13,875.4
Belgium	4,966.2	5,818.6	6,960.3	7,716.9	9,011.0	11,277.0	15,338.0	17,953.1	19,378.7	15,319.8
Cyprus	660.5	1,089.3	1,606.9	2,713.6	2,561.0	2,657.0	2,711.0	2,941.7	2,785.1	3,011.9
Denmark	2,963.5	2,975.1	4,173.1	4,950.8	5,466.0	5,669.0	5,658.0	5,872.6	6,128.0	6,952.0
Finland	2,019.1	2,728.9	4,716.4	6,852.8	8,731.0	9,575.0	10,716.0	7,800.0	7,634.9	8,194.8
France	34,099.2	40,015.4	53,600.3	69,913.5	81,594.0	84,675.0	90,903.0	97,884.8	113,438.1	113,278.7
Germany	25,150.8	30,761.8	46,018.6	72,105.8	77,765.0	86,189.0	90,393.0	97,153.0	112,795.0	111,302.8
Gibraltar										
Greece	4,792.3	5,878.4	7,478.6	7,864.9	8,533.0	9,261.0	8,556.0	9,960.0	9,841.2	9,800.9
Iceland	2,292.1	2,761.5	1,876.7	2,643.0	2,872.0	3,216.0	3,774.0	3,944.6	3,937.2	3,713.7
Ireland	2,550.3	2,522.8	4,938.7	5,652.1	6,732.0	8,964.0	10,401.0	11,315.3	13,664.3	13,917.3
Italy	11,891.8	14,099.1	22,209.8	32,796.5	36,157.0	38,180.0	38,122.0	40,913.8	44,389.3	40,950.0
Liechtenstein										
Luxembourg		101.9	130.3	340.8	421.0	281.0	454.0	521.3	557.3	586.0
Malta	565.9	542.8	709.3	1,559.1	1,663.0	1,681.0	1,888.0	2,028.8	2,383.8	2,359.2
Monaco					1.0	1.0	1.0	1.0	2.5	2.3
Netherlands	23,490.6	28,498.5	43,401.4	57,333.8	62,397.0	66,666.0	69,084.0	70,236.0	74,425.9	69,317.1
Norway	4,261.8	4,078.7	6,440.6	8,348.1	8,688.0	9,158.0	9,480.0	9,945.5	10,366.7	10,460.9
Portugal	4,919.9	5,311.1	7,863.8	8,238.7	8,423.0	10,466.0	12,120.0	12,072.0	11,216.5	11,182.4
Spain	20,358.2	23,416.0	30,641.9	24,168.0	25,812.0	28,140.0	32,472.0	44,100.0	52,427.3	55,323.7
Sweden	4,368.5	5,137.0	7,006.3	8,580.0	8,424.0	8,748.0	9,852.0	10,140.0	11,192.2	11,277.4
Switzerland	10,390.8	13,157.5	17,420.6	20,813.8	21,324.0	25,404.0	28,032.0	31,920.0	36,624.8	33,469.6
Turkey			5,097.8	10,276.6	10,947.0	12,379.0	13,032.0	13,356.0	17,282.1	16,057.6
United Kingdom	83,589.4	80,111.0	133,847.8	161,337.0	167,577.0	157,895.0	182,352.0	192,420.0	170,686.7	159,020.8
Eastern Europe										
Albania					9.0	35.0	86.3	95.9	101.3	92.6
Belarus						399.0	397.0	282.8	316.5	339.2
Bosnia-Herzegovina									48.1	44.3
Bulgaria			1,349.9	2,084.4	1,812.0	1,796.0	2,026.0	2,311.9	834.5	361.7
Croatia				486.0	486.0	469.0	624.0	643.0	643.8	735.9
Czech Republic				2,188.6	2,368.0	2,442.0	3,168.0	3,444.0	3,313.1	3,575.7
Estonia				138.0	158.0	209.0	227.3	297.6	235.0	246.8
Georgia				301.9	288.0	206.0	340.0	376.2	230.1	234.9
Hungary	1,027.3	1,284.1	1,475.6	1,768.8	2,077.0	2,346.0	2,510.0	2,662.0	3,572.6	2,951.9
Latvia				131.1	260.0	217.0	174.0	164.5	236.4	180.4
Lithuania				202.9	304.0	301.0	307.0	324.0	321.6	347.0
Macedonia									740.3	377.4
Moldova									125.0	146.1
Montenegro										65.5
Poland	2,259.5	1,732.7	3,014.6	3,599.9	3,917.0	4,204.0	4,255.0	4,568.8	4,757.5	4,914.6
Romania	772.0	898.4	1,077.8	1,692.0	1,823.0	1,702.0	1,709.0	1,795.7	2,097.9	1,854.2
Russia				60,482.2	52,713.0	49,278.0	50,304.0	47,684.0	42,950.3	48,320.8
Serbia										831.8
Slovakia				68.6	84.0	72.0	84.0	72.0	107.8	84.8
Slovenia				325.6	380.0	375.0	408.0	516.0	562.5	656.7
Ukraine				2,029.8	1,792.0	1,853.0	2,064.0	1,560.0	1,387.4	1,418.2

Source: Euromonitor International from International Civil Aviation Authority/national statistics

Automotives and Transport Statistics

Airline Passengers 1980-2009 *(continued)*

Million passenger-kilometres

	2002	2003	2004	2005	2006	2007	2008	2009
Western Europe								
Austria	13,794.3	14,558.4	17,529.5	18,835.3	19,921.3	17,407.9	16,460.1	14,623.6
Belgium	2,606.1	3,958.3	4,737.9	4,918.3	5,311.8	7,858.9	8,346.5	8,045.8
Cyprus	3,436.3	3,934.5	4,229.6	4,183.9	4,293.1	4,478.3	4,478.3	4,079.3
Denmark	7,453.0	7,201.6	8,101.5	7,832.5	7,943.2	7,816.7	7,705.9	6,890.1
Finland	8,807.2	9,055.9	11,142.5	11,899.7	13,417.6	16,416.2	17,909.8	16,661.2
France	117,273.4	115,571.1	123,984.0	135,016.8	144,096.0	151,011.6	143,990.6	139,284.6
Germany	124,245.6	149,671.8	170,628.0	182,507.6	204,117.8	214,654.7	173,841.2	168,302.6
Gibraltar								
Greece	8,586.7	7,353.6	9,166.2	9,410.5	9,225.3	9,646.6	8,816.9	7,039.7
Iceland	3,187.6	2,997.5	3,634.9	4,307.7	4,253.4	4,280.1	3,752.6	3,411.4
Ireland	18,575.2	27,440.9	34,597.0	44,791.9	54,272.0	67,667.3	72,695.6	69,974.2
Italy	34,327.6	41,176.9	43,237.0	51,127.4	50,039.5	50,486.2	51,649.9	50,808.6
Liechtenstein								
Luxembourg	436.8	548.5	572.6	565.7	610.9	665.9	680.6	653.6
Malta	2,305.5	2,174.0	2,281.8	2,292.2	2,475.5	2,698.3	2,829.4	2,761.0
Monaco	6.9	6.0	3.8	4.9	4.9	5.1	5.3	5.1
Netherlands	69,492.9	69,236.4	76,310.7	82,268.9	86,833.4	90,914.5	94,619.6	90,130.4
Norway	10,546.3	10,506.4	10,321.1	10,309.7	10,437.5	10,401.0	10,930.1	9,201.4
Portugal	12,109.1	13,562.3	16,092.9	16,833.6	19,010.1	21,381.3	23,178.1	23,392.5
Spain	54,044.3	57,594.3	64,140.6	70,975.5	77,100.4	88,404.4	86,820.4	74,372.9
Sweden	11,662.5	11,411.1	11,976.2	12,330.2	11,939.8	13,273.7	13,794.2	11,986.9
Switzerland	26,712.0	23,294.8	20,602.2	20,476.5	22,139.8	25,150.1	26,165.5	25,390.6
Turkey	16,931.9	16,451.0	20,499.8	24,297.4	27,889.6	33,689.5	35,844.3	34,565.6
United Kingdom	156,594.4	164,208.4	182,736.1	200,332.8	213,335.5	227,501.7	232,601.8	226,169.4
Eastern Europe								
Albania	95.9	121.1	135.6	149.1	161.1	175.6	188.9	181.1
Belarus	308.1	337.8	398.8	383.3	414.0	451.2	479.6	459.4
Bosnia-Herzegovina	43.4	47.3						
Bulgaria	56.7	457.3	747.1	1,122.6	1,345.6	1,442.5	1,622.9	1,261.4
Croatia	783.3	869.2	940.5	973.5	1,004.5	1,084.0	1,216.5	1,227.5
Czech Republic	3,855.1	4,938.0	5,988.0	6,605.4	6,651.8	6,310.9	6,298.9	6,265.5
Estonia	282.6	415.3	547.3	660.1	682.1	754.2	754.2	762.2
Georgia	521.1	634.5	472.7	520.0	505.3	612.1	606.5	596.4
Hungary	3,076.1	3,316.3	3,509.7	3,806.4	4,139.9	4,435.3	4,575.2	4,442.0
Latvia	183.8	244.8	581.2	1,161.2	1,510.3	1,501.1	1,492.0	1,482.8
Lithuania	355.1	394.8	556.8	700.3	622.7	576.9	939.2	909.7
Macedonia	235.6	280.2	275.6	248.7	268.6	253.1	246.4	239.0
Moldova	161.1	222.8	257.3	325.0	363.2	434.3	530.8	493.7
Montenegro	111.4	157.2	190.8	210.6	246.8	283.1	298.8	289.8
Poland	5,111.4	5,433.8	5,860.7	6,222.9	6,719.7	7,288.0	5,946.0	5,504.8
Romania	1,593.0	1,696.1	1,532.2	1,967.1	2,430.3	3,695.2	3,983.2	3,901.6
Russia	49,889.9	53,893.9	62,010.1	63,192.3	69,499.3	82,331.6	89,614.1	76,926.8
Serbia	1,080.9	1,041.5	1,095.0	958.6	1,088.0	1,136.7	1,136.7	851.5
Slovakia	93.8	220.4	847.9	949.4	2,289.9	2,202.4	2,760.0	2,683.9
Slovenia	675.1	700.3	711.0	706.8	772.9	863.3	1,007.2	904.6
Ukraine	1,578.1	2,580.3	3,826.1	4,086.9	4,928.8	2,622.7	6,605.4	5,196.5

Source: *Euromonitor International from International Civil Aviation Authority/national statistics*

Automotives and Transport Statistics

Table 3.16

Scheduled Flights: Distance Flown 1980-2009
Million kilometres

	1980	1985	1990	1995	1996	1997	1998	1999	2000	2001
Western Europe										
Austria	44.1	50.2	69.8	101.5	110.5	118.0	125.5	133.6	139.1	134.2
Belgium	71.8	65.6	91.4	141.9	152.5	159.2	197.4	209.7	215.7	186.2
Cyprus	6.6	8.2	9.6	16.8	18.9	19.5	19.8	21.2	20.9	22.0
Denmark	41.2	42.3	63.4	78.2	79.3	84.5	85.6	85.5	85.4	91.7
Finland	33.1	38.8	58.1	70.6	82.2	92.0	94.8	100.7	101.6	95.2
France	345.3	335.4	431.2	597.9	608.8	680.5	742.5	842.7	961.0	902.0
Germany	228.7	266.2	419.0	619.6	652.7	703.6	735.6	781.3	839.5	860.8
Gibraltar										
Greece	40.5	46.4	52.5	62.5	65.8	68.4	68.3	70.5	89.9	95.3
Iceland	17.9	20.2	19.0	25.3	26.2	27.8	32.7	34.0	34.0	31.7
Ireland	31.8	27.4	55.5	55.6	59.2	69.9	78.5	83.5	106.0	118.6
Italy	160.8	159.9	211.6	298.9	299.6	338.3	343.7	358.5	392.1	392.6
Liechtenstein										
Luxembourg									60.7	66.3
Malta	3.8	3.5	5.8	14.5	20.4	20.0	20.1	22.5	26.0	25.3
Monaco					0.4	0.4	0.4	0.4	0.6	0.5
Netherlands	139.2	158.3	210.9	351.1	386.3	370.6	397.5	420.5	463.9	434.2
Norway	64.2	64.3	89.3	115.3	121.2	129.8	134.0	139.8	148.9	148.8
Portugal	49.3	46.8	65.8	85.7	96.4	105.7	107.2	112.3	104.8	111.9
Spain	193.0	187.3	224.5	279.8	285.3	304.9	331.1	343.0	418.3	459.6
Sweden	63.0	72.9	105.4	115.3	119.8	131.8	143.1	153.1	166.8	166.9
Switzerland	113.1	124.8	161.7	210.1	211.4	230.2	263.5	275.8	317.0	303.6
Turkey	25.2	27.9	44.4	96.8	100.9	113.4	123.4	135.5	148.1	143.0
United Kingdom	575.4	535.9	672.1	917.7	940.8	917.8	939.7	1,013.2	1,016.2	1,052.7
Eastern Europe										
Albania					0.4	1.1	1.6	2.1	2.6	2.1
Belarus						8.5	8.6	5.4	7.1	7.3
Bosnia-Herzegovina									1.5	1.5
Bulgaria	10.7	22.0	27.3	22.0	21.4	20.4	22.2	23.6	13.9	6.3
Croatia				6.5	9.0	9.5	10.1	10.2	10.3	10.9
Czech Republic				29.1	28.2	29.6	32.2	32.3	39.4	42.1
Estonia				3.9	3.9	4.9	6.1	6.7	6.2	6.1
Georgia				4.4	4.5	3.1	5.4	6.2	3.7	3.8
Hungary	16.9	18.7	21.6	27.4	30.0	32.5	35.2	37.1	42.1	38.1
Latvia				8.5	9.1	6.4	6.3	9.4	6.7	5.7
Lithuania				5.7	8.1	8.9	10.1	11.4	9.9	10.2
Macedonia									9.6	5.3
Moldova									4.1	4.6
Montenegro										1.3
Poland	34.6	22.8	37.8	38.4	40.1	45.1	44.5	46.8	55.4	70.2
Romania	12.7	12.2	14.1	18.7	23.5	26.1	21.6	22.3	30.1	25.6
Russia				777.3	723.8	608.6	578.8	523.3	533.7	568.2
Serbia										11.5
Slovakia				2.4	2.1	2.3	3.3	3.5	2.0	1.6
Slovenia				6.5	6.8	6.8	7.8	9.1	9.8	11.1
Ukraine				53.8	36.2	36.4	35.8	24.0	31.5	30.3

Source: *Euromonitor International from International Civil Aviation Authority/national statistics*

Automotives and Transport Statistics

Scheduled Flights: Distance Flown 1980-2009 *(continued)*
Million kilometres

	2002	2003	2004	2005	2006	2007	2008	2009
Western Europe								
Austria	129.9	130.3	148.7	158.9	170.0	159.8	151.0	134.4
Belgium	114.6	103.0	125.3	124.1	131.6	162.6	174.2	167.9
Cyprus	25.0	29.5	32.4	31.7	32.0	34.2	34.0	31.2
Denmark	80.9	78.3	85.4	83.3	84.1	81.8	81.5	73.0
Finland	90.9	96.9	107.8	108.6	118.7	139.7	151.8	140.3
France	880.4	856.5	911.3	925.1	960.1	1,001.6	965.0	924.4
Germany	927.3	1,069.3	1,198.4	1,285.2	1,397.1	1,484.0	1,188.1	1,136.6
Gibraltar								
Greece	81.7	75.8	95.7	88.0	88.9	92.6	84.0	67.0
Iceland	26.5	25.1	29.2	32.2	33.8	37.2	32.2	29.0
Ireland	138.1	196.9	235.7	292.3	349.6	442.0	475.5	462.8
Italy	350.7	404.3	406.6	448.0	427.9	440.7	453.0	444.4
Liechtenstein								
Luxembourg	70.3	73.7	78.3	90.7	93.5	97.3	98.9	94.0
Malta	22.5	22.2	22.5	23.8	25.2	27.5	28.6	27.9
Monaco	0.7	0.7	0.6	0.6	0.7	0.8	0.8	0.8
Netherlands	433.3	438.1	469.8	481.3	502.6	520.8	547.2	518.3
Norway	129.4	127.4	128.0	127.7	125.7	123.5	129.5	108.8
Portugal	116.8	128.4	148.8	158.1	171.3	198.6	215.4	218.4
Spain	442.3	473.4	520.3	561.1	575.1	638.5	625.5	541.7
Sweden	129.6	125.3	133.1	133.3	137.3	141.3	146.8	129.1
Switzerland	256.1	217.7	171.9	165.7	164.5	180.5	188.2	181.6
Turkey	140.5	141.5	161.2	186.4	227.1	263.2	278.5	267.5
United Kingdom	1,048.0	1,086.7	1,204.7	1,324.2	1,399.8	1,472.0	1,498.4	1,469.1
Eastern Europe								
Albania	2.0	2.5	2.7	2.9	3.1	3.3	3.6	3.4
Belarus	6.5	6.7	7.1	6.3	6.7	7.3	7.8	7.5
Bosnia-Herzegovina	1.4	1.5						
Bulgaria	1.4	7.3	10.7	14.0	18.9	18.3	20.6	15.9
Croatia	11.4	11.7	12.2	13.5	13.3	13.4	15.2	15.3
Czech Republic	44.4	53.0	66.5	75.3	73.9	73.1	72.6	73.1
Estonia	5.9	6.9	8.1	9.2	9.1	9.5	9.5	9.7
Georgia	8.2	9.8	7.3	7.8	6.9	9.0	8.8	8.7
Hungary	38.7	44.5	52.3	53.7	56.8	58.4	60.0	58.5
Latvia	5.8	6.9	12.8	21.2	26.1	25.7	25.3	24.8
Lithuania	9.8	10.3	12.5	14.4	13.8	13.1	21.0	20.5
Macedonia	2.8	3.1	3.1	2.9	3.1	3.3	3.3	3.2
Moldova	4.6	5.1	5.5	5.6	5.3	5.9	7.1	6.6
Montenegro	2.1	2.8	2.9	3.0	3.5	3.9	4.1	4.0
Poland	65.6	67.9	72.9	77.0	81.1	91.8	75.0	70.2
Romania	20.6	26.2	28.0	36.0	40.5	50.5	54.0	52.5
Russia	653.2	601.8	694.4	680.0	748.7	868.4	940.7	810.6
Serbia	16.5	15.5	16.8	14.7	16.6	16.9	17.0	12.7
Slovakia	2.7	5.0	11.8	13.0	22.3	18.4	23.1	22.7
Slovenia	12.1	12.9	13.7	14.6	15.4	18.4	21.2	18.9
Ukraine	31.7	43.8	54.4	56.5	61.6	35.4	88.4	68.7

Source: Euromonitor International from International Civil Aviation Authority/national statistics

Automotives and Transport Statistics

Table 3.17

Merchant Shipping Fleet 1980-2009

'000 gross tons

	1980	1985	1990	1995	1996	1997	1998	1999	2000	2001
Western Europe										
Austria	88.8	134.2	139.3	91.9	94.7	83.4	68.0	71.1	53.2	35.3
Belgium	1,809.8	2,400.3	1,954.5	72.0	277.9	168.6	127.0	132.1	141.5	151.0
Cyprus	2,091.1	8,196.1	18,335.9	24,652.5	23,798.9	23,652.6	23,301.5	23,641.0	23,206.4	22,761.8
Denmark	5,390.4	4,942.2	5,188.1	5,747.2	5,632.0	5,753.8	5,686.7	5,353.6	6,357.8	7,109.0
Finland	2,346.2	1,649.7	1,093.6	1,581.4	1,543.7	1,558.8	1,629.1	1,658.4	1,620.4	1,595.4
France	11,924.6	8,237.4	3,832.4	4,194.3	4,236.0	4,570.4	4,737.7	4,766.4	4,681.2	4,677.7
Germany	9,887.8	7,611.4	5,737.8	5,626.2	5,842.1	6,949.6	8,083.6	6,513.8	6,552.2	6,300.2
Gibraltar	2.3	583.3	2,008.5	307.1	306.0	421.0	530.0	628.0	722.0	816.3
Greece	39,471.7	31,031.5	20,521.6	29,434.7	29,070.0	25,288.5	25,224.5	24,833.3	26,401.7	28,678.2
Iceland	188.2	180.3	176.6	190.2	205.9	214.9	198.4	192.1	192.7	193.4
Ireland	209.0	194.0	180.8	213.4	190.8	235.0	183.8	218.9	259.6	300.3
Italy	11,095.7	8,843.2	7,991.4	6,905.0	6,246.0	6,193.7	6,818.6	8,048.5	9,048.7	9,655.0
Liechtenstein										
Luxembourg			3.3	880.8	878.5	820.4	931.8	1,343.0	1,406.1	1,469.2
Malta	132.9	1,855.8	4,518.7	17,678.3	19,479.4	22,984.2	24,074.7	28,205.5	28,170.0	27,052.6
Monaco										
Netherlands	5,723.8	4,301.3	3,784.8	2,903.0	2,795.0	3,879.5	4,263.3	4,813.8	5,167.7	5,605.0
Norway										22,590.8
Portugal										1,199.2
Spain	8,112.2	6,256.2	3,807.1	1,618.6	1,062.0	1,141.5	1,206.8	1,269.0	1,552.6	2,147.5
Sweden	4,234.0	2,620.0	2,782.0	2,880.0	2,945.0	2,754.1	2,552.4	2,946.9	2,887.0	2,957.9
Switzerland	310.8	342.0	287.5	381.0	381.0	433.9	383.3	439.1	470.6	502.0
Turkey	1,454.8	3,684.4	3,718.6	6,267.6	6,069.0	6,567.3	6,251.4	6,324.6	5,832.7	5,896.7
United Kingdom	27,135.2	14,343.5	9,836.0	8,935.0	8,100.0	8,247.5	8,289.8	9,061.5	9,702.5	12,143.1
Eastern Europe										
Albania	56.1	56.1	55.8	63.0	43.4	30.4	28.7	21.4	23.3	25.2
Belarus										
Bosnia-Herzegovina										
Bulgaria	1,233.3	1,322.2	1,360.5	1,166.1	1,149.7	1,128.2	1,091.2	1,035.8	989.6	955.3
Croatia						871.0	896.4	868.9	822.0	775.2
Czech Republic	155.3	184.3	325.8	140.3	78.1	16.4				
Estonia				597.7	545.3	602.0	521.9	452.6	399.6	346.6
Georgia				282.0	206.0	128.1	117.8	132.2	204.4	276.6
Hungary	75.0	77.2	98.3	45.1	50.2	26.7	15.3	11.9	11.9	
Latvia				798.1	723.4	318.8	118.0	118.1	93.2	68.3
Lithuania				610.2	571.5	510.3	481.1	424.3	408.8	393.3
Macedonia										
Moldova										
Montenegro										
Poland	3,639.1	3,315.3	3,369.2	2,358.0	2,292.6	1,877.7	1,424.2	1,319.1	1,119.2	618.3
Romania	1,856.3	3,023.8	4,004.6	2,536.4	2,567.5	2,344.7	2,088.2	1,220.6	766.9	637.7
Russia				10,818.0	13,755.4	12,282.4	11,089.9	10,649.0	10,485.9	10,247.8
Serbia										
Slovakia				19.3	19.4	15.2	15.2	15.2	15.2	15.2
Slovenia				2.1	1.0	2.3	1.8	1.8	1.8	1.9
Ukraine				4,613.0	3,825.4	2,690.0	2,033.2	1,775.2	1,546.3	1,407.7

Source: *Euromonitor International from Lloyd's Register/national statistics*
Notes: *Ships of 100 gross tons or more. Gross tonnage (gt) is a measure of the total volume within the hull, and above deck, available for cargo, passengers, crew, fuel, stores etc. 1gt = 100 cu ft*

Automotives and Transport Statistics

Merchant Shipping Fleet 1980-2009 *(continued)*

'000 gross tons

	2002	2003	2004	2005	2006	2007	2008	2009
Western Europe								
Austria	29.9	32.0	34.1	34.1	34.1	14.0	14.0	9.9
Belgium	186.7	1,392.9	3,973.3	4,058.4	4,312.7	4,091.3	4,241.8	4,301.0
Cyprus	22,997.0	22,054.2	21,283.4	19,019.1	19,032.2	18,954.3	20,109.4	20,168.9
Denmark	7,602.9	7,726.7	7,763.1	8,290.4	8,799.6	9,476.3	10,570.0	11,336.5
Finland	1,545.2	1,452.1	1,428.9	1,475.2	1,422.6	1,570.1	1,564.9	1,459.3
France	4,731.5	4,859.2	4,974.9	5,611.1	6,164.8	6,350.2	6,323.5	6,842.3
Germany	6,545.8	6,111.8	8,246.4	11,497.2	11,364.3	12,934.2	15,282.8	15,157.1
Gibraltar	960.9	993.0	1,142.4	1,156.6	1,297.4	1,515.4	1,607.1	2,026.8
Greece	28,782.8	32,203.1	32,040.7	30,744.7	32,048.1	35,704.5	36,822.3	38,910.6
Iceland	187.3	187.4	194.1	188.5	184.2	180.0	168.7	161.6
Ireland	279.6	471.0	496.8	309.8	193.4	187.2	185.5	183.4
Italy	9,595.9	10,245.8	10,956.0	11,616.0	12,571.2	12,971.7	13,599.9	15,530.6
Liechtenstein								
Luxembourg	1,493.8	1,006.0	689.7	570.0	779.9	883.5	729.9	935.0
Malta	26,331.4	25,134.3	22,352.6	23,015.6	24,849.8	27,754.4	31,633.3	35,037.0
Monaco								
Netherlands	5,664.3	5,702.6	5,622.9	5,669.4	5,818.8	6,139.8	6,684.2	6,966.2
Norway	22,194.5	20,509.3	18,936.2	17,531.9	18,222.3	18,156.0	18,311.3	16,614.3
Portugal	1,099.7	1,156.3	1,136.5	1,239.6	1,223.6	1,070.1	1,095.7	1,287.6
Spain	2,371.2	2,651.0	2,869.1	2,901.7	3,004.6	3,061.8	3,054.9	2,880.4
Sweden	3,177.5	3,579.3	3,666.9	3,765.7	3,876.5	4,044.9	4,389.3	4,044.9
Switzerland	559.1	588.7	487.5	479.6	510.0	588.6	640.4	640.6
Turkey	5,658.8	4,950.6	4,678.9	5,044.7	4,848.8	4,995.1	5,181.0	5,450.5
United Kingdom	13,773.0	17,314.2	18,344.3	19,652.0	20,835.7	21,947.2	24,262.0	17,007.9
Eastern Europe								
Albania	48.7	70.0	72.8	74.8	74.7	67.5	65.7	67.2
Belarus								
Bosnia-Herzegovina								
Bulgaria	889.3	747.9	789.5	894.2	875.5	911.1	876.1	522.8
Croatia	834.7	847.7	1,016.1	1,135.2	1,157.2	1,373.5	1,444.7	1,389.7
Czech Republic								
Estonia	357.4	358.2	334.9	292.5	416.7	389.8	363.5	374.9
Georgia	569.3	814.9	974.3	1,091.9	1,129.3	1,048.4	678.4	707.9
Hungary	3.8	7.6						
Latvia	88.7	90.9	294.3	304.8	333.3	261.8	289.7	263.9
Lithuania	435.3	442.1	453.4	476.7	448.6	425.8	423.7	433.7
Macedonia								
Moldova			3.7	11.4	15.7	50.1	178.7	351.2
Montenegro					10.5	13.1	14.3	7.7
Poland	585.6	282.4	162.7	190.1	193.4	193.3	212.9	203.8
Romania	622.0	563.1	426.7	336.5	272.1	269.5	261.8	246.0
Russia	10,380.0	10,430.8	8,638.9	8,334.5	8,046.0	7,587.3	7,527.0	7,650.0
Serbia								
Slovakia	7.4	29.2	126.4	211.2	232.7	233.3	189.9	146.8
Slovenia	2.3	1.7	1.5	1.1	1.6	1.6	2.1	2.1
Ukraine	1,349.9	1,378.8	1,144.8	1,154.0	1,136.5	1,144.6	1,087.1	905.0

Source: *Euromonitor International from Lloyd's Register/national statistics*
Notes: *Ships of 100 gross tons or more. Gross tonnage (gt) is a measure of the total volume within the hull, and above deck, available for cargo, passengers, crew, fuel, stores etc. 1gt = 100 cu ft*

Automotives and Transport Statistics

Table 3.18

Public Railway Network 1980-2009

Kilometres at end-year

	1980	1985	1990	1995	1996	1997	1998	1999	2000	2001
Western Europe										
Austria			5,624	5,672	5,672	5,672	5,643	5,618	5,563	5,603
Belgium	3,978	3,712	3,479	3,368	3,380	3,422	3,470	3,472	3,471	3,454
Cyprus										
Denmark	2,461	2,471	2,344	2,303	2,275	2,248	2,264	2,756	2,768	2,768
Finland			5,846	5,859	5,860	5,865	5,867	5,836	5,854	5,850
France	34,382	34,678	34,260	31,940	31,852	31,821	31,735	29,113	29,272	29,445
Germany	28,517	27,634	40,980	41,718	40,826	38,450	38,150	37,589	36,642	36,050
Gibraltar										
Greece	2,461	2,461	2,484	2,474	2,474	2,503	2,299	2,299	2,385	2,377
Iceland										
Ireland	1,987	1,944	1,944	1,945	1,954	1,908	1,909	1,919	1,919	1,919
Italy	16,133	16,183	16,016	16,005	16,014	16,030	16,080	16,092	16,295	16,357
Liechtenstein										
Luxembourg	270	270	271	275	275	274	274	271	271	274
Malta										
Monaco										
Netherlands	2,760	2,794	2,780	2,813	2,813	2,805	2,808	2,808	2,802	2,809
Norway			4,044	4,023	4,021	4,021	4,021	4,021	4,179	4,178
Portugal	3,588	3,607	3,126	3,065	3,071	3,038	2,794	2,814	2,814	2,814
Spain	13,542	12,710	12,560	12,280	12,284	12,303	12,303	12,319	12,310	12,310
Sweden			10,801	9,782	9,821	9,798	9,855	9,884	9,877	11,021
Switzerland			2,978	2,987	2,989	3,450	4,000	5,108	5,062	5,053
Turkey	8,193	8,169	8,429	8,549	8,607	8,607	8,607	8,682	8,671	8,671
United Kingdom	18,028	17,122	16,924	16,999	17,001	16,991	16,994	16,994	16,994	16,994
Eastern Europe										
Albania			674	674	447	447	447	440	440	447
Belarus	5,512	5,540	5,569	5,543	5,543	5,542	5,533	5,523	5,512	5,509
Bosnia-Herzegovina			944	1,032	539	539	607	607	519	608
Bulgaria	4,267	4,297	4,299	4,293	4,293	4,291	4,290	4,290	4,320	4,320
Croatia		2,441	2,573	2,296	2,726	2,726	2,726	2,726	2,726	2,726
Czech Republic			9,451	9,327	9,435	9,430	9,430	9,444	9,444	9,523
Estonia	993	1,009	1,026	1,021	1,020	966	966	968	968	967
Georgia		1,465	1,583	1,575	1,575	1,576	1,576	1,545	1,562	1,565
Hungary	7,826	7,406	7,838	7,988	7,988	7,988	7,988	7,988	8,005	7,736
Latvia	2,384	2,384	2,397	2,413	2,413	2,413	2,413	2,413	2,331	2,305
Lithuania	2,008	2,014	2,007	2,002	1,997	1,997	1,997	1,905	1,905	1,695
Macedonia			696	699	697	699	699	699	699	699
Moldova			1,150			1,312	1,240	1,185	1,139	1,121
Montenegro									250	250
Poland	27,181	25,848	26,228	23,986	23,420	23,424	23,210	22,891	22,560	21,119
Romania	11,110	11,269	11,348	11,376	11,385	11,380	11,010	10,981	11,015	11,015
Russia			87,000	87,000	87,000	87,000	86,700	86,200	86,075	85,835
Serbia									3,809	3,809
Slovakia			3,660	3,665	3,673	3,673	3,665	3,665	3,662	3,662
Slovenia	1,229	1,228	1,196	1,201	1,201	1,201	1,201	1,201	1,201	1,229
Ukraine	22,553	22,698	22,799	22,756	22,757	22,702	22,600	22,472	22,301	22,218

Source: *Euromonitor International from national statistics*

Automotives and Transport Statistics

Public Railway Network 1980-2009 *(continued)*

Kilometres at end-year

	2002	2003	2004	2005	2006	2007	2008	2009
Western Europe								
Austria	5,642	5,656	5,675	5,691	5,702	5,712	5,726	5,730
Belgium	3,518	3,521	3,536	3,544	3,560	3,568	3,580	3,582
Cyprus								
Denmark	2,768	2,779	2,785	2,644	2,644	2,663	2,667	2,667
Finland	5,850	5,851	5,741	5,732	5,905	5,899	5,911	5,910
France	29,352	29,269	29,246	28,412	29,463	29,989	30,168	30,284
Germany	35,868	36,054	34,725	34,228	34,128	33,694	33,103	32,833
Gibraltar								
Greece	2,383	2,414	2,449	2,576	2,509	2,487	2,505	2,508
Iceland								
Ireland	1,919	1,919	1,919	1,919	1,919	1,919	1,919	1,919
Italy	16,307	16,288	16,236	16,543	16,627	16,655	16,747	16,789
Liechtenstein								
Luxembourg	274	275	275	275	275	275	275	275
Malta								
Monaco								
Netherlands	2,806	2,811	2,811	2,813	2,776	2,766	2,754	2,745
Norway	4,077	4,077	4,077	4,087	4,114	4,114	4,123	4,126
Portugal	2,881	2,818	2,849	2,839	2,839	2,839	2,844	2,843
Spain	12,298	12,298	13,117	12,824	12,991	13,075	13,269	13,307
Sweden	11,095	11,037	11,050	11,017	11,020	10,972	10,956	10,932
Switzerland	5,049	5,028	5,062	5,062	5,062	5,062	5,071	5,073
Turkey	8,671	8,697	8,697	8,697	8,697	8,697	8,697	8,697
United Kingdom	17,020	16,652	16,652	16,116	15,810	15,814	15,605	15,474
Eastern Europe								
Albania	447	447	447	423	423	423	417	410
Belarus	5,512	5,502	5,498	5,498	5,494	5,492	5,490	5,488
Bosnia-Herzegovina	608	608	608	608	608	608	608	608
Bulgaria	4,318	4,318	4,259	4,154	4,146	4,143	4,131	4,129
Croatia	2,726	2,726	2,726	2,726	2,722	2,722	2,721	2,720
Czech Republic	9,600	9,602	9,612	9,614	9,597	9,588	9,585	9,578
Estonia	967	967	959	959	962	961	960	960
Georgia	1,565	1,564	1,336	1,336	1,336	1,336	1,279	1,265
Hungary	7,950	7,950	7,950	7,950	7,960	7,964	7,968	7,969
Latvia	2,270	2,270	2,270	2,270	2,269	2,265	2,264	2,262
Lithuania	1,775	1,774	1,782	1,771	1,771	1,766	1,764	1,760
Macedonia	699	699	699	699	699	699	699	699
Moldova	1,121	1,111	1,075	1,115	1,154	1,182	1,200	1,208
Montenegro	250	250	250	250	250	250	250	
Poland	21,073	20,665	20,250	20,253	20,176	20,107	19,968	19,897
Romania	11,002	11,077	11,053	10,948	10,789	10,777	10,702	10,644
Russia	85,542	85,394	85,000	85,000	92,217	95,104	97,531	98,314
Serbia	3,809	3,809	3,809	3,809	3,809	3,809	3,809	
Slovakia	3,657	3,657	3,660	3,658	3,658	3,658	3,658	3,658
Slovenia	1,229	1,229	1,229	1,228	1,228	1,228	1,228	1,228
Ukraine	22,078	22,051	21,990	21,980	21,870	21,852	21,655	21,627

Source: *Euromonitor International from national statistics*

Automotives and Transport Statistics

Table 3.19

Railway Statistics of Major National Carriers 2009
As stated

	Locomotives (number)	Rail motor vehicles (number)	Passengers carried (million)	Average journey length (km)	Total goods carried (million tonnes)
Western Europe					
Austria	1,364	254	209.2	48.3	119.0
Belgium	660	1,485	219.2	48.0	78.9
Cyprus					
Denmark	144	671	169.2	36.1	6.3
Finland	474		70.6	58.2	39.0
France	4,378		1,102.5	79.4	96.4
Germany	3,847	5,240	2,352.8	35.0	365.5
Gibraltar					
Greece	184		16.5	100.0	5.1
Iceland					
Ireland	93		43.9	44.5	0.7
Italy	3,329		595.6	76.7	106.2
Liechtenstein			0.2	8.3	2.3
Luxembourg	100		17.9	19.5	10.4
Malta					
Monaco					
Netherlands	171		336.3	49.0	41.7
Norway	157	190	58.1	52.6	25.6
Portugal	124	220	158.8	26.8	10.8
Spain	792	1,981	646.1	37.8	30.0
Sweden	702		180.4	61.5	68.5
Switzerland	1,904		322.7	51.8	55.7
Turkey	586		78.5	64.5	21.3
United Kingdom	1,677		1,310.7	40.6	128.8
Eastern Europe					
Albania	58		1.6	47.3	0.5
Belarus	355		56.0	125.0	141.0
Bosnia-Herzegovina	169		0.5	78.6	6.7
Bulgaria	544	75	33.1	68.7	22.1
Croatia	216	193	72.9	24.7	15.8
Czech Republic	2,384		176.5	38.5	98.9
Estonia	345		5.3	52.6	45.1
Georgia	317		3.6	206.4	21.8
Hungary	1,004	262	142.4	56.3	52.7
Latvia	187	385	26.4	34.8	52.9
Lithuania	252	67	4.0	62.0	53.9
Macedonia	56		1.1	103.5	4.3
Moldova	153		5.5	104.3	10.4
Montenegro					
Poland	4,477	990	273.8	72.5	237.1
Romania	1,592		69.5	92.6	67.0
Russia			1,362.7	130.2	1,364.8
Serbia					
Slovakia	985		48.1	48.1	51.8
Slovenia	171	108	16.3	46.0	17.7
Ukraine	4,199		443.2	121.9	391.2

Source: Euromonitor International from International Road Federation/national statistics

Automotives and Transport Statistics

Table 3.20

Railway Freight 1980-2009

Million net tonne-kilometres

	1980	1985	1990	1995	1996	1997	1998	1999	2000	2001
Western Europe										
Austria	11,200	11,292	12,158	13,714	13,909	14,791	15,358	15,566	17,095	17,357
Belgium	8,037	8,277	8,354	8,407	8,454	8,700	8,764	8,468	8,734	8,174
Cyprus										
Denmark	1,619	1,749	1,801	1,998	1,767	1,992	2,065	1,974	2,025	1,961
Finland	8,300	8,066	8,400	9,559	8,800	9,900	9,900	9,800	10,107	9,857
France	68,815	55,121	50,670	48,136	49,506	53,855	53,967	53,438	55,448	50,396
Germany				69,483	68,490	72,389	73,273	71,494	75,884	76,092
Gibraltar										
Greece	814	733	647	306	337	243	226	234	426	379
Iceland										
Ireland	624	601	589	602	570	522	466	526	491	516
Italy	18,384	16,853	13,259	24,050	23,314	25,228	24,707	23,781	25,017	24,655
Liechtenstein										
Luxembourg	660	648	615	564	570	609	622	660	678	628
Malta										
Monaco										
Netherlands	3,468	3,269	3,070	3,097	3,123	3,406	3,793	3,988	3,819	3,834
Norway	3,084	2,928	2,559	2,715	3,108	2,399	2,421	2,456	2,399	2,451
Portugal	1,001	1,196	1,444	2,343	2,177	2,632	2,340	2,562	2,569	2,498
Spain	10,528	11,415	10,142	10,074	9,790	11,030	11,325	11,470	11,620	11,752
Sweden	15,914	17,331	19,102	19,391	18,840	18,605	18,597	18,503	19,468	18,954
Switzerland	7,799	7,434	8,958	8,686	8,710	8,505	9,128	9,825	9,937	10,091
Turkey	5,029	7,747	8,031	8,632	9,018	9,717	8,466	8,446	9,895	7,562
United Kingdom	17,640	16,047	16,778	13,000	13,300	15,100	16,900	17,300	18,200	19,700
Eastern Europe										
Albania				53	42	23	25	27	28	19
Belarus	66,264	73,243	75,373	25,510	26,018	30,636	30,370	30,529	31,425	29,727
Bosnia-Herzegovina				16	18	47	73	120	140	159
Bulgaria	17,663	18,172	14,132	8,560	7,517	7,353	6,070	5,176	5,538	4,905
Croatia	7,561	8,674	6,535	1,971	1,712	1,876	2,001	1,685	1,928	2,249
Czech Republic			41,150	22,634	22,333	20,733	18,288	16,457	18,983	18,302
Estonia				6,977	3,851	4,177	5,143	6,058	7,277	7,788	8,222
Georgia	14,656	13,487	12,354		2,394	2,006	2,694	3,160	3,912	4,481
Hungary	24,041	21,929	16,593	8,132	7,409	7,873	7,852	6,642	8,093	7,730
Latvia		19,933	18,538	9,757	12,400	13,970	13,000	12,210	13,310	14,179
Lithuania			19,258	7,220	8,103	8,622	8,265	8,341	8,919	7,741
Macedonia	712	992	769	169	271	280	408	380	509	462
Moldova	15,200		15,007	3,134	2,785	2,818	2,652	1,232	1,538	2,049
Montenegro										
Poland	132,576	118,863	83,530	69,116	68,332	68,651	61,760	55,471	54,448	47,913
Romania	78,390	64,090	57,253	27,179	26,877	24,789	19,708	15,927	16,354	16,102
Russia	2,316,000	2,506,000	2,523,000	1,214,000	1,131,251	1,100,000	1,020,000	1,205,000	1,373,178	1,433,617
Serbia									1,937	1,989
Slovakia			23,176	13,764	12,017	12,373	11,753	9,859	11,234	10,929
Slovenia	3,851	4,292	4,209	3,076	2,551	2,852	2,859	2,784	2,857	2,837
Ukraine			488,243	195,762	163,364	160,433	158,693	156,336	172,840	177,465

Source: Euromonitor International from national statistics

Automotives and Transport Statistics

Railway Freight 1980-2009 *(continued)*
Million net tonne-kilometres

	2002	2003	2004	2005	2006	2007	2008	2009
Western Europe								
Austria	17,633	17,864	18,757	18,957	20,980	21,371	22,248	21,811
Belgium	8,363	8,306	8,725	9,157	9,835	9,258	9,496	9,400
Cyprus								
Denmark	1,906	1,985	2,321	1,976	1,892	1,779	1,728	1,579
Finland	9,664	10,047	10,105	9,706	11,060	10,434	10,531	10,428
France	50,295	46,835	45,121	40,701	41,190	38,914	36,933	34,887
Germany	76,300	78,463	86,409	95,420	107,007	114,615	123,653	117,135
Gibraltar								
Greece	327	456	592	613	662	835	930	871
Iceland								
Ireland	426	398	399	303	205	129	95	70
Italy	23,299	20,299	22,183	22,761	24,151	25,285	26,532	25,771
Liechtenstein			21	17	18	18	23	21
Luxembourg	612	525	559	392	441	427	403	363
Malta								
Monaco								
Netherlands	3,685	4,705	5,831	5,865	6,289	7,216	7,844	7,492
Norway	2,191	2,627	2,845	3,182	3,351	3,456	3,663	3,520
Portugal	2,585	2,073	2,282	2,422	2,430	2,586	2,714	2,639
Spain	11,673	11,743	11,874	11,635	11,634	11,064	10,894	10,813
Sweden	19,197	20,170	20,856	21,675	22,271	23,250	24,020	23,466
Switzerland	9,639	9,534	10,800	11,500	12,000	12,300	12,452	12,253
Turkey	7,224	8,612	9,332	9,077	9,544	9,755	10,041	9,917
United Kingdom	18,700	18,734	22,552	22,322	27,365	26,384	28,297	27,291
Eastern Europe								
Albania	21	31	32	26	36	38	39	38
Belarus	34,169	38,402	40,331	43,559	45,723	47,933	50,316	49,068
Bosnia-Herzegovina	177	212	445	762	682	629	733	723
Bulgaria	4,627	5,274	5,212	5,163	5,396	5,241	5,233	5,238
Croatia	2,420	2,745	2,493	2,835	3,305	3,574	3,781	3,524
Czech Republic	17,042	17,069	16,214	15,973	15,779	16,304	16,113	16,087
Estonia	9,330	9,670	10,488	10,639	10,418	8,430	8,120	7,528
Georgia	5,065	5,539	4,862	6,127	6,760	6,997	7,361	6,924
Hungary	7,751	8,028	8,749	9,090	10,167	10,048	9,989	9,679
Latvia	15,020	17,955	18,618	19,779	16,831	18,313	18,403	18,349
Lithuania	9,767	11,457	11,637	12,457	12,896	14,373	15,102	14,409
Macedonia	334	376	426	530	614	779	880	789
Moldova	2,715	3,000	2,968	2,980	3,655	3,930	4,162	3,923
Montenegro								
Poland	47,756	49,595	52,332	49,972	53,622	54,253	55,418	54,878
Romania	15,218	15,039	17,022	16,582	15,791	15,757	15,937	15,846
Russia	1,510,203	1,668,921	1,802,000	1,858,000	1,951,000	2,090,000	2,195,270	2,126,448
Serbia	2,262	2,591	3,164	3,482	4,232	4,779	5,317	
Slovakia	10,383	10,113	9,702	9,463	9,988	9,647	9,531	9,561
Slovenia	3,078	3,018	3,149	3,245	3,373	3,603	3,749	3,644
Ukraine	193,141	225,288	233,961	223,980	240,810	255,698	231,911	210,928

Source: *Euromonitor International from national statistics*

Automotives and Transport Statistics

Table 3.21

Railway Passenger 1985-2009
Million passenger-kilometres

	1985	1990	1995	2000	2004	2005	2006	2007	2008	2009
Western Europe										
Austria	7,290	8,575	9,628	8,318	8,295	8,470	8,651	8,927	10,160	10,113
Belgium	6,572	6,540	6,757	7,755	8,670	9,117	9,627	9,929	10,401	10,509
Cyprus										
Denmark	4,546	4,851	4,783	5,343	5,745	5,760	5,903	5,968	6,092	6,109
Finland	3,224	3,300	3,184	3,405	3,346	3,468	3,582	3,789	4,053	4,112
France	62,070	63,740	55,560	69,571	74,293	76,884	79,809	81,961	86,516	87,535
Germany			60,514	74,015	72,563	74,947	77,803	78,820	81,762	82,337
Gibraltar										
Greece	1,732	1,978	1,568	1,886	1,698	1,854	1,826	1,933	1,657	1,647
Iceland										
Ireland	1,023	1,226	1,291	1,389	1,582	1,781	1,872	1,997	1,975	1,953
Italy	37,401	45,512	43,859	43,752	45,578	46,145	46,438	45,985	45,767	45,673
Liechtenstein					1	1	1	1	1	1
Luxembourg	288	264	304	332	267	272	297	317	345	350
Malta										
Monaco										
Netherlands	9,007	11,060	13,977	14,666	14,097	14,983	15,696	15,883	16,343	16,483
Norway	2,232	2,430	2,676	2,635	2,664	2,700	2,740	2,991	3,031	3,054
Portugal	5,725	5,664	4,809	3,632	3,691	3,752	3,876	3,987	4,212	4,255
Spain	15,979	15,476	15,318	18,547	19,015	19,802	20,310	19,989	23,337	24,418
Sweden	6,586	6,353	6,345	8,301	8,634	8,910	9,617	10,260	10,956	11,101
Switzerland	10,163	12,678	13,408	12,620	15,000	15,200	16,200	17,100	16,630	16,732
Turkey	6,489	6,410	5,797	5,833	5,237	5,036	5,278	5,553	5,097	5,062
United Kingdom	30,400	33,200	30,000	38,200	43,349	44,416	46,776	50,105	52,675	53,258
Eastern Europe										
Albania			197	125	89	73	80	85	80	78
Belarus	13,761	16,852	12,505	17,722	13,893	10,351	9,968	9,366	8,381	7,002
Bosnia-Herzegovina			63	9	19	23	30	34	38	39
Bulgaria	7,785	7,793	4,693	3,472	2,628	2,389	2,422	2,378	2,343	2,272
Croatia	4,063	3,429	943	1,252	1,213	1,227	1,322	1,573	1,769	1,804
Czech Republic		13,313	8,023	7,300	6,590	6,667	6,922	6,899	6,803	6,789
Estonia		1,510	421	261	193	247	256	274	274	278
Georgia	4,214	2,497	371	378	615	720	790	836	785	752
Hungary	10,464	11,400	5,880	9,693	10,406	9,743	9,200	8,751	8,284	8,019
Latvia		5,364	1,373	715	811	889	986	982	941	919
Lithuania		3,640	1,130	611	307	280	268	246	258	246
Macedonia	417	354	65	170	94	94	105	109	112	114
Moldova		1,464	1,019	315	346	355	471	521	563	577
Montenegro										
Poland	51,978	50,373	26,635	19,706	18,210	17,679	18,389	19,148	19,658	19,839
Romania	31,082	30,582	18,879	11,632	8,633	7,960	8,066	7,417	6,877	6,438
Russia		274,400	192,117	167,054	164,300	172,000	178,000	173,000	176,850	177,478
Serbia				1,189	821	713	684	642	583	
Slovakia		6,381	4,202	2,870	2,228	2,181	2,213	2,164	2,297	2,314
Slovenia	1,667	1,429	595	705	763	775	793	812	765	751
Ukraine		81,998	63,752	51,767	51,726	52,655	53,230	53,606	53,868	54,002

Source: Euromonitor International from national statistics

Automotives and Transport Statistics

Table 3.22

Car Traffic 1980-2009

Million car-kilometres

	1980	1985	1990	1995	1996	1997	1998	1999	2000	2001
Western Europe										
Austria	25,840	27,500							811,944	812,374
Belgium	40,861	42,101	50,467	85,200	92,416	94,033	95,659	92,189	88,719	85,250
Cyprus										
Denmark	19,928	22,608	26,885	29,423	30,036	30,800	31,255	32,026	31,759	31,363
Finland	22,180	25,970	33,430	35,760	36,000	36,790	38,080	39,190	39,815	40,680
France		222,503	290,315	341,169	349,364	361,000	371,000	383,000	383,000	398,000
Germany				514,900	519,000	524,800	528,000	541,900	555,800	569,700
Gibraltar										
Greece	9,392				37,271	39,683	42,317	47,457	48,573	50,909
Iceland	986									2,039
Ireland	14,798	20,540	24,800		23,200		23,775	25,212	26,204	27,505
Italy				329,000	335,000	341,000	342,000	348,000	362,000	380,000
Liechtenstein										
Luxembourg	1,382	2,191	2,971	2,954	3,074	3,192	3,269	3,339	3,408	3,478
Malta									1,507	
Monaco				1						
Netherlands	61,400	65,000	76,960	89,094	89,973	89,661	90,400	93,185	93,185	95,185
Norway	22,743	22,565			25,388	25,512	27,500	27,643	28,113	27,563
Portugal		22,500	30,300	44,250	41,250	44,250	47,250	49,463	52,339	53,192
Spain	52,780	56,300	81,344	107,994	112,895	149,412	158,562	169,000	180,908	189,167
Sweden		52,900		57,400	56,571	56,596	54,700	56,000	56,400	56,600
Switzerland	32,071	36,468	42,649	43,794	44,962	45,142	47,069	48,166	49,585	50,765
Turkey	7,444	9,415	14,755	28,837	25,157	28,837	30,683	30,791	36,224	34,047
United Kingdom	201,100	228,000	329,700	353,200	362,400	370,900	375,600	377,444	376,798	382,756
Eastern Europe										
Albania				2						
Belarus				935	942	1,036	1,083	1,114	966	889
Bosnia-Herzegovina										
Bulgaria			10,597	11,230	12,055	12,117	12,696	12,718	13,189	13,529
Croatia						9,282	10,436	11,454	11,158	12,337
Czech Republic				24,540	24,200	25,900	26,240	27,320	28,400	31,707
Estonia					4,339	4,690	4,763	5,094	5,116	5,238
Georgia				17						248
Hungary			17,155				15,620	15,840	16,000	16,300
Latvia			5,853	1,834	2,208	3,352	4,108	4,161	4,789	5,359
Lithuania										
Macedonia			2,400	2,621	2,659					
Moldova				180	188	179	170	141	143	157
Montenegro										
Poland	20,494	20,193	34,194	75,150	80,500	85,350	88,900	92,800	94,600	94,600
Romania			19,681	24,019	26,048	26,919	27,918	28,895	27,545	29,029
Russia				14,711	13,882	15,319	14,833	16,317	17,099	17,495
Serbia										
Slovakia				8,251	8,627	9,003	9,378	9,754	9,754	9,817
Slovenia			4,749	5,640	7,089	7,581	7,577	8,021	8,130	8,515
Ukraine							3,383	3,362	3,347	3,636

Source: *Euromonitor International from International Road Federation/national statistics*

Automotives and Transport Statistics

Car Traffic 1980-2009 *(continued)*

Million car-kilometres

	2002	2003	2004	2005	2006	2007	2008	2009
Western Europe								
Austria	812,533			59,414	60,679	61,944	62,209	63,017
Belgium	77,990	78,310	79,550	78,416	80,334	81,009	81,495	81,725
Cyprus			6,384					
Denmark	31,540	31,971	32,811	33,152	33,907	35,013	35,214	35,317
Finland	41,675	42,565	43,530	44,220	44,610	45,560	45,628	45,695
France	401,000	404,000	403,000	398,000	396,000	398,000	394,000	393,067
Germany	583,600	577,800	590,400	578,200	583,900	587,500	590,400	592,821
Gibraltar								
Greece	54,465	59,241	65,236	67,939	71,787	75,093	79,547	81,178
Iceland	2,062	2,085	2,108	2,131	2,154	2,177	2,200	2,223
Ireland	28,463	29,342	29,776	29,955	30,287	30,497	30,737	30,750
Italy	397,000	411,000	422,000	426,000	427,208	428,164	429,241	430,191
Liechtenstein								
Luxembourg	3,548	3,532	3,623	3,729	3,841	3,944	4,051	4,148
Malta								
Monaco								
Netherlands	98,812	101,151	103,709	104,767	106,090	107,188	108,348	109,466
Norway	28,507	29,162	29,395	29,543	30,701	31,859	32,652	33,810
Portugal	55,072	56,278	57,066	57,392	57,907	58,269	58,671	58,937
Spain	197,597	204,211	209,389	213,883	217,503	220,456	224,145	227,344
Sweden	44,092	60,000	60,500	63,000	63,000	64,400	67,313	69,083
Switzerland	51,758	52,000	53,768	54,338	52,415	52,800	52,850	53,023
Turkey	33,204	33,802	38,403	40,490	43,188	47,124	49,808	51,638
United Kingdom	392,926	393,049	398,056	397,191	419,726	421,813	424,523	428,843
Eastern Europe								
Albania								
Belarus	760	861	731	744	784	796	836	867
Bosnia-Herzegovina								
Bulgaria	13,897	14,698	15,033	15,368	15,694	15,916	16,151	16,278
Croatia	13,432	14,600	17,800	20,900	25,001	25,955	26,461	26,991
Czech Republic	33,445	34,298	35,013	35,309	35,705	36,017	36,352	36,672
Estonia	5,431	5,898	6,263	6,373	6,420	6,446	6,481	6,510
Georgia	252							
Hungary	15,800	17,200	19,400	22,100	24,556	25,917	27,241	28,165
Latvia	6,160	6,763	7,309	8,547	10,936	13,142	13,611	13,783
Lithuania		6,472	7,051	6,753	7,206	8,383	8,423	8,441
Macedonia								
Moldova	191	198	202	204	206	208	210	212
Montenegro								
Poland	95,000	95,120	95,320	95,658	95,893	96,098	96,305	96,513
Romania	30,593	31,159	32,800	35,800	39,200	43,600	49,900	55,344
Russia	18,086	18,479	18,786	19,073	19,292	19,473	19,656	19,839
Serbia								
Slovakia	9,854	9,862	9,891	9,911	9,926	9,943	9,960	9,969
Slovenia	8,762	8,918	9,334	9,490	9,768	10,133	10,374	10,532
Ukraine	3,786	4,241	4,697	4,788	4,995	5,303	5,544	5,650

Source: *Euromonitor International from International Road Federation/national statistics*

Automotives and Transport Statistics

Table 3.23

Road-Transported Goods 1980-2009

Million car-kilometres

	1980	1985	1990	1995	1996	1997	1998	1999	2000	2001
Western Europe										
Austria	7,931	9,099	15,317	26,824	28,224	29,674	31,673	34,198	35,124	37,529
Belgium	16,738	19,124	25,979	27,500	29,822	32,144	34,466	36,788	32,450	38,682
Cyprus										
Denmark	9,600	9,500	10,664	10,786	9,976	10,307	10,740	11,087	11,696	11,619
Finland	18,400	20,800	26,300	23,200	24,100	25,400	26,500	26,500	28,500	27,600
France		84,422	114,830	157,100	158,126	160,177	166,970	181,430	183,696	188,514
Germany				199,196	199,196	203,119	210,402	278,427	280,708	288,964
Gibraltar										
Greece			12,485	16,700	13,383	13,851	13,522	13,909	18,360	19,104
Iceland										
Ireland					5,700	5,700	5,900	6,100	6,500	12,405
Italy	119,629	144,129	177,945	174,432	175,450	181,687	191,482	173,578	184,756	186,510
Liechtenstein										
Luxembourg	278	431			412	431	400	3,517	6,797	8,699
Malta										
Monaco										
Netherlands	17,663	19,249	23,300	23,491	21,300	21,600	29,200	48,600	45,700	56,167
Norway	5,252	6,418	7,692	10,395	10,651	11,838	12,636	15,094	12,483	13,287
Portugal	11,800		11,712	11,457	11,917	13,500	14,200	14,714	20,470	23,085
Spain	94,800	108,100	102,544	101,874	102,167	109,841	125,268	134,259	148,715	161,042
Sweden	21,362	21,177	26,519	29,324	31,185	33,126	36,500	33,739	32,419	34,161
Switzerland	7,287	8,640	11,214	12,868	16,289	17,863	19,504	20,487	21,949	23,500
Turkey	39,233	62,480	97,843	152,210	135,781	139,789	152,210	150,974	161,552	151,421
United Kingdom	95,900	102,100	136,300	149,600	153,900	157,100	159,500	164,562	165,827	165,284
Eastern Europe										
Albania					1,120	1,340	1,830	2,015	2,200	2,249
Belarus			22,361	9,539	8,658	9,065	9,686	9,232	9,745	10,241
Bosnia-Herzegovina										
Bulgaria										5,423
Croatia			2,458	1,251	1,117	1,091	1,151	1,093	1,090	6,783
Czech Republic				31,267	30,052	40,640	33,911	36,964	39,036	40,260
Estonia			2,097	1,549	1,897	2,773	3,791	3,929	3,689	4,677
Georgia				98	131	303	385	420	475	520
Hungary					13,000	13,000	14,000	13,100	13,329	15,356
Latvia			5,853	1,100	1,019	3,352	4,108	4,161	4,789	5,359
Lithuania			7,336	5,160	4,191	8,622	5,611	7,740	7,769	8,274
Macedonia			3,510	1,178	1,210	1,719	1,812	2,076	2,436	3,131
Moldova			6,305	1,121	944	946	940	952	1,001	964
Montenegro									60	64
Poland	44,546	36,593	49,800	71,600	79,200	95,500	69,543	70,452	72,843	74,403
Romania			28,993	19,748	19,807	21,750	15,785	13,456	14,288	18,544
Russia				158,868	149,404	139,394	127,587	125,820	154,404	161,408
Serbia									388	410
Slovakia				5,158	5,171	3,779	4,750	18,516	14,340	13,799
Slovenia					2,287	2,777	3,844	4,240	5,252	7,035
Ukraine			79,668	34,478	22,201	20,532	18,266	18,206	16,811	14,405

Source: *Euromonitor International from International Road Federation/national statistics*

Automotives and Transport Statistics

Road-Transported Goods 1980-2009 *(continued)*

Million car-kilometres

	2002	2003	2004	2005	2006	2007	2008	2009
Western Europe								
Austria	38,495	39,556	36,769	37,043	39,186	37,401	34,312	33,797
Belgium	44,915	51,147	54,856	48,944	51,572	52,989	53,611	53,973
Cyprus			1,100	1,374	1,144	1,184	1,204	1,224
Denmark	11,810	11,174	10,538	11,058	11,495	11,799	11,860	11,921
Finland	29,000	27,800	28,100	27,800	26,400	26,900	27,170	27,310
France	188,093	188,871	197,031	192,879	198,546	206,731	206,304	207,124
Germany	285,214	290,745	303,752	310,103	330,016	343,447	341,532	341,867
Gibraltar								
Greece	19,241	19,362	19,452	19,489	19,544	19,585	19,629	19,674
Iceland	800	800						
Ireland	14,448	15,900	16,483	16,991	17,687	19,146	20,034	19,701
Italy	192,700	195,887	197,742	199,614	200,179	200,626	201,130	201,575
Liechtenstein								
Luxembourg	9,142	9,493	9,692	9,829	9,913	9,968	10,029	10,127
Malta								
Monaco								
Netherlands	66,634	77,100	82,333	86,694	90,037	92,193	94,384	95,551
Norway	13,614	14,115	14,966	15,414	15,894	16,313	16,518	16,657
Portugal	23,187	23,311	23,435	25,231	45,032	46,406	48,320	50,936
Spain	179,519	187,044	214,717	227,381	235,792	252,041	264,483	279,463
Sweden	36,620	36,603	36,926	38,556	39,899	40,525	41,325	42,248
Switzerland	24,500	14,582	15,000	15,753	16,337	16,900	17,563	17,831
Turkey	150,912	152,163	156,853	166,831	177,399	181,330	195,464	196,131
United Kingdom	164,741	159,000	163,000	163,000	166,728	173,077	174,878	176,017
Eastern Europe								
Albania	2,292	2,349	2,414	2,448	2,491	2,526	2,578	2,629
Belarus	11,400	12,710	13,969	15,045	15,779	19,200	20,434	20,845
Bosnia-Herzegovina	221	221	483	657	809	1,005	1,179	1,203
Bulgaria	6,603	6,840	9,015	11,843	12,760	13,250	13,721	13,982
Croatia	7,413	8,241	8,819	9,328	10,175	10,502	10,886	11,232
Czech Republic	45,100	46,564	46,010	43,447	50,369	51,637	53,513	54,984
Estonia	4,387	6,364	6,837	7,641	8,183	8,486	8,682	8,849
Georgia	543	562	570	578	586	596	602	608
Hungary	18,074	20,813	23,237	25,138	30,495	35,804	35,743	35,945
Latvia	1,930	2,324	2,330	2,767	2,729	2,959	3,042	3,075
Lithuania	10,709	11,462	12,279	15,908	18,134	20,278	21,111	21,488
Macedonia	4,291	5,451	5,341	5,577	8,299	5,938	6,071	6,235
Moldova	1,153	1,577	1,673	1,791	1,880	1,931	2,017	2,030
Montenegro	71	71	65	61	73	74	77	82
Poland	74,679	85,989	110,481	119,740	136,490	159,527	174,386	180,709
Romania	25,350	30,854	37,220	51,531	60,258	70,059	81,006	84,387
Russia	168,877	174,707	183,565	195,573	200,917	208,742	221,079	222,666
Serbia	459	452	277	680	798	913	1,125	1,212
Slovakia	14,929	16,859	18,517	22,550	22,114	21,676	21,413	21,298
Slovenia	6,609	7,040	9,007	11,033	12,112	13,737	14,713	14,755
Ukraine	12,000	14,100	15,300	19,700	25,300	29,400	31,750	32,503

Source: *Euromonitor International from International Road Federation/national statistics*

Automotives and Transport Statistics

Table 3.24

Passenger Cars: Average Annual Distance Travelled 1980-2009

Kilometres

	1980	1985	1990	1995	1996	1997	1998	1999	2000	2001
Western Europe										
Austria	11,500	10,866							198,175	194,255
Belgium	12,936	12,840	13,165	20,099	21,454	21,503	21,458	20,274	19,166	18,198
Cyprus										
Denmark	14,342	15,063	16,902	17,464	17,220	17,228	17,157	17,340	17,233	16,724
Finland	18,093	16,797	17,242	18,812	18,530	18,885	18,841	18,818	18,774	18,954
France		10,550	12,328	13,592	13,701	13,837	13,838	13,937	13,649	13,868
Germany				12,714	12,645	12,699	12,657	12,774	12,698	12,836
Gibraltar										
Greece	10,675				15,932	15,873	15,815	16,308	15,420	14,870
Iceland	12,325									12,695
Ireland	20,150	28,950	31,140		21,941		19,864	19,864	19,862	19,864
Italy				10,858	10,939	10,962	10,902	10,862	11,110	11,432
Liechtenstein										
Luxembourg	9,376	14,414	16,199	12,897	13,268	13,478	13,390	13,176	13,218	12,968
Malta									7,969	
Monaco				48						
Netherlands	13,599	13,263	14,811	15,816	15,675	15,432	15,242	15,226	14,691	14,557
Norway	18,436	14,904			15,282	14,512	15,394	15,242	15,180	14,717
Portugal		18,987	18,589	16,948	14,685	14,647	14,588	14,259	14,567	14,200
Spain	6,985	6,071	6,781	7,599	7,652	9,767	9,879	10,031	10,368	10,422
Sweden		16,787		15,809	15,478	15,291	14,430	14,395	14,105	14,085
Switzerland	14,274	13,934	14,286	13,562	13,758	13,583	13,912	13,892	13,986	13,986
Turkey	10,028	9,574	8,943	9,428	7,683	8,077	7,994	7,561	8,191	7,508
United Kingdom	13,027	11,717	14,994	14,458	14,185	14,093	13,906	13,974	13,476	13,364
Eastern Europe										
Albania				34						
Belarus				995	909	915	847	824	697	621
Bosnia-Herzegovina										
Bulgaria			8,300	6,816	7,328	7,353	7,455	7,242	7,289	7,068
Croatia						9,956	10,435	10,770	9,920	10,320
Czech Republic				8,064	7,580	7,637	7,512	7,943	8,258	8,983
Estonia					10,671	10,966	10,563	11,105	11,028	12,860
Georgia				47						1,000
Hungary			9,239				7,042	7,023	6,766	6,565
Latvia				5,527	5,812	7,763	8,510	7,917	8,601	9,142
Lithuania										
Macedonia			10,399	9,168	9,680					
Moldova				1,085	1,060	869	792	628	619	631
Montenegro										
Poland	9,029	5,853	6,500	9,997	9,995	10,002	9,841	9,997	9,468	9,007
Romania			15,230	10,930	11,198	11,000	10,760	10,690	9,917	10,075
Russia				1,036	878	869	835	943	1,003	915
Serbia										
Slovakia				8,123	8,151	7,926	7,840	7,889	7,822	7,605
Slovenia			8,212	8,078	9,744	9,912	9,497	9,668	9,387	9,660
Ukraine							694	645	623	666

Source: *Euromonitor International from national statistics*

Automotives and Transport Statistics

Passenger Cars: Average Annual Distance Travelled 1980-2009 *(continued)*
Kilometres

	2002	2003	2004	2005	2006	2007	2008	2009
Western Europe								
Austria	203,790			14,294	14,430	14,590	14,586	14,742
Belgium	16,506	16,408	16,509	16,130	16,297	16,181	16,206	16,212
Cyprus			19,023					
Denmark	16,688	16,878	17,139	16,904	16,836	17,006	16,938	16,903
Finland	19,117	18,839	18,673	18,314	17,921	17,841	17,668	17,639
France	13,752	13,667	13,478	13,223	13,026	12,964	12,781	12,700
Germany	13,068	12,833	13,011	12,545	12,538	14,265	14,288	14,402
Gibraltar								
Greece	15,664	16,025	16,473	16,159	16,145	15,575	16,173	16,470
Iceland	12,750	12,495	12,016	11,369	10,917	10,491	10,423	10,453
Ireland	19,658	19,469	18,812	18,021	17,026	16,197	16,051	15,951
Italy	11,778	11,979	12,422	12,288	12,103	12,000	11,959	11,917
Liechtenstein								
Luxembourg	12,562	12,296	12,348	12,441	12,614	12,549	12,701	12,876
Malta								
Monaco								
Netherlands	14,726	14,756	14,503	14,354	14,311	14,109	14,173	14,317
Norway	15,006	15,082	14,862	14,561	14,726	14,792	14,957	15,310
Portugal	14,176	14,190	13,919	13,665	13,498	13,307	13,291	13,337
Spain	10,548	10,927	10,715	10,562	10,331	10,131	10,136	10,191
Sweden	10,906	14,722	14,708	15,167	14,991	15,123	15,718	16,077
Switzerland	13,985	13,852	14,107	14,072	13,440	13,348	13,279	13,290
Turkey	7,218	7,191	7,111	7,014	7,033	7,281	7,557	7,744
United Kingdom	13,795	13,550	13,549	13,352	14,047	13,978	14,002	14,068
Eastern Europe								
Albania								
Belarus	501	531	437	428	432	432	448	466
Bosnia-Herzegovina								
Bulgaria	7,123	7,386	7,366	7,447	7,573	7,543	7,591	7,590
Croatia	10,795	11,288	13,308	15,094	17,413	17,407	17,505	17,723
Czech Republic	9,170	9,255	9,177	8,919	8,690	8,415	8,325	8,393
Estonia	13,553	13,591	13,292	12,906	11,588	12,306	12,519	12,635
Georgia	1,000							
Hungary	6,009	6,193	6,859	7,650	8,314	8,604	8,971	9,219
Latvia	9,950	10,422	10,653	11,513	13,304	14,466	14,402	14,537
Lithuania		5,149	5,358	4,640	4,710	5,247	5,151	5,155
Macedonia								
Moldova	732	770	746	729	716	713	713	718
Montenegro								
Poland	8,449	8,460	7,960	7,752	7,165	6,587	6,447	6,413
Romania	10,289	10,092	10,169	10,643	12,154	12,392	14,027	15,462
Russia	855	790	776	746	754	719	717	720
Serbia								
Slovakia	7,426	7,273	7,125	7,602	7,442	6,934	6,869	6,811
Slovenia	9,795	9,795	9,994	9,884	9,964	9,992	10,097	10,233
Ukraine	685	759	838	826	834	873	904	920

Source: *Euromonitor International from national statistics*

Automotives and Transport Statistics

Table 3.25

Road Network 2009

Kilometres

	Total	Motorway	National Highway	Secondary Regional	Other Local	% Paved	Density (km per sq km of land)	Motorway Intensity (% of total road network)
Western Europe								
Austria	107,411	1,680	10,432	23,670	71,629	100.00	1.30	1.56
Belgium	153,947	1,770	12,605	1,350	138,222	78.51	5.08	1.15
Cyprus	12,374	259	5,365	2,753	3,997	67.30	1.34	2.09
Denmark	73,331	1,128	379	9,695	62,129	100.00	1.73	1.54
Finland	78,970	742	13,275	13,482	51,471	65.43	0.26	0.94
France	1,030,227	11,089	26,052	377,592	615,494	100.00	1.88	1.08
Germany	644,833	12,717	40,450	178,192	413,474	100.00	1.85	1.97
Gibraltar								
Greece	118,936	880	10,764	31,692	75,600	91.82	0.92	0.74
Iceland	13,082		4,236	4,013	4,833	37.12	0.13	
Ireland	97,648	256	5,310	11,666	80,416	100.00	1.42	0.26
Italy	489,982	6,783	21,683	148,776	312,740	100.00	1.67	1.38
Liechtenstein	380		139	241		100.00	2.38	
Luxembourg	5,254	179	845	1,880	2,350	100.00	2.03	3.41
Malta	3,096		185		2,911	87.53	9.68	
Monaco	77					100.00	38.50	
Netherlands	140,111	2,500	6,788	57,953	72,870	90.00	4.15	1.78
Norway	93,241	288	27,470	27,106	38,377	79.62	0.31	0.31
Portugal	86,748	2,688	15,491	4,500	64,069	86.00	0.95	3.10
Spain	680,347	12,580	22,841	139,705	505,221	99.00	1.36	1.85
Sweden	430,546	1,778	15,425	83,515	329,828	80.56	1.05	0.41
Switzerland	71,419	1,786	18,171	51,462		100.00	1.79	2.50
Turkey	427,235	2,003	31,289	30,743	363,200	40.00	0.56	0.47
United Kingdom	398,156	12,226	38,217	114,784	232,929	100.00	1.65	3.07
Eastern Europe								
Albania	18,000		3,220	4,300	10,480	72.00	0.66	
Belarus	99,146		15,444	71,863	11,839	89.72	0.48	
Bosnia-Herzegovina	21,846		3,722	4,104	14,020	52.29	0.43	
Bulgaria	43,456	334	2,958	4,198	35,966	98.80	0.40	0.77
Croatia	29,095	984	7,192	10,544	10,375	89.39	0.54	3.38
Czech Republic	129,143	710	6,215	48,695	73,522	100.00	1.67	0.55
Estonia	58,268	100	3,946	12,447	41,775	29.45	1.37	0.17
Georgia	20,370		1,495	3,354	15,521	38.63	0.29	
Hungary	162,028	680	31,460	54,448	75,440	37.08	1.81	0.42
Latvia	69,777		6,980	13,237	49,560	100.00	1.12	
Lithuania	81,102	309	6,384	14,624	59,785	88.24	1.29	0.38
Macedonia	14,187	225	677	3,962	9,323	63.80	0.56	1.59
Moldova	12,786		3,329	6,027	3,430	85.59	0.39	
Montenegro	7,414					64.81	0.55	
Poland	383,505	801	18,543	155,414	208,747	90.50	1.26	0.21
Romania	199,298	228	14,862	36,146	148,062	30.29	0.87	0.11
Russia	952,957		690,222	262,735		81.20	0.06	
Serbia	39,372	379	5,149	10,494	23,350		0.45	0.96
Slovakia	44,138	327	3,380	3,759	36,672	87.06	0.92	0.74
Slovenia	38,767	617	942	4,938	32,270	100.00	1.92	1.59
Ukraine	169,533	15	20,514	79,429	69,575	97.93	0.29	0.01

Source: *Euromonitor International from International Road Federation/national statistics*

Banking and Finance

Banking and Finance Statistics

Table 4.1

Private Sector Bank Claims 1980-2009

National currency billion / US$ billion

	1980	1985	1990	1995	1996	1997	1998	1999	2000	2001
Western Europe										
Austria	54.8	83.7	122.3	162.0	172.7	188.7	188.7	197.1	213.0	224.1
Belgium	53.0	66.5	126.5	151.2	158.7	167.3	177.1	192.3	196.6	197.3
Cyprus	0.9	1.7	4.9	9.9	11.2	12.5	13.9	16.3	18.1	19.9
Denmark	94.0	190.4	429.2	312.9	331.1	357.7	405.4	420.6	1,749.3	1,902.2
Finland	15.2	34.2	75.7	58.9	58.5	56.7	60.3	65.0	70.1	77.8
France	321.2	555.8	969.3	1,028.3	1,014.2	1,034.3	1,007.8	1,115.3	1,225.2	1,314.3
Germany	649.8	889.9	1,250.7	1,856.4	1,994.1	2,115.6	2,286.5	2,326.4	2,445.7	2,497.1
Gibraltar										
Greece	2.6	7.0	14.2	26.8	30.4	34.9	40.3	52.0	63.9	83.1
Iceland	4.3	46.9	157.1	209.0	236.7	348.9	376.3	461.0	663.6	772.5
Ireland	5.5	10.4	17.3	37.0	43.1	55.9	68.6	91.8	110.7	129.1
Italy	111.2	212.5	385.2	530.8	547.7	580.3	632.3	788.2	896.8	966.6
Liechtenstein										
Luxembourg	4.0	5.6	11.1	13.0	13.7	15.3	13.6	19.8	22.5	29.1
Malta	0.3	0.6	1.3	2.6	2.9	3.2	3.5	3.9	4.3	4.6
Monaco										
Netherlands	102.0	122.9	193.8	284.4	317.1	357.8	409.2	484.0	560.8	605.7
Norway	96.8	241.3	461.7	527.5	599.8	708.0	801.6	849.7	969.6	1,075.5
Portugal	5.4	14.3	24.9	55.6	65.3	78.7	98.3	129.3	160.5	179.2
Spain	71.5	118.8	250.3	323.1	346.7	394.2	459.3	519.6	615.9	688.5
Sweden	219.2	340.6	791.2	596.7	623.2	711.1	771.7	848.4	958.7	2,298.0
Switzerland	195.8	335.2	532.8	611.7	608.2	625.6	635.7	676.5	668.9	660.9
Turkey			0.1	1.4	3.4	7.6	12.1	17.4	29.6	36.9
United Kingdom	63.7	167.4	645.3	829.1	911.9	973.0	1,016.8	1,094.4	1,254.3	1,367.8
Eastern Europe										
Albania				8.3	10.9	13.0	14.9	18.2	24.4	34.9
Belarus				7.4	12.3	30.3	113.0	279.7	802.5	1,400.8
Bosnia-Herzegovina						3.8	4.2	4.1	4.4	3.3
Bulgaria				0.4	1.1	1.6	2.4	2.9	3.4	4.4
Croatia				30.7	31.6	46.1	56.7	52.7	56.8	69.7
Czech Republic				1,036.6	1,153.9	1,250.4	1,176.3	1,098.5	1,029.9	916.4
Estonia				7.0	12.4	22.4	25.1	26.7	34.8	42.5
Georgia				0.1	0.1	0.2	0.2	0.3	0.4	0.5
Hungary		208.6	971.3	1,263.2	1,520.7	2,076.9	2,440.4	2,968.0	4,247.6	5,025.9
Latvia				0.2	0.2	0.4	0.6	0.7	0.9	1.4
Lithuania				3.9	3.7	4.4	5.6	6.3	6.0	6.6
Macedonia				39.2	46.8	50.7	34.5	43.6	42.2	41.2
Moldova				0.4	0.6	0.6	1.3	1.5	2.0	2.8
Montenegro										
Poland		0.6	11.8	56.9	81.2	107.3	135.5	169.8	197.8	212.6
Romania			0.1		1.3	2.1	4.3	4.4	5.8	10.2
Russia				133.8	166.5	250.1	410.7	631.1	969.4	1,473.1
Serbia						31.5	44.7	59.2	188.7	257.6
Slovakia				5.5	7.2	10.5	10.7	10.4	11.3	8.8
Slovenia				4.1	4.4	4.7	5.8	7.0	7.8	8.7
Ukraine				0.8	1.1	2.3	7.9	11.0	18.8	26.6

Source: International Monetary Fund (IMF), International Financial Statistics

Banking and Finance Statistics

Private Sector Bank Claims 1980-2009 *(continued)*

National currency billion / US$ billion

	2002	2003	2004	2005	2006	2007	2008	2009	US$ billion 2009
Western Europe									
Austria	229.5	234.9	247.7	276.8	292.4	309.0	333.8	340.8	473.5
Belgium	198.9	203.8	207.4	223.8	261.5	305.2	325.3	332.1	461.5
Cyprus	20.4	21.7	23.4	25.0	27.5	34.0	43.6	45.7	63.5
Denmark	1,996.8	2,123.2	2,318.4	2,654.0	3,029.2	3,432.5	3,791.9	3,703.3	690.8
Finland	83.8	93.4	102.9	118.1	130.6	146.6	159.6	161.4	224.3
France	1,325.9	1,407.6	1,499.8	1,591.8	1,769.2	1,991.3	2,102.0	2,102.9	2,922.2
Germany	2,505.8	2,497.4	2,479.7	2,504.6	2,536.1	2,556.0	2,686.9	2,692.9	3,742.0
Gibraltar									
Greece	94.5	110.4	129.7	153.4	177.5	209.3	226.8	217.5	302.2
Iceland	858.9	1,097.2	1,531.3	2,542.8	3,733.2	5,205.1	5,941.0	6,696.2	54.2
Ireland	142.4	160.2	200.3	260.7	321.8	377.7	396.5	376.7	523.4
Italy	1,030.8	1,110.8	1,178.9	1,271.5	1,403.1	1,555.9	1,646.2	1,681.2	2,336.3
Liechtenstein									
Luxembourg	24.9	26.5	29.1	39.1	52.5	69.3	72.4	70.0	97.3
Malta	4.7	4.4	4.7	5.1	5.8	6.3	7.3	7.8	10.8
Monaco									
Netherlands	656.6	705.8	775.2	847.3	903.2	1,075.3	1,148.3	1,227.6	1,705.9
Norway	1,144.6	1,232.5	1,354.1	1,583.5	1,879.2	2,027.1	2,176.6	2,308.4	367.0
Portugal	190.8	194.0	202.7	216.9	244.2	275.0	298.6	314.6	437.2
Spain	770.9	886.2	1,050.4	1,324.4	1,645.7	1,978.0	2,205.5	2,219.1	3,083.7
Sweden	2,421.7	2,540.3	2,696.3	2,986.9	3,321.5	3,797.3	4,090.1	4,220.5	551.4
Switzerland	662.9	687.0	716.8	762.3	831.6	904.8	896.2	935.4	860.9
Turkey	50.9	66.2	96.6	144.4	196.7	248.7	309.8	321.8	206.9
United Kingdom	1,479.4	1,624.6	1,807.6	1,994.9	2,256.2	2,625.9	3,030.3	2,973.2	4,636.8
Eastern Europe									
Albania	39.5	51.9	71.1	123.6	194.7	288.9	381.8	411.0	4.3
Belarus	2,364.1	4,283.5	6,928.0	10,063.7	15,437.8	22,988.5	35,331.2	46,097.6	16.5
Bosnia-Herzegovina	4.2	5.1	5.9	7.5	9.2	11.8	14.3	13.7	9.8
Bulgaria	6.3	9.4	14.0	18.6	23.2	37.7	49.6	50.2	35.7
Croatia	91.0	104.7	119.9	140.1	172.2	198.2	222.2	220.1	41.7
Czech Republic	720.6	782.5	886.8	1,076.9	1,312.9	1,686.4	1,937.9	1,957.5	102.7
Estonia	54.3	69.0	92.1	121.9	173.4	229.6	244.8	236.0	21.0
Georgia	0.6	0.7	1.0	1.7	2.7	4.8	6.3	5.5	3.3
Hungary	5,989.2	7,988.9	9,480.0	11,271.3	13,152.2	15,624.5	18,518.2	17,886.9	88.4
Latvia	1.9	2.6	3.8	6.2	9.8	13.1	14.7	14.0	27.7
Lithuania	8.4	13.0	18.0	29.5	41.4	59.2	69.9	65.3	26.3
Macedonia	43.1	47.2	58.6	70.9	92.7	129.0	173.1	175.5	4.0
Moldova	3.9	5.6	6.8	8.9	12.3	19.7	22.9	21.3	1.9
Montenegro	0.1	0.2	0.2	0.3	0.8	2.2	2.7	2.3	3.2
Poland	221.8	236.7	260.1	284.4	352.8	464.1	633.1	647.8	207.6
Romania	15.4	27.1	38.6	57.5	89.1	144.7	193.9	195.9	64.2
Russia	1,915.1	2,772.5	4,109.0	5,557.6	8,312.0	12,539.9	17,100.2	17,164.3	540.4
Serbia	167.9	216.7	316.8	487.4	571.5	801.1	1,069.7	1,166.2	17.3
Slovakia	10.2	9.1	10.1	13.5	17.2	23.2	27.4	30.5	42.4
Slovenia	9.5	10.7	13.1	16.2	20.5	27.2	31.8	32.8	45.6
Ukraine	39.8	65.6	86.7	142.0	241.2	419.0	700.0	685.1	87.9

Source: *International Monetary Fund (IMF), International Financial Statistics*

Banking and Finance Statistics

Table 4.2

Deposit Money Bank Assets 1980-2009

US$ billion

	1980	1985	1990	1995	1996	1997	1998	1999	2000	2001
Western Europe										
Austria	21.71	36.75	65.99	92.04	89.54			62.99	69.68	74.78
Belgium	60.77	92.67	192.03	273.06	267.76	262.47	277.35	112.05	108.17	126.96
Cyprus	0.05	0.12	2.53	5.34	6.44	16.74	12.13	11.97	15.96	16.37
Denmark	4.83	14.16	45.55	56.59	62.39	65.68	76.75	68.43	70.56	60.06
Finland	2.76	7.67	27.00	24.17	26.99	21.36	21.84	15.72	19.91	35.26
France	160.21	184.38	455.78	705.08	684.06	736.80		430.98	435.49	447.01
Germany	85.17	112.93	395.49	578.20	606.02	650.29	828.89	513.97	579.53	641.34
Gibraltar										
Greece	1.19	1.98	3.46	8.96	12.66	15.99	15.55	13.85	12.63	16.39
Iceland	0.03	0.06	0.13	0.09	0.11	0.13	0.12	0.22	0.27	0.32
Ireland	8.78	3.21	13.45	46.68	70.32	101.45	142.09	78.11	135.34	173.20
Italy	35.09	50.44	102.73	145.84	193.22	177.15	193.74	90.84	85.89	75.04
Liechtenstein										
Luxembourg	104.83	130.95	355.12	504.84	496.51	471.90	498.62	178.65	174.95	207.51
Malta	0.16	0.21	0.96	2.24	2.88	3.42	5.85	6.81	8.60	6.89
Monaco										
Netherlands	62.63	72.88	185.92	234.14	238.73	263.59		155.62	163.90	211.40
Norway	0.63	3.64	7.82	7.47	9.09	9.78	12.32	12.42	15.28	15.09
Portugal	1.13	1.43	6.16	35.92	37.50	47.45	54.67	25.17	29.90	26.87
Spain	12.79	20.04	39.11	146.06	129.73	111.18	126.79	61.25	77.37	82.00
Sweden	8.04	8.94	34.92	36.16	44.71	44.94	50.85	53.09	67.36	62.01
Switzerland	66.45	85.24	153.25	212.37	263.36	314.44	369.71	463.67	465.83	446.49
Turkey	0.55	2.01	5.51	10.97	10.37	11.57	12.73	16.07	18.18	13.33
United Kingdom	356.32	590.07	1,068.96	1,350.86	1,460.35	1,685.14	1,868.89	1,802.43	2,059.96	2,168.52
Eastern Europe										
Albania										
Belarus				0.29	0.33	0.37	0.31	0.34	0.33	0.30
Bosnia-Herzegovina										
Bulgaria				1.06	0.97	1.36	1.47	1.49	1.94	2.10
Croatia				1.75	2.27	2.57	2.04	1.62	2.42	3.93
Czech Republic				3.78	5.77	8.58	11.79	13.30	13.26	15.61
Estonia				0.32	0.32	0.56	0.48	0.56	0.62	0.87
Georgia				0.03	0.03	0.04	0.05	0.05	0.05	0.08
Hungary		0.34	1.16	0.92	1.68	2.49	3.31	3.59	2.74	4.44
Latvia				0.60	1.02	1.55	1.26	1.49	2.11	2.27
Lithuania				0.12	0.29	0.37	0.30	0.42	0.69	0.75
Macedonia				0.25	0.23	0.29	0.34	0.40	0.43	0.64
Moldova				0.17	0.20	0.15				
Montenegro									0.10	0.12
Poland	1.48	2.30	6.09	7.15	6.13	7.28	5.41	7.87	11.32	15.31
Romania	0.26	1.00	0.68	0.07	0.07	0.08	0.09	0.09	0.10	1.61
Russia				9.95	13.11	12.51	11.25	14.28	17.44	18.15
Serbia						0.80	0.90	0.77	0.82	0.98
Slovakia				1.82	2.51	3.62	3.79	1.62	2.35	2.39
Slovenia				2.40	2.58	1.87	2.00	1.81	2.01	3.27
Ukraine				1.04	0.94	0.96	0.91	0.85	0.92	0.77

Source: *International Monetary Fund (IMF), International Financial Statistics*

Banking and Finance Statistics

Deposit Money Bank Assets 1980-2009 *(continued)*
US$ billion

	2002	2003	2004	2005	2006	2007	2008	2009
Western Europe								
Austria	91.22	122.77	157.55	167.08	228.71	296.68	303.34	281.84
Belgium	164.25	194.31	236.40	274.52	314.10	399.43	331.54	287.77
Cyprus	14.49	17.72	23.85	33.10	49.06	69.22	48.96	56.54
Denmark	71.59	103.18	128.55	134.42	177.44	252.82	247.49	227.43
Finland	41.88	51.76	66.70	61.33	82.53	98.95	101.32	114.77
France	538.48	635.90	829.48	1,003.06	1,268.93	1,478.58	1,288.90	1,299.44
Germany	774.43	1,018.88	1,223.06	1,172.69	1,544.88	1,972.33	1,780.81	1,571.61
Gibraltar								
Greece	21.77	32.37	39.51	41.06	62.81	94.20	117.10	138.09
Iceland	0.57	1.59	2.86	8.55	18.58	22.30	25.74	27.52
Ireland	236.53	324.81	433.63	509.69	747.61	991.46	957.94	958.49
Italy	94.26	117.86	122.63	110.30	140.81	156.31	128.90	141.27
Liechtenstein								
Luxembourg	237.00	301.44	332.05	355.16	471.20	594.55	548.11	550.12
Malta	9.42	12.94	16.75	20.74	27.95	40.34	35.45	34.17
Monaco								
Netherlands	256.24	308.25	376.87	413.18	576.25	749.83	579.51	555.16
Norway	17.64	28.59	25.18	34.06	63.11	77.63	91.61	106.96
Portugal	28.93	34.88	37.67	36.83	46.10	49.35	44.23	49.36
Spain	95.10	101.13	153.24	167.65	226.89	293.58	276.02	276.57
Sweden	72.53	102.26	157.44	160.90	229.17	303.92	299.71	310.96
Switzerland	557.85	616.29	680.72	709.24	803.01	1,116.56	834.81	739.49
Turkey	13.59	14.55	21.01	23.47	37.47	43.99	52.41	60.13
United Kingdom	2,477.29	3,023.60	3,643.33	3,937.75	4,914.15	5,539.19	5,851.71	6,362.10
Eastern Europe								
Albania								
Belarus	0.26	0.33	0.46	0.69	0.43	1.24	1.28	1.44
Bosnia-Herzegovina								
Bulgaria	2.02	1.94	3.13	3.27	5.57	5.91	5.51	5.64
Croatia	3.64	5.78	7.78	5.77	7.19	9.41	9.80	10.88
Czech Republic	14.64	15.32	20.53	24.10	27.07	38.35	36.00	35.14
Estonia	1.10	1.38	2.49	3.47	3.66	5.93	5.51	6.27
Georgia	0.09	0.11	0.16	0.16	0.22	0.39	0.69	0.83
Hungary	4.36	5.94	7.20	6.97	12.43	17.04	19.86	21.66
Latvia	3.02	4.04	5.78	5.63	6.68	11.17	9.73	9.91
Lithuania	0.72	0.93	1.86	2.54	3.75	5.03	4.49	5.91
Macedonia	0.56	0.67	0.82	0.73	0.86	0.92	0.55	0.50
Moldova								
Montenegro	0.09	0.07	0.08	0.20	0.37	0.50	0.35	0.47
Poland	13.71	14.92	24.96	25.51	29.54	29.93	20.39	15.27
Romania	1.19	1.08	1.81	1.45	1.81	2.47	2.43	4.94
Russia	19.03	20.66	25.48	37.97	62.49	93.44	159.26	191.60
Serbia	0.74	1.09	1.12	0.93	0.93	2.07	2.38	2.77
Slovakia	2.05	2.33	2.87	3.03	3.94	5.93	6.69	4.94
Slovenia	2.26	2.58	2.89	4.19	6.51	6.12	6.22	6.33
Ukraine	0.85	1.36	2.30	2.83	4.07	6.06	7.49	8.74

Source: *International Monetary Fund (IMF), International Financial Statistics*

Banking and Finance Statistics

Table 4.3

Deposit Money Bank Liabilities 1980-2009
US$ billion

	1980	1985	1990	1995	1996	1997	1998	1999	2000	2001
Western Europe										
Austria	24.95	38.03	74.31	99.15	102.74			49.42	49.93	58.52
Belgium	72.95	112.93	239.79	302.86	293.66	280.03	297.91	181.82	163.88	176.33
Cyprus	0.18	0.41	3.24	6.00	7.49	17.79	13.40	13.33	17.14	17.84
Denmark	4.88	14.85	44.80	33.25	40.17	50.35	61.48	63.34	62.55	58.81
Finland	4.57	12.81	59.91	29.27	25.88	17.92	19.99	9.37	15.47	28.04
France	146.68	197.18	519.81	662.47	671.76	694.58	723.56	337.03	384.58	399.22
Germany	72.09	75.77	226.37	482.24	490.21	561.59	760.83	491.34	559.07	571.75
Gibraltar										
Greece	5.15	7.59	16.46	34.29	38.54	42.28	46.85	41.73	39.65	9.64
Iceland	0.18	0.42	0.71	0.42	0.75	0.88	1.48	1.99	2.65	2.50
Ireland	10.72	6.32	17.74	49.10	70.17	99.23	142.77	77.73	141.51	191.25
Italy	51.41	72.83	205.38	216.81	237.87	223.25	236.90	136.37	146.78	150.86
Liechtenstein										
Luxembourg	98.45	117.21	308.09	434.11	415.57	389.82		164.24	159.29	163.50
Malta	0.02	0.07	0.49	1.58	2.33	2.97	5.24	6.34	7.91	6.16
Monaco										
Netherlands	64.35	65.68	153.43	220.96	245.75	290.78		194.07	206.13	250.06
Norway	2.74	9.16	22.17	9.62	19.89	25.62	29.85	31.82	37.02	39.76
Portugal	0.81	1.64	5.78	32.43	36.98	48.28	60.98	31.35	47.62	50.01
Spain	24.50	20.94	63.99	109.25	123.36	135.02	179.18	125.66	147.33	157.56
Sweden	12.52	17.20	99.36	55.10	56.67	60.38	86.85	76.77	102.35	78.87
Switzerland	47.95	63.40	133.57	184.87	223.84	268.97	300.78	395.02	440.01	415.25
Turkey	0.70	3.06	4.46	6.11	8.93	12.16	15.51	20.10	25.17	11.74
United Kingdom	377.71	625.74	1,201.03	1,429.20	1,533.44	1,748.76	1,893.68	1,871.71	2,160.04	2,305.83
Eastern Europe										
Albania										
Belarus				0.12	0.14	0.16	0.14	0.12	0.11	0.19
Bosnia-Herzegovina										
Bulgaria				0.58	0.40	0.10	0.13	0.17	0.26	0.31
Croatia				2.85	2.25	2.19	2.59	2.25	2.18	2.62
Czech Republic				6.43	9.05	9.12	10.80	9.68	8.42	7.71
Estonia				0.14	0.34	0.91	0.88	0.88	0.98	0.99
Georgia				0.05	0.00	0.01	0.04	0.05	0.06	0.07
Hungary		1.20	1.69	2.88	3.08	4.48	5.46	5.58	5.51	5.97
Latvia				0.45	0.85	1.30	1.34	1.77	2.14	2.65
Lithuania				0.09	0.20	0.30	0.45	0.54	0.52	0.62
Macedonia				0.08	0.14	0.19	0.25	0.26	0.23	0.20
Moldova				0.06	0.24	0.29				
Montenegro									0.20	0.21
Poland	25.32	26.68	1.92	2.07	2.75	4.28	5.21	6.75	6.61	7.77
Romania	8.38	6.05	1.72	0.82	1.24	1.15	0.93	0.61	0.51	0.66
Russia				6.46	10.59	18.03	10.73	9.41	10.11	11.36
Serbia						3.37	3.13	2.98	2.86	3.07
Slovakia				0.98	2.16	2.85	2.63	0.64	0.64	0.84
Slovenia				1.48	1.46	1.22	1.33	1.44	1.57	1.76
Ukraine				0.30	0.33	0.95	0.51	0.34	0.46	0.65

Source: *International Monetary Fund (IMF), International Financial Statistics*

Banking and Finance Statistics

Deposit Money Bank Liabilities 1980-2009 *(continued)*
US$ billion

	2002	2003	2004	2005	2006	2007	2008	2009
Western Europe								
Austria	56.53	70.38	81.78	85.74	103.95	114.25	106.65	110.75
Belgium	199.01	236.31	274.68	328.34	350.61	477.40	332.58	317.80
Cyprus	16.76	19.37	25.24	24.63	33.72	52.69	33.41	39.18
Denmark	75.60	110.79	129.87	128.69	165.11	239.00	213.75	210.99
Finland	26.34	25.27	34.95	39.52	48.61	69.02	82.53	98.79
France	464.83	547.13	701.86	899.66	1,237.77	1,611.18	1,380.99	1,400.73
Germany	629.90	719.20	787.91	740.01	842.36	974.61	928.19	860.76
Gibraltar								
Greece	18.56	27.72	44.53	53.22	76.86	115.46	103.53	102.65
Iceland	2.81	3.05	3.66	5.34	9.50	30.63	33.83	38.58
Ireland	255.23	338.47	428.83	487.80	696.75	918.17	871.00	884.31
Italy	153.43	201.52	214.47	212.37	253.35	310.24	270.40	289.10
Liechtenstein								
Luxembourg	173.27	198.97	221.67	235.53	284.00	332.35	292.49	227.67
Malta	8.36	10.92	14.27	18.40	24.70	35.82	24.55	25.40
Monaco								
Netherlands	305.75	328.22	392.49	427.83	564.21	717.98	624.57	680.77
Norway	52.76	69.46	76.04	93.24	140.23	163.73	183.21	203.20
Portugal	62.15	84.36	93.12	86.53	120.58	135.43	111.25	118.79
Spain	176.27	231.74	244.31	241.05	257.68	311.49	375.67	388.50
Sweden	91.64	109.49	157.60	139.93	184.51	196.71	228.79	217.40
Switzerland	498.61	546.82	608.31	634.71	717.63	1,044.11	810.24	752.44
Turkey	11.17	15.58	21.34	36.19	46.13	55.82	57.48	52.81
United Kingdom	2,684.13	3,276.43	4,033.35	4,251.40	5,254.85	5,959.07	6,311.18	6,768.91
Eastern Europe								
Albania								
Belarus	0.27	0.40	0.62	0.85	1.38	2.48	3.08	3.72
Bosnia-Herzegovina								
Bulgaria	0.47	0.96	3.38	3.22	4.25	8.87	13.27	12.61
Croatia	4.90	8.16	10.99	10.88	13.74	13.21	14.98	15.90
Czech Republic	7.66	10.09	10.27	9.79	12.05	19.69	22.70	19.65
Estonia	1.58	2.81	3.07	4.50	7.08	12.72	13.65	16.02
Georgia	0.09	0.10	0.12	0.29	0.52	1.20	1.73	1.32
Hungary	7.43	12.50	16.39	19.00	25.80	34.60	47.68	49.95
Latvia	3.74	5.30	8.06	10.00	15.68	25.66	25.79	22.85
Lithuania	0.85	1.88	2.81	5.07	8.14	13.83	17.15	16.24
Macedonia	0.21	0.20	0.24	0.28	0.37	0.57	0.55	0.74
Moldova								
Montenegro	0.02	0.05	0.11	0.15	0.42	1.18	1.75	1.50
Poland	9.07	12.64	13.72	12.65	19.68	37.93	58.55	62.41
Romania	1.00	2.22	4.98	8.15	16.42	29.90	36.73	33.83
Russia	12.89	23.16	32.17	51.45	105.26	167.99	170.61	135.17
Serbia	0.29	0.43	1.44	2.65	5.13	5.58	6.96	7.52
Slovakia	1.50	3.15	5.83	10.01	7.09	13.23	17.02	2.38
Slovenia	2.79	4.59	6.26	9.75	14.02	4.54	3.62	3.23
Ukraine	0.74	1.63	2.25	5.24	12.83	28.61	36.86	28.13

Source: International Monetary Fund (IMF), International Financial Statistics

Banking and Finance Statistics

Table 4.4

Annual Lending Rates 1980-2009

% per annum

	1980	1985	1990	1995	1996	1997	1998	1999	2000	2001
Western Europe										
Austria							6.42	5.64	6.33	
Belgium		12.54	13.00	8.42	7.17	7.06	7.25	6.71	7.98	8.46
Cyprus	9.00	9.00	9.00	8.50	8.50	8.08	8.00	8.00	8.00	7.52
Denmark	17.20	14.65	14.10	10.33	8.70	7.73	7.90	7.13	8.08	8.20
Finland	9.77	10.41	11.62	7.75	6.16	5.29	5.35	4.71	5.61	5.79
France	12.54	11.09	10.57	8.12	6.77	6.34	6.55	6.36	6.70	6.98
Germany	12.04	9.53	11.59	10.94	10.02	9.13	9.02	8.81	9.63	10.01
Gibraltar										
Greece	21.25	20.50	27.62	23.05	20.96	18.92	18.56	15.00	12.32	8.59
Iceland	45.00	32.60	16.18	11.58	12.43	12.89	12.78	13.30	16.80	17.95
Ireland	15.96	12.44	11.29	6.56	5.85	6.57	6.22	3.34	4.77	4.84
Italy	19.03	18.06	14.85	13.24	12.82	10.51	8.64	6.35	7.02	7.29
Liechtenstein										
Luxembourg	9.25	8.75	8.23	6.50	5.50	5.50	5.27			
Malta	8.00	8.00	8.50	7.38	7.77	7.99	8.09	7.70	7.28	6.90
Monaco										
Netherlands	13.50	9.25	11.75	7.21	5.90	6.13	6.50	3.46	4.79	5.00
Norway	13.00	13.41	14.15	7.60	6.68	6.00	9.80	7.61	8.93	8.69
Portugal	18.75	27.29	21.78	13.80	11.73	9.15	7.24	5.19	5.45	
Spain	16.85	13.52	16.01	10.05	8.50	6.08	5.01	3.95	5.18	5.16
Sweden	15.18	16.89	16.69	11.11	7.38	7.01	5.94	5.53	5.83	5.55
Switzerland		5.49	7.42	5.48	4.97	4.47	4.07	3.90	4.29	4.30
Turkey	25.67	53.50		88.00	74.70			82.00	33.00	
United Kingdom	16.17	12.33	14.75	6.69	5.96	6.58	7.21	5.33	5.98	5.08
Eastern Europe										
Albania				19.65	23.96	29.28		21.62	22.10	19.65
Belarus				175.00	62.33	31.80	26.99	51.04	67.67	46.97
Bosnia-Herzegovina							73.50	24.29	30.50	30.99
Bulgaria				79.36	291.06	213.02	14.08	13.50	11.34	11.11
Croatia				20.24	22.52	15.47	15.75	14.94	12.07	9.55
Czech Republic				12.80	12.54	13.20	12.81	8.68	7.16	7.20
Estonia				19.01	14.87	11.76	15.06	11.09	7.43	7.78
Georgia				85.62	58.24	50.64	46.00	33.42	32.75	27.25
Hungary			28.78	32.61	27.31	21.77	19.28	16.34	12.60	12.12
Latvia				34.56	25.78	15.25	14.29	14.20	11.87	11.17
Lithuania				27.08	21.56	14.39	12.21	13.09	12.14	9.63
Macedonia				45.95	21.58	21.42	21.03	20.45	18.93	19.35
Moldova				39.60	36.67	33.33	30.83	35.54	33.78	28.69
Montenegro										
Poland	10.23	15.34	644.50	33.45	26.08	25.21	24.48	16.94	20.01	18.36
Romania				50.72	55.13	72.53	55.32	65.64	53.85	45.40
Russia				320.31	146.81	32.04	41.79	39.72	24.43	17.91
Serbia					77.97	60.86	46.06	6.30	34.50	
Slovakia				16.85	13.92	18.65	21.17	21.07	14.89	11.24
Slovenia				23.36	22.60	20.02	16.09	12.38	15.77	15.05
Ukraine				122.70	79.88	49.12	54.50	54.95	41.53	32.28

Source: *International Monetary Fund (IMF), International Financial Statistics*

Banking and Finance Statistics

Annual Lending Rates 1980-2009 *(continued)*
% per annum

	2002	2003	2004	2005	2006	2007	2008	2009
Western Europe								
Austria		5.50	5.28	5.00	5.51	6.30	6.82	5.00
Belgium	7.71	6.89	6.70	6.72	7.49	8.57	9.15	9.50
Cyprus	7.15	6.95	7.57	7.09	6.69	6.74	6.42	6.20
Denmark	7.10							
Finland	4.82	4.13	3.69	3.56	3.39	3.35		
France	6.60	6.60	6.60					
Germany	9.70	9.62						
Gibraltar								
Greece	7.41	6.79						
Iceland	15.37	11.95	12.02	14.78	17.91	19.29	20.26	18.99
Ireland	3.83	2.85	2.57	2.65	3.08	3.21		
Italy	6.54	5.83	5.51	5.31	5.62	6.33	6.84	4.76
Liechtenstein								
Luxembourg								
Malta	6.04	5.85	5.32	5.51	5.65	6.24	5.89	4.47
Monaco								
Netherlands	3.96	3.00	2.75	2.77	3.54	4.60	4.60	1.98
Norway	8.71	4.73	4.04	4.04	4.70	6.65	7.28	4.28
Portugal								
Spain	4.31	3.88						
Sweden	5.64	4.79	4.00	3.31	3.72	4.00		
Switzerland	3.93	3.27	3.20	3.12	3.03	3.15	3.34	2.75
Turkey								
United Kingdom	4.00	3.69	4.40	4.65	4.65	5.52	4.63	0.63
Eastern Europe								
Albania	15.30	14.27	11.76	13.08	12.94	14.10	13.02	12.66
Belarus	36.88	23.98	16.91	11.36	8.84	8.58	8.55	11.68
Bosnia-Herzegovina	12.70	10.87	10.28	9.61	8.01	7.17	6.98	7.93
Bulgaria	9.21	8.54	8.87	8.66	8.89	10.00	10.86	11.34
Croatia	12.84	11.58	11.75	11.19	9.93	9.33	10.07	11.55
Czech Republic	6.72	5.95	6.03	5.78	5.59	5.79	6.25	5.99
Estonia	6.70	5.51	5.66	4.93	5.03	6.46	8.55	9.39
Georgia	31.83	32.27	31.23	21.63	18.75	20.41	21.24	25.52
Hungary	10.17	9.60	12.82	8.54	8.08	9.09	10.18	11.04
Latvia	7.97	5.38	7.45	6.11	7.29	10.91	11.85	16.23
Lithuania	6.84	5.84	5.74	5.27	5.11	6.86	8.41	8.39
Macedonia	18.36	16.00	12.44	12.13	11.29	10.23	9.68	10.07
Moldova	23.52	19.29	20.94	19.26	18.13	18.83	21.06	20.54
Montenegro				12.11	11.15	9.20	9.24	9.36
Poland	12.03	7.30	7.56	6.83	5.48	6.16		
Romania	35.43	25.44	25.61	19.60	13.98	13.35	14.99	17.28
Russia	15.70	12.98	11.44	10.68	10.43	10.03	12.23	15.31
Serbia	19.71	15.48	15.53	16.83	16.56	11.13	18.11	5.06
Slovakia	10.25	8.46	9.07	6.68	7.67	7.99	5.80	7.00
Slovenia	13.17	10.75	8.65	7.80	7.41	5.91	6.66	5.97
Ukraine	25.35	17.89	17.40	16.17	15.17	13.90	17.49	20.86

Source: International Monetary Fund (IMF), International Financial Statistics

Banking and Finance Statistics

Table 4.5

Deposit Money Bank Reserves 1980-2009

National currency million

	1980	1985	1990	1995	1996	1997	1998	1999	2000	2001
Western Europe										
Austria	3,151.82	4,023.47	4,494.33	5,374.78	5,821.66	5,629.14		3,305.00	3,878.00	7,975.00
Belgium	520.58	545.37	629.65	939.52	6,093.22	5,666.85	5,556.00	3,509.00	7,130.00	5,945.00
Cyprus	61.06	146.32	306.97	344.10	296.36	280.72	284.55	425.00	472.88	582.63
Denmark	1,138.00	25,797.00	8,704.00	39,573.40	51,617.10	70,630.50	54,196.80	96,258.00	23,816.00	17,368.00
Finland	667.84	2,044.96	3,767.45	7,732.63	4,306.34	3,651.58	3,493.95	4,884.00	2,475.00	4,111.00
France	7,149.83	17,104.70	13,933.78	7,149.83	7,759.62	7,256.54		24,371.00	28,083.00	29,467.00
Germany	36,010.84	40,009.20	60,169.75	44,503.53	45,322.12	45,779.22	47,082.52	45,641.00	51,003.00	56,439.00
Gibraltar										
Greece	393.50	2,087.07	4,354.78	14,674.81	14,908.73	16,386.44	21,904.89	24,053.50	20,645.14	11,521.00
Iceland	1,045.00	7,365.00	15,042.00	10,325.00	13,418.00	14,100.00	13,990.00	29,026.00	25,731.00	20,701.40
Ireland	977.26	1,049.73	1,445.21	1,823.18	1,711.53	2,140.68	3,435.75	2,486.00		4,324.00
Italy	20,176.42	43,240.35	67,125.45	40,958.13	42,195.05	45,350.60	12,214.72	9,896.00	8,158.00	25,732.00
Liechtenstein										
Luxembourg	27.52	46.85	79.82	91.72	473.48	337.14		4,182.73	4,911.69	5,981.17
Malta	227.20	351.21	138.54	209.91	204.42	275.77	311.42	405.07	380.16	430.47
Monaco										
Netherlands	467.40	953.40	1,304.17	1,401.73	1,533.33	1,524.71		7,138.00	9,242.00	9,676.00
Norway	2,652.00	4,314.00	3,000.00	5,153.00	28,058.00	17,275.00	14,066.00	38,362.00	27,815.00	29,747.00
Portugal	854.34	5,288.85	11,108.23	10,426.77	9,433.66	8,220.84	8,070.20	4,247.00	3,447.00	2,757.00
Spain	3,778.14	23,536.48	31,027.85	22,388.30	19,606.82	18,587.50	17,981.08	15,793.00	8,391.00	14,725.00
Sweden	5,646.00	7,708.00	24,908.00	9,415.00	11,133.00	10,167.00	13,515.00	30,668.00	9,803.00	16,010.00
Switzerland	16,500.00	15,775.00	8,274.00	8,270.00	9,608.00	9,829.00	10,954.00	17,169.00	12,511.00	12,741.00
Turkey	0.22	1.83	13.38	171.69	365.51	725.57	1,428.70	2,516.35	3,272.62	4,807.40
United Kingdom	2,385.00	2,884.00	5,972.00	7,558.00	7,714.00	8,261.00	8,393.00	11,536.00	9,752.00	8,556.00
Eastern Europe										
Albania				10,301.50	12,904.40	16,442.00	21,565.50	28,150.20	30,161.90	33,814.60
Belarus				2,841.79	5,693.16	11,889.00	35,688.20	92,002.20	158,118.00	312,321.00
Bosnia-Herzegovina						71.37	90.29	274.67	287.41	871.93
Bulgaria				67.64	118.64	800.25	643.84	745.27	598.06	864.44
Croatia				3,508.33	4,573.90	5,056.70	5,908.10	8,987.90	10,588.90	15,002.70
Czech Republic				160,933.00	158,503.00	214,936.00	288,853.00	296,541.00	310,927.00	333,319.00
Estonia				1,293.06	1,922.52	3,885.31	4,509.51	5,790.89	6,787.13	4,896.57
Georgia				38.00	30.39	39.62	45.01	56.37	76.65	82.45
Hungary		117,700.00	118,367.00	273,721.00	154,003.00	291,124.00	365,637.00	447,525.00	646,928.00	520,074.00
Latvia				64.15	71.69	107.23	129.93	144.46	135.11	153.25
Lithuania				522.70	583.60	742.10	1,447.50	1,342.30	1,282.40	1,343.10
Macedonia				1,836.00	1,125.00	2,158.00	2,379.00	3,861.00	6,192.00	6,195.00
Moldova				54.38	36.54	52.05	200.66	360.92	465.22	652.38
Montenegro										
Poland	112.51	131.43	3,908.89	8,806.00	10,632.90	15,049.10	23,335.90	14,866.60	14,660.80	21,485.30
Romania	8.13	3.59	0.87	329.32	363.21	534.73	1,304.97	3,501.43	5,103.77	8,712.49
Russia				36,712.00	48,301.00	74,981.00	75,438.00	168,180.00	310,781.00	356,771.00
Serbia										
Slovakia				195.73	278.24	328.97	261.65	277.32	1,204.46	1,039.70
Slovenia				76.66	99.77	183.07	181.97	170.19	178.66	269.25
Ukraine				960.25	848.63	925.50	1,454.57	2,613.25	4,749.59	3,687.92

Source: *International Monetary Fund (IMF), International Financial Statistics*

Banking and Finance Statistics

Deposit Money Bank Reserves 1980-2009 *(continued)*

National currency million

	2002	2003	2004	2005	2006	2007	2008	2009
Western Europe								
Austria	3,729.00	4,864.00	3,819.00	4,819.00	5,068.00	8,398.00	15,373.00	16,309.00
Belgium	4,482.00	8,325.00	5,416.00	6,786.00	7,928.00	17,789.00	10,804.00	14,777.00
Cyprus	898.49	684.54	714.88	862.69	1,203.03	1,453.51	1,304.00	3,050.00
Denmark	32,474.00	18,907.00	27,703.00	25,793.00	22,539.00	18,067.00	44,838.00	9,577.96
Finland	3,759.00	2,146.00	3,156.00	3,535.00	3,766.00	5,910.00	8,110.00	13,543.00
France	33,293.00	25,995.00	26,384.00	25,692.00	26,320.00	73,610.00	90,762.00	61,044.00
Germany	45,585.00	46,857.00	41,248.00	47,942.00	49,495.00	64,986.00	102,611.00	78,968.00
Gibraltar								
Greece	4,841.00	2,479.00	5,387.00	4,354.00	4,625.00	7,248.00	7,936.00	8,187.00
Iceland	25,293.80	13,293.50	29,412.50	36,906.50	47,358.80	80,214.15	101,423.19	120,614.89
Ireland	4,909.00	4,303.00	4,760.00	8,720.00	13,473.00	22,428.00	20,215.00	16,123.00
Italy	10,344.00	10,384.00	13,126.00	11,624.00	14,716.00	41,918.00	34,930.00	35,017.00
Liechtenstein								
Luxembourg	4,638.04	6,765.57	5,063.32	6,810.32	9,741.90	10,779.70	45,531.70	13,488.50
Malta	724.20	612.25	396.98	376.73	458.27	421.14	489.18	519.17
Monaco								
Netherlands	8,365.00	12,539.00	11,215.00	15,681.00	13,010.00	20,116.00	21,252.00	62,284.00
Norway	65,871.80	39,492.90	47,702.00	53,372.90	30,448.80	41,910.85	40,366.54	36,898.18
Portugal	1,884.00	964.00						
Spain	9,291.00	14,409.00	13,091.00	16,531.00	20,559.00	52,321.00	54,315.00	35,089.00
Sweden	12,085.00	20,564.00	15,819.00	10,701.00	11,762.00	15,012.00	219,934.00	275,729.47
Switzerland	13,619.00	14,328.00	13,166.00	13,603.00	15,320.00	19,505.00	50,894.00	53,863.00
Turkey	19,548.40	21,772.50	23,104.90	35,188.40	38,653.70	43,938.20	64,879.10	46,283.12
United Kingdom	8,919.00	9,731.00	12,998.00	13,375.00	29,734.00	32,245.00	60,788.00	155,346.00
Eastern Europe								
Albania	32,175.90	35,245.20	40,626.60	49,967.80	60,303.10	72,660.00	76,560.60	71,070.87
Belarus	438,923.00	772,808.00	1,134,530.00	1,810,240.00	2,349,290.00	2,410,680.00	3,516,910.00	2,802,650.00
Bosnia-Herzegovina	595.25	1,004.55	1,566.58	2,233.86	3,061.92	4,022.28	3,394.50	3,631.86
Bulgaria	1,071.15	1,388.25	2,428.00	2,955.00	4,244.00	6,733.00	6,135.00	5,054.56
Croatia	20,373.50	26,783.70	33,743.40	41,789.30	48,402.70	50,201.50	40,721.50	44,412.19
Czech Republic	60,197.00	56,563.00	49,989.00	45,561.00	60,208.00	66,665.00	147,168.00	80,904.58
Estonia	4,677.98	6,243.01	8,876.00	13,328.00	18,782.00	19,411.00	27,646.00	19,860.88
Georgia	126.13	148.91	220.40	268.93	442.26	627.62	558.09	601.98
Hungary	464,058.00	406,811.00	677,319.00	599,145.00	595,805.00	723,774.00	467,332.00	659,322.75
Latvia	213.73	205.00	311.00	594.00	1,317.00	1,557.00	1,221.00	916.81
Lithuania	1,391.80	1,897.10	1,868.00	2,819.00	3,419.00	4,789.00	4,216.00	3,096.13
Macedonia	6,364.00	7,090.00	7,192.00	11,454.00	15,247.00	19,912.00	24,581.00	32,487.37
Moldova	979.20	1,155.98	2,842.09	3,526.31	2,411.82	4,673.69	7,020.37	4,945.99
Montenegro								
Poland	19,857.00	16,902.70	18,398.00	13,579.00	18,302.00	25,765.00	36,297.00	38,820.06
Romania	14,395.60	16,912.80	26,853.50	34,068.30	55,519.20	68,545.60	77,650.00	39,289.93
Russia	471,563.00	768,914.00	837,433.00	873,086.00	1,236,500.00	1,717,000.00	2,580,600.00	3,035,937.07
Serbia								
Slovakia	1,139.63	899.92	755.88	1,053.08	1,336.62	2,338.91	2,999.88	1,198.00
Slovenia	375.72	400.85	357.31	400.02	301.98	351.00	984.00	1,220.00
Ukraine	4,516.01	7,127.74	11,629.30	22,559.50	22,429.70	30,471.70	31,547.20	29,796.95

Source: International Monetary Fund (IMF), International Financial Statistics

Banking and Finance Statistics   **Table 4.6**

Credit Cards in Circulation 1998-2009
'000

	1998	1999	2000	2001	2002	2003	2004	2005	2006	2007	2008	2009
Western Europe												
Austria	711.6	762.7	820.6	875.0	946.5	961.8	948.2	1,031.7	1,094.8	1,176.0	1,255.7	1,314.3
Belgium	113.2	125.8	144.2	170.1	224.5	312.9	381.2	488.8	581.9	753.8	925.8	1,093.5
Cyprus												
Denmark	398.0	421.0	458.0	497.0	541.0	590.0	789.9	957.1	1,021.4	941.5	1,115.1	1,215.5
Finland												
France	2,468.3	2,750.0	3,000.0	3,242.6	3,500.0	3,800.0	4,005.0	4,166.6	4,326.4	4,499.2	5,068.5	8,362.6
Germany	929.6	1,214.0	1,722.6	2,428.0	3,199.2	3,857.7	4,078.2	5,233.0	6,574.0	6,776.1	7,047.2	7,168.7
Gibraltar												
Greece	1,513.0	2,014.0	3,030.1	4,144.1	5,157.1	5,579.9	5,641.9	6,045.5	6,284.8	6,707.3	6,945.6	6,734.3
Iceland												
Ireland												
Italy	1,456.8	1,542.0	1,696.9	2,699.6	3,965.0	7,270.0	8,500.0	10,159.1	12,199.7	13,900.4	14,612.4	15,752.1
Liechtenstein												
Luxembourg												
Malta												
Monaco												
Netherlands	3,740.8	4,136.2	4,630.1	4,636.8	4,626.7	5,331.9	5,416.8	5,653.8	5,839.2	5,635.9	5,334.9	5,409.0
Norway	849.0	1,102.0	1,161.0	1,543.0	1,811.0	2,130.0	2,351.0	2,729.0	3,340.0	3,913.0	4,434.0	4,535.0
Portugal	1,961.4	2,072.8	2,310.2	2,667.7	3,150.0	3,351.5	3,817.2	4,503.2	5,161.9	5,540.0	5,550.3	5,411.7
Spain	2,584.0	3,310.2	3,564.0	4,259.0	5,663.2	6,680.0	8,972.2	11,304.0	14,250.0	17,384.0	18,059.3	17,413.4
Sweden	2,727.7	2,766.9	2,801.7	2,318.7	2,583.9	2,826.8	3,305.7	2,824.9	3,089.9	3,327.4	3,637.4	3,760.5
Switzerland	2,470.0	2,844.0	2,945.7	3,109.2	3,158.2	3,179.4	3,202.8	3,249.9	3,661.8	4,102.7	4,303.6	4,441.0
Turkey	7,200.0	10,046.0	13,409.0	13,997.0	15,706.0	19,863.0	26,681.0	29,978.0	32,433.0	37,335.2	43,394.0	45,206.3
United Kingdom	38,302.5	41,430.9	47,089.7	51,718.1	58,818.9	66,856.2	69,924.1	69,927.4	69,437.8	67,231.1	66,014.0	58,303.7
Eastern Europe												
Albania												
Belarus												
Bosnia-Herzegovina												
Bulgaria												
Croatia												
Czech Republic	47.0	80.2	125.7	165.4	268.3	376.8	1,048.4	1,626.6	2,333.4	2,754.4	3,507.9	3,388.0
Estonia												
Georgia												
Hungary	22.8	96.0	245.8	407.7	598.4	880.7	972.4	1,217.7	1,477.0	1,617.7	1,681.1	1,505.4
Latvia												
Lithuania												
Macedonia												
Moldova												
Montenegro												
Poland	90.9	179.8	371.7	600.1	806.4	1,172.6	1,996.3	3,386.8	5,124.0	6,996.2	9,010.0	10,744.1
Romania			48.4	82.8	137.2	219.8	308.0	721.5	1,287.1	1,848.2	2,719.1	2,248.7
Russia						206.0	1,319.0	2,480.0	5,660.0	8,940.0	9,300.0	8,601.0
Serbia												
Slovakia												
Slovenia												
Ukraine						461.2	2,341.7	3,717.0	6,078.0	10,045.0	9,032.6	5,188.2

Source: *Euromonitor International from trade sources*

Banking and Finance Statistics

Table 4.7

Charge Cards in Circulation 1998-2009
'000

	1998	1999	2000	2001	2002	2003	2004	2005	2006	2007	2008	2009
Western Europe												
Austria	799.2	832.1	932.0	1,019.1	1,049.1	1,062.6	1,051.6	1,065.2	1,121.0	1,172.4	1,267.3	1,338.2
Belgium	2,308.2	2,417.6	2,535.9	2,665.9	2,581.5	2,816.2	2,794.8	2,770.2	2,841.1	3,015.2	3,099.3	3,207.3
Cyprus												
Denmark												
Finland												
France	10,181.0	10,906.0	11,753.0	12,836.0	13,628.0	14,719.0	17,661.3	19,727.0	25,278.1	27,557.1	27,315.5	27,450.1
Germany	16,037.0	17,198.0	19,061.0	18,228.9	19,106.9	19,308.4	19,650.1	20,300.7	20,689.7	20,899.0	21,357.5	21,753.2
Gibraltar												
Greece	275.0	315.0	342.0	305.6	306.3	297.9	76.5	69.5	60.5	60.6	60.1	59.3
Iceland												
Ireland												
Italy	11,654.4	12,336.0	15,272.1	17,296.4	17,792.0	18,375.0	18,520.0	18,732.9	19,074.4	20,604.6	21,371.6	23,315.2
Liechtenstein												
Luxembourg												
Malta												
Monaco												
Netherlands	359.2	363.8	369.9	367.2	363.3	378.1	377.2	394.3	401.6	391.2	387.5	399.2
Norway	422.0	450.0	480.0	505.0	526.0	552.0	597.0	708.0	832.0	987.0	1,083.0	1,030.5
Portugal	206.9	265.3	316.3	330.2	394.3	451.9	581.9	646.0	729.0	751.4	794.9	825.2
Spain	10,338.0	12,461.8	12,493.0	13,487.0	15,273.8	17,177.0	19,989.8	21,855.2	24,031.0	25,743.0	26,760.7	26,360.6
Sweden	876.9	942.3	1,009.0	1,025.0	807.0	839.0	807.0	813.0	850.0	968.0	1,030.0	1,042.6
Switzerland	184.0	197.0	185.3	172.0	174.8	179.6	188.2	204.1	210.6	207.7	197.1	224.0
Turkey												
United Kingdom	3,306.5	3,495.1	3,840.3	4,511.9	4,425.1	4,546.8	4,544.0	4,845.6	4,957.2	5,544.2	6,220.6	5,760.3
Eastern Europe												
Albania												
Belarus												
Bosnia-Herzegovina												
Bulgaria												
Croatia												
Czech Republic	253.3	267.2	294.4	286.8	294.9	335.2	327.0	357.3	376.8	436.5	434.4	452.7
Estonia												
Georgia												
Hungary	5.2	6.0	6.4	6.2	5.3	10.8	17.2	18.2	20.0	19.9	18.8	17.4
Latvia												
Lithuania												
Macedonia												
Moldova												
Montenegro												
Poland	456.1	846.6	1,040.5	1,124.2	1,204.4	861.2	884.2	891.8	853.4	778.3	827.3	797.5
Romania				0.1	0.7	1.8	4.2	7.8	14.0	13.5	13.9	11.3
Russia												
Serbia												
Slovakia												
Slovenia												
Ukraine												

Source: Euromonitor International from trade sources

Banking and Finance Statistics

Table 4.8

Credit Card Expenditure 1998-2009

US$ million

	1998	1999	2000	2001	2002	2003	2004	2005	2006	2007	2008	2009
Western Europe												
Austria	1,790.8	1,739.2	1,644.9	1,888.0	2,140.4	2,616.2	3,371.2	3,705.5	4,027.1	4,735.6	5,344.2	5,359.6
Belgium	542.3	566.9	537.8	551.1	708.7	1,056.8	1,398.7	1,843.2	2,418.3	3,511.9	4,013.1	3,668.1
Cyprus												
Denmark	1,396.2	1,455.5	1,358.2	1,434.3	1,651.7	1,980.0	4,500.1	5,066.1	5,545.5	6,767.1	8,393.2	7,437.8
Finland												
France	4,248.9	4,528.4	4,331.1	4,609.4	5,274.9	6,909.0	8,085.7	8,513.4	9,032.7	10,381.7	12,234.6	14,830.1
Germany	5,281.6	5,181.2	4,718.0	5,386.4	6,688.8	9,090.4	10,761.7	11,743.1	12,315.6	14,315.0	15,938.6	15,328.8
Gibraltar												
Greece	982.4	1,590.4	2,049.7	1,897.5	2,062.9	4,843.1	6,744.3	8,082.4	8,518.7	10,222.8	11,563.4	10,316.6
Iceland												
Ireland												
Italy	2,464.1	2,696.4	2,744.3	3,300.3	3,857.8	5,423.9	7,275.3	8,918.7	10,908.0	14,225.0	15,632.6	14,752.6
Liechtenstein												
Luxembourg												
Malta												
Monaco												
Netherlands	4,620.5	5,362.5	4,716.9	4,768.0	5,088.9	6,070.1	7,119.4	7,677.8	8,768.0	10,509.4	12,584.6	10,840.1
Norway	796.5	1,012.5	1,141.3	1,472.3	2,103.1	3,071.0	4,101.2	5,124.4	6,000.0	8,308.2	9,524.4	10,267.8
Portugal	5,898.8	7,079.8	7,822.6	7,673.4	9,370.3	11,997.2	14,924.9	16,726.2	18,941.3	21,726.0	26,358.7	23,199.5
Spain	3,729.8	4,405.3	4,245.5	4,864.9	7,995.4	11,570.5	16,268.4	19,716.0	22,285.5	26,958.0	28,466.6	25,683.2
Sweden	1,593.5	1,621.7	1,808.1	2,217.8	1,925.0	2,852.7	4,916.0	3,443.6	5,050.5	10,948.1	13,354.3	11,717.2
Switzerland	8,268.7	9,059.0	8,441.3	9,071.4	10,030.1	11,428.4	12,897.5	13,725.8	14,939.7	18,179.1	20,335.1	19,628.8
Turkey	15,725.4	12,739.5	16,790.9	9,922.6	14,577.0	23,774.7	41,047.6	57,621.0	69,171.0	91,482.9	118,745.7	114,415.2
United Kingdom	90,886.6	103,429.7	108,405.7	111,851.7	131,718.7	160,931.3	195,945.3	194,450.6	193,129.2	219,567.1	208,718.5	168,059.4
Eastern Europe												
Albania												
Belarus												
Bosnia-Herzegovina												
Bulgaria												
Croatia												
Czech Republic	31.1	36.6	43.6	51.7	102.9	183.9	594.5	1,032.0	1,517.5	1,856.1	2,710.8	2,468.2
Estonia												
Georgia												
Hungary	12.8	19.0	42.2	75.8	142.6	236.9	349.9	485.2	699.8	1,025.0	1,243.1	1,058.7
Latvia												
Lithuania												
Macedonia												
Moldova												
Montenegro												
Poland	230.8	332.7	425.7	546.2	1,065.4	1,417.6	1,957.8	3,063.2	3,689.5	5,562.3	8,116.7	6,608.2
Romania			4.6	26.6	58.7	103.8	133.8	209.6	420.6	856.3	942.2	746.1
Russia						123.8	537.9	1,019.5	1,703.9	2,260.4	3,369.6	2,811.2
Serbia												
Slovakia												
Slovenia												
Ukraine						17.2	109.7	203.0	306.8	659.9	1,148.7	435.9

Source: Euromonitor International from trade sources

Banking and Finance Statistics

Table 4.9

Charge Card Expenditure 1998-2009

US$ million

	1998	1999	2000	2001	2002	2003	2004	2005	2006	2007	2008	2009
Western Europe												
Austria	1,589.6	1,594.6	1,548.2	1,863.2	2,143.6	2,545.0	3,311.3	3,481.8	3,813.8	4,653.5	5,831.9	6,118.8
Belgium	5,635.9	5,751.7	5,426.3	5,783.3	6,105.6	7,397.1	8,382.6	8,810.8	9,983.4	12,096.6	13,983.2	13,392.9
Cyprus												
Denmark												
Finland												
France	25,433.0	30,254.2	30,746.5	40,276.4	47,097.6	65,477.2	73,280.9	93,212.6	122,945.6	164,240.9	200,496.0	195,909.7
Germany	28,653.4	21,274.6	20,844.3	21,774.5	25,123.4	32,827.2	40,119.5	42,242.2	44,361.4	50,323.3	54,955.2	53,008.2
Gibraltar												
Greece	361.7	553.7	707.7	489.7	528.1	683.3	230.1	202.7	242.4	269.7	296.9	273.7
Iceland												
Ireland												
Italy	18,680.9	20,232.6	20,643.9	23,138.9	27,980.2	34,161.6	44,928.0	49,013.6	49,730.5	57,433.3	67,083.0	67,228.5
Liechtenstein												
Luxembourg												
Malta												
Monaco												
Netherlands	2,388.8	2,327.1	2,014.9	2,003.5	2,173.6	2,632.5	2,992.3	2,973.5	2,829.0	2,855.7	3,316.0	2,676.3
Norway	2,312.8	2,295.1	2,073.4	2,079.8	2,385.4	2,642.4	3,021.7	3,314.7	3,783.7	5,787.1	6,176.3	5,110.8
Portugal	857.8	928.9	922.9	963.2	1,039.7	1,293.5	1,560.6	1,688.9	1,806.3	2,058.0	2,365.1	2,366.4
Spain	8,703.0	9,361.2	8,241.1	9,034.9	14,526.7	20,569.8	27,700.2	33,141.8	37,142.4	50,098.3	59,107.7	53,546.4
Sweden	5,087.9	5,086.1	5,583.1	5,041.2	5,102.8	6,675.5	7,293.5	7,573.7	8,186.1	22,384.0	23,977.0	21,938.0
Switzerland	1,939.6	2,124.9	1,980.1	2,127.9	2,352.7	2,680.7	3,025.3	3,219.6	3,324.1	3,397.7	3,640.6	3,574.4
Turkey												
United Kingdom	22,646.6	26,325.4	29,793.1	33,427.8	34,829.7	38,675.0	46,129.2	47,997.3	55,614.6	66,672.7	61,385.8	44,682.4
Eastern Europe												
Albania												
Belarus												
Bosnia-Herzegovina												
Bulgaria												
Croatia												
Czech Republic	233.6	231.1	232.8	243.2	291.0	401.0	440.0	526.9	602.0	806.4	965.9	919.2
Estonia												
Georgia												
Hungary	6.5	7.0	8.6	12.0	17.0	25.0	32.9	43.7	70.8	102.1	124.3	80.7
Latvia												
Lithuania												
Macedonia												
Moldova												
Montenegro												
Poland	432.9	676.8	855.7	1,264.7	2,350.8	2,685.9	2,816.2	3,456.9	4,756.6	5,921.7	7,705.0	5,622.3
Romania				0.2	1.0	2.5	4.7	10.7	20.9	25.1	26.4	19.0
Russia												
Serbia												
Slovakia												
Slovenia												
Ukraine												

Source: *Euromonitor International from trade sources*

Banking and Finance Statistics

Table 4.10

Credit Card Transactions 1998-2009

Million

	1998	1999	2000	2001	2002	2003	2004	2005	2006	2007	2008	2009
Western Europe												
Austria	13.7	13.6	14.2	17.5	19.3	19.0	26.8	28.5	30.2	31.8	33.1	35.2
Belgium	3.8	4.3	4.6	4.8	5.5	7.1	9.4	11.9	15.5	21.9	23.8	24.7
Cyprus												
Denmark	12.0	12.5	13.0	13.0	14.0	15.0	36.8	44.6	49.4	57.2	68.2	65.0
Finland												
France	52.3	59.2	66.0	73.0	80.0	88.0	93.9	98.9	104.0	109.6	122.0	153.8
Germany	24.2	26.4	28.9	31.8	36.3	40.3	44.1	47.9	52.5	56.1	58.9	60.1
Gibraltar												
Greece	24.9	37.6	50.4	41.9	39.3	50.5	59.9	60.7	64.4	69.3	75.3	71.6
Iceland												
Ireland												
Italy	23.3	24.6	27.9	34.3	38.0	47.8	55.9	69.5	70.0	99.8	102.1	103.0
Liechtenstein												
Luxembourg												
Malta												
Monaco												
Netherlands	43.0	45.0	46.8	49.1	51.8	55.1	57.7	65.0	69.1	75.4	80.6	77.7
Norway	5.8	7.6	9.3	12.7	16.5	21.6	27.0	31.8	39.0	42.9	55.6	66.6
Portugal	64.5	90.9	121.0	171.5	190.3	204.2	219.8	236.9	258.6	280.2	291.5	286.1
Spain	36.5	40.3	41.5	48.7	75.8	88.4	115.0	135.0	178.6	259.3	320.0	327.0
Sweden	16.6	17.9	21.0	23.0	30.0	36.0	100.0	111.0	134.0	123.0	148.0	155.0
Switzerland	63.1	77.0	80.1	87.1	90.1	88.8	90.7	94.8	100.8	117.8	120.5	124.0
Turkey	299.9	359.9	465.0	511.9	594.1	787.2	1,079.2	1,240.4	1,273.4	1,368.4	1,603.4	1,768.9
United Kingdom	1,127.7	1,247.8	1,345.1	1,434.4	1,571.2	1,702.0	1,850.9	1,675.2	1,669.2	1,681.2	1,810.5	1,866.4
Eastern Europe												
Albania												
Belarus												
Bosnia-Herzegovina												
Bulgaria												
Croatia												
Czech Republic	0.6	0.7	0.9	1.0	2.0	3.2	8.7	15.1	24.7	32.0	44.6	48.9
Estonia												
Georgia												
Hungary	0.4	0.5	1.2	2.0	3.2	4.7	6.9	9.4	15.2	19.8	23.1	25.5
Latvia												
Lithuania												
Macedonia												
Moldova												
Montenegro												
Poland	2.0	5.5	9.6	12.9	27.3	34.1	45.1	67.5	81.5	107.9	138.1	157.0
Romania			0.0	0.5	0.8	1.6	2.8	5.2	9.8	15.0	17.4	16.6
Russia						1.4	3.0	5.5	9.4	18.0	27.6	31.6
Serbia												
Slovakia												
Slovenia												
Ukraine						0.3	1.6	2.7	5.8	11.0	20.2	13.8

Source: *Euromonitor International from trade sources*

Banking and Finance Statistics

Table 4.11

Charge Card Transactions 1998-2009
Million

	1998	1999	2000	2001	2002	2003	2004	2005	2006	2007	2008	2009
Western Europe												
Austria	13.2	13.1	13.7	16.9	18.7	18.4	25.9	27.5	29.2	31.5	36.7	40.2
Belgium	55.9	58.8	62.3	65.7	66.2	64.7	66.2	69.5	80.0	93.9	101.6	107.3
Cyprus												
Denmark												
Finland												
France	166.0	260.0	309.0	426.0	497.0	584.0	632.0	813.0	1,077.0	1,328.0	1,529.0	1,593.0
Germany	252.8	278.6	271.3	289.0	299.0	346.0	366.4	369.5	377.0	382.5	386.3	388.4
Gibraltar												
Greece	3.6	5.7	8.4	5.9	6.0	6.4	1.8	1.5	1.9	1.9	1.9	1.9
Iceland												
Ireland												
Italy	179.2	201.2	244.4	280.1	320.3	326.2	377.7	394.1	395.9	404.1	420.5	442.2
Liechtenstein												
Luxembourg												
Malta												
Monaco												
Netherlands	11.2	11.0	11.2	11.6	12.3	12.8	13.3	14.7	14.2	13.1	13.6	11.9
Norway	15.4	16.0	16.6	17.3	16.8	17.4	18.9	19.9	22.4	30.7	32.0	29.5
Portugal	27.3	33.8	37.4	41.5	41.8	47.2	53.1	57.7	62.0	66.9	73.9	79.5
Spain	152.5	178.7	180.5	210.3	325.2	376.7	463.0	540.0	641.9	777.8	824.0	842.0
Sweden	36.5	40.0	47.0	52.0	51.0	64.0	59.0	59.0	63.0	73.0	97.0	107.8
Switzerland	6.6	9.4	10.0	11.2	11.6	11.6	11.9	12.6	12.4	12.0	11.4	11.0
Turkey												
United Kingdom	169.7	185.0	198.0	235.7	230.8	240.7	240.7	247.3	268.8	279.5	294.3	298.0
Eastern Europe												
Albania												
Belarus												
Bosnia-Herzegovina												
Bulgaria												
Croatia												
Czech Republic	6.7	7.2	8.1	8.0	8.2	9.7	9.7	10.8	11.5	14.0	14.1	15.1
Estonia												
Georgia												
Hungary	0.1	0.1	0.1	0.1	0.1	0.1	0.1	0.1	0.2	0.3	0.4	0.3
Latvia												
Lithuania												
Macedonia												
Moldova												
Montenegro												
Poland	10.7	17.9	29.7	52.1	89.0	96.1	91.0	97.7	107.1	132.0	153.1	149.5
Romania				0.0	0.0	0.0	0.1	0.2	0.4	0.5	0.6	0.2
Russia												
Serbia												
Slovakia												
Slovenia												
Ukraine												

Source: *Euromonitor International from trade sources*

Banking and Finance Statistics

Table 4.12

Average Expenditure per Credit Card 1998-2009

US$ per card

	1998	1999	2000	2001	2002	2003	2004	2005	2006	2007	2008	2009
Western Europe												
Austria	2,516.6	2,280.4	2,004.6	2,157.6	2,261.3	2,720.0	3,555.3	3,591.7	3,678.4	4,026.8	4,256.1	4,077.8
Belgium	4,790.4	4,506.0	3,729.5	3,239.7	3,156.9	3,377.4	3,669.1	3,771.0	4,155.8	4,658.9	4,334.8	3,354.5
Cyprus												
Denmark	3,508.0	3,457.3	2,965.4	2,885.8	3,053.0	3,356.0	5,697.1	5,293.2	5,429.3	7,187.5	7,526.8	6,119.1
Finland												
France	1,721.4	1,646.7	1,443.7	1,421.5	1,507.1	1,818.2	2,018.9	2,043.3	2,087.8	2,307.5	2,413.9	1,773.4
Germany	5,681.3	4,267.8	2,738.9	2,218.4	2,090.8	2,356.4	2,638.8	2,244.0	1,873.4	2,112.6	2,261.7	2,138.3
Gibraltar												
Greece	649.3	789.7	676.4	457.9	400.0	868.0	1,195.4	1,336.9	1,355.5	1,524.1	1,664.9	1,531.9
Iceland												
Ireland												
Italy	1,691.4	1,748.6	1,617.2	1,222.5	973.0	746.1	855.9	877.9	894.1	1,023.4	1,069.8	936.5
Liechtenstein												
Luxembourg												
Malta												
Monaco												
Netherlands	1,235.2	1,296.5	1,018.7	1,028.3	1,099.9	1,138.5	1,314.3	1,358.0	1,501.6	1,864.7	2,358.9	2,004.1
Norway	938.2	918.8	983.0	954.2	1,161.3	1,441.8	1,744.5	1,877.8	1,796.4	2,123.2	2,148.0	2,264.1
Portugal	3,007.4	3,415.6	3,386.1	2,876.4	2,974.7	3,579.6	3,909.9	3,714.3	3,669.5	3,921.7	4,749.1	4,286.9
Spain	1,443.4	1,330.8	1,191.2	1,142.3	1,411.8	1,732.1	1,813.2	1,744.2	1,563.9	1,550.7	1,576.3	1,474.9
Sweden	584.2	586.1	645.3	956.5	745.0	1,009.2	1,487.1	1,219.0	1,634.5	3,290.3	3,671.4	3,115.9
Switzerland	3,347.6	3,185.3	2,865.6	2,917.6	3,175.9	3,594.4	4,027.0	4,223.5	4,079.8	4,431.0	4,725.1	4,419.9
Turkey	2,184.1	1,268.1	1,252.2	708.9	928.1	1,196.9	1,538.5	1,922.1	2,132.7	2,450.3	2,736.5	2,531.0
United Kingdom	2,372.9	2,496.4	2,302.1	2,162.7	2,239.4	2,407.1	2,802.3	2,780.7	2,781.3	3,265.9	3,161.7	2,882.5
Eastern Europe												
Albania												
Belarus												
Bosnia-Herzegovina												
Bulgaria												
Croatia												
Czech Republic	661.4	456.5	346.8	312.9	383.6	488.0	567.0	634.5	650.3	673.9	772.8	728.5
Estonia												
Georgia												
Hungary	559.6	197.9	171.8	185.9	238.4	268.9	359.8	398.5	473.8	633.6	739.4	703.2
Latvia												
Lithuania												
Macedonia												
Moldova												
Montenegro												
Poland	2,538.7	1,850.6	1,145.2	910.1	1,321.2	1,208.9	980.7	904.4	720.0	795.0	900.9	615.1
Romania			95.8	321.8	427.9	472.5	434.5	290.4	326.8	463.3	346.5	331.8
Russia						601.0	407.8	411.1	301.0	252.8	362.3	326.8
Serbia												
Slovakia												
Slovenia												
Ukraine						37.4	46.8	54.6	50.5	65.7	127.2	84.0

Source: *Euromonitor International from trade sources*

Banking and Finance Statistics

Table 4.13

Average Expenditure per Charge Card 1998-2009

US$ per card

	1998	1999	2000	2001	2002	2003	2004	2005	2006	2007	2008	2009
Western Europe												
Austria	1,988.9	1,916.5	1,661.1	1,828.4	2,043.4	2,395.1	3,148.9	3,268.7	3,402.2	3,969.1	4,601.9	4,572.4
Belgium	2,441.7	2,379.1	2,139.8	2,169.4	2,365.2	2,626.6	2,999.4	3,180.6	3,513.9	4,011.9	4,511.7	4,175.7
Cyprus												
Denmark												
Finland												
France	2,498.1	2,774.1	2,616.1	3,137.8	3,455.9	4,448.5	4,149.2	4,725.1	4,863.7	5,960.0	7,340.0	7,136.9
Germany	1,786.7	1,237.0	1,093.6	1,194.5	1,314.9	1,700.1	2,041.7	2,080.8	2,144.1	2,407.9	2,573.1	2,436.8
Gibraltar												
Greece	1,315.2	1,757.7	2,069.4	1,602.2	1,724.1	2,294.1	3,007.4	2,915.2	4,007.3	4,450.6	4,944.0	4,613.7
Iceland												
Ireland												
Italy	1,602.9	1,640.1	1,351.7	1,337.8	1,572.6	1,859.1	2,425.9	2,616.4	2,607.2	2,787.4	3,138.9	2,883.5
Liechtenstein												
Luxembourg												
Malta												
Monaco												
Netherlands	6,649.5	6,396.8	5,447.5	5,456.3	5,983.2	6,961.8	7,933.4	7,541.7	7,044.8	7,300.4	8,557.3	6,703.5
Norway	5,480.5	5,100.3	4,319.6	4,118.4	4,535.0	4,786.9	5,061.5	4,681.7	4,547.7	5,863.3	5,702.9	4,959.7
Portugal	4,145.5	3,501.4	2,918.3	2,916.7	2,636.7	2,862.6	2,682.1	2,614.6	2,477.9	2,738.9	2,975.4	2,867.8
Spain	841.8	751.2	659.7	669.9	951.1	1,197.5	1,385.7	1,516.4	1,545.6	1,946.1	2,208.8	2,031.3
Sweden	5,802.3	5,397.8	5,533.3	4,918.2	6,323.2	7,956.5	9,037.8	9,315.8	9,630.7	23,123.9	23,278.6	21,042.2
Switzerland	10,541.1	10,786.5	10,688.6	12,371.2	13,459.6	14,930.2	16,071.7	15,772.4	15,787.0	16,358.5	18,470.8	15,957.2
Turkey												
United Kingdom	6,849.2	7,532.1	7,758.0	7,408.7	7,870.9	8,506.0	10,151.8	9,905.4	11,218.9	12,025.6	9,868.1	7,756.9
Eastern Europe												
Albania												
Belarus												
Bosnia-Herzegovina												
Bulgaria												
Croatia												
Czech Republic	922.2	864.7	790.7	847.9	986.7	1,196.2	1,345.3	1,474.9	1,597.7	1,847.6	2,223.6	2,030.6
Estonia												
Georgia												
Hungary	1,246.8	1,162.5	1,333.0	1,936.4	3,223.6	2,324.1	1,909.9	2,404.2	3,539.6	5,142.7	6,595.1	4,626.7
Latvia												
Lithuania												
Macedonia												
Moldova												
Montenegro												
Poland	949.1	799.4	822.4	1,125.0	1,951.8	3,118.8	3,185.0	3,876.3	5,573.4	7,608.5	9,313.4	7,050.0
Romania				1,564.1	1,385.1	1,389.1	1,128.7	1,362.2	1,495.2	1,866.3	1,906.0	1,683.2
Russia												
Serbia												
Slovakia												
Slovenia												
Ukraine												

Source: *Euromonitor International from trade sources*

Banking and Finance Statistics   **Table 4.14**

Average Expenditure per Credit Card Transaction 1998-2009

US$ per transaction

	1998	1999	2000	2001	2002	2003	2004	2005	2006	2007	2008	2009
Western Europe												
Austria	130.9	128.0	115.8	108.1	110.9	137.6	125.7	130.2	133.3	148.8	161.6	152.1
Belgium	144.6	132.8	116.9	114.8	128.9	148.8	148.8	154.9	156.0	160.4	168.6	148.5
Cyprus												
Denmark	116.3	116.6	104.4	110.3	118.3	131.8	122.2	113.6	112.3	118.3	123.0	114.4
Finland												
France	81.2	76.5	65.6	63.1	65.9	78.5	86.1	86.1	86.9	94.7	100.3	96.4
Germany	218.3	196.0	163.3	169.6	184.5	225.7	244.2	245.1	234.6	255.2	270.6	255.1
Gibraltar												
Greece	39.5	42.2	40.7	45.3	52.5	95.9	112.6	133.2	132.4	147.6	153.6	144.0
Iceland												
Ireland												
Italy	105.8	109.6	98.4	96.2	101.5	113.5	130.1	128.3	155.8	142.5	153.1	143.2
Liechtenstein												
Luxembourg												
Malta												
Monaco												
Netherlands	107.6	119.2	100.7	97.2	98.3	110.1	123.4	118.1	126.9	139.4	156.1	139.5
Norway	138.3	132.7	122.5	116.3	127.6	142.3	152.0	161.1	153.8	193.7	171.3	154.2
Portugal	91.5	77.9	64.6	44.7	49.3	58.7	67.9	70.6	73.3	77.6	90.4	81.1
Spain	102.2	109.3	102.3	99.9	105.5	131.0	141.4	146.0	124.8	104.0	89.0	78.5
Sweden	96.0	90.8	86.1	96.5	64.2	79.3	49.2	31.0	37.7	89.0	90.2	75.6
Switzerland	131.1	117.6	105.3	104.2	111.3	128.6	142.2	144.9	148.2	154.3	168.7	158.3
Turkey	52.4	35.4	36.1	19.4	24.5	30.2	38.0	46.5	54.3	66.9	74.1	64.7
United Kingdom	80.6	82.9	80.6	78.0	83.8	94.6	105.9	116.1	115.7	130.6	115.3	90.0
Eastern Europe												
Albania												
Belarus												
Bosnia-Herzegovina												
Bulgaria												
Croatia												
Czech Republic	56.4	54.4	49.1	49.6	52.7	57.9	68.0	68.3	61.4	57.9	60.8	50.4
Estonia												
Georgia												
Hungary	36.1	41.7	35.8	37.6	44.1	50.6	50.8	51.4	46.1	51.8	53.9	41.5
Latvia												
Lithuania												
Macedonia												
Moldova												
Montenegro												
Poland	115.4	60.5	44.3	42.3	39.0	41.6	43.4	45.4	45.3	51.6	58.8	42.1
Romania			463.0	51.4	72.3	64.0	47.7	40.1	42.9	57.0	54.1	44.9
Russia						88.4	179.3	185.4	181.3	125.5	122.0	89.0
Serbia												
Slovakia												
Slovenia												
Ukraine						61.5	66.6	75.2	52.7	60.0	56.8	31.6

Source: Euromonitor International from trade sources

Banking and Finance Statistics

Table 4.15

Average Expenditure per Charge Card Transaction 1998-2009

US$ per transaction

	1998	1999	2000	2001	2002	2003	2004	2005	2006	2007	2008	2009
Western Europe												
Austria	120.2	121.3	112.7	110.3	114.8	138.4	127.7	126.5	130.7	147.7	159.0	152.3
Belgium	100.8	97.8	87.1	88.0	92.2	114.3	126.6	126.8	124.8	128.8	137.6	124.8
Cyprus												
Denmark												
Finland												
France	153.2	116.4	99.5	94.5	94.8	112.1	116.0	114.7	114.2	123.7	131.1	123.0
Germany	113.3	76.4	76.8	75.4	84.0	94.9	109.5	114.3	117.7	131.6	142.3	136.5
Gibraltar												
Greece	101.9	97.2	84.5	82.7	87.7	105.9	125.0	132.0	129.0	141.9	153.2	145.0
Iceland												
Ireland												
Italy	104.2	100.6	84.5	82.6	87.3	104.7	118.9	124.4	125.6	142.1	159.5	152.0
Liechtenstein												
Luxembourg												
Malta												
Monaco												
Netherlands	213.2	212.4	180.0	172.4	177.4	206.4	225.6	202.0	199.8	217.9	243.7	224.7
Norway	150.2	143.4	124.9	120.2	142.0	151.9	159.9	166.6	168.9	188.5	193.0	173.5
Portugal	31.4	27.5	24.7	23.2	24.9	27.4	29.4	29.3	29.2	30.8	32.0	29.8
Spain	57.1	52.4	45.7	43.0	44.7	54.6	59.8	61.4	57.9	64.4	71.7	63.6
Sweden	139.4	127.2	118.8	96.9	100.1	104.3	123.6	128.4	130.0	306.7	247.2	203.5
Switzerland	292.8	226.3	198.7	189.4	202.7	231.9	254.2	254.6	268.1	284.1	318.5	325.2
Turkey												
United Kingdom	133.4	142.3	150.5	141.8	150.9	160.7	191.7	194.1	206.9	238.6	208.6	149.9
Eastern Europe												
Albania												
Belarus												
Bosnia-Herzegovina												
Bulgaria												
Croatia												
Czech Republic	34.9	32.3	28.9	30.3	35.3	41.3	45.4	48.8	52.1	57.7	68.5	60.7
Estonia												
Georgia												
Hungary	108.4	99.5	107.0	133.9	189.0	312.4	365.0	336.2	292.7	329.5	355.0	278.2
Latvia												
Lithuania												
Macedonia												
Moldova												
Montenegro												
Poland	40.6	37.8	28.8	24.3	26.4	27.9	30.9	35.4	44.4	44.9	50.3	37.6
Romania				28.7	48.5	69.5	50.4	51.9	47.1	50.0	43.9	95.1
Russia												
Serbia												
Slovakia												
Slovenia												
Ukraine												

Source: *Euromonitor International from trade sources*

Consumer Expenditure

Consumer Expenditure Statistics

Table 5.1

Consumer Expenditure 1990-2009
Million units of national currency / as stated

	1990	1995	1996	1997	1998	1999	2000
Western Europe							
Austria	81,015	98,984	103,089	104,419	107,213	109,927	115,859
Belgium	89,929	108,999	111,808	115,910	120,179	122,918	130,579
Cyprus	3,562	5,602	5,904	6,178	6,647	7,157	7,915
Denmark	419,184	515,752	535,160	560,603	580,505	589,504	608,142
Finland	43,440	48,241	50,391	53,124	56,682	58,834	62,783
France	584,670	668,678	689,717	700,252	728,862	751,860	797,959
Germany	791,111	1,013,340	1,039,580	1,062,500	1,081,860	1,113,840	1,149,690
Gibraltar	133	167	176	165	166	163	164
Greece	34,237	71,896	79,455	87,585	94,786	99,025	105,097
Iceland	205,144	244,504	262,382	288,385	318,569	357,755	383,732
Ireland	21,189	27,767	30,676	33,920	38,099	42,580	49,397
Italy	404,844	564,870	592,371	624,969	657,391	685,715	727,205
Liechtenstein	1,158	1,784	1,946	2,112	2,266	2,547	2,626
Luxembourg	4,943	6,541	6,825	7,479	7,806	8,362	9,160
Malta	1,456	2,148	2,341	2,535	2,673	2,867	3,010
Monaco							
Netherlands	118,207	147,673	157,095	166,785	178,839	191,745	205,578
Norway	343,426	446,752	481,081	507,696	533,969	565,189	605,588
Portugal	36,736	57,763	60,997	65,360	70,732	76,163	81,954
Spain	194,086	280,748	296,920	316,311	339,069	366,095	397,750
Sweden	688,830	869,666	890,622	926,608	960,366	1,014,258	1,064,071
Switzerland	185,251	218,123	222,454	227,938	233,216	239,738	248,020
Turkey	283	5,805	10,665	21,459	49,694	74,994	124,768
United Kingdom	342,613	448,267	481,702	511,577	544,519	576,993	609,617
Eastern Europe							
Albania	11,890	198,129	334,910	330,996	377,018	408,032	410,367
Belarus	2	70,254	114,185	207,159	403,784	1,773,389	5,211,536
Bosnia-Herzegovina	1	3,206	4,197	5,770	8,447	10,157	10,400
Bulgaria	30	637	1,340	12,929	15,866	17,623	19,533
Croatia	207	76,349	80,524	94,309	100,220	100,473	109,419
Czech Republic	311,302	759,693	896,017	1,002,251	1,092,486	1,137,889	1,193,313
Estonia		25,528	36,783	44,873	50,169	52,193	57,876
Georgia		3,304	4,006	4,690	4,363	4,617	5,430
Hungary	1,159,524	3,165,857	3,821,099	4,640,638	5,550,415	6,462,198	7,361,600
Latvia	49	1,640	2,038	2,335	2,466	2,601	2,884
Lithuania	76	17,051	21,792	25,025	28,132	29,220	30,001
Macedonia	344	119,688	127,455	135,734	142,104	150,786	181,870
Moldova	8	3,556	5,021	5,796	6,631	8,736	13,379
Montenegro		648	493	542	562	586	739
Poland	27,674	205,751	265,144	325,160	375,347	419,854	474,790
Romania	56	4,799	7,443	18,456	27,729	39,089	54,870
Russia	286	688,038	1,000,861	1,222,135	1,452,024	2,459,553	3,167,498
Serbia		37,000	67,826	84,967	124,387	157,803	293,461
Slovakia	5,460	10,324	11,552	12,793	14,212	15,751	17,461
Slovenia	424	6,318	7,297	8,181	8,870	9,967	10,924
Ukraine	1	28,022	45,361	52,840	61,170	74,560	96,425

Source: National statistical offices/OECD/Eurostat/Euromonitor International

Consumer Expenditure 1990-2009 *(continued)*

Million units of national currency / as stated

	2004	2005	2006	2007	2008	2009	Total US$ million 2009	US$ per capita 2009
Western Europe								
Austria	130,039	136,373	141,764	146,595	151,707	152,756	212,269	25,321
Belgium	145,276	150,620	158,050	165,329	173,381	172,092	239,139	22,245
Cyprus	9,144	9,619	10,158	11,166	12,631	12,868	17,881	20,528
Denmark	696,488	735,377	774,854	807,478	830,281	802,349	149,668	27,156
Finland	74,852	77,807	82,315	86,992	91,442	90,095	125,197	23,511
France	927,529	967,566	1,012,077	1,059,189	1,090,223	1,090,862	1,515,862	24,274
Germany	1,234,490	1,256,910	1,291,187	1,309,712	1,341,051	1,339,485	1,861,349	22,699
Gibraltar	210	211	217	235	229	244	380	12,989
Greece	137,594	147,657	160,585	170,375	180,711	179,371	249,254	22,152
Iceland	496,490	560,976	626,252	689,294	698,547	645,509	5,221	16,179
Ireland	65,199	70,601	76,904	83,574	84,266	75,139	104,414	23,464
Italy	826,694	853,236	887,964	917,575	938,393	919,911	1,278,310	21,286
Liechtenstein	2,726	2,895	3,097	3,203	3,323	3,302	3,039	84,922
Luxembourg	10,523	10,969	11,420	11,874	12,980	11,913	16,555	34,051
Malta	3,303	3,441	3,489	3,659	3,940	3,876	5,386	13,179
Monaco								
Netherlands	237,424	245,144	249,660	259,142	265,186	257,275	357,509	21,786
Norway	735,379	770,229	819,419	875,399	916,912	941,066	149,618	31,175
Portugal	96,713	100,607	105,644	111,618	116,694	112,888	156,870	14,702
Spain	508,494	546,739	586,034	626,109	642,527	614,154	853,429	18,748
Sweden	1,235,312	1,287,641	1,347,172	1,418,909	1,456,913	1,484,129	193,916	21,074
Switzerland	264,804	270,492	278,805	289,759	301,277	303,301	279,150	36,925
Turkey	423,620	490,692	564,898	628,733	695,620	716,786	460,871	6,444
United Kingdom	737,927	772,181	808,061	849,935	877,596	859,099	1,339,795	21,746
Eastern Europe								
Albania	580,309	629,224	689,443	775,187	847,459	860,124	9,056	2,870
Belarus	27,001,692	34,170,019	41,158,150	50,862,554	68,224,331	77,244,627	27,691	2,863
Bosnia-Herzegovina	15,701	17,259	18,790	20,640	21,948	20,721	14,717	3,828
Bulgaria	28,081	31,606	36,822	41,579	48,665	46,591	33,121	4,405
Croatia	151,544	163,354	174,088	190,571	204,052	191,613	36,263	8,189
Czech Republic	1,448,801	1,515,653	1,627,403	1,750,428	1,882,104	1,886,236	98,936	9,452
Estonia	90,084	101,800	120,625	140,266	145,074	116,735	10,370	7,793
Georgia	7,104	7,589	10,544	11,614	13,488	14,313	8,568	1,954
Hungary	11,297,869	12,037,887	12,646,048	13,461,271	14,108,321	13,622,107	67,322	6,719
Latvia	4,550	5,463	6,972	8,807	9,749	7,720	15,298	6,788
Lithuania	41,271	47,060	53,686	63,121	71,321	61,788	24,874	7,430
Macedonia	212,252	227,494	248,793	278,814	327,784	330,783	7,501	3,675
Moldova	27,325	33,547	39,473	46,947	60,819	55,652	5,009	1,390
Montenegro	1,210	1,257	1,648	2,142	2,440	2,380	3,308	5,267
Poland	592,705	617,291	657,474	706,814	779,806	819,394	262,538	6,884
Romania	168,338	197,810	233,834	274,213	328,819	303,859	99,648	4,649
Russia	8,104,309	10,262,259	12,600,159	15,681,304	19,677,455	20,802,072	654,947	4,615
Serbia	1,057,080	1,286,733	1,498,988	1,723,239	2,036,304	2,135,935	31,606	4,290
Slovakia	25,504	27,784	30,960	33,908	37,647	37,771	52,487	9,728
Slovenia	15,373	16,364	17,230	19,130	20,934	20,878	29,012	14,342
Ukraine	184,236	255,628	322,282	427,245	581,361	595,561	76,441	1,663

Source: National statistical offices/OECD/Eurostat/Euromonitor International

Consumer Expenditure Statistics

Table 5.2

Consumer Expenditure by Object 2009

US$ million

	Food and Non-alcoholic Beverages	Alcoholic Beverages and Tobacco	Clothing and Footwear	Housing	Household Goods and Services	Health Goods and Medical Services
Western Europe						
Austria	23,623.2	6,274.9	12,005.0	44,911.8	14,162.2	7,189.2
Belgium	30,900.5	8,559.3	12,098.9	57,755.0	13,363.6	13,519.0
Cyprus						
Denmark	17,258.8	4,900.1	6,888.1	40,733.6	8,347.4	3,875.9
Finland	15,493.6	6,758.1	5,892.4	30,785.4	6,684.8	5,631.0
France	204,092.5	45,160.2	64,463.7	384,592.3	88,162.2	55,153.3
Germany	206,550.9	62,064.6	88,313.1	452,185.6	118,923.0	92,614.0
Gibraltar						
Greece	34,863.6	12,060.9	23,028.1	37,135.8	15,735.3	15,926.0
Iceland						
Ireland	11,071.0	5,237.4	5,065.1	22,735.3	6,347.7	3,913.1
Italy	190,545.6	33,553.2	97,353.2	273,553.9	94,949.1	37,780.5
Liechtenstein						
Luxembourg						
Malta						
Monaco						
Netherlands	41,285.1	10,189.0	19,178.4	82,352.3	25,021.0	4,480.7
Norway	20,539.2	6,346.1	8,630.4	29,635.7	9,021.3	4,444.7
Portugal	24,411.3	5,628.1	10,248.3	22,717.6	9,908.1	9,228.1
Spain	112,880.6	26,761.6	39,673.5	146,990.1	41,002.7	32,443.8
Sweden	24,494.9	6,988.8	9,834.5	52,411.3	10,345.8	6,644.6
Switzerland	29,257.6	9,568.4	10,243.8	68,655.7	11,552.7	42,982.2
Turkey	102,827.7	17,425.6	23,774.1	102,186.7	31,796.3	17,924.6
United Kingdom	118,562.1	44,611.0	73,784.4	295,009.1	72,966.5	23,157.0
Eastern Europe						
Albania						
Belarus	11,964.7	1,570.7	2,219.9	3,578.1	1,335.5	712.6
Bosnia-Herzegovina	4,833.8	803.6	702.7	1,953.1	1,005.6	646.9
Bulgaria	6,043.3	1,349.5	949.3	5,779.5	1,583.5	1,356.2
Croatia	9,348.7	958.6	2,350.5	11,071.5	1,462.5	822.1
Czech Republic	15,880.7	7,524.6	3,980.6	21,209.8	5,082.1	2,778.6
Estonia	1,518.1	852.4	801.8	1,867.5	598.3	318.3
Georgia	3,487.7	440.0	368.2	1,056.0	339.8	796.8
Hungary	10,949.4	5,321.8	2,398.5	13,124.1	5,186.3	2,814.4
Latvia	2,912.4	930.4	998.3	3,057.5	563.1	901.8
Lithuania	5,431.2	1,418.1	1,527.0	3,017.6	1,474.7	1,104.5
Macedonia	2,478.6	292.6	450.4	1,241.1	399.4	162.1
Moldova						
Montenegro	1,137.1	109.3	207.3	656.1	156.4	85.1
Poland	53,371.5	17,180.1	11,585.9	63,744.7	11,428.4	10,761.5
Romania	34,140.3	4,809.3	3,202.1	24,438.9	5,114.9	3,515.9
Russia	194,519.3	13,927.9	63,457.3	72,111.8	49,776.0	16,676.1
Serbia	7,882.5	1,449.0	1,576.1	6,676.5	1,836.3	1,594.6
Slovakia	9,511.8	2,283.1	2,083.0	13,437.4	3,032.1	1,962.1
Slovenia	4,339.3	1,329.5	1,422.6	5,454.0	1,777.6	1,050.9
Ukraine	32,193.9	4,865.1	11,709.8	6,675.5	3,091.7	3,292.4

Source: National statistical offices/OECD/Eurostat/Euromonitor International

Consumer Expenditure Statistics

Consumer Expenditure by Object 2009 *(continued)*

US$ million

	Transport	Communi- cations	Leisure and Recreation	Education	Hotels and Catering	Miscellaneous Goods and Services	Total
Western Europe							
Austria	25,836.5	5,427.1	24,045.2	1,859.7	24,863.6	22,071.1	212,269.4
Belgium	28,101.0	6,495.3	22,432.7	1,198.8	13,775.5	30,939.4	239,139.0
Cyprus							17,881.1
Denmark	17,727.4	3,098.7	16,635.7	1,087.5	9,855.9	19,258.8	149,667.8
Finland	13,448.4	3,881.7	15,280.7	349.9	8,005.4	12,985.1	125,196.5
France	218,422.4	39,463.5	136,045.5	12,643.6	94,103.2	173,560.0	1,515,862.4
Germany	263,914.2	57,842.1	177,575.5	15,809.9	106,016.1	219,537.6	1,861,349.5
Gibraltar							379.9
Greece	18,531.7	7,411.3	15,723.0	5,008.3	48,032.3	15,797.8	249,254.0
Iceland							5,221.0
Ireland	12,075.6	3,097.4	7,601.1	1,309.0	13,973.8	11,989.5	104,413.6
Italy	161,078.9	32,711.5	87,389.8	11,762.4	126,508.6	131,123.2	1,278,309.8
Liechtenstein							3,039.2
Luxembourg							16,554.9
Malta							5,386.3
Monaco							
Netherlands	44,226.8	15,748.2	37,294.5	1,841.3	18,664.3	57,227.4	357,509.1
Norway	19,839.6	4,036.3	19,496.3	736.8	9,139.0	17,752.3	149,617.7
Portugal	21,472.6	4,461.9	10,851.5	1,875.6	16,305.0	19,761.8	156,869.9
Spain	101,350.0	25,229.9	83,148.7	10,955.2	166,030.2	66,962.4	853,428.5
Sweden	23,793.9	6,277.3	22,063.3	591.5	10,330.1	20,139.6	193,915.5
Switzerland	22,663.7	7,644.0	22,495.5	1,448.8	21,231.1	31,406.3	279,149.7
Turkey	55,442.9	25,272.3	18,821.1	6,009.8	29,663.5	29,726.5	460,871.3
United Kingdom	203,579.9	27,648.8	144,719.1	21,467.7	137,239.1	177,050.4	1,339,795.2
Eastern Europe							
Albania							9,056.0
Belarus	2,073.6	1,127.0	963.7	394.2	662.4	1,088.8	27,691.3
Bosnia-Herzegovina	1,390.8	413.2	689.8	180.0	1,054.5	1,043.4	14,717.4
Bulgaria	6,910.7	2,089.1	2,139.3	219.4	3,115.4	1,586.0	33,121.0
Croatia	3,387.3	1,500.2	1,817.0	186.7	1,023.4	2,334.7	36,263.2
Czech Republic	11,457.2	3,261.4	10,428.6	705.8	7,239.9	9,386.6	98,936.1
Estonia	1,320.1	365.8	909.8	114.6	873.5	829.7	10,369.8
Georgia	568.3	243.6	271.2	117.5	402.5	476.8	8,568.3
Hungary	11,120.8	3,399.9	5,463.7	874.5	3,530.8	3,138.2	67,322.4
Latvia	1,785.6	812.5	1,543.0	597.7	650.2	544.9	15,297.5
Lithuania	4,961.5	602.3	2,052.5	264.4	843.0	2,177.4	24,874.3
Macedonia	907.0	602.0	225.1	132.8	233.3	376.2	7,500.6
Moldova							5,009.4
Montenegro	356.3	179.5	108.1	61.4	76.3	174.9	3,307.8
Poland	21,567.9	9,195.3	18,872.8	3,335.9	7,322.1	34,172.4	262,538.5
Romania	11,022.3	2,300.6	4,218.9	1,309.9	3,184.7	2,390.1	99,647.9
Russia	105,351.2	22,567.6	47,330.9	11,782.1	19,908.3	37,794.1	654,947.1
Serbia	4,363.7	1,511.8	1,915.6	395.3	762.3	1,642.1	31,605.7
Slovakia	4,257.7	1,735.6	5,263.8	779.6	3,375.3	4,763.6	52,486.9
Slovenia	4,880.9	734.7	2,930.0	403.1	2,083.2	2,605.9	29,011.7
Ukraine	3,625.8	2,365.6	2,966.3	1,626.5	2,095.5	1,932.8	76,440.9

Source: National statistical offices/OECD/Eurostat/Euromonitor International

Consumer Expenditure Statistics

Table 5.3

Food and Non-alcoholic Beverages Consumer Expenditure 1990-2009

Million units of national currency / as stated

	1990	1995	1996	1997	1998	1999	2000
Western Europe							
Austria	10,144	11,288	11,447	11,708	11,863	11,893	12,275
Belgium	13,471	16,606	16,549	16,790	16,840	16,837	16,984
Cyprus							
Denmark	59,706	68,186	69,386	72,033	73,139	71,953	74,403
Finland	7,098	7,442	7,091	7,201	7,360	7,681	7,923
France	91,014	99,625	100,480	103,048	105,971	107,962	112,679
Germany	109,205	124,900	125,340	125,130	126,670	128,480	132,140
Gibraltar							
Greece	7,372	12,956	14,032	15,087	15,963	16,452	17,112
Iceland							
Ireland	3,876	4,254	4,517	4,544	4,723	4,854	5,453
Italy	76,483	94,327	98,268	100,888	103,451	104,927	109,549
Liechtenstein							
Luxembourg							
Malta							
Monaco							
Netherlands	16,442	19,221	19,828	20,750	21,661	22,363	22,992
Norway	58,883	71,160	73,056	76,566	80,808	84,769	88,832
Portugal	6,809	10,577	11,042	11,386	12,364	12,938	13,424
Spain	38,522	48,226	50,166	51,454	52,535	54,643	56,813
Sweden	103,144	123,438	117,765	120,079	122,298	125,527	128,579
Switzerland	22,255	24,384	24,188	24,538	24,950	25,500	26,200
Turkey	84	1,637	2,971	5,589	13,909	20,160	29,500
United Kingdom	42,285	49,700	53,025	53,787	55,162	57,040	58,628
Eastern Europe							
Albania							
Belarus	1	35,395	61,069	116,376	213,036	1,011,114	3,060,851
Bosnia-Herzegovina		1,114	1,442	1,961	2,842	3,383	3,432
Bulgaria	8	192	404	4,936	5,237	5,196	5,560
Croatia	73	24,489	25,265	28,941	30,138	28,887	27,382
Czech Republic	73,302	147,982	170,392	185,987	202,846	213,690	221,837
Estonia		8,762	10,865	12,891	12,979	12,529	11,913
Georgia		1,867	2,268	2,597	2,503	2,658	2,738
Hungary	251,015	765,971	863,467	1,032,025	1,207,965	1,292,269	1,404,448
Latvia	15	605	718	736	732	696	725
Lithuania	33	6,716	8,466	8,795	9,057	9,149	9,195
Macedonia	131	42,408	43,991	47,734	49,689	49,791	53,464
Moldova							
Montenegro		307	229	248	252	258	320
Poland	9,307	56,518	69,900	79,991	85,015	87,926	108,406
Romania	19	1,685	2,656	6,597	9,798	13,532	19,042
Russia	95	337,129	496,606	603,091	705,183	1,171,374	1,481,340
Serbia		16,437	29,335	35,669	50,474	61,771	109,883
Slovakia	1,203	2,889	3,031	3,475	3,728	3,899	4,099
Slovenia	89	1,126	1,264	1,423	1,574	1,699	1,850
Ukraine	0	11,769	19,074	22,378	26,303	32,498	44,837

Source: *National statistical offices/OECD/Eurostat/Euromonitor International*

Consumer Expenditure Statistics

Food and Non-alcoholic Beverages Consumer Expenditure 1990-2009 *(continued)*

Million units of national currency / as stated

	2004	2005	2006	2007	2008	2009	Total US$ million 2009	US$ per capita 2009
Western Europe								
Austria	13,923	14,397	14,915	15,884	16,867	17,000	23,623	2,818
Belgium	19,915	20,122	20,293	21,208	22,143	22,237	30,901	2,874
Cyprus								
Denmark	80,799	82,133	85,504	89,952	95,012	92,522	17,259	3,131
Finland	9,166	9,403	9,808	10,458	11,405	11,150	15,494	2,910
France	130,625	132,836	136,031	140,017	146,426	146,871	204,093	3,268
Germany	138,050	138,330	141,986	145,404	152,328	148,640	206,551	2,519
Gibraltar								
Greece	20,816	21,958	23,749	24,728	25,748	25,089	34,864	3,098
Iceland								
Ireland	6,150	6,441	7,047	7,562	8,110	7,967	11,071	2,488
Italy	123,436	126,188	130,486	133,375	137,528	137,123	190,546	3,173
Liechtenstein								
Luxembourg								
Malta								
Monaco								
Netherlands	26,211	25,985	27,190	28,445	30,279	29,710	41,285	2,516
Norway	99,878	103,806	107,902	114,218	122,960	129,188	20,539	4,280
Portugal	16,148	16,284	16,937	17,727	18,326	17,567	24,411	2,288
Spain	72,112	77,092	81,301	85,239	86,123	81,232	112,881	2,480
Sweden	151,148	154,283	162,148	170,498	180,079	187,472	24,495	2,662
Switzerland	28,308	28,900	29,598	30,147	30,907	31,789	29,258	3,870
Turkey	97,683	112,018	125,083	135,615	153,810	159,926	102,828	1,438
United Kingdom	65,156	67,138	69,718	72,559	78,235	76,024	118,562	1,924
Eastern Europe								
Albania								
Belarus	12,284,901	15,546,259	18,725,634	22,687,513	30,037,828	33,375,333	11,965	1,237
Bosnia-Herzegovina	5,009	5,446	5,950	6,529	7,097	6,806	4,834	1,257
Bulgaria	6,579	6,890	7,664	8,310	9,259	8,501	6,043	804
Croatia	39,265	44,216	46,312	50,089	53,197	49,398	9,349	2,111
Czech Republic	242,159	243,450	251,863	274,311	307,171	302,769	15,881	1,517
Estonia	16,762	18,522	20,609	22,561	22,242	17,089	1,518	1,141
Georgia	3,468	3,467	4,806	5,024	5,676	5,826	3,488	795
Hungary	2,009,498	2,105,365	2,220,222	2,299,535	2,343,921	2,215,518	10,949	1,093
Latvia	1,010	1,143	1,354	1,695	1,869	1,470	2,912	1,292
Lithuania	11,683	12,469	13,963	15,806	16,308	13,491	5,431	1,622
Macedonia	70,290	77,347	81,784	91,548	108,126	109,308	2,479	1,214
Moldova								
Montenegro	479	484	637	747	855	818	1,137	1,811
Poland	125,780	129,952	137,310	145,555	159,278	166,575	53,371	1,400
Romania	58,717	68,369	80,468	94,074	112,545	104,105	34,140	1,593
Russia	2,917,551	3,407,070	3,981,650	4,453,490	5,726,139	6,178,215	194,519	1,371
Serbia	309,801	362,705	411,154	444,811	538,798	532,704	7,882	1,070
Slovakia	4,946	5,057	5,378	6,028	6,846	6,845	9,512	1,763
Slovenia	2,421	2,445	2,524	2,779	3,047	3,123	4,339	2,145
Ukraine	80,850	109,624	136,275	180,656	245,509	250,827	32,194	700

Source: *National statistical offices/OECD/Eurostat/Euromonitor International*

Consumer Expenditure Statistics

Table 5.4

Alcoholic Beverages and Tobacco Consumer Expenditure 1990-2009

Million units of national currency / as stated

	1990	1995	1996	1997	1998	1999	2000
Western Europe							
Austria	3,436	3,364	3,339	3,428	3,633	3,722	3,797
Belgium	3,041	3,645	3,809	4,004	4,234	4,529	4,685
Cyprus							
Denmark	24,617	24,725	25,255	25,498	25,403	25,917	26,514
Finland	2,851	2,921	3,031	3,183	3,247	3,255	3,466
France	16,826	22,180	23,120	23,787	24,873	26,010	27,103
Germany	35,802	38,190	38,640	38,740	39,210	40,140	40,240
Gibraltar							
Greece	1,248	3,048	3,425	3,847	4,270	4,582	4,822
Iceland							
Ireland	1,296	1,823	1,995	2,160	2,359	2,658	3,066
Italy	10,404	13,942	15,002	15,494	16,368	17,317	18,228
Liechtenstein							
Luxembourg							
Malta							
Monaco							
Netherlands	4,105	4,926	5,112	5,349	5,441	5,741	5,915
Norway	17,370	20,787	22,274	24,732	25,539	27,408	28,566
Portugal	1,512	2,222	2,334	2,437	2,699	2,909	3,012
Spain	4,402	7,471	7,707	8,946	10,185	11,125	12,065
Sweden	34,573	39,494	39,401	39,091	38,380	40,709	41,433
Switzerland	8,158	8,474	8,474	8,617	8,808	9,044	9,213
Turkey	6	125	226	476	1,122	1,435	3,556
United Kingdom	14,753	18,776	20,439	21,553	22,459	24,458	24,617
Eastern Europe							
Albania							
Belarus	0	6,756	8,479	17,148	33,263	119,613	350,424
Bosnia-Herzegovina		226	291	395	570	676	684
Bulgaria	1	17	35	312	421	499	654
Croatia	8	2,850	2,978	3,451	3,638	3,484	3,303
Czech Republic	39,622	73,261	80,709	83,581	91,771	97,372	99,016
Estonia		1,913	2,786	3,295	3,834	4,257	4,428
Georgia		109	124	139	131	139	166
Hungary	118,060	260,921	309,974	376,722	472,852	532,248	597,861
Latvia	3	126	152	176	179	193	238
Lithuania	8	1,606	1,881	2,188	2,263	2,366	2,264
Macedonia	16	6,682	6,838	6,142	6,619	7,043	9,207
Moldova							
Montenegro		37	28	30	30	30	37
Poland	2,632	17,062	22,058	25,757	28,627	30,415	32,994
Romania	3	253	398	1,016	1,500	2,264	2,943
Russia	18	24,797	35,043	43,125	52,564	91,316	118,388
Serbia		2,791	5,022	6,170	8,837	10,909	19,793
Slovakia	332	680	709	742	823	857	887
Slovenia	17	361	398	417	425	450	525
Ukraine	0	1,704	2,758	3,294	3,734	4,497	5,785

Source: *National statistical offices/OECD/Eurostat/Euromonitor International*

Consumer Expenditure Statistics

Alcoholic Beverages and Tobacco Consumer Expenditure 1990-2009 *(continued)*

Million units of national currency / as stated

	2004	2005	2006	2007	2008	2009	Total US$ million 2009	US$ per capita 2009
Western Europe								
Austria	4,244	4,509	4,448	4,487	4,577	4,516	6,275	749
Belgium	5,646	5,745	5,999	6,083	6,038	6,160	8,559	796
Cyprus								
Denmark	27,269	27,428	27,299	25,939	27,189	26,269	4,900	889
Finland	3,914	3,928	4,058	4,198	4,381	4,863	6,758	1,269
France	29,877	29,733	30,157	30,598	31,091	32,499	45,160	723
Germany	43,030	43,830	43,237	43,723	43,318	44,664	62,065	757
Gibraltar								
Greece	6,513	7,053	7,651	8,176	8,716	8,679	12,061	1,072
Iceland								
Ireland	3,484	3,688	3,889	4,198	4,115	3,769	5,237	1,177
Italy	21,649	22,335	23,484	23,932	24,475	24,146	33,553	559
Liechtenstein								
Luxembourg								
Malta								
Monaco								
Netherlands	6,965	6,992	7,163	7,353	7,421	7,332	10,189	621
Norway	31,766	32,528	33,741	35,539	38,447	39,916	6,346	1,322
Portugal	3,515	3,547	3,846	4,053	4,214	4,050	5,628	527
Spain	15,654	16,902	18,130	19,541	20,112	19,258	26,762	588
Sweden	45,051	44,801	45,159	47,487	49,385	53,489	6,989	760
Switzerland	9,493	9,515	9,599	9,782	9,897	10,396	9,568	1,266
Turkey	15,991	18,642	20,532	24,820	26,065	27,102	17,426	244
United Kingdom	28,579	28,853	29,349	29,946	30,287	28,605	44,611	724
Eastern Europe								
Albania								
Belarus	1,624,636	2,055,939	2,476,401	2,979,144	3,888,434	4,381,532	1,571	162
Bosnia-Herzegovina	969	1,085	1,163	1,180	1,161	1,131	804	209
Bulgaria	1,057	1,163	1,418	1,636	1,940	1,898	1,349	179
Croatia	5,062	5,325	5,206	5,494	5,659	5,065	959	216
Czech Republic	111,129	115,888	121,623	132,742	143,120	143,458	7,525	719
Estonia	7,263	8,187	9,681	11,345	11,873	9,596	852	641
Georgia	354	376	550	602	695	735	440	100
Hungary	919,447	971,101	1,014,941	1,077,806	1,120,587	1,076,824	5,322	531
Latvia	325	362	448	553	603	470	930	413
Lithuania	2,908	3,098	3,342	3,711	4,292	3,523	1,418	424
Macedonia	7,172	7,823	9,359	10,046	12,851	12,905	293	143
Moldova								
Montenegro	51	50	60	70	79	79	109	174
Poland	38,763	40,798	43,308	46,342	51,051	53,620	17,180	450
Romania	8,027	9,885	11,721	13,602	16,151	14,665	4,809	224
Russia	243,129	277,081	340,204	376,351	452,581	442,369	13,928	98
Serbia	61,568	65,310	77,138	86,984	97,687	97,922	1,449	197
Slovakia	1,234	1,287	1,369	1,523	1,579	1,643	2,283	423
Slovenia	661	734	778	839	934	957	1,329	657
Ukraine	12,080	16,447	20,294	26,929	36,785	37,905	4,865	106

Source: National statistical offices/OECD/Eurostat/Euromonitor International

Consumer Expenditure Statistics

Table 5.5

Clothing and Footwear Consumer Expenditure 1990-2009

Million units of national currency / as stated

	1990	1995	1996	1997	1998	1999	2000
Western Europe							
Austria	7,440	7,412	7,648	7,767	7,841	7,860	7,978
Belgium	5,776	7,045	7,251	7,427	7,348	6,949	6,763
Cyprus							
Denmark	22,196	26,312	26,960	28,831	29,972	29,679	30,350
Finland	2,439	2,227	2,551	2,729	2,861	2,890	2,894
France	39,510	38,755	38,982	39,652	40,280	40,798	42,345
Germany	63,665	67,310	68,230	68,070	67,820	68,140	69,530
Gibraltar							
Greece	4,177	7,925	8,883	9,595	10,396	10,880	11,370
Iceland							
Ireland	1,493	2,008	2,182	2,397	2,684	2,870	3,303
Italy	40,269	51,453	52,939	55,979	60,168	62,001	64,471
Liechtenstein							
Luxembourg							
Malta							
Monaco							
Netherlands	9,078	9,527	9,786	10,322	11,235	11,871	12,493
Norway	23,148	27,328	28,224	30,037	31,169	32,817	34,072
Portugal	3,323	4,873	5,103	5,439	5,868	6,003	6,303
Spain	13,340	18,538	19,501	20,475	21,764	23,599	24,643
Sweden	36,141	40,465	40,356	41,315	43,416	46,778	49,656
Switzerland	11,429	10,499	10,161	10,373	10,465	10,684	10,634
Turkey	37	750	1,328	2,841	5,980	6,909	10,852
United Kingdom	21,259	28,000	29,535	30,901	31,947	33,375	35,479
Eastern Europe							
Albania							
Belarus	0	5,374	9,225	14,119	35,442	179,333	440,577
Bosnia-Herzegovina		185	238	324	468	554	557
Bulgaria	2	40	85	648	811	841	711
Croatia	5	2,919	3,371	4,302	4,954	5,699	8,584
Czech Republic	21,346	40,762	45,566	51,166	55,369	57,915	61,899
Estonia		1,572	2,108	2,622	2,929	2,792	3,825
Georgia		235	276	288	305	322	364
Hungary	96,467	163,233	188,386	229,784	269,662	309,775	330,967
Latvia	2	106	138	180	219	224	241
Lithuania	3	896	1,363	1,537	1,791	1,823	1,822
Macedonia	30	7,474	7,901	8,103	8,476	8,945	9,621
Moldova							
Montenegro		48	36	39	40	41	51
Poland	1,812	11,802	15,024	18,037	19,734	21,334	24,308
Romania	3	222	329	787	1,141	1,524	1,996
Russia	73	102,515	151,708	194,153	240,099	407,648	488,593
Serbia		2,274	4,095	5,033	7,203	8,927	16,174
Slovakia	385	776	882	939	953	963	977
Slovenia	33	394	429	476	540	592	668
Ukraine	0	4,355	7,042	8,132	9,318	11,244	13,709

Source: National statistical offices/OECD/Eurostat/Euromonitor International

Consumer Expenditure Statistics

Clothing and Footwear Consumer Expenditure 1990-2009 *(continued)*
Million units of national currency / as stated

	2004	2005	2006	2007	2008	2009	Total US$ million 2009	US$ per capita 2009
Western Europe								
Austria	8,062	8,203	8,359	8,537	8,618	8,639	12,005	1,432
Belgium	7,279	7,575	7,773	8,330	8,597	8,707	12,099	1,125
Cyprus								
Denmark	33,734	34,847	36,913	38,833	38,592	36,926	6,888	1,250
Finland	3,585	3,780	4,026	4,302	4,489	4,240	5,892	1,107
France	46,182	46,667	47,471	48,744	47,748	46,390	64,464	1,032
Germany	64,940	65,930	66,733	69,750	70,976	63,553	88,313	1,077
Gibraltar								
Greece	13,723	14,447	15,610	16,313	17,010	16,572	23,028	2,047
Iceland								
Ireland	3,154	3,555	3,765	4,000	3,821	3,645	5,065	1,138
Italy	67,825	68,703	69,942	71,550	71,415	70,058	97,353	1,621
Liechtenstein								
Luxembourg								
Malta								
Monaco								
Netherlands	12,762	12,819	13,700	14,400	14,243	13,801	19,178	1,169
Norway	40,451	42,964	45,683	50,223	51,183	54,283	8,630	1,798
Portugal	7,039	7,130	7,292	7,565	7,752	7,375	10,248	960
Spain	27,974	28,973	29,861	31,029	30,902	28,550	39,673	872
Sweden	59,125	62,421	67,383	70,366	72,366	75,269	9,835	1,069
Switzerland	10,329	10,759	10,973	11,587	10,740	11,130	10,244	1,355
Turkey	38,475	35,975	37,498	38,986	39,988	36,976	23,774	332
United Kingdom	42,339	43,532	44,624	45,752	46,150	47,312	73,784	1,198
Eastern Europe								
Albania								
Belarus	2,133,872	2,700,365	3,252,619	4,128,188	5,537,174	6,192,489	2,220	230
Bosnia-Herzegovina	789	988	892	985	1,019	989	703	183
Bulgaria	916	1,015	1,143	1,252	1,432	1,335	949	126
Croatia	10,047	10,274	11,352	12,307	13,137	12,420	2,350	531
Czech Republic	70,806	73,408	73,963	74,985	78,523	75,891	3,981	380
Estonia	6,051	7,396	8,935	10,449	10,960	9,026	802	603
Georgia	422	427	550	551	610	615	368	84
Hungary	450,880	466,696	491,540	508,759	518,041	485,319	2,399	239
Latvia	312	386	487	607	653	504	998	443
Lithuania	2,678	3,812	4,348	5,198	4,194	3,793	1,527	456
Macedonia	12,743	13,903	15,938	17,249	19,629	19,865	450	221
Moldova								
Montenegro	78	81	119	150	157	149	207	330
Poland	28,226	28,446	30,157	31,954	34,831	36,160	11,586	304
Romania	6,038	7,061	8,303	9,408	10,899	9,764	3,202	149
Russia	940,100	1,098,062	1,373,417	1,630,856	2,046,455	2,015,497	63,457	447
Serbia	48,953	59,577	71,325	86,652	100,416	106,512	1,576	214
Slovakia	1,067	1,180	1,254	1,340	1,587	1,499	2,083	386
Slovenia	916	936	936	1,054	1,203	1,024	1,423	703
Ukraine	27,138	38,507	49,253	65,248	88,856	91,233	11,710	255

Source: National statistical offices/OECD/Eurostat/Euromonitor International

Consumer Expenditure Statistics | Table 5.6

Housing Consumer Expenditure 1990-2009

Million units of national currency / as stated

	1990	1995	1996	1997	1998	1999	2000
Western Europe							
Austria	13,584	18,912	20,273	20,289	20,765	21,449	22,484
Belgium	20,675	24,794	26,386	27,326	28,061	28,719	30,562
Cyprus							
Denmark	109,404	135,539	142,028	145,944	151,320	155,216	162,042
Finland	7,918	11,939	12,622	13,588	14,275	14,958	15,566
France	116,943	153,129	160,777	164,388	170,996	176,488	183,170
Germany	148,642	227,650	239,330	248,030	251,550	257,270	266,460
Gibraltar							
Greece	5,549	12,661	14,212	15,360	16,526	15,892	16,730
Iceland							
Ireland	3,188	4,362	4,864	5,683	6,645	7,512	8,766
Italy	64,579	103,294	108,461	113,158	119,081	126,915	134,172
Liechtenstein							
Luxembourg							
Malta							
Monaco							
Netherlands	22,002	31,547	34,102	35,650	37,316	39,295	41,962
Norway	82,569	97,440	102,412	105,783	107,749	111,292	119,134
Portugal	5,171	7,791	8,252	8,798	9,276	9,856	10,468
Spain	27,231	40,084	42,952	45,567	48,263	51,273	60,945
Sweden	216,817	268,162	282,084	288,737	289,340	289,576	292,907
Switzerland	38,608	50,791	52,283	52,834	53,366	54,640	56,578
Turkey	30	633	1,207	2,511	5,383	10,799	19,655
United Kingdom	58,588	83,126	87,700	91,977	98,114	103,193	108,050
Eastern Europe							
Albania							
Belarus	0	6,373	11,620	17,393	32,844	89,003	290,529
Bosnia-Herzegovina		566	735	1,000	1,450	1,724	1,744
Bulgaria	9	172	361	3,117	4,131	4,745	4,611
Croatia	60	23,293	24,685	29,096	30,946	34,932	35,600
Czech Republic	51,217	157,156	177,601	196,198	217,733	228,314	247,479
Estonia		5,303	8,263	10,480	12,653	13,558	12,585
Georgia		219	289	362	334	341	455
Hungary	160,163	604,568	772,569	941,513	1,089,837	1,265,192	1,391,860
Latvia	19	337	418	473	516	560	619
Lithuania	18	3,606	4,192	4,717	4,865	4,907	5,112
Macedonia	62	21,895	23,265	25,361	26,216	27,616	31,632
Moldova							
Montenegro		121	93	102	107	112	143
Poland	4,935	42,500	53,703	70,544	82,430	94,535	97,182
Romania	8	840	1,357	3,520	5,389	8,231	12,314
Russia	16	43,345	60,199	69,355	79,130	135,340	189,836
Serbia		7,728	14,378	18,303	27,247	35,110	66,462
Slovakia	1,235	1,816	2,115	2,352	2,675	3,274	3,918
Slovenia	88	1,154	1,358	1,523	1,673	1,861	2,090
Ukraine	0	3,084	4,987	5,758	6,598	7,962	9,707

Source: *National statistical offices/OECD/Eurostat/Euromonitor International*

Consumer Expenditure Statistics

Housing Consumer Expenditure 1990-2009 *(continued)*

Million units of national currency / as stated

	2004	2005	2006	2007	2008	2009	Total US$ million 2009	US$ per capita 2009
Western Europe								
Austria	26,326	28,828	30,103	30,615	32,059	32,320	44,912	5,357
Belgium	34,412	35,725	37,417	38,037	41,378	41,562	57,755	5,373
Cyprus								
Denmark	188,073	198,739	205,500	209,595	220,251	218,367	40,734	7,391
Finland	19,027	19,686	20,601	21,506	22,843	22,154	30,785	5,781
France	220,424	235,602	249,159	260,962	274,744	276,765	384,592	6,159
Germany	292,300	301,140	310,120	312,023	326,130	325,407	452,186	5,514
Gibraltar								
Greece	21,487	22,975	24,909	26,029	27,160	26,724	37,136	3,300
Iceland								
Ireland	13,200	14,171	15,352	17,281	18,919	16,361	22,735	5,109
Italy	166,209	174,671	181,798	188,297	198,502	196,858	273,554	4,555
Liechtenstein								
Luxembourg								
Malta								
Monaco								
Netherlands	51,343	53,893	56,630	58,380	59,490	59,263	82,352	5,018
Norway	152,288	156,639	168,671	167,831	181,163	186,403	29,636	6,175
Portugal	13,537	14,311	14,925	15,855	16,719	16,348	22,718	2,129
Spain	81,608	88,815	96,088	104,044	108,516	105,779	146,990	3,229
Sweden	338,885	349,041	359,313	372,634	387,093	401,129	52,411	5,696
Switzerland	61,821	63,734	65,965	68,107	71,949	74,596	68,656	9,082
Turkey	67,064	81,982	100,252	119,517	141,245	158,929	102,187	1,429
United Kingdom	139,116	149,309	161,313	172,340	185,112	189,165	295,009	4,788
Eastern Europe								
Albania								
Belarus	3,321,916	4,203,809	5,063,532	6,348,151	8,697,990	9,981,137	3,578	370
Bosnia-Herzegovina	2,437	2,544	2,753	2,831	2,902	2,750	1,953	508
Bulgaria	5,858	6,333	7,132	7,735	8,760	8,130	5,779	769
Croatia	43,114	48,250	51,570	56,812	61,857	58,501	11,071	2,500
Czech Republic	318,713	338,112	357,450	375,373	410,254	404,368	21,210	2,026
Estonia	17,829	19,496	22,519	26,775	26,999	21,022	1,867	1,403
Georgia	633	748	1,091	1,312	1,583	1,764	1,056	241
Hungary	2,197,695	2,360,791	2,483,080	2,630,555	2,752,857	2,655,541	13,124	1,310
Latvia	972	1,117	1,398	1,765	1,952	1,543	3,058	1,357
Lithuania	6,016	6,714	7,576	8,557	8,786	7,496	3,018	901
Macedonia	44,684	45,139	44,202	48,851	55,435	54,732	1,241	608
Moldova								
Montenegro	244	252	337	443	488	472	656	1,045
Poland	135,405	146,777	155,815	169,479	188,145	198,950	63,745	1,672
Romania	38,929	46,056	54,544	65,175	79,618	74,522	24,439	1,140
Russia	875,265	1,159,635	1,524,619	1,819,031	2,046,455	2,290,376	72,112	508
Serbia	259,858	308,102	346,164	382,712	434,103	451,204	6,677	906
Slovakia	6,545	7,150	8,201	8,813	9,502	9,670	13,437	2,491
Slovenia	2,887	3,124	3,285	3,473	3,905	3,925	5,454	2,696
Ukraine	16,395	23,263	29,756	38,741	51,751	52,009	6,675	145

Source: National statistical offices/OECD/Eurostat/Euromonitor International

Consumer Expenditure Statistics

Table 5.7

Household Goods and Services Consumer Expenditure 1990-2009

Million units of national currency / as stated

	1990	1995	1996	1997	1998	1999	2000
Western Europe							
Austria	6,122	7,519	7,721	7,790	7,824	8,069	8,468
Belgium	5,958	7,226	7,378	7,676	7,971	8,072	8,487
Cyprus							
Denmark	24,534	29,896	30,357	32,413	33,703	34,570	35,138
Finland	2,336	2,141	2,297	2,504	2,779	2,813	3,050
France	39,042	41,034	42,124	43,007	44,663	46,193	48,418
Germany	65,776	83,960	84,210	85,800	87,600	86,750	90,530
Gibraltar							
Greece	2,437	4,611	5,026	5,423	5,931	6,297	6,859
Iceland							
Ireland	1,552	1,948	2,233	2,448	2,733	3,164	3,576
Italy	37,507	49,131	50,844	52,853	55,642	58,684	60,003
Liechtenstein							
Luxembourg							
Malta							
Monaco							
Netherlands	9,071	10,427	10,988	11,787	13,104	14,012	15,152
Norway	21,018	27,464	29,300	31,783	33,342	34,183	37,995
Portugal	2,691	4,082	4,455	4,840	5,376	5,701	6,119
Spain	12,173	16,956	17,588	18,580	20,253	22,000	23,013
Sweden	30,400	35,787	35,389	37,315	39,289	42,789	46,735
Switzerland	11,595	11,155	10,844	10,829	11,075	11,443	11,712
Turkey	30	592	1,067	2,093	4,655	6,615	10,377
United Kingdom	19,936	26,287	27,758	29,492	31,002	32,846	35,675
Eastern Europe							
Albania							
Belarus	0	2,524	4,174	7,237	15,982	69,014	168,869
Bosnia-Herzegovina		249	323	440	638	761	771
Bulgaria	1	16	35	272	402	513	678
Croatia	12	3,988	4,169	4,817	4,983	4,489	4,185
Czech Republic	14,865	46,526	55,049	59,485	64,686	66,433	70,998
Estonia		1,286	1,918	2,154	2,233	2,297	2,879
Georgia		129	144	147	148	142	213
Hungary	106,708	227,300	256,677	310,514	380,953	435,634	488,055
Latvia	1	44	55	64	66	81	91
Lithuania	2	603	825	1,204	1,302	1,313	1,282
Macedonia	16	4,727	4,443	4,986	5,185	5,435	6,718
Moldova							
Montenegro		27	21	23	24	25	32
Poland	1,221	9,391	12,606	15,825	18,106	19,976	20,757
Romania	4	261	383	901	1,323	1,672	2,270
Russia	17	24,769	31,727	35,493	43,033	86,338	149,379
Serbia		1,651	3,034	3,801	5,564	7,114	13,084
Slovakia	312	524	565	625	740	787	821
Slovenia	23	367	404	452	494	570	642
Ukraine	0	795	1,286	1,485	1,702	2,053	2,504

Source: National statistical offices/OECD/Eurostat/Euromonitor International

Consumer Expenditure Statistics

Household Goods and Services Consumer Expenditure 1990-2009 *(continued)*

Million units of national currency / as stated

	2004	2005	2006	2007	2008	2009	Total US$ million 2009	US$ per capita 2009
Western Europe								
Austria	9,130	9,248	9,380	9,915	10,054	10,192	14,162	1,689
Belgium	8,576	8,764	9,057	9,585	9,829	9,617	13,364	1,243
Cyprus								
Denmark	39,997	41,652	45,015	46,819	46,824	44,749	8,347	1,515
Finland	3,868	4,157	4,423	4,751	4,925	4,811	6,685	1,255
France	55,753	58,075	60,201	63,587	63,861	63,444	88,162	1,412
Germany	86,700	85,970	88,187	88,919	91,006	85,581	118,923	1,450
Gibraltar								
Greece	8,731	9,315	10,157	10,783	11,430	11,324	15,735	1,398
Iceland								
Ireland	4,448	4,670	5,243	5,664	5,069	4,568	6,348	1,426
Italy	64,127	65,704	67,004	68,500	70,077	68,328	94,949	1,581
Liechtenstein								
Luxembourg								
Malta								
Monaco								
Netherlands	15,521	15,513	16,322	16,869	18,757	18,006	25,021	1,525
Norway	44,755	47,504	51,041	55,132	56,340	56,742	9,021	1,880
Portugal	6,671	6,876	6,951	7,264	7,482	7,130	9,908	929
Spain	26,996	28,428	29,924	31,440	31,609	29,507	41,003	901
Sweden	58,945	63,655	68,940	74,659	77,008	79,181	10,346	1,124
Switzerland	12,048	12,295	12,557	13,074	12,644	12,552	11,553	1,528
Turkey	31,409	40,237	45,720	48,989	49,849	49,452	31,796	445
United Kingdom	43,492	44,475	45,352	46,369	45,842	46,787	72,967	1,184
Eastern Europe								
Albania								
Belarus	1,184,118	1,498,474	1,804,928	2,308,192	3,176,542	3,725,436	1,336	138
Bosnia-Herzegovina	1,128	1,230	1,296	1,500	1,486	1,416	1,006	262
Bulgaria	1,044	1,250	1,533	1,829	2,237	2,227	1,583	211
Croatia	6,668	6,779	7,260	7,854	8,283	7,728	1,463	330
Czech Republic	74,806	79,596	86,123	93,361	96,426	96,892	5,082	486
Estonia	4,924	5,739	6,805	7,637	8,118	6,735	598	450
Georgia	265	280	377	444	528	568	340	77
Hungary	835,908	916,710	965,369	1,031,395	1,082,532	1,049,405	5,186	518
Latvia	157	186	239	309	353	284	563	250
Lithuania	2,149	2,676	2,948	3,496	4,218	3,663	1,475	440
Macedonia	8,323	9,772	13,483	15,569	17,641	17,614	399	196
Moldova								
Montenegro	53	56	74	93	116	113	156	249
Poland	25,406	26,892	28,618	30,815	33,911	35,669	11,428	300
Romania	7,998	9,771	12,174	14,228	17,037	15,597	5,115	239
Russia	559,197	738,883	919,812	1,144,735	1,475,809	1,580,957	49,776	351
Serbia	47,034	65,351	72,490	94,232	113,420	124,096	1,836	249
Slovakia	1,295	1,505	1,700	1,877	2,342	2,182	3,032	562
Slovenia	904	976	1,012	1,160	1,204	1,279	1,778	879
Ukraine	6,502	9,225	11,800	16,142	22,780	24,088	3,092	67

Source: National statistical offices/OECD/Eurostat/Euromonitor International

Consumer Expenditure Statistics

Table 5.8

Health Goods and Medical Services Consumer Expenditure 1990-2009

Million units of national currency / as stated

	1990	1995	1996	1997	1998	1999	2000
Western Europe							
Austria	2,244	3,154	3,284	3,380	3,551	3,664	3,792
Belgium	4,420	5,399	5,286	5,697	5,858	6,543	6,913
Cyprus							
Denmark	10,010	12,226	12,936	13,847	14,359	14,790	15,315
Finland	1,277	1,638	1,833	1,965	2,053	2,172	2,402
France	16,896	22,239	22,789	23,073	23,650	24,466	25,257
Germany	21,630	38,820	38,990	43,030	42,780	45,540	47,370
Gibraltar							
Greece	1,512	4,051	4,316	4,717	5,140	5,395	5,635
Iceland							
Ireland	600	838	892	964	1,034	1,141	1,279
Italy	9,553	18,960	20,385	21,956	23,280	23,736	24,373
Liechtenstein							
Luxembourg							
Malta							
Monaco							
Netherlands	5,618	6,095	7,216	7,349	7,796	8,371	8,736
Norway	8,789	11,313	12,355	13,247	14,176	15,074	16,454
Portugal	1,111	2,841	2,896	3,137	3,209	3,543	3,868
Spain	6,308	8,989	9,504	9,983	10,754	11,714	12,941
Sweden	14,867	21,305	21,556	23,846	25,383	26,846	30,355
Switzerland	19,596	27,512	28,764	29,763	31,352	32,390	33,917
Turkey	6	131	250	525	1,283	2,256	3,873
United Kingdom	4,432	7,000	7,432	7,757	8,306	8,775	9,208
Eastern Europe							
Albania							
Belarus	0	1,574	1,838	2,202	5,812	25,471	81,523
Bosnia-Herzegovina		88	121	174	266	335	357
Bulgaria	1	15	32	253	260	397	546
Croatia	2	949	1,011	1,202	1,321	1,394	1,784
Czech Republic	5,473	12,725	14,906	16,889	18,024	17,709	16,303
Estonia		329	504	589	663	847	1,690
Georgia		91	124	161	131	173	294
Hungary	21,602	89,192	109,162	137,528	165,653	212,204	244,046
Latvia	1	59	72	93	94	105	125
Lithuania	2	460	603	757	988	1,018	1,042
Macedonia	4	3,390	3,869	3,458	3,960	4,427	6,356
Moldova							
Montenegro		15	12	13	14	15	20
Poland	622	6,354	8,667	11,513	14,219	16,641	16,873
Romania	1	113	176	450	694	957	1,303
Russia	9	19,781	32,452	45,876	59,444	98,584	102,114
Serbia		433	880	1,223	1,983	2,807	5,758
Slovakia	87	257	287	281	292	351	392
Slovenia	5	152	191	228	256	290	355
Ukraine	0	1,403	2,270	2,621	3,003	3,624	4,418

Source: National statistical offices/OECD/Eurostat/Euromonitor International

Consumer Expenditure Statistics

Health Goods and Medical Services Consumer Expenditure 1990-2009 *(continued)*

Million units of national currency / as stated

	2004	2005	2006	2007	2008	2009	Total US$ million 2009	US$ per capita 2009
Western Europe								
Austria	4,465	4,587	4,777	4,945	5,085	5,174	7,189	858
Belgium	7,787	8,054	8,708	9,273	10,069	9,729	13,519	1,258
Cyprus								
Denmark	18,713	19,538	20,408	21,100	21,604	20,778	3,876	703
Finland	3,138	3,375	3,571	3,852	4,120	4,052	5,631	1,057
France	30,995	32,696	35,130	36,817	39,047	39,690	55,153	883
Germany	58,940	58,250	60,637	61,408	63,458	66,648	92,614	1,129
Gibraltar								
Greece	8,190	9,032	9,852	10,586	11,378	11,461	15,926	1,415
Iceland								
Ireland	2,268	2,464	2,636	2,729	3,196	2,816	3,913	879
Italy	26,613	27,285	27,841	28,429	28,892	27,188	37,780	629
Liechtenstein								
Luxembourg								
Malta								
Monaco								
Netherlands	12,189	12,733	5,909	6,485	5,094	3,224	4,481	273
Norway	21,585	23,090	23,556	24,622	26,121	27,956	4,445	926
Portugal	5,264	5,565	5,923	6,338	6,747	6,641	9,228	865
Spain	17,792	19,479	21,288	23,071	24,041	23,348	32,444	713
Sweden	38,735	41,183	43,088	45,208	47,623	50,854	6,645	722
Switzerland	39,352	40,280	40,815	42,687	46,543	46,701	42,982	5,686
Turkey	15,374	18,973	22,931	25,596	28,481	27,878	17,925	251
United Kingdom	11,881	12,183	12,798	13,822	13,713	14,849	23,157	376
Eastern Europe								
Albania								
Belarus	587,254	743,156	895,140	1,187,293	1,663,897	1,987,710	713	74
Bosnia-Herzegovina	627	712	811	918	1,003	911	647	168
Bulgaria	1,113	1,259	1,482	1,681	1,980	1,908	1,356	180
Croatia	2,985	3,054	3,552	4,059	4,453	4,344	822	186
Czech Republic	26,986	28,716	34,135	41,906	51,854	52,974	2,779	265
Estonia	2,795	2,840	3,686	4,307	4,441	3,583	318	239
Georgia	445	559	855	998	1,210	1,331	797	182
Hungary	420,233	461,278	486,840	533,017	576,038	569,470	2,814	281
Latvia	224	302	398	505	568	455	902	400
Lithuania	1,724	2,338	2,268	2,574	3,023	2,744	1,105	330
Macedonia	4,464	4,770	4,628	6,087	7,072	7,148	162	79
Moldova								
Montenegro	36	40	46	72	62	61	85	135
Poland	24,858	24,731	26,295	28,578	31,748	33,587	10,762	282
Romania	5,313	6,434	7,776	9,408	11,412	10,721	3,516	164
Russia	194,503	256,556	378,005	486,120	570,646	529,656	16,676	118
Serbia	31,079	45,471	60,525	81,704	96,933	107,766	1,595	216
Slovakia	804	916	1,046	1,251	1,359	1,412	1,962	364
Slovenia	525	570	593	668	733	756	1,051	520
Ukraine	7,915	11,231	14,365	18,823	25,323	25,651	3,292	72

Source: *National statistical offices/OECD/Eurostat/Euromonitor International*

Consumer Expenditure Statistics

Table 5.9

Transport Consumer Expenditure 1990-2009

Million units of national currency / as stated

	1990	1995	1996	1997	1998	1999	2000
Western Europe							
Austria	10,194	12,198	13,131	13,070	13,195	13,622	14,677
Belgium	10,200	12,252	12,947	13,251	14,006	15,028	16,277
Cyprus							
Denmark	48,453	68,181	72,710	76,220	77,891	78,062	73,916
Finland	6,296	5,920	6,442	6,856	7,441	7,618	8,115
France	89,636	97,909	103,051	100,231	106,279	113,592	120,484
Germany	122,081	137,050	145,740	146,330	150,050	156,210	157,680
Gibraltar							
Greece	3,642	6,437	6,933	7,636	8,227	9,066	8,754
Iceland							
Ireland	2,492	3,113	3,516	4,133	4,640	5,298	6,684
Italy	50,489	72,342	76,573	86,454	91,249	94,441	99,957
Liechtenstein							
Luxembourg							
Malta							
Monaco							
Netherlands	13,783	16,911	17,659	18,818	19,963	22,134	23,675
Norway	42,715	62,912	74,367	77,700	81,142	83,504	92,495
Portugal	4,999	8,186	8,822	9,623	10,708	12,051	13,056
Spain	18,291	31,569	34,467	38,277	42,137	47,414	49,471
Sweden	81,807	110,515	115,069	124,476	131,022	144,084	154,035
Switzerland	14,973	17,109	17,203	17,885	18,291	19,283	20,317
Turkey	23	493	931	1,960	4,642	7,646	14,386
United Kingdom	51,852	64,087	70,380	77,204	82,506	87,237	93,052
Eastern Europe							
Albania							
Belarus	0	4,351	6,456	12,920	25,693	101,886	318,085
Bosnia-Herzegovina		192	262	374	569	710	753
Bulgaria	4	74	156	1,411	1,584	1,953	2,613
Croatia	25	8,681	8,993	10,238	10,599	8,381	10,398
Czech Republic	39,145	81,985	99,621	107,817	114,686	118,326	129,855
Estonia		2,062	3,841	4,508	5,010	5,198	5,995
Georgia		151	206	266	222	262	360
Hungary	151,911	397,613	494,416	598,326	728,922	938,267	1,109,781
Latvia	2	129	173	244	264	256	265
Lithuania	5	1,351	1,861	2,428	3,249	3,647	4,271
Macedonia	31	14,598	15,591	15,116	16,047	17,553	25,832
Moldova							
Montenegro		18	15	19	22	25	35
Poland	1,588	15,673	23,188	28,026	34,691	42,064	43,477
Romania	9	659	993	2,399	3,506	4,593	6,268
Russia	14	47,473	70,018	85,630	101,482	172,116	230,552
Serbia		1,824	3,550	4,762	7,540	10,414	21,263
Slovakia	404	877	945	1,025	1,206	1,406	1,552
Slovenia	66	1,085	1,247	1,367	1,420	1,640	1,750
Ukraine	0	1,403	2,270	2,621	3,003	3,624	4,418

Source: National statistical offices/OECD/Eurostat/Euromonitor International

Consumer Expenditure Statistics

Transport Consumer Expenditure 1990-2009 *(continued)*

Million units of national currency / as stated

	2004	2005	2006	2007	2008	2009	Total US$ million 2009	US$ per capita 2009
Western Europe								
Austria	16,429	17,068	17,930	18,142	19,105	18,593	25,836	3,082
Belgium	17,390	17,998	19,286	19,850	20,749	20,222	28,101	2,614
Cyprus								
Denmark	85,663	96,510	104,366	110,935	105,574	95,034	17,727	3,216
Finland	9,427	9,917	10,215	10,180	10,709	9,678	13,448	2,525
France	134,619	142,746	147,238	154,594	158,508	157,184	218,422	3,498
Germany	174,520	177,970	188,096	183,763	185,541	189,921	263,914	3,218
Gibraltar								
Greece	10,862	11,517	12,549	13,137	13,732	13,336	18,532	1,647
Iceland								
Ireland	7,578	8,606	9,643	10,542	10,356	8,690	12,076	2,714
Italy	110,933	114,632	119,208	122,694	120,828	115,917	161,079	2,682
Liechtenstein								
Luxembourg								
Malta								
Monaco								
Netherlands	27,189	28,289	29,824	30,895	32,485	31,827	44,227	2,695
Norway	108,051	113,991	121,945	134,084	131,568	124,787	19,840	4,134
Portugal	13,448	14,320	14,816	15,587	16,177	15,452	21,473	2,012
Spain	60,886	65,257	70,680	75,418	77,055	72,935	101,350	2,226
Sweden	172,518	185,798	188,053	198,724	191,812	182,106	23,794	2,586
Switzerland	20,651	21,625	22,484	23,239	24,599	24,624	22,664	2,998
Turkey	49,329	60,741	74,506	81,385	88,326	86,229	55,443	775
United Kingdom	109,472	116,186	120,279	130,906	135,085	130,539	203,580	3,304
Eastern Europe								
Albania								
Belarus	1,978,146	2,503,298	3,015,249	3,733,677	5,018,617	5,784,308	2,074	214
Bosnia-Herzegovina	1,299	1,461	1,661	1,901	2,203	1,958	1,391	362
Bulgaria	4,526	5,675	6,873	8,065	9,859	9,721	6,911	919
Croatia	14,776	14,472	16,192	17,752	18,837	17,898	3,387	765
Czech Republic	163,426	174,943	192,704	206,158	216,851	218,434	11,457	1,095
Estonia	10,685	12,319	14,699	17,232	18,133	14,860	1,320	992
Georgia	478	542	686	759	886	949	568	130
Hungary	1,752,997	1,882,857	1,978,833	2,150,434	2,301,943	2,250,193	11,121	1,110
Latvia	488	623	808	1,019	1,127	901	1,786	792
Lithuania	6,262	6,995	8,763	10,525	13,340	12,325	4,961	1,482
Macedonia	22,405	22,650	27,074	31,753	39,051	39,999	907	444
Moldova								
Montenegro	85	98	130	200	255	256	356	567
Poland	53,527	53,709	56,307	59,798	65,101	67,314	21,568	566
Romania	19,533	23,001	26,999	31,115	36,701	33,611	11,022	514
Russia	826,640	1,251,996	1,575,020	2,603,097	3,050,006	3,346,107	105,351	742
Serbia	125,719	156,971	188,798	210,706	264,111	294,901	4,364	592
Slovakia	2,187	2,408	2,602	2,803	3,179	3,064	4,258	789
Slovenia	2,351	2,564	2,767	3,108	3,420	3,512	4,881	2,413
Ukraine	8,480	12,033	15,391	20,334	27,606	28,249	3,626	79

Source: National statistical offices/OECD/Eurostat/Euromonitor International

Consumer Expenditure Statistics

Table 5.10

Communications Consumer Expenditure 1990-2009

Million units of national currency / as stated

	1990	1995	1996	1997	1998	1999	2000
Western Europe							
Austria	1,451	1,819	1,948	2,156	2,344	2,714	3,178
Belgium	1,593	1,833	1,988	2,295	2,567	2,908	3,227
Cyprus							
Denmark	6,861	9,123	9,323	10,516	10,635	11,393	11,898
Finland	625	783	945	1,177	1,434	1,765	1,972
France	10,321	12,514	13,090	13,515	14,343	16,284	18,652
Germany	13,001	19,910	20,650	22,840	24,140	25,570	28,670
Gibraltar							
Greece	309	1,043	1,358	1,544	1,695	2,616	2,730
Iceland							
Ireland	333	530	622	710	749	859	1,115
Italy	6,315	10,443	11,697	13,239	15,163	17,223	19,281
Liechtenstein							
Luxembourg							
Malta							
Monaco							
Netherlands	2,188	3,280	4,068	4,725	5,748	6,787	7,997
Norway	7,095	8,179	9,105	9,484	11,259	14,342	15,922
Portugal	702	1,143	1,255	1,458	1,577	1,819	2,065
Spain	2,545	4,894	5,518	6,056	7,052	8,248	9,397
Sweden	11,353	18,905	22,092	25,118	29,246	32,178	32,891
Switzerland	3,554	4,707	4,771	4,901	5,035	5,141	5,394
Turkey	10	245	474	1,019	2,437	4,013	7,492
United Kingdom	6,510	9,067	9,359	9,984	10,902	12,005	13,356
Eastern Europe							
Albania							
Belarus	0	943	1,579	2,773	5,047	24,267	73,412
Bosnia-Herzegovina		66	89	127	193	239	251
Bulgaria	0	11	23	232	357	523	848
Croatia	1	585	776	1,133	1,483	1,622	2,352
Czech Republic	3,548	11,740	16,936	19,155	20,554	20,861	23,990
Estonia		409	672	827	995	1,212	1,753
Georgia		61	82	114	95	92	118
Hungary	7,155	63,940	98,447	138,194	190,000	261,812	312,361
Latvia	0	24	31	29	42	70	94
Lithuania	0	142	203	421	527	606	794
Macedonia	4	1,259	1,321	3,155	3,979	6,749	8,981
Moldova							
Montenegro		16	14	17	20	22	30
Poland	518	4,674	5,940	5,603	8,015	11,540	12,885
Romania	0	26	52	210	630	1,080	1,651
Russia	4	7,705	11,583	14,916	18,694	32,900	42,699
Serbia		430	1,030	1,585	2,785	3,969	8,838
Slovakia	71	217	246	275	360	476	565
Slovenia	4	116	143	161	176	218	246
Ukraine	0	608	984	1,136	1,301	1,570	1,915

Source: *National statistical offices/OECD/Eurostat/Euromonitor International*

Consumer Expenditure Statistics

Communications Consumer Expenditure 1990-2009 *(continued)*

Million units of national currency / as stated

	2004	2005	2006	2007	2008	2009	Total US$ million 2009	US$ per capita 2009
Western Europe								
Austria	3,642	3,744	3,715	3,610	3,526	3,905	5,427	647
Belgium	4,546	4,667	4,552	4,522	4,468	4,674	6,495	604
Cyprus								
Denmark	14,863	14,844	15,817	16,573	17,076	16,612	3,099	562
Finland	2,460	2,190	2,198	2,239	2,222	2,793	3,882	729
France	25,447	26,880	27,370	28,592	29,213	28,399	39,464	632
Germany	35,590	36,430	36,830	37,256	37,543	41,625	57,842	705
Gibraltar								
Greece	3,620	3,908	4,239	4,737	5,312	5,333	7,411	659
Iceland								
Ireland	2,203	2,490	2,787	2,826	2,670	2,229	3,097	696
Italy	23,481	23,876	24,406	24,548	23,988	23,540	32,711	545
Liechtenstein								
Luxembourg								
Malta								
Monaco								
Netherlands	11,009	11,366	11,545	11,675	12,245	11,333	15,748	960
Norway	23,869	24,869	25,860	25,464	25,608	25,388	4,036	841
Portugal	2,845	2,856	2,869	3,080	3,276	3,211	4,462	418
Spain	13,642	14,731	15,735	17,452	18,496	18,156	25,230	554
Sweden	46,053	45,906	45,863	47,317	47,641	48,043	6,277	682
Switzerland	6,997	7,382	7,669	7,763	8,549	8,305	7,644	1,011
Turkey	27,166	29,868	31,195	34,297	40,261	39,306	25,272	353
United Kingdom	17,217	17,939	18,320	18,559	18,664	17,729	27,649	449
Eastern Europe								
Albania								
Belarus	989,951	1,252,760	1,508,963	1,943,481	2,691,946	3,143,846	1,127	117
Bosnia-Herzegovina	447	468	518	583	625	582	413	107
Bulgaria	1,695	1,929	2,276	2,581	3,046	2,939	2,089	278
Croatia	6,668	7,089	7,260	8,036	8,535	7,927	1,500	339
Czech Republic	49,910	52,578	61,067	62,334	65,525	62,180	3,261	312
Estonia	2,707	2,915	3,612	4,438	4,877	4,117	366	275
Georgia	205	232	294	325	380	407	244	56
Hungary	518,955	565,858	597,581	657,211	703,002	687,937	3,400	339
Latvia	205	253	365	463	515	410	812	361
Lithuania	1,209	1,233	1,343	1,541	1,757	1,496	602	180
Macedonia	15,522	16,575	17,664	18,528	25,132	26,550	602	295
Moldova								
Montenegro	59	65	85	111	115	129	179	286
Poland	18,411	20,780	21,780	23,844	26,830	28,699	9,195	241
Romania	3,942	4,345	5,009	6,024	7,408	7,015	2,301	107
Russia	235,025	379,704	504,006	595,890	728,066	716,780	22,568	159
Serbia	39,389	50,128	59,762	84,476	93,935	102,167	1,512	205
Slovakia	925	1,003	1,090	1,183	1,248	1,249	1,736	322
Slovenia	492	575	624	603	652	529	735	363
Ukraine	5,088	7,220	9,235	12,671	17,582	18,431	2,366	51

Source: National statistical offices/OECD/Eurostat/Euromonitor International

Consumer Expenditure Statistics

Table 5.11

Leisure and Recreation Consumer Expenditure 1990-2009

Million units of national currency / as stated

	1990	1995	1996	1997	1998	1999	2000
Western Europe							
Austria	8,963	11,258	11,791	11,898	12,542	13,067	13,805
Belgium	8,245	9,950	10,132	10,802	11,298	11,953	12,362
Cyprus							
Denmark	41,163	52,489	56,376	59,805	61,322	63,642	66,673
Finland	4,850	5,108	5,581	5,838	6,328	6,574	7,097
France	49,550	57,796	59,018	60,701	64,970	67,891	72,866
Germany	74,673	93,780	96,680	101,340	105,840	110,880	115,940
Gibraltar							
Greece	1,489	3,660	4,194	4,551	4,947	5,535	5,897
Iceland							
Ireland	1,776	2,148	2,414	2,500	2,712	2,899	3,629
Italy	30,696	40,101	43,100	45,395	47,901	50,260	53,397
Liechtenstein							
Luxembourg							
Malta							
Monaco							
Netherlands	13,650	15,921	16,928	18,267	19,820	21,738	22,826
Norway	32,814	50,781	56,520	60,970	65,774	71,897	76,821
Portugal	2,205	3,212	3,600	4,003	4,444	4,828	5,263
Spain	15,939	23,170	24,405	25,773	28,330	30,316	36,101
Sweden	71,914	91,417	93,911	99,979	107,639	116,994	125,864
Switzerland	17,640	20,322	20,222	20,510	20,807	21,349	21,725
Turkey	19	375	670	1,312	2,930	3,907	6,402
United Kingdom	35,494	49,274	53,575	58,012	63,246	67,481	70,154
Eastern Europe							
Albania							
Belarus	0	1,216	2,044	3,343	8,335	32,872	82,563
Bosnia-Herzegovina		72	104	155	246	318	348
Bulgaria	1	22	45	368	538	680	942
Croatia	6	2,759	3,012	3,656	4,058	4,362	5,712
Czech Republic	26,899	80,215	98,061	115,539	124,994	129,676	132,569
Estonia		1,270	2,264	2,937	3,426	3,573	4,738
Georgia		101	103	111	102	99	140
Hungary	107,327	252,962	300,676	356,894	415,600	481,513	555,610
Latvia	1	60	79	104	112	142	192
Lithuania	1	512	862	1,104	1,633	1,705	1,727
Macedonia	14	3,579	4,621	5,819	5,515	5,289	6,218
Moldova							
Montenegro		13	11	12	13	14	19
Poland	2,262	16,427	22,772	26,779	32,318	34,187	42,236
Romania	3	242	368	893	1,316	1,893	2,735
Russia	10	25,691	38,985	50,406	63,447	112,705	149,080
Serbia		487	1,030	1,466	2,433	3,498	7,139
Slovakia	576	739	871	977	1,118	1,277	1,480
Slovenia	40	568	686	809	908	1,029	1,115
Ukraine	0	889	1,437	1,660	1,902	2,295	2,798

Source: *National statistical offices/OECD/Eurostat/Euromonitor International*

Consumer Expenditure Statistics

Leisure and Recreation Consumer Expenditure 1990-2009 *(continued)*

Million units of national currency / as stated

	2004	2005	2006	2007	2008	2009	Total US$ million 2009	US$ per capita 2009
Western Europe								
Austria	14,993	15,527	16,119	16,738	17,171	17,304	24,045	2,868
Belgium	13,702	14,259	14,895	15,931	16,365	16,143	22,433	2,087
Cyprus								
Denmark	80,215	84,512	90,905	94,039	92,810	89,182	16,636	3,018
Finland	8,605	9,115	9,967	10,644	10,934	10,996	15,281	2,870
France	87,084	89,936	93,936	97,640	97,531	97,903	136,045	2,179
Germany	116,860	117,680	120,332	124,541	125,893	127,789	177,575	2,165
Gibraltar								
Greece	8,139	8,861	9,711	10,461	11,277	11,315	15,723	1,397
Iceland								
Ireland	4,886	5,238	5,571	6,095	5,913	5,470	7,601	1,708
Italy	59,231	58,636	61,260	63,542	64,165	62,888	87,390	1,455
Liechtenstein								
Luxembourg								
Malta								
Monaco								
Netherlands	24,427	24,795	25,972	27,410	28,077	26,838	37,295	2,273
Norway	95,365	98,890	105,711	114,154	117,153	122,628	19,496	4,062
Portugal	6,334	6,695	7,145	7,613	8,017	7,809	10,851	1,017
Spain	47,181	50,854	54,725	59,303	61,654	59,836	83,149	1,827
Sweden	144,707	146,858	154,953	165,853	165,913	168,861	22,063	2,398
Switzerland	22,555	22,771	22,760	23,377	23,774	24,442	22,496	2,976
Turkey	21,002	24,170	26,318	26,564	27,420	29,272	18,821	263
United Kingdom	88,447	90,130	93,912	99,396	102,068	92,796	144,719	2,349
Eastern Europe								
Albania								
Belarus	904,596	1,144,746	1,378,858	1,726,662	2,338,211	2,688,329	964	100
Bosnia-Herzegovina	652	784	862	969	1,054	971	690	179
Bulgaria	1,450	1,710	2,092	2,489	3,029	3,009	2,139	285
Croatia	8,153	8,281	8,810	9,680	10,248	9,601	1,817	410
Czech Republic	167,634	177,025	180,426	190,531	200,872	198,824	10,429	996
Estonia	7,636	8,089	9,782	11,630	12,363	10,241	910	684
Georgia	134	158	241	324	397	453	271	62
Hungary	892,625	962,650	1,009,224	1,077,244	1,136,039	1,105,531	5,464	545
Latvia	379	493	679	868	975	779	1,543	685
Lithuania	2,784	3,023	3,329	4,847	5,750	5,098	2,052	613
Macedonia	5,631	6,568	8,276	9,334	9,909	9,927	225	110
Moldova								
Montenegro	36	38	45	71	81	78	108	172
Poland	46,519	46,770	48,183	51,359	56,611	58,903	18,873	495
Romania	7,571	8,671	10,079	11,745	14,013	12,865	4,219	197
Russia	510,571	728,620	806,410	1,003,603	1,515,164	1,503,299	47,331	334
Serbia	40,207	55,659	73,094	94,122	117,887	129,456	1,916	260
Slovakia	2,173	2,431	2,684	3,103	3,578	3,788	5,264	976
Slovenia	1,667	1,757	1,831	1,966	2,041	2,109	2,930	1,448
Ukraine	6,784	9,627	12,313	16,376	22,400	23,111	2,966	65

Source: *National statistical offices/OECD/Eurostat/Euromonitor International*

Consumer Expenditure Statistics

Table 5.12

Education Consumer Expenditure 1990-2009

Million units of national currency / as stated

	1990	1995	1996	1997	1998	1999	2000
Western Europe							
Austria	428	651	644	720	746	817	845
Belgium	458	552	562	625	618	629	669
Cyprus							
Denmark	2,331	3,718	4,019	4,099	4,600	4,662	4,652
Finland	123	229	243	301	315	305	298
France	3,608	4,119	4,195	4,759	4,860	4,970	4,983
Germany	3,628	6,040	6,240	6,900	7,290	7,530	7,890
Gibraltar							
Greece	555	1,471	1,488	1,610	1,646	1,459	1,554
Iceland							
Ireland	183	365	440	370	328	359	466
Italy	4,022	5,702	5,976	6,177	6,311	6,602	6,804
Liechtenstein							
Luxembourg							
Malta							
Monaco							
Netherlands	896	946	952	999	1,052	1,108	1,161
Norway	1,722	1,927	2,253	2,402	2,466	2,748	2,883
Portugal	378	711	761	814	838	879	956
Spain	2,774	4,602	5,108	5,499	5,895	6,208	6,202
Sweden	40	40	45	46	42	39	33
Switzerland	701	900	948	975	1,023	1,047	1,078
Turkey	1	34	67	139	332	583	943
United Kingdom	3,222	6,197	6,565	7,440	7,814	8,943	9,534
Eastern Europe							
Albania							
Belarus	0	60	162	1,062	3,288	11,703	34,730
Bosnia-Herzegovina		29	39	54	82	100	105
Bulgaria	0	3	6	60	142	149	150
Croatia	1	321	351	433	486	536	626
Czech Republic	1,244	3,443	4,304	5,153	3,785	4,062	6,264
Estonia		199	349	425	549	531	635
Georgia		40	45	48	44	43	60
Hungary	8,556	43,851	53,678	59,076	66,838	73,954	79,231
Latvia	0	5	9	19	32	41	53
Lithuania	0	57	61	133	148	173	182
Macedonia	1	1,364	1,590	861	1,017	1,080	1,833
Moldova							
Montenegro		7	5	6	6	7	9
Poland	203	2,154	2,654	3,470	4,550	5,871	5,651
Romania	1	46	71	131	236	461	489
Russia	3	6,192	8,156	8,997	10,146	18,116	28,009
Serbia		339	654	861	1,322	1,762	3,406
Slovakia	37	60	71	74	82	83	109
Slovenia	7	57	62	71	77	82	96
Ukraine	0	561	908	1,048	1,201	1,449	1,767

Source: *National statistical offices/OECD/Eurostat/Euromonitor International*

Consumer Expenditure Statistics

Education Consumer Expenditure 1990-2009 *(continued)*
Million units of national currency / as stated

	2004	2005	2006	2007	2008	2009	Total US$ million 2009	US$ per capita 2009
Western Europe								
Austria	1,069	1,137	1,204	1,263	1,315	1,338	1,860	222
Belgium	782	791	806	832	853	863	1,199	112
Cyprus								
Denmark	5,007	5,184	5,400	5,609	5,835	5,830	1,088	197
Finland	351	334	361	385	402	252	350	66
France	6,202	6,655	7,422	8,047	8,794	9,099	12,644	202
Germany	9,090	9,230	9,470	11,189	11,779	11,377	15,810	193
Gibraltar								
Greece	2,459	2,757	3,059	3,269	3,516	3,604	5,008	445
Iceland								
Ireland	679	812	1,070	1,102	1,028	942	1,309	294
Italy	7,652	7,849	8,141	8,440	8,687	8,465	11,762	196
Liechtenstein								
Luxembourg								
Malta								
Monaco								
Netherlands	1,491	1,316	1,356	1,388	1,342	1,325	1,841	112
Norway	4,057	4,432	3,892	4,091	4,373	4,635	737	154
Portugal	1,167	1,225	1,263	1,330	1,391	1,350	1,876	176
Spain	7,445	7,840	8,174	8,512	8,490	7,884	10,955	241
Sweden	3,124	3,382	3,626	3,976	4,274	4,527	591	64
Switzerland	1,394	1,411	1,433	1,535	1,614	1,574	1,449	192
Turkey	4,294	5,771	7,098	8,199	8,888	9,347	6,010	84
United Kingdom	10,763	11,050	11,800	12,485	12,652	13,765	21,468	348
Eastern Europe								
Albania								
Belarus	352,580	446,181	537,430	688,946	932,910	1,099,478	394	41
Bosnia-Herzegovina	177	189	225	259	277	253	180	47
Bulgaria	251	267	291	308	341	309	219	29
Croatia	924	1,013	958	1,053	1,099	986	187	42
Czech Republic	8,997	10,318	10,987	12,091	13,805	13,457	706	67
Estonia	959	1,089	1,297	1,527	1,586	1,291	115	86
Georgia	57	68	103	139	171	196	118	27
Hungary	136,782	150,417	161,167	171,559	180,932	176,956	875	87
Latvia	105	151	241	331	366	302	598	265
Lithuania	296	361	513	689	670	657	264	79
Macedonia	2,958	3,710	3,980	4,746	5,769	5,858	133	65
Moldova								
Montenegro	17	19	18	42	45	44	61	98
Poland	8,067	7,727	8,510	9,148	10,022	10,411	3,336	87
Romania	1,951	2,480	2,973	3,577	4,322	3,994	1,310	61
Russia	137,773	184,721	252,003	282,263	314,839	374,216	11,782	83
Serbia	14,687	18,922	20,637	22,792	24,990	26,715	395	54
Slovakia	362	420	470	495	525	561	780	144
Slovenia	157	183	198	247	267	290	403	199
Ukraine	3,675	5,214	6,670	8,903	12,227	12,672	1,626	35

Source: National statistical offices/OECD/Eurostat/Euromonitor International

Consumer Expenditure Statistics

Table 5.13

Hotels and Catering Consumer Expenditure 1990-2009

Million units of national currency / as stated

	1990	1995	1996	1997	1998	1999	2000
Western Europe							
Austria	8,838	11,087	11,180	11,286	11,805	11,946	12,663
Belgium	4,879	5,913	6,035	6,342	6,504	6,651	7,109
Cyprus							
Denmark	22,077	25,798	25,946	27,514	29,569	29,728	31,118
Finland	3,321	3,397	3,600	3,653	3,742	3,822	4,021
France	34,196	39,403	39,151	40,655	43,429	45,944	49,559
Germany	45,852	57,420	57,650	58,890	59,930	61,890	65,700
Gibraltar							
Greece	4,267	10,541	11,827	14,068	15,312	15,444	17,643
Iceland							
Ireland	2,785	4,027	4,406	5,036	5,783	6,420	7,149
Italy	33,039	48,724	52,056	54,415	57,837	61,153	68,738
Liechtenstein							
Luxembourg							
Malta							
Monaco							
Netherlands	6,369	8,318	8,789	9,397	10,051	10,713	11,517
Norway	15,690	28,102	30,473	33,281	35,685	38,179	39,437
Portugal	3,937	6,112	6,327	6,743	7,441	7,749	8,482
Spain	35,888	51,418	53,788	57,587	61,839	67,425	71,984
Sweden	28,386	39,063	41,620	43,446	46,853	50,035	52,875
Switzerland	14,840	18,420	18,725	19,150	19,255	19,683	20,177
Turkey	20	395	712	1,420	3,273	4,404	7,820
United Kingdom	40,603	50,381	55,071	57,164	61,807	64,387	68,557
Eastern Europe							
Albania							
Belarus	0	3,388	4,034	7,394	12,732	55,934	149,944
Bosnia-Herzegovina		271	350	474	683	810	818
Bulgaria	3	57	119	997	1,540	1,651	1,683
Croatia	4	1,735	1,877	2,246	2,405	2,082	3,131
Czech Republic	19,112	55,987	65,599	76,622	83,248	80,709	88,664
Estonia		1,231	1,634	1,875	2,264	2,498	3,617
Georgia		99	139	179	181	200	243
Hungary	53,425	152,169	186,669	224,529	268,170	313,012	357,379
Latvia	2	66	79	101	96	133	143
Lithuania	2	514	672	901	961	1,014	968
Macedonia	10	6,051	6,739	6,888	6,719	6,755	9,405
Moldova							
Montenegro		16	12	13	13	13	16
Poland	912	6,634	8,268	9,661	11,773	12,641	14,736
Romania	4	347	500	1,156	1,602	1,991	2,672
Russia	14	21,466	24,682	22,540	20,667	33,589	58,258
Serbia		1,363	2,475	3,070	4,436	5,542	10,177
Slovakia	528	762	838	896	1,057	1,193	1,334
Slovenia	32	441	501	569	622	656	699
Ukraine	0	515	832	961	1,101	1,329	1,620

Source: *National statistical offices/OECD/Eurostat/Euromonitor International*

Consumer Expenditure Statistics

Hotels and Catering Consumer Expenditure 1990-2009 *(continued)*

Million units of national currency / as stated

	2004	2005	2006	2007	2008	2009	Total US$ million 2009	US$ per capita 2009
Western Europe								
Austria	14,940	15,207	16,158	16,869	17,949	17,893	24,864	2,966
Belgium	8,283	8,493	8,828	9,368	10,016	9,913	13,776	1,281
Cyprus								
Denmark	33,803	36,137	38,697	45,105	52,891	52,836	9,856	1,788
Finland	4,953	5,271	5,535	5,843	6,072	5,761	8,005	1,503
France	57,971	60,402	63,350	66,504	67,715	67,720	94,103	1,507
Germany	66,930	68,370	71,148	74,913	76,761	76,293	106,016	1,293
Gibraltar								
Greece	24,927	27,025	29,504	31,727	34,133	34,566	48,032	4,269
Iceland								
Ireland	9,167	9,802	10,372	11,301	11,086	10,056	13,974	3,140
Italy	80,597	83,215	87,899	92,239	94,096	91,040	126,509	2,107
Liechtenstein								
Luxembourg								
Malta								
Monaco								
Netherlands	12,294	12,540	13,116	13,868	13,568	13,431	18,664	1,137
Norway	41,826	43,589	48,469	53,125	56,990	57,483	9,139	1,904
Portugal	10,095	10,460	10,964	11,592	12,108	11,734	16,305	1,528
Spain	94,807	103,432	112,470	120,709	124,479	119,480	166,030	3,647
Sweden	60,039	64,703	69,491	74,316	80,240	79,061	10,330	1,123
Switzerland	21,422	21,549	22,413	23,340	23,972	23,068	21,231	2,808
Turkey	25,549	29,213	34,361	37,753	41,618	46,135	29,664	415
United Kingdom	82,886	85,473	87,857	91,124	94,034	88,000	137,239	2,227
Eastern Europe								
Albania								
Belarus	688,212	870,917	1,049,029	1,257,921	1,657,062	1,847,720	662	68
Bosnia-Herzegovina	1,177	1,254	1,388	1,532	1,539	1,485	1,055	274
Bulgaria	2,507	2,826	3,345	3,830	4,526	4,382	3,115	414
Croatia	4,258	4,508	4,649	5,333	5,729	5,407	1,023	231
Czech Republic	93,190	99,809	117,657	124,888	128,608	138,031	7,240	692
Estonia	5,958	7,801	9,765	11,485	12,022	9,833	873	656
Georgia	329	352	491	542	631	672	402	92
Hungary	573,387	618,535	650,236	696,077	734,389	714,428	3,531	352
Latvia	189	233	297	375	421	328	650	289
Lithuania	1,271	1,460	1,575	1,723	2,667	2,094	843	252
Macedonia	6,956	8,582	9,781	11,102	11,255	10,287	233	114
Moldova								
Montenegro	22	20	28	50	61	55	76	121
Poland	17,169	17,640	18,736	19,940	21,891	22,853	7,322	192
Romania	6,484	7,172	8,284	9,353	10,848	9,711	3,185	149
Russia	283,651	297,606	327,604	470,439	590,324	632,316	19,908	140
Serbia	32,164	37,643	42,925	48,647	51,483	51,520	762	103
Slovakia	1,684	1,877	2,253	2,331	2,441	2,429	3,375	626
Slovenia	1,027	1,071	1,147	1,413	1,527	1,499	2,083	1,030
Ukraine	4,523	6,418	8,209	11,109	15,490	16,326	2,095	46

Source: *National statistical offices/OECD/Eurostat/Euromonitor International*

Consumer Expenditure Statistics

Table 5.14

Miscellaneous Goods and Services Consumer Expenditure 1990-2009

Million units of national currency / as stated

	1990	1995	1996	1997	1998	1999	2000
Western Europe							
Austria	8,172	10,324	10,682	10,926	11,105	11,104	11,899
Belgium	11,213	13,785	13,486	13,676	14,876	14,101	16,542
Cyprus							
Denmark	47,832	59,560	59,864	63,885	68,594	69,894	76,125
Finland	4,306	4,496	4,155	4,129	4,847	4,981	5,981
France	77,129	79,974	82,941	83,437	84,548	81,264	92,443
Germany	87,287	118,310	117,880	117,400	118,980	125,440	127,540
Gibraltar							
Greece	1,681	3,492	3,761	4,146	4,732	5,405	5,991
Iceland							
Ireland	1,616	2,351	2,595	2,975	3,709	4,546	4,910
Italy	41,489	56,449	57,070	58,961	60,941	62,456	68,229
Liechtenstein							
Luxembourg							
Malta							
Monaco							
Netherlands	15,005	20,554	21,667	23,372	25,652	27,612	31,152
Norway	31,612	39,360	40,742	41,710	44,862	48,977	52,977
Portugal	3,897	6,013	6,150	6,683	6,933	7,887	8,937
Spain	16,673	24,831	26,215	28,115	30,062	32,129	34,175
Sweden	59,389	81,076	81,334	83,162	87,457	98,704	108,708
Switzerland	21,902	23,850	25,872	27,562	28,791	29,533	31,074
Turkey	16	395	763	1,574	3,748	6,268	9,913
United Kingdom	43,679	56,372	60,863	66,306	71,254	77,253	83,307
Eastern Europe							
Albania							
Belarus	0	2,299	3,504	5,192	12,311	53,180	160,030
Bosnia-Herzegovina		150	204	291	441	548	580
Bulgaria	1	19	40	322	442	475	535
Croatia	9	3,781	4,036	4,792	5,210	4,604	6,361
Czech Republic	15,527	47,911	67,273	84,659	94,788	102,824	94,439
Estonia		1,192	1,579	2,268	2,635	2,901	3,818
Georgia		202	206	277	167	147	278
Hungary	77,136	144,138	186,978	235,535	293,964	346,317	490,001
Latvia	1	77	113	117	115	100	99
Lithuania	3	588	802	840	1,347	1,500	1,341
Macedonia	24	6,262	7,287	8,111	8,682	10,104	12,600
Moldova							
Montenegro		23	18	20	21	22	28
Poland	1,662	16,561	20,364	29,954	35,869	42,724	55,284
Romania	1	105	161	395	593	893	1,187
Russia	11	27,177	39,703	48,553	58,136	99,528	129,251
Serbia		1,241	2,342	3,024	4,562	5,980	11,485
Slovakia	291	728	993	1,134	1,178	1,187	1,327
Slovenia	22	498	613	682	707	879	890
Ukraine	0	936	1,513	1,747	2,002	2,416	2,945

Source: National statistical offices/OECD/Eurostat/Euromonitor International

Consumer Expenditure Statistics

Miscellaneous Goods and Services Consumer Expenditure 1990-2009 *(continued)*

Million units of national currency / as stated

	2004	2005	2006	2007	2008	2009	Total US$ million 2009	US$ per capita 2009
Western Europe								
Austria	12,816	13,917	14,656	15,590	15,381	15,883	22,071	2,633
Belgium	16,958	18,427	20,437	22,308	22,877	22,265	30,939	2,878
Cyprus								
Denmark	88,352	93,852	99,030	102,981	106,624	103,244	19,259	3,494
Finland	6,359	6,651	7,553	8,633	8,942	9,344	12,985	2,438
France	102,349	105,338	114,612	123,090	125,544	124,899	173,560	2,779
Germany	147,540	153,780	154,409	156,824	156,318	157,986	219,538	2,677
Gibraltar								
Greece	8,127	8,810	9,594	10,430	11,298	11,369	15,798	1,404
Iceland								
Ireland	7,981	8,665	9,528	10,275	9,984	8,628	11,989	2,694
Italy	74,944	80,142	86,496	92,029	95,739	94,360	131,123	2,183
Liechtenstein								
Luxembourg								
Malta								
Monaco								
Netherlands	36,023	38,903	40,933	41,974	42,186	41,183	57,227	3,487
Norway	71,487	77,926	82,950	96,916	105,006	111,659	17,752	3,699
Portugal	10,649	11,338	12,714	13,614	14,486	14,221	19,762	1,852
Spain	42,398	44,934	47,658	50,351	51,048	48,188	66,962	1,471
Sweden	116,983	125,611	139,156	147,872	153,481	154,138	20,140	2,189
Switzerland	30,435	30,272	32,542	35,121	36,089	34,123	31,406	4,154
Turkey	30,284	33,103	39,403	47,011	49,670	46,233	29,726	416
United Kingdom	98,579	105,913	112,737	116,677	115,753	113,528	177,050	2,874
Eastern Europe								
Albania								
Belarus	951,510	1,204,115	1,450,369	1,873,386	2,583,720	3,037,309	1,089	113
Bosnia-Herzegovina	992	1,098	1,271	1,452	1,582	1,469	1,043	271
Bulgaria	1,085	1,289	1,572	1,862	2,258	2,231	1,586	211
Croatia	9,623	10,094	10,969	12,101	13,017	12,336	2,335	527
Czech Republic	121,045	121,810	139,405	161,748	169,095	178,958	9,387	897
Estonia	6,515	7,407	9,234	10,881	11,460	9,340	830	624
Georgia	314	380	499	595	722	797	477	109
Hungary	589,462	575,630	587,014	627,678	658,038	634,984	3,138	313
Latvia	184	215	257	317	346	275	545	242
Lithuania	2,291	2,880	3,719	4,453	6,315	5,409	2,177	650
Macedonia	11,105	10,656	12,623	14,001	15,915	16,591	376	184
Moldova								
Montenegro	50	55	68	92	128	126	175	278
Poland	70,573	73,069	82,456	90,002	100,386	106,653	34,172	896
Romania	3,833	4,564	5,504	6,504	7,863	7,288	2,390	112
Russia	380,903	482,326	617,408	815,428	1,160,970	1,200,395	37,794	266
Serbia	46,621	60,893	74,975	85,402	102,541	110,973	1,642	223
Slovakia	2,283	2,550	2,914	3,160	3,460	3,428	4,764	883
Slovenia	1,365	1,429	1,537	1,819	2,002	1,875	2,606	1,288
Ukraine	4,806	6,819	8,722	11,314	15,052	15,058	1,933	42

Source: *National statistical offices/OECD/Eurostat/Euromonitor International*

Consumer Market Sizes

Consumer Market Statistics

Table 6.1

Alcoholic Drinks: Per Capita Retail Sales 2009

Litres per capita

	Alcoholic Drinks	Beer	Wine	Spirits
Western Europe				
Austria	92.75	68.78	18.81	2.53
Belgium	67.49	43.03	21.06	2.71
Denmark	90.60	56.73	28.12	2.36
Finland	99.34	67.93	11.07	5.51
France	53.33	19.67	26.92	4.79
Germany	98.90	66.89	21.49	4.52
Greece	30.52	14.67	13.75	2.03
Ireland	63.52	40.40	13.28	3.21
Italy	46.70	18.83	26.23	1.26
Netherlands	76.15	52.13	20.74	2.36
Norway	59.45	41.61	13.19	2.65
Portugal	53.17	21.53	30.33	1.24
Spain	39.70	25.37	10.35	2.13
Sweden	66.75	41.35	18.88	2.10
Switzerland	65.32	29.36	32.39	2.26
Turkey	10.43	9.65	0.30	0.47
United Kingdom	68.92	38.38	18.23	3.87
Eastern Europe				
Bulgaria	62.15	52.11	5.10	4.93
Czech Republic	95.72	79.63	11.00	5.04
Hungary	72.71	49.33	19.58	3.75
Poland	82.37	67.22	6.96	8.10
Romania	77.28	64.07	11.13	2.06
Russia	88.94	67.48	7.30	11.61
Slovakia	84.33	69.12	10.62	4.38
Ukraine	64.59	47.89	5.42	9.70

Source: *Euromonitor International from industry sources/national statistics*
Notes: *Alcoholic drinks data are off-trade*

Table 6.2

Beauty and Personal Care: Per Capita Retail Sales 2009

US$ per capita

	Baby Care	Bath & Shower Products	Deodorants	Hair Care	Colour Cosmetics
Western Europe					
Austria	5.19	19.07	8.69	35.19	27.14
Belgium	4.01	20.03	13.78	33.49	25.76
Denmark	4.93	15.39	15.39	81.01	34.65
Finland	2.35	12.43	8.70	46.84	31.73
France	3.83	18.32	13.48	38.08	27.53
Germany	2.84	16.96	11.05	35.36	22.38
Greece	4.57	12.35	7.97	50.27	15.80
Ireland	6.99	22.93	16.85	43.44	28.65
Italy	4.73	25.03	10.76	30.20	21.85
Netherlands	4.38	22.11	13.82	41.96	29.38
Norway	5.13	32.29	16.10	77.16	55.35
Portugal	3.85	14.86	8.20	35.75	12.55
Spain	4.81	13.08	9.82	35.45	21.94
Sweden	3.26	13.62	8.26	43.95	36.04
Switzerland	5.53	27.37	10.23	39.64	37.09
Turkey	0.77	3.18	1.55	7.89	3.56
United Kingdom	3.91	20.14	20.90	33.53	35.03
Eastern Europe					
Bulgaria	0.93	6.33	3.51	9.72	5.21
Czech Republic	3.00	11.56	7.79	23.23	16.90
Hungary	1.57	13.28	8.64	17.30	8.56
Poland	1.83	7.87	8.43	18.04	9.22
Romania	0.48	5.87	4.63	8.00	7.17
Russia	1.48	6.42	2.75	12.30	9.60
Slovakia	1.33	10.85	7.85	19.91	16.37
Ukraine	0.98	3.62	2.15	9.50	5.02

Source: *Euromonitor International from industry sources/national statistics*

Consumer Market Statistics

Beauty and Personal Care: Per Capita Retail Sales 2009 *(continued)*
US$ per capita

	Men's Grooming	Oral Care	Fragrances	Skin Care	Sun Care
Western Europe					
Austria	29.41	28.18	21.90	56.06	6.10
Belgium	19.99	18.70	40.10	49.03	6.36
Denmark	23.02	21.79	44.00	42.06	11.91
Finland	11.90	14.80	15.84	53.18	5.45
France	21.87	17.73	38.27	66.41	7.36
Germany	20.92	21.97	31.29	52.42	2.50
Greece	14.49	11.04	16.00	47.18	8.81
Ireland	33.03	27.30	26.94	31.82	7.37
Italy	16.15	23.62	23.38	43.48	8.55
Netherlands	27.31	25.72	44.27	44.78	7.08
Norway	27.11	27.88	24.72	76.55	11.21
Portugal	17.74	20.76	26.04	29.13	7.13
Spain	17.06	18.85	38.64	49.66	11.92
Sweden	13.43	16.70	18.10	53.02	5.02
Switzerland	22.18	28.74	56.79	38.42	12.43
Turkey	3.65	3.61	3.42	4.96	0.40
United Kingdom	21.68	22.26	24.97	49.79	8.76
Eastern Europe					
Bulgaria	2.51	4.22	5.49	9.73	1.13
Czech Republic	8.37	9.84	18.91	21.30	1.85
Hungary	10.65	9.01	11.16	20.14	1.20
Poland	9.38	7.01	18.58	16.98	0.99
Romania	2.43	2.80	16.26	11.92	0.64
Russia	6.28	6.10	14.32	14.27	0.70
Slovakia	9.25	8.22		24.43	0.78
Ukraine	4.27	3.86	9.91	7.93	0.40

Source: Euromonitor International from industry sources/national statistics

Table 6.3

Major Appliances: Per Capita Retail Sales 2009

Units per '000 inhabitants

	Refrigeration Appliances	Fridge-freezers	Freezers	Large Cooking Appliances	Microwaves	Home Laundry Appliances	Dishwashers
Western Europe							
Austria	30.67	10.38	7.07	37.60	14.87	30.83	13.20
Belgium	49.66	23.83	17.11	47.92	28.83	44.81	16.21
Denmark	55.50	21.22	13.96	65.94	24.66	59.42	30.43
Finland	48.40	16.86	14.40	53.48	23.36	33.67	17.49
France	43.12	19.59	10.26	59.15	32.15	46.29	20.33
Germany	54.76	21.23	13.69	61.54	18.41	50.34	21.71
Greece	36.67	11.04	4.50	43.44	7.96	30.19	8.44
Ireland	65.99	29.99	17.96	93.21	58.95	102.30	18.52
Italy	39.32	28.47	7.74	42.20	14.05	32.93	15.17
Netherlands	54.04	35.23	14.26	56.87	30.65	60.47	22.74
Norway	65.49	31.48	16.59	88.20	28.93	63.65	32.97
Portugal	41.42	17.59	7.62	60.75	22.28	27.91	11.98
Spain	32.75	24.26	5.57	60.67	27.02	36.25	13.83
Sweden	61.29	21.19	16.08	65.16	33.31	43.88	26.04
Switzerland	40.30	13.68	9.31	49.52	19.59	40.63	17.38
Turkey	26.72	22.06	3.63	28.38	2.82	35.94	17.41
United Kingdom	54.42	26.95	14.42	56.57	45.13	72.31	14.64
Eastern Europe							
Bulgaria	24.34	17.65	4.35	12.81	10.30	22.23	2.08
Czech Republic	37.98	22.05	6.79	43.08	28.74	33.64	9.38
Hungary	37.50	26.84	6.46	25.14	21.61	32.95	6.92
Poland	34.05	29.52	1.42	50.06	16.18	35.83	9.63
Romania	17.83	12.93	3.18	9.38	7.54	16.28	1.47
Russia	21.15	16.91	1.11	16.86	14.34	27.48	0.58
Slovakia	30.60	17.45	5.02	34.25	20.03	25.37	6.15
Ukraine	5.84	5.52	0.02	3.05	5.96	11.69	1.19

Source: Euromonitor International from industry sources/national statistics

Consumer Market Statistics

Table 6.4

Small Appliances 2009: Per Capita Retail Sales 2009

Units per '000 inhabitants

	Food Preparation Appliances	Small Cooking Appliances	Hair Care Appliances	Irons	Body Shavers	Vacuum Cleaners
Western Europe						
Austria	43.94	137.37	45.77	28.46	27.73	68.42
Belgium	19.99	181.46	54.35	46.70	40.96	77.93
Denmark	105.52	152.16	83.53	24.22	12.38	69.11
Finland	65.40	115.46	46.81	25.48	28.34	35.26
France	88.81	193.77	65.89	49.57	35.97	50.75
Germany	58.83	226.16	101.34	43.25	52.45	64.54
Greece	91.62	62.92	94.49	54.85	13.90	41.76
Ireland	70.95	183.85	194.28	71.17	40.36	92.10
Italy	51.18	69.44	54.30	55.26	26.22	55.02
Netherlands	16.10	134.15	61.23	55.54	23.30	74.12
Norway	73.39	144.22	100.49	27.65	26.59	93.94
Portugal	97.44	111.80	50.51	44.87	32.52	46.24
Spain	100.16	96.54	70.88	48.68	24.44	26.90
Sweden	116.41	146.03	106.66	27.93	19.11	73.99
Switzerland	57.92	181.01	60.32	37.49	36.55	72.13
Turkey	44.68	69.99	32.68	36.09	12.03	36.28
United Kingdom	65.50	147.79	175.46	82.53	37.37	108.04
Eastern Europe						
Bulgaria	4.53	19.17	52.48	32.76	9.11	14.68
Czech Republic	33.54	37.94	43.13	30.53	26.81	57.29
Hungary	13.18	35.03	76.04	43.65	12.52	19.99
Poland	56.29	23.18	59.32	28.65	42.13	36.38
Romania	3.31	14.04	38.43	23.99	6.67	10.75
Russia	25.27	17.19	29.24	32.14	15.83	26.91
Slovakia	44.40	36.74	59.66	31.85	25.00	43.24
Ukraine	3.30	1.63	3.38	3.49	1.49	2.91

Source: *Euromonitor International from industry sources/national statistics*

Table 6.5

Clothing and Footwear: Per Capita Retail Sales 2009

US$ per capita

	Total Clothing	Men's Outerwear	Women's Outerwear	Footwear
Western Europe				
Austria				
Belgium	735.31	186.82	308.17	156.41
Denmark				
Finland				
France	551.70	137.90	214.82	169.71
Germany	640.08	181.59	304.50	135.70
Greece	939.94	261.97	367.26	152.74
Ireland				
Italy	879.17	265.50	287.56	355.14
Netherlands	788.83	265.03	298.52	193.70
Norway				
Portugal	266.07	77.76	154.21	59.45
Spain	414.42	104.43	160.14	110.63
Sweden	720.50	193.23	321.62	129.19
Switzerland				
Turkey	52.44	21.24	16.43	9.99
United Kingdom	722.50	213.98	282.45	128.60
Eastern Europe				
Bulgaria				
Czech Republic				
Hungary	81.19	30.64	37.01	34.34
Poland	188.79	59.91	75.65	68.24
Romania				
Russia	215.16	61.88	86.50	35.49
Slovakia				
Ukraine				

Source: *Euromonitor International from industry sources/national statistics*

Consumer Market Statistics

Table 6.6

Consumer Electronics: Per Capita Retail Sales 2009

US$ per capita

	Digital Televisions	DVD Players	Home Audio & Cinema	Computers	Cameras	Camcorders	Portable Media Players	Mobile Phone	In-Car Media Players
Western Europe									
Austria	89.12	3.65	18.96	102.35	34.79	6.69	11.26	61.05	2.83
Belgium	110.43	15.59	16.48	188.83	15.45	7.10	28.88	78.00	2.19
Denmark									
Finland									
France	97.10	3.76	19.52	79.54	27.57	4.86	15.53	56.08	1.09
Germany	104.78	3.98	15.94	80.45	30.38	4.19	12.91	49.42	3.17
Greece	48.47	0.31	11.62	60.79	11.59	2.14	7.01	80.52	0.11
Ireland									
Italy	76.84	5.52	10.14	20.31	11.40	3.52	13.75	41.74	2.61
Netherlands	68.15	4.57	20.70	118.56	37.78	12.23	26.54	42.37	6.63
Norway									
Portugal	33.99	3.91	4.18	102.55	13.01	4.93	8.50	71.32	1.67
Spain	122.61	10.08	6.28	113.44	19.39	6.90	6.36	93.63	2.51
Sweden	86.33	3.63	17.68	111.51	22.19	6.26	19.17	42.32	1.76
Switzerland									
Turkey	3.67	1.00	1.68	30.75	2.10	0.32	0.76	18.67	0.21
United Kingdom	109.50	1.26	18.10	105.09	27.99	5.23	33.10	50.37	2.92
Eastern Europe									
Bulgaria									
Czech Republic	39.69	0.13	4.37	60.76	8.88	6.18	1.55	37.55	1.58
Hungary	21.01	2.62	8.53	32.71	12.13	6.97	3.34	61.93	1.98
Poland	38.08	0.49	4.24	54.61	9.96	2.33	2.66	20.63	1.52
Romania	18.07	0.84	1.85	18.57	3.32	3.88	0.55	25.40	0.39
Russia	30.42	0.59	7.27	25.65	7.66	8.87	2.01	28.63	0.64
Slovakia									
Ukraine	7.24	0.08	0.96	10.73	2.39	0.64	1.25	12.46	0.03

Source: *Euromonitor International from industry sources/national statistics*

Table 6.7

Consumer Health: Per Capita Retail Sales 2009

US$ per capita

	Analgesics	Cough, Cold and Allergy Remedies	Digestive Remedies	Medicated Skin Care	Vitamins & Dietary Supplements
Western Europe					
Austria	9.06	21.00	6.90	8.74	25.27
Belgium	19.01	20.86	11.81	6.73	30.42
Denmark	16.59	16.64	12.20	7.05	30.56
Finland	19.27	15.40	13.38	9.22	30.28
France	9.36	13.31	7.06	8.03	16.65
Germany	13.75	24.41	8.41	8.29	25.73
Greece	9.63	8.96	4.03	7.14	18.85
Ireland	19.84	21.27	9.95	10.98	18.02
Italy	12.89	13.13	8.63	9.70	36.17
Netherlands	7.92	16.74	2.55	4.82	20.76
Norway	16.71	20.84	10.19	8.46	102.28
Portugal	10.99	7.50	5.78	6.37	8.57
Spain	8.67	11.55	6.07	5.65	7.49
Sweden	19.31	19.02	7.35	7.21	28.57
Switzerland	19.07	37.41	14.96	21.70	24.17
Turkey	4.62	4.32	1.68	1.12	2.13
United Kingdom	13.55	15.91	7.53	10.43	17.93
Eastern Europe					
Bulgaria	8.99	5.22	1.25	1.48	7.57
Czech Republic	8.25	12.86	4.14	4.21	9.99
Hungary	7.41	8.81	4.20	4.34	14.47
Poland	9.30	9.78	6.38	2.62	8.87
Romania	3.59	3.08	1.83	0.91	4.61
Russia	2.94	5.71	3.18	1.89	8.24
Slovakia	6.74	10.50	4.76	3.94	8.23
Ukraine	1.83	4.94	2.06	1.39	4.09

Source: *Euromonitor International from industry sources/national statistics*

Consumer Market Statistics

Table 6.8

Fresh Foods: Per Capita Retail Sales 2009

Kg per capita

	Meat	Fish and Seafood	Pulses	Vegetables	Starchy Roots	Fruits	Eggs	Sugar and Sweeteners
Western Europe								
Austria	102.56	14.75	0.31	74.05	64.68	75.31	10.35	7.10
Belgium	63.45	20.52	1.74	154.16	97.44	63.27	13.11	8.57
Denmark	73.92	9.06	0.69	81.17	71.20	99.25	14.16	6.68
Finland	37.46	22.40	1.23	61.06	52.92	54.25	7.86	4.24
France	54.23	5.29	1.12	41.96	41.29	41.18	15.00	7.64
Germany	60.78	4.70	0.12	63.63	26.78	61.61	13.27	6.72
Greece	101.51	23.70	3.44	256.91	56.49	139.15	7.86	22.59
Ireland	79.34	12.78	1.33	76.11	50.09	56.59	6.35	30.95
Italy	49.20	9.15	2.83	62.06	11.43	81.34	11.18	9.34
Netherlands	60.21	4.39	1.37	55.68	66.78	69.67	7.95	5.04
Norway	38.33	35.67	0.81	51.00	51.80	94.42	8.38	6.24
Portugal	104.78	44.66	2.36	103.06	96.48	66.38	11.59	23.74
Spain	48.63	20.19	4.65	55.18	31.89	99.07	11.81	7.05
Sweden	40.18	19.71	1.86	50.80	30.87	72.89	12.64	5.62
Switzerland	54.30	15.42	0.68	78.39	41.52	47.97	10.89	7.33
Turkey	20.53	8.83	11.61	251.63	68.78	90.83	6.61	19.77
United Kingdom	53.01	13.35	0.34	69.40	42.01	44.29	11.49	8.10
Eastern Europe								
Bulgaria	54.97	1.90	3.81	171.86	33.51	40.50	16.90	18.04
Czech Republic	57.13	10.29	1.04	82.79	56.15	44.04	18.32	16.39
Hungary	58.24	3.33	4.76	121.19	60.86	40.98	15.72	32.96
Poland	73.95	7.65	1.85	111.32	118.22	41.69	12.05	20.80
Romania	52.17	2.66	1.39	191.07	101.43	48.17	14.38	13.75
Russia	43.70	13.03	0.45	80.36	71.51	40.06	14.30	24.45
Slovakia	44.47	2.68	3.25	83.19	79.09	52.01	12.20	23.85
Ukraine	24.42	9.04	2.44	123.12	123.05	21.42	10.27	26.26

Source: Euromonitor International from industry sources/national statistics

Consumer Market Statistics

Table 6.9

Home Care Products: Per Capita Retail Sales 2009

US$ per capita

	Laundry Care	Fabric Softeners	Hand Dishwashing	Automatic Dishwashing	Surface Care	Air Care
Western Europe						
Austria	41.78	5.69	3.72	7.10	11.05	7.71
Belgium	36.66	8.92	3.09	7.87	12.68	6.16
Denmark	32.64	5.93	5.42	5.48	11.43	1.04
Finland	23.51	4.92	4.47	5.31	9.05	1.03
France	37.67	3.96	4.83	6.17	11.28	8.65
Germany	30.28	5.14	3.51	5.80	12.41	3.56
Greece	46.53	6.57	4.83	3.74	12.45	2.65
Ireland	31.06	5.84	3.73	5.92	10.56	7.64
Italy	42.95	6.70	6.27	4.66	15.34	6.00
Netherlands	29.78	3.99	3.26	6.25	8.88	4.80
Norway	31.74	6.70	5.55	6.75	15.03	1.39
Portugal	30.28	4.14	4.74	5.14	12.91	6.80
Spain	40.41	7.90	4.79	5.16	12.89	9.04
Sweden	21.00	4.95	3.83	4.44	6.64	1.34
Switzerland	51.14	4.99	3.93	9.66	12.51	7.44
Turkey	12.45	1.75	3.10	2.16	2.14	0.27
United Kingdom	41.88	8.63	5.77	6.63	12.42	10.46
Eastern Europe						
Bulgaria	16.22	2.22	2.19	0.58	4.09	1.92
Czech Republic	24.22	2.67	4.29	1.37	4.90	2.15
Hungary	24.46	6.10	4.09	1.28	5.17	1.75
Poland	16.66	2.87	3.23	1.01	6.39	2.46
Romania	18.07	2.94	1.65	0.21	2.18	1.27
Russia	16.40	1.78	2.82	0.09	3.28	0.84
Slovakia	21.94	5.73	2.98	0.17	4.98	0.97
Ukraine	15.51	0.91	1.48	0.24	3.47	0.87

Source: *Euromonitor International from industry sources/national statistics*

Consumer Market Statistics

Table 6.10

Hot and Soft Drinks: Per Capita Retail Sales 2009

As stated

	Coffee (Grams)	Tea (Grams)	Bottled Water (Litres)	Carbonates (Litres)
Western Europe				
Austria	5,029.47	274.20	65.90	51.78
Belgium	4,169.34	111.72	99.91	85.34
Denmark	4,822.25	122.83	26.39	51.55
Finland	8,407.25	208.96	14.53	41.94
France	2,910.37	191.42	121.13	34.29
Germany	4,835.91	602.39	118.33	65.71
Greece	1,763.34	20.33	44.07	37.46
Ireland	693.16	2,233.87	44.49	72.11
Italy	2,433.03	104.07	141.15	30.00
Netherlands	4,984.76	572.28	19.54	57.12
Norway	6,704.03	213.16	19.68	96.21
Portugal	1,078.96	51.59	60.93	28.79
Spain	1,544.58	84.16	118.05	59.33
Sweden	6,321.39	359.98	18.20	52.82
Switzerland	3,452.87	383.43	78.92	53.29
Turkey	268.45	1,680.79	66.00	26.02
United Kingdom	1,037.74	1,889.05	37.59	60.22
Eastern Europe				
Bulgaria	1,532.43	77.55	64.78	43.64
Czech Republic	2,350.05	376.27	118.11	42.85
Hungary	3,457.04	208.01	96.59	49.26
Poland	2,896.42	1,017.91	56.53	48.86
Romania	1,467.18	57.31	51.81	52.30
Russia	730.73	1,258.04	20.51	21.85
Slovakia	2,403.38	306.47	78.82	54.57
Ukraine	906.77	448.49	30.60	26.64

Source: Euromonitor International from industry sources/national statistics

Table 6.11

Dairy Products and Ice Cream: Per Capita Retail Sales 2009

US$ per capita

	Drinking Milk Products	Cheese	Yoghurt and Sour Milk Drinks	Other Dairy Products	Ice Cream
Western Europe					
Austria	69.42	87.92	44.60	52.25	45.82
Belgium	78.88	145.56	54.45	54.77	48.72
Denmark	105.67	174.99	59.04	51.63	65.97
Finland	145.08	183.42	120.97	85.54	92.10
France	55.42	170.26	54.94	66.60	36.07
Germany	44.81	102.83	45.23	60.17	51.14
Greece	83.65	101.09	45.33	34.26	37.69
Ireland	136.58	56.21	82.14	36.05	53.54
Italy	60.59	125.17	43.03	15.58	112.92
Netherlands	59.17	129.99	68.58	75.53	35.23
Norway	187.66	234.67	79.48	79.40	77.07
Portugal	88.61	96.71	59.19	18.69	52.42
Spain	113.92	69.95	61.54	27.08	49.32
Sweden	88.57	148.63	60.83	55.80	65.84
Switzerland	87.63	248.85	94.97	85.75	75.36
Turkey	11.19	12.09	28.98	0.82	14.18
United Kingdom	95.00	55.92	39.77	38.46	39.28
Eastern Europe					
Bulgaria	7.39	55.77	15.77	1.48	8.71
Czech Republic	28.91	82.41	37.08	46.92	31.56
Hungary	62.07	44.24	31.32	43.70	21.99
Poland	27.91	32.57	23.15	27.12	10.60
Romania	11.74	9.89	15.91	13.58	11.11
Russia	25.58	37.52	20.50	18.69	13.91
Slovakia	24.91	56.25	33.42	29.78	16.86
Ukraine	7.95	20.43	7.17	10.43	7.95

Source: *Euromonitor International from industry sources/national statistics*

Consumer Market Statistics

Table 6.12

Bakery Products: Per Capita Retail Sales 2009

US$ per capita

	Bread	Pastries	Cakes	Biscuits	Breakfast Cereals
Western Europe					
Austria	301.00	37.72	55.16	42.79	10.29
Belgium	175.42	69.37	85.38	70.81	23.08
Denmark	229.59	15.92	37.22	26.91	28.22
Finland	239.43	31.73	48.88	32.75	27.47
France	156.21	59.78	77.80	44.06	14.66
Germany	159.31	19.82	45.14	24.72	11.87
Greece	148.35	124.38	24.88	18.64	14.04
Ireland	150.34	12.14	40.48	61.18	66.17
Italy	139.68	154.33	80.57	42.42	8.92
Netherlands	159.06	6.60	63.20	60.35	8.30
Norway	197.28	26.10	68.07	34.41	20.29
Portugal	73.67	15.61	11.77	25.41	16.74
Spain	149.97	28.49	12.17	26.76	9.89
Sweden	138.05	15.76	36.19	26.86	20.05
Switzerland	275.71	25.04	42.03	50.50	23.30
Turkey	226.98	2.95	13.34	11.79	0.99
United Kingdom	67.39	19.54	47.53	41.91	41.09
Eastern Europe					
Bulgaria	85.48	10.56	3.64	6.46	2.23
Czech Republic	82.48	8.53	8.76	28.16	4.38
Hungary	73.56	4.44	11.87	17.93	6.56
Poland	62.35	1.03	11.12	13.94	5.89
Romania	88.49	3.42	16.84	9.90	4.15
Russia	44.98	2.59	5.31	11.49	2.41
Slovakia	101.97	1.80	8.53	20.50	5.38
Ukraine	19.05	0.95	4.12	11.85	1.41

Source: *Euromonitor International from industry sources/national statistics*

Consumer Market Statistics   **Table 6.13**

Confectionery: Per Capita Retail Sales 2009

US$ per capita

	Total Confectionery	Chocolate Confectionery	Sugar Confectionery	Gum
Western Europe				
Austria	149.70	107.59	34.93	7.19
Belgium	137.26	89.60	34.62	13.04
Denmark	214.01	102.43	95.12	16.45
Finland	201.07	97.66	82.19	21.22
France	119.29	83.73	21.13	14.43
Germany	152.51	98.94	42.44	11.13
Greece	66.78	41.01	6.03	19.74
Ireland	246.24	177.47	50.36	18.40
Italy	97.11	55.94	24.45	16.71
Netherlands	128.12	59.46	51.58	17.08
Norway	277.99	162.39	85.60	29.99
Portugal	60.90	37.39	17.47	6.04
Spain	62.81	29.59	23.49	9.73
Sweden	168.75	87.10	63.99	17.66
Switzerland	214.03	150.78	48.92	14.33
Turkey	24.62	14.92	5.17	4.53
United Kingdom	185.66	133.23	43.38	9.04
Eastern Europe				
Bulgaria	36.73	25.57	4.40	6.76
Czech Republic	65.92	44.98	13.71	7.23
Hungary	66.32	45.28	12.13	8.91
Poland	62.20	44.04	11.05	7.11
Romania	26.10	17.05	3.06	5.98
Russia	65.96	46.79	13.15	6.02
Slovakia	65.18	46.63	12.61	5.94
Ukraine	32.63	22.18	7.31	3.14

Source: *Euromonitor International from industry sources/national statistics*

Consumer Market Statistics

Table 6.14

Other Selected Packaged Foods: Per Capita Retail Sales 2009

US$ per capita

	Canned Preserved Food	Frozen Processed Food	Dried Processed Food	Chilled Processed Food	Oils and Fats	Sauces, Dressings & Condiments	Sweet and Savoury Snacks
Western Europe							
Austria	34.59	83.61	37.74	122.76	56.60	62.07	30.25
Belgium	83.44	93.16	40.47	226.11	62.63	50.93	32.86
Denmark	67.51	157.83	36.01	271.48	75.12	73.58	47.94
Finland	44.65	97.54	28.32	291.53	73.68	65.87	37.38
France	84.19	82.67	27.40	219.78	51.11	40.42	24.37
Germany	66.91	107.43	34.33	170.11	58.54	54.15	30.68
Greece	23.17	31.00	29.45	41.97	55.60	35.86	46.95
Ireland	40.68	129.58	43.33	140.20	58.15	57.82	124.45
Italy	45.66	52.90	52.55	280.08	48.95	48.91	16.94
Netherlands	37.40	59.96	32.11	168.36	49.45	47.60	44.39
Norway	86.70	178.85	54.41	268.97	80.55	100.45	128.55
Portugal	43.54	29.73	26.44	27.23	60.55	28.70	19.79
Spain	103.18	32.49	19.42	97.42	52.48	35.11	59.34
Sweden	64.36	132.46	31.51	196.34	62.12	71.49	53.64
Switzerland	89.51	95.10	47.52	238.89	75.40	48.92	48.70
Turkey	1.59	1.24	13.30	8.83	46.90	8.35	17.34
United Kingdom	67.21	113.99	28.64	260.08	37.93	61.97	97.14
Eastern Europe							
Bulgaria	11.29	17.97	15.51	54.69	30.79	11.99	4.96
Czech Republic	34.26	45.35	31.06	54.30	55.91	30.31	15.31
Hungary	40.03	26.23	27.75	72.81	37.27	26.31	15.44
Poland	18.88	14.28	21.98	17.52	40.69	29.18	19.76
Romania	8.85	0.83	17.03	39.34	19.68	3.34	11.98
Russia	30.07	39.22	21.24	34.34	36.34	21.99	20.23
Slovakia	35.75	22.81	23.06	66.71	42.50	32.09	19.94
Ukraine	14.55	10.22	8.76	34.23	17.91	16.85	16.40

Source: *Euromonitor International from industry sources/national statistics*

Table 6.15

Tissue and Hygiene: Per Capita Retail Sales 2009

US$ per capita

	Sanitary Protection	Nappies, Diapers & Pants	Toilet Paper	Tissues	Kitchen Towels
Western Europe					
Austria	10.32	13.58	22.86	8.68	7.77
Belgium	12.32	21.03	19.45	3.83	8.18
Denmark	18.08	18.98	19.59	1.72	10.33
Finland	13.27	19.77	23.29	1.90	9.36
France	10.18	15.89	17.74	5.07	7.05
Germany	10.91	11.46	21.93	5.33	5.69
Greece	10.88	17.94	17.04	2.26	8.87
Ireland	13.32	22.25	23.37	3.32	5.93
Italy	9.48	14.21	16.47	4.60	7.54
Netherlands	11.52	19.23	23.51	3.68	6.62
Norway	17.58	18.78	37.22	1.89	13.94
Portugal	9.03	12.59	18.27	1.88	5.20
Spain	13.57	13.23	17.12	2.81	5.83
Sweden	9.32	16.32	22.72	3.46	9.60
Switzerland	11.95	14.68	25.50	8.40	8.01
Turkey	2.79	6.43	3.49	0.37	1.62
United Kingdom	8.55	14.33	27.07	5.50	8.63
Eastern Europe					
Bulgaria	3.57	2.81	4.82	3.46	0.75
Czech Republic	9.02	6.94	11.14	4.09	1.39
Hungary	6.83	7.27	10.99	5.21	2.91
Poland	7.01	6.54	7.66	2.73	2.36
Romania	3.23	7.03	4.64	0.69	1.16
Russia	6.28	8.64	2.36	0.20	0.16
Slovakia	8.43	4.27	10.19	2.69	0.77
Ukraine	3.91	4.28	2.59	0.17	0.41

Source: *Euromonitor International from industry sources/national statistics*

Consumer Market Statistics

Table 6.16

Tobacco: Per Capita Retail Sales 2009

US$ per capita

	Total Tobacco	Cigarettes	Cigars	Smoking Tobacco
Western Europe				
Austria	416.51	385.52	22.16	8.83
Belgium	453.21	330.38	32.04	90.79
Denmark	437.80	388.03	21.01	26.61
Finland	344.37	278.98	22.10	43.29
France	352.07	313.46	11.22	27.39
Germany	475.66	347.87	84.48	42.86
Greece	618.98	582.19	18.20	18.59
Ireland	613.33	579.01	13.75	20.57
Italy	421.00	410.45	6.88	3.68
Netherlands	378.84	256.70	19.01	103.13
Norway	524.13	309.72	7.79	122.03
Portugal	295.19	279.30	9.93	5.96
Spain	451.16	420.98	16.88	13.30
Sweden	311.79	187.84	6.54	17.24
Switzerland	560.32	487.19	62.45	10.68
Turkey	215.75	215.56	0.02	0.18
United Kingdom	340.68	298.28	15.33	27.08
Eastern Europe				
Bulgaria	274.00	272.40	1.40	0.19
Czech Republic	397.35	376.34	5.77	15.24
Hungary	221.09	199.22	3.84	18.02
Poland	218.48	191.67	0.95	25.87
Romania	197.42	196.65	0.75	0.02
Russia	107.37	105.55	1.67	0.16
Slovakia	255.23	251.35	3.68	0.21
Ukraine	84.05	83.84	0.19	0.02

Source: *Euromonitor International from industry sources/national statistics*

Consumer Market Statistics

Table 6.17

Toys and Games: Per Capita Retail Sales 2009

US$ per capita

	Toys and Games	Traditional Toys and Games	Video Games Hardware	Video Games Software
Western Europe				
Austria				
Belgium	106.06	47.83	24.73	33.51
Denmark				
Finland				
France	138.27	60.72	28.30	49.25
Germany	70.77	39.13	11.25	20.39
Greece	39.40	23.99	9.40	6.01
Ireland				
Italy	82.42	48.71	15.23	18.48
Netherlands	141.79	67.42	34.78	39.59
Norway				
Portugal	47.34	24.00	11.27	12.07
Spain	74.01	34.91	16.83	22.27
Sweden	98.54	41.93	13.88	42.72
Switzerland				
Turkey	4.05	2.99	0.56	0.50
United Kingdom	160.30	53.74	33.55	73.01
Eastern Europe				
Bulgaria				
Czech Republic				
Hungary	15.86	11.81	0.99	3.07
Poland	14.06	6.97	0.86	6.23
Romania	5.84	4.88	0.32	0.64
Russia	5.58	4.35	0.47	0.76
Slovakia				
Ukraine				

Source: *Euromonitor International from industry sources/national statistics*

Consumer Prices and Costs

Consumer Prices Statistics

Table 7.1

Consumer Prices Indices 1990-2009

1995 = 100

	1990	1995	2000	2004	2005	2006	2007	2008	2009
Western Europe									
Austria	85.3	100.0	107.2	115.9	118.5	120.2	122.8	126.8	127.4
Belgium	88.6	100.0	108.6	117.3	120.6	122.7	125.0	130.6	130.5
Cyprus	79.3	100.0	115.4	128.9	132.2	135.5	138.7	145.2	145.7
Denmark	90.7	100.0	112.1	121.4	123.6	125.9	128.0	132.4	134.2
Finland	89.8	100.0	107.6	113.3	114.0	115.8	118.7	123.6	123.6
France	89.6	100.0	106.2	114.7	116.7	118.6	120.4	123.8	123.9
Germany	84.3	100.0	106.5	113.1	114.9	116.7	119.3	122.5	122.9
Gibraltar	72.2	100.0	117.3	126.6	127.7	129.2	131.6	133.7	135.8
Greece	52.3	100.0	126.7	144.6	149.7	154.5	159.0	165.6	167.6
Iceland	83.8	100.0	114.9	135.3	140.7	150.2	157.7	177.8	199.1
Ireland	88.3	100.0	113.4	131.6	134.8	140.1	147.0	152.9	146.1
Italy	78.3	100.0	112.8	124.6	127.1	129.8	132.1	136.6	137.6
Liechtenstein	86.5	100.0	104.2	108.2	108.8	109.4	109.8	110.4	111.4
Luxembourg	87.1	100.0	108.1	118.2	121.1	124.4	127.2	131.6	132.0
Malta	84.7	100.0	112.6	123.4	127.1	130.6	132.2	137.9	140.8
Monaco	88.7	100.0	107.5	111.6	112.6	113.4	114.5	115.7	117.2
Netherlands	87.4	100.0	111.2	123.7	125.8	127.2	129.3	132.5	134.1
Norway	88.9	100.0	112.0	120.4	122.2	125.1	126.0	130.7	133.6
Portugal	70.9	100.0	113.9	130.1	133.1	137.2	140.6	144.2	143.0
Spain	77.7	100.0	113.8	129.0	133.3	138.0	141.9	147.7	147.3
Sweden	81.5	100.0	102.2	109.4	109.9	111.4	113.9	117.8	117.5
Switzerland	85.6	100.0	103.8	107.0	108.3	109.4	110.2	112.9	112.4
Turkey	5.5	100.0	1,579.6	4,725.5	5,112.5	5,602.6	6,094.7	6,730.6	7,153.2
United Kingdom	83.1	100.0	108.2	114.0	116.3	119.0	121.8	126.2	128.9
Eastern Europe									
Albania	9.2	100.0	181.9	207.8	212.7	217.7	224.1	231.6	236.8
Belarus	0.0	100.0	4,576.7	15,940.7	17,588.8	18,825.8	20,411.2	23,439.8	26,474.3
Bosnia-Herzegovina		100.0	100.7	106.5	110.3	117.0	118.8	127.6	127.1
Bulgaria	2.2	100.0	3,446.6	4,258.3	4,472.7	4,797.9	5,200.9	5,847.4	6,011.3
Croatia		100.0	125.8	137.8	142.4	147.0	151.2	160.4	164.3
Czech Republic	39.6	100.0	138.7	152.2	155.0	158.9	163.5	173.9	175.7
Estonia	1.8	100.0	158.2	181.0	188.4	196.7	209.7	231.5	231.3
Georgia	0.0	100.0	191.6	234.5	253.9	277.2	302.8	333.0	338.9
Hungary	32.4	100.0	201.7	258.9	268.2	278.7	300.9	319.1	332.6
Latvia	5.7	100.0	140.2	160.2	171.0	182.1	200.5	231.5	239.9
Lithuania	0.2	100.0	145.1	147.5	151.4	157.1	166.1	184.3	192.6
Macedonia	0.2	100.0	109.8	120.6	120.8	124.8	129.3	138.6	138.2
Moldova	0.1	100.0	271.8	395.1	442.3	498.8	560.5	632.1	631.8
Montenegro	100.1	100.0	85.3	140.0	144.9	147.9	153.1	166.9	172.8
Poland	16.7	100.0	181.9	204.2	208.5	210.8	215.9	225.3	233.9
Romania	0.9	100.0	1,154.4	2,466.6	2,688.6	2,866.7	3,005.0	3,241.0	3,421.4
Russia	0.0	100.0	485.6	862.3	971.9	1,066.1	1,161.9	1,325.7	1,481.2
Serbia		100.0	765.3	2,175.3	2,526.0	2,822.1	3,002.5	3,389.0	3,652.7
Slovakia	40.2	100.0	148.5	192.0	197.2	206.0	211.7	221.4	225.0
Slovenia	8.9	100.0	148.5	189.2	193.9	198.7	205.9	217.6	219.4
Ukraine	0.0	100.0	363.6	470.6	534.3	582.9	657.3	823.4	955.3

Source:National statistical offices/OECD/Eurostat/Euromonitor International

Table 7.2

Food and Non-Alcoholic Beverage Price Indices 1990-2009

1995 = 100

	1990	1995	2000	2004	2005	2006	2007	2008	2009
Western Europe									
Austria	93.3	100.0	104.2	112.7	113.1	115.1	123.0	126.3	128.9
Belgium	97.9	100.0	105.5	116.0	118.1	121.4	126.4	133.9	131.5
Cyprus	78.2	100.0	115.9	134.7	139.5	144.4	149.3	157.9	160.1
Denmark	95.5	100.0	104.6	111.6	112.0	114.9	120.4	129.6	131.9
Finland	106.1	100.0	102.2	111.0	111.2	112.4	114.8	124.6	120.8
France	95.3	100.0	107.0	119.2	119.5	121.6	123.2	129.2	129.3
Germany	93.9	100.0	101.0	106.1	106.2	108.0	111.8	119.1	121.1
Gibraltar	87.9	100.0	110.2	126.9	129.4	132.8	137.1	145.6	147.9
Greece	60.2	100.0	122.9	144.4	145.8	149.3	151.0	152.9	154.2
Iceland	93.3	100.0	117.4	128.8	125.3	135.8	133.6	155.3	173.4
Ireland	94.6	100.0	107.6	113.5	111.6	111.9	115.8	125.1	120.8
Italy	80.7	100.0	107.6	121.3	121.4	123.2	126.8	133.8	136.0
Liechtenstein									
Luxembourg	92.6	100.0	107.7	121.7	123.7	126.6	130.9	137.9	138.1
Malta	87.3	100.0	109.9	120.3	122.4	124.9	130.3	140.7	143.7
Monaco									
Netherlands	93.5	100.0	107.6	116.2	114.9	117.0	118.6	125.7	123.9
Norway	94.0	100.0	114.0	119.0	121.0	123.0	126.0	135.0	142.0
Portugal	80.6	100.0	111.6	134.7	132.8	136.5	138.2	139.3	137.8
Spain	95.5	100.0	112.5	135.4	139.8	145.3	150.4	158.8	157.1
Sweden	95.6	100.0	96.4	102.4	101.9	102.9	105.0	112.3	115.9
Switzerland	94.8	100.0	101.9	107.3	106.6	106.7	107.3	110.7	110.4
Turkey	5.7	100.0	1,413.8	4,493.1	4,858.4	5,309.3	5,774.2	6,377.2	6,776.0
United Kingdom	88.7	100.0	103.8	109.4	111.0	113.6	118.8	129.5	132.6
Eastern Europe									
Albania		100.0	213.7	245.5	244.3	246.9	254.3	268.2	273.5
Belarus		100.0	5,442.0	13,345.4	15,471.0	16,535.5	17,924.4	19,284.7	21,747.0
Bosnia-Herzegovina		100.0	97.1	102.1	105.8	108.9	111.2	113.7	122.7
Bulgaria	2.2	100.0	3,475.2	3,891.0	3,909.7	4,137.2	4,294.6	4,430.7	4,506.0
Croatia		100.0	115.1	121.2	126.9	132.8	136.7	141.1	144.3
Czech Republic	38.7	100.0	108.0	112.7	112.6	114.1	115.6	116.5	117.1
Estonia		100.0	126.8	146.9	153.9	157.4	163.0	167.9	166.3
Georgia		100.0	173.7	217.4	227.2	247.2	269.1	295.2	298.4
Hungary	33.7	100.0	182.9	221.6	221.9	230.2	236.0	240.4	248.7
Latvia	2.9	100.0	120.4	144.5	161.6	174.0	176.0	203.6	213.3
Lithuania	0.6	100.0	88.5	92.9	91.4	97.2	107.8	123.8	125.8
Macedonia	0.2	100.0	105.2	109.4	107.0	109.3	113.5	120.9	120.6
Moldova		100.0	240.8	356.2	404.7	441.6	489.8	565.4	565.7
Montenegro		100.0	76.0	113.4	112.5	117.1	121.1	133.0	136.8
Poland	21.0	100.0	140.4	154.6	157.7	160.1	167.1	176.1	184.0
Romania	0.6	100.0	845.9	1,723.3	1,773.4	1,875.0	1,970.6	2,044.6	2,150.1
Russia	0.1	100.0	404.7	462.2	540.8	617.2	720.3	1,173.8	1,019.1
Serbia		100.0	673.7	1,630.9	1,886.9	2,078.8	2,230.5	2,249.2	2,466.3
Slovakia	30.5	100.0	132.6	148.4	145.6	148.2	154.4	167.0	160.6
Slovenia	10.0	100.0	141.5	175.4	174.0	178.0	191.9	210.7	216.6
Ukraine		100.0	840.6	1,522.9	1,870.4	1,915.0	2,105.8	2,282.5	2,604.2

Source:National statistical offices/OECD/Eurostat/Euromonitor International

Consumer Prices Statistics

Table 7.3

Food and Drink Costs: Selected Items 2009

US$

	Apples (Kg)	Beer (33cl)	Butter (250g)	Flour (Kg)	Fresh Chicken (Kg)	Instant Coffee (250g)
Western Europe						
Austria	2.45	0.70	2.13	1.44	6.29	
Belgium	1.98	0.62	2.13	0.93	5.57	8.05
Cyprus	2.64	0.86	2.93	1.72	5.54	10.68
Denmark	2.98	1.07	2.76	1.56		12.69
Finland	2.85	1.06	2.25	0.90	2.46	10.81
France	3.12	0.69	2.30	1.51	12.58	8.95
Germany	2.69	0.62	1.61	0.94		15.99
Gibraltar	3.51	1.27	1.92	2.75	4.83	10.54
Greece	2.21	0.99	2.11	2.04	4.56	9.68
Iceland	2.08	1.09	1.07	0.49	4.33	6.85
Ireland	5.47	1.65	1.87	1.46	6.46	
Italy	3.07	0.77	3.01	0.97	6.44	
Liechtenstein						
Luxembourg	3.50	0.96	2.31	1.33	8.11	10.98
Malta	2.15	1.12	2.45	1.36	3.33	6.96
Monaco						
Netherlands	2.16	0.74	1.58	0.72	5.74	9.32
Norway	3.73	2.37	2.34	1.64	7.65	17.69
Portugal	1.78	0.66	2.34	1.45	3.21	10.81
Spain	2.57	0.70	2.91	1.18	4.07	8.67
Sweden	2.81	1.12	1.43	0.81	4.99	10.99
Switzerland	3.75	1.08	4.29	1.93	9.66	13.46
Turkey	0.97	0.91	2.63	1.10	2.67	9.10
United Kingdom	2.40	2.23	1.72	0.78	5.12	8.23
Eastern Europe						
Albania	1.97		2.05		4.20	
Belarus	1.12	0.32	1.08	0.64	2.62	6.41
Bosnia-Herzegovina						
Bulgaria	1.31	0.39	1.48	0.79	3.43	9.05
Croatia	1.59	0.66	3.00	1.10	4.57	12.91
Czech Republic	1.39	0.64	1.41	0.74	3.28	10.17
Estonia	2.20	0.61	2.16	0.90	4.00	8.08
Georgia	0.73	0.46	1.06	0.87	3.53	7.21
Hungary	0.87	0.47	2.60	0.68	3.74	12.08
Latvia	1.63	0.67	2.31	1.05	4.00	7.75
Lithuania	1.66	0.63	1.94	0.99	3.67	9.33
Macedonia	0.85	0.46	1.51	0.59	2.73	8.92
Moldova	1.01	0.76	1.64	0.88	4.12	10.67
Montenegro						
Poland	0.66	0.59	1.41	0.71	1.94	9.98
Romania	1.33	0.53	1.93	0.67	3.30	10.10
Russia	1.89	0.46	1.42	0.70	3.10	7.77
Serbia	0.79	0.28	1.76	0.72	3.25	
Slovakia	1.66	0.49	2.44	0.65	3.34	12.93
Slovenia	1.98	0.71	2.78	1.32	4.92	11.81
Ukraine	1.00	0.25	0.96	0.44	2.17	5.76

Source:*Euromonitor International from International Labour Organisation*
Notes: *Note: 'Cost' refers to national average retail prices paid by consumers, including related costs, such as sales or value-added, taxes.*

Consumer Prices Statistics

Food and Drink Costs: Selected Items 2009 *(continued)*
US$

	Milk (Litre)	Potatoes (Kg)	Red Table Wine (Litre)	Soft Drinks (Cola etc.) (33cl)	Sugar (Kg)	Tea (100g)
Western Europe						
Austria	1.38	1.26	7.81	0.36	1.48	5.85
Belgium	1.25	1.32	10.29	0.40	1.31	
Cyprus	1.55	1.85	6.46	0.39	1.61	1.81
Denmark	1.61	1.99		1.06	1.82	2.95
Finland	1.31	1.18	12.52	0.59	1.47	4.27
France	1.78	1.91	2.60	0.37	1.98	
Germany	1.07	1.23	3.77	0.44	1.60	6.71
Gibraltar	1.54	0.74	13.18	0.70	1.15	0.87
Greece	1.91	1.09	6.05		1.17	2.10
Iceland	0.78	1.58	16.94	0.57	1.22	5.18
Ireland	1.65	1.93	16.80		1.43	2.44
Italy	2.38	1.59	3.27	0.44	1.30	4.97
Liechtenstein						
Luxembourg	1.74	1.74	2.15	0.42	1.96	4.06
Malta	1.00	0.68	3.12	0.74	1.13	1.28
Monaco						
Netherlands	1.36	1.05	6.16	0.36	1.27	1.81
Norway	2.16	1.47	19.16	1.85	2.33	6.26
Portugal	1.15	0.87	2.18	0.67	1.33	5.33
Spain	1.34	1.15	1.51	0.28	1.28	3.65
Sweden	1.06	1.59	8.56	0.68	1.31	3.03
Switzerland	1.71	2.08	11.41	0.83	1.80	4.80
Turkey	1.24	0.52	9.68	0.70	1.63	0.75
United Kingdom	1.30	1.97	8.41	0.63	1.32	1.16
Eastern Europe						
Albania	0.77	0.74			1.05	
Belarus	0.47	0.26	4.49	0.18	0.76	1.19
Bosnia-Herzegovina						
Bulgaria	1.08	0.64	4.96	0.22	1.54	2.08
Croatia	1.13	0.72	4.61	0.44	1.11	1.65
Czech Republic	1.39	0.49	3.63	0.11	1.06	2.30
Estonia	1.20	0.69	7.62	0.62	1.32	1.36
Georgia	1.59	0.37	3.67	0.17	0.77	0.90
Hungary	1.12	0.38	1.59	0.77	0.99	1.70
Latvia	1.18	0.63		0.35	1.41	1.22
Lithuania	1.07	0.50	9.35	0.57	1.30	3.36
Macedonia	0.99	0.58	1.71	0.33	0.84	1.71
Moldova	0.83	0.47	3.93	0.59	1.05	1.17
Montenegro						
Poland	0.35	0.33	6.81	0.48	0.83	0.93
Romania	0.83	0.42	2.29	0.40	1.07	
Russia	0.90	0.54	5.04	0.21	0.76	0.95
Serbia	1.08	0.33	1.81	0.33	0.87	1.75
Slovakia	0.94	0.51	3.37	0.26	1.38	2.36
Slovenia	1.08	0.71	2.53	0.35	1.19	5.82
Ukraine	0.56	0.35	0.95	0.14	0.53	0.42

Source: *Euromonitor International from International Labour Organisation*
Notes: *Note: 'Cost' refers to national average retail prices paid by consumers, including related costs, such as sales or value-added, taxes.*

Consumer Prices Statistics | **Table 7.4**

Alcoholic Beverage and Tobacco Price Indices 1990-2009
1995 = 100

	1990	1995	2000	2004	2005	2006	2007	2008	2009
Western Europe									
Austria	91.0	100.0	106.7	119.5	124.0	121.6	127.3	129.9	131.3
Belgium	95.3	100.0	111.9	131.1	135.2	137.8	146.3	152.1	150.3
Cyprus									
Denmark	95.8	100.0	108.5	109.7	112.6	113.3	115.1	120.2	121.7
Finland	82.9	100.0	109.9	103.1	101.6	102.5	104.0	109.6	108.5
France	74.9	100.0	119.3	156.7	156.8	157.5	160.5	166.5	166.4
Germany	86.7	100.0	107.3	125.0	134.0	137.7	142.1	144.9	146.0
Gibraltar									
Greece	43.5	100.0	139.9	174.6	178.8	185.6	191.0	195.9	198.0
Iceland									
Ireland	72.6	100.0	119.8	149.1	150.7	152.8	164.4	179.4	190.8
Italy	65.7	100.0	120.2	144.8	154.0	161.1	166.5	173.6	180.1
Liechtenstein									
Luxembourg									
Malta									
Monaco									
Netherlands	83.8	100.0	119.4	148.2	151.9	153.1	155.9	167.2	163.2
Norway	75.0	100.0	132.0	154.0	159.0	163.0	165.0	178.0	184.0
Portugal	72.7	100.0	122.1	153.8	159.4	168.8	175.5	174.5	173.2
Spain	121.5	100.0	134.7	159.6	168.0	171.1	183.4	190.4	207.2
Sweden	89.0	100.0	110.0	113.9	114.7	115.5	121.9	130.6	134.0
Switzerland	89.0	100.0	111.1	119.9	125.6	126.9	129.6	132.9	136.6
Turkey	5.2	100.0	1,772.1	7,590.7	8,615.0	10,402.6	11,435.5	12,243.6	13,799.5
United Kingdom	70.7	100.0	126.0	138.0	139.7	141.7	145.1	149.2	151.9
Eastern Europe									
Albania									
Belarus		100.0	3,575.4	11,597.5	14,273.2	15,255.3	16,973.1	18,575.9	21,011.0
Bosnia-Herzegovina		100.0	105.3	112.3	128.9	112.3	113.1	113.8	124.8
Bulgaria	2.5	100.0	3,762.2	6,298.0	6,537.7	6,918.3	7,504.4	7,894.5	8,066.9
Croatia		100.0	140.4	158.4	168.3	175.0	182.0	188.8	193.2
Czech Republic	38.7	100.0	150.4	164.5	166.9	171.3	174.7	177.8	179.0
Estonia		100.0	193.5	206.5	222.8	231.0	237.0	246.1	244.0
Georgia									
Hungary	41.1	100.0	227.9	326.0	330.1	343.3	357.8	367.6	381.1
Latvia	3.7	100.0	159.7	181.3	186.6	203.4	229.2	283.2	347.1
Lithuania	0.5	100.0	145.8	149.0	148.5	147.9	155.7	177.9	204.6
Macedonia	0.2	100.0	108.4	113.1	121.6	150.4	153.7	155.8	161.5
Moldova									
Montenegro		100.0	95.2	173.9	181.4	182.8	182.2	187.4	194.7
Poland	17.4	100.0	176.7	194.7	200.0	204.6	211.8	227.2	252.0
Romania	1.7	100.0	1,008.3	2,221.2	2,415.9	2,554.2	2,751.4	2,910.7	3,070.1
Russia	0.4	100.0	265.9	401.7	498.9	575.1	617.2	939.1	869.3
Serbia		100.0	729.9	2,003.1	2,120.7	2,477.0	2,762.0	2,777.7	3,050.7
Slovakia	32.3	100.0	116.1	157.7	157.5	162.9	171.9	186.4	202.6
Slovenia	6.0	100.0	143.3	174.2	171.0	176.9	186.5	195.3	197.9
Ukraine		100.0	353.3	714.6	911.5	947.4	1,053.2	1,155.8	1,322.9

Source:National statistical offices/OECD/Eurostat/Euromonitor International

Table 7.5

Clothing and Footwear Prices Indices 1990-2009

1995 = 100

	1990	1995	2000	2004	2005	2006	2007	2008	2009
Western Europe									
Austria	85.9	100.0	100.9	101.6	101.9	99.7	99.3	99.9	98.1
Belgium	98.8	100.0	103.7	107.7	108.0	108.3	108.8	109.9	112.7
Cyprus	81.1	100.0	113.8	102.9	100.7	100.3	100.6	99.3	99.7
Denmark	94.6	100.0	100.9	102.7	102.0	100.3	98.1	97.4	97.8
Finland	86.2	100.0	100.5	100.2	99.9	98.0	97.8	98.2	101.0
France	93.0	100.0	101.3	102.3	102.7	102.8	103.5	104.2	103.8
Germany	90.5	100.0	102.1	101.8	99.6	99.3	100.7	101.3	100.1
Gibraltar	90.8	100.0	102.1	98.8	100.2	101.9	101.7	100.2	101.8
Greece	60.3	100.0	131.8	149.0	156.2	162.1	167.5	173.1	175.1
Iceland	87.9	100.0	94.9	93.4	92.3	92.3	93.6	103.1	115.2
Ireland	88.3	100.0	69.8	58.7	56.9	55.5	53.5	50.7	44.7
Italy	80.9	100.0	114.5	127.1	129.1	130.9	132.7	135.0	135.6
Liechtenstein									
Luxembourg			87.6	92.7	93.2	93.3	93.8	94.2	94.5
Malta	89.7	100.0	95.2	81.5	81.1	79.6	79.9	83.5	85.3
Monaco									
Netherlands	95.9	100.0	107.2	110.2	108.6	108.7	109.3	109.3	112.3
Norway	89.0	100.0	91.0	74.0	71.0	69.0	66.0	66.0	69.0
Portugal	94.7	100.0	95.7	107.6	105.4	106.9	107.0	106.9	105.5
Spain	96.2	100.0	113.2	129.4	131.6	133.3	134.4	135.5	133.3
Sweden	91.9	100.0	105.8	105.6	104.6	106.2	108.8	108.3	110.8
Switzerland	90.3	100.0	102.6	93.0	94.7	96.1	96.4	100.2	102.6
Turkey	5.7	100.0	1,102.6	3,453.6	3,615.4	3,920.6	4,165.5	4,627.5	4,830.5
United Kingdom	97.3	100.0	93.2	81.1	79.3	78.6	78.0	75.0	75.7
Eastern Europe									
Albania		100.0	188.4	157.9	153.8	156.7	148.2	143.9	140.7
Belarus		100.0	5,523.0	19,424.2	23,165.0	24,758.9	27,174.8	29,481.8	33,294.9
Bosnia-Herzegovina		100.0	104.6	118.2	117.0	117.7	115.4	115.8	127.5
Bulgaria	1.7	100.0	2,883.9	2,821.8	2,749.8	2,909.9	2,950.9	2,999.3	3,041.0
Croatia		100.0	128.1	135.5	136.3	136.1	136.1	136.0	138.0
Czech Republic	38.7	100.0	112.9	98.7	93.2	89.4	85.5	81.5	80.8
Estonia		100.0	157.8	175.9	181.4	189.4	193.7	199.0	197.3
Georgia									
Hungary	38.7	100.0	210.7	236.9	234.4	242.1	245.7	248.4	256.6
Latvia	2.4	100.0	177.8	189.3	185.8	191.0	248.2	243.8	243.5
Lithuania	0.5	100.0	157.1	135.9	136.5	133.2	126.5	121.7	111.6
Macedonia	0.3	100.0	105.2	116.1	119.1	121.2	123.6	133.4	132.6
Moldova									
Montenegro		100.0	83.6	141.9	144.5	145.2	146.6	148.8	153.8
Poland	21.9	100.0	166.4	162.2	153.7	144.1	133.9	129.0	119.9
Romania	0.9	100.0	990.7	1,778.5	1,807.9	1,911.4	1,995.3	2,060.0	2,164.5
Russia	0.7	100.0	410.8	672.8	809.7	932.0	942.1	1,226.3	1,274.4
Serbia		100.0	695.3	1,732.8	1,885.1	2,095.4	2,188.6	2,406.7	2,638.9
Slovakia	35.2	100.0	131.9	140.4	138.7	139.4	141.3	141.3	140.1
Slovenia	8.9	100.0	136.0	154.4	152.7	151.9	155.2	162.1	161.0
Ukraine		100.0	415.2	668.0	838.6	861.6	954.5	1,041.3	1,189.8

Source:National statistical offices/OECD/Eurostat/Euromonitor International

Consumer Prices Statistics

Table 7.6

Housing Price Indices 1990-2009

1995 = 100

	1990	1995	2000	2004	2005	2006	2007	2008	2009
Western Europe									
Austria	80.1	100.0	114.4	125.5	132.0	136.5	141.4	142.9	143.1
Belgium	96.6	100.0	110.2	119.6	123.8	128.8	130.9	139.8	137.6
Cyprus									
Denmark	87.4	100.0	117.9	131.9	136.2	140.9	144.6	150.4	152.7
Finland	78.1	100.0	119.2	135.0	138.1	141.5	145.8	152.4	151.0
France	85.2	100.0	107.2	116.4	121.3	126.0	130.1	134.3	134.6
Germany	74.9	100.0	110.3	117.2	120.3	123.5	125.6	129.9	130.7
Gibraltar									
Greece	49.6	100.0	124.6	145.2	158.8	169.0	177.8	187.6	190.6
Iceland									
Ireland	75.1	100.0	152.0	191.7	194.8	201.9	218.2	230.8	213.2
Italy	66.9	100.0	124.5	148.8	154.5	162.1	168.0	175.3	175.3
Liechtenstein									
Luxembourg									
Malta									
Monaco									
Netherlands	81.6	100.0	121.0	139.5	145.2	150.6	154.1	157.5	158.5
Norway	87.0	100.0	115.0	143.0	145.0	154.0	151.0	163.0	168.0
Portugal	75.4	100.0	115.6	143.6	148.6	157.1	163.2	169.1	168.2
Spain	80.7	100.0	110.6	129.1	135.6	143.3	150.3	159.2	161.2
Sweden	89.3	100.0	107.6	121.3	124.1	126.9	129.2	133.6	137.9
Switzerland	81.1	100.0	104.8	109.1	111.0	113.4	115.7	122.2	119.1
Turkey	5.4	100.0	1,938.1	5,778.5	6,710.0	7,847.0	9,054.8	10,357.9	11,391.3
United Kingdom	70.7	100.0	121.9	150.6	159.1	170.2	181.2	194.8	200.1
Eastern Europe									
Albania									
Belarus		100.0	2,987.0	40,081.2	50,860.3	54,359.7	60,433.9	66,507.4	75,250.1
Bosnia-Herzegovina		100.0	99.8	102.8	107.1	109.1	104.2	108.4	116.0
Bulgaria	2.2	100.0	4,495.6	6,621.5	6,745.2	7,137.8	7,449.3	7,724.2	7,861.6
Croatia		100.0	143.2	166.9	174.4	183.9	190.6	197.5	202.2
Czech Republic	38.7	100.0	167.3	203.8	213.4	220.8	227.1	234.3	236.4
Estonia		100.0	184.1	232.6	242.5	256.0	265.5	275.4	273.6
Georgia									
Hungary	31.8	100.0	239.5	328.5	347.0	360.4	380.2	396.0	411.3
Latvia	7.0	100.0	146.8	174.2	191.1	214.0	220.6	321.1	299.3
Lithuania	0.5	100.0	209.5	218.8	232.7	248.0	300.8	337.5	376.4
Macedonia	0.2	100.0	128.8	154.3	154.7	159.2	182.2	181.6	183.4
Moldova									
Montenegro		100.0	99.6	193.9	196.2	197.6	214.0	235.6	245.5
Poland	18.5	100.0	218.3	257.4	266.2	273.8	285.8	307.4	328.6
Romania	0.9	100.0	1,729.5	4,650.4	5,372.3	5,680.1	6,238.4	6,716.4	7,101.3
Russia	0.2	100.0	222.2	1,388.3	1,777.8	2,011.8	2,124.9	2,491.3	2,731.1
Serbia		100.0	862.0	2,811.5	3,281.6	3,713.3	4,028.3	4,115.6	4,532.7
Slovakia	50.4	100.0	155.0	226.6	245.3	276.7	287.6	308.0	318.6
Slovenia	8.2	100.0	164.2	209.1	220.2	227.7	235.1	252.0	255.5
Ukraine		100.0	308.9	578.1	736.8	782.6	859.3	944.5	1,082.1

Source:National statistical offices/OECD/Eurostat/Euromonitor International

Consumer Prices Statistics **Table 7.7**

Household Goods and Services Price Indices 1990-2009
1995 = 100

	1990	1995	2000	2004	2005	2006	2007	2008	2009
Western Europe									
Austria	88.2	100.0	103.0	107.0	105.4	105.9	106.5	107.6	106.3
Belgium	98.9	100.0	104.0	110.6	111.4	112.3	114.5	117.4	118.6
Cyprus									
Denmark	90.4	100.0	109.3	115.5	117.0	117.9	119.3	121.7	123.0
Finland	88.8	100.0	102.8	107.4	108.5	108.9	110.2	111.9	113.7
France	91.7	100.0	105.6	111.7	112.4	113.1	114.3	116.2	116.0
Germany	89.5	100.0	103.6	106.4	106.1	106.2	107.6	109.2	108.4
Gibraltar									
Greece	55.2	100.0	125.2	134.3	137.2	139.9	142.1	144.4	145.6
Iceland									
Ireland	88.1	100.0	104.6	111.9	111.1	110.4	109.1	107.8	104.4
Italy	79.3	100.0	111.8	120.9	122.7	124.5	127.2	131.0	133.2
Liechtenstein									
Luxembourg									
Malta									
Monaco									
Netherlands	92.7	100.0	108.2	118.8	119.3	119.8	121.3	123.9	125.2
Norway	92.0	100.0	105.0	110.0	110.0	110.0	111.0	111.0	110.0
Portugal	78.9	100.0	111.9	133.7	134.2	139.0	142.1	144.6	143.3
Spain	83.2	100.0	116.5	124.9	127.1	129.9	133.1	136.6	138.6
Sweden	92.5	100.0	104.4	108.6	107.1	105.3	106.6	108.5	110.3
Switzerland	89.7	100.0	102.6	104.5	104.5	104.5	104.8	105.7	106.5
Turkey	5.7	100.0	1,069.7	2,535.4	2,658.1	2,867.4	2,988.9	3,256.6	3,247.7
United Kingdom	89.5	100.0	104.8	108.5	109.1	110.2	113.1	116.5	118.7
Eastern Europe									
Albania									
Belarus		100.0	3,011.7	14,864.9	18,321.8	19,582.4	21,946.7	24,058.8	27,229.1
Bosnia-Herzegovina		100.0	108.1	113.5	113.4	114.0	114.5	115.6	126.2
Bulgaria	2.2	100.0	2,474.5	2,468.4	2,420.6	2,561.5	2,590.4	2,635.5	2,671.8
Croatia		100.0	140.6	137.7	141.1	141.6	142.6	143.8	146.1
Czech Republic	38.7	100.0	131.3	126.4	123.7	122.2	120.2	118.3	118.2
Estonia		100.0	126.1	128.2	129.5	130.9	131.6	132.6	130.7
Georgia									
Hungary	33.0	100.0	185.2	195.1	191.9	195.1	195.4	195.5	201.4
Latvia	3.3	100.0	137.1	145.8	151.3	156.0	185.2	189.6	199.8
Lithuania	0.5	100.0	120.0	106.3	106.8	107.0	108.8	112.6	114.9
Macedonia	0.4	100.0	130.1	132.1	128.1	129.5	129.7	142.0	140.7
Moldova									
Montenegro		100.0	75.0	110.7	110.5	110.7	111.1	113.0	115.9
Poland	16.3	100.0	177.9	195.4	198.2	199.1	201.4	207.8	212.1
Romania	0.9	100.0	839.1	1,519.9	1,557.4	1,646.6	1,722.0	1,782.3	1,873.3
Russia	0.6	100.0	224.0	514.9	640.4	717.8	735.7	912.6	973.9
Serbia		100.0	631.6	1,432.4	1,577.9	1,663.2	1,693.8	1,999.3	2,188.0
Slovakia	49.6	100.0	124.9	121.9	117.0	116.5	116.8	116.5	114.4
Slovenia	7.5	100.0	125.4	154.7	160.1	166.2	173.3	183.5	186.2
Ukraine		100.0	326.9	638.2	775.1	775.7	863.9	932.4	1,062.4

Source:National statistical offices/OECD/Eurostat/Euromonitor International

Consumer Prices Statistics

Table 7.8

Health Goods and Medical Services Price Indices 1990-2009

1995 = 100

	1990	1995	2000	2004	2005	2006	2007	2008	2009
Western Europe									
Austria	78.3	100.0	111.7	136.6	141.6	143.2	150.2	151.6	152.5
Belgium	95.5	100.0	111.2	112.4	114.4	121.8	126.7	137.3	132.9
Cyprus									
Denmark	95.6	100.0	104.6	108.7	111.7	112.8	114.0	116.1	117.4
Finland	77.5	100.0	114.4	127.5	130.2	130.9	130.9	133.2	135.7
France	92.8	100.0	102.8	104.8	105.6	105.8	106.3	106.9	106.6
Germany	86.0	100.0	106.5	116.0	118.1	119.1	120.4	121.7	120.8
Gibraltar									
Greece	41.8	100.0	95.4	113.1	118.2	124.1	128.9	133.6	135.3
Iceland									
Ireland	59.0	100.0	123.3	173.9	188.2	196.5	202.5	216.4	224.2
Italy	81.2	100.0	120.2	123.9	124.6	123.2	122.1	121.3	125.3
Liechtenstein									
Luxembourg									
Malta									
Monaco									
Netherlands	92.7	100.0	113.6	131.4	131.6	132.9	139.1	141.7	141.9
Norway	81.0	100.0	123.0	145.0	149.0	154.0	157.0	166.0	179.0
Portugal	71.1	100.0	120.9	147.5	147.5	152.6	155.8	158.3	156.8
Spain	72.1	100.0	112.3	125.1	128.0	131.2	131.4	133.1	132.2
Sweden	83.8	100.0	129.0	151.5	154.6	155.5	158.6	159.7	160.9
Switzerland	81.4	100.0	103.0	106.5	107.4	107.9	108.1	108.0	108.4
Turkey	5.1	100.0	1,761.5	5,098.2	5,105.2	5,110.7	4,888.5	5,040.3	5,007.8
United Kingdom	67.2	100.0	134.9	153.5	154.8	156.8	160.7	162.8	165.7
Eastern Europe									
Albania									
Belarus		100.0	4,457.9	29,487.6	37,121.7	39,675.9	44,043.1	48,385.5	54,733.9
Bosnia-Herzegovina		100.0	96.0	92.6	92.5	100.0	93.2	92.7	94.9
Bulgaria	1.2	100.0	4,621.4	8,067.9	8,494.6	8,989.0	9,305.4	9,710.6	9,882.1
Croatia		100.0	123.9	164.7	170.1	178.5	184.0	189.6	193.8
Czech Republic	38.7	100.0	78.9	93.1	99.5	104.9	108.9	113.8	115.1
Estonia		100.0	164.5	229.6	235.5	251.0	259.2	268.1	266.5
Georgia									
Hungary	18.0	100.0	343.8	458.9	489.4	509.7	532.8	555.5	576.6
Latvia	3.6	100.0	122.5	161.4	179.2	192.1	170.7	189.1	229.7
Lithuania	0.6	100.0	115.9	130.2	140.1	148.1	157.0	173.9	204.5
Macedonia	0.2	100.0	108.2	110.0	132.9	135.8	140.6	150.0	149.5
Moldova									
Montenegro		100.0	70.2	102.2	102.5	102.5	102.7	104.0	106.4
Poland	20.4	100.0	248.1	284.9	293.1	298.5	304.7	318.1	328.8
Romania	1.3	100.0	1,268.9	2,352.9	2,327.3	2,460.6	2,492.6	2,533.7	2,653.5
Russia	0.1	100.0	331.5	1,021.3	1,297.6	1,470.5	1,604.2	2,122.6	2,130.1
Serbia		100.0	572.5	1,383.5	1,520.1	1,721.3	1,846.1	2,125.6	2,330.3
Slovakia	26.5	100.0	141.5	179.3	195.0	216.5	215.4	233.1	251.9
Slovenia	6.1	100.0	144.8	185.9	188.0	189.4	192.5	199.3	197.8
Ukraine		100.0	436.1	820.7	1,076.2	1,149.8	1,284.6	1,425.2	1,636.9

Source: *National statistical offices/OECD/Eurostat/Euromonitor International*

Table 7.9

Transport Price Indices 1990-2009

1995 = 100

	1990	1995	2000	2004	2005	2006	2007	2008	2009
Western Europe									
Austria	87.5	100.0	110.8	118.2	122.0	125.9	122.1	125.1	122.3
Belgium	96.3	100.0	114.1	124.3	130.9	133.6	134.4	140.2	140.7
Cyprus									
Denmark	90.5	100.0	110.2	117.6	121.5	123.4	124.9	128.2	129.7
Finland	82.7	100.0	112.4	114.9	119.0	121.5	122.5	125.2	126.8
France	88.2	100.0	109.3	117.3	122.3	125.9	129.1	136.0	136.3
Germany	83.9	100.0	110.5	119.0	122.6	126.0	130.5	135.1	136.7
Gibraltar									
Greece	65.6	100.0	120.7	131.1	137.5	142.9	147.6	152.6	154.4
Iceland									
Ireland	84.9	100.0	106.0	116.8	120.6	125.3	128.2	131.3	125.3
Italy	76.1	100.0	114.3	123.0	128.1	132.0	134.3	142.1	138.8
Liechtenstein									
Luxembourg									
Malta									
Monaco									
Netherlands	89.6	100.0	115.4	129.1	134.9	138.3	140.8	145.4	145.5
Norway	80.0	100.0	115.0	126.0	132.0	137.0	140.0	137.0	129.0
Portugal	74.0	100.0	120.4	154.7	162.3	172.8	180.7	188.5	187.8
Spain	102.1	100.0	116.2	130.5	138.3	144.7	148.0	156.3	147.6
Sweden	89.2	100.0	107.9	115.9	120.1	122.2	123.6	128.4	129.1
Switzerland	82.4	100.0	107.1	108.0	112.3	115.4	116.8	120.0	115.8
Turkey	5.2	100.0	1,612.8	3,016.9	3,505.9	4,002.4	4,072.4	4,420.5	4,571.0
United Kingdom	80.9	100.0	117.4	125.5	128.5	130.8	134.0	140.0	142.8
Eastern Europe									
Albania									
Belarus		100.0	3,933.2	20,554.2	25,266.5	27,005.0	30,119.1	32,971.0	37,299.9
Bosnia-Herzegovina		100.0	109.6	123.6	134.1	130.8	130.0	137.1	156.0
Bulgaria	2.2	100.0	3,586.9	4,124.0	4,445.9	4,704.6	4,943.1	5,207.4	5,309.2
Croatia		100.0	143.3	172.1	175.9	183.6	188.3	192.9	197.0
Czech Republic	38.7	100.0	125.4	128.9	131.6	134.9	137.7	140.4	141.4
Estonia		100.0	213.0	226.2	241.0	256.5	268.0	280.6	279.3
Georgia									
Hungary	33.0	100.0	224.3	246.1	255.9	265.4	274.5	283.2	293.5
Latvia	2.1	100.0	164.2	185.9	211.7	223.8	239.2	262.4	265.8
Lithuania	0.5	100.0	172.9	173.5	188.3	198.7	211.5	237.1	233.9
Macedonia	0.2	100.0	131.5	138.0	150.3	157.6	159.3	171.2	171.2
Moldova									
Montenegro		100.0	80.5	129.3	169.3	175.1	180.1	206.5	214.6
Poland	19.2	100.0	204.5	245.6	255.4	257.3	259.9	269.9	266.7
Romania	0.9	100.0	1,143.6	2,804.5	3,100.6	3,278.2	3,522.5	3,738.3	3,943.2
Russia	0.2	100.0	292.5	711.9	883.2	827.9	1,043.9	842.2	1,126.9
Serbia		100.0	742.9	2,239.0	2,672.0	2,827.1	2,879.8	3,234.8	3,556.9
Slovakia	35.6	100.0	141.2	159.4	160.9	162.3	158.5	164.8	156.0
Slovenia	8.4	100.0	158.0	203.7	209.7	211.8	212.3	219.8	217.6
Ukraine		100.0	291.4	430.0	524.5	542.1	585.4	632.5	720.8

Source:National statistical offices/OECD/Eurostat/Euromonitor International

Consumer Prices Statistics

Table 7.10

Communications Price Indices 1990-2009

1995 = 100

	1990	1995	2000	2004	2005	2006	2007	2008	2009
Western Europe									
Austria	103.6	100.0	75.0	68.8	63.0	62.8	60.9	58.6	55.4
Belgium	91.4	100.0	101.0	97.9	98.5	95.5	92.6	89.9	95.9
Cyprus									
Denmark	98.7	100.0	92.3	76.7	76.0	75.6	76.1	76.9	77.6
Finland	98.9	100.0	87.3	75.1	65.9	60.4	63.8	62.1	64.0
France	103.3	100.0	72.4	66.0	65.3	61.1	60.0	59.8	59.1
Germany	92.6	100.0	77.0	73.4	71.9	69.1	68.7	66.6	63.9
Gibraltar									
Greece	50.9	100.0	95.7	81.7	81.6	79.2	77.4	76.0	75.9
Iceland									
Ireland	97.3	100.0	78.8	84.4	85.9	86.4	88.0	90.1	90.5
Italy	85.6	100.0	95.6	85.2	80.5	77.3	70.8	67.2	67.0
Liechtenstein									
Luxembourg									
Malta									
Monaco									
Netherlands	88.9	100.0	92.4	97.6	95.7	92.8	91.0	88.0	93.3
Norway	131.0	100.0	79.0	77.0	76.0	74.0	72.0	72.0	72.0
Portugal	90.1	100.0	90.2	93.9	92.9	93.9	94.2	94.3	93.1
Spain	79.6	100.0	95.7	89.9	88.6	87.5	87.6	87.0	86.4
Sweden	89.6	100.0	89.5	81.2	77.6	72.9	70.2	67.3	65.0
Switzerland	82.6	100.0	64.8	61.5	58.0	54.1	52.5	51.0	48.5
Turkey	4.2	100.0	1,835.0	5,887.9	6,030.2	6,190.0	6,138.2	6,249.1	6,464.4
United Kingdom	97.1	100.0	87.7	84.2	82.1	81.7	78.4	75.9	76.5
Eastern Europe									
Albania									
Belarus		100.0	6,917.2	60,493.3	71,955.8	76,906.8	86,115.5	93,747.5	106,044.3
Bosnia-Herzegovina		100.0	105.9	112.7	111.7	114.3	115.3	117.3	128.3
Bulgaria	2.2	100.0	3,040.0	4,000.2	4,063.4	4,299.9	4,453.3	4,604.9	4,683.0
Croatia		100.0	183.2	258.1	257.6	256.2	255.3	254.0	257.5
Czech Republic	38.7	100.0	38.8	45.3	46.3	48.2	50.4	51.9	52.5
Estonia		100.0	199.4	204.5	199.9	210.4	211.7	213.8	211.5
Georgia									
Hungary	33.0	100.0	248.5	261.6	257.9	262.0	261.8	261.9	269.6
Latvia	3.7	100.0	220.6	189.1	205.7	175.9	269.5	250.5	257.9
Lithuania	0.1	100.0	305.7	319.8	306.1	300.5	284.3	250.9	248.3
Macedonia	0.3	100.0	274.7	616.9	621.4	596.5	535.7	643.9	622.7
Moldova									
Montenegro		100.0	128.5	226.6	268.2	266.7	275.9	339.0	354.4
Poland	30.7	100.0	110.6	115.3	115.2	114.7	114.7	116.2	115.8
Romania	0.9	100.0	3,570.8	6,869.1	6,530.8	6,904.9	7,137.2	7,214.9	7,564.0
Russia	0.1	100.0	514.4	2,095.2	2,515.2	2,805.7	2,933.4	3,706.7	3,882.8
Serbia		100.0	1,606.4	4,474.3	4,869.9	4,930.0	5,408.1	6,139.7	6,748.3
Slovakia	23.6	100.0	184.5	254.8	252.3	251.0	251.4	252.1	252.6
Slovenia	5.2	100.0	140.2	172.6	172.3	172.8	173.3	174.6	171.1
Ukraine		100.0	380.2	745.7	913.5	936.5	1,057.8	1,152.4	1,318.5

Source:National statistical offices/OECD/Eurostat/Euromonitor International

Table 7.11

Leisure and Recreation Price Indices 1990-2009

1995 = 100

	1990	1995	2000	2004	2005	2006	2007	2008	2009
Western Europe									
Austria	87.7	100.0	97.9	100.1	100.6	97.9	95.7	95.9	93.0
Belgium	98.0	100.0	105.7	111.3	111.4	111.7	112.0	113.3	116.2
Cyprus									
Denmark	97.2	100.0	103.4	109.1	107.4	108.9	109.7	110.8	112.0
Finland	88.1	100.0	104.9	111.3	110.4	109.1	107.6	107.0	111.3
France	94.6	100.0	94.2	90.5	88.7	87.3	85.1	83.6	82.9
Germany	92.4	100.0	98.3	96.4	95.4	94.5	94.1	93.1	90.9
Gibraltar									
Greece	64.0	100.0	122.6	137.1	139.4	142.8	145.6	148.1	149.4
Iceland									
Ireland	82.4	100.0	96.5	105.4	104.5	104.9	104.0	104.2	103.8
Italy	79.5	100.0	106.7	115.0	115.6	116.1	117.2	118.1	119.0
Liechtenstein									
Luxembourg									
Malta									
Monaco									
Netherlands	95.2	100.0	104.7	108.0	106.8	105.4	102.8	102.5	106.6
Norway	90.0	100.0	102.0	101.0	101.0	101.0	101.0	101.0	104.0
Portugal	84.5	100.0	103.8	122.3	123.3	127.6	130.7	133.2	132.0
Spain	89.0	100.0	103.4	112.2	112.7	113.6	113.6	113.9	113.5
Sweden	94.5	100.0	94.6	90.9	88.7	87.5	86.2	84.4	84.7
Switzerland	92.5	100.0	98.1	97.4	97.1	97.2	97.0	98.3	97.5
Turkey	6.0	100.0	948.3	2,206.7	2,556.8	2,886.3	2,969.3	3,294.6	3,790.3
United Kingdom	88.0	100.0	96.9	90.2	88.1	87.0	85.1	82.4	83.2
Eastern Europe									
Albania									
Belarus		100.0	3,891.9	38,580.9	41,148.7	43,980.0	49,776.1	53,093.6	60,018.0
Bosnia-Herzegovina		100.0	97.2	102.4	102.1	103.8	102.0	104.2	110.4
Bulgaria	2.2	100.0	4,003.9	4,599.2	4,544.3	4,808.8	4,912.7	5,023.3	5,098.6
Croatia		100.0	110.3	129.8	133.4	136.8	140.1	143.0	145.8
Czech Republic	38.7	100.0	166.5	178.6	181.3	184.1	186.2	188.6	189.6
Estonia		100.0	159.4	170.7	171.0	176.1	177.7	179.7	177.6
Georgia									
Hungary	33.0	100.0	200.9	237.2	238.6	244.3	249.2	253.0	261.3
Latvia	4.1	100.0	140.4	160.3	168.1	178.0	192.2	203.0	217.3
Lithuania	0.5	100.0	122.5	113.5	113.6	115.9	117.9	120.9	122.5
Macedonia	0.3	100.0	132.4	141.5	135.2	135.4	132.9	148.0	146.0
Moldova									
Montenegro		100.0	127.2	276.2	276.6	278.6	283.0	293.1	306.4
Poland	16.3	100.0	297.6	321.7	327.1	326.5	327.7	331.8	338.4
Romania	0.9	100.0	1,157.8	1,980.3	2,059.4	2,177.3	2,295.4	2,389.7	2,514.1
Russia	0.6	100.0	289.5	1,336.3	1,438.3	1,530.0	1,563.0	1,592.0	1,942.2
Serbia		100.0	829.7	2,207.0	2,553.6	2,697.1	2,863.5	3,477.5	3,821.0
Slovakia	58.1	100.0	153.2	170.2	169.5	172.9	175.5	174.3	173.8
Slovenia	9.5	100.0	144.5	181.1	184.0	186.4	191.1	197.1	196.3
Ukraine		100.0	339.8	696.1	859.3	901.3	997.2	1,088.4	1,245.7

Source:National statistical offices/OECD/Eurostat/Euromonitor International

Consumer Prices Statistics

Table 7.12

Education Price Indices 1990-2009

1995 = 100

	1990	1995	2000	2004	2005	2006	2007	2008	2009
Western Europe									
Austria	64.9	100.0	119.1	164.1	166.6	179.6	188.8	189.8	190.8
Belgium	96.7	100.0	110.4	118.8	121.3	124.5	127.3	129.7	131.5
Cyprus									
Denmark	89.0	100.0	113.4	128.5	134.6	140.6	147.1	153.0	155.6
Finland	87.4	100.0	113.6	135.8	141.3	143.5	149.0	154.0	153.3
France	83.9	100.0	105.1	118.1	123.8	130.6	136.0	144.4	145.2
Germany	63.2	100.0	119.2	131.9	133.5	135.2	157.3	168.3	176.4
Gibraltar									
Greece	36.1	100.0	136.5	160.1	166.9	174.4	180.5	186.6	188.9
Iceland									
Ireland	83.1	100.0	117.4	153.7	164.7	169.6	178.2	111.9	119.1
Italy	76.3	100.0	112.5	127.7	132.1	135.9	139.0	142.3	146.2
Liechtenstein									
Luxembourg									
Malta									
Monaco									
Netherlands	82.5	100.0	123.0	141.6	144.4	149.6	151.3	154.3	156.1
Norway	85.0	100.0	121.0	154.0	163.0	161.0	162.0	166.0	168.0
Portugal	79.0	100.0	119.2	167.0	177.2	194.2	207.4	219.6	219.5
Spain	102.1	100.0	127.0	149.3	155.3	161.3	167.8	174.7	180.8
Sweden	100.7	100.0	105.7	99.3	102.5	105.5	110.5	113.5	115.8
Switzerland	77.6	100.0	113.1	122.3	123.0	124.7	126.9	128.9	131.0
Turkey	4.3	100.0	2,217.3	7,648.4	8,641.3	9,295.4	10,140.3	10,563.2	11,164.3
United Kingdom	68.5	100.0	129.3	162.1	170.0	179.5	192.8	205.6	211.1
Eastern Europe									
Albania									
Belarus		100.0	9,588.5	94,478.5	106,737.9	114,082.1	124,485.3	133,390.0	150,448.4
Bosnia-Herzegovina		100.0	98.5	104.5	105.5	107.1	109.6	108.3	116.2
Bulgaria	1.7	100.0	6,332.9	9,396.1	9,642.0	10,203.1	10,600.2	10,999.2	11,191.7
Croatia		100.0	133.5	136.8	142.2	142.1	142.1	143.5	145.7
Czech Republic	38.7	100.0	169.0	193.1	199.0	207.4	213.5	219.8	221.8
Estonia		100.0	244.7	305.8	329.1	362.9	385.2	409.1	409.1
Georgia									
Hungary	28.7	100.0	229.5	333.8	356.2	397.8	426.9	455.2	476.3
Latvia	4.3	100.0	150.9	190.6	205.6	222.6	225.4	268.5	334.4
Lithuania	0.3	100.0	198.0	205.0	205.3	206.4	220.7	245.7	271.9
Macedonia	0.5	100.0	129.1	151.4	153.4	166.1	189.8	186.4	190.2
Moldova									
Montenegro		100.0	87.2	134.3	133.7	133.1	132.0	132.7	136.8
Poland	22.7	100.0	183.7	215.5	222.0	225.3	229.1	238.3	245.5
Romania	1.7	100.0	3,796.3	8,213.7	8,453.8	8,938.0	9,443.0	9,810.8	10,321.7
Russia	0.1	100.0	713.1	3,272.4	3,730.9	4,598.5	5,266.4	6,983.7	6,894.7
Serbia		100.0	928.2	2,994.6	3,772.3	4,071.4	4,361.5	4,486.0	4,942.0
Slovakia	44.5	100.0	164.0	226.0	300.7	320.6	330.6	347.8	366.8
Slovenia	13.1	100.0	155.8	206.2	222.0	229.1	233.0	248.3	250.2
Ukraine		100.0	443.6	971.9	1,223.4	1,216.3	1,373.4	1,495.0	1,705.9

Source:National statistical offices/OECD/Eurostat/Euromonitor International

Consumer Prices Statistics

Table 7.13

Hotel and Catering Price Indices 1990-2009

1995 = 100

	1990	1995	2000	2004	2005	2006	2007	2008	2009
Western Europe									
Austria	83.0	100.0	109.8	121.9	124.7	129.8	133.6	135.7	135.8
Belgium	97.3	100.0	109.7	124.6	128.1	131.6	135.0	140.5	140.3
Cyprus									
Denmark	91.3	100.0	114.2	126.3	129.8	132.7	136.1	142.8	144.9
Finland	86.5	100.0	113.1	123.0	125.5	128.1	131.2	138.6	136.6
France	84.0	100.0	109.4	122.6	125.5	128.4	132.0	135.8	136.0
Germany	83.0	100.0	106.8	114.2	115.0	116.4	119.7	122.5	122.8
Gibraltar									
Greece	46.4	100.0	142.8	174.6	180.3	188.0	193.9	199.7	202.0
Iceland									
Ireland	76.0	100.0	111.8	138.8	143.2	147.7	153.1	157.9	157.8
Italy	73.9	100.0	117.2	136.1	139.5	142.9	146.7	150.4	152.0
Liechtenstein									
Luxembourg									
Malta									
Monaco									
Netherlands	87.0	100.0	114.0	134.9	137.3	140.2	145.0	150.6	149.4
Norway	86.0	100.0	117.0	136.0	139.0	144.0	150.0	159.0	165.0
Portugal	76.9	100.0	116.4	152.8	153.6	162.4	168.2	172.9	171.9
Spain	92.8	100.0	123.5	149.0	155.3	162.1	169.4	177.2	180.6
Sweden	89.0	100.0	109.9	123.2	126.0	129.2	133.4	139.6	143.2
Switzerland	75.8	100.0	106.0	114.1	115.3	116.6	118.1	121.0	122.8
Turkey	5.3	100.0	1,548.3	4,704.6	5,359.6	6,151.8	6,617.7	7,443.4	7,938.4
United Kingdom	76.9	100.0	120.6	136.4	141.5	146.8	152.1	158.2	161.7
Eastern Europe									
Albania									
Belarus		100.0	2,778.1	8,652.6	10,991.5	11,747.8	13,210.2	14,570.8	16,501.4
Bosnia-Herzegovina		100.0	99.4	106.4	106.7	110.6	112.2	112.9	122.1
Bulgaria	2.2	100.0	4,279.5	5,186.1	5,245.4	5,550.7	5,737.1	5,922.4	6,021.2
Croatia		100.0	115.3	134.4	137.4	141.6	145.1	148.1	151.1
Czech Republic	38.7	100.0	141.8	163.1	169.4	177.2	183.5	189.8	191.7
Estonia		100.0	167.2	199.6	209.0	220.4	228.7	237.5	236.0
Georgia									
Hungary	33.0	100.0	218.5	315.0	328.1	338.2	353.2	364.9	378.2
Latvia	3.9	100.0	127.2	144.5	167.3	189.2	157.7	179.4	191.0
Lithuania	0.5	100.0	135.1	150.7	153.6	159.6	174.5	199.9	214.0
Macedonia	0.2	100.0	127.7	129.3	131.0	134.8	143.6	150.0	150.2
Moldova									
Montenegro		100.0	84.4	137.0	139.5	143.0	147.6	161.1	166.5
Poland	19.6	100.0	185.6	204.7	210.6	214.5	221.4	235.1	246.9
Romania	0.9	100.0	1,961.1	4,822.6	5,292.0	5,595.1	6,015.2	6,373.5	6,722.4
Russia	0.6	100.0	206.6	299.7	384.2	464.9	530.5	632.5	668.8
Serbia		100.0	761.7	2,088.7	2,489.7	3,031.1	3,231.2	3,202.8	3,523.0
Slovakia	44.9	100.0	156.5	206.3	215.0	219.3	225.8	232.0	243.7
Slovenia	7.0	100.0	148.1	191.8	199.5	207.5	221.4	241.8	248.7
Ukraine		100.0	355.6	697.9	861.6	890.7	992.2	1,081.5	1,236.8

Source:National statistical offices/OECD/Eurostat/Euromonitor International

Consumer Prices Statistics

Table 7.14

Miscellaneous Goods and Services Price Indices 1990-2009

1995 = 100

	1990	1995	2000	2004	2005	2006	2007	2008	2009
Western Europe									
Austria	92.9	100.0	112.4	112.5	117.6	121.1	130.3	132.3	134.9
Belgium	101.5	100.0	100.3	103.0	108.0	115.9	127.1	126.1	127.2
Cyprus									
Denmark	84.3	100.0	105.1	109.7	109.1	110.5	112.2	114.4	115.7
Finland	91.5	100.0	122.7	109.3	109.1	115.5	126.9	129.8	127.7
France	102.7	100.0	99.6	103.4	104.0	109.5	115.9	118.5	119.1
Germany	85.5	100.0	91.0	104.0	107.0	105.7	105.5	105.0	102.7
Gibraltar									
Greece	38.0	100.0	135.5	150.0	154.9	158.9	162.3	166.0	167.6
Iceland									
Ireland	83.5	100.0	111.2	134.7	141.9	149.8	154.7	154.0	160.9
Italy	77.3	100.0	112.0	123.1	127.1	134.7	140.4	142.9	146.5
Liechtenstein									
Luxembourg									
Malta									
Monaco									
Netherlands	81.7	100.0	119.6	133.3	140.3	143.1	145.6	145.6	149.0
Norway	97.0	100.0	118.0	114.0	112.0	109.0	117.0	125.0	132.0
Portugal	73.6	100.0	120.8	154.6	156.5	164.0	168.9	173.2	172.0
Spain	93.9	100.0	120.0	126.7	129.4	134.9	142.1	143.6	146.7
Sweden	85.3	100.0	109.1	111.5	113.7	118.8	120.7	124.9	122.7
Switzerland	105.7	100.0	108.2	110.1	106.7	111.9	117.3	118.2	118.9
Turkey	4.8	100.0	1,283.7	2,831.1	2,687.3	2,989.8	3,108.9	3,277.0	3,119.5
United Kingdom	82.0	100.0	114.4	120.1	124.6	129.2	133.5	130.0	132.2
Eastern Europe									
Albania									
Belarus		100.0	4,647.0	22,313.1	7,598.7	8,121.6	3,216.2	1,940.3	2,136.3
Bosnia-Herzegovina		100.0	98.9	104.5	107.8	109.5	105.5	108.3	116.2
Bulgaria	2.2	100.0	3,547.4	3,995.0	3,967.2	4,198.1	4,293.1	4,397.0	4,463.9
Croatia		100.0	142.3	149.6	152.6	154.8	157.1	159.1	161.9
Czech Republic	38.7	100.0	118.3	138.8	141.2	146.8	150.8	154.5	155.9
Estonia		100.0	160.7	178.4	183.3	191.1	195.9	201.2	199.4
Georgia									
Hungary	33.0	100.0	212.0	255.3	258.7	264.2	270.4	275.0	284.2
Latvia	1.0	100.0	123.5	132.4	154.1	167.2	179.6	195.6	220.0
Lithuania	0.5	100.0	158.4	155.6	150.5	157.7	169.7	187.9	206.7
Macedonia	0.3	100.0	121.9	138.7	141.2	149.4	155.6	163.5	164.3
Moldova									
Montenegro		100.0	84.5	137.1	139.5	143.0	147.6	161.1	166.6
Poland	16.5	100.0	180.8	184.1	187.9	190.8	194.8	194.8	204.2
Romania	0.9	100.0	1,161.9	2,299.2	2,376.0	2,512.1	2,642.2	2,744.8	2,886.9
Russia	0.4	100.0	345.6	449.3	466.6	473.5	483.9	490.8	600.4
Serbia		100.0	792.4	2,213.4	2,478.3	2,716.1	2,858.7	3,309.2	3,636.5
Slovakia	34.9	100.0	142.1	199.4	206.3	213.8	221.1	229.0	235.0
Slovenia	6.0	100.0	133.4	185.0	187.0	191.9	210.2	216.8	220.5
Ukraine		100.0	207.3	248.0	252.8	245.5	246.4	245.9	274.4

Source:National statistical offices/OECD/Eurostat/Euromonitor International

Economic Indicators

Economic Statistics

Table 8.1

Gross Domestic Product in National Currencies 1980-2009

Billion units of national currency

	1980	1985	1990	1995	1996	1997	1998	1999	2000	2001
Western Europe										
Austria	76.60	103.42	136.21	174.61	180.15	183.48	190.85	197.98	207.53	212.50
Belgium	90.70	125.27	167.80	207.65	211.40	221.20	229.69	238.57	252.22	259.43
Cyprus	1.35	2.62	4.52	7.09	7.45	7.81	8.45	9.06	9.88	10.63
Denmark	392.88	648.54	840.65	1,019.55	1,069.49	1,125.64	1,163.62	1,213.47	1,293.96	1,335.61
Finland	33.24	57.27	89.29	95.99	99.07	107.31	116.55	122.22	132.11	139.20
France	445.23	743.89	1,033.03	1,194.60	1,227.25	1,267.43	1,323.65	1,367.97	1,441.41	1,497.21
Germany	766.60	955.30	1,274.90	1,848.45	1,876.18	1,915.58	1,965.38	2,012.00	2,062.50	2,113.16
Gibraltar				0.37	0.39	0.36	0.38	0.41	0.43	0.45
Greece	6.84	18.65	43.82	89.56	98.40	108.89	118.40	126.16	136.28	146.43
Iceland	16.14	122.42	365.05	445.11	477.69	526.32	586.80	630.73	683.75	771.90
Ireland	13.10	25.00	36.56	53.11	58.71	67.93	78.54	90.38	104.83	116.93
Italy	203.38	429.65	701.35	947.34	1,003.78	1,048.77	1,091.36	1,127.09	1,191.06	1,248.65
Liechtenstein	0.90	1.30	1.97	2.87	3.09	3.34	3.60	4.00	4.19	4.21
Luxembourg	3.76	5.84	9.18	15.11	15.80	16.42	17.41	19.89	22.00	22.57
Malta	1.01	1.22	1.89	2.94	3.08	3.27	3.45	3.63	3.97	4.04
Monaco	0.89	1.48	2.06	2.38	2.45	2.53	2.64	2.73	2.87	2.99
Netherlands	163.09	200.83	243.65	305.26	319.76	342.24	362.46	386.19	417.96	447.73
Norway	314.70	552.43	736.30	943.44	1,032.99	1,119.18	1,140.36	1,240.43	1,481.24	1,536.89
Portugal	8.10	22.71	55.17	87.75	93.09	100.98	110.10	118.37	127.01	134.14
Spain	95.34	175.63	312.42	447.21	473.86	503.92	539.49	579.94	630.26	680.68
Sweden	558.58	914.77	1,446.64	1,809.58	1,853.92	1,932.99	2,025.02	2,138.42	2,265.45	2,348.42
Switzerland	184.08	244.42	330.93	373.60	376.67	383.99	395.26	402.91	422.06	430.32
Turkey	0.01	0.05	0.53	10.43	19.86	38.76	70.20	104.60	166.66	240.22
United Kingdom	233.18	361.76	570.28	733.27	781.73	830.09	879.10	928.73	976.53	1,021.83
Eastern Europe										
Albania	15.53	16.86	16.81	229.79	346.40	346.20	409.21	471.58	523.04	583.37
Belarus			0.00	121.40	191.84	366.83	702.16	3,026.06	9,133.80	17,173.20
Bosnia-Herzegovina			0.00	2.86	4.19	6.37	7.24	8.99	10.71	11.60
Bulgaria	0.03	0.03	0.05	0.88	1.76	17.43	22.42	23.79	26.75	29.71
Croatia			0.28	115.70	127.05	145.39	160.60	164.05	176.69	190.80
Czech Republic	443.86	512.78	617.56	1,466.52	1,683.29	1,811.09	1,996.48	2,080.80	2,189.17	2,352.21
Estonia			0.80	43.28	56.89	70.12	78.74	83.84	96.38	109.07
Georgia			0.00	3.69	3.87	4.55	5.02	5.67	6.02	6.65
Hungary	817.50	1,171.96	2,318.13	5,755.36	7,112.34	8,812.93	10,451.21	11,650.64	13,345.30	15,288.75
Latvia			0.06	2.62	3.13	3.63	3.97	4.27	4.75	5.22
Lithuania			0.13	25.96	32.74	40.00	44.70	43.67	45.74	48.64
Macedonia			0.44	169.52	176.44	186.02	194.98	209.01	236.39	233.84
Moldova			0.01	6.48	7.80	8.92	9.12	12.32	16.02	19.05
Montenegro			1.77	0.89	0.67	0.75	0.77	0.79	1.07	1.30
Poland	0.25	1.04	56.03	337.22	422.44	515.35	600.90	665.69	744.38	779.56
Romania	0.06	0.08	0.09	7.26	10.97	25.47	37.38	55.19	80.98	117.95
Russia			0.64	1,428.50	2,007.80	2,342.50	2,629.60	4,823.20	7,305.65	8,943.58
Serbia				51.36	92.24	120.88	162.54	205.62	384.23	762.18
Slovakia			9.23	19.31	21.51	23.85	26.15	28.09	31.15	33.86
Slovenia			0.82	10.29	11.87	13.51	14.97	16.81	18.48	20.65
Ukraine			0.00	54.52	81.52	93.37	102.59	130.44	170.07	204.19

Source: *Euromonitor International from International Monetary Fund (IMF), International Financial Statistics*

Economic Statistics

Gross Domestic Product in National Currencies 1980-2009 *(continued)*

Billion units of national currency

	2002	2003	2004	2005	2006	2007	2008	2009	Total US$ billion 2009	US$ per capita 2009
Western Europe										
Austria	218.85	223.30	232.78	243.58	256.95	272.01	283.09	274.32	381.20	45,472.0
Belgium	268.26	275.72	290.83	302.85	318.15	335.08	345.01	339.16	471.30	43,841.7
Cyprus	10.98	11.76	12.65	13.46	14.44	15.88	17.25	16.95	23.55	27,035.3
Denmark	1,372.74	1,400.69	1,466.18	1,545.26	1,631.66	1,691.47	1,737.45	1,662.37	310.09	56,263.5
Finland	143.54	145.42	152.15	157.31	165.64	179.70	184.65	171.32	238.06	44,705.0
France	1,548.64	1,594.80	1,660.18	1,726.05	1,806.42	1,895.23	1,948.50	1,907.14	2,650.17	42,437.3
Germany	2,143.18	2,163.80	2,210.90	2,242.20	2,326.50	2,432.40	2,481.20	2,397.10	3,331.01	40,620.9
Gibraltar	0.47	0.51	0.56	0.57	0.57	0.58	0.60	0.61	0.94	32,274.9
Greece	156.61	172.43	185.81	195.37	210.46	226.44	239.14	237.49	330.02	29,330.3
Iceland	816.56	841.48	928.66	1,026.72	1,168.58	1,308.52	1,477.65	1,500.16	12.13	37,600.9
Ireland	130.26	139.76	149.10	162.09	176.76	189.75	181.82	163.54	227.26	51,069.2
Italy	1,295.23	1,335.35	1,391.53	1,429.48	1,485.38	1,546.18	1,567.85	1,520.87	2,113.40	35,192.0
Liechtenstein	4.19	4.14	4.30	4.56	5.00	5.26	5.45	5.45	5.01	140,083.0
Luxembourg	23.99	25.83	27.46	30.28	34.15	37.47	39.35	37.65	52.31	107,597.4
Malta	4.28	4.39	4.49	4.79	5.11	5.46	5.70	5.71	7.94	19,420.2
Monaco	3.09	3.18	3.31	3.44	3.72	4.37	4.72	4.82	6.70	203,465.7
Netherlands	465.21	476.95	491.18	513.41	540.22	571.77	596.23	571.98	794.82	48,434.6
Norway	1,532.31	1,593.83	1,743.04	1,945.72	2,159.57	2,271.61	2,516.80	2,380.72	378.50	78,867.3
Portugal	140.14	143.01	148.83	153.73	160.27	168.74	171.92	167.63	232.94	21,831.1
Spain	729.21	782.93	841.04	908.79	984.28	1,053.54	1,088.12	1,053.91	1,464.52	32,172.6
Sweden	2,443.63	2,544.87	2,660.96	2,769.38	2,944.48	3,126.02	3,213.66	3,108.00	406.09	44,133.1
Switzerland	434.26	437.73	451.38	463.80	490.54	521.10	544.20	535.28	492.66	65,167.8
Turkey	350.48	454.78	559.03	648.93	758.39	843.18	950.53	953.97	613.38	8,576.6
United Kingdom	1,075.56	1,139.75	1,202.96	1,254.06	1,328.36	1,404.85	1,445.58	1,392.71	2,171.97	35,252.3
Eastern Europe										
Albania	622.71	694.10	750.79	814.80	882.21	966.65	1,087.87	1,124.88	11.84	3,753.6
Belarus	26,138.30	36,564.80	49,991.80	65,067.10	79,267.00	97,165.30	129,791.00	136,790.00	49.04	5,070.1
Bosnia-Herzegovina	12.83	14.51	16.68	18.18	21.37	24.71	27.93	27.26	19.36	5,036.4
Bulgaria	32.40	34.63	38.82	42.80	49.36	56.52	66.73	66.26	47.10	6,264.1
Croatia	208.22	227.01	245.55	264.37	286.34	314.22	342.16	333.06	63.03	14,233.4
Czech Republic	2,464.43	2,577.11	2,814.76	2,983.86	3,222.37	3,535.46	3,688.99	3,628.08	190.30	18,179.9
Estonia	121.67	136.42	151.54	174.96	207.00	244.50	251.49	214.83	19.08	14,342.2
Georgia	7.46	8.56	9.82	11.62	13.79	16.99	19.07	17.95	10.74	2,450.1
Hungary	17,219.44	18,814.99	20,803.80	21,988.59	23,755.49	25,408.08	26,543.25	26,094.82	128.96	12,871.0
Latvia	5.76	6.39	7.43	9.06	11.17	14.78	16.19	13.08	25.93	11,504.6
Lithuania	52.07	56.96	62.70	72.06	82.79	98.67	111.19	92.02	37.04	11,064.4
Macedonia	243.97	251.49	265.26	286.62	310.92	354.32	398.49	406.65	9.22	4,518.1
Moldova	22.56	27.62	32.03	37.65	44.75	53.43	62.92	60.04	5.40	1,499.8
Montenegro	1.36	1.51	1.67	1.81	2.15	2.68	3.09	2.94	4.09	6,507.5
Poland	808.58	843.16	924.54	983.30	1,060.03	1,176.74	1,275.43	1,344.04	430.64	11,292.2
Romania	152.02	197.43	247.37	288.95	344.65	416.01	514.65	491.27	161.11	7,516.1
Russia	10,819.21	13,208.23	17,027.19	21,609.77	26,917.20	33,247.51	41,428.56	39,100.65	1,231.07	8,675.4
Serbia	972.90	1,133.03	1,384.25	1,687.83	1,980.24	2,362.85	2,750.90	2,898.96	42.90	5,822.6
Slovakia	36.78	40.58	45.13	49.28	55.05	61.55	67.22	63.33	88.01	16,311.5
Slovenia	23.13	25.11	27.07	28.75	31.05	34.57	37.30	35.38	49.17	24,308.1
Ukraine	225.81	267.34	345.11	441.45	544.15	720.73	949.86	902.66	115.86	2,520.7

Source: *Euromonitor International from International Monetary Fund (IMF), International Financial Statistics*

Economic Statistics

Table 8.2

Gross Domestic Product in US$ 1980-2009

US$ million

	1980	1985	1990	1995	1996	1997	1998	1999	2000	2001
Western Europe										
Austria	106,646.5	78,918.0	173,457.6	228,395.2	228,745.0	208,074.0	213,960.9	210,948.5	191,241.8	190,192.8
Belgium	126,282.8	95,589.1	213,685.8	271,609.6	268,418.8	250,851.9	257,503.2	254,198.2	232,421.0	232,201.4
Cyprus	1,872.8	1,998.8	5,757.6	9,270.2	9,458.7	8,857.1	9,467.9	9,656.3	9,107.5	9,512.3
Denmark	69,708.9	61,203.8	135,839.0	181,984.6	184,436.8	170,436.5	173,652.5	173,943.7	159,985.0	160,514.5
Finland	46,281.0	43,702.8	113,705.8	125,550.6	125,787.8	121,696.1	130,660.8	130,229.1	121,741.9	124,586.5
France	619,910.8	567,654.0	1,315,485.0	1,562,549.1	1,558,304.1	1,437,310.9	1,483,934.1	1,457,584.7	1,328,283.4	1,340,047.3
Germany	1,067,360.2	728,978.0	1,623,495.9	2,417,791.1	2,382,279.6	2,172,344.3	2,203,367.9	2,143,810.9	1,900,633.5	1,891,343.4
Gibraltar				590.4	606.9	592.6	634.8	655.4	648.7	645.3
Greece	9,524.9	14,232.4	55,804.2	117,138.8	124,939.6	123,481.1	132,734.8	134,419.7	125,584.5	131,057.2
Iceland	3,363.5	2,949.4	6,263.2	6,880.4	7,183.3	7,423.0	8,269.6	8,719.6	8,697.3	7,923.0
Ireland	18,234.0	19,074.9	46,556.6	69,471.2	74,551.8	77,039.5	88,045.4	96,298.9	96,603.0	104,656.5
Italy	283,176.3	327,860.0	893,122.7	1,239,128.9	1,274,547.1	1,189,343.7	1,223,515.0	1,200,929.4	1,097,582.1	1,117,578.6
Liechtenstein	534.7	529.1	1,421.5	2,428.5	2,504.0	2,298.4	2,479.7	2,664.1	2,483.9	2,491.8
Luxembourg	5,228.2	4,458.0	11,689.5	19,764.4	20,057.7	18,621.7	19,523.3	21,189.6	20,274.0	20,202.9
Malta	1,400.6	932.2	2,401.3	3,845.4	3,914.7	3,704.6	3,864.8	3,869.1	3,661.5	3,613.2
Monaco	1,236.1	1,131.9	2,623.0	3,115.6	3,107.2	2,865.9	2,958.9	2,906.4	2,648.5	2,672.0
Netherlands	227,076.5	153,248.7	310,273.8	399,284.4	406,008.9	388,110.4	406,354.8	411,493.4	385,158.2	400,733.1
Norway	63,714.1	64,257.0	117,623.9	148,920.8	160,158.2	158,223.8	151,139.1	159,046.4	168,287.5	170,931.6
Portugal	11,272.1	17,332.4	70,250.6	114,771.3	118,197.0	114,516.6	123,436.6	126,124.7	117,039.9	120,056.8
Spain	132,738.5	134,017.6	397,847.9	584,948.6	601,677.4	571,466.6	604,820.2	617,935.4	580,799.5	609,227.8
Sweden	132,065.3	106,319.8	244,414.7	253,681.0	276,457.8	253,178.2	254,724.2	258,812.6	247,259.1	227,358.6
Switzerland	109,852.0	99,474.1	238,219.6	315,947.9	304,749.1	264,582.2	272,630.6	268,218.7	249,912.5	254,987.5
Turkey	92,476.6	90,379.0	202,545.9	227,606.6	243,933.0	255,243.2	269,262.5	249,761.8	266,559.6	196,007.4
United Kingdom	541,916.6	464,241.1	1,012,617.7	1,157,176.9	1,219,621.3	1,358,947.4	1,455,891.1	1,502,660.8	1,477,511.6	1,470,986.3
Eastern Europe										
Albania	2,218.9	2,409.0	2,170.6	2,479.0	3,314.9	2,324.5	2,716.6	3,424.9	3,639.6	4,065.7
Belarus			18,833.0	13,845.2	14,500.4	14,097.7	15,222.1	12,138.5	10,417.8	12,354.8
Bosnia-Herzegovina			7,754.8	2,042.9	2,794.7	3,671.7	4,116.7	4,897.0	5,046.5	5,306.9
Bulgaria	18,620.1	16,418.1	20,726.0	13,105.7	9,900.4	10,364.9	12,736.7	12,955.1	12,599.4	13,598.7
Croatia			24,813.7	22,119.0	23,380.3	23,600.7	25,239.0	23,068.1	21,345.3	22,873.0
Czech Republic			34,398.1	55,255.6	62,011.2	57,135.2	61,846.6	60,192.2	56,716.5	61,842.9
Estonia			5,634.6	4,379.6	4,725.9	5,051.4	5,594.3	5,712.2	5,679.9	6,240.4
Georgia			8,427.0	2,701.3	3,063.4	3,510.4	3,613.5	2,800.0	3,044.0	3,206.9
Hungary	25,128.9	23,383.3	36,675.8	45,793.4	46,593.4	47,181.2	48,745.9	49,128.6	47,293.7	53,365.7
Latvia			8,855.9	4,956.7	5,681.8	6,252.0	6,732.8	7,288.5	7,833.0	8,313.2
Lithuania			9,767.3	6,489.1	8,184.9	9,999.4	11,174.7	10,916.7	11,434.2	12,159.2
Macedonia			3,853.9	4,475.0	4,413.2	3,720.1	3,580.1	3,673.2	3,586.9	3,437.0
Moldova			3,968.6	1,765.6	1,693.5	1,928.6	1,698.5	1,171.7	1,288.3	1,480.9
Montenegro			2,258.8	1,164.4	853.7	850.9	866.3	836.7	982.1	1,159.2
Poland	56,788.5	70,985.9	58,975.9	139,061.8	156,684.1	157,153.8	172,901.5	167,801.7	171,275.9	190,420.9
Romania	34,599.3	48,140.8	38,510.5	35,726.4	35,563.0	35,533.3	42,115.3	35,995.6	37,305.1	40,585.9
Russia			614,173.3	399,159.4	392,084.9	404,938.4	270,950.9	195,906.6	259,717.9	306,617.6
Serbia				17,499.7	18,662.4	18,150.3	16,966.7	10,856.6	8,728.4	11,390.5
Slovakia			11,751.1	25,256.1	27,318.4	27,049.3	29,321.1	29,927.6	28,707.0	30,301.5
Slovenia			1,045.6	13,465.0	15,067.1	15,319.1	16,781.7	17,907.9	17,030.3	18,486.2
Ukraine			108,108.1	48,608.4	44,558.8	50,151.5	41,882.6	31,580.7	31,261.5	38,008.9

Source: Euromonitor International from International Monetary Fund (IMF), International Financial Statistics

Economic Statistics

Gross Domestic Product in US$ 1980-2009 *(continued)*

US$ million

	2002	2003	2004	2005	2006	2007	2008	2009	US$ per capita 2009
Western Europe									
Austria	206,143.9	252,090.0	289,126.5	302,735.7	322,356.5	372,293.1	414,288.2	381,196.0	45,472.0
Belgium	252,684.1	311,260.8	361,220.4	376,387.6	399,136.5	458,620.7	504,908.8	471,298.5	43,841.7
Cyprus	10,342.3	13,277.4	15,716.4	16,731.4	18,109.6	21,733.3	25,241.7	23,548.7	27,035.3
Denmark	174,110.6	212,967.9	244,871.3	257,710.7	274,550.9	310,774.3	340,663.7	310,093.3	56,263.5
Finland	135,208.7	164,162.8	188,975.4	195,506.7	207,806.8	245,953.4	270,229.0	238,059.5	44,705.0
France	1,458,739.9	1,800,402.0	2,062,020.0	2,145,199.2	2,266,240.4	2,593,946.3	2,851,582.3	2,650,167.8	42,437.3
Germany	2,018,771.5	2,442,753.0	2,746,047.8	2,786,684.8	2,918,702.4	3,329,162.3	3,631,172.1	3,331,012.6	40,620.9
Gibraltar	710.7	830.2	1,030.3	1,029.4	1,051.2	1,164.6	1,112.1	943.9	32,274.9
Greece	147,523.6	194,660.7	230,788.5	242,807.7	264,030.4	309,918.1	349,977.4	330,021.2	29,330.3
Iceland	8,908.4	10,969.8	13,230.3	16,301.9	16,651.2	20,428.1	16,801.4	12,133.5	37,600.9
Ireland	122,696.7	157,781.2	185,187.1	201,452.4	221,752.1	259,707.5	266,083.5	227,259.5	51,069.2
Italy	1,220,039.4	1,507,505.1	1,728,349.7	1,776,606.9	1,863,474.9	2,116,213.4	2,294,509.6	2,113,402.5	35,192.0
Liechtenstein	2,688.6	3,070.8	3,454.4	3,658.4	3,988.8	4,381.2	5,028.2	5,013.3	140,083.0
Luxembourg	22,599.6	29,164.8	34,101.6	37,635.9	42,843.3	51,278.5	57,585.4	52,311.8	107,597.4
Malta	4,027.4	4,954.1	5,578.8	5,952.1	6,411.9	7,471.4	8,337.2	7,937.2	19,420.2
Monaco	2,908.5	3,589.9	4,111.6	4,277.5	4,663.7	5,974.4	6,912.9	6,700.3	203,465.7
Netherlands	438,209.0	538,431.8	610,075.0	638,080.2	677,726.1	782,570.8	872,561.3	794,822.6	48,434.6
Norway	191,924.4	225,116.1	258,563.6	302,008.1	336,722.1	387,583.4	446,319.6	378,503.8	78,867.3
Portugal	132,007.0	161,452.0	184,851.0	191,059.2	201,070.3	230,945.9	251,601.2	232,942.8	21,831.1
Spain	686,876.6	883,862.7	1,044,616.0	1,129,478.6	1,234,830.0	1,441,948.6	1,592,441.4	1,464,520.0	32,172.6
Sweden	250,960.0	314,713.2	362,089.8	370,579.7	399,075.7	462,512.9	487,685.3	406,089.9	44,133.1
Switzerland	278,619.5	325,051.7	362,991.9	372,476.7	391,232.6	434,118.2	502,487.2	492,659.3	65,167.8
Turkey	232,530.5	303,008.2	392,156.2	482,239.0	527,882.2	645,763.7	728,466.9	613,376.3	8,576.6
United Kingdom	1,612,000.0	1,860,893.3	2,202,490.0	2,280,112.4	2,444,150.1	2,810,973.7	2,656,827.8	2,171,971.6	35,252.3
Eastern Europe									
Albania	4,443.0	5,695.7	7,304.8	8,158.5	8,992.6	10,689.7	12,967.1	11,843.6	3,753.6
Belarus	14,594.9	17,825.4	23,141.6	30,210.1	36,961.9	45,275.7	60,752.2	49,037.6	5,070.1
Bosnia-Herzegovina	6,173.2	8,370.2	10,589.5	11,558.1	13,704.4	17,290.8	20,921.0	19,362.4	5,036.4
Bulgaria	15,600.4	19,985.6	24,647.5	27,187.7	31,656.4	39,550.9	49,900.4	47,100.6	6,264.1
Croatia	26,452.1	33,857.2	40,692.1	44,437.2	49,049.4	58,574.1	69,332.5	63,033.1	14,233.4
Czech Republic	75,276.2	91,357.7	109,524.9	124,548.6	142,610.6	174,214.9	216,088.7	190,298.6	18,179.9
Estonia	7,324.5	9,845.4	12,031.3	13,903.3	16,605.5	21,384.2	23,516.2	19,083.7	14,342.2
Georgia	3,396.0	3,991.4	5,125.8	6,410.9	7,745.3	10,172.9	12,791.6	10,744.5	2,450.1
Hungary	66,771.3	83,880.7	102,610.2	110,172.9	112,911.7	138,368.8	154,219.6	128,964.3	12,871.0
Latvia	9,314.6	11,186.3	13,761.6	16,041.8	19,934.9	28,766.3	33,668.1	25,925.3	11,504.6
Lithuania	14,161.2	18,608.9	22,548.4	25,976.8	30,082.1	39,096.6	47,172.8	37,043.0	11,064.4
Macedonia	3,791.3	4,629.5	5,368.5	5,815.7	6,371.0	7,921.4	9,517.9	9,221.0	4,518.1
Moldova	1,662.1	1,980.6	2,597.9	2,988.3	3,408.3	4,401.2	6,054.8	5,404.6	1,499.8
Montenegro	1,281.4	1,704.8	2,074.0	2,255.7	2,696.0	3,668.0	4,516.3	4,086.8	6,507.5
Poland	198,179.3	216,801.2	252,768.9	303,912.2	341,597.8	425,129.4	529,230.8	430,637.2	11,292.2
Romania	45,988.5	59,466.0	75,794.7	99,172.6	122,695.9	170,617.0	204,320.3	161,109.0	7,516.1
Russia	345,127.1	430,347.4	590,939.9	764,016.0	989,932.1	1,299,703.6	1,666,952.5	1,231,072.5	8,675.4
Serbia	15,107.6	19,675.6	23,710.5	25,299.6	29,491.6	40,422.7	49,367.0	42,896.4	5,822.6
Slovakia	34,645.3	45,814.4	56,051.6	61,246.9	69,057.1	84,237.8	98,376.3	88,005.8	16,311.5
Slovenia	21,785.9	28,351.8	33,626.5	35,731.0	38,954.2	47,312.7	54,594.5	49,170.2	24,308.1
Ukraine	42,392.7	50,133.0	64,880.7	86,141.7	107,753.1	142,719.0	180,335.0	115,856.9	2,520.7

Source:Euromonitor International from International Monetary Fund (IMF), International Financial Statistics

Economic Statistics

Table 8.3

Gross Domestic Product by Origin 2009

US$ million

	Agriculture, Forestry & Fishing	Mining & Quarrying	Manufacturing	Electricity, Gas & Water	Construction	Hotels and Restaurants
Western Europe						
Austria	6,152.4	1,591.7	71,272.3	10,966.6	24,259.7	15,190.9
Belgium	2,713.7	414.0	65,095.3	8,164.5	22,632.0	6,842.6
Cyprus						
Denmark	2,697.4	12,463.1	37,397.9	3,907.2	15,603.6	3,958.8
Finland	6,314.6	742.3	45,461.4	5,288.4	14,553.1	3,010.0
France	45,657.0	3,950.5	275,115.5	40,068.9	166,224.7	54,109.3
Germany	27,361.5	8,186.4	698,847.6	65,106.5	129,637.3	51,318.6
Gibraltar						
Greece	9,082.4	1,275.4	30,911.6	8,113.9	16,991.9	19,215.5
Iceland						
Ireland	2,626.6	1,179.6	44,116.8	3,199.5	16,540.0	5,041.0
Italy	37,195.5	6,742.8	347,478.0	43,137.2	117,712.1	73,155.5
Liechtenstein						
Luxembourg						
Malta						
Monaco						
Netherlands	11,921.7	31,483.0	94,258.7	14,998.7	41,571.8	11,736.8
Norway	3,184.5	103,932.9	30,376.2	9,665.3	16,217.8	4,655.0
Portugal	4,244.7	967.7	25,455.3	5,068.4	12,027.2	9,463.5
Spain	33,725.4	3,197.1	200,186.6	31,031.4	158,316.5	100,888.7
Sweden	6,251.8	2,138.1	72,067.8	6,550.9	17,875.7	4,682.8
Switzerland	5,464.9	742.1	100,163.9	6,550.4	25,359.5	9,988.1
Turkey	51,793.4	10,270.8	109,396.8	15,585.0	32,339.2	15,689.2
United Kingdom	15,732.8	39,793.3	190,361.7	53,223.1	111,808.8	51,528.4
Eastern Europe						
Albania						
Belarus	3,556.5		12,679.4		4,709.8	
Bosnia-Herzegovina	1,397.3	399.6	2,197.9	499.0	935.1	536.9
Bulgaria	2,225.4	1,723.7	7,460.2	1,079.4	2,694.4	1,116.7
Croatia	2,868.6	592.9	7,986.1	1,947.1	4,518.6	2,384.5
Czech Republic	4,117.1	2,663.8	41,406.5	8,748.0	11,474.3	3,029.6
Estonia	436.1	172.1	2,713.2	509.7	1,406.6	235.5
Georgia	777.3	71.2	1,093.4	215.7	480.3	201.4
Hungary	3,942.0	175.9	24,287.1	2,973.8	4,940.3	1,766.0
Latvia	664.5	99.3	2,312.9	672.8	2,255.2	377.9
Lithuania	1,395.7	134.7	5,183.0	944.0	3,493.5	434.3
Macedonia	765.2	88.8	1,903.7	200.1	598.1	168.2
Moldova						
Montenegro	279.6	31.7	244.4	97.2	143.8	167.3
Poland	15,631.5	5,527.4	78,936.4	8,993.3	28,777.3	4,101.0
Romania	7,590.3	971.7	30,586.7	2,261.5	13,890.6	3,432.6
Russia	49,270.6	91,024.4	179,186.2	30,121.5	70,980.6	10,666.2
Serbia	3,057.2	545.5	6,844.1	1,593.2	1,824.1	546.7
Slovakia	2,351.5	472.4	19,006.3	4,287.3	6,945.6	1,171.9
Slovenia	969.7	171.5	9,330.2	1,291.4	3,811.2	1,011.5
Ukraine	6,625.9	6,103.8	20,429.2	3,300.3	3,982.4	725.6

Source:*Euromonitor International from national statistics*

Economic Statistics

Gross Domestic Product by Origin 2009 *(continued)*

US$ million

	Wholesale & Retail Trade, Repair of Motor vehicles/goods	Transport, Storage & Communications	Financial Inter-mediation, Real Estate, Renting and Business	Public Admin and Defence, Compulsory Social Security	Education, Health, Social Work and Other Community Activities	Activities of Households	GDP by origin
Western Europe							
Austria	41,381.5	20,749.7	84,763.4	18,743.9	50,001.3	109.2	345,182.4
Belgium	53,986.2	34,899.3	124,607.2	30,346.8	70,874.0	629.5	421,205.3
Cyprus							
Denmark	31,725.1	21,204.1	64,624.6	15,554.6	54,859.9	394.3	264,390.8
Finland	20,819.6	20,426.8	45,677.0	9,878.7	35,854.6	157.1	208,183.5
France	233,538.5	152,443.1	809,470.7	175,232.4	412,149.2	13,594.5	2,381,554.2
Germany	309,151.9	166,318.8	880,626.9	166,317.3	476,135.3	9,587.5	2,988,595.5
Gibraltar							
Greece	49,991.7	29,109.1	53,550.6	24,335.8	45,661.6	2,564.7	290,804.2
Iceland							
Ireland	17,626.0	11,481.4	59,688.7	9,918.7	31,840.4	282.5	203,541.0
Italy	199,738.9	139,496.4	535,792.5	122,468.1	255,877.2	20,432.2	1,899,226.5
Liechtenstein							
Luxembourg							
Malta							
Monaco							
Netherlands	88,435.6	45,349.0	201,108.9	47,646.1	114,264.9	2,832.2	705,607.6
Norway	26,655.4	20,583.3	60,285.8	14,747.0	50,713.7	259.7	341,276.4
Portugal	25,004.7	13,898.2	44,864.6	20,609.4	36,189.5	1,596.0	199,389.2
Spain	139,353.9	90,661.5	330,650.9	87,887.8	206,192.3	10,877.2	1,392,969.3
Sweden	39,282.9	24,794.0	91,071.8	19,530.4	71,361.3	144.7	355,752.2
Switzerland	58,269.9	28,297.7	133,799.1	51,852.3	42,150.2	1,684.3	464,322.3
Turkey	84,536.1	99,181.1	54,577.4	26,171.1	43,509.4	1,269.6	544,319.2
United Kingdom	214,731.1	125,211.5	644,453.0	88,326.5	338,327.5	8,892.9	1,882,390.5
Eastern Europe							
Albania							
Belarus	5,231.8	3,777.6	4,075.8	2,378.9	4,751.6		41,161.5
Bosnia-Herzegovina	2,620.9	1,285.0	2,174.7	1,532.2	2,006.0		15,584.8
Bulgaria	4,237.4	4,253.2	8,038.8	2,468.6	2,843.2		38,141.1
Croatia	8,236.1	6,502.8	10,200.9	2,474.3	6,164.8	52.4	53,929.1
Czech Republic	22,195.8	18,264.4	31,162.9	9,224.2	19,027.6	20.5	171,334.7
Estonia	2,258.2	1,595.4	3,959.2	1,095.9	2,004.1	1.7	16,387.7
Georgia	1,542.2	997.0	844.7	1,849.4	1,225.8	7.7	9,306.0
Hungary	13,326.9	9,270.1	25,407.4	8,991.7	14,789.4		109,870.8
Latvia	3,848.6	2,281.1	5,800.3	1,941.0	3,036.0		23,289.5
Lithuania	5,784.3	4,287.4	5,744.3	2,160.8	3,601.3	31.9	33,195.1
Macedonia	1,253.0	763.6	1,158.1	569.7	785.9		8,254.5
Moldova							
Montenegro	543.6	430.7	671.3	376.7	301.1		3,287.6
Poland	68,990.1	23,815.3	71,398.1	22,474.2	46,829.4	2,024.6	377,498.5
Romania	19,187.3	15,030.9	28,440.4	6,657.3	14,794.3		142,843.9
Russia	220,337.8	95,456.5	168,991.0	51,163.4	78,239.8		1,045,438.0
Serbia	5,836.8	2,744.5	7,096.4	714.1	5,053.3	20.4	35,876.4
Slovakia	13,866.2	5,671.9	14,929.0	4,922.3	6,264.5		79,888.9
Slovenia	5,557.7	3,329.2	9,719.7	2,418.9	5,540.0	30.0	43,181.1
Ukraine	15,317.7	10,123.9	15,553.8	5,396.1	13,307.2	1.4	100,867.3

Source: *Euromonitor International from national statistics*

Economic Statistics

Table 8.4

Gross Domestic Product by Origin 2009 (% Analysis)

% of total GDP

	Agriculture, Forestry & Fishing	Mining & Quarrying	Manufacturing	Electricity, Gas & Water	Construction	Hotels and Restaurants
Western Europe						
Austria	1.78	0.46	20.65	3.18	7.03	4.4
Belgium	0.64	0.10	15.45	1.94	5.37	1.6
Cyprus						
Denmark	1.02	4.71	14.14	1.48	5.90	1.5
Finland	3.03	0.36	21.84	2.54	6.99	1.4
France	1.92	0.17	11.55	1.68	6.98	2.3
Germany	0.92	0.27	23.38	2.18	4.34	1.7
Gibraltar						
Greece	3.12	0.44	10.63	2.79	5.84	6.6
Iceland						
Ireland	1.29	0.58	21.67	1.57	8.13	2.5
Italy	1.96	0.36	18.30	2.27	6.20	3.9
Liechtenstein						
Luxembourg						
Malta						
Monaco						
Netherlands	1.69	4.46	13.36	2.13	5.89	1.7
Norway	0.93	30.45	8.90	2.83	4.75	1.4
Portugal	2.13	0.49	12.77	2.54	6.03	4.7
Spain	2.42	0.23	14.37	2.23	11.37	7.2
Sweden	1.76	0.60	20.26	1.84	5.02	1.3
Switzerland	1.18	0.16	21.57	1.41	5.46	2.2
Turkey	9.52	1.89	20.10	2.86	5.94	2.9
United Kingdom	0.84	2.11	10.11	2.83	5.94	2.7
Eastern Europe						
Albania						
Belarus	8.64		30.80		11.44	
Bosnia-Herzegovina	8.97	2.56	14.10	3.20	6.00	3.4
Bulgaria	5.83	4.52	19.56	2.83	7.06	2.9
Croatia	5.32	1.10	14.81	3.61	8.38	4.4
Czech Republic	2.40	1.55	24.17	5.11	6.70	1.8
Estonia	2.66	1.05	16.56	3.11	8.58	1.4
Georgia	8.35	0.77	11.75	2.32	5.16	2.2
Hungary	3.59	0.16	22.11	2.71	4.50	1.6
Latvia	2.85	0.43	9.93	2.89	9.68	1.6
Lithuania	4.20	0.41	15.61	2.84	10.52	1.3
Macedonia	9.27	1.08	23.06	2.42	7.25	2.0
Moldova						
Montenegro	8.51	0.97	7.43	2.96	4.37	5.1
Poland	4.14	1.46	20.91	2.38	7.62	1.1
Romania	5.31	0.68	21.41	1.58	9.72	2.4
Russia	4.71	8.71	17.14	2.88	6.79	1.0
Serbia	8.52	1.52	19.08	4.44	5.08	1.5
Slovakia	2.94	0.59	23.79	5.37	8.69	1.5
Slovenia	2.25	0.40	21.61	2.99	8.83	2.3
Ukraine	6.57	6.05	20.25	3.27	3.95	0.7

Source: Euromonitor International from national statistics

Economic Statistics

Gross Domestic Product by Origin 2009 (% Analysis) *(continued)*
% of total GDP

	Wholesale & Retail Trade, Restaurants & Hotels	Transport, Storage & Commun- ications	Financial Inter- mediation, real estate, renting and business	Public Admin and Defence, Compulsory Social Security	Education, Health, Social Work and Other Community Activities	Activities of Households	GDP by origin
Western Europe							
Austria	11.99	6.01	24.56	5.43	3.74	0.03	100.0
Belgium	12.82	8.29	29.58	7.20	2.67	0.15	100.0
Cyprus							
Denmark	12.00	8.02	24.44	5.88	4.44	0.15	100.0
Finland	10.00	9.81	21.94	4.75	3.72	0.08	100.0
France	9.81	6.40	33.99	7.36	3.53	0.57	100.0
Germany	10.34	5.57	29.47	5.57	4.58	0.32	100.0
Gibraltar							
Greece	17.19	10.01	18.41	8.37	4.22	0.88	100.0
Iceland							
Ireland	8.66	5.64	29.33	4.87	2.92	0.14	100.0
Italy	10.52	7.34	28.21	6.45	2.78	1.08	100.0
Liechtenstein							
Luxembourg							
Malta							
Monaco							
Netherlands	12.53	6.43	28.50	6.75	2.87	0.40	100.0
Norway	7.81	6.03	17.66	4.32	2.49	0.08	100.0
Portugal	12.54	6.97	22.50	10.34	2.94	0.80	100.0
Spain	10.00	6.51	23.74	6.31	3.81	0.78	100.0
Sweden	11.04	6.97	25.60	5.49	4.10	0.04	100.0
Switzerland	12.55	6.09	28.82	11.17	2.11	0.36	100.0
Turkey	15.53	18.22	10.03	4.81	2.13	0.23	100.0
United Kingdom	11.41	6.65	34.24	4.69	4.95	0.47	100.0
Eastern Europe							
Albania							
Belarus	12.71	9.18	9.90	5.78	1.83		100.0
Bosnia-Herzegovina	16.82	8.25	13.95	9.83	3.29		100.0
Bulgaria	11.11	11.15	21.08	6.47	2.45		100.0
Croatia	15.27	12.06	18.92	4.59	3.07	0.10	100.0
Czech Republic	12.95	10.66	18.19	5.38	3.07	0.01	100.0
Estonia	13.78	9.74	24.16	6.69	3.58	0.01	100.0
Georgia	16.57	10.71	9.08	19.87		0.08	100.0
Hungary	12.13	8.44	23.12	8.18	4.75		100.0
Latvia	16.52	9.79	24.91	8.33	5.02		100.0
Lithuania	17.43	12.92	17.30	6.51	2.48	0.10	100.0
Macedonia	15.18	9.25	14.03	6.90			100.0
Moldova							
Montenegro	16.54	13.10	20.42	11.46	2.11		100.0
Poland	18.28	6.31	18.91	5.95	3.93	0.54	100.0
Romania	13.43	10.52	19.91	4.66	3.03		100.0
Russia	21.08	9.13	16.16	4.89	1.76		100.0
Serbia	16.27	7.65	19.78	1.99	3.48	0.06	100.0
Slovakia	17.36	7.10	18.69	6.16	2.40		100.0
Slovenia	12.87	7.71	22.51	5.60	3.16	0.07	100.0
Ukraine	15.19	10.04	15.42	5.35	3.76	0.00	100.0

Source: *Euromonitor International from national statistics*

Economic Statistics

Table 8.5

Gross Domestic Product Usage 2009

US$ million

	Government Final Consumption	Private Final Consumption	Increases in Stocks	Gross Fixed Capital Formation	Exports of Goods & Services	Imports of Goods & Services	Total
Western Europe							
Austria	76,411.1	207,058.6	469.8	79,876.9	192,412.5	-174,627.0	381,196.0
Belgium	115,410.5	247,054.4	-3,964.5	99,840.1	344,022.1	-330,916.8	471,298.5
Cyprus	4,675.2	16,188.6	-761.4	4,814.6	9,268.5	-10,636.7	23,548.7
Denmark	92,593.6	152,509.3	-3,511.2	57,550.9	146,473.1	-135,522.1	310,093.3
Finland	59,595.8	130,679.5	-6,503.3	46,664.2	86,329.0	-80,200.8	238,059.5
France	652,744.2	1,546,354.9	-41,754.7	544,836.2	610,842.2	-662,425.6	2,650,167.8
Germany	658,031.7	1,960,810.4	-26,305.1	595,888.7	1,358,223.8	-1,202,171.6	3,331,012.6
Gibraltar		210.8					943.9
Greece	62,764.2	239,485.2	4,366.4	55,445.1	62,148.7	-94,188.5	330,021.2
Iceland	3,167.0	6,264.8	15.0	1,713.3	6,341.7	-5,368.3	12,133.5
Ireland	43,661.4	112,498.9	-3,172.5	34,364.8	201,189.2	-167,280.2	227,259.5
Italy	455,530.7	1,266,639.1	-580.6	399,274.1	505,614.7	-513,982.8	2,113,402.5
Liechtenstein	522.8	2,891.9	-13.9	1,102.6	2,935.3	-2,366.8	5,013.3
Luxembourg	8,731.0	17,586.2	-798.9	9,139.7	84,289.6	-66,635.8	52,311.8
Malta	1,731.9	5,052.6	-157.7	1,131.0	5,758.3	-5,642.5	7,937.2
Monaco	1,535.6	3,815.6	12.5	1,500.1	1,770.3	-1,964.0	6,700.3
Netherlands	226,024.2	364,888.4	-4,905.3	151,335.9	550,211.1	-492,731.7	794,822.6
Norway	85,042.4	161,413.8	-307.2	81,947.7	159,858.7	-104,583.4	378,503.8
Portugal	49,197.4	155,531.1	683.8	45,410.2	65,135.3	-83,015.6	232,942.8
Spain	308,948.6	828,791.4	6,892.4	356,670.3	345,849.5	-375,799.5	1,464,520.0
Sweden	112,849.4	198,072.8	-5,327.9	72,579.0	196,963.9	-169,073.3	406,089.9
Switzerland	56,337.2	285,738.1	995.9	100,774.3	249,308.6	-198,998.3	492,659.3
Turkey	90,130.2	439,339.9	-12,179.4	103,269.3	142,116.2	-149,300.1	613,376.3
United Kingdom	510,694.6	1,417,286.3	-22,911.1	302,248.7	606,406.3	-657,055.3	2,171,971.6
Eastern Europe							
Albania	1,064.6	9,700.5	-58.7	4,784.2	3,605.2	-6,930.8	11,843.6
Belarus	8,190.4	27,339.6	682.0	18,103.8	24,884.0	-30,461.6	49,037.6
Bosnia-Herzegovina	3,257.4	14,362.6		4,443.9	6,578.5	-11,856.9	19,362.4
Bulgaria	7,601.6	30,809.8	659.8	11,672.8	23,537.2	-27,180.7	47,100.6
Croatia	12,138.9	36,177.5	1,244.0	15,567.9	22,747.6	-24,842.8	63,033.1
Czech Republic	41,986.1	96,349.7	-1,310.1	42,704.3	131,495.1	-120,926.7	190,298.6
Estonia	4,230.7	10,102.8	-475.1	4,172.2	13,473.0	-12,449.0	19,083.7
Georgia	2,618.1	8,886.9	-246.9	1,549.7	3,172.5	-5,266.7	10,744.5
Hungary	27,050.4	68,429.7	-2,372.5	25,824.0	100,416.9	-91,375.8	128,964.3
Latvia	4,836.6	15,980.7	-265.3	5,562.0	11,192.8	-11,381.3	25,925.3
Lithuania	8,056.0	25,339.2	-2,226.9	6,283.8	19,938.5	-20,347.6	37,043.0
Macedonia	1,702.6	7,340.4	419.8	2,083.7	5,004.0	-7,353.7	9,221.0
Moldova	1,302.8	4,794.5	69.3	1,214.3	2,060.3	-4,962.8	5,404.6
Montenegro	1,304.2	3,329.5	81.4	962.5	2,053.0	-3,198.4	4,086.8
Poland	79,233.5	264,224.3	-3,983.8	90,900.4	167,704.9	-167,441.8	430,637.2
Romania	29,179.2	101,103.2	-863.7	41,263.6	50,292.1	-59,865.4	161,109.0
Russia	247,700.9	671,184.6	-33,422.0	264,077.3	341,517.7	-250,632.4	1,231,072.5
Serbia	9,601.2	31,810.2	1,087.7	9,064.4	13,025.1	-23,202.1	42,896.4
Slovakia	17,249.1	53,238.1	-2,638.9	20,766.2	61,734.4	-61,929.0	88,005.8
Slovenia	9,803.1	27,246.2	-255.8	11,629.4	28,567.4	-27,829.7	49,170.2
Ukraine	22,509.8	76,775.5	-1,089.8	21,174.2	54,365.0	-56,397.4	115,856.9

Source: *International Monetary Fund (IMF), International Financial Statistics*
Notes: *The difference between the sum of GDP by usage components and Total GDP (usually production approach measured GDP) appears due to the statistical discrepancies*

Economic Statistics   **Table 8.6**

Gross Domestic Product Usage 2009 (% Analysis)

% of total GDP

	Government Final Consumption	Private Final Consumption	Increases in Stocks	Gross Fixed Capital Formation	Exports of Goods & Services	Imports of Goods & Services	Total
Western Europe							
Austria	20.05	54.32	0.12	20.95	50.48	-45.81	100.00
Belgium	24.49	52.42	-0.84	21.18	72.99	-70.21	100.00
Cyprus	19.85	68.74	-3.23	20.45	39.36	-45.17	100.00
Denmark	29.86	49.18	-1.13	18.56	47.24	-43.70	100.00
Finland	25.03	54.89	-2.73	19.60	36.26	-33.69	100.00
France	24.63	58.35	-1.58	20.56	23.05	-25.00	100.00
Germany	19.75	58.87	-0.79	17.89	40.78	-36.09	100.00
Gibraltar		22.33					100.00
Greece	19.02	72.57	1.32	16.80	18.83	-28.54	100.00
Iceland	26.10	51.63	0.12	14.12	52.27	-44.24	100.00
Ireland	19.21	49.50	-1.40	15.12	88.53	-73.61	100.00
Italy	21.55	59.93	-0.03	18.89	23.92	-24.32	100.00
Liechtenstein	10.43	57.68	-0.28	21.99	58.55	-47.21	100.00
Luxembourg	16.69	33.62	-1.53	17.47	161.13	-127.38	100.00
Malta	21.82	63.66	-1.99	14.25	72.55	-71.09	100.00
Monaco	22.92	56.95	0.19	22.39	26.42	-29.31	100.00
Netherlands	28.44	45.91	-0.62	19.04	69.22	-61.99	100.00
Norway	22.47	42.65	-0.08	21.65	42.23	-27.63	100.00
Portugal	21.12	66.77	0.29	19.49	27.96	-35.64	100.00
Spain	21.10	56.59	0.47	24.35	23.62	-25.66	100.00
Sweden	27.79	48.78	-1.31	17.87	48.50	-41.63	100.00
Switzerland	11.44	58.00	0.20	20.46	50.60	-40.39	100.00
Turkey	14.69	71.63	-1.99	16.84	23.17	-24.34	100.00
United Kingdom	23.51	65.25	-1.05	13.92	27.92	-30.25	100.00
Eastern Europe							
Albania	8.99	81.91	-0.50	40.40	30.44	-58.52	100.00
Belarus	16.70	55.75	1.39	36.92	50.74	-62.12	100.00
Bosnia-Herzegovina	16.82	74.18		22.95	33.98	-61.24	100.00
Bulgaria	16.14	65.41	1.40	24.78	49.97	-57.71	100.00
Croatia	19.26	57.39	1.97	24.70	36.09	-39.41	100.00
Czech Republic	22.06	50.63	-0.69	22.44	69.10	-63.55	100.00
Estonia	22.17	52.94	-2.49	21.86	70.60	-65.23	100.00
Georgia	24.37	82.71	-2.30	14.42	29.53	-49.02	100.00
Hungary	20.98	53.06	-1.84	20.02	77.86	-70.85	100.00
Latvia	18.66	61.64	-1.02	21.45	43.17	-43.90	100.00
Lithuania	21.75	68.40	-6.01	16.96	53.83	-54.93	100.00
Macedonia	18.46	79.61	4.55	22.60	54.27	-79.75	100.00
Moldova	24.10	88.71	1.28	22.47	38.12	-91.82	100.00
Montenegro	31.91	81.47	1.99	23.55	50.24	-78.26	100.00
Poland	18.40	61.36	-0.93	21.11	38.94	-38.88	100.00
Romania	18.11	62.75	-0.54	25.61	31.22	-37.16	100.00
Russia	20.12	54.52	-2.71	21.45	27.74	-20.36	100.00
Serbia	22.38	74.16	2.54	21.13	30.36	-54.09	100.00
Slovakia	19.60	60.49	-3.00	23.60	70.15	-70.37	100.00
Slovenia	19.94	55.41	-0.52	23.65	58.10	-56.60	100.00
Ukraine	19.43	66.27	-0.94	18.28	46.92	-48.68	100.00

Source: *International Monetary Fund (IMF), International Financial Statistics*
Notes: *The difference between the sum of GDP by usage components and Total GDP (usually production approach measured GDP) appears due to the statistical discrepancies*

Economic Statistics

Table 8.7

Gross National Income in National Currencies 1980-2009

Million units of national currency

	1980	1985	1990	1995	1996	1997	1998	1999	2000	2001
Western Europe										
Austria	75,470	102,016	135,860	172,515	180,033	182,390	189,362	194,448	204,010	207,952
Belgium	88,334	122,081	163,855	211,663	215,836	226,054	230,332	243,212	257,990	263,598
Cyprus	1,514	3,086	4,232	6,612	6,894	7,288	8,645	8,850	9,419	10,209
Denmark	382,155	615,288	818,974	1,008,640	1,055,830	1,109,710	1,150,470	1,203,240	1,266,610	1,316,780
Finland	32,767	56,401	86,923	94,269	98,048	107,317	116,222	120,634	131,100	139,005
France	442,342	725,315	1,006,426	1,198,118	1,235,481	1,278,181	1,335,968	1,387,940	1,462,700	1,515,300
Germany	755,394	937,979	1,251,764	1,834,789	1,866,321	1,901,738	1,945,051	1,990,460	2,043,160	2,092,160
Gibraltar										
Greece	5,543	14,374	41,542	88,102	96,485	106,803	116,077	122,003	136,648	147,352
Iceland	15,675	117,211	359,053	441,303	476,310	514,338	575,682	620,011	664,837	747,638
Ireland	11,510	20,460	32,396	46,953	51,763	59,359	68,008	76,831	89,530	98,162
Italy	199,501	415,559	673,202	909,863	970,707	1,016,867	1,062,682	1,122,160	1,182,140	1,240,430
Liechtenstein										
Luxembourg	3,989	6,535	9,990	14,046	14,815	15,690	16,979	17,868	19,170	20,050
Malta	1,315	1,254	1,743	3,188	3,263	3,358	3,471	3,679	3,722	3,896
Monaco										
Netherlands	154,449	193,089	241,845	309,796	322,610	346,800	358,704	390,395	426,980	451,110
Norway	305,071	542,876	715,315	931,980	1,021,240	1,107,440	1,127,500	1,230,020	1,461,260	1,538,260
Portugal	1,225,400	3,327,500	9,741,840	17,034,800	18,046,900	19,390,100	21,043,400			
Spain	90,627	167,502	298,661	436,695	461,370	489,277	521,558	559,562	603,252	644,093
Sweden	549,779	883,312	1,396,300	1,767,190	1,812,620	1,890,940	1,995,270	2,118,870	2,246,400	2,331,320
Switzerland	177,345	241,355	327,585	377,560						
Turkey	4	28	287	7,855	15,064					
United Kingdom	228,084	352,581	560,449	727,497	776,504	827,707	887,495	924,587	974,732	1,027,910
Eastern Europe										
Albania										
Belarus			4	121,351	192,046	366,300	701,810	3,028,910	9,096,100	17,113,100
Bosnia-Herzegovina										
Bulgaria				852	1,692	16,844	21,911	23,464	26,078	29,045
Croatia										
Czech Republic				1,463,500	1,660,040	1,782,880	1,959,310	2,031,710	2,139,690	2,273,220
Estonia				43,305	57,125	68,312	77,796	82,690	93,230	104,624
Georgia										
Hungary	583,000	842,000	2,080,000							
Latvia				2,631	3,149	3,657	3,994	4,225	4,739	5,233
Lithuania				25,928	32,364	39,252	43,685	42,870	44,937	47,995
Macedonia										
Moldova				6,480	8,070	9,207	9,279	12,678	16,814	20,484
Montenegro										
Poland	199	859	50,630							
Romania	62	82	86	7,214	10,839	24,975	38,145			
Russia										
Serbia										
Slovakia										
Slovenia			2,576	15,852	16,469	17,524	18,818	20,313	20,996	22,156
Ukraine				53,639	80,472	92,166	100,524	126,934	164,942	200,610

Source:*International Monetary Fund (IMF), International Financial Statistics*

Economic Statistics

Gross National Income in National Currencies 1980-2009 *(continued)*

Million units of national currency

	2002	2003	2004	2005	2006	2007	2008	2009	Total US$ million 2009	US$ per capita 2009
Western Europe										
Austria	216,117	221,132	231,033	241,205	253,321	265,352	277,386	274,203	381,032.8	45,452.5
Belgium	271,864	279,969	293,980	304,816	320,971	338,153	346,972	340,041	472,521.3	43,955.5
Cyprus	10,780	11,487	12,182	13,174	14,081	15,606	16,125	16,642	23,126.2	26,550.1
Denmark	1,356,520	1,392,120	1,472,920	1,566,810	1,662,100	1,708,840	1,761,750	1,706,400	318,306.7	57,753.7
Finland	143,780	144,313	153,298	158,032	167,215	179,613	185,138	168,868	234,659.1	44,066.5
France	1,553,820	1,605,650	1,670,500	1,735,230	1,825,760	1,918,010	1,966,340	1,922,930	2,672,105.5	42,788.6
Germany	2,116,630	2,148,680	2,232,070	2,268,820	2,374,350	2,477,700	2,536,980	2,443,960	3,396,129.3	41,415.0
Gibraltar										
Greece	157,028	171,412	184,438	192,067	205,923	219,809	231,252	230,938	320,911.7	28,520.7
Iceland	815,123	828,135	891,145	989,764	1,093,440	1,236,760	1,249,840	1,338,920	10,829.4	33,559.5
Ireland	106,767	118,283	126,466	138,053	154,078	162,853	154,672	131,242	182,374.0	40,982.6
Italy	1,285,100	1,324,400	1,383,510	1,425,440	1,484,290	1,536,350	1,543,420	1,494,050	2,076,133.4	34,571.4
Liechtenstein										
Luxembourg	19,898	20,028	23,986	26,005	26,032	29,688	29,716	25,930	36,031.9	74,112.2
Malta	4,172	4,346	4,439	4,567	4,885	5,268	5,512	5,359	7,446.5	18,219.6
Monaco										
Netherlands	469,468	482,368	504,333	515,885	554,741	576,875	580,214	557,115	774,167.6	47,175.9
Norway	1,537,010	1,603,730	1,746,400	1,959,170	2,161,140	2,264,340	2,550,040	2,452,850	389,972.4	81,256.9
Portugal										
Spain	687,643	735,064	793,300	858,790	933,564	990,081	1,013,823	968,896	1,346,379.4	29,577.3
Sweden	2,434,050	2,576,240	2,660,470	2,789,270	2,982,310	3,197,270	3,321,310	3,163,970	413,402.6	44,927.8
Switzerland										
Turkey										
United Kingdom	1,091,480	1,155,260	1,220,160	1,275,060	1,334,090	1,417,880	1,476,870	1,423,810	2,220,481.0	36,039.6
Eastern Europe										
Albania										
Belarus	26,084,300	36,616,300	49,951,600	65,186,600	79,020,900	96,283,300	128,108,000	133,688,000	47,925.6	4,955.1
Bosnia-Herzegovina										
Bulgaria	33,154	35,125	39,317	43,189	48,130	55,830	65,741	64,762	46,038.7	6,122.8
Croatia										
Czech Republic	2,352,130	2,466,090	2,660,120	2,849,950	3,062,350	3,288,160	3,426,040	3,413,530	179,045.1	17,104.8
Estonia	116,669	129,352	144,256	168,300	196,064	227,361	236,325	209,828	18,639.5	14,008.3
Georgia										
Hungary										
Latvia	5,775	6,372	7,274	8,945	10,842	14,305	16,029	14,105	27,951.7	12,403.9
Lithuania	51,524	55,535	61,362	70,821	80,943	94,826	108,347	92,533	37,251.0	11,126.5
Macedonia										
Moldova	24,805	30,838	36,414	42,740	50,026	58,410	69,098	60,563	5,451.4	1,512.8
Montenegro										
Poland										
Romania										
Russia										
Serbia										
Slovakia										
Slovenia	23,537	24,676	25,941	27,371	30,644	33,854	36,278	34,381	47,775.6	23,618.6
Ukraine	222,585	264,247	341,686	436,411	535,459	717,406	939,356	895,681	114,961.5	2,501.2

Source:International Monetary Fund (IMF), International Financial Statistics

Economic Statistics

Table 8.8

Gross National Income in US$1980-2009

US$ million

	1980	1985	1990	1995	1996	1997	1998	1999	2000	2001
Western Europe										
Austria	105,079	77,847	173,009	225,652	228,597	206,837	212,292	207,187	187,999	186,123
Belgium	122,990	93,158	208,658	276,857	274,058	256,355	258,223	259,145	237,743	235,928
Cyprus	2,108	2,355	5,389	8,649	8,754	8,265	9,692	9,430	8,680	9,138
Denmark	67,807	58,066	132,337	180,038	182,081	168,024	171,691	172,477	156,603	158,251
Finland	45,623	43,039	110,690	123,304	124,497	121,702	130,295	128,537	120,811	124,414
France	615,885	553,479	1,281,613	1,567,151	1,568,752	1,449,508	1,497,740	1,478,867	1,347,906	1,356,240
Germany	1,051,758	715,761	1,594,034	2,399,922	2,369,761	2,156,647	2,180,577	2,120,860	1,882,811	1,872,548
Gibraltar										
Greece	7,717	10,968	52,900	115,238	122,512	121,119	130,133	129,996	125,924	131,885
Iceland	3,267	2,824	6,160	6,822	7,163	7,254	8,113	8,571	8,457	7,674
Ireland	16,026	15,613	41,254	61,415	65,726	67,315	76,243	81,864	82,504	87,858
Italy	277,771	317,108	857,275	1,190,110	1,232,555	1,153,168	1,191,363	1,195,675	1,089,365	1,110,223
Liechtenstein										
Luxembourg	5,554	4,987	12,721	18,372	18,811	17,793	19,035	19,039	17,666	17,946
Malta	1,831	957	2,219	4,170	4,143	3,808	3,891	3,920	3,430	3,487
Monaco										
Netherlands	215,044	147,344	307,973	405,216	409,634	393,285	402,139	415,971	393,470	403,757
Norway	61,765	63,145	114,272	147,112	158,336	156,564	149,435	157,712	166,017	171,084
Portugal	1,706,161	2,539,175	12,405,551	22,281,689	22,915,051	21,989,149	23,591,545			
Spain	126,183	127,819	380,324	571,202	585,824	554,860	584,713	596,220	555,908	576,483
Sweden	129,985	102,664	235,910	247,739	270,300	247,671	250,981	256,446	245,180	225,703
Switzerland	105,833	98,226	235,815	319,298						
Turkey	58,326	53,253	110,116	171,335	185,055					
United Kingdom	530,064	452,464	995,156	1,148,073	1,211,474	1,355,040	1,469,791	1,495,957	1,474,787	1,479,742
Eastern Europe										
Albania										
Belarus			18,833	13,839	14,516	14,077	15,215	12,150	10,375	12,312
Bosnia-Herzegovina										
Bulgaria				12,679	9,511	10,015	12,447	12,777	12,281	13,295
Croatia										
Czech Republic				55,142	61,155	56,245	60,695	58,772	55,435	59,766
Estonia				4,382	4,745	4,921	5,527	5,634	5,494	5,986
Georgia										
Hungary	17,921	16,800	32,908							
Latvia				4,988	5,718	6,295	6,771	7,220	7,814	8,333
Lithuania				6,482	8,091	9,813	10,921	10,718	11,234	11,999
Macedonia										
Moldova				1,766	1,753	1,991	1,728	1,206	1,352	1,592
Montenegro										
Poland	45,051	58,352	53,295							
Romania	34,273	47,683	38,242	35,478	35,144	34,843	42,977			
Russia										
Serbia										
Slovakia										
Slovenia			3,281	20,734	20,912	19,873	21,097	21,644	19,348	19,831
Ukraine				47,826	43,987	49,507	41,038	30,731	30,319	37,343

Source:*International Monetary Fund (IMF), International Financial Statistics*

Economic Statistics

Gross National Income in US$1980-2009 *(continued)*

US$ million

	2002	2003	2004	2005	2006	2007	2008	2009	US$ per capita 2009
Western Europe									
Austria	203,572	249,640	286,954	299,778	317,803	363,180	405,947	381,032.8	45,452.5
Belgium	256,083	316,062	365,138	378,836	402,673	462,821	507,785	472,521.3	43,955.5
Cyprus	10,154	12,968	15,130	16,373	17,665	21,360	23,599	23,126.2	26,550.1
Denmark	172,054	211,665	245,997	261,305	279,673	313,965	345,429	318,306.7	57,753.7
Finland	135,434	162,918	190,404	196,408	209,779	245,832	270,945	234,659.1	44,066.5
France	1,463,623	1,812,647	2,074,844	2,156,605	2,290,501	2,625,130	2,877,688	2,672,105.5	42,788.6
Germany	1,993,763	2,425,684	2,772,342	2,819,769	2,978,732	3,391,163	3,712,805	3,396,129.3	41,415.0
Gibraltar									
Greece	147,913	193,510	229,081	238,708	258,340	300,847	338,431	320,911.7	28,520.7
Iceland	8,893	10,796	12,696	15,715	15,581	19,308	14,211	10,829.4	33,559.5
Ireland	100,569	133,532	157,077	171,577	193,298	222,893	226,358	182,374.0	40,982.6
Italy	1,210,502	1,495,139	1,718,388	1,771,587	1,862,111	2,102,762	2,258,755	2,076,133.4	34,571.4
Liechtenstein									
Luxembourg	18,743	22,610	29,792	32,320	32,659	40,634	43,488	36,031.9	74,112.2
Malta	3,930	4,906	5,514	5,676	6,129	7,211	8,067	7,446.5	18,219.6
Monaco									
Netherlands	442,216	544,554	626,407	641,160	695,948	789,554	849,128	774,167.6	47,175.9
Norway	192,513	226,515	259,062	304,097	336,966	386,343	452,214	389,972.4	81,256.9
Portugal									
Spain	647,726	829,827	985,317	1,067,335	1,171,199	1,355,098	1,483,704	1,346,379.4	29,577.3
Sweden	249,976	318,593	362,024	373,242	404,203	473,055	504,022	413,402.6	44,927.8
Switzerland									
Turkey									
United Kingdom	1,635,854	1,886,223	2,233,989	2,318,298	2,454,688	2,837,056	2,714,336	2,220,481.0	36,039.6
Eastern Europe									
Albania									
Belarus	14,565	17,851	23,123	30,266	36,847	44,865	59,964	47,925.6	4,955.1
Bosnia-Herzegovina									
Bulgaria	15,962	20,273	24,961	27,437	30,867	39,068	49,162	46,038.7	6,122.8
Croatia									
Czech Republic	71,846	87,422	103,508	118,959	135,529	162,029	200,686	179,045.1	17,104.8
Estonia	7,023	9,335	11,453	13,374	15,729	19,885	22,098	18,639.5	14,008.3
Georgia									
Hungary									
Latvia	9,342	11,150	13,465	15,839	19,346	27,843	33,337	27,951.7	12,403.9
Lithuania	14,013	18,143	22,068	25,530	29,410	37,574	45,967	37,251.0	11,126.5
Macedonia									
Moldova	1,828	2,211	2,953	3,392	3,810	4,811	6,649	5,451.4	1,512.8
Montenegro									
Poland									
Romania									
Russia									
Serbia									
Slovakia									
Slovenia	22,170	27,857	32,220	34,018	38,445	46,334	53,092	47,775.6	23,618.6
Ukraine	41,787	49,552	64,236	85,158	106,031	142,061	178,340	114,961.5	2,501.2

Source:International Monetary Fund (IMF), International Financial Statistics

Economic Statistics

Table 8.9

Money Supply 1985-2009

Billion units of national currency

	1985	1990	1995	2000	2004	2005	2006	2007	2008	2009	Total US$ billion 2009
Western Europe											
Austria	6.9	9.1	12.3	14.5	14.1	15.9	17.7	19.0	21.4	19.8	27.5
Belgium	10.1	11.1	11.5	13.5	17.2	19.4	21.6	23.2	26.0	24.2	33.6
Cyprus	0.6	0.7	1.0	1.8	2.5	2.9	3.5	3.9	3.9	3.9	5.4
Denmark	156.5	244.5	292.0	386.0	536.6	643.6	699.5	755.2	755.3	900.5	168.0
Finland	1.4	2.4	2.6	3.3	8.6	9.7	10.8	11.6	13.0	12.0	16.7
France	33.1	41.1	41.9	49.2	97.8	110.2	122.3	131.1	147.3	136.5	189.7
Germany	58.7	91.9	134.7	142.2	141.3	159.1	176.7	190.1	213.3	197.8	274.9
Gibraltar											
Greece	1.6	3.7	6.0	9.1	12.8	14.4	16.0	16.9	19.0	17.6	24.5
Iceland	6.7	24.6	38.3	72.3	141.7	174.0	202.6	410.8	474.8	432.1	3.5
Ireland	1.4	2.0	2.7	5.4	6.4	7.2	8.0	8.6	9.6	9.0	12.4
Italy	29.3	42.7	58.7	76.4	86.8	97.9	108.7	115.6	129.8	120.3	167.2
Liechtenstein											
Luxembourg				0.7	1.1	1.3	1.4	1.6	1.8	1.6	2.3
Malta	0.9	0.9	1.0	1.5	3.7	3.9	3.9	4.2	4.2	4.2	5.8
Monaco											
Netherlands	14.0	17.9	18.7	18.7	26.5	29.7	32.9	35.5	39.8	36.9	51.3
Norway	98.6	237.6	358.7	565.1	801.0	842.0	879.1	917.2	942.5	925.6	147.2
Portugal	1.6	3.1	4.2	6.5	11.8	13.3	14.7	15.8	17.7	16.5	22.9
Spain	12.5	27.3	45.3	59.8	52.7	59.4	65.9	70.9	79.4	73.8	102.5
Sweden	46.8				995.8	1,133.5	1,274.5	1,391.9	1,448.1	1,522.6	198.9
Switzerland	73.9	84.3	100.6	160.0	224.1	238.6	232.6	241.7	292.0	364.4	335.4
Turkey	0.0	0.0	0.4	7.3	28.6	63.0	67.2	74.7	81.5	87.7	56.4
United Kingdom	145.5	523.1	514.6	1,037.9	1,434.7	1,490.3	1,529.2	1,595.5	1,639.8	1,610.3	2,511.3
Eastern Europe											
Albania			59.3	124.0	158.8	182.9	214.2	224.4	266.2	277.8	2.9
Belarus			10.0	508.4	3,111.4	4,945.8	7,023.2	8,739.9	10,718.5	8,465.6	3.0
Bosnia-Herzegovina				1.5	3.8	4.4	5.6	6.8	6.3	6.4	4.5
Bulgaria			0.2	4.8	10.3	12.4	16.1	20.7	19.9	18.0	12.8
Croatia			8.3	18.0	34.6	38.9	48.6	57.9	55.3	48.2	9.1
Czech Republic			431.1	499.0	1,026.3	1,162.8	1,325.6	1,526.6	1,675.0	1,791.8	94.0
Estonia			8.2	20.9	42.3	57.6	72.3	76.2	67.8	63.4	5.6
Georgia			0.2	0.4	0.8	1.0	1.3	1.8	1.6	1.9	1.2
Hungary	239.7	517.5	1,011.2	2,379.7	4,169.3	5,188.8	5,833.3	6,348.3	6,161.9	5,988.1	29.6
Latvia			0.4	0.8	2.0	2.9	4.1	3.9	3.3	2.7	5.3
Lithuania			3.5	5.7	15.1	20.9	24.8	27.9	23.3	20.1	8.1
Macedonia			11.5	21.4	28.8	31.4	36.8	48.9	56.9	57.4	1.3
Moldova			0.9	2.0	5.6	7.3	8.3	10.9	11.6	11.7	1.1
Montenegro				0.0	0.1	0.2	0.5	0.8	0.6	0.5	0.7
Poland	0.2	9.4	37.4	82.6	175.7	220.6	275.8	335.3	349.9	360.3	115.4
Romania	0.0	0.0	0.7	4.6	15.3	24.6	38.0	61.9	71.6	67.2	22.0
Russia			150.1	863.5	2,812.2	3,815.0	5,473.8	7,456.7	7,419.7	7,444.4	234.4
Serbia				26.9	111.3	144.9	200.1	248.9	241.0	252.6	3.7
Slovakia			3.9	4.4	10.1	12.1	14.2	16.3	14.9	16.7	23.2
Slovenia			0.7	1.3	5.0	6.2	7.1	7.1	6.8	7.4	10.2
Ukraine			4.7	20.8	67.1	98.6	123.3	181.7	225.1	217.3	27.9

Source: *International Monetary Fund (IMF), International Financial Statistics*
Notes: *The money supply refers to the total amount of money held by the nonbank public at a point in time in an economy. M1: Physical currency + demand deposits, which are checking accounts*

Economic Statistics | **Table 8.10**

Inflation Rates (Annual) 1985-2009
% growth

	1985	1990	1995	2000	2004	2005	2006	2007	2008	2009
Western Europe										
Austria	3.19	3.26	2.25	2.34	2.06	2.30	1.44	2.17	3.22	0.51
Belgium	4.87	3.45	1.47	2.54	2.08	2.80	1.79	1.82	4.49	-0.04
Cyprus	5.03	4.50	2.62	4.14	2.29	2.56	2.50	2.37	4.67	0.37
Denmark	4.65	2.65	2.10	2.91	1.16	1.81	1.89	1.71	3.40	1.33
Finland	5.87	6.10	0.99	3.04	0.19	0.63	1.57	2.51	4.06	0.02
France	5.83	3.38	1.78	1.69	2.13	1.74	1.68	1.49	2.82	0.09
Germany	2.10	2.70	1.72	1.47	1.67	1.56	1.58	2.29	2.63	0.32
Gibraltar	6.00	5.90	4.70	3.30	1.45	0.82	1.17	1.87	1.64	1.55
Greece	19.30	20.40	8.94	3.15	2.89	3.57	3.20	2.89	4.16	1.21
Iceland	31.69	15.51	1.65	5.12	3.16	3.99	6.69	5.05	12.69	12.00
Ireland	5.44	3.27	2.52	5.55	2.20	2.41	3.94	4.92	4.06	-4.46
Italy	9.21	6.50	5.24	2.54	2.21	1.98	2.09	1.83	3.35	0.78
Liechtenstein	3.40	5.40	1.88	0.70	0.77	0.56	0.58	0.31	0.52	0.94
Luxembourg	4.09	3.70	1.92	3.15	2.23	2.49	2.68	2.30	3.40	0.37
Malta	-0.24	2.98	4.43	2.37	2.79	3.01	2.77	1.25	4.26	2.09
Monaco		3.62	1.79	1.07	0.90	0.87	0.75	0.94	1.08	1.24
Netherlands	2.22	2.45	1.92	2.37	1.24	1.67	1.17	1.61	2.49	1.19
Norway	5.67	4.11	2.46	3.09	0.47	1.52	2.33	0.73	3.77	2.17
Portugal	19.65	13.37	4.12	2.86	2.36	2.29	3.10	2.45	2.57	-0.82
Spain	8.82	6.72	4.67	3.43	3.04	3.37	3.52	2.78	4.09	-0.28
Sweden	7.36	10.47	2.53	0.90	0.37	0.45	1.36	2.21	3.44	-0.27
Switzerland	3.43	5.38	1.80	1.56	0.80	1.17	1.06	0.73	2.43	-0.48
Turkey	44.96	60.31	88.11	54.92	8.60	8.19	9.59	8.78	10.43	6.28
United Kingdom	5.20	7.00	2.60	0.79	1.34	2.05	2.33	2.32	3.61	2.17
Eastern Europe										
Albania	0.57	-0.20	7.79	0.05	2.28	2.37	2.37	2.93	3.36	2.23
Belarus			709.35	168.62	18.11	10.34	7.03	8.42	14.84	12.95
Bosnia-Herzegovina			12.90	5.03	0.28	3.58	6.10	1.50	7.40	-0.38
Bulgaria	2.80	23.80	62.05	10.30	6.16	5.03	7.27	8.40	12.43	2.80
Croatia			4.04	4.62	2.03	3.34	3.21	2.87	6.08	2.39
Czech Republic	2.30	9.50	9.47	3.90	2.78	1.84	2.55	2.86	6.35	1.04
Estonia			28.78	4.01	3.05	4.09	4.43	6.58	10.40	-0.05
Georgia			162.72	4.02	5.68	8.30	9.16	9.25	9.98	1.74
Hungary	7.01	28.97	28.30	9.80	6.75	3.56	3.92	7.97	6.06	4.21
Latvia			24.98	2.65	6.18	6.74	6.54	10.07	15.48	3.62
Lithuania			39.66	0.98	1.18	2.66	3.74	5.72	10.94	4.51
Macedonia			16.37	6.61	0.93	0.16	3.27	3.61	7.22	-0.27
Moldova			9.91	31.30	12.52	11.96	12.78	12.37	12.77	-0.05
Montenegro			10.66	21.74	3.10	3.45	2.12	3.52	8.99	3.56
Poland	11.52	555.38	28.07	10.06	3.57	2.12	1.11	2.39	4.35	3.83
Romania	-0.20	127.90	32.24	40.71	11.91	9.00	6.62	4.82	7.85	5.57
Russia			197.47	20.78	10.88	12.70	9.69	8.99	14.10	11.73
Serbia			82.66	71.12	11.03	16.12	11.72	6.39	12.87	7.78
Slovakia			9.92	12.17	7.56	2.71	4.48	2.76	4.60	1.62
Slovenia			13.41	8.88	3.59	2.48	2.46	3.60	5.68	0.87
Ukraine			376.75	28.20	9.04	13.54	9.08	12.78	25.27	16.02

Source:*Euromonitor International from International Monetary Fund (IMF), International Financial Statistics and World Economic Outlook/UN/national statistics*

Economic Statistics

Table 8.11

Public Consumption 1985-2009

Billion units of national currency

	1985	1990	1995	2000	2004	2005	2006	2007	2008	2009	Total US$ billion 2009
Western Europe											
Austria	20.1	25.6	35.7	39.7	43.4	45.1	47.4	49.4	52.6	55.0	76.4
Belgium	28.6	33.1	44.4	53.7	65.9	69.0	71.5	74.7	79.8	83.1	115.4
Cyprus	0.3	0.7	1.0	1.6	2.3	2.4	2.7	2.8	3.1	3.4	4.7
Denmark	164.2	211.2	257.2	325.1	389.0	402.5	422.6	439.1	463.8	496.4	92.6
Finland	11.8	19.5	21.9	27.1	33.7	35.4	36.7	38.6	41.6	42.9	59.6
France	171.6	224.5	283.0	330.3	393.5	408.4	422.4	436.5	451.2	469.7	652.7
Germany	220.6	272.3	361.8	391.9	415.9	419.6	426.3	435.6	451.8	473.5	658.0
Gibraltar											
Greece	3.1	6.7	13.8	24.3	31.9	33.2	34.3	38.5	40.3	45.2	62.8
Iceland	21.1	73.1	99.0	160.2	233.1	252.6	285.4	316.8	367.3	391.6	3.2
Ireland	4.8	6.0	8.6	14.3	22.7	24.5	27.2	30.3	32.2	31.4	43.7
Italy	80.3	141.2	170.2	219.7	276.2	290.8	299.3	304.2	317.3	327.8	455.5
Liechtenstein	0.1	0.2	0.3	0.5	0.5	0.5	0.6	0.6	0.6	0.6	0.5
Luxembourg	1.1	1.7	2.4	3.3	4.7	5.0	5.2	5.6	5.9	6.3	8.7
Malta	0.2	0.3	0.6	0.7	0.9	0.9	1.0	1.0	1.2	1.2	1.7
Monaco	0.3	0.4	0.6	0.7	0.8	0.8	0.9	1.0	1.1	1.1	1.5
Netherlands	47.7	56.1	72.7	91.9	118.9	121.7	135.4	143.9	152.3	162.7	226.0
Norway	102.1	155.9	203.7	286.1	373.3	387.2	413.0	446.5	491.8	534.9	85.0
Portugal	3.1	8.4	15.3	23.8	29.8	32.1	32.4	33.0	33.9	35.4	49.2
Spain	27.4	52.1	80.9	108.4	149.8	163.7	177.5	193.5	209.3	222.3	308.9
Sweden	251.2	389.6	482.1	585.5	704.9	725.2	765.3	797.4	837.0	863.7	112.8
Switzerland	25.2	37.0	44.2	46.8	53.0	54.2	55.2	56.4	58.6	61.2	56.3
Turkey	0.0	0.0	0.8	19.5	66.8	76.5	93.5	107.8	121.7	140.2	90.1
United Kingdom	75.7	112.5	143.0	182.0	251.1	268.1	285.2	294.7	313.6	327.5	510.7
Eastern Europe											
Albania	1.6	1.7	30.7	49.5	82.5	88.5	89.4	98.4	99.9	101.1	1.1
Belarus		0.0	24.9	1,779.1	10,299.9	13,524.4	15,225.1	17,998.1	21,447.9	22,846.9	8.2
Bosnia-Herzegovina		0.0	0.7	2.3	3.5	3.7	4.1	4.5	4.8	4.6	3.3
Bulgaria	0.0	0.0	0.1	4.8	7.2	7.7	8.2	9.1	10.9	10.7	7.6
Croatia		0.1	28.3	38.4	45.7	48.6	51.8	56.9	62.0	64.1	12.1
Czech Republic		159.9	306.3	460.9	621.6	658.5	687.0	718.2	753.2	800.5	42.0
Estonia		0.1	11.0	19.0	26.7	30.1	33.9	41.2	48.8	47.6	4.2
Georgia		0.0	0.3	0.5	1.4	2.0	2.1	3.7	4.9	4.4	2.6
Hungary	245.4	504.2	1,341.7	2,833.7	4,636.8	4,958.1	5,423.2	5,390.8	5,743.1	5,473.4	27.1
Latvia		0.0	0.6	1.0	1.5	1.6	1.9	2.6	3.2	2.4	4.8
Lithuania		0.0	6.6	10.4	12.2	13.5	16.0	17.6	21.5	20.0	8.1
Macedonia		0.1	31.5	43.0	53.1	54.0	57.6	62.0	74.5	75.1	1.7
Moldova		0.0	1.8	2.5	4.8	6.2	8.9	10.7	12.8	14.5	1.3
Montenegro		0.4	0.2	0.2	0.4	0.5	0.6	0.8	0.9	0.9	1.3
Poland	0.2	10.5	63.0	129.8	162.7	177.8	193.7	211.0	236.1	247.3	79.2
Romania	0.0	0.0	1.0	14.1	40.3	50.2	57.4	66.6	87.1	89.0	29.2
Russia		0.1	272.5	1,102.5	2,847.5	3,590.7	4,589.2	5,745.2	7,191.0	7,867.3	247.7
Serbia			11.8	75.2	273.8	316.2	371.3	467.6	594.5	648.9	9.6
Slovakia		2.0	4.2	6.3	8.6	9.0	10.4	10.6	11.7	12.4	17.2
Slovenia		0.1	1.9	3.5	5.1	5.5	5.8	6.0	6.7	7.1	9.8
Ukraine		0.0	11.6	31.7	60.6	80.5	100.4	129.0	169.2	175.4	22.5

Source:*International Monetary Fund (IMF), International Financial Statistics*

Economic Statistics

Table 8.12

Private Consumption 1985-2009

Billion units of national currency

	1985	1990	1995	2000	2004	2005	2006	2007	2008	2009	Total US$ billion 2009
Western Europe											
Austria	60.4	76.9	96.9	113.8	127.7	133.8	139.1	143.8	148.2	149.0	207.1
Belgium	73.1	92.6	112.2	134.4	150.1	155.8	163.3	171.0	179.1	177.8	247.1
Cyprus	1.7	2.7	4.6	6.4	8.2	8.7	9.3	10.5	12.0	11.6	16.2
Denmark	346.0	423.2	521.8	616.7	707.2	745.1	786.6	821.7	845.5	817.6	152.5
Finland	30.3	45.6	50.0	65.3	78.0	81.1	85.8	90.7	95.4	94.0	130.7
France	436.2	589.8	676.3	803.3	940.0	981.5	1,026.1	1,074.2	1,110.8	1,112.8	1,546.4
Germany	639.1	817.5	1,067.2	1,214.2	1,303.1	1,325.4	1,357.8	1,378.9	1,413.2	1,411.1	1,960.8
Gibraltar	0.1	0.1	0.1	0.1	0.1	0.1	0.1	0.1	0.1	0.1	0.2
Greece	12.5	32.9	68.6	98.6	130.0	140.4	152.9	162.7	173.3	172.3	239.5
Iceland	77.2	218.1	258.2	414.5	530.3	609.4	679.9	751.6	789.5	774.6	6.3
Ireland	15.5	21.8	28.9	50.9	68.7	74.6	81.4	88.9	90.6	81.0	112.5
Italy	251.7	402.1	553.3	713.7	815.8	844.0	877.4	907.5	929.1	911.5	1,266.6
Liechtenstein	0.8	1.1	1.7	2.5	2.6	2.7	2.9	3.0	3.1	3.1	2.9
Luxembourg	3.5	4.8	6.5	9.0	10.2	10.7	11.3	11.8	12.7	12.7	17.6
Malta	0.9	1.3	1.9	2.6	3.0	3.2	3.3	3.4	3.6	3.6	5.1
Monaco	0.9	1.2	1.3	1.6	1.9	2.0	2.1	2.5	2.7	2.7	3.8
Netherlands	102.9	121.1	151.1	210.8	242.8	250.3	254.9	264.1	270.8	262.6	364.9
Norway	266.5	366.5	470.9	640.0	786.0	826.2	881.8	940.1	988.8	1,015.3	161.4
Portugal	15.5	35.5	57.3	81.0	95.6	99.8	104.7	110.6	115.7	111.9	155.5
Spain	109.0	188.1	268.4	376.0	487.1	525.1	564.6	604.4	622.0	596.4	828.8
Sweden	450.0	708.1	894.2	1,113.7	1,286.3	1,336.1	1,389.3	1,460.2	1,500.5	1,515.9	198.1
Switzerland	148.3	188.4	223.0	252.7	272.3	278.2	286.4	296.8	308.6	310.5	285.7
Turkey	0.0	0.3	5.5	117.5	398.6	465.4	534.8	601.2	663.9	683.3	439.3
United Kingdom	215.4	354.8	465.3	640.1	779.1	815.0	852.0	896.0	928.0	908.8	1,417.3
Eastern Europe											
Albania	9.9	12.2	203.1	400.4	585.7	635.7	681.7	776.8	874.4	921.3	9.7
Belarus		0.0	71.7	5,198.1	26,858.8	33,827.0	40,803.1	50,342.4	67,435.7	76,263.5	27.3
Bosnia-Herzegovina		0.0	3.1	10.0	15.1	16.7	18.2	20.0	21.4	20.2	14.4
Bulgaria	0.0	0.0	0.6	18.5	26.9	30.0	34.8	39.1	45.5	43.3	30.8
Croatia		0.2	78.0	111.0	151.7	163.4	174.0	190.3	203.7	191.2	36.2
Czech Republic		308.6	746.0	1,149.2	1,416.9	1,464.5	1,561.8	1,686.8	1,834.0	1,836.9	96.3
Estonia		0.5	23.6	53.5	85.4	97.1	115.4	135.2	140.6	113.7	10.1
Georgia		0.0	3.4	5.5	7.2	7.8	10.9	12.0	14.0	14.8	8.9
Hungary	594.6	1,135.2	3,126.7	7,073.2	11,358.3	12,174.7	12,800.2	13,644.0	14,331.8	13,846.2	68.4
Latvia		0.0	1.6	3.0	4.7	5.7	7.3	9.2	10.2	8.1	16.0
Lithuania		0.1	17.1	29.6	40.7	46.5	53.4	63.7	72.4	62.9	25.3
Macedonia		0.3	119.4	176.0	209.1	222.7	243.1	273.3	321.0	323.7	7.3
Moldova		0.0	3.6	14.0	28.5	35.2	42.0	50.0	58.6	53.3	4.8
Montenegro		1.3	0.7	0.7	1.2	1.3	1.7	2.2	2.5	2.4	3.3
Poland	0.6	27.2	203.8	477.4	598.1	623.4	662.3	711.9	785.1	824.7	264.2
Romania	0.0	0.1	4.9	55.4	170.8	200.9	237.5	278.4	333.7	308.3	101.1
Russia		0.3	744.1	3,374.3	8,554.0	10,728.2	13,040.5	16,192.7	20,226.3	21,317.8	671.2
Serbia			37.3	298.3	1,066.8	1,297.7	1,512.1	1,738.3	2,050.5	2,149.8	31.8
Slovakia		5.3	10.0	17.5	25.9	28.3	31.4	34.5	38.2	38.3	53.2
Slovenia		0.4	6.1	10.6	14.9	15.6	16.4	18.2	19.8	19.6	27.2
Ukraine		0.0	30.1	96.3	184.9	257.4	324.6	429.6	584.2	598.2	76.8

Source:International Monetary Fund (IMF), International Financial Statistics

Economic Statistics

Table 8.13

Government Finance and International Liquidity 2009

US$ million / as stated

	Budget Expenditure	Budget Revenue	Budget Surplus/ Deficit	Foreign Debt	Foreign Exchange Reserves	Gold Reserves (million troy oz)
Western Europe						
Austria	171,883.7	115,197.6	-56,686.2	209,530.1	4,781.4	9.0
Belgium	107,424.7	59,365.0	-48,059.7	280,908.6	7,800.9	7.3
Cyprus	9,660.2	7,308.8	-2,351.4	5,049.1	562.9	0.4
Denmark				51,668.6	71,259.0	2.1
Finland	66,215.9	54,294.5	-11,921.4	81,130.5	7,403.2	1.6
France	1,615,040.3	1,392,219.3	-222,821.0	1,131,892.0	27,728.7	78.3
Germany	523,866.1	469,692.2	-54,173.9	1,281,121.8	36,928.3	109.5
Gibraltar						
Greece	97,284.8	71,221.2	-26,063.6	310,816.2	198.8	3.6
Iceland	4,151.8	3,353.4	-798.5	5,324.4	3,638.7	0.1
Ireland	68,748.2	52,178.6	-16,569.6	97,998.6	516.7	0.2
Italy	1,064,812.3	970,496.0	-94,316.4	983,157.8	34,521.1	78.8
Liechtenstein						
Luxembourg	14,666.5	15,506.7	840.2	1,909,224.2	267.5	0.1
Malta	3,029.5	3,048.0	18.5		329.7	0.0
Monaco						
Netherlands	278,168.9	291,691.1	13,522.2	353,735.7	8,613.4	19.7
Norway	154,853.3	163,121.1	8,267.8	104,699.9	45,718.6	
Portugal	80,128.1	80,260.0	132.0	130,347.4	811.4	12.3
Spain	263,077.9	141,792.1	-121,285.8	352,540.4	12,786.8	9.1
Sweden	115,722.2	92,708.1	-23,014.1	51,214.5	38,543.0	4.0
Switzerland	52,823.9	47,321.9	-5,502.1	17,590.9	91,614.0	33.4
Turkey	124,272.3	71,691.4	-52,580.9	75,473.1	69,177.5	3.7
United Kingdom				345,258.5	38,026.0	10.0
Eastern Europe						
Albania	2,801.5	3,271.2	469.6	2,279.6	2,229.6	0.1
Belarus	10,925.8	11,569.0	643.2	22,060.6	4,253.0	0.7
Bosnia-Herzegovina					3,240.9	
Bulgaria	15,321.4	16,662.1	1,340.7	4,574.0	16,116.8	1.3
Croatia	21,669.5	20,677.2	-992.2	5,763.7	14,419.0	
Czech Republic	52,458.6	53,035.5	576.9	20,951.7	39,669.8	0.4
Estonia				987.7	3,874.7	0.0
Georgia	3,230.8	3,151.5	-79.3	3,412.5	1,891.6	
Hungary	46,453.5	41,899.8	-4,553.6	50,367.1	42,479.0	0.1
Latvia	9,420.0	7,758.6	-1,661.4	7,763.2	6,445.0	0.2
Lithuania	13,756.8	11,236.0	-2,520.8	6,130.9	6,237.9	0.2
Macedonia				1,587.0	1,959.9	0.2
Moldova	1,444.4	1,593.2	148.8		1,476.7	
Montenegro				1,340.8		
Poland	146,478.9	125,854.4	-20,624.5	55,364.1	73,393.6	3.3
Romania	54,544.2	51,179.5	-3,364.7	10,965.6	39,344.3	3.3
Russia	253,130.7	230,770.3	-22,360.4	28,592.8	405,825.0	20.9
Serbia				8,019.4	14,749.9	0.4
Slovakia	30,374.4	28,932.4	-1,442.0	11,564.1	50.4	1.0
Slovenia	20,644.7	17,756.0	-2,888.7	7,872.1	589.5	0.1
Ukraine	33,294.0	32,126.4	-1,167.6	108,350.0	25,493.3	0.9

Source: *Euromonitor International from industry sources/national statistics*

Economic Statistics

Table 8.14

Government Expenditure by Object 2009

US$ million

	General Public Services	Defence	Education	Health	Social Security & Welfare	Housing/ Amenities	Other Community/ Social	Economic Services	Other
Western Europe									
Austria	20,804	3,150	12,716	24,456	79,810	2,512	1,016	10,666	5,187
Belgium	66,601	4,712	5,595	34,128	86,904	1	335	7,462	5,054
Cyprus	2,686	399	1,741	664	2,156	463	254	928	499
Denmark	48,193	4,829	12,973	139	37,642	929	2,303	6,473	3,729
Finland	11,990	3,490	8,902	9,622	48,826	488	1,034	8,000	2,985
France	169,264	45,073	110,147	191,543	576,198	8,945	11,258	79,817	25,937
Germany	117,574	34,230	6,820	196,482	671,602	7,150	2,829	68,340	7,803
Gibraltar									
Greece	23,156	7,131	9,678	16,495	62,999	637	848	38,788	4,570
Iceland	572	8	365	844	711	16	147	446	195
Ireland	9,147	1,145	11,423	16,838	24,484	2,563	1,038	10,505	3,380
Italy	179,095	27,949	78,162	75,693	502,434	11,747	9,271	49,013	38,030
Liechtenstein									
Luxembourg	2,410	113	1,836	2,150	11,344	186	625	1,556	611
Malta	492	52	413	493	1,145	60	38	284	259
Monaco									
Netherlands	65,290	10,271	33,970	47,427	144,486	890	2,275	22,049	15,242
Norway	21,771	6,234	6,890	21,064	51,276	144	1,677	11,329	3,330
Portugal	26,081	2,190	10,065	13,698	41,403	207	840	5,194	3,211
Spain	137,973	14,180	1,892	5,739	167,801	453	5,120	32,072	16,454
Sweden	36,766	7,161	8,622	6,292	73,764	487	1,549	15,583	6,272
Switzerland	16,749	3,754	4,053	147	48,943	501	369	10,834	404
Turkey	107,052	6,758	5,897	4,271	6,035	4,212	637	2,452	3,696
United Kingdom	158,737	59,794	124,887	177,546	324,865	11,734	13,156	113,133	55,768
Eastern Europe									
Albania	245	131	362	157	509	120	27	298	56
Belarus	4,089	492	333	346	4,864	2	108	4,519	946
Bosnia-Herzegovina									
Bulgaria	7,705	469	650	673	5,657	218	156	1,595	1,565
Croatia	2,908	685	2,121	3,395	9,394	709	396	2,124	1,675
Czech Republic	7,588	1,916	6,449	12,700	21,475	1,089	823	8,402	3,693
Estonia	922	258	514	1,122	1,854	10	216	762	589
Georgia	137	1,332	292	144	427	2	69	43	558
Hungary	11,312	1,630	4,846	9,461	26,009	34	1,094	9,632	3,194
Latvia	500	472	1,045	981	1,811	140	422	1,611	1,018
Lithuania	2,089	843	802	2,632	4,712	13	292	1,442	600
Macedonia									
Moldova	497	31	135	304	569	11	32	327	98
Montenegro									
Poland	21,626	9,010	23,116	22,480	84,089	783	1,702	17,312	8,901
Romania	5,932	4,899	4,615	11,918	17,348	1,303	1,198	10,392	5,599
Russia	87,545	40,581	17,472	32,601	69,651	9,652	3,714	9,233	34,321
Serbia									
Slovakia	2,171	1,260	1,745	5,749	7,331	335	235	4,335	1,833
Slovenia	2,498	694	2,200	4,006	8,787	113	290	1,675	987
Ukraine	9,790	1,520	2,272	1,246	16,541	314	406	4,988	2,828

Source:*Euromonitor International/International Monetary Fund (IMF), Government Finance Statistics/national statistics*

Economic Statistics

Table 8.15

Government Expenditure by Object 2009 (% Analysis)

% of total expenditure

	General Public Services	Defence	Education	Health	Social Security & Welfare	Housing/ Amenities	Other Community/ Social	Economic Services	Other
Western Europe									
Austria	12.98	1.97	7.93	15.25	49.78	1.57	0.63	6.65	3.24
Belgium	31.60	2.24	2.65	16.19	41.23	0.00	0.16	3.54	2.40
Cyprus	27.43	4.07	17.78	6.78	22.03	4.73	2.60	9.48	5.10
Denmark	41.12	4.12	11.07	0.12	32.11	0.79	1.97	5.52	3.18
Finland	12.58	3.66	9.34	10.09	51.21	0.51	1.08	8.39	3.13
France	13.89	3.70	9.04	15.72	47.30	0.73	0.92	6.55	2.13
Germany	10.57	3.08	0.61	17.66	60.35	0.64	0.25	6.14	0.70
Gibraltar									
Greece	14.09	4.34	5.89	10.04	38.34	0.39	0.52	23.61	2.78
Iceland	17.32	0.24	11.06	25.54	21.52	0.49	4.44	13.49	5.91
Ireland	11.36	1.42	14.19	20.91	30.41	3.18	1.29	13.05	4.20
Italy	18.44	2.88	8.05	7.79	51.72	1.21	0.95	5.05	3.92
Liechtenstein									
Luxembourg	11.57	0.54	8.82	10.32	54.45	0.90	3.00	7.47	2.93
Malta	15.21	1.60	12.76	15.23	35.40	1.84	1.16	8.78	8.02
Monaco									
Netherlands	19.10	3.00	9.94	13.87	42.26	0.26	0.67	6.45	4.46
Norway	17.60	5.04	5.57	17.03	41.45	0.12	1.36	9.16	2.69
Portugal	25.35	2.13	9.78	13.31	40.24	0.20	0.82	5.05	3.12
Spain	36.15	3.72	0.50	1.50	43.96	0.12	1.34	8.40	4.31
Sweden	23.49	4.58	5.51	4.02	47.13	0.31	0.99	9.96	4.01
Switzerland	19.53	4.38	4.73	0.17	57.07	0.58	0.43	12.63	0.47
Turkey	75.92	4.79	4.18	3.03	4.28	2.99	0.45	1.74	2.62
United Kingdom	15.27	5.75	12.01	17.08	31.25	1.13	1.27	10.88	5.36
Eastern Europe									
Albania	12.86	6.85	19.02	8.24	26.73	6.29	1.41	15.66	2.95
Belarus	26.05	3.13	2.12	2.20	30.99	0.01	0.69	28.79	6.02
Bosnia-Herzegovina									
Bulgaria	41.23	2.51	3.48	3.60	30.27	1.17	0.83	8.54	8.38
Croatia	12.42	2.93	9.06	14.50	40.13	3.03	1.69	9.07	7.16
Czech Republic	11.83	2.99	10.06	19.80	33.48	1.70	1.28	13.10	5.76
Estonia	14.76	4.14	8.23	17.96	29.67	0.16	3.46	12.20	9.43
Georgia	4.57	44.34	9.71	4.78	14.22	0.08	2.29	1.43	18.59
Hungary	16.83	2.43	7.21	14.08	38.70	0.05	1.63	14.33	4.75
Latvia	6.25	5.90	13.07	12.27	22.64	1.75	5.27	20.14	12.72
Lithuania	15.56	6.28	5.98	19.60	35.10	0.10	2.18	10.74	4.47
Macedonia									
Moldova	24.80	1.55	6.73	15.16	28.39	0.53	1.62	16.31	4.91
Montenegro									
Poland	11.44	4.77	12.23	11.89	44.49	0.41	0.90	9.16	4.71
Romania	9.39	7.75	7.30	18.86	27.45	2.06	1.90	16.44	8.86
Russia	28.73	13.32	5.73	10.70	22.85	3.17	1.22	3.03	11.26
Serbia									
Slovakia	8.69	5.04	6.98	23.00	29.33	1.34	0.94	17.35	7.33
Slovenia	11.76	3.27	10.35	18.85	41.35	0.53	1.36	7.88	4.65
Ukraine	24.53	3.81	5.69	3.12	41.45	0.79	1.02	12.50	7.09

Source:*Euromonitor International/International Monetary Fund (IMF), Government Finance Statistics/national statistics*

Economic Statistics

Table 8.16

Current Account Balance 1998-2009

US$ million / as stated

	1998	1999	2000	2001	2002	2003	2004	2005	2006	2007	2008	2009	Current account balance as % of total GDP 2009
Western Europe													
Austria	-3,396	-3,451	-1,334	-1,513	5,472	4,192	6,451	6,724	9,044	13,190	13,434	8,730	2.3
Belgium	13,255	20,070	9,356	7,889	11,574	12,927	12,447	9,993	8,028	6,868	-14,295	1,400	0.3
Cyprus	292	-170	-489	-316	-393	-297	-788	-995	-1,283	-2,565	-4,484	-2,206	-9.4
Denmark	-1,485	3,328	2,507	4,145	4,997	7,338	5,702	11,033	8,224	4,767	7,547	12,762	4.1
Finland	7,292	7,763	9,355	10,436	11,631	8,050	11,962	6,395	8,837	10,615	8,159	3,455	1.5
France	38,554	45,891	19,704	23,545	18,210	12,872	11,141	-10,335	-13,153	-26,638	-54,566	-52,150	-2.0
Germany	-16,330	-26,858	-32,241	277	41,286	47,311	128,051	142,505	189,194	254,775	246,025	168,066	5.0
Gibraltar													
Greece	-3,682	-7,295	-9,973	-9,520	-10,051	-12,829	-13,543	-18,377	-29,719	-44,928	-50,914	-37,060	-11.2
Iceland	-561	-593	-883	-342	139	-523	-1,302	-2,625	-4,259	-3,327	-2,651	460	3.8
Ireland	704	241	-356	-692	-1,106	74	-1,079	-7,134	-7,865	-13,837	-15,286	-6,485	-2.9
Italy	19,791	8,208	-5,714	-769	-9,336	-19,509	-16,734	-29,906	-47,871	-51,686	-82,181	-68,115	-3.2
Liechtenstein													
Luxembourg	1,648	2,272	2,688	1,770	2,386	2,378	4,046	4,141	4,415	4,985	3,091	2,967	5.7
Malta	-229	-136	-488	-148	104	-156	-335	-523	-595	-466	-453	-310	-3.9
Monaco													
Netherlands	12,970	15,643	7,269	9,810	11,036	29,903	46,130	46,235	60,627	64,572	40,577	39,572	5.0
Norway	-475	8,916	25,097	27,542	24,263	27,708	33,007	49,010	58,479	55,470	83,871	41,132	10.9
Portugal	-8,372	-10,311	-12,160	-12,427	-10,870	-10,472	-15,518	-19,835	-21,541	-23,549	-31,798	-23,993	-10.3
Spain	-7,074	-18,100	-23,186	-24,064	-22,245	-30,890	-54,860	-83,387	-110,875	-144,539	-156,277	-78,692	-5.4
Sweden	9,672	10,588	10,165	11,347	11,619	22,334	23,970	25,416	31,215	38,178	45,942	29,966	7.4
Switzerland	26,090	29,378	30,129	20,937	24,892	43,431	48,601	52,327	59,523	38,863	10,125	41,453	8.4
Turkey	2,152	-925	-9,920	3,760	-626	-7,515	-14,431	-22,198	-32,193	-38,311	-41,946	-13,959	-2.3
United Kingdom	-5,266	-35,365	-38,844	-30,347	-27,892	-29,995	-45,523	-59,251	-81,109	-75,239	-40,015	-28,838	-1.3
Eastern Europe													
Albania	-89	77	-134	-125	-318	-286	-292	-498	-508	-1,109	-1,975	-1,709	-14.4
Belarus	-1,017	-194	-338	-401	-334	-426	-1,193	435	-1,448	-3,032	-5,209	-6,326	-12.9
Bosnia-Herzegovina	-420	-502	-397	-746	-1,183	-1,627	-1,639	-1,938	-1,025	-1,920	-2,765	-1,283	-6.6
Bulgaria	-62	-652	-711	-767	-373	-1,108	-1,672	-3,343	-5,858	-10,707	-11,906	-4,335	-9.2
Croatia	-1,472	-1,536	-533	-729	-1,926	-2,162	-1,875	-2,555	-3,313	-4,445	-6,251	-3,247	-5.2
Czech Republic	-1,308	-1,464	-2,687	-3,274	-4,266	-5,810	-5,757	-1,569	-3,533	-5,734	-1,277	-2,208	-1.2
Estonia	-478	-247	-297	-326	-779	-1,117	-1,370	-1,388	-2,585	-3,722	-2,347	897	4.7
Georgia	-462	-281	-239	-205	-216	-383	-354	-710	-1,175	-2,009	-2,915	-1,312	-12.2
Hungary	-3,400	-3,762	-4,002	-3,203	-4,692	-6,721	-8,476	-7,936	-8,056	-9,037	-10,863	376	0.3
Latvia	-595	-654	-371	-626	-624	-920	-1,762	-1,992	-4,522	-6,424	-4,484	2,532	9.8
Lithuania	-1,298	-1,194	-675	-574	-733	-1,279	-1,722	-1,839	-3,220	-5,697	-5,788	1,492	4.0
Macedonia	-311	-98	-68	-248	-356	-190	-451	-151	-56	-569	-1,253	-673	-7.3
Moldova	-335	-68	-98	-27	-20	-130	-46	-226	-389	-674	-987	-428	-7.9
Montenegro						-114	-149	-192	-650	-1,450	-2,382	-1,119	-27.4
Poland	-6,901	-12,487	-10,352	-5,946	-5,525	-5,502	-10,046	-3,713	-9,399	-20,260	-26,846	-7,371	-1.7
Romania	-2,892	-1,446	-1,355	-2,229	-1,525	-3,311	-6,382	-8,435	-12,943	-23,268	-24,002	-7,298	-4.5
Russia	219	24,616	46,839	33,935	29,116	35,410	59,513	84,602	94,686	77,768	103,661	49,519	4.0
Serbia	-469	-455	-153	-285	-1,247	-1,420	-2,871	-2,194	-2,986	-6,287	-8,646	-2,429	-5.7
Slovakia	-1,983	-983	-667	-1,743	-1,953	-1,977	-3,299	-4,002	-4,418	-4,103	-6,262	-2,827	-3.2
Slovenia	-156	-878	-548	37	244	-215	-892	-620	-997	-2,243	-3,624	-733	-1.5
Ukraine	-1,296	1,658	1,481	1,402	3,173	2,891	6,909	2,531	-1,617	-5,272	-12,763	-1,801	-1.6

Source:Euromonitor International from International Monetary Fund (IMF), International Financial Statistics

Economic Statistics

Table 8.17

Corruption Perception Index 1998-2009

Score

	1998	1999	2000	2001	2002	2003	2004	2005	2006	2007	2008	2009
Western Europe												
Austria	7.5	7.6	7.7	7.8	7.8	8.0	8.4	8.7	8.6	8.1	8.1	7.9
Belgium	5.4	5.3	6.1	6.6	7.1	7.6	7.5	7.4	7.3	7.1	7.3	7.1
Cyprus						6.1	5.4	5.7	5.6	5.3	6.4	6.6
Denmark	10.0	10.0	9.8	9.5	9.5	9.5	9.5	9.5	9.5	9.4	9.3	9.3
Finland	9.6	9.8	10.0	9.9	9.7	9.7	9.7	9.6	9.6	9.4	9.0	8.9
France	6.7	6.6	6.7	6.7	6.3	6.9	7.1	7.5	7.4	7.3	6.9	6.9
Germany	7.9	8.0	7.6	7.4	7.3	7.7	8.2	8.2	8.0	7.8	7.9	8.0
Gibraltar												
Greece	4.9	4.9	4.9	4.2	4.2	4.3	4.3	4.3	4.4	4.6	4.7	3.8
Iceland	9.3	9.2	9.1	9.2	9.4	9.6	9.5	9.7	9.6	9.2	8.9	8.7
Ireland	8.2	7.7	7.2	7.5	6.9	7.5	7.5	7.4	7.4	7.5	7.7	8.0
Italy	4.6	4.7	4.6	5.5	5.2	5.3	4.8	5.0	4.9	5.2	4.8	4.3
Liechtenstein												
Luxembourg	8.7	8.8	8.6	8.7	9.0	8.7	8.4	8.5	8.6	8.4	8.3	8.2
Malta							6.8	6.6	6.4	5.8	5.8	5.2
Monaco												
Netherlands	9.0	9.0	8.9	8.8	9.0	8.9	8.7	8.6	8.7	9.0	8.9	8.9
Norway	9.0	8.9	9.1	8.6	8.5	8.8	8.9	8.9	8.8	8.7	7.9	8.6
Portugal	6.5	6.7	6.4	6.3	6.3	6.6	6.3	6.5	6.6	6.5	6.1	5.8
Spain	6.1	6.6	7.0	7.0	7.1	6.9	7.1	7.0	6.8	6.7	6.5	6.1
Sweden	9.5	9.4	9.4	9.0	9.3	9.3	9.2	9.2	9.2	9.3	9.3	9.2
Switzerland	8.9	8.9	8.6	8.4	8.5	8.8	9.1	9.1	9.1	9.0	9.0	9.0
Turkey	3.4	3.6	3.8	3.6	3.2	3.1	3.2	3.5	3.8	4.1	4.6	4.4
United Kingdom	8.7	8.6	8.7	8.3	8.7	8.7	8.6	8.6	8.6	8.4	7.7	7.7
Eastern Europe												
Albania		2.3			2.5	2.5	2.5	2.4	2.6	2.9	3.4	3.2
Belarus	3.9	3.4	4.1		4.8	4.2	3.3	2.6	2.1	2.1	2.0	2.4
Bosnia-Herzegovina						3.3	3.1	2.9	2.9	3.3	3.2	3.0
Bulgaria	2.9	3.3	3.5	3.9	4.0	3.9	4.1	4.0	4.0	4.1	3.6	3.8
Croatia		2.7	3.7	3.9	3.8	3.7	3.5	3.4	3.4	4.1	4.4	4.1
Czech Republic	4.8	4.6	4.3	3.9	3.7	3.9	4.2	4.3	4.8	5.2	5.2	4.9
Estonia	5.7	5.7	5.7	5.6	5.6	5.5	6.0	6.4	6.7	6.5	6.6	6.6
Georgia		2.3			2.4	1.8	2.0	2.3	2.8	3.4	3.9	4.1
Hungary	5.0	5.2	5.2	5.3	4.9	4.8	4.8	5.0	5.2	5.3	5.1	5.1
Latvia	2.7	3.4	3.4	3.4	3.7	3.8	4.0	4.2	4.7	4.8	5.0	4.5
Lithuania		3.8	4.1	4.8	4.8	4.7	4.6	4.8	4.8	4.8	4.6	4.9
Macedonia		3.3				2.3	2.7	2.7	2.7	3.3	3.6	3.8
Moldova		2.6	2.6	3.1	2.1	2.4	2.3	2.9	3.2	2.8	2.9	3.3
Montenegro										3.3	3.4	3.9
Poland	4.6	4.2	4.1	4.1	4.0	3.6	3.5	3.4	3.7	4.2	4.6	5.0
Romania	3.0	3.3	2.9	2.8	2.6	2.8	2.9	3.0	3.1	3.7	3.8	3.8
Russia	2.4	2.4	2.1	2.3	2.7	2.7	2.8	2.4	2.5	2.3	2.1	2.2
Serbia	3.0	2.0	1.3			2.3	2.7	2.8	3.0	3.4	3.4	3.5
Slovakia	3.9	3.7	3.5	3.7	3.7	3.7	4.0	4.3	4.7	4.9	5.0	4.5
Slovenia		6.0	5.5	5.2	6.0	5.9	6.0	6.1	6.4	6.6	6.7	6.6
Ukraine	2.8	2.6	1.5	2.1	2.4	2.3	2.2	2.6	2.8	2.7	2.5	2.2

Source: International Monetary Fund (IMF), International Financial Statistics

Economic Statistics

Table 8.18

Minimum Wage (Monthly) 1998-2008

US$ per month

	1998	1999	2000	2001	2002	2003	2004	2005	2006	2007	2008	2009
Western Europe												
Austria												
Belgium	1,204.1	1,167.8	1,030.3	1,020.3	1,095.5	1,338.9	1,473.1	1,503.8	1,548.1	1,756.0	1,954.9	1,928.1
Cyprus												
Denmark												
Finland												
France	1,150.3	1,117.7	996.1	970.6	1,030.1	1,256.7	1,445.7	1,513.6	1,573.6	1,751.9	1,933.2	1,835.7
Germany												
Gibraltar												
Greece	472.1	538.1	492.1	494.1	548.2	683.0	783.5	829.8	837.7	900.5	996.6	974.1
Iceland												
Ireland			870.8	903.1	950.4	1,211.3	1,469.3	1,607.0	1,622.1	2,001.0	2,139.6	2,031.6
Italy												
Liechtenstein												
Luxembourg	1,285.9	1,269.0	1,125.2	1,154.6	1,245.3	1,545.5	1,742.6	1,823.2	1,886.1	2,148.8	2,355.5	2,281.3
Malta		514.9	467.3	483.6	506.8	606.2	681.9	699.7	727.6	800.3	895.6	875.4
Monaco												
Netherlands	1,158.1	1,133.7	1,006.3	1,056.1	1,160.5	1,428.1	1,571.2	1,572.2	1,612.1	1,802.5	1,985.9	1,920.4
Norway												
Portugal	384.5	380.4	341.9	349.1	382.4	469.6	529.1	543.1	564.8	643.3	727.3	729.5
Spain	458.4	443.3	391.6	387.5	486.0	593.8	711.7	744.5	791.6	911.5	1,024.4	1,011.6
Sweden												
Switzerland												
Turkey	176.4	223.5	190.0	137.0	166.5	203.9	311.6	363.2	369.6	448.0	489.5	428.2
United Kingdom		983.7	945.6	997.6	1,038.6	1,159.2	1,393.3	1,512.7	1,586.1	1,832.8	1,670.6	1,425.1
Eastern Europe												
Albania												
Belarus			4.1	2.6	9.5	21.9	40.3	54.8	73.2	83.4	97.7	82.1
Bosnia-Herzegovina												
Bulgaria		34.9	35.3	39.8	48.1	63.5	76.2	95.3	102.6	126.0	164.5	170.6
Croatia	215.3	210.9	205.4	203.8	228.7	277.2	323.4	349.8	371.7	428.4	494.7	532.6
Czech Republic	82.1	104.1	110.1	131.5	174.1	219.8	260.7	299.9	352.1	394.2	468.6	419.6
Estonia		85.1	82.7	91.5	111.4	155.9	196.9	213.8	240.7	314.9	406.8	386.4
Georgia		9.9	10.1	9.6	9.1	9.3	10.4	11.0	11.2	12.0	13.4	
Hungary	91.0	94.9	90.4	139.6	193.9	222.9	261.4	285.6	297.1	356.7	400.9	353.4
Latvia		85.4	82.4	95.6	97.1	122.5	148.1	141.7	160.6	233.6	332.8	356.7
Lithuania		107.5	107.5	107.5	116.9	140.5	179.8	198.3	218.0	277.4	339.4	322.1
Macedonia												
Moldova											38.5	69.0
Montenegro												
Poland	142.7	163.8	161.1	185.6	186.3	205.7	225.3	262.4	289.7	338.2	467.2	360.8
Romania		29.3	32.2	48.2	52.9	75.3	85.8	106.4	117.5	160.0	198.5	196.8
Russia		3.4	4.7	15.4	14.4	19.5	25.0	28.3	40.5	43.0	80.5	136.3
Serbia												
Slovakia	3,363.3	3,835.8	3,686.1	4,403.6	5,246.7	200.9	241.0	258.5	277.3	332.6	379.0	411.3
Slovenia	375.6	373.8	343.5	346.6	423.9	501.2	578.8	610.2	641.8	714.2	829.1	818.5
Ukraine		17.8	21.7	22.0	26.3	30.9	49.3	64.4	79.2	91.1	97.8	80.2

Source: International Monetary Fund (IMF), International Financial Statistics

Economic Statistics

Table 8.19

Foreign Direct Investment Intensity 1998-2009
% of total GDP

	1998	1999	2000	2001	2002	2003	2004	2005	2006	2007	2008	2009
Western Europe												
Austria	2.1	1.4	4.6	3.1	0.2	2.8	1.3	3.6	2.5	8.4	2.7	1.8
Belgium					6.4	10.8	12.1	9.1	14.8	25.8	21.8	7.2
Cyprus	3.6	8.4	9.2	9.8	10.0	6.7	6.9	7.0	10.1	10.2	15.9	24.6
Denmark	4.3	9.6	21.1	7.2	3.8	1.3	-4.3	5.0	1.0	3.8	0.8	2.5
Finland	9.3	3.5	7.3	3.0	6.0	2.0	1.5	2.4	3.7	5.0	-0.7	1.1
France	2.1	3.2	3.3	3.8	3.4	2.4	1.6	4.0	3.2	3.7	2.2	2.2
Germany	1.1	2.6	10.4	1.4	2.7	1.3	-0.4	1.7	1.9	2.3	0.7	1.1
Gibraltar	-25.5	19.9	21.2	1.9	11.6	7.5	17.7	11.9	13.1	14.2	14.3	18.3
Greece	0.1	0.4	0.9	1.2	0.0	0.7	0.9	0.3	2.0	0.7	1.3	1.0
Iceland	1.8	0.8	2.0	2.3	1.0	2.9	4.9	14.3	23.1	33.4	5.5	-0.7
Ireland	10.1	18.9	26.7	9.2	23.9	14.4	-5.7	-15.7	-2.5	9.5	-7.5	11.0
Italy	0.3	0.6	1.2	1.3	1.2	1.1	1.0	1.1	2.1	1.9	0.7	1.4
Liechtenstein												
Luxembourg	116.2	564.9	437.7	436.6	18.0	10.0	15.2	15.9	74.2	-56.8	16.1	52.1
Malta	7.2	22.4	15.9	6.5	-10.4	19.4	7.1	11.4	29.2	13.7	11.3	11.3
Monaco												
Netherlands	9.1	10.0	16.6	13.0	5.7	3.9	0.8	7.5	1.2	14.7	-0.9	3.4
Norway	2.6	4.3	4.2	1.2	0.4	1.5	1.0	1.8	1.9	1.5	1.8	1.8
Portugal	2.4	0.9	5.7	5.2	1.4	4.4	1.0	2.1	5.4	1.3	1.9	1.2
Spain	2.3	3.0	6.8	4.7	5.7	2.9	2.4	2.2	2.5	4.5	4.6	1.0
Sweden	7.8	23.6	9.5	4.8	4.9	1.6	3.0	2.7	6.8	5.9	6.9	2.7
Switzerland	3.3	4.4	7.7	3.5	2.3	5.1	0.3	-0.3	8.0	11.9	1.0	2.0
Turkey	0.3	0.3	0.4	1.7	0.5	0.6	0.7	2.1	3.8	3.4	2.5	1.2
United Kingdom	5.1	5.9	8.0	3.6	1.5	0.9	2.5	7.7	6.4	6.6	3.4	2.1
Eastern Europe												
Albania	1.7	1.2	4.0	5.1	3.0	3.1	4.7	3.2	3.6	6.2	7.6	8.3
Belarus	1.3	3.7	1.0	0.8	1.7	1.0	0.7	1.0	1.0	3.9	3.6	3.8
Bosnia-Herzegovina	1.6	3.6	2.9	2.2	4.3	4.6	6.6	5.3	5.6	12.0	5.1	2.6
Bulgaria	4.2	6.3	8.1	5.9	5.9	10.5	13.8	14.4	24.7	31.3	19.6	9.5
Croatia	3.7	6.3	4.9	5.7	4.0	5.9	2.9	4.1	7.1	8.6	8.9	4.1
Czech Republic	6.0	10.5	8.8	9.1	11.3	2.3	4.5	9.4	3.8	6.0	3.0	1.4
Estonia	10.3	5.3	6.9	8.6	3.9	9.4	8.0	20.6	10.8	12.7	7.3	8.8
Georgia	7.3	2.9	4.3	3.4	4.7	8.4	9.6	7.1	15.1	17.2	12.2	7.1
Hungary	6.8	6.7	5.8	7.4	4.5	2.5	4.4	7.0	17.5	51.7	40.2	-4.3
Latvia	5.3	4.8	5.3	1.6	2.7	2.7	4.6	4.4	8.3	8.1	3.7	0.3
Lithuania	8.3	4.5	3.3	3.7	5.1	1.0	3.4	4.0	6.0	5.2	3.9	0.9
Macedonia	4.2	2.4	6.0	13.0	2.8	2.5	6.0	1.7	6.7	8.8	6.2	2.7
Moldova	4.4	3.2	9.9	7.0	5.1	3.7	5.6	6.4	6.8	12.2	11.7	1.6
Montenegro											20.3	32.1
Poland	3.7	4.3	5.5	3.0	2.1	2.1	5.1	3.4	5.7	5.5	2.8	2.6
Romania	4.8	2.9	2.8	2.9	2.5	3.7	8.5	6.5	9.3	5.8	6.8	3.9
Russia	1.0	1.7	1.0	0.9	1.0	1.8	2.6	1.7	3.0	4.2	4.5	3.1
Serbia	0.7	1.0	0.6	1.6	3.8	7.1	4.3	8.1	14.7	8.6	6.1	4.5
Slovakia	2.5	1.4	6.7	5.2	12.0	4.7	5.4	4.0	6.8	4.3	3.5	-0.1
Slovenia	1.3	0.6	0.8	2.0	7.6	1.1	2.5	1.6	1.7	3.2	3.5	-0.1
Ukraine	1.8	1.6	1.9	2.1	1.6	2.8	2.6	9.1	5.2	6.9	6.1	4.2

Source:Euromonitor International from national statistics

Economic Statistics

Table 8.20

Exchange Rates Against the US$ 1985-2009

Units of national currency per US$

	1985	1990	1995	2000	2004	2005	2006	2007	2008	2009
Western Europe										
Austria	1.31	0.79	0.76	1.09	0.81	0.80	0.80	0.73	0.68	0.72
Belgium	1.31	0.79	0.76	1.09	0.81	0.80	0.80	0.73	0.68	0.72
Cyprus	1.31	0.79	0.76	1.09	0.81	0.80	0.80	0.73	0.68	0.72
Denmark	10.60	6.19	5.60	8.09	5.99	6.00	5.94	5.44	5.10	5.36
Finland	1.31	0.79	0.76	1.09	0.81	0.80	0.80	0.73	0.68	0.72
France	1.31	0.79	0.76	1.09	0.81	0.80	0.80	0.73	0.68	0.72
Germany	1.31	0.79	0.76	1.09	0.81	0.80	0.80	0.73	0.68	0.72
Gibraltar	0.78	0.56	0.63	0.66	0.55	0.55	0.54	0.50	0.54	0.64
Greece	1.31	0.79	0.76	1.09	0.81	0.80	0.80	0.73	0.68	0.72
Iceland	41.51	58.28	64.69	78.62	70.19	62.98	70.18	64.06	87.95	123.64
Ireland	1.31	0.79	0.76	1.09	0.81	0.80	0.80	0.73	0.68	0.72
Italy	1.31	0.79	0.76	1.09	0.81	0.80	0.80	0.73	0.68	0.72
Liechtenstein	2.46	1.39	1.18	1.69	1.24	1.25	1.25	1.20	1.08	1.09
Luxembourg	1.31	0.79	0.76	1.09	0.81	0.80	0.80	0.73	0.68	0.72
Malta	1.31	0.79	0.76	1.09	0.81	0.80	0.80	0.73	0.68	0.72
Monaco	1.31	0.79	0.76	1.09	0.81	0.80	0.80	0.73	0.68	0.72
Netherlands	1.31	0.79	0.76	1.09	0.81	0.80	0.80	0.73	0.68	0.72
Norway	8.60	6.26	6.34	8.80	6.74	6.44	6.41	5.86	5.64	6.29
Portugal	1.31	0.79	0.76	1.09	0.81	0.80	0.80	0.73	0.68	0.72
Spain	1.31	0.79	0.76	1.09	0.81	0.80	0.80	0.73	0.68	0.72
Sweden	8.60	5.92	7.13	9.16	7.35	7.47	7.38	6.76	6.59	7.65
Switzerland	2.46	1.39	1.18	1.69	1.24	1.25	1.25	1.20	1.08	1.09
Turkey	0.00	0.00	0.05	0.63	1.43	1.35	1.44	1.31	1.30	1.56
United Kingdom	0.78	0.56	0.63	0.66	0.55	0.55	0.54	0.50	0.54	0.64
Eastern Europe										
Albania	7.00	7.75	92.70	143.71	102.78	99.87	98.10	90.43	83.89	94.98
Belarus		0.00	8.77	876.75	2,160.26	2,153.82	2,144.56	2,146.08	2,136.40	2,789.49
Bosnia-Herzegovina		0.00	1.40	2.12	1.58	1.57	1.56	1.43	1.34	1.41
Bulgaria	0.00	0.00	0.07	2.12	1.58	1.57	1.56	1.43	1.34	1.41
Croatia		0.01	5.23	8.28	6.03	5.95	5.84	5.36	4.94	5.28
Czech Republic		17.95	26.54	38.60	25.70	23.96	22.60	20.29	17.07	19.07
Estonia		0.14	9.88	16.97	12.60	12.58	12.47	11.43	10.69	11.26
Georgia		0.00	1.37	1.98	1.92	1.81	1.78	1.67	1.49	1.67
Hungary	50.12	63.21	125.68	282.18	202.75	199.58	210.39	183.63	172.11	202.34
Latvia		0.01	0.53	0.61	0.54	0.56	0.56	0.51	0.48	0.50
Lithuania		0.01	4.00	4.00	2.78	2.77	2.75	2.52	2.36	2.48
Macedonia		0.11	37.88	65.90	49.41	49.28	48.80	44.73	41.87	44.10
Moldova		0.00	3.67	12.43	12.33	12.60	13.13	12.14	10.39	11.11
Montenegro	1.31	0.79	0.76	1.09	0.81	0.80	0.80	0.73	0.68	0.72
Poland	0.01	0.95	2.42	4.35	3.66	3.24	3.10	2.77	2.41	3.12
Romania	0.00	0.00	0.20	2.17	3.26	2.91	2.81	2.44	2.52	3.05
Russia		0.00	3.58	28.13	28.81	28.28	27.19	25.58	24.85	31.76
Serbia		0.00	2.93	44.02	58.38	66.71	67.15	58.45	55.72	67.58
Slovakia	1.31	0.79	0.76	1.09	0.81	0.80	0.80	0.73	0.68	0.72
Slovenia	1.31	0.79	0.76	1.09	0.81	0.80	0.80	0.73	0.68	0.72
Ukraine		0.00	1.12	5.44	5.32	5.12	5.05	5.05	5.27	7.79

Source: *International Monetary Fund (IMF)/Euromonitor International research*
Notes: *Annual average market exchange rates*

Economic Statistics

Table 8.21

Exchange Rates Against the EUR 1985-2009

Units of national currency per EUR

	1985	1990	1995	2000	2004	2005	2006	2007	2008	2009
Western Europe										
Austria	1.00	1.00	1.00	1.00	1.00	1.00	1.00	1.00	1.00	1.00
Belgium	1.00	1.00	1.00	1.00	1.00	1.00	1.00	1.00	1.00	1.00
Cyprus	1.00	1.00	1.00	1.00	1.00	1.00	1.00	1.00	1.00	1.00
Denmark	8.09	7.88	7.33	7.45	7.44	7.45	7.46	7.45	7.46	7.45
Finland	1.00	1.00	1.00	1.00	1.00	1.00	1.00	1.00	1.00	1.00
France	1.00	1.00	1.00	1.00	1.00	1.00	1.00	1.00	1.00	1.00
Germany	1.00	1.00	1.00	1.00	1.00	1.00	1.00	1.00	1.00	1.00
Gibraltar	0.59	0.72	0.83	0.61	0.68	0.68	0.68	0.68	0.80	0.89
Greece	1.00	1.00	1.00	1.00	1.00	1.00	1.00	1.00	1.00	1.00
Iceland	31.67	74.22	84.62	72.45	87.18	78.28	88.04	87.67	128.71	171.81
Ireland	1.00	1.00	1.00	1.00	1.00	1.00	1.00	1.00	1.00	1.00
Italy	1.00	1.00	1.00	1.00	1.00	1.00	1.00	1.00	1.00	1.00
Liechtenstein	1.88	1.77	1.55	1.56	1.54	1.55	1.57	1.64	1.58	1.51
Luxembourg	1.00	1.00	1.00	1.00	1.00	1.00	1.00	1.00	1.00	1.00
Malta	1.00	1.00	1.00	1.00	1.00	1.00	1.00	1.00	1.00	1.00
Monaco	1.00	1.00	1.00	1.00	1.00	1.00	1.00	1.00	1.00	1.00
Netherlands	1.00	1.00	1.00	1.00	1.00	1.00	1.00	1.00	1.00	1.00
Norway	6.56	7.97	8.29	8.11	8.37	8.01	8.05	8.02	8.25	8.74
Portugal	1.00	1.00	1.00	1.00	1.00	1.00	1.00	1.00	1.00	1.00
Spain	1.00	1.00	1.00	1.00	1.00	1.00	1.00	1.00	1.00	1.00
Sweden	6.57	7.54	9.33	8.44	9.13	9.29	9.26	9.25	9.64	10.64
Switzerland	1.88	1.77	1.55	1.56	1.54	1.55	1.57	1.64	1.58	1.51
Turkey	0.00	0.00	0.06	0.58	1.77	1.67	1.80	1.79	1.91	2.16
United Kingdom	0.59	0.72	0.83	0.61	0.68	0.68	0.68	0.68	0.80	0.89
Eastern Europe										
Albania	5.34	9.86	121.25	132.43	127.66	124.12	123.08	123.77	122.78	131.98
Belarus		0.00	11.47	807.94	2,683.15	2,676.84	2,690.45	2,937.28	3,126.57	3,876.28
Bosnia-Herzegovina		0.00	1.83	1.96	1.96	1.95	1.96	1.96	1.95	1.96
Bulgaria	0.00	0.00	0.09	1.96	1.96	1.96	1.96	1.96	1.96	1.95
Croatia		0.01	6.84	7.63	7.49	7.39	7.32	7.34	7.22	7.34
Czech Republic		22.86	34.72	35.57	31.92	29.78	28.35	27.78	24.98	26.49
Estonia		0.18	12.93	15.64	15.64	15.64	15.64	15.65	15.65	15.64
Georgia		0.00	1.79	1.82	2.38	2.25	2.23	2.29	2.18	2.32
Hungary	38.25	80.49	164.39	260.03	251.82	248.05	263.94	251.32	251.88	281.17
Latvia		0.01	0.69	0.56	0.67	0.70	0.70	0.70	0.70	0.70
Lithuania		0.02	5.23	3.69	3.45	3.45	3.45	3.45	3.45	3.45
Macedonia		0.14	49.55	60.73	61.37	61.25	61.22	61.22	61.27	61.28
Moldova		0.00	4.80	11.46	15.31	15.66	16.47	16.62	15.21	15.44
Montenegro	1.00	1.00	1.00	1.00	1.00	1.00	1.00	1.00	1.00	1.00
Poland	0.01	1.21	3.17	4.00	4.54	4.02	3.89	3.79	3.53	4.34
Romania	0.00	0.00	0.27	2.00	4.05	3.62	3.52	3.34	3.69	4.24
Russia		0.00	4.68	25.92	35.79	35.15	34.11	35.01	36.37	44.14
Serbia		0.00	3.84	40.57	72.51	82.91	84.24	80.00	81.55	93.91
Slovakia	1.00	1.00	1.00	1.00	1.00	1.00	1.00	1.00	1.00	1.00
Slovenia	1.00	1.00	1.00	1.00	1.00	1.00	1.00	1.00	1.00	1.00
Ukraine		0.00	1.47	5.01	6.61	6.37	6.34	6.91	7.71	10.83

Source: *European Central Bank/Euromonitor International research*
Notes: *Annual average market exchange rates*

Education

Education Statistics

Table 9.1

Education Statistcs 2009

As stated

	literacy rate (% of population aged 15+)	Compulsory education commencement (years)	School leaving age (years)
Western Europe			
Austria	99.9	6	14
Belgium	99.9	6	18
Cyprus	98.0	6	14
Denmark	99.2	7	16
Finland	99.0	7	16
France	99.0	6	16
Germany	99.9	6	18
Gibraltar	99.9	4	15
Greece	97.3	6	14
Iceland	99.9	6	16
Ireland	99.0	6	15
Italy	99.0	6	14
Liechtenstein	99.9	6	14
Luxembourg	99.9	6	15
Malta	92.2	5	15
Monaco	99.0	6	16
Netherlands	99.6	5	17
Norway	99.9	6	16
Portugal	95.5	6	14
Spain	97.6	6	16
Sweden	99.2	7	16
Switzerland	99.9	7	15
Turkey	89.5	6	14
United Kingdom	99.8	5	16
Eastern Europe			
Albania	99.1	6	13
Belarus	99.7	6	14
Bosnia-Herzegovina			
Bulgaria	98.3	7	14
Croatia	98.9	7	14
Czech Republic		6	15
Estonia	99.8	7	15
Georgia	99.0	6	14
Hungary	98.9	7	16
Latvia	99.8	7	15
Lithuania	99.7	7	15
Macedonia	97.3	6	18
Moldova	99.4	7	15
Montenegro		7	14
Poland	99.3	7	15
Romania	97.7	7	14
Russia	99.6	6	15
Serbia		7	14
Slovakia		6	15
Slovenia	99.7	6	14
Ukraine	99.7	6	17

Source:*Euromonitor International from UNESCO/national statistics*

Table 9.2

Pre-primary Education 2009

As stated

	Pre-Primary Schools	Staff ('000)	Pupils ('000)	Pupil to Staff Ratio
Western Europe				
Austria	4,780	16.8	221.8	13.2
Belgium	5,019	30.2	414.2	13.7
Cyprus	687	1.3	22.3	17.8
Denmark	1,922	42.4	253.1	6.0
Finland	3,002	13.0	147.1	11.3
France	16,888	143.5	2,535.4	17.7
Germany	1,341	217.2	2,469.0	11.4
Gibraltar		0.0	0.7	16.3
Greece	6,033	12.5	145.7	11.7
Iceland	282	1.8	18.6	10.1
Ireland		5.1		
Italy	24,803	145.6	1,658.1	11.4
Liechtenstein		0.1	0.7	9.4
Luxembourg		1.2	14.4	12.1
Malta	29	0.8	7.9	9.9
Monaco		0.1	0.9	13.6
Netherlands	7,498		412.0	
Norway	6,676		167.2	
Portugal	6,833	17.8	268.1	15.0
Spain	5,212	126.9	1,680.1	13.2
Sweden	9,960	37.5	380.9	10.2
Switzerland		11.3	152.8	13.5
Turkey	23,653	29.3	804.8	27.4
United Kingdom	3,209	46.7	1,092.0	23.4
Eastern Europe				
Albania		3.7	77.9	21.0
Belarus	3,938	44.2	273.5	6.2
Bosnia-Herzegovina	196			
Bulgaria	2,291	18.5	212.5	11.5
Croatia	1,210	6.1	95.5	15.5
Czech Republic	4,809	20.4	298.0	14.6
Estonia	635	5.5	48.5	8.8
Georgia	1,180	5.7	82.7	14.5
Hungary	4,355	29.9	325.7	10.9
Latvia	586	6.8	71.0	10.5
Lithuania	642	13.0	89.4	6.9
Macedonia	52	3.5	36.9	10.6
Moldova	1,350	11.2	109.6	9.8
Montenegro	90	0.8	13.1	15.7
Poland	17,272	64.8	929.1	14.3
Romania	1,615	37.7	652.8	17.3
Russia	45,361	651.1	5,113.7	7.9
Serbia	2,038	10.7	181.9	17.0
Slovakia	2,852	13.6	140.2	10.3
Slovenia	863	2.7	49.2	18.5
Ukraine	15,500	135.1	1,195.0	8.8

Source:*Euromonitor International from UNESCO*

Education Statistics

Table 9.3

Primary Education 2009

As stated

	Primary Schools	Staff ('000)	Pupils ('000)	Pupil to Staff Ratio
Western Europe				
Austria	3,207	29.6	334.6	11.3
Belgium	4,327	65.9	729.6	11.1
Cyprus	371	3.9	57.6	14.9
Denmark	2,442	70.9	418.2	5.9
Finland	3,065	24.3	351.1	14.4
France	37,841	215.7	4,169.8	19.3
Germany	16,391	245.9	2,997.0	12.2
Gibraltar		0.2	3.3	15.9
Greece	5,804	63.4	638.8	10.1
Iceland		2.9	29.8	10.3
Ireland	3,303	29.2	501.4	17.1
Italy	18,100	275.1	2,845.9	10.3
Liechtenstein	14	0.3	2.0	7.6
Luxembourg		3.3	36.3	11.0
Malta	115	2.2	27.7	12.6
Monaco		0.2	1.8	10.8
Netherlands	7,220	142.3	1,284.6	9.0
Norway	1,758	47.3	423.2	9.0
Portugal	9,054	62.4	748.0	12.0
Spain	13,737	210.5	2,591.4	12.3
Sweden	4,755	58.1	613.9	10.6
Switzerland		40.0	497.7	12.4
Turkey	33,769	453.3	8,163.6	18.0
United Kingdom	21,568	252.8	4,340.9	17.2
Eastern Europe				
Albania		10.5	245.6	23.3
Belarus	521	23.7	350.4	14.8
Bosnia-Herzegovina				
Bulgaria	1,900	16.3	241.1	14.7
Croatia	2,127	11.5	188.8	16.4
Czech Republic	4,133	23.8	446.9	18.8
Estonia	71	5.6	71.0	12.8
Georgia	2,438	36.1	300.1	8.3
Hungary	3,363	37.2	386.0	10.4
Latvia	503	6.6	71.9	10.8
Lithuania	92	10.6	129.5	12.3
Macedonia	1,046	5.5	97.0	17.7
Moldova	91	9.5	164.0	17.3
Montenegro	440	5.0	74.0	14.8
Poland	13,972	170.5	2,211.6	13.0
Romania	4,789	54.4	860.4	15.8
Russia	3,908	281.2	4,907.6	17.5
Serbia	3,521	22.3	277.6	12.4
Slovakia	2,224	15.3	202.0	13.2
Slovenia	460	6.2	97.2	15.7
Ukraine	24,922	99.5	1,544.3	15.5

Source: Euromonitor International from UNESCO

Table 9.4

Secondary Education 2009

As stated

	Staff ('000)	Total Pupils ('000)	Pupils in Technical Colleges ('000)	Pupil to Staff Ratio
Western Europe				
Austria	72.1	776.9	302.3	10.8
Belgium	84.2	228.2	349.7	2.7
Cyprus	6.3	65.1	4.1	10.3
Denmark	73.6	480.4	125.2	6.5
Finland	20.8	433.4	128.5	20.8
France	489.4	3,070.3	1,459.3	6.3
Germany	590.9	7,883.2	1,702.8	13.3
Gibraltar	0.3	1.7		5.7
Greece	86.6	672.9	101.8	7.8
Iceland	3.5	35.6	6.8	10.2
Ireland	13.5	184.3	103.7	13.7
Italy	467.0	4,577.5	1,698.0	9.8
Liechtenstein	0.4	3.3	1.1	8.3
Luxembourg	3.9	39.5	12.1	10.1
Malta	4.3	36.2	6.2	8.4
Monaco	0.5	3.0	0.6	6.0
Netherlands	108.8	1,453.0	693.4	13.4
Norway	48.9	436.2	4.4	8.9
Portugal	92.7	685.0	129.3	7.4
Spain	288.7	3,042.2	497.5	10.5
Sweden	80.1	773.2	234.6	9.7
Switzerland	57.5	601.9	197.5	10.5
Turkey	206.9	4,240.1	1,819.5	20.5
United Kingdom	379.0	4,991.2	994.1	13.2
Eastern Europe				
Albania	24.3	423.0	38.3	17.4
Belarus	100.4	1,006.8	166.0	10.0
Bosnia-Herzegovina	7.9	104.0		13.2
Bulgaria	50.5	555.0	183.7	11.0
Croatia	23.8	181.9	130.8	7.6
Czech Republic	46.7	564.3	371.4	12.1
Estonia	11.3	152.0	18.1	13.5
Georgia	39.5	643.3	2.6	16.3
Hungary	37.9	514.1	271.4	13.6
Latvia	26.7	165.6	38.8	6.2
Lithuania	41.1	333.3	36.9	8.1
Macedonia	15.6	205.3	58.1	13.2
Moldova	30.1	58.5	24.3	1.9
Montenegro				
Poland	229.5	3,140.7	948.8	13.7
Romania	138.0	1,752.0	189.0	12.7
Russia	1,219.2	9,934.9	2,244.0	8.1
Serbia	61.6	604.1	218.1	9.8
Slovakia	46.7	585.4	44.1	12.5
Slovenia	16.1	162.7	98.2	10.1
Ukraine	522.0	4,495.0	424.3	8.6

Source: Euromonitor International from UNESCO

Education Statistics

Table 9.5

Higher and University Education 2009

As stated

	Establish-ments	Teaching Staff ('000)	Students ('000)	Student to Staff Ratio	University Teachers ('000)	University Teachers (% of total)	University Students ('000)	University Students (% of total)	University Students to Staff Ratio
Western Europe									
Austria	170	48.4	275.6	5.7	17.8	36.8	252.5	91.6	14.2
Belgium		26.9	410.9	15.3	26.6	98.9	195.5	47.6	7.3
Cyprus	43	2.0	22.0	11.0	0.3	15.0	5.8	26.4	19.3
Denmark	103	20.5	237.3	11.6			201.9	85.1	
Finland	20	19.4	316.3	16.3	8.3	42.8	316.2	100.0	38.1
France	312	148.1	2,235.1	15.1	76.8	51.9	1,678.8	75.1	21.9
Germany	409	291.1	2,328.2	8.0	250.1	85.9	2,264.8	97.3	9.1
Gibraltar									
Greece	20	32.4	719.7	22.2	18.0	55.6	437.7	60.8	24.3
Iceland		2.1	16.8	8.0	1.1	52.4	16.7	99.4	15.2
Ireland	32	12.8	188.3	14.7	8.1	63.3	134.0	71.2	16.5
Italy		106.9	2,062.0	19.3	105.0	98.2	2,051.3	99.5	19.5
Liechtenstein			0.8				0.8	100.0	
Luxembourg		0.3	2.4	8.0			1.7	70.8	
Malta		0.8	9.2	11.5	0.6	75.0	7.9	85.9	13.2
Monaco									
Netherlands	64	45.1	630.3	14.0			226.8	36.0	
Norway	68	18.0	216.7	12.0	11.5	63.9	215.4	99.4	18.7
Portugal	301	37.2	337.3	9.1	32.4	87.1	329.9	97.8	10.2
Spain	77	151.0	1,741.3	11.5	111.9	74.1	1,504.5	86.4	13.4
Sweden		34.6	413.8	12.0	38.1	110.1	394.4	95.3	10.4
Switzerland		31.4	216.0	6.9	11.2	35.7	181.2	83.9	16.2
Turkey	1,155	92.8	2,638.3	28.4	85.2	91.8	1,887.1	71.5	22.1
United Kingdom	166	134.1	2,402.2	17.9	45.8	34.2	2,003.0	83.4	43.7
Eastern Europe									
Albania	26	2.8	100.8	36.0	1.2	42.9	69.5	68.9	57.9
Belarus	54	43.0	595.6	13.9	30.2	70.2	441.3	74.1	14.6
Bosnia-Herzegovina			74.5						
Bulgaria	53	24.5	263.4	10.8	25.6	104.5	231.0	87.7	9.0
Croatia	126	10.7	148.6	13.9	8.0	74.8	102.2	68.8	12.8
Czech Republic	257	20.4	356.6	17.5	20.8	102.0	326.7	91.6	15.7
Estonia	34	6.3	71.4	11.3	3.1	49.2	48.8	68.3	15.7
Georgia	129	9.8	116.0	11.8	14.0	142.9	116.0	100.0	8.3
Hungary	71	29.6	457.4	15.5	22.0	74.3	427.8	93.5	19.4
Latvia	61	6.5	134.9	20.8	6.3	96.9	114.2	84.7	18.1
Lithuania	46	13.8	218.0	15.8	10.6	76.8	156.1	71.6	14.7
Macedonia		3.5	63.4	18.1	3.4	97.1	62.5	98.5	18.4
Moldova	33	8.9	161.9	18.2	6.8	76.4	145.9	90.1	21.5
Montenegro			23.1						
Poland	454	107.5	2,271.1	21.1	23.7	22.0	2,246.5	98.9	94.8
Romania	107	33.3	1,072.6	32.2	33.3	100.0	1,065.6	99.3	32.0
Russia	1,134	727.5	9,872.5	13.6			7,922.3	80.2	
Serbia		14.3	270.5	18.9	9.2	64.3			
Slovakia	33	14.5	246.2	17.0	14.3	98.6	246.2	100.0	17.2
Slovenia	59	5.1	127.4	25.0	4.2	82.4	75.9	59.6	18.1
Ukraine	350	206.5	3,138.7	15.2			2,703.4	86.1	

Source: *Euromonitor International from UNESCO*

Education Statistics

Table 9.6

Foreign Students in Higher and University Education 1985-2009

'000

	1985	1990	1995	2000	2004	2005	2006	2007	2008	2009
Western Europe										
Austria		17.9	26.3	30.4	33.7	34.7	36.1	37.3	38.6	39.7
Belgium		20.7	32.4	38.8	37.1	36.3	35.4	33.2	31.9	30.4
Cyprus				2.0	6.7	7.4	8.1	9.0	9.8	10.6
Denmark		7.7	11.1	16.5	24.0	25.9	27.4	28.6	29.6	30.7
Finland		1.6	3.4	5.6	7.9	8.5	9.2	9.7	10.0	10.4
France		136.0	138.2	137.1	237.6	249.7	258.9	267.6	277.6	286.2
Germany		107.0	159.9	187.0	246.1	246.3	248.4	250.1	251.4	252.9
Gibraltar										
Greece		1.5	2.5	3.2	14.4	16.3	17.6	18.7	19.5	20.6
Iceland				0.4	0.5	0.5	0.4	0.4	0.3	0.3
Ireland		3.3	5.8	7.4	12.7	13.9	14.6	15.4	16.0	16.7
Italy		21.4	22.4	24.9	40.6	44.1	47.9	51.6	54.6	57.9
Liechtenstein					0.4	0.5	0.5	0.5	0.6	0.6
Luxembourg				0.7	0.7	0.7	0.7	0.7	0.7	0.8
Malta				0.4	0.4	0.5	0.5	0.6	0.6	0.6
Monaco										
Netherlands		8.9	9.7	14.0	21.3	22.8	24.1	25.1	26.4	27.6
Norway		6.9	11.2	8.7	12.4	13.6	14.6	15.5	16.3	17.1
Portugal		3.8	7.2	11.2	16.2	17.1	17.9	18.5	19.2	19.7
Spain		10.3	19.1	40.7	41.7	38.8	36.7	35.0	32.8	31.0
Sweden		14.6	19.4	25.5	36.5	39.1	43.4	46.0	48.6	51.4
Switzerland		22.6	24.1	26.0	35.7	37.0	39.6	41.2	43.0	44.9
Turkey		7.7	14.1	17.7	15.3	16.4	17.1	17.4	17.9	18.3
United Kingdom		80.2	197.2	222.9	300.1	327.6	360.5	384.1	412.1	438.8
Eastern Europe										
Albania				0.7	0.5	0.4	0.4	0.4	0.3	0.3
Belarus			1.8	2.7	2.4	3.0	3.3	3.6	3.8	4.1
Bosnia-Herzegovina										
Bulgaria		7.3	8.2	8.1	8.3	8.4	8.5	8.5	8.6	8.6
Croatia			0.3	1.2	3.4	3.8	4.3	4.6	5.1	5.5
Czech Republic			3.3	5.7	14.9	18.4	22.9	25.6	29.3	32.7
Estonia			0.4	0.9	0.8	0.8	0.8	0.8	0.8	0.8
Georgia				0.2	1.1	1.2	1.3	1.4	1.5	1.5
Hungary		3.3	6.9	9.9	12.9	12.9	12.5	12.3	12.0	11.7
Latvia			0.6	6.0	1.3	1.2	1.0	0.9	0.8	0.6
Lithuania			0.3	0.6	0.8	0.9	0.9	0.9	1.0	1.0
Macedonia				0.2	0.1	0.3	0.2	0.9	1.3	1.3
Moldova					2.4	2.5	2.6	2.6	2.6	2.5
Montenegro										
Poland		4.3	5.6	6.0	8.1	8.8	9.4	9.8	10.3	10.8
Romania		8.1	12.9	12.6	11.6	12.7	14.8	16.5	18.5	20.3
Russia			27.4	50.6	75.8	80.7	84.6	87.8	91.4	94.7
Serbia										
Slovakia			1.8	1.6	1.6	1.6	1.9	2.1	2.2	2.4
Slovenia			0.4	0.7	0.9	1.0	1.0	1.1	1.2	1.2
Ukraine			19.1	16.1	15.6	14.9	14.3	13.6	12.9	12.1

Source: Euromonitor International from UNESCO

Education Statistics

Table 9.7

Foreign Students' Share of All Higher and University Education Students 1985-2009
%

	1985	1990	1995	2000	2004	2005	2006	2007	2008	2009
Western Europe										
Austria		9.0	11.3	11.6	14.1	14.2	14.3	14.3	14.4	14.4
Belgium		7.9	9.2	10.9	9.6	9.3	9.0	8.3	7.9	7.4
Cyprus				19.5	32.1	36.6	39.3	42.3	45.6	48.3
Denmark		5.7	6.5	8.7	11.1	11.2	12.0	12.2	12.5	13.0
Finland		1.0	1.7	2.1	2.6	2.8	3.0	3.1	3.2	3.3
France		8.6	6.7	6.8	11.0	11.4	11.8	12.1	12.5	12.8
Germany			7.4	9.1	10.6	10.9	10.8	10.8	10.9	10.9
Gibraltar										
Greece		0.5	0.9	0.8	2.4	2.5	2.7	2.7	2.8	2.9
Iceland				4.2	3.3	3.0	2.6	2.3	2.1	1.8
Ireland		4.0	4.8	4.6	6.7	7.4	7.8	8.2	8.5	8.9
Italy		1.5	1.2	1.4	2.0	2.2	2.4	2.5	2.7	2.8
Liechtenstein					77.4	85.6	77.0	77.1	77.0	74.4
Luxembourg				27.8	24.0	26.0	27.2	28.9	30.0	31.2
Malta				5.6	5.6	5.1	5.8	6.2	6.4	6.8
Monaco										
Netherlands		1.9	1.9	2.9	3.9	4.0	4.2	4.2	4.3	4.4
Norway		5.2	6.5	4.6	5.8	6.4	6.8	7.2	7.5	7.9
Portugal		2.3	2.4	3.0	4.1	4.5	4.9	5.2	5.5	5.9
Spain		0.9	1.3	2.2	2.3	2.1	2.1	2.0	1.9	1.8
Sweden		8.1	7.9	7.4	8.5	9.2	10.3	11.0	11.7	12.4
Switzerland		16.9	16.3	16.6	18.2	18.5	19.3	19.7	20.3	20.8
Turkey		1.1	1.2	1.2	0.8	0.8	0.7	0.7	0.7	0.7
United Kingdom		7.0	10.9	11.0	13.4	14.3	15.4	16.3	17.4	18.3
Eastern Europe										
Albania				1.7	0.9	0.7	0.6	0.5	0.4	0.3
Belarus			0.6	0.7	0.5	0.6	0.6	0.6	0.7	0.7
Bosnia-Herzegovina										
Bulgaria		3.9	3.7	3.1	3.6	3.5	3.5	3.4	3.3	3.3
Croatia			0.4	1.2	2.7	2.8	3.1	3.3	3.5	3.7
Czech Republic			1.8	2.2	4.7	5.5	6.8	7.4	8.3	9.2
Estonia			1.6	1.6	1.3	1.2	1.2	1.2	1.1	1.1
Georgia				0.1	0.7	0.7	0.9	1.0	1.2	1.3
Hungary		3.3	4.1	3.2	3.1	3.0	2.8	2.8	2.7	2.6
Latvia			1.4	6.6	1.0	0.9	0.8	0.7	0.6	0.5
Lithuania			0.4	0.5	0.5	0.5	0.5	0.5	0.5	0.5
Macedonia				0.7	0.3	0.6	0.4	1.6	2.1	2.1
Moldova					2.0	1.9	1.8	1./	1.7	1.6
Montenegro										
Poland		0.9	0.8	0.4	0.4	0.4	0.4	0.4	0.5	0.5
Romania		4.6	5.1	2.8	1.7	1.7	1.8	1.8	1.9	1.9
Russia			0.6	0.8	0.9	0.9	0.9	0.9	0.9	1.0
Serbia										
Slovakia			2.2	1.1	1.0	0.9	1.0	1.0	1.0	1.0
Slovenia			0.8	0.8	0.8	0.9	0.9	0.9	0.9	1.0
Ukraine			1.2	0.9	0.6	0.6	0.5	0.5	0.4	0.4

Source: Euromonitor International from UNESCO

Energy Resources and Output

Energy Statistics   **Table 10.1**

Refinery Product Consumption 2009

'000 metric tonnes

	Motor Gasoline	Liquefied Gases	Aviation Fuels	Diesel/ Gasoil	Biofuels
Western Europe					
Austria	1,608	142	690	7,327	391
Belgium	1,115	552	732	10,036	126
Cyprus	377	50	281	448	
Denmark	1,669	59	853	3,816	19
Finland	1,754	350	649	3,996	1
France	7,874	3,063	6,892	45,274	2,183
Germany	17,784	2,598	8,914	44,188	5,904
Gibraltar	23		4	66	
Greece	3,850	269	1,244	6,447	96
Iceland	140	2	142	340	
Ireland	1,700	119	879	3,774	38
Italy	10,568	2,857	3,703	31,013	389
Liechtenstein					
Luxembourg	396	9	297	1,834	50
Malta	62	21	83	97	
Monaco					
Netherlands	4,013	1,569	3,553	7,439	634
Norway	1,372	1,672	637	3,748	
Portugal	1,273	826	957	5,185	172
Spain	5,226	1,863	5,774	33,084	565
Sweden	3,662	979	893	4,340	485
Switzerland	3,196	202	1,336	5,943	21
Turkey	2,296	4,284	1,037	11,965	12
United Kingdom	15,666	4,932	12,010	25,813	640
Eastern Europe					
Albania	136	96	104	623	
Belarus	976	275		2,419	
Bosnia-Herzegovina	282	25	5	559	
Bulgaria	549	409	213	1,673	
Croatia	671	233	100	1,868	
Czech Republic	1,957	166	370	4,218	32
Estonia	301	6	43	620	
Georgia	327	36	52	370	
Hungary	1,454	275	249	3,104	125
Latvia	415	46	85	957	5
Lithuania	337	243	65	1,118	100
Macedonia	135	66	7	325	
Moldova	213	48	20	338	
Montenegro					
Poland	3,941	2,794	501	10,400	184
Romania	1,742	660	152	3,441	
Russia	29,720	8,392	10,143	22,881	
Serbia	522	391	36	1,363	
Slovakia	657	106	40	1,236	144
Slovenia	625	88	27	1,519	22
Ukraine	5,055	786	303	5,683	

Source: *Euromonitor International from OECD*

Energy Statistics

Table 10.2

Motor Gasoline Consumption 1985-2009

'000 metric tonnes

	1985	1990	1995	2000	2004	2005	2006	2007	2008	2009
Western Europe										
Austria	2,430	2,552	2,394	1,981	2,160	2,078	2,007	1,936	1,710	1,608
Belgium	2,502	2,727	2,833	2,245	1,932	1,762	1,465	1,394	1,277	1,115
Cyprus	124	163	183	206	282	303	323	352	372	377
Denmark	1,530	1,581	1,893	1,966	1,925	1,868	1,828	1,808	1,784	1,669
Finland	1,521	1,986	1,897	1,785	1,878	1,876	1,861	1,859	1,833	1,754
France	18,006	18,231	15,613	13,803	11,447	10,721	9,973	9,302	8,495	7,874
Germany	26,212	31,274	30,134	28,806	24,993	23,171	22,092	20,832	18,863	17,784
Gibraltar	5	12	16	20	22	22	23	24	24	23
Greece	1,795	2,423	2,774	3,280	3,763	3,918	3,959	4,137	3,999	3,850
Iceland	99	134	136	143	149	149	161	160	149	140
Ireland	841	885	1,037	1,493	1,627	1,712	1,877	1,821	1,804	1,700
Italy	11,820	14,055	18,496	16,863	14,940	13,936	13,090	12,321	11,618	10,568
Liechtenstein										
Luxembourg	303	412	516	582	530	486	450	432	418	396
Malta	20	65	120	71	58	68	76	64	62	62
Monaco										
Netherlands	3,395	3,445	4,023	4,031	4,158	4,097	4,169	4,171	4,118	4,013
Norway	1,587	1,785	1,664	1,619	1,637	1,580	1,519	1,441	1,475	1,372
Portugal	855	1,369	1,890	2,123	1,927	1,808	1,672	1,587	1,455	1,273
Spain	5,894	8,145	8,534	8,524	7,534	7,260	6,928	6,669	6,136	5,226
Sweden	3,750	4,166	4,251	3,977	3,926	3,862	3,741	3,602	3,632	3,662
Switzerland	3,058	3,724	3,590	3,983	3,708	3,595	3,484	3,450	3,426	3,196
Turkey	1,916	3,196	4,330	3,619	2,415	2,673	2,723	2,463	2,413	2,296
United Kingdom	20,403	24,312	21,953	21,603	19,484	18,731	18,144	17,591	16,882	15,666
Eastern Europe										
Albania	121	60	133	101	175	181	173	157	146	136
Belarus		2,363	1,154	987	965	1,033	1,121	1,094	990	976
Bosnia-Herzegovina		349	118	321	275	264	282	301	290	282
Bulgaria	1,213	1,391	1,083	659	559	544	605	597	566	549
Croatia		764	575	784	723	709	710	724	710	671
Czech Republic	1,069	1,161	1,637	1,858	2,092	2,055	2,010	2,099	2,066	1,957
Estonia		523	247	282	287	290	308	323	315	301
Georgia		894	134	272	290	334	328	409	369	327
Hungary	1,336	1,790	1,427	1,336	1,442	1,482	1,510	1,533	1,529	1,454
Latvia		608	412	337	349	344	381	416	429	415
Lithuania		980	603	381	344	338	356	419	368	337
Macedonia		161	207	144	121	117	107	115	135	135
Moldova		774	223	117	210	212	198	203	192	213
Montenegro										
Poland	2,944	3,079	4,372	5,001	4,095	3,955	4,058	4,049	4,305	3,941
Romania	1,405	2,083	1,022	1,326	1,715	1,695	1,552	1,607	1,699	1,742
Russia		30,436	24,836	23,259	26,451	26,260	27,893	28,757	30,476	29,720
Serbia		647	396	340	671	630	530	608	587	522
Slovakia	408	438	504	592	614	643	604	613	650	657
Slovenia		565	821	807	666	655	640	620	661	625
Ukraine		10,960	4,355	3,825	4,184	4,756	4,742	5,231	5,545	5,055

Source: *Euromonitor International from OECD*

Energy Statistics

Table 10.3

Aviation Fuels Consumption 1985-2009

'000 metric tonnes

	1985	1990	1995	2000	2004	2005	2006	2007	2008	2009
Western Europe										
Austria		302	449	571	582	657	686	726	678	690
Belgium		927	920	1,481	1,387	1,247	1,146	986	854	732
Cyprus		236	260	268	295	291	300	287	285	281
Denmark		662	694	823	863	918	893	934	885	853
Finland	245	447	397	492	534	550	592	658	666	649
France		3,735	4,565	6,507	6,606	6,615	6,866	7,052	7,075	6,892
Germany		5,417	5,804	7,142	7,512	8,085	8,497	8,808	9,032	8,914
Gibraltar		7	4	4	4	4	4	4	4	4
Greece		1,231	1,213	1,290	1,176	1,150	1,261	1,277	1,296	1,244
Iceland		80	73	137	121	136	181	168	156	142
Ireland		355	380	597	705	814	841	992	983	879
Italy		2,238	2,692	3,579	3,611	3,781	4,014	4,231	4,043	3,703
Liechtenstein										
Luxembourg		128	184	312	414	420	394	423	343	297
Malta		70	72	84	98	85	75	87	87	83
Monaco										
Netherlands		1,561	2,529	3,255	3,466	3,573	3,603	3,627	3,650	3,553
Norway		489	551	636	587	618	678	680	663	637
Portugal		565	604	769	818	858	898	974	986	957
Spain		2,391	3,023	4,368	4,864	5,183	5,422	5,704	5,954	5,774
Sweden		740	827	904	821	824	843	911	901	893
Switzerland		1,115	1,273	1,576	1,166	1,182	1,239	1,321	1,361	1,336
Turkey		467	1,120	1,228	1,812	1,957	1,723	2,119	1,147	1,037
United Kingdom		6,590	7,716	10,838	11,636	12,497	12,641	12,633	12,240	12,010
Eastern Europe										
Albania		27	31	40	57	69	83	100	107	104
Belarus										
Bosnia-Herzegovina		25	37	10	5	5	5	5	5	5
Bulgaria		269	322	98	167	195	199	217	219	213
Croatia		160	85	72	78	93	96	100	103	100
Czech Republic		169	180	192	322	335	339	368	389	370
Estonia		35	18	19	27	41	28	49	50	43
Georgia		197	4	15	37	37	37	47	50	52
Hungary		160	177	224	225	261	264	242	261	249
Latvia		71	27	26	48	57	66	79	89	85
Lithuania		131	40	26	38	49	55	70	74	65
Macedonia		5	31	28	5	6	4	7	7	7
Moldova		72	12	21	14	15	17	20	21	20
Montenegro										
Poland		215	262	269	275	312	417	434	519	501
Romania		227	179	123	133	110	135	174	171	152
Russia		17,323	9,189	8,717	9,283	10,036	10,602	10,699	10,514	10,143
Serbia		140	35	29	46	47	45	40	39	36
Slovakia		26	39	26	26	38	39	48	43	40
Slovenia		26	19	24	19	22	24	31	29	27
Ukraine		2,009	155	255	366	364	325	348	309	303

Source: *Euromonitor International from OECD*

Energy Statistics

Table 10.4

Biofuels Consumption 1998-2009

'000 metric tonnes

	1998	1999	2000	2001	2002	2003	2004	2005	2006	2007	2008	2009
Western Europe												
Austria	16	18	20	22	23	23	25	77	160	294	347	391
Belgium								1	13	110	118	126
Denmark									6	9	14	19
Finland					1	6	7		1	2	2	1
France	318	338	399	393	411	378	412	474	912	1,747	1,952	2,183
Germany	100	130	250	350	550	800	1,115	2,256	4,034	4,616	5,303	5,904
Greece									51	94	85	96
Ireland								1	3	27	32	38
Italy							286	200	223	202	317	389
Netherlands									53	384	483	634
Norway												
Portugal									79	153	140	172
Spain			80	80	187	257	229	339	242	480	516	565
Sweden				22	49	102	194	207	273	398	439	485
Switzerland								3	8	9	14	18	21
Turkey									22	14	15	12
United Kingdom					3	17	18	96	224	426	535	640
Eastern Europe												
Belarus												
Bulgaria												
Croatia												
Czech Republic	36	45	64	46	66	70	36	3	21	34	32	32
Estonia												
Hungary								4	17	44	95	125
Latvia								3	3	4	5	5
Lithuania							1	4	23	64	81	100
Montenegro												
Poland						44	21	70	126	140	162	184
Romania												
Russia												
Serbia												
Slovakia				33	3	2	1	11	46	102	131	144
Slovenia									2	15	19	22
Ukraine												

Source:International Energy Association

Energy Statistics

Table 10.5

Energy Intensity 1998-2009

US$ per tonne of energy consumed

	1998	1999	2000	2001	2002	2003	2004	2005	2006	2007	2008	2009
Western Europe												
Austria	6,858	6,572	6,014	5,781	6,285	7,480	8,761	8,983	9,858	11,598	12,866	11,912
Belgium	4,120	3,991	3,527	3,651	3,924	4,571	5,124	5,249	5,460	6,308	7,152	6,791
Denmark	8,430	8,785	8,510	8,630	9,463	10,866	13,381	14,811	14,080	17,170	19,806	19,260
Finland	5,104	5,067	4,682	4,719	5,064	5,680	6,608	7,462	7,557	8,944	10,083	9,522
France	6,018	5,814	5,240	5,202	5,732	6,967	7,849	8,248	8,791	10,180	11,161	10,956
Germany	6,605	6,542	5,768	5,642	6,134	7,380	8,344	8,612	8,904	10,767	11,702	11,494
Greece	4,625	4,451	3,937	4,108	4,498	5,990	6,768	7,184	7,631	8,957	10,203	10,092
Ireland	7,217	7,351	7,051	7,168	8,521	11,270	12,772	13,612	14,686	16,864	17,621	16,350
Italy	7,322	6,974	6,275	6,364	7,004	8,384	9,455	9,708	10,245	11,842	12,993	12,934
Netherlands	4,709	4,864	4,417	4,443	4,847	5,904	6,483	6,661	7,082	8,059	9,137	8,519
Norway	3,741	3,832	3,666	4,169	4,474	5,878	6,630	6,696	8,114	8,594	9,682	8,906
Portugal	5,438	5,413	4,719	4,802	5,280	6,382	7,454	7,704	8,241	9,623	11,133	10,446
Spain	5,139	5,061	4,513	4,601	5,130	6,291	7,209	7,726	8,440	9,658	10,900	11,045
Sweden	4,937	5,016	5,088	4,364	5,174	6,812	7,497	7,295	8,366	9,636	10,245	9,400
Switzerland	9,434	9,001	8,588	8,199	9,575	11,247	12,737	13,545	13,679	15,340	17,091	16,757
Turkey	3,719	3,518	3,480	2,741	3,096	3,802	4,652	5,388	5,516	6,381	7,156	6,595
United Kingdom	6,558	6,812	6,629	6,526	7,317	8,315	9,780	10,125	11,000	13,086	12,598	10,920
Eastern Europe												
Belarus	689	578	491	575	673	829	976	1,275	1,467	1,863	2,355	2,052
Bulgaria	615	720	708	739	839	999	1,277	1,366	1,537	1,987	2,559	2,707
Croatia												
Czech Republic	1,550	1,563	1,418	1,490	1,814	2,095	2,450	2,793	3,226	4,023	5,182	4,806
Estonia												
Hungary	2,048	2,073	2,056	2,214	2,853	3,481	4,275	4,321	4,481	5,602	6,346	5,757
Latvia												
Lithuania	1,215	1,400	1,633	1,501	1,647	2,045	2,451	3,092	3,714	4,494	5,485	4,517
Montenegro												
Poland	1,837	1,842	1,938	2,149	2,275	2,450	2,781	3,351	3,619	4,470	5,612	4,666
Romania	1,020	975	1,008	1,088	1,191	1,573	1,943	2,492	3,022	4,550	5,293	4,656
Russia	450	322	423	491	551	669	908	1,177	1,485	1,922	2,448	1,938
Serbia												
Slovakia	1,666	1,710	1,586	1,629	1,853	2,531	3,185	3,275	3,774	4,786	5,496	5,238
Slovenia												
Ukraine	318	235	232	282	320	371	472	633	784	1,056	1,361	1,030

Source: *Euromonitor International from national statistics*

Table 10.6

Biofuel Production 1998-2009

Thousand tonnes of oil equivalent

	1998	1999	2000	2001	2002	2003	2004	2005	2006	2007	2008	2009
Western Europe												
Austria	14	16	17	19	20	20	37	53	89	212	328	402
Belgium								17	29	161	182	196
Denmark				22	36	40	58	64	88	88	88	95
Finland												
France	262	275	331	330	354	388	407	463	684	1,145	2,024	2,307
Germany	89	116	222	318	499	750	994	2,229	3,855	5,218	4,056	5,480
Greece									43	83	75	85
Ireland								1	3	15	19	23
Italy							255	179	199	180	566	696
Netherlands							2	53	106	137	160	208
Norway												
Portugal									70	163	148	188
Spain			72	72	139	191	176	259	172	382	468	538
Sweden				15	32	67	144	218	319	430	452	499
Switzerland							2	6	7	11	11	13
Turkey									19	12	13	10
United Kingdom								8	225	384	784	963
Eastern Europe												
Belarus												
Bulgaria												
Croatia												
Czech Republic	41	51	70	52	73	103	77	113	97	74	86	88
Estonia												
Hungary								3	11	17	159	239
Latvia								2	9	16	21	24
Lithuania							3	11	15	32	39	47
Montenegro												
Poland							28	13	116	166	111	308	363
Romania												
Russia												
Serbia												
Slovakia				36	3	2	11	33	42	59	81	98
Slovenia									5	4	4	4
Ukraine												

Source: *International Energy Association*

Energy Statistics | **Table 10.7**

Crude Oil Production 1998-2009

Million tonnes of oil equivalent

	1998	1999	2000	2001	2002	2003	2004	2005	2006	2007	2008	2009
Western Europe												
Austria												
Belgium												
Denmark	11.6	14.6	17.7	17.0	18.1	17.9	19.1	18.4	16.7	15.2	14.0	12.9
Finland												
France												
Germany												
Greece												
Ireland												
Italy	5.6	5.0	4.6	4.1	5.5	5.6	5.5	6.1	5.8	5.9	5.2	4.6
Netherlands												
Norway	149.6	149.7	160.2	162.0	157.3	153.0	149.9	138.2	128.7	118.6	114.1	108.3
Portugal												
Spain												
Sweden												
Switzerland												
Turkey												
United Kingdom	132.6	137.4	126.2	116.7	115.9	106.1	95.4	84.7	76.6	76.8	71.7	68.0
Eastern Europe												
Belarus	1.7	1.7	2.0	2.0	2.3	2.4	2.8	3.0	3.2	3.4	3.5	3.7
Bulgaria												
Croatia												
Czech Republic												
Estonia												
Hungary												
Latvia												
Lithuania												
Montenegro												
Poland	0.4	0.4	0.4	0.4								
Romania	6.6	6.4	6.3	6.2	6.1	5.9	5.7	5.4	5.0	4.7	4.7	4.5
Russia	304.3	304.8	323.3	348.1	379.6	421.4	458.8	470.0	480.5	491.3	488.5	494.2
Serbia												
Slovakia												
Slovenia												
Ukraine												

Source: *BP Amoco, BP Statistical Review of World Energy*
Notes: *Million tonnes of oil equivalent = the amount of oil required to fuel an oil-fired plant in order to generate the same amount of electricity*

Energy Statistics | **Table 10.8**

Electricity Production 2009

GWh/% shares

	Net Total Production	% Fossil Fuels	% Combustible Renewables and Waste	% Geothermal	% Hydroelectric	% Nuclear	% Wind Powered
Western Europe							
Austria	67,955	30.59	9.12	0.00	56.79		3.46
Belgium	90,541	38.66	5.60		1.86	53.32	0.56
Denmark	38,057	71.62	9.28		0.06		19.03
Finland	76,451	45.07	10.82		15.44	28.22	0.22
France	583,154	9.85	1.02		10.34	78.18	0.51
Germany	648,041	60.02	5.14		4.15	25.25	5.06
Greece	58,298	85.69	0.46		10.62		3.23
Ireland	28,370	88.58	0.43		3.83		7.15
Italy	294,649	80.52	2.24	1.73	14.02		1.20
Netherlands	111,115	86.34	6.62		0.10	3.60	3.16
Norway	144,083	0.77	0.27		98.21		0.71
Portugal	48,292	61.65	4.17	0.15	26.99		7.03
Spain	310,977	61.62	1.31		10.38	17.59	8.96
Sweden	149,531	2.06	6.84		44.43	45.91	0.76
Switzerland	69,025	1.60	3.85		49.79	44.68	0.03
Turkey	226,498	75.91	0.10	0.05	23.87		0.07
United Kingdom	370,255	74.27	3.03		2.15	19.06	1.49
Eastern Europe							
Belarus	33,828	99.80	0.09		0.11		0.00
Bulgaria	44,872	45.22	0.01		10.86	43.84	0.06
Croatia	13,102	48.54	0.18		51.10		0.18
Czech Republic	84,464	66.02	1.75		2.93	29.22	0.07
Estonia	9,331	98.60	0.35		0.16		0.89
Hungary	30,646	55.42	5.59		0.51	38.33	0.14
Latvia	5,784	43.19	0.84		55.07		0.89
Lithuania	12,760	24.74	0.44		5.14	69.57	0.12
Montenegro							
Poland	155,311	95.53	2.49		1.81		0.17
Romania	61,746	60.85	0.06		30.68	8.42	
Russia	1,030,045	67.20	0.20	0.05	16.98	15.58	0.00
Serbia	40,157	72.11			27.89		
Slovakia	27,466	24.37	1.78		16.35	57.31	0.02
Slovenia	16,153	39.19	0.72		23.41	36.68	
Ukraine	188,133	46.29			6.88	46.81	0.02

Source: Euromonitor International from OECD

Energy Statistics

Table 10.9

Natural Gas Production 1985-2009

Million tonnes of oil equivalent

	1985	1990	1995	2000	2004	2005	2006	2007	2008	2009
Western Europe										
Austria										
Belgium										
Denmark	1.00	2.80	4.80	7.30	8.50	9.40	9.40	8.30	9.10	7.60
Finland										
France			2.40	2.00	1.50	1.00	1.00	0.80	0.60	0.50
Germany	15.70	14.30	14.50	15.20	14.70	14.20	14.10	12.90	11.70	11.00
Greece			16.10							
Ireland			16.40							
Italy	11.50	14.00	16.30	13.70	10.70	10.00	9.10	8.00	7.60	6.70
Netherlands	61.60	54.90	61.00	52.30	61.60	56.30	55.40	54.50	60.00	56.40
Norway	23.60	22.90	25.00	44.80	70.60	76.50	78.90	80.70	89.30	93.10
Portugal										
Spain			0.40							
Sweden										
Switzerland										
Turkey			0.20							
United Kingdom	35.70	40.90	63.70	97.50	86.70	79.40	72.00	64.90	62.70	53.70
Eastern Europe										
Belarus		0.30	0.20	0.20	0.20	0.20	0.20	0.20	0.20	0.20
Bulgaria										
Croatia			1.70	1.40	1.20	1.30	1.30	1.30	1.30	1.40
Czech Republic										
Estonia										
Hungary	5.80	3.80	3.70	2.40	2.40	2.40	2.30	2.30	2.20	2.10
Latvia										
Lithuania										
Montenegro										
Poland	4.10	2.40	3.10	3.30	3.90	3.90	3.90	3.90	3.70	3.70
Romania	31.30	25.50	16.20	12.40	11.50	11.20	10.70	10.40	10.20	9.80
Russia	376.30	531.00	479.30	475.70	516.00	522.10	535.60	532.80	541.50	474.80
Serbia										
Slovakia			3.00	2.80	3.30	3.10	2.90	2.70	2.50	2.30
Slovenia										
Ukraine	34.90	22.90	14.80	14.60	16.50	16.70	16.90	16.90	17.10	17.30

Source: BP Amoco, BP Statistical Review of World Energy
Notes: Million tonnes of oil equivalent = the amount of oil required to fuel an oil-fired plant in order to generate the same amount of electricity

Table 10.10

Refinery Output 1990-2009

'000 tonnes per year

	1990	1995	2000	2004	2005	2006	2007	2008	2009
Western Europe									
Austria	8,779	9,271	8,770	8,846	9,182	8,988	8,997	9,248	9,160
Belgium	29,372	29,643	38,092	43,233	37,046	36,386	38,097	37,316	37,003
Cyprus	638	830	1,181	279					
Denmark	7,848	9,778	8,231	7,954	7,499	7,853	7,622	7,314	7,489
Finland	10,344	11,533	12,893	13,506	12,839	13,827	14,503	15,052	14,892
France	81,320	83,694	88,576	88,406	86,293	86,839	86,060	89,160	87,439
Germany	3,480	114,414	115,973	119,954	122,675	120,571	118,469	115,810	111,923
Gibraltar									
Greece	16,678	17,651	22,232	20,991	21,240	22,245	23,047	21,813	20,774
Iceland									
Ireland	1,526	2,273	3,286	2,895	3,120	3,231	3,255	3,093	2,944
Italy	91,020	91,171	94,771	98,140	100,598	99,199	100,704	94,536	92,884
Liechtenstein									
Luxembourg									
Malta									
Monaco									
Netherlands	67,905	80,123	80,185	83,486	84,900	80,881	66,121	65,447	61,939
Norway	13,018	13,109	15,196	14,093	15,424	16,403	16,216	14,676	12,903
Portugal	11,144	13,346	12,308	13,293	13,563	13,664	12,621	12,111	12,648
Spain	52,954	55,312	59,830	59,483	60,310	61,350	59,855	60,543	61,839
Sweden	17,239	19,105	22,712	20,308	19,800	19,861	17,903	20,857	21,943
Switzerland	3,047	4,638	4,647	5,214	4,855	5,500	4,740	5,095	5,289
Turkey	22,884	27,140	23,745	26,002	25,638	26,235	25,554	24,805	22,883
United Kingdom	88,120	92,617	86,341	89,826	85,763	82,841	81,210	79,827	80,993
Eastern Europe									
Albania	675	501	311	399	443	502	542	580	587
Belarus	855	12,147	11,490	15,646	17,582	18,492	18,788	18,400	18,489
Bosnia-Herzegovina			512	170	143	145	116	134	140
Bulgaria	6,974	7,255	5,181	5,779	6,297	7,136	6,929	7,121	6,900
Croatia		5,234	5,214	5,321	5,141	4,823	5,312	5,370	5,442
Czech Republic		7,260	6,131	6,999	8,132	8,179	7,753	8,662	8,794
Estonia		313							
Georgia		40	19	24	13	12	39	42	49
Hungary	8,316	7,837	7,483	7,149	8,234	8,512	8,639	8,485	8,249
Latvia									
Lithuania		3,269	4,903	8,629	9,206	8,257	5,776	5,301	5,491
Macedonia		111	936	991	1,147	1,026	1,050	1,018	1,066
Moldova									
Montenegro									
Poland	12,686	13,860	18,480	18,564	18,465	20,947	21,570	22,254	22,673
Romania	22,709	14,559	10,990	13,077	14,867	14,407	13,835	13,746	13,431
Russia	267,723	178,148	176,803	193,929	205,702	216,548	223,731	229,668	219,434
Serbia	4,674	1,155	1,215	3,368	3,162	2,661	3,426	3,319	3,190
Slovakia		4,954	5,810	6,575	6,191	6,276	6,628	6,508	6,392
Slovenia		593	184						
Ukraine		16,554	9,788	22,068	19,222	15,175	14,708	13,579	13,667

Source: *Euromonitor International from OECD*

Energy Statistics

Table 10.11

Primary Energy Consumption: Selected Materials 2009

Million tonnes of oil equivalent

	Crude Oil	Hydroelectricity	Natural Gas	Nuclear Energy	Coal	Total
Western Europe						
Austria	13.0	8.3	8.4		2.3	32.0
Belgium	38.5	0.1	15.6	10.7	4.6	69.4
Denmark	8.2		4.0		4.0	16.1
Finland	9.9	2.9	3.2	5.4	3.7	25.0
France	87.5	13.1	38.4	92.9	10.1	241.9
Germany	113.9	4.2	70.2	30.5	71.0	289.8
Greece	20.2	1.6	3.0		7.9	32.7
Ireland	8.0	0.2	4.3		1.3	13.9
Italy	75.1	10.5	64.5		13.4	163.4
Netherlands	49.4		35.0	1.0	7.9	93.3
Norway	9.7	28.8	3.7		0.3	42.5
Portugal	12.9	2.0	3.9		3.6	22.3
Spain	72.9	6.1	31.1	12.0	10.6	132.6
Sweden	13.7	14.9	1.0	11.9	1.6	43.2
Switzerland	12.3	8.1	2.7	6.2	0.1	29.4
Turkey	28.8	8.1	28.9		27.2	93.0
United Kingdom	74.4	1.2	77.9	15.7	29.7	198.9
Eastern Europe						
Belarus	9.3		14.5		0.0	23.9
Bulgaria	4.4	0.9	2.2	3.5	6.3	17.4
Croatia						
Czech Republic	9.7	0.7	7.4	6.1	15.8	39.6
Estonia						
Hungary	7.3	0.1	9.1	3.5	2.5	22.4
Latvia						
Lithuania	2.9	0.3	2.5	2.5	0.2	8.2
Montenegro						
Poland	25.5	0.7	12.3		53.9	92.3
Romania	9.9	3.6	12.2	2.7	6.2	34.6
Russia	124.9	39.8	350.7	37.0	82.9	635.3
Serbia						
Slovakia	3.9	1.1	5.1	3.2	3.6	16.8
Slovenia						
Ukraine	16.0	2.7	42.3	18.6	35.0	112.5

Source: *BP Amoco, BP Statistical Review of World Energy*

Energy Statistics

Table 10.12

Coal Consumption 1985-2009

Million tonnes of oil equivalent

	1985	1990	1995	2000	2004	2005	2006	2007	2008	2009
Western Europe										
Austria	3.5	3.6	2.4	3.2	2.9	2.8	2.8	3.1	2.2	2.3
Belgium	10.9	10.4	9.8	7.6	6.4	6.1	6.1	5.5	4.8	4.6
Denmark	7.1	6.0	6.6	4.0	4.6	3.7	5.6	4.7	4.1	4.0
Finland	3.5	3.3	3.1	3.5	5.3	3.1	5.2	4.6	3.4	3.7
France	23.0	19.1	14.5	13.9	12.8	13.3	12.1	12.3	11.9	10.1
Germany	147.6	129.6	90.6	84.9	85.4	82.1	83.5	85.7	80.1	71.0
Greece	6.0	8.0	8.2	9.2	9.0	8.8	8.1	8.5	8.1	7.9
Ireland	1.1	2.1	1.8	1.8	1.8	1.8	1.6	1.5	1.4	1.3
Italy	15.1	14.1	12.5	13.0	17.1	17.0	17.2	17.2	16.7	13.4
Netherlands	7.0	9.5	9.8	8.6	9.1	8.7	8.5	9.0	8.5	7.9
Norway	0.5	0.5	0.7	0.7	0.6	0.5	0.4	0.4	0.5	0.3
Portugal	0.8	2.8	4.2	4.5	3.7	3.8	3.8	3.3	3.2	3.6
Spain	19.2	19.0	18.5	21.6	21.0	21.2	18.5	20.2	15.6	10.6
Sweden	2.9	2.2	2.1	1.9	2.3	2.2	2.3	2.2	2.0	1.6
Switzerland	0.4	0.3	0.2	0.1	0.1	0.1	0.1	0.1	0.1	0.1
Turkey	10.6	16.8	17.5	25.5	23.0	26.1	28.8	31.0	30.9	27.2
United Kingdom	62.9	64.9	47.5	36.7	36.6	37.4	40.8	38.2	35.5	29.7
Eastern Europe										
Belarus	1.1	1.2	0.3	0.1	0.1	0.1	0.1	0.1	0.0	0.0
Bulgaria	10.1	8.9	7.8	6.3	6.9	6.9	7.1	7.8	7.5	6.3
Croatia										
Czech Republic	38.2	33.5	23.5	21.0	20.5	19.8	19.4	19.3	17.4	15.8
Estonia										
Hungary	7.6	5.6	3.6	3.2	3.1	2.7	2.9	2.9	2.8	2.5
Latvia										
Lithuania	0.6	0.6	0.1	0.1	0.2	0.2	0.2	0.2	0.2	0.2
Montenegro										
Poland	99.9	80.2	71.7	57.6	57.3	55.7	58.0	57.9	56.0	53.9
Romania	16.9	11.7	9.7	7.0	7.4	7.6	8.5	7.4	7.4	6.2
Russia	195.6	180.6	119.4	105.2	99.5	94.2	96.7	93.5	100.4	82.9
Serbia										
Slovakia	7.2	6.9	5.1	4.0	4.1	3.9	3.8	3.8	3.7	3.6
Slovenia										
Ukraine	76.5	74.8	42.1	38.8	39.1	37.5	39.8	39.7	40.3	35.0

Source: *BP Amoco, BP Statistical Review of World Energy*
Notes: *Million tonnes of oil equivalent = the amount of oil required to fuel an oil-fired plant in order to generate the same amount of electricity*

Energy Statistics

Table 10.13

Crude Oil Consumption 1985-2009

Million metric tonnes

	1985	1990	1995	2000	2004	2005	2006	2007	2008	2009
Western Europe										
Austria	9.8	10.8	11.3	11.8	13.8	14.2	14.2	13.4	13.5	13.0
Belgium	20.8	24.8	26.4	33.9	38.4	39.9	41.1	41.0	40.1	38.5
Denmark	10.7	9.0	10.5	10.4	9.1	9.2	9.3	9.3	8.9	8.2
Finland	10.8	11.0	9.9	10.7	10.6	11.0	10.6	10.6	10.5	9.9
France	84.3	89.4	89.0	94.9	94.0	93.1	93.0	91.4	90.8	87.5
Germany	126.3	127.3	135.1	129.8	124.0	122.4	123.6	112.5	118.9	113.9
Greece	12.0	15.7	17.6	19.9	21.4	21.2	22.2	21.7	21.4	20.2
Ireland	3.9	4.4	5.7	8.2	8.9	9.4	9.3	9.4	9.0	8.0
Italy	84.4	93.6	95.5	93.5	89.7	86.7	86.7	84.0	80.4	75.1
Netherlands	29.7	35.9	39.0	42.7	47.3	50.8	52.2	53.8	51.4	49.4
Norway	9.0	9.2	9.6	9.4	9.6	9.7	10.0	10.2	9.9	9.7
Portugal	8.8	11.1	13.0	15.5	15.4	16.0	14.4	14.4	13.6	12.9
Spain	42.9	48.7	56.3	70.0	77.6	78.8	78.1	78.8	77.1	72.9
Sweden	18.4	16.4	16.1	15.2	15.3	15.1	15.5	14.7	14.5	13.7
Switzerland	12.0	12.8	11.8	12.2	12.0	12.2	12.6	11.3	12.1	12.3
Turkey	16.8	22.1	28.4	31.1	31.0	30.2	29.5	30.5	30.9	28.8
United Kingdom	77.4	82.9	81.9	78.6	81.7	83.0	82.3	79.2	77.9	74.4
Eastern Europe										
Belarus	25.2	24.8	10.4	7.0	7.4	7.1	8.0	7.3	8.4	9.3
Bulgaria	10.4	8.8	5.6	3.9	4.7	4.9	5.2	5.1	4.6	4.4
Croatia										
Czech Republic	10.6	8.4	8.0	7.9	9.5	9.9	9.8	9.7	9.9	9.7
Estonia										
Hungary	10.3	9.3	7.7	6.8	6.5	7.5	7.8	7.7	7.5	7.3
Latvia										
Lithuania	8.6	7.5	3.2	2.4	2.6	2.8	2.8	2.8	3.1	2.9
Montenegro										
Poland	16.4	15.8	14.9	20.0	21.1	21.9	23.3	24.2	25.3	25.5
Romania	15.0	18.7	13.5	10.0	10.9	10.5	10.3	10.3	10.4	9.9
Russia	244.5	249.7	146.1	123.5	123.3	121.9	127.1	126.3	131.6	124.9
Serbia										
Slovakia	6.2	5.0	3.2	3.4	3.2	3.8	4.0	4.1	4.3	3.9
Slovenia										
Ukraine	63.0	63.0	18.9	12.0	13.9	13.9	15.0	15.3	15.5	16.0

Source: *BP Amoco, BP Statistical Review of World Energy*

Table 10.14

Natural Gas Consumption 1985-2009

Million tonnes of oil equivalent

	1985	1990	1995	2000	2004	2005	2006	2007	2008	2009
Western Europe										
Austria	5.0	5.8	7.1	7.3	8.5	9.0	8.5	8.0	8.6	8.4
Belgium	8.4	9.5	10.6	13.4	14.9	14.9	15.3	15.2	15.3	15.6
Denmark	0.6	1.8	3.2	4.4	4.7	4.5	4.6	4.1	4.1	4.0
Finland	0.8	2.3	2.9	3.4	3.9	3.6	3.8	3.5	3.6	3.2
France	23.3	26.4	29.7	35.4	40.5	39.6	37.9	38.2	39.4	38.4
Germany	49.2	53.9	67.0	71.5	77.3	77.6	78.5	74.6	73.1	70.2
Greece	0.1	0.1		1.8	2.4	2.5	2.9	3.6	3.8	3.0
Ireland	2.0	1.9	2.3	3.4	3.7	3.5	4.0	4.3	4.5	4.3
Italy	27.2	39.1	44.9	58.4	66.5	71.2	69.7	70.0	70.0	64.5
Netherlands	32.9	31.1	34.6	35.1	36.8	35.3	34.3	33.3	34.7	35.0
Norway	1.1	1.9	2.7	3.6	4.1	4.0	4.0	3.8	3.9	3.7
Portugal				2.1	3.4	3.8	3.7	3.9	4.2	3.9
Spain	2.1	5.0	7.5	15.2	24.7	29.1	30.3	31.6	34.8	31.1
Sweden	0.1	0.6	0.7	0.7	0.7	0.7	0.8	0.9	0.8	1.0
Switzerland	1.3	1.6	2.2	2.4	2.7	2.8	2.7	2.6	2.8	2.7
Turkey		3.0	6.1	13.1	19.9	24.2	27.4	31.6	32.4	28.9
United Kingdom	46.6	47.2	63.5	87.2	87.7	85.2	80.9	81.9	84.4	77.9
Eastern Europe										
Belarus	8.1	12.1	10.8	14.2	16.1	16.5	17.1	17.0	17.3	14.5
Bulgaria	4.6	5.3	4.5	2.9	2.5	2.8	2.9	3.0	3.0	2.2
Croatia										
Czech Republic	3.7	4.9	6.5	7.5	8.2	8.6	8.4	7.8	7.8	7.4
Estonia										
Hungary	8.6	8.7	9.2	9.7	11.7	12.1	11.5	10.7	10.6	9.1
Latvia										
Lithuania	3.8	5.0	2.1	2.5	2.8	2.9	2.9	3.3	2.9	2.5
Montenegro										
Poland	8.9	8.9	8.9	10.0	11.8	12.3	12.3	12.3	12.5	12.3
Romania	31.9	27.7	21.6	15.4	15.7	15.8	16.3	14.5	14.4	12.2
Russia	315.4	366.8	329.9	318.6	354.7	360.2	367.7	379.9	374.4	350.7
Serbia										
Slovakia	4.2	5.3	5.1	5.8	5.5	5.9	5.4	5.1	5.2	5.1
Slovenia										
Ukraine	78.4	111.6	66.5	63.9	61.7	62.1	60.3	56.9	54.0	42.3

Source: BP Amoco, BP Statistical Review of World Energy
Notes: Million tonnes of oil equivalent = the amount of oil required to fuel an oil-fired plant in order to generate the same amount of electricity

Energy Statistics　　　　　　　　　　　　　　　　　　　　　　　　　　　　　　**Table 10.15**

Nuclear Energy Consumption 1985-2009

Million tonnes of oil equivalent

	1985	1990	1995	2000	2004	2005	2006	2007	2008	2009
Western Europe										
Austria										
Belgium	7.8	9.7	9.4	10.9	10.7	10.8	10.5	10.9	10.4	10.7
Denmark										
Finland	4.3	4.3	4.3	5.1	5.5	5.5	5.4	5.6	5.4	5.4
France	50.7	71.1	85.4	94.0	101.7	102.4	102.1	99.7	99.6	92.9
Germany	31.4	34.5	34.9	38.4	37.8	36.9	37.9	31.8	33.7	30.5
Greece										
Ireland										
Italy	1.6									
Netherlands	0.9	0.8	0.9	0.9	0.9	0.9	0.8	1.0	0.9	1.0
Norway										
Portugal										
Spain	6.3	12.3	12.5	14.1	14.4	13.0	13.6	12.5	13.3	12.0
Sweden	13.3	15.4	15.8	13.0	17.3	16.4	15.2	15.2	14.6	11.9
Switzerland	5.1	5.3	5.6	6.0	6.1	5.2	6.3	6.3	6.2	6.2
Turkey										
United Kingdom	13.8	14.9	20.1	19.3	18.1	18.5	17.1	14.3	11.9	15.7
Eastern Europe										
Belarus										
Bulgaria	3.0	3.3	3.9	4.1	4.4	4.2	4.4	3.3	3.6	3.5
Croatia										
Czech Republic	0.5	2.8	2.8	3.1	6.0	5.6	5.9	5.9	6.0	6.1
Estonia										
Hungary	1.5	3.1	3.2	3.2	2.7	3.1	3.0	3.3	3.4	3.5
Latvia										
Lithuania	2.1	3.9	2.7	1.9	3.4	2.3	2.0	2.2	2.2	2.5
Montenegro										
Poland										
Romania				1.2	1.3	1.3	1.3	1.7	2.5	2.7
Russia	22.5	26.8	22.5	29.5	32.7	33.4	35.4	36.2	36.9	37.0
Serbia										
Slovakia	2.1	2.7	2.6	3.7	3.9	4.0	4.1	3.5	3.8	3.2
Slovenia										
Ukraine	12.1	17.2	16.0	17.5	19.7	20.1	20.4	20.9	20.3	18.6

Source: *BP Amoco, BP Statistical Review of World Energy*
Notes: *Million tonnes of oil equivalent = the amount of oil required to fuel an oil-fired plant in order to generate the same amount of electricity*

Energy Statistics

Table 10.16

Hydroelectricity Consumption 1985-2009

Million tonnes of oil equivalent

	1985	1990	1995	2000	2004	2005	2006	2007	2008	2009
Western Europe										
Austria	7.0	7.1	8.4	9.5	7.7	7.7	7.2	7.7	7.9	8.3
Belgium	0.1	0.1	0.1	0.1	0.1	0.1	0.1	0.1	0.1	0.1
Denmark										
Finland	2.8	2.5	2.9	3.3	3.4	3.1	2.6	3.2	3.9	2.9
France	14.1	12.2	16.5	15.3	13.5	11.8	12.7	13.2	13.7	13.1
Germany	3.9	3.9	4.5	4.9	4.7	4.6	4.4	4.6	4.5	4.2
Greece	0.6	0.5	0.9	0.9	1.2	1.3	1.5	0.8	0.9	1.6
Ireland	0.2	0.2	0.2	0.2	0.1	0.1	0.2	0.2	0.2	0.2
Italy	9.3	7.2	8.6	10.0	9.6	8.2	8.4	7.4	9.4	10.5
Netherlands										
Norway	23.3	27.5	27.7	32.2	24.7	30.9	27.1	30.6	31.8	28.8
Portugal	2.4	2.1	1.9	2.7	2.3	1.2	2.6	2.3	1.7	2.0
Spain	7.1	5.8	5.2	7.7	7.2	4.0	5.8	6.2	5.3	6.1
Sweden	16.2	16.5	15.3	17.8	12.7	16.5	14.0	15.0	15.6	14.9
Switzerland	7.3	6.7	8.0	8.3	7.6	7.1	7.0	8.0	8.2	8.1
Turkey	2.7	5.2	8.0	7.0	10.4	9.0	10.0	8.1	7.5	8.1
United Kingdom	0.9	1.2	1.1	1.2	1.1	1.1	1.0	1.2	1.2	1.2
Eastern Europe										
Belarus										
Bulgaria	0.5	0.4	0.5	0.6	0.7	1.1	1.0	0.7	0.8	0.9
Croatia										
Czech Republic	0.4	0.3	0.5	0.5	0.6	0.7	0.7	0.6	0.5	0.7
Estonia										
Hungary	0.1	0.1	0.1	0.1	0.1	0.1	0.1	0.1	0.1	0.1
Latvia										
Lithuania	0.1	0.1	0.2	0.1	0.2	0.2	0.2	0.2	0.2	0.3
Montenegro										
Poland	0.9	0.8	0.9	0.9	0.8	0.9	0.7	0.7	0.6	0.7
Romania	2.7	2.5	3.8	3.3	3.7	4.6	4.2	3.6	3.9	3.6
Russia	36.1	37.8	40.1	37.4	40.8	39.6	39.6	40.4	37.7	39.8
Serbia										
Slovakia	0.6	0.6	1.2	1.1	1.0	1.1	1.0	1.0	1.0	1.1
Slovenia										
Ukraine	2.4	2.4	2.3	2.6	2.7	2.8	2.9	2.3	2.6	2.7

Source: *BP Amoco, BP Statistical Review of World Energy*
Notes: *Million tonnes of oil equivalent = the amount of oil required to fuel an oil-fired plant in order to generate the same amount of electricity*

Energy Statistics

Table 10.17

Electricity Residential Consumption 1985-2009

'000 GWh

	1985	1990	1995	2000	2004	2005	2006	2007	2008	2009
Western Europe										
Austria	8.3	11.9	13.6	14.2	14.8	15.2	15.4	14.9	14.9	14.8
Belgium	15.5	18.4	22.1	23.7	26.5	26.0	22.7	21.9	21.3	20.9
Cyprus	0.3	0.4	0.8	1.1	1.3	1.4	1.5	1.6	1.7	1.6
Denmark	9.1	9.7	10.3	10.2	10.3	10.4	10.6	10.3	10.4	10.4
Finland	12.2	14.6	16.3	18.1	20.4	20.6	21.1	21.5	21.8	21.5
France	85.8	96.9	108.8	128.7	147.1	144.5	147.1	145.8	146.8	146.7
Germany	132.6	137.1	127.2	128.9	140.4	141.3	141.5	140.1	140.2	139.9
Gibraltar										
Greece	7.7	9.1	11.5	14.2	16.9	16.9	17.7	18.0	18.2	18.1
Iceland	0.5	0.6	0.6	0.6	0.7	0.7	0.8	0.8	0.8	0.8
Ireland	4.0	4.1	5.0	6.4	7.3	7.5	8.1	8.1	8.3	8.2
Italy	44.5	52.7	57.2	61.1	66.6	67.0	67.6	67.2	67.8	67.7
Liechtenstein										
Luxembourg	0.6	0.6	0.7	0.7	0.7	0.7	0.7	0.7	0.8	0.8
Malta	0.2	0.3	0.4	0.6	0.6	0.6	0.7	0.7	0.7	0.7
Monaco										
Netherlands	16.0	16.5	19.7	21.8	23.5	24.2	24.8	24.3	24.5	24.0
Norway	28.9	30.3	34.6	34.6	32.4	34.0	33.6	35.4	36.3	36.1
Portugal	4.5	5.9	7.9	10.1	12.4	13.2	13.4	13.9	14.4	14.3
Spain	23.3	30.2	36.0	43.6	58.0	62.6	70.7	71.6	75.9	71.5
Sweden	39.7	38.1	42.4	42.0	41.4	42.7	41.5	39.6	39.0	38.8
Switzerland	12.0	13.6	15.2	15.7	17.1	17.6	17.7	17.5	17.7	17.6
Turkey	5.0	9.1	14.5	23.9	27.6	30.9	34.5	36.5	38.4	36.5
United Kingdom	88.2	93.8	102.2	111.8	115.5	116.8	116.4	115.1	114.9	114.7
Eastern Europe										
Albania		0.7	0.9	2.5	2.8	2.7	2.0	2.1	2.0	1.9
Belarus		3.5	4.9	5.6	6.1	6.0	5.7	6.0	6.1	6.0
Bosnia-Herzegovina		3.0	2.5	3.7	3.8	4.1	4.1	4.1	4.2	4.1
Bulgaria	9.6	10.5	11.0	9.9	8.8	9.0	9.3	9.4	9.4	9.3
Croatia		4.5	4.6	5.7	6.1	6.3	6.5	6.4	6.6	6.5
Czech Republic	8.0	9.6	14.8	13.8	14.5	14.7	15.2	14.6	14.7	14.6
Estonia		0.9	1.1	1.5	1.6	1.6	1.7	1.8	1.8	1.7
Georgia		2.9	4.6	2.7	2.8	3.0	2.7	2.8	2.8	2.8
Hungary	7.4	9.2	9.8	9.8	11.0	11.1	11.5	11.3	11.3	11.3
Latvia		1.3	1.2	1.2	1.5	1.6	1.7	1.8	1.8	1.8
Lithuania		1.8	1.5	1.8	2.1	2.1	2.4	2.5	2.5	2.5
Macedonia		1.7	2.4	2.7	2.9	3.0	3.0	3.0	3.1	3.1
Moldova		1.7	1.9	1.2	1.6	1.7	1.8	1.3	1.3	1.2
Montenegro										
Poland	14.9	20.2	18.1	21.0	25.5	25.1	26.0	26.6	27.0	27.0
Romania	4.8	5.4	7.1	7.7	8.0	9.2	10.0	10.4	10.7	10.5
Russia		106.9	126.1	140.7	143.3	108.9	112.5	115.9	109.3	105.1
Serbia		10.7	16.1	16.3	13.6	14.2	14.1	13.9	13.3	13.4
Slovakia	2.9	3.7	5.0	5.4	4.8	4.7	4.6	4.6	4.5	4.4
Slovenia		2.2	2.6	2.6	3.0	3.0	3.1	3.0	3.0	3.0
Ukraine		17.2	36.0	30.1	24.2	26.1	27.7	28.3	29.5	28.5

Source: *Euromonitor International from OECD*

Table 10.18

Gas Residential Consumption 1985-2009

'000 TJ

	1985	1990	1995	2000	2004	2005	2006	2007	2008	2009
Western Europe										
Austria	32.6	36.2	47.5	63.3	67.8	71.4	64.5	59.3	57.4	54.9
Belgium		115.5	145.5	153.2	175.2	173.3	160.8	152.5	148.8	142.2
Denmark		19.3	29.9	30.6	33.2	32.8	31.7	29.6	28.7	27.5
Finland		1.3	0.8	1.0	1.3	1.4	1.6	1.7	1.8	1.7
France		306.5	365.0	589.0	686.8	672.3	679.8	602.0	599.5	577.7
Germany		671.9	978.4	1,090.5	1,320.4	1,350.4	1,340.4	1,310.2	1,324.9	1,319.2
Greece		0.1	0.1	0.2	1.6	3.4	6.5	8.2	9.1	8.2
Ireland	1.4	5.4	11.7	20.4	27.9	28.2	29.3	27.5	28.2	28.0
Italy		534.9	636.8	696.6	836.6	874.1	793.0	743.3	728.2	701.1
Netherlands		365.8	400.9	370.7	367.5	349.9	342.9	308.6	300.6	292.2
Norway				0.0	0.1	0.2	0.2	0.2	0.2	0.2
Portugal		1.9	1.9	4.6	8.4	9.3	9.4	10.2	11.0	10.5
Spain		29.6	46.6	94.0	141.2	148.3	170.4	177.7	182.6	177.5
Sweden		2.4	4.1	4.8	3.2	3.3	2.6	2.5	2.5	2.3
Switzerland		28.3	37.5	40.2	46.1	47.4	45.7	43.7	43.5	42.9
Turkey		2.4	52.2	125.4	181.3	222.6	287.6	321.1	339.6	311.9
United Kingdom	1,021.5	1,081.4	1,173.6	1,331.7	1,427.1	1,382.4	1,313.5	1,259.8	1,243.3	1,220.4
Eastern Europe										
Belarus		35.0	42.6	46.7	52.1	54.2	55.4	55.8	56.7	56.5
Bulgaria				0.0	0.3	0.7	1.1	1.5	1.7	1.4
Croatia		8.4	14.7	19.1	24.2	26.4	25.1	23.9	23.8	22.9
Czech Republic		50.0	76.2	95.3	109.4	107.5	105.9	94.7	90.5	88.1
Estonia		2.6	2.2	2.0	1.8	2.1	2.1	2.3	2.4	2.3
Hungary		76.4	134.5	140.7	166.0	182.7	169.5	147.7	138.7	135.3
Latvia		4.4	4.6	3.0	4.4	4.7	4.8	5.1	5.2	5.1
Lithuania		10.3	8.6	4.8	5.9	6.3	6.5	6.8	7.0	6.8
Montenegro										
Poland		139.2	177.6	142.0	140.5	150.2	154.2	147.4	148.8	144.7
Romania		105.0	83.3	103.1	118.3	107.0	118.5	96.2	90.4	86.9
Russia		2,192.7	2,011.8	2,006.1	1,987.3	1,774.4	1,840.6	1,806.0	1,767.2	1,712.2
Serbia			6.7	8.7	11.6	9.7	10.0	3.8	2.5	1.7
Slovakia		50.8	47.5	76.4	69.2	65.9	59.7	51.6	48.7	46.2
Slovenia		1.3	2.5	2.7	4.6	4.6	4.3	4.0	4.0	3.9
Ukraine		406.4	524.6	596.3	619.9	667.5	692.4	621.7	605.2	601.5

Source: Euromonitor International from OECD

Environmental Data

Environmental Statistics

Table 11.1

Carbon Dioxide Emissions 2009

'000 metric tonnes / as stated

	Fossil Fuels	Natural Gases	Coal	Petroleum	CO2 emissions per unit of output (grams per US$)
Western Europe					
Austria	73,286.8	18,077.0	14,849.4	40,360.4	192.3
Belgium	157,174.9	35,588.3	20,485.0	101,101.6	333.5
Cyprus	10,318.6		439.0	9,879.6	438.2
Denmark	53,797.9	10,022.2	17,120.3	26,655.4	173.5
Finland	56,355.1	9,132.0	16,214.0	31,009.1	236.7
France	416,005.6	103,523.3	50,328.8	262,153.5	157.0
Germany	822,120.3	180,198.1	321,414.6	320,507.6	246.8
Gibraltar	4,796.4			4,796.4	5,081.6
Greece	107,088.4	8,365.0	32,350.1	66,373.2	324.5
Iceland	3,490.5		364.9	3,125.6	287.7
Ireland	45,021.4	10,569.9	6,369.6	28,081.9	198.1
Italy	454,527.0	162,991.5	62,700.6	228,835.0	215.1
Liechtenstein					
Luxembourg	11,456.4	2,458.7	197.2	8,800.5	219.0
Malta	3,267.3		28.4	3,238.9	411.6
Monaco					
Netherlands	267,798.4	80,932.6	47,218.2	139,647.6	336.9
Norway	40,927.9	9,130.9	3,140.7	28,656.4	108.1
Portugal	58,036.5	10,481.4	9,007.6	38,547.5	249.1
Spain	370,317.4	85,998.8	52,492.6	231,826.0	252.9
Sweden	55,444.1	1,942.8	8,054.7	45,446.6	136.5
Switzerland	46,383.8	6,632.0	497.6	39,254.1	94.1
Turkey	280,968.4	74,208.4	120,983.9	85,776.1	458.1
United Kingdom	577,726.5	194,514.0	152,616.0	230,596.6	266.0
Eastern Europe					
Albania	4,949.9	58.6	124.8	4,766.5	417.9
Belarus	68,459.8	42,600.2	431.6	25,428.0	1,396.1
Bosnia-Herzegovina	20,602.0	594.3	15,892.3	4,115.4	1,064.0
Bulgaria	53,675.2	6,213.0	31,915.1	15,547.2	1,139.6
Croatia	24,538.5	5,716.2	3,160.7	15,661.7	389.3
Czech Republic	99,559.9	16,783.0	55,211.5	27,565.5	523.2
Estonia	20,842.4	2,916.5	13,435.2	4,490.6	1,092.2
Georgia	5,653.0	3,372.8	80.8	2,199.4	526.1
Hungary	56,004.0	24,697.3	12,716.7	18,590.0	434.3
Latvia	10,181.4	3,991.8	299.6	5,890.0	392.7
Lithuania	18,378.5	6,646.7	990.8	10,740.9	496.1
Macedonia	7,203.6	125.5	4,070.4	3,007.7	781.2
Moldova	7,815.5	5,264.2	233.4	2,317.8	1,446.1
Montenegro	1,955.5		1,379.1	576.4	478.5
Poland	299,399.4	30,067.2	202,854.0	66,478.2	695.2
Romania	103,012.7	31,363.7	42,126.2	29,522.9	639.4
Russia	1,749,023.7	918,645.6	455,545.2	374,833.0	1,420.7
Serbia	47,764.6		33,995.8	13,768.8	1,113.5
Slovakia	37,694.5	11,895.9	14,984.7	10,813.9	428.3
Slovenia	16,734.4	1,940.5	6,584.8	8,209.1	340.3
Ukraine	355,919.7	160,319.4	144,098.2	51,502.1	3,072.1

Source: Energy Information Administration of the US Government, International Energy Annual

Environmental Statistics

Table 11.2

Air and Water Pollutant Emissions 2009

'000 metric tonnes / as stated

	Carbon Monoxide	Nitrogen Oxide	Daily Organic Water Pollutants (kg)	Particulate Matter	Sulphur Oxide
Western Europe					
Austria	756	224	82,975	43	25
Belgium	815	272	93,128	36	143
Cyprus	24	17	7,706	1	40
Denmark	598	181	55,406	38	19
Finland	487	189	58,814	54	61
France	4,885	1,321	557,025	475	450
Germany	3,880	1,346	917,013	192	542
Gibraltar					
Greece	885	310	60,034	62	608
Iceland	18	37	9,478		11
Ireland	167	117	36,440	11	65
Italy	3,370	1,015	480,509	167	473
Liechtenstein	2	0		0	0
Luxembourg	0	0	3,792	3	3
Malta	0	8	4,519	1	14
Monaco					
Netherlands	502	300	111,639	37	61
Norway	399	189	43,593	53	24
Portugal	601	259	100,368	145	206
Spain	2,334	1,454	378,307	173	1,339
Sweden	560	169	100,106	48	38
Switzerland	307	80	99,282	19	17
Turkey	3,514	1,101	167,276	369	1,347
United Kingdom	2,112	1,567	488,239	151	606
Eastern Europe					
Albania			4,123		
Belarus	135	47		41	128
Bosnia-Herzegovina			17,583		600
Bulgaria	983	256	103,904	121	878
Croatia	310	68	41,486	10	56
Czech Republic	457	271	152,268	31	213
Estonia	139	28	14,476	16	71
Georgia					
Hungary	560	215	106,469	51	94
Latvia	317	44	28,764	18	3
Lithuania	199	64	41,679	11	44
Macedonia	121	41	17,761		84
Moldova			21,975		
Montenegro					
Poland	2,688	920	338,673	282	1,163
Romania	1,613	364	233,788	46	642
Russia	15,979	2,785	1,234,496	1,649	3,907
Serbia					
Slovakia	284	82	50,996	44	84
Slovenia	103	47	29,197	8	33
Ukraine	1,169	395	523,765	708	925

Source: Euromonitor International from national statistics/World Resources Institute/World Bank

Environmental Statistics

Table 11.3

Waste Generation 2009

'000 tonnes / Kg per capita

	Municipal Waste	Municipal Waste per capita	Nuclear Waste: Spent Fuel Arising	Nuclear Waste per capita	Hazardous Industrial Waste	Hazardous Industrial Waste per capita
Western Europe						
Austria	4,703	561			960	115
Belgium	5,054	470	0.12	0.01	3,668	341
Cyprus	596	684				
Denmark	4,158	754			546	99
Finland	2,541	477	0.08	0.01	3,252	611
France	33,841	542	1.15	0.02	9,863	158
Germany	47,924	584	0.32	0.00	22,668	276
Gibraltar						
Greece	4,974	442			244	22
Iceland	170	525			13	40
Ireland	2,909	654			654	147
Italy	32,309	538			8,036	134
Liechtenstein						
Luxembourg	318	654			257	529
Malta	280	686				
Monaco						
Netherlands	9,586	584	0.01	0.00	6,230	380
Norway	2,163	451			766	160
Portugal	4,853	455			7,609	713
Spain	26,069	573	0.16	0.00	4,369	96
Sweden	4,529	492	0.24	0.03	3,050	331
Switzerland	5,553	735	0.06	0.01	1,361	180
Turkey	30,083	421				
United Kingdom	34,487	560	0.30	0.00	9,147	148
Eastern Europe						
Albania						
Belarus						
Bosnia-Herzegovina						
Bulgaria	3,558	473			849	113
Croatia	2,340	528				
Czech Republic	3,201	306	0.09	0.01	1,295	124
Estonia	577	433			5,575	4,190
Georgia						
Hungary	4,542	453	0.06	0.01	1,307	130
Latvia	553	246			79	35
Lithuania	1,081	323			140	42
Macedonia						
Moldova						
Montenegro						
Poland	12,400	325			2,685	70
Romania	7,351	343			647	30
Russia					256,369	1,807
Serbia						
Slovakia	1,658	307	0.04	0.01	338	63
Slovenia	848	419			125	62
Ukraine					2,625	57

Source: *Euromonitor International from OECD/national statistics*

Environmental Statistics

Table 11.4

Recycling Levels of Packaging Waste 2009

% of total consumption

	Aluminium	Glass	Paper and Cardboard
Western Europe			
Austria	55	90	77
Belgium	25	92	67
Cyprus		12	41
Denmark		94	63
Finland	99	96	78
France	40	65	62
Germany	74	86	71
Gibraltar			
Greece	34	11	41
Iceland		85	15
Ireland	9	100	98
Italy	55	66	53
Liechtenstein	100	63	90
Luxembourg			
Malta		14	11
Monaco			
Netherlands	24	82	74
Norway	78	88	85
Portugal	17	44	48
Spain	31	53	59
Sweden	70	95	77
Switzerland	99	95	76
Turkey	57	31	43
United Kingdom	32	60	62
Eastern Europe			
Albania			
Belarus			
Bosnia-Herzegovina			
Bulgaria		82	98
Croatia			
Czech Republic	31	63	50
Estonia		63	60
Georgia			
Hungary	54	21	51
Latvia			
Lithuania		36	69
Macedonia			
Moldova			
Montenegro			
Poland	88	42	35
Romania		19	68
Russia			
Serbia			
Slovakia	38	58	53
Slovenia		44	67
Ukraine			

Source: *Euromonitor International from national statistics/World Resources Institute*

External Trade

External Trade Statistics

Table 12.1

Imports (cif) 1980-2009

US$ million

	1980	1985	1990	1995	1996	1997	1998	1999	2000	2001
Western Europe										
Austria	24,444	20,986	49,088	66,386	67,331	64,776	68,183	69,555	68,987	70,493
Belgium			120,068	159,683	163,604	157,260	164,669	164,607	177,008	178,721
Cyprus	1,202	1,247	2,568	3,694	3,983	3,698	3,685	3,618	3,846	3,923
Denmark	19,340	18,245	33,248	45,728	45,004	44,406	46,330	44,519	44,329	44,136
Finland	15,635	13,232	27,001	28,114	29,264	29,784	32,301	31,617	33,900	32,115
France	134,889	108,337	234,447	281,440	281,750	271,914	290,241	294,921	305,113	298,426
Germany	188,002	158,488	346,153	464,271	458,783	445,616	471,418	473,539	495,351	485,969
Gibraltar		25	33	26	199	811	618	776	865	388
Greece	10,548	10,134	19,777	26,795	29,672	27,899	29,388	28,720	28,323	28,126
Iceland	999	905	1,680	1,756	2,032	1,993	2,489	2,503	2,591	2,252
Ireland	11,153	10,015	20,682	33,064	35,897	39,225	44,631	47,194	51,475	51,444
Italy	100,741	87,692	181,968	206,040	208,092	210,268	218,445	220,323	230,677	229,315
Liechtenstein										
Luxembourg	3,612	3,144	7,596	9,748	9,667	9,379	10,237	11,045	10,716	11,151
Malta	938	759	1,961	2,943	2,795	2,552	2,668	2,846	3,400	2,726
Monaco										
Netherlands	88,419	73,123	126,475	176,874	180,639	178,130	187,747	190,279	198,929	195,574
Norway	16,926	15,556	27,221	32,968	35,615	35,709	37,473	34,167	34,391	32,954
Portugal	9,309	7,652	25,264	33,306	35,177	35,064	38,536	39,825	42,129	41,666
Spain	34,078	29,963	87,554	113,319	121,782	122,711	133,149	144,436	152,870	153,607
Sweden	33,438	28,548	54,245	64,741	66,925	65,676	68,590	68,755	73,317	64,326
Switzerland	36,342	30,696	69,681	76,985	74,462	71,064	73,877	75,438	76,092	77,070
Turkey	7,910	11,343	22,303	35,710	43,628	48,560	45,921	40,226	54,503	41,399
United Kingdom	115,559	109,643	224,416	265,176	287,514	306,487	313,940	317,970	334,263	331,579
Eastern Europe										
Albania		261	423	714	937	646	842	1,154	1,090	1,327
Belarus				5,564	6,939	8,689	8,549	6,674	8,646	8,286
Bosnia-Herzegovina				950	1,941	2,400	2,910	3,294	3,101	3,354
Bulgaria		3,237	3,097	5,661	6,861	5,224	4,949	5,453	6,504	7,263
Croatia			5,188	7,352	7,784	9,101	8,276	7,799	7,922	9,054
Czech Republic				26,385	29,366	28,837	30,338	29,482	32,104	36,453
Estonia				2,546	3,209	4,437	4,787	4,110	4,237	4,300
Georgia				489	751	995	882	690	709	753
Hungary	9,245	8,224	8,671	15,380	18,058	21,115	25,679	27,923	31,955	33,724
Latvia				1,818	2,320	2,721	3,191	2,945	3,184	3,505
Lithuania				3,013	3,883	5,025	5,364	4,627	5,219	6,060
Macedonia				1,719	1,627	1,779	1,915	1,776	2,094	1,694
Moldova				841	1,072	1,171	1,024	586	776	893
Montenegro									322	459
Poland	16,690	11,855	8,413	29,050	37,137	42,308	46,495	45,903	48,197	49,314
Romania	13,043	11,267	9,843	10,278	11,435	11,280	11,821	10,392	13,055	15,552
Russia				68,863	74,879	79,076	63,817	43,588	49,125	59,140
Serbia									3,330	4,261
Slovakia				9,648	12,030	12,892	14,380	12,453	16,306	18,846
Slovenia			4,727	9,492	9,423	9,357	10,110	10,083	10,120	10,152
Ukraine				15,484	17,603	17,128	14,676	11,846	14,943	16,893

Source: *Euromonitor International from International Monetary Fund (IMF), International Financial Statistics*
Notes: *US$ totals in this table may differ from the totals given for Imports (cif) by Origin and Imports (cif) by Commodity*

External Trade Statistics

Imports (cif) 1980-2009 *(Continued)*

US$ million

	2002	2003	2004	2005	2006	2007	2008	2009
Western Europe								
Austria	72,839	91,600	113,344	119,873	130,945	156,761	176,063	136,118
Belgium	198,225	234,968	285,611	318,547	351,570	412,011	467,379	352,302
Cyprus	3,863	4,288	5,659	6,282	6,951	8,687	10,791	7,855
Denmark	48,956	56,310	66,926	74,265	85,343	97,341	109,715	81,926
Finland	33,661	41,603	50,679	58,433	69,449	81,757	92,108	60,884
France	308,598	364,926	427,551	471,397	525,613	608,418	687,886	534,253
Germany	490,023	604,626	715,679	780,444	922,343	1,055,997	1,185,453	930,395
Gibraltar	146	259	686	541	538			
Greece	31,318	44,870	52,539	54,456	63,642	76,255	90,122	59,731
Iceland	2,274	2,789	3,553	4,557	5,084	6,107	5,649	3,598
Ireland	52,281	54,174	63,605	71,455	76,433	87,049	84,878	62,620
Italy	239,245	286,811	341,296	371,797	430,647	511,870	556,207	412,286
Liechtenstein								
Luxembourg	11,597	13,691	16,826	17,564	19,433	22,092	25,067	24,291
Malta	2,839	3,368	4,133	3,877	4,376	4,899	5,009	3,798
Monaco								
Netherlands	194,235	234,027	284,025	310,382	358,511	421,084	494,736	382,374
Norway	34,873	40,057	48,533	55,480	64,276	80,389	90,308	69,274
Portugal	42,627	50,329	61,287	63,879	70,712	82,280	94,668	71,510
Spain	163,501	208,512	257,587	287,617	326,033	384,955	416,636	290,804
Sweden	67,644	84,199	100,864	111,566	127,666	153,463	169,014	120,061
Switzerland	82,377	95,582	110,321	119,770	132,021	153,171	173,323	147,796
Turkey	51,554	69,340	97,540	116,774	139,576	170,063	201,964	140,919
United Kingdom	351,540	387,294	461,239	509,131	588,563	622,067	642,494	485,645
Eastern Europe								
Albania	1,503	1,864	2,309	2,618	3,058	4,188	5,251	4,548
Belarus	9,092	11,558	16,491	16,708	22,351	28,693	39,483	28,559
Bosnia-Herzegovina	3,873	4,745	5,908	7,108	7,305	9,726	12,197	10,890
Bulgaria	7,987	10,902	14,467	18,162	23,269	30,087	37,015	23,552
Croatia	10,722	14,209	16,590	18,560	21,488	25,839	30,728	21,203
Czech Republic	40,735	51,239	68,245	76,340	93,430	118,467	142,172	105,242
Estonia	4,810	6,480	8,334	10,212	13,472	15,686	16,058	10,132
Georgia	796	1,141	1,846	2,490	3,678	5,217	6,066	4,386
Hungary	37,787	47,602	59,637	65,783	77,206	94,888	108,685	77,369
Latvia	4,053	5,242	7,048	8,592	11,430	15,182	15,775	9,362
Lithuania	7,526	9,668	12,386	15,510	19,413	24,445	31,295	18,341
Macedonia	1,995	2,306	2,932	3,228	3,752	5,177	6,844	5,032
Moldova	1,039	1,403	1,773	2,293	2,693	3,690	4,081	3,278
Montenegro	585	603	967	1,080	1,222	2,032	2,388	2,112
Poland	53,987	66,712	87,459	99,218	124,450	162,401	204,735	144,438
Romania	17,862	24,003	32,664	40,463	51,114	69,787	82,931	54,359
Russia	67,063	83,677	107,120	137,977	181,161	245,837	321,170	210,984
Serbia	5,614	7,477	10,753	10,461	13,172	18,554	21,154	18,023
Slovakia	21,227	28,874	38,808	43,793	54,950	66,096	74,081	53,855
Slovenia	10,939	13,858	17,585	19,618	23,065	29,531	33,987	23,887
Ukraine	16,977	23,020	28,997	36,136	45,040	60,619	85,533	45,487

Source: Euromonitor International from International Monetary Fund (IMF), International Financial Statistics
Notes: US$ totals in this table may differ from the totals given for Imports (cif) by Origin and Imports (cif) by Commodity

External Trade Statistics

Table 12.2

Imports (cif) by Origin 2009

US$ million

	France	Germany	Italy	Netherlands	Sweden	UK	Total EU	Norway	Switzerland	Russia	Poland
Western Europe											
Austria	4,285	61,351	9,070	5,485	1,474	2,097	106,201	607	9,206	2,080	1,894
Belgium	41,185	60,385	11,666	63,163	5,833	17,851	250,464	3,533	3,772	3,880	3,457
Cyprus	315	690	838	381	72	703	5,647	11	74	19	30
Denmark	2,833	17,264	2,810	5,719	10,769	4,524	57,184	5,755	882	605	2,130
Finland	2,556	9,622	1,519	4,259	8,968	1,936	39,582	1,243	461	8,199	1,181
France		103,723	42,559	38,172	6,417	26,201	368,559	5,481	14,847	11,260	8,381
Germany	77,196		54,722	118,268	14,345	44,258	603,253	21,949	37,816	31,635	33,153
Gibraltar											
Greece	3,638	8,193	7,584	3,591	573	2,295	38,464	107	1,079	2,862	679
Iceland	70	299	99	310	289	164	1,864	467	99		42
Ireland	2,986	4,256	1,126	3,670	494	22,161	39,911	1,021	616		519
Italy	36,472	68,810		23,265	4,018	13,410	236,141	2,936	14,564	16,751	9,387
Liechtenstein											
Luxembourg	2,150	5,622	479	1,230	137	276	17,460	3	121	1	167
Malta	303	352	922	143	10	448	2,617	2	154		27
Monaco											
Netherlands	16,804	65,639	7,827		5,016	21,860	187,801	11,808	2,291	13,497	4,563
Norway	2,529	8,928	2,150	2,703	9,600	4,160	45,935		778		1,889
Portugal	6,132	8,874	3,966	3,800	761	2,308	54,565	840	477		425
Spain	37,288	43,664	20,845	15,185	2,915	13,664	178,838	2,195	4,206		3,325
Sweden	6,071	21,479	3,706	7,414		6,684	81,809	10,450	1,135	3,872	3,652
Switzerland	11,296	39,938	15,270	6,393	1,043	5,427	100,691	492			936
Turkey	7,092	14,098	7,674	2,543	1,891	3,474	56,591	772	2,002	21,573	1,817
United Kingdom	32,147	62,692	19,360	33,771	8,582		253,397	23,504	6,665	8,326	7,326
Eastern Europe											
Albania	86	314	1,363	76	16	32	3,254	1	32	201	31
Belarus	393	2,215	708	232	151	256	6,549	92	185	16,012	787
Bosnia-Herzegovina	132	1,533	1,294	222	54	55	7,365	5	96	207	216
Bulgaria	832	2,880	1,833	653	137	324	14,148	30	229	3,193	524
Croatia	632	2,876	3,279	427	197	368	13,311	75	474	2,246	398
Czech Republic	3,789	32,279	4,187	6,308	940	2,880	81,502	210	980	5,957	7,340
Estonia	257	1,053	227	375	850	228	8,153	126	47	1,002	576
Georgia	72	271	129	76	15	49	1,228	3	47	315	44
Hungary	3,492	19,378	3,199	3,661	656	1,450	53,233	34	559	6,181	3,151
Latvia	290	1,062	367	370	328	168	7,072	127	160	967	754
Lithuania	458	2,047	705	744	498	304	10,780	87	63	5,767	1,827
Macedonia	85	762	384	159	18	64	3,917	2	65		66
Moldova	48	283	184	61	7	44	1,606	4	18	743	114
Montenegro											
Poland	6,632	40,509	9,385	8,065	3,180	4,459	103,925	1,303	980	13,950	
Romania	3,337	9,404	6,404	2,086	350	1,202	39,859	115	501		1,933
Russia	6,661	34,510	10,333		2,009	3,671	88,362	978	2,088		5,218
Serbia	379	2,130	1,686	467		180	11,576	12	241	1,445	263
Slovakia	2,558	9,638	2,306	1,304	312	1,372	40,232	36	330	4,583	2,657
Slovenia	1,192	3,947	3,809	713	138	277	16,956	19	313		453
Ukraine	975	3,856	1,141	678	452	652	15,411	260	443	12,871	2,173

Source: *International Monetary Fund (IMF), Direction of Trade Statistics*

External Trade Statistics

Imports (cif) by Origin 2009 *(Continued)*
US$ million

	Africa & Middle East	Asia/ Pacific	of which: Japan	China	Australasia	Latin America	of which: Brazil	USA	Canada	Total, including Others
Western Europe										
Austria	2,306	7,467	986	3,354	91	508	178	2,159	367	136,118
Belgium	13,524	36,420	9,053	14,422	1,405	8,513	2,540	20,227	1,917	352,302
Cyprus	778	840	170	434	24	89	17	119	11	7,855
Denmark	487	9,419	415	5,112	230	1,528	309	2,664	473	81,926
Finland	408	5,211	592	3,204	284	1,011	415	1,311	363	60,884
France	33,045	48,382	6,055	23,712	1,380	7,774	3,272	25,198	2,562	534,253
Germany	21,158	117,680	19,197	64,124	2,380	18,309	7,037	39,575	3,527	930,395
Gibraltar										
Greece	2,046	6,950	962	4,227	162	1,302	242	1,819	138	59,731
Iceland	30	379	123	179	61	273	147	250	68	3,598
Ireland	958	5,467	679	2,398	136	650	176	10,519	523	62,620
Italy	45,901	51,192	5,388	26,787	1,226	10,221	3,351	13,202	1,640	412,286
Liechtenstein										
Luxembourg	41	5,521	71	4,522	6	93	8	528	76	24,291
Malta	44	527	63	173	16	25	15	113	119	3,798
Monaco										
Netherlands	20,978	79,406	10,376	44,281	1,663	17,773	6,657	29,690	2,011	382,374
Norway	1,448	9,152	1,719	5,405	126	1,800	854	4,269	1,533	69,274
Portugal	5,366	3,350	402	1,593	47	2,283	1,270	1,233	166	71,510
Spain	33,476	30,250	3,332	16,851	760	14,860	3,102	9,509	1,069	290,804
Sweden	1,694	10,717	2,146	5,756	387	1,618	492	4,470	468	120,061
Switzerland	6,265	14,068	5,056	2,148	358	2,847	1,830	14,119	842	147,796
Turkey	14,161	25,425	2,782	12,678	651	2,753	1,106	8,579	937	140,919
United Kingdom	20,222	82,612	9,810	43,110	4,403	11,321	4,042	47,241	8,135	485,645
Eastern Europe										
Albania	44	299	3	246	3	67	57	56	23	4,548
Belarus	149	1,742	205	1,081	13	298	118	431	40	28,559
Bosnia-Herzegovina	12	89	2	64	4	55	31	38	5	10,890
Bulgaria	329	1,165	107	638	12	653	173	199	65	23,552
Croatia	197	2,477	289	1,448	12	343	191	546	106	21,203
Czech Republic	362	11,860	1,832	6,003	24	274	118	1,182	206	105,242
Estonia	24	397	30	252	3	90	13	129	17	10,132
Georgia	233	906	61	186	24	113	86	289	17	4,386
Hungary	212	10,972	1,902	6,624	17	315	103	1,213	107	77,369
Latvia	30	311	12	191	2	16	4	78	9	9,362
Lithuania	73	762	25	453	4	100	31	204	36	18,341
Macedonia	38	163	5	76	2	62	39	47	19	5,032
Moldova	12	178	7	68		22	17	25	2	3,278
Montenegro										
Poland	1,362	11,636	1,342	7,604	227	1,664	368	2,082	155	144,438
Romania	692	5,908	262	2,666	27	657	430	696	114	54,359
Russia	1,759	40,062	4,366	17,707	565	1,475		5,427	997	190,566
Serbia	76	765	13	389	6	152	25	139	0	18,023
Slovakia	141	3,161	481	1,927	15	53	27	313	45	53,855
Slovenia	406	1,233	80	693	6	533	184	409	41	23,887
Ukraine	718	9,268	520	2,737	149	770	376	1,291	136	45,487

Source: International Monetary Fund (IMF), Direction of Trade Statistics
Notes: US$ totals in this table may differ from the totals given for Imports (cif) by Commodity and Total Imports (cif)

External Trade Statistics

Table 12.3

Imports (cif) by Origin 2009 (% Analysis)
% of total imports

	France	Germany	Italy	Netherlands	Sweden	UK	Total EU	Norway	Switzerland	Russia	Poland
Western Europe											
Austria	3.15	45.07	6.66	4.03	1.08	1.54	78.02	0.45	6.76	1.53	1.39
Belgium	11.69	17.14	3.31	17.93	1.66	5.07	71.09	1.00	1.07	1.10	0.98
Cyprus	4.01	8.79	10.67	4.85	0.91	8.95	71.89	0.14	0.94	0.25	0.39
Denmark	3.46	21.07	3.43	6.98	13.15	5.52	69.80	7.02	1.08	0.74	2.60
Finland	4.20	15.80	2.50	7.00	14.73	3.18	65.01	2.04	0.76	13.47	1.94
France		19.41	7.97	7.14	1.20	4.90	68.99	1.03	2.78	2.11	1.57
Germany	8.30		5.88	12.71	1.54	4.76	64.84	2.36	4.06	3.40	3.56
Gibraltar											
Greece	6.09	13.72	12.70	6.01	0.96	3.84	64.40	0.18	1.81	4.79	1.14
Iceland	1.94	8.30	2.76	8.62	8.03	4.55	51.81	12.97	2.75		1.17
Ireland	4.77	6.80	1.80	5.86	0.79	35.39	63.74	1.63	0.98		0.83
Italy	8.85	16.69		5.64	0.97	3.25	57.28	0.71	3.53	4.06	2.28
Liechtenstein											
Luxembourg	8.85	23.14	1.97	5.06	0.56	1.13	71.88	0.01	0.50	0.00	0.69
Malta	7.99	9.28	24.27	3.78	0.26	11.79	68.89	0.05	4.05		0.70
Monaco											
Netherlands	4.39	17.17	2.05		1.31	5.72	49.11	3.09	0.60	3.53	1.19
Norway	3.65	12.89	3.10	3.90	13.86	6.01	66.31		1.12		2.73
Portugal	8.58	12.41	5.55	5.31	1.06	3.23	76.30	1.17	0.67		0.59
Spain	12.82	15.01	7.17	5.22	1.00	4.70	61.50	0.75	1.45		1.14
Sweden	5.06	17.89	3.09	6.18		5.57	68.14	8.70	0.95	3.23	3.04
Switzerland	7.64	27.02	10.33	4.33	0.71	3.67	68.13	0.33			0.63
Turkey	5.03	10.00	5.45	1.80	1.34	2.47	40.16	0.55	1.42	15.31	1.29
United Kingdom	6.62	12.91	3.99	6.95	1.77		52.18	4.84	1.37	1.71	1.51
Eastern Europe											
Albania	1.89	6.91	29.96	1.67	0.35	0.71	71.55	0.03	0.71	4.43	0.69
Belarus	1.38	7.76	2.48	0.81	0.53	0.90	22.93	0.32	0.65	56.07	2.75
Bosnia-Herzegovina	1.21	14.08	11.88	2.04	0.50	0.50	67.64	0.05	0.88	1.90	1.99
Bulgaria	3.53	12.23	7.78	2.77	0.58	1.38	60.07	0.13	0.97	13.56	2.22
Croatia	2.98	13.57	15.46	2.01	0.93	1.73	62.78	0.35	2.23	10.59	1.88
Czech Republic	3.60	30.67	3.98	5.99	0.89	2.74	77.44	0.20	0.93	5.66	6.97
Estonia	2.54	10.40	2.24	3.70	8.39	2.25	80.46	1.25	0.46	9.89	5.68
Georgia	1.65	6.18	2.94	1.72	0.35	1.12	28.00	0.06	1.07	7.19	1.00
Hungary	4.51	25.05	4.13	4.73	0.85	1.87	68.80	0.04	0.72	7.99	4.07
Latvia	3.09	11.34	3.93	3.95	3.50	1.80	75.54	1.35	1.71	10.33	8.06
Lithuania	2.50	11.16	3.85	4.06	2.72	1.66	58.78	0.48	0.34	31.44	9.96
Macedonia	1.69	15.14	7.63	3.15	0.36	1.28	77.85	0.04	1.29		1.31
Moldova	1.47	8.62	5.62	1.85	0.21	1.33	48.98	0.13	0.53	22.66	3.48
Montenegro											
Poland	4.59	28.05	6.50	5.58	2.20	3.09	71.95	0.90	0.68	9.66	
Romania	6.14	17.30	11.78	3.84	0.64	2.21	73.33	0.21	0.92		3.56
Russia	3.50	18.11	5.42		1.05	1.93	46.37	0.51	1.10		2.74
Serbia	2.10	11.82	9.35	2.59		1.00	64.23	0.07	1.33	8.02	1.46
Slovakia	4.75	17.90	4.28	2.42	0.58	2.55	74.71	0.07	0.61	8.51	4.93
Slovenia	4.99	16.52	15.95	2.98	0.58	1.16	70.98	0.08	1.31		1.90
Ukraine	2.14	8.48	2.51	1.49	0.99	1.43	33.88	0.57	0.97	28.30	4.78

Source: International Monetary Fund (IMF), Direction of Trade Statistics

External Trade Statistics

Imports (cif) by Origin 2009 (% Analysis) *(Continued)*
% of total imports

	Africa & Middle East	Asia/ Pacific	of which: Japan	China	Australasia	Latin America	of which: Brazil	USA	Canada	Total, including Others
Western Europe										
Austria	1.69	5.49	0.72	2.46	0.07	0.37	0.13	1.59	0.27	100.00
Belgium	3.84	10.34	2.57	4.09	0.40	2.42	0.72	5.74	0.54	100.00
Cyprus	9.91	10.70	2.17	5.52	0.30	1.14	0.21	1.52	0.14	100.00
Denmark	0.59	11.50	0.51	6.24	0.28	1.86	0.38	3.25	0.58	100.00
Finland	0.67	8.56	0.97	5.26	0.47	1.66	0.68	2.15	0.60	100.00
France	6.19	9.06	1.13	4.44	0.26	1.46	0.61	4.72	0.48	100.00
Germany	2.27	12.65	2.06	6.89	0.26	1.97	0.76	4.25	0.38	100.00
Gibraltar										
Greece	3.43	11.64	1.61	7.08	0.27	2.18	0.41	3.05	0.23	100.00
Iceland	0.82	10.53	3.43	4.98	1.69	7.60	4.09	6.94	1.90	100.00
Ireland	1.53	8.73	1.08	3.83	0.22	1.04	0.28	16.80	0.83	100.00
Italy	11.13	12.42	1.31	6.50	0.30	2.48	0.81	3.20	0.40	100.00
Liechtenstein										
Luxembourg	0.17	22.73	0.29	18.62	0.03	0.38	0.03	2.17	0.31	100.00
Malta	1.16	13.87	1.65	4.55	0.41	0.66	0.39	2.97	3.12	100.00
Monaco										
Netherlands	5.49	20.77	2.71	11.58	0.43	4.65	1.74	7.76	0.53	100.00
Norway	2.09	13.21	2.48	7.80	0.18	2.60	1.23	6.16	2.21	100.00
Portugal	7.50	4.69	0.56	2.23	0.07	3.19	1.78	1.72	0.23	100.00
Spain	11.51	10.40	1.15	5.79	0.26	5.11	1.07	3.27	0.37	100.00
Sweden	1.41	8.93	1.79	4.79	0.32	1.35	0.41	3.72	0.39	100.00
Switzerland	4.24	9.52	3.42	1.45	0.24	1.93	1.24	9.55	0.57	100.00
Turkey	10.05	18.04	1.97	9.00	0.46	1.95	0.78	6.09	0.67	100.00
United Kingdom	4.16	17.01	2.02	8.88	0.91	2.33	0.83	9.73	1.67	100.00
Eastern Europe										
Albania	0.96	6.57	0.07	5.41	0.07	1.48	1.24	1.24	0.51	100.00
Belarus	0.52	6.10	0.72	3.79	0.05	1.04	0.41	1.51	0.14	100.00
Bosnia-Herzegovina	0.11	0.82	0.02	0.59	0.04	0.50	0.28	0.35	0.05	100.00
Bulgaria	1.40	4.95	0.46	2.71	0.05	2.77	0.74	0.85	0.27	100.00
Croatia	0.93	11.68	1.36	6.83	0.05	1.62	0.90	2.57	0.50	100.00
Czech Republic	0.34	11.27	1.74	5.70	0.02	0.26	0.11	1.12	0.20	100.00
Estonia	0.23	3.92	0.29	2.49	0.03	0.89	0.12	1.27	0.17	100.00
Georgia	5.31	20.66	1.38	4.24	0.55	2.59	1.96	6.59	0.40	100.00
Hungary	0.27	14.18	2.46	8.56	0.02	0.41	0.13	1.57	0.14	100.00
Latvia	0.32	3.32	0.12	2.04	0.02	0.17	0.04	0.83	0.10	100.00
Lithuania	0.40	4.16	0.14	2.47	0.02	0.55	0.17	1.11	0.19	100.00
Macedonia	0.76	3.24	0.10	1.50	0.03	1.22	0.77	0.94	0.38	100.00
Moldova	0.38	5.44	0.21	2.07	0.01	0.67	0.53	0.77	0.07	100.00
Montenegro										
Poland	0.94	8.06	0.93	5.26	0.16	1.15	0.25	1.44	0.11	100.00
Romania	1.27	10.87	0.48	4.91	0.05	1.21	0.79	1.28	0.21	100.00
Russia	0.92	21.02	2.29	9.29	0.30	0.77		2.85	0.52	100.00
Serbia	0.42	4.24	0.07	2.16	0.03	0.85	0.14	0.77	0.00	100.00
Slovakia	0.26	5.87	0.89	3.58	0.03	0.10	0.05	0.58	0.08	100.00
Slovenia	1.70	5.16	0.34	2.90	0.02	2.23	0.77	1.71	0.17	100.00
Ukraine	1.58	20.37	1.14	6.02	0.33	1.69	0.83	2.84	0.30	100.00

Source: International Monetary Fund (IMF), Direction of Trade Statistics

External Trade Statistics

Table 12.4

Imports (cif) by Commodity: SITC Classification 2009

US$ million

	Food and live animals	Beverages and tobacco	Crude materials excluding fuels	Mineral fuels etc	Oils and fats
Western Europe					
Austria	8,755	998	5,253	14,195	475
Belgium	25,893	3,849	11,413	41,641	1,923
Cyprus	890	291	85	1,387	39
Denmark	9,012	1,134	2,189	5,276	600
Finland	3,674	645	3,743	10,205	202
France	41,006	5,591	11,364	71,113	2,307
Germany	58,350	7,818	28,289	104,324	3,363
Gibraltar					
Greece	5,115	729	1,669	12,136	311
Iceland	338	57	488	447	18
Ireland	6,136	1,063	808	6,200	255
Italy	32,757	4,700	13,807	72,782	3,400
Liechtenstein					
Luxembourg	2,137	742	1,487	1,946	24
Malta	497	80	39	400	9
Monaco					
Netherlands	27,997	3,164	14,665	60,345	3,968
Norway	4,356	753	4,006	3,445	500
Portugal	7,820	594	1,767	9,230	415
Spain	20,827	3,141	12,191	59,089	1,403
Sweden	9,852	1,296	3,448	13,905	638
Switzerland	7,149	1,803	2,188	10,608	297
Turkey	3,590	479	9,936	19,932	1,123
United Kingdom	42,122	7,775	10,963	50,044	1,764
Eastern Europe					
Albania	551	172	104	536	54
Belarus	1,776	307	837	11,291	129
Bosnia-Herzegovina	1,536	405	273	1,663	80
Bulgaria	1,866	341	1,453	4,741	98
Croatia	1,871	182	339	3,585	84
Czech Republic	5,574	713	2,306	9,623	292
Estonia	970	237	249	1,921	53
Georgia	518	94	103	777	43
Hungary	2,848	365	985	6,400	169
Latvia	1,148	225	252	1,538	62
Lithuania	2,009	373	614	5,123	130
Macedonia	559	52	88	259	46
Moldova	346	136	66	703	7
Montenegro	221	55	52	351	12
Poland	8,109	733	4,343	16,367	596
Romania	4,121	438	1,226	5,069	224
Russia	29,384	3,920	6,753	3,122	1,638
Serbia	843	131	518	2,676	52
Slovakia	2,426	312	1,456	6,877	161
Slovenia	1,816	230	1,147	2,700	69
Ukraine	2,544	390	1,938	11,942	299

Source: *United Nations, UN Trade Statistics*

External Trade Statistics

Imports (cif) by Commodity: SITC Classification 2009 *(Continued)*

US$ million

	Chemicals	Basic manufactures	Machinery and transport equipment	Miscellaneous manufactured goods	Others	Total
Western Europe						
Austria	16,955	20,734	44,822	20,624	3,307	136,118
Belgium	93,331	48,333	85,281	36,452	4,188	352,302
Cyprus	821	1,022	2,024	1,282	14	7,855
Denmark	9,334	11,510	27,621	13,310	1,942	81,926
Finland	7,120	7,328	19,563	6,470	1,932	60,884
France	77,317	66,797	179,826	78,377	555	534,253
Germany	119,302	107,404	307,154	108,516	85,875	930,395
Gibraltar						
Greece	8,091	7,865	16,040	7,665	110	59,731
Iceland	371	411	1,055	408	4	3,598
Ireland	10,234	4,750	19,895	8,423	4,856	62,620
Italy	58,243	52,817	113,497	48,417	11,866	412,286
Liechtenstein						
Luxembourg	2,438	4,132	7,197	2,681	1,504	24,291
Malta	405	373	1,509	452	34	3,798
Monaco						
Netherlands	40,599	37,209	105,190	36,738	52,499	382,374
Norway	6,868	10,463	27,648	10,826	410	69,274
Portugal	8,361	9,436	20,314	7,419	6,153	71,510
Spain	34,206	35,446	91,539	31,841	1,120	290,804
Sweden	14,597	15,411	41,054	14,522	5,339	120,061
Switzerland	32,081	22,862	39,683	30,655	471	147,796
Turkey	20,077	23,179	41,062	9,110	12,432	140,919
United Kingdom	60,190	57,153	149,181	79,736	26,717	485,645
Eastern Europe						
Albania	452	1,151	1,026	500	3	4,548
Belarus	2,789	3,699	5,589	1,150	992	28,559
Bosnia-Herzegovina	1,366	2,152	2,281	1,124	10	10,890
Bulgaria	2,604	3,956	5,841	1,796	858	23,552
Croatia	2,620	3,844	6,049	2,605	24	21,203
Czech Republic	11,432	18,146	42,921	12,114	2,121	105,242
Estonia	1,114	1,471	2,490	1,056	571	10,132
Georgia	397	728	1,282	415	29	4,386
Hungary	7,102	10,168	34,964	4,727	9,641	77,369
Latvia	1,194	1,285	1,825	877	955	9,362
Lithuania	2,696	2,166	3,421	1,388	421	18,341
Macedonia	565	1,199	1,036	384	845	5,032
Moldova	462	599	626	334	2	3,278
Montenegro	171	327	434	223	266	2,112
Poland	18,122	26,066	50,408	12,916	6,777	144,438
Romania	7,451	11,348	17,884	4,988	1,609	54,359
Russia	29,468	25,891	83,152	22,970	4,685	210,984
Serbia	2,285	2,972	3,652	1,453	3,440	18,023
Slovakia	4,586	9,063	23,614	5,166	192	53,855
Slovenia	3,212	4,394	7,646	2,592	83	23,887
Ukraine	5,091	6,113	13,866	2,492	811	45,487

Source: *United Nations, UN Trade Statistics*
Notes: *US$ totals in this table may differ from the totals given for Imports (cif) by Origin and Total Imports (cif)*

External Trade Statistics   **Table 12.5**

Imports (cif) by Commodity: SITC Classification 2009 (% Analysis)
% of total imports

	Food and live animals	Beverages and tobacco	Crude materials excluding fuels	Mineral fuels etc	Oils and fats
Western Europe					
Austria	6.43	0.73	3.86	10.43	0.35
Belgium	7.35	1.09	3.24	11.82	0.55
Cyprus	11.32	3.71	1.09	17.66	0.49
Denmark	11.00	1.38	2.67	6.44	0.73
Finland	6.03	1.06	6.15	16.76	0.33
France	7.68	1.05	2.13	13.31	0.43
Germany	6.27	0.84	3.04	11.21	0.36
Gibraltar					
Greece	8.56	1.22	2.79	20.32	0.52
Iceland	9.39	1.59	13.56	12.43	0.51
Ireland	9.80	1.70	1.29	9.90	0.41
Italy	7.95	1.14	3.35	17.65	0.82
Liechtenstein					
Luxembourg	8.80	3.06	6.12	8.01	0.10
Malta	13.10	2.10	1.02	10.53	0.24
Monaco					
Netherlands	7.32	0.83	3.84	15.78	1.04
Norway	6.29	1.09	5.78	4.97	0.72
Portugal	10.94	0.83	2.47	12.91	0.58
Spain	7.16	1.08	4.19	20.32	0.48
Sweden	8.21	1.08	2.87	11.58	0.53
Switzerland	4.84	1.22	1.48	7.18	0.20
Turkey	2.55	0.34	7.05	14.14	0.80
United Kingdom	8.67	1.60	2.26	10.30	0.36
Eastern Europe					
Albania	12.11	3.78	2.28	11.78	1.18
Belarus	6.22	1.08	2.93	39.54	0.45
Bosnia-Herzegovina	14.11	3.72	2.51	15.27	0.74
Bulgaria	7.92	1.45	6.17	20.13	0.41
Croatia	8.82	0.86	1.60	16.91	0.40
Czech Republic	5.30	0.68	2.19	9.14	0.28
Estonia	9.57	2.34	2.46	18.96	0.52
Georgia	11.81	2.15	2.34	17.71	0.98
Hungary	3.68	0.47	1.27	8.27	0.22
Latvia	12.27	2.41	2.70	16.43	0.66
Lithuania	10.96	2.03	3.35	27.93	0.71
Macedonia	11.11	1.03	1.76	5.15	0.91
Moldova	10.56	4.14	2.00	21.43	0.21
Montenegro	10.48	2.62	2.44	16.63	0.55
Poland	5.61	0.51	3.01	11.33	0.41
Romania	7.58	0.81	2.26	9.32	0.41
Russia	13.93	1.86	3.20	1.48	0.78
Serbia	4.68	0.73	2.87	14.85	0.29
Slovakia	4.51	0.58	2.70	12.77	0.30
Slovenia	7.60	0.96	4.80	11.30	0.29
Ukraine	5.59	0.86	4.26	26.25	0.66

Source: United Nations, UN Trade Statistics

Imports (cif) by Commodity: SITC Classification 2009 (% Analysis) *(Continued)*

% of total imports

	Chemicals	Basic manufactures	Machinery and transport equipment	Miscellaneous manufactured goods	Others	Total
Western Europe						
Austria	12.46	15.23	32.93	15.15	2.43	100.00
Belgium	26.49	13.72	24.21	10.35	1.19	100.00
Cyprus	10.46	13.01	25.77	16.32	0.18	100.00
Denmark	11.39	14.05	33.71	16.25	2.37	100.00
Finland	11.70	12.04	32.13	10.63	3.17	100.00
France	14.47	12.50	33.66	14.67	0.10	100.00
Germany	12.82	11.54	33.01	11.66	9.23	100.00
Gibraltar						
Greece	13.55	13.17	26.85	12.83	0.18	100.00
Iceland	10.31	11.43	29.32	11.35	0.12	100.00
Ireland	16.34	7.59	31.77	13.45	7.76	100.00
Italy	14.13	12.81	27.53	11.74	2.88	100.00
Liechtenstein						
Luxembourg	10.04	17.01	29.63	11.04	6.19	100.00
Malta	10.65	9.83	39.74	11.90	0.90	100.00
Monaco						
Netherlands	10.62	9.73	27.51	9.61	13.73	100.00
Norway	9.91	15.10	39.91	15.63	0.59	100.00
Portugal	11.69	13.20	28.41	10.38	8.60	100.00
Spain	11.76	12.19	31.48	10.95	0.39	100.00
Sweden	12.16	12.84	34.19	12.10	4.45	100.00
Switzerland	21.71	15.47	26.85	20.74	0.32	100.00
Turkey	14.25	16.45	29.14	6.46	8.82	100.00
United Kingdom	12.39	11.77	30.72	16.42	5.50	100.00
Eastern Europe						
Albania	9.94	25.30	22.55	11.00	0.06	100.00
Belarus	9.77	12.95	19.57	4.03	3.47	100.00
Bosnia-Herzegovina	12.54	19.76	20.95	10.32	0.09	100.00
Bulgaria	11.06	16.79	24.80	7.63	3.64	100.00
Croatia	12.36	18.13	28.53	12.29	0.11	100.00
Czech Republic	10.86	17.24	40.78	11.51	2.02	100.00
Estonia	10.99	14.52	24.58	10.42	5.64	100.00
Georgia	9.06	16.60	29.23	9.46	0.67	100.00
Hungary	9.18	13.14	45.19	6.11	12.46	100.00
Latvia	12.75	13.72	19.50	9.36	10.20	100.00
Lithuania	14.70	11.81	18.65	7.57	2.30	100.00
Macedonia	11.22	23.83	20.58	7.63	16.78	100.00
Moldova	14.08	18.27	19.08	10.18	0.05	100.00
Montenegro	8.08	15.49	20.54	10.55	12.61	100.00
Poland	12.55	18.05	34.90	8.94	4.69	100.00
Romania	13.71	20.88	32.90	9.18	2.96	100.00
Russia	13.97	12.27	39.41	10.89	2.22	100.00
Serbia	12.68	16.49	20.26	8.06	19.09	100.00
Slovakia	8.52	16.83	43.85	9.59	0.36	100.00
Slovenia	13.45	18.39	32.01	10.85	0.35	100.00
Ukraine	11.19	13.44	30.48	5.48	1.78	100.00

Source: United Nations, UN Trade Statistics

External Trade Statistics

Table 12.6

Exports (fob) 1980-2009

US$ million

	1980	1985	1990	1995	1996	1997	1998	1999	2000	2001
Western Europe										
Austria	17,489	17,239	41,135	57,643	57,818	58,590	62,742	64,124	64,170	66,494
Belgium			118,296	175,849	175,356	171,881	179,078	178,972	187,890	190,356
Cyprus	532	476	957	1,229	1,395	1,101	1,061	995	951	976
Denmark	16,749	17,090	37,037	51,478	51,480	49,119	48,839	50,399	50,349	51,083
Finland	14,150	13,617	26,571	39,573	38,435	39,316	42,963	41,841	45,482	42,803
France	116,030	101,671	216,591	286,738	287,667	289,736	305,641	302,493	301,391	298,594
Germany	192,860	183,933	410,104	523,802	524,198	512,427	543,397	542,870	550,112	571,358
Gibraltar		1	0	35	41	34	21	38	30	18
Greece	5,153	4,539	8,105	10,961	11,948	11,128	10,732	10,475	10,964	9,706
Iceland	918	815	1,592	1,804	1,639	1,852	2,045	2,005	1,892	2,022
Ireland	8,398	10,357	23,747	44,635	48,668	53,512	64,477	71,219	77,098	82,985
Italy	78,104	76,717	170,486	233,998	252,039	240,404	245,700	235,175	240,338	244,753
Liechtenstein										
Luxembourg	3,005	2,831	6,305	7,750	7,210	6,999	7,922	7,895	7,946	8,238
Malta	483	400	1,130	1,914	1,731	1,630	1,834	1,983	2,443	1,958
Monaco										
Netherlands	84,948	77,873	131,775	196,276	197,417	194,905	201,374	200,778	213,427	216,186
Norway	18,543	19,985	34,049	41,992	49,645	48,542	40,399	45,455	60,058	59,218
Portugal	4,640	5,685	16,422	23,207	24,605	23,973	24,814	25,227	25,089	24,930
Spain	20,720	24,247	55,521	91,046	101,996	104,359	109,228	109,964	113,325	115,155
Sweden	30,906	30,461	57,538	79,801	84,896	82,946	84,969	84,812	87,724	78,208
Switzerland	29,632	27,433	63,784	78,040	76,196	72,493	75,431	76,122	74,856	78,066
Turkey	2,910	7,957	12,959	21,599	23,245	26,260	26,881	26,587	27,775	31,334
United Kingdom	110,144	101,299	185,107	241,976	262,009	281,037	271,718	268,178	284,416	272,301
Eastern Europe										
Albania		198	224	202	211	139	208	351	258	307
Belarus				4,803	5,652	7,301	7,070	5,909	7,326	7,451
Bosnia-Herzegovina				52	181	381	593	750	1,067	1,032
Bulgaria		1,773	1,708	5,359	6,602	5,323	4,195	3,964	4,822	5,115
Croatia			4,020	4,517	4,643	3,981	4,517	4,303	4,422	4,659
Czech Republic				21,686	21,916	22,747	26,418	26,241	28,996	33,358
Estonia				1,840	2,077	2,932	3,244	3,018	3,167	3,312
Georgia				155	203	244	191	238	323	318
Hungary	8,671	8,538	9,598	12,801	15,631	18,990	22,992	24,950	28,016	30,530
Latvia				1,305	1,443	1,672	1,811	1,723	1,865	2,001
Lithuania				2,039	2,656	3,200	3,235	2,754	3,548	4,279
Macedonia				1,204	1,147	1,237	1,311	1,191	1,323	1,158
Moldova				739	823	890	644	474	472	568
Montenegro									228	253
Poland	14,191	11,489	13,627	22,895	24,440	25,751	27,191	27,397	35,895	41,651
Romania	11,209	12,167	5,775	7,910	8,085	8,431	8,300	8,505	10,367	11,385
Russia				82,913	90,563	89,008	74,884	75,665	105,565	101,884
Serbia									1,558	1,721
Slovakia				8,579	8,831	9,645	10,720	10,234	15,894	16,899
Slovenia			4,118	8,316	8,312	8,372	9,048	8,546	8,741	9,261
Ukraine				13,128	14,401	14,232	12,637	11,582	15,722	17,091

Source: *Euromonitor International from International Monetary Fund (IMF), International Financial Statistics*
Notes: *US$ totals in this table may differ from the totals given for Exports (fob) by Destination and Exports (fob) by Commodity*

External Trade Statistics

Exports (fob) 1980-2009 *(Continued)*

US$ million

	2002	2003	2004	2005	2006	2007	2008	2009
Western Europe								
Austria	73,156	89,264	111,723	117,647	130,376	157,316	173,302	130,826
Belgium	215,972	255,637	306,807	335,625	366,758	431,119	473,348	370,029
Cyprus	770	834	1,081	1,303	1,153	1,254	1,744	1,338
Denmark	56,385	65,376	75,665	83,570	91,635	101,973	115,648	92,843
Finland	44,702	52,518	60,920	65,193	77,288	90,092	96,837	62,888
France	313,654	367,212	420,853	441,754	488,585	552,289	608,183	474,861
Germany	615,435	751,685	909,237	977,883	1,122,067	1,323,818	1,450,009	1,121,500
Gibraltar	43	22	32	31	31			
Greece	10,328	13,641	15,218	17,239	20,775	23,608	25,670	20,044
Iceland	2,227	2,385	2,896	2,942	3,239	4,350	5,216	4,026
Ireland	88,237	92,929	104,963	107,848	109,006	122,253	126,961	116,990
Italy	252,681	298,256	352,092	372,278	418,134	500,240	537,411	405,439
Liechtenstein								
Luxembourg	8,495	9,979	12,175	12,696	14,174	16,048	17,590	12,761
Malta	2,225	2,440	2,623	2,436	2,831	3,131	2,976	2,184
Monaco								
Netherlands	219,974	264,864	318,072	349,599	400,667	472,649	545,549	431,796
Norway	59,661	68,324	82,524	103,750	122,118	136,392	172,648	120,848
Portugal	26,897	33,104	38,452	38,720	44,782	52,515	57,535	44,180
Spain	123,507	155,995	182,099	191,100	213,341	248,917	277,424	220,896
Sweden	82,918	102,420	123,312	130,898	147,904	168,979	183,930	131,327
Switzerland	87,358	100,724	117,816	126,083	141,669	164,797	191,415	166,703
Turkey	36,059	47,253	63,167	73,476	85,535	107,272	132,027	102,135
United Kingdom	279,764	307,615	349,722	384,470	447,625	442,260	468,576	358,040
Eastern Europe								
Albania	340	448	605	658	798	1,078	1,355	1,088
Belarus	8,021	9,946	13,774	15,979	19,734	24,275	32,902	21,278
Bosnia-Herzegovina	1,005	1,364	1,790	2,406	3,312	4,155	5,027	4,704
Bulgaria	5,749	7,540	9,931	11,739	15,101	18,575	22,484	16,378
Croatia	4,903	6,187	8,025	8,806	10,376	12,364	14,112	10,464
Czech Republic	38,504	48,709	67,194	77,985	95,143	122,760	146,406	113,161
Estonia	3,444	4,539	5,934	7,698	9,705	11,018	12,468	9,048
Georgia	346	461	647	865	993	1,240	1,507	1,140
Hungary	34,512	42,532	54,892	62,179	74,216	94,745	108,220	82,663
Latvia	2,284	2,893	3,982	5,108	5,893	7,892	9,278	7,185
Lithuania	5,232	6,970	9,307	11,782	14,153	17,162	23,770	16,496
Macedonia	1,116	1,367	1,676	2,041	2,398	3,302	3,920	2,691
Moldova	644	789	980	1,091	1,052	1,342	1,335	1,288
Montenegro	303	405	506	562	578	860	984	878
Poland	46,732	60,977	81,849	96,450	117,418	145,300	178,702	139,944
Romania	13,876	17,618	23,485	27,730	32,335	40,234	49,622	40,724
Russia	107,301	135,929	183,207	243,799	303,926	354,403	471,765	303,388
Serbia	2,075	2,756	3,523	4,482	6,428	8,825	10,592	8,960
Slovakia	19,352	29,340	36,738	40,765	51,487	65,039	73,005	55,563
Slovenia	10,360	12,768	15,892	17,891	21,055	26,615	29,229	22,348
Ukraine	17,957	23,067	32,666	34,231	38,368	49,296	66,954	39,782

Source: *Euromonitor International from International Monetary Fund (IMF), International Financial Statistics*
Notes: *US$ totals in this table may differ from the totals given for Exports (fob) by Destination and Exports (fob) by Commodity*

External Trade Statistics

Table 12.7

Exports (fob) by Destination 2009

US$ million

	France	Germany	Italy	Netherlands	Sweden	UK	Total EU	Norway	Switzerland	Russia	Poland
Western Europe											
Austria	5,166.5	40,503.9	10,689.1	2,296.8	1,253.3	4,208.9	93,920.4	623.8	6,527.4	3,570.2	3,658.4
Belgium	65,515.2	72,436.2	17,654.7	43,798.6	4,991.0	26,672.8	280,728.5	1,850.4	4,313.9	3,664.9	5,743.7
Cyprus	12.7	123.2	27.2	19.1	16.0	117.5	741.5	2.3	3.1	41.3	4.8
Denmark	4,235.8	16,282.8	2,953.9	4,481.1	11,805.1	7,784.1	62,392.4	5,594.6	852.3	1,222.4	2,276.4
Finland	2,303.4	6,505.1	1,895.2	3,704.9	6,156.2	3,292.1	34,905.5	1,880.4	736.6	5,969.5	2,001.8
France		75,423.6	38,760.7	18,948.6	5,653.7	33,411.8	292,423.2	1,959.6	13,747.9	7,531.2	7,138.1
Germany	113,470.2		70,574.6	74,508.7	21,944.4	73,678.2	702,462.6	8,501.2	49,534.1	32,950.1	43,764.0
Gibraltar											
Greece	748.8	2,222.7	2,209.6	518.5	164.9	879.7	12,536.9	43.5	400.6	316.9	262.7
Iceland	141.7	451.4	40.8	1,236.3	32.3	512.7	3,128.8	231.6	52.2	30.4	42.7
Ireland	6,520.2	6,652.5	3,961.0	4,043.5	965.4	19,139.4	71,835.5	658.7	3,465.0	258.3	895.3
Italy	47,081.8	51,239.8		9,871.2	3,819.5	20,872.8	232,273.2	1,749.0	18,941.9	9,821.4	11,010.0
Liechtenstein											
Luxembourg	2,024.9	2,524.6	955.4	549.9	343.8	1,016.4	10,530.7	68.6	276.2	67.1	228.4
Malta	264.3	264.4	83.3	26.3	4.7	132.6	901.1	3.8	14.7	0.3	16.6
Monaco											
Netherlands	40,041.6	110,337.4	21,896.6		7,143.9	35,273.2	332,684.9	4,331.2	6,867.7	5,378.7	7,937.0
Norway	10,326.5	16,192.0	3,620.2	13,134.5	6,960.2	29,346.4	97,145.4		610.9	1,071.1	1,557.3
Portugal	5,320.2	5,737.5	1,653.7	1,582.9	514.5	2,448.1	32,304.3	118.5	410.4	152.4	369.1
Spain	42,563.4	24,546.8	18,190.4	6,640.0	1,716.8	13,644.7	150,989.8	1,136.1	3,724.9	2,499.3	3,519.8
Sweden	6,634.0	13,389.3	4,021.8	6,133.5		9,782.0	76,535.2	13,933.6	1,294.0	2,215.3	3,329.2
Switzerland	14,207.5	34,583.9	13,306.4	2,440.1	1,036.9	6,043.1	95,107.5	702.5		3,012.3	911.3
Turkey	6,206.1	9,779.3	5,886.8	2,121.7	748.0	5,912.6	46,945.0	383.9	3,933.4	3,171.1	1,319.8
United Kingdom	28,653.8	39,579.7	13,169.4	27,966.8	6,536.0		197,109.2	4,228.1	6,828.7	4,137.7	4,324.3
Eastern Europe											
Albania	12.2	35.5	637.5	8.3	1.2	2.8	910.5	1.9	1.6		0.7
Belarus	67.5	986.8	187.0	3,680.0	72.7	799.3	9,287.8	111.5	5.9	9,899.7	823.4
Bosnia-Herzegovina	100.9	633.0	797.8	47.5	39.0	29.4	3,398.5	13.3	28.3	22.9	51.4
Bulgaria	726.0	1,834.6	1,511.8	257.1	90.4	318.4	10,509.0	31.3	123.0	470.7	255.1
Croatia	211.5	1,157.0	1,998.6	140.3	45.8	224.3	6,343.5	22.6	156.6	109.9	114.4
Czech Republic	6,362.8	36,499.1	4,959.3	4,382.3	1,753.4	5,581.2	95,746.6	668.1	1,830.9	3,151.0	6,563.9
Estonia	209.4	552.4	101.8	223.5	1,129.5	183.4	6,248.3	288.8	29.7	899.0	159.2
Georgia	6.2	19.0	17.6	6.5	0.2	84.5	379.6	0.6	1.3		3.5
Hungary	4,441.1	21,115.1	4,689.4	3,060.4	859.7	4,468.8	65,178.1	222.7	933.1	2,923.0	3,106.1
Latvia	124.1	585.7	109.6	173.2	411.2	214.3	4,861.0	179.4	34.2	962.5	256.7
Lithuania	522.6	1,598.5	331.4	839.5	592.9	725.3	10,599.4	411.2	73.7	2,033.0	1,189.5
Macedonia	15.6	545.6	297.4	78.4	13.4	49.5	1,950.8	6.8	27.8	50.0	7.7
Moldova	28.6	88.5	179.9	10.9	7.0	40.0	644.4	1.0	2.6	167.0	33.0
Montenegro											
Poland	9,481.6	36,464.6	9,577.6	5,794.2	3,764.1	8,928.7	110,901.8	2,653.2	1,206.5	5,883.5	
Romania	3,338.1	7,640.2	6,277.7	1,329.5	347.8	1,363.7	30,295.1	563.0	356.1	801.6	901.3
Russia	11,796.3	27,306.9			4,315.5	6,976.4	105,177.1	761.6			12,558.6
Serbia	204.7	885.5	979.6	144.8		122.1	5,159.5	5.2	47.8	608.1	78.7
Slovakia	4,289.2	11,062.1	3,366.4	1,784.9	1,058.8	2,617.3	47,710.6	130.7	557.2	2,278.5	4,033.8
Slovenia	1,645.3	4,335.2	2,539.7	344.2	171.3	459.6	15,485.5	47.4	203.2	857.5	732.1
Ukraine	446.2	1,250.6	1,232.8	596.0	81.3	347.0	9,529.0	154.1	454.0	10,493.7	1,215.5

Source: International Monetary Fund (IMF), Direction of Trade Statistics

External Trade Statistics

Exports (fob) by Destination 2009 *(Continued)*

US$ million

	Africa & Middle East	Asia/ Pacific	of which: Japan	China	Australasia	Latin America	of which: Brazil	USA	Canada	Total, including Others
Western Europe										
Austria	4,532.7	7,194.8	1,029.5	2,551.5	840.4	2,005.6	855.3	5,220.2	728.4	130,826.3
Belgium	17,376.1	22,430.6	3,102.2	6,057.9	1,914.9	4,880.8	2,072.0	19,863.5	2,774.8	370,028.6
Cyprus	223.3	80.0	0.8	17.1	8.8	2.9	0.3	19.4	1.3	1,338.1
Denmark	2,691.8	7,092.5	1,857.1	2,117.3	1,091.5	1,745.1	401.0	5,633.0	917.5	92,842.8
Finland	3,033.4	6,188.4	1,027.0	2,578.7	527.3	1,788.1	830.8	4,958.1	643.2	62,887.7
France	49,425.9	39,382.2	6,540.3	10,785.5	3,747.6	10,744.1	3,495.0	26,845.1	3,283.6	474,861.2
Germany	55,001.1	107,864.7	15,041.7	51,023.3	9,641.4	26,113.7	10,031.2	74,656.6	7,196.2	1,121,499.6
Gibraltar										
Greece	1,663.3	584.8	40.1	129.6	143.6	188.1	32.6	989.8	102.2	20,043.7
Iceland	94.3	189.6	74.5	99.7	7.7	13.0	3.2	157.7	18.4	4,026.1
Ireland	2,855.3	8,620.2	2,474.2	2,310.8	1,164.9	1,459.2	304.2	24,003.3	566.6	116,990.5
Italy	42,823.9	32,030.8	5,175.5	9,252.9	3,790.4	12,628.1	3,774.5	23,854.7	2,898.6	405,438.9
Liechtenstein										
Luxembourg	235.8	304.2	29.1	114.1	23.2	109.1	14.5	272.3	45.8	12,761.4
Malta	265.1	613.4	83.4	39.1	6.5	32.3	7.1	220.0	16.1	2,183.8
Monaco										
Netherlands	20,030.4	19,473.9	2,979.5	5,762.5	1,750.0	6,522.8	1,400.8	17,143.9	1,709.0	431,796.1
Norway	1,760.7	6,530.9	1,256.2	2,436.3	230.6	1,104.1	458.6	5,826.3	2,595.8	120,848.2
Portugal	5,398.7	853.4	122.8	317.9	74.3	1,186.1	425.5	1,445.0	195.9	44,179.6
Spain	18,130.7	9,160.4	1,696.1	2,790.3	1,297.4	10,884.3	1,895.2	8,081.3	1,003.4	220,896.5
Sweden	7,520.7	11,112.7	1,639.4	4,108.5	1,792.7	2,805.9	876.5	8,355.1	1,134.6	131,326.6
Switzerland	12,055.5	25,961.9	5,724.7	6,345.0	2,158.8	5,071.7	2,030.6	14,978.6	3,005.9	166,703.2
Turkey	27,103.7	7,743.6	232.6	1,597.7	458.6	1,064.3	387.8	3,425.3	338.0	102,135.0
United Kingdom	28,568.4	34,744.3	5,318.8	8,137.9	5,001.5	7,268.2	2,764.8	52,632.6	6,258.5	358,039.6
Eastern Europe										
Albania	1.5	70.2	1.6	63.7	0.3	1.9	1.2	15.7	3.5	1,087.9
Belarus	528.6	1,735.9	2.8	173.9	12.7	775.3	449.8	41.3	4.9	21,277.8
Bosnia-Herzegovina	57.1	37.5	6.6	21.6	3.8	3.3	2.6	41.7	13.2	4,703.6
Bulgaria	928.5	766.6	19.9	163.3	40.0	95.0	40.9	259.3	44.4	16,377.6
Croatia	697.1	239.2	62.2	41.4	26.2	91.8	13.5	239.0	15.4	10,464.1
Czech Republic	2,804.1	3,010.8	423.4	845.5	223.9	1,017.1	277.2	1,799.0	147.7	113,160.7
Estonia	383.0	247.5	54.1	76.6	13.2	34.8	21.0	385.9	177.7	9,048.4
Georgia	29.4	233.2	3.5	12.0	0.7	18.9	0.5	56.3	99.1	1,140.2
Hungary	2,177.9	2,809.5	476.6	1,233.9	268.5	418.7	106.0	1,857.4	212.5	82,662.7
Latvia	408.8	242.4	33.7	21.7	5.9	41.4	1.7	111.3	9.7	7,185.3
Lithuania	431.3	668.5	17.7	30.6	18.0	58.6	2.7	487.2	86.0	16,496.3
Macedonia	30.9	48.6	17.9	25.7	5.4	6.9	3.0	54.4	9.7	2,690.7
Moldova	33.0	54.1	4.5	2.9	0.5	20.4	14.7	7.9	1.6	1,287.5
Montenegro										
Poland	3,173.0	3,919.0	318.4	1,531.4	272.5	994.4	209.4	2,597.4	655.3	139,944.0
Romania	2,297.9	1,108.6	113.1	300.0	21.7	326.2	60.4	480.6	30.9	40,723.7
Russia	3,367.7	45,606.1	7,199.4	13,035.3		2,935.5	2,076.0	21,825.2	2,347.4	301,931.0
Serbia	143.4	85.5	4.9	32.6	5.5	11.0	1.9	73.8		8,960.2
Slovakia	552.4	1,181.3	35.8	774.7	82.7	239.4	44.1	592.5	118.1	55,562.9
Slovenia	606.6	491.3	22.2	102.0	28.0	95.7	30.0	256.6	49.1	22,347.6
Ukraine	6,804.5	7,704.2	111.4	1,437.2	21.6	813.6	115.4	251.1	61.8	39,782.0

Source: *International Monetary Fund (IMF), Direction of Trade Statistics*
Notes: *US$ totals in this table may differ from the totals given for Exports (fob) by Commodity and Total Exports (fob)*

External Trade Statistics

Table 12.8

Exports (fob) by Destination 2009 (% Analysis)
% of total exports

	France	Germany	Italy	Netherlands	Sweden	UK	Total EU	Norway	Switzerland	Russia	Poland
Western Europe											
Austria	3.95	30.96	8.17	1.76	0.96	3.22	71.79	0.48	4.99	2.73	2.80
Belgium	17.71	19.58	4.77	11.84	1.35	7.21	75.87	0.50	1.17	0.99	1.55
Cyprus	0.95	9.20	2.04	1.43	1.20	8.78	55.42	0.18	0.23	3.09	0.36
Denmark	4.56	17.54	3.18	4.83	12.72	8.38	67.20	6.03	0.92	1.32	2.45
Finland	3.66	10.34	3.01	5.89	9.79	5.23	55.50	2.99	1.17	9.49	3.18
France		15.88	8.16	3.99	1.19	7.04	61.58	0.41	2.90	1.59	1.50
Germany	10.12		6.29	6.64	1.96	6.57	62.64	0.76	4.42	2.94	3.90
Gibraltar											
Greece	3.74	11.09	11.02	2.59	0.82	4.39	62.55	0.22	2.00	1.58	1.31
Iceland	3.52	11.21	1.01	30.71	0.80	12.73	77.71	5.75	1.30	0.75	1.06
Ireland	5.57	5.69	3.39	3.46	0.83	16.36	61.40	0.56	2.96	0.22	0.77
Italy	11.61	12.64		2.43	0.94	5.15	57.29	0.43	4.67	2.42	2.72
Liechtenstein											
Luxembourg	15.87	19.78	7.49	4.31	2.69	7.96	82.52	0.54	2.16	0.53	1.79
Malta	12.10	12.11	3.82	1.21	0.21	6.07	41.26	0.17	0.67	0.01	0.76
Monaco											
Netherlands	9.27	25.55	5.07		1.65	8.17	77.05	1.00	1.59	1.25	1.84
Norway	8.55	13.40	3.00	10.87	5.76	24.28	80.39		0.51	0.89	1.29
Portugal	12.04	12.99	3.74	3.58	1.16	5.54	73.12	0.27	0.93	0.34	0.84
Spain	19.27	11.11	8.23	3.01	0.78	6.18	68.35	0.51	1.69	1.13	1.59
Sweden	5.05	10.20	3.06	4.67		7.45	58.28	10.61	0.99	1.69	2.54
Switzerland	8.52	20.75	7.98	1.46	0.62	3.63	57.05	0.42		1.81	0.55
Turkey	6.08	9.57	5.76	2.08	0.73	5.79	45.96	0.38	3.85	3.10	1.29
United Kingdom	8.00	11.05	3.68	7.81	1.83		55.05	1.18	1.91	1.16	1.21
Eastern Europe											
Albania	1.12	3.26	58.60	0.77	0.11	0.26	83.69	0.17	0.15		0.07
Belarus	0.32	4.64	0.88	17.29	0.34	3.76	43.65	0.52	0.03	46.53	3.87
Bosnia-Herzegovina	2.15	13.46	16.96	1.01	0.83	0.63	72.25	0.28	0.60	0.49	1.09
Bulgaria	4.43	11.20	9.23	1.57	0.55	1.94	64.17	0.19	0.75	2.87	1.56
Croatia	2.02	11.06	19.10	1.34	0.44	2.14	60.62	0.22	1.50	1.05	1.09
Czech Republic	5.62	32.25	4.38	3.87	1.55	4.93	84.61	0.59	1.62	2.78	5.80
Estonia	2.31	6.11	1.13	2.47	12.48	2.03	69.05	3.19	0.33	9.94	1.76
Georgia	0.54	1.67	1.55	0.57	0.02	7.41	33.29	0.05	0.12		0.31
Hungary	5.37	25.54	5.67	3.70	1.04	5.41	78.85	0.27	1.13	3.54	3.76
Latvia	1.73	8.15	1.53	2.41	5.72	2.98	67.65	2.50	0.48	13.39	3.57
Lithuania	3.17	9.69	2.01	5.09	3.59	4.40	64.25	2.49	0.45	12.32	7.21
Macedonia	0.58	20.28	11.05	2.91	0.50	1.84	72.50	0.25	1.03	1.86	0.29
Moldova	2.22	6.87	13.97	0.84	0.55	3.10	50.05	0.08	0.20	12.97	2.56
Montenegro											
Poland	6.78	26.06	6.84	4.14	2.69	6.38	79.25	1.90	0.86	4.20	
Romania	8.20	18.76	15.42	3.26	0.85	3.35	74.39	1.38	0.87	1.97	2.21
Russia	3.91	9.04			1.43	2.31	34.83	0.25			4.16
Serbia	2.28	9.88	10.93	1.62		1.36	57.58	0.06	0.53	6.79	0.88
Slovakia	7.72	19.91	6.06	3.21	1.91	4.71	85.87	0.24	1.00	4.10	7.26
Slovenia	7.36	19.40	11.36	1.54	0.77	2.06	69.29	0.21	0.91	3.84	3.28
Ukraine	1.12	3.14	3.10	1.50	0.20	0.87	23.95	0.39	1.14	26.38	3.06

Source: International Monetary Fund (IMF), Direction of Trade Statistics

External Trade Statistics

Exports (fob) by Destination 2009 (% Analysis) *(Continued)*

% of total exports

	Africa & Middle East	Asia/ Pacific	of which: Japan	China	Australasia	Latin America	of which: Brazil	USA	Canada	Total, including Others
Western Europe										
Austria	3.46	5.50	0.79	1.95	0.64	1.53	0.65	3.99	0.56	100.00
Belgium	4.70	6.06	0.84	1.64	0.52	1.32	0.56	5.37	0.75	100.00
Cyprus	16.69	5.98	0.06	1.28	0.66	0.21	0.02	1.45	0.10	100.00
Denmark	2.90	7.64	2.00	2.28	1.18	1.88	0.43	6.07	0.99	100.00
Finland	4.82	9.84	1.63	4.10	0.84	2.84	1.32	7.88	1.02	100.00
France	10.41	8.29	1.38	2.27	0.79	2.26	0.74	5.65	0.69	100.00
Germany	4.90	9.62	1.34	4.55	0.86	2.33	0.89	6.66	0.64	100.00
Gibraltar										
Greece	8.30	2.92	0.20	0.65	0.72	0.94	0.16	4.94	0.51	100.00
Iceland	2.34	4.71	1.85	2.48	0.19	0.32	0.08	3.92	0.46	100.00
Ireland	2.44	7.37	2.11	1.98	1.00	1.25	0.26	20.52	0.48	100.00
Italy	10.56	7.90	1.28	2.28	0.93	3.11	0.93	5.88	0.71	100.00
Liechtenstein										
Luxembourg	1.85	2.38	0.23	0.89	0.18	0.86	0.11	2.13	0.36	100.00
Malta	12.14	28.09	3.82	1.79	0.30	1.48	0.32	10.07	0.74	100.00
Monaco										
Netherlands	4.64	4.51	0.69	1.33	0.41	1.51	0.32	3.97	0.40	100.00
Norway	1.46	5.40	1.04	2.02	0.19	0.91	0.38	4.82	2.15	100.00
Portugal	12.22	1.93	0.28	0.72	0.17	2.68	0.96	3.27	0.44	100.00
Spain	8.21	4.15	0.77	1.26	0.59	4.93	0.86	3.66	0.45	100.00
Sweden	5.73	8.46	1.25	3.13	1.37	2.14	0.67	6.36	0.86	100.00
Switzerland	7.23	15.57	3.43	3.81	1.30	3.04	1.22	8.99	1.80	100.00
Turkey	26.54	7.58	0.23	1.56	0.45	1.04	0.38	3.35	0.33	100.00
United Kingdom	7.98	9.70	1.49	2.27	1.40	2.03	0.77	14.70	1.75	100.00
Eastern Europe										
Albania	0.14	6.45	0.15	5.86	0.03	0.17	0.11	1.44	0.32	100.00
Belarus	2.48	8.16	0.01	0.82	0.06	3.64	2.11	0.19	0.02	100.00
Bosnia-Herzegovina	1.21	0.80	0.14	0.46	0.08	0.07	0.06	0.89	0.28	100.00
Bulgaria	5.67	4.68	0.12	1.00	0.24	0.58	0.25	1.58	0.27	100.00
Croatia	6.66	2.29	0.59	0.40	0.25	0.88	0.13	2.28	0.15	100.00
Czech Republic	2.48	2.66	0.37	0.75	0.20	0.90	0.24	1.59	0.13	100.00
Estonia	4.23	2.74	0.60	0.85	0.15	0.38	0.23	4.26	1.96	100.00
Georgia	2.57	20.46	0.30	1.05	0.07	1.66	0.04	4.94	8.69	100.00
Hungary	2.63	3.40	0.58	1.49	0.32	0.51	0.13	2.25	0.26	100.00
Latvia	5.69	3.37	0.47	0.30	0.08	0.58	0.02	1.55	0.13	100.00
Lithuania	2.61	4.05	0.11	0.19	0.11	0.36	0.02	2.95	0.52	100.00
Macedonia	1.15	1.81	0.67	0.95	0.20	0.26	0.11	2.02	0.36	100.00
Moldova	2.56	4.20	0.35	0.23	0.04	1.59	1.14	0.61	0.13	100.00
Montenegro										
Poland	2.27	2.80	0.23	1.09	0.19	0.71	0.15	1.86	0.47	100.00
Romania	5.64	2.72	0.28	0.74	0.05	0.80	0.15	1.18	0.08	100.00
Russia	1.12	15.10	2.38	4.32		0.97	0.69	7.23	0.78	100.00
Serbia	1.60	0.95	0.05	0.36	0.06	0.12	0.02	0.82	0.00	100.00
Slovakia	0.99	2.13	0.06	1.39	0.15	0.43	0.08	1.07	0.21	100.00
Slovenia	2.71	2.20	0.10	0.46	0.13	0.43	0.13	1.15	0.22	100.00
Ukraine	17.10	19.37	0.28	3.61	0.05	2.05	0.29	0.63	0.16	100.00

Source: International Monetary Fund (IMF), Direction of Trade Statistics

External Trade Statistics

Table 12.9

Exports (fob) by Commodity: SITC Classification 2009

US$ million

	Food and live animals	Beverages and tobacco	Crude materials excluding fuels	Mineral fuels etc	Oils and fats
Western Europe					
Austria	7,138.1	2,102.0	3,327.6	4,501.4	181.7
Belgium	30,828.9	3,377.8	8,519.6	26,004.5	1,329.0
Cyprus	226.2	89.2	67.0	187.6	1.8
Denmark	15,935.7	1,074.9	3,147.2	7,189.7	510.8
Finland	1,394.7	192.1	3,041.0	4,030.5	117.5
France	42,734.5	13,866.6	8,979.8	16,769.0	1,372.5
Germany	50,819.6	9,593.5	17,122.3	23,016.4	2,182.0
Gibraltar					
Greece	3,162.5	647.2	881.5	2,252.6	352.3
Iceland	1,665.2	5.7	47.2	39.9	78.9
Ireland	8,781.6	1,499.4	1,287.6	835.4	28.2
Italy	23,795.5	6,734.4	4,446.8	14,657.4	1,916.1
Liechtenstein					
Luxembourg	815.5	256.9	188.5	157.0	1.6
Malta	92.9	9.2	12.9	33.6	0.0
Monaco					
Netherlands	43,442.5	6,497.8	17,412.5	48,531.1	5,285.3
Norway	7,379.8	72.4	1,187.5	78,348.2	165.8
Portugal	2,969.0	1,709.5	1,792.7	2,241.7	299.8
Spain	24,849.6	3,252.0	4,506.2	15,252.1	3,228.4
Sweden	5,252.7	900.8	7,862.4	8,072.5	301.2
Switzerland	4,550.6	1,969.6	1,377.5	4,580.5	30.0
Turkey	9,126.1	932.9	2,223.3	3,901.0	427.2
United Kingdom	14,422.9	8,476.0	7,061.0	39,860.5	610.0
Eastern Europe					
Albania	56.5	4.7	125.2	126.2	0.4
Belarus	2,127.9	26.5	463.2	7,969.2	62.9
Bosnia-Herzegovina	279.9	44.7	504.0	620.5	36.4
Bulgaria	1,672.0	481.5	1,201.0	2,060.8	109.7
Croatia	1,031.4	228.3	643.5	1,347.4	25.6
Czech Republic	3,859.1	842.5	2,911.6	4,050.0	146.7
Estonia	718.4	140.2	564.2	1,492.7	35.3
Georgia	63.2	86.5	255.8	33.1	1.8
Hungary	5,011.5	276.8	1,533.6	2,620.4	250.7
Latvia	905.2	243.3	944.7	349.4	9.2
Lithuania	2,624.7	313.4	613.4	3,516.0	56.2
Macedonia	283.4	197.0	90.4	30.1	8.2
Moldova	317.0	174.2	87.6	5.5	50.9
Montenegro	36.3	46.6	57.3	66.3	0.5
Poland	11,487.0	1,345.1	3,022.3	5,738.0	312.8
Romania	1,791.9	591.0	2,241.6	2,400.4	110.4
Russia	8,024.6	851.4	9,821.1	202,384.2	831.1
Serbia	1,621.1	267.4	312.7	418.8	133.6
Slovakia	1,661.0	74.9	1,247.5	2,722.5	39.4
Slovenia	827.2	100.9	673.0	772.2	14.3
Ukraine	4,051.1	420.2	3,440.9	2,201.0	1,218.0

Source: United Nations, UN Trade Statistics

External Trade Statistics

Exports (fob) by Commodity: SITC Classification 2009 *(Continued)*
US$ million

	Chemicals	Basic manufactures	Machinery and transport equipment	Miscellaneous manufactured goods	Others	Total
Western Europe						
Austria	15,211.9	28,045.8	49,051.8	15,726.5	5,539.3	130,826.3
Belgium	116,013.6	59,202.2	79,789.8	35,692.1	9,271.1	370,028.6
Cyprus	262.4	45.8	264.2	191.4	2.5	1,338.1
Denmark	13,586.8	9,370.8	23,360.0	14,078.1	4,588.8	92,842.8
Finland	6,349.2	17,694.4	25,466.2	3,721.6	880.6	62,887.7
France	88,492.9	57,278.7	179,044.9	53,807.5	12,514.9	474,861.2
Germany	171,120.5	143,715.7	499,127.2	118,307.2	86,495.2	1,121,499.6
Gibraltar						
Greece	2,622.9	4,613.9	2,870.8	2,109.8	530.1	20,043.7
Iceland	109.9	1,576.6	403.2	78.6	20.9	4,026.1
Ireland	66,071.1	1,730.5	19,257.3	12,906.9	4,592.6	116,990.5
Italy	44,883.2	75,205.3	148,463.3	71,322.8	14,014.2	405,438.9
Liechtenstein						
Luxembourg	961.0	5,397.1	3,248.7	1,299.2	435.9	12,761.4
Malta	260.2	118.8	1,254.1	375.1	27.1	2,183.8
Monaco						
Netherlands	56,609.7	35,643.1	114,502.0	31,793.9	72,078.4	431,796.1
Norway	3,863.1	9,405.4	13,618.9	3,234.2	3,572.8	120,848.2
Portugal	3,150.0	9,640.7	11,842.4	7,246.8	3,287.0	44,179.6
Spain	27,823.7	40,609.4	77,142.8	18,840.8	5,391.5	220,896.5
Sweden	16,654.0	24,265.3	47,912.1	12,801.1	7,304.4	131,326.6
Switzerland	65,326.1	15,831.3	36,323.4	36,351.9	362.2	166,703.2
Turkey	4,836.5	28,599.8	28,802.5	17,377.1	5,908.7	102,135.0
United Kingdom	69,648.6	38,673.7	112,978.5	43,398.6	22,909.7	358,039.6
Eastern Europe						
Albania	7.1	176.0	51.8	538.9	1.1	1,087.9
Belarus	2,949.3	2,869.1	3,086.0	1,278.8	444.9	21,277.8
Bosnia-Herzegovina	243.4	1,132.5	631.3	1,078.2	132.7	4,703.6
Bulgaria	1,242.5	3,730.2	2,762.3	2,774.9	342.7	16,377.6
Croatia	1,013.4	1,579.0	3,096.3	1,495.0	4.3	10,464.1
Czech Republic	6,894.5	19,527.3	59,673.8	12,888.3	2,366.9	113,160.7
Estonia	531.3	1,387.8	2,419.2	1,327.1	432.2	9,048.4
Georgia	127.3	323.1	139.7	26.0	83.6	1,140.2
Hungary	6,238.7	7,694.8	46,634.0	5,823.7	6,578.5	82,662.7
Latvia	638.6	1,516.2	1,414.6	712.9	451.2	7,185.3
Lithuania	2,216.8	1,638.2	2,758.9	2,449.6	309.3	16,496.3
Macedonia	120.5	371.6	142.7	740.8	706.1	2,690.7
Moldova	63.3	99.0	154.3	335.5	0.3	1,287.5
Montenegro	15.9	558.2	47.7	12.9	36.4	878.2
Poland	11,091.5	29,737.4	58,203.7	16,744.4	2,261.7	139,944.0
Romania	2,034.2	6,162.1	17,352.4	7,132.3	907.5	40,723.7
Russia	13,283.2	39,511.3	11,561.9	2,439.9	14,679.2	303,388.0
Serbia	707.0	2,343.0	1,595.1	1,426.8	134.7	8,960.2
Slovakia	2,332.5	10,517.1	30,884.4	4,802.1	1,281.5	55,562.9
Slovenia	3,627.8	4,645.3	8,989.8	2,635.6	61.5	22,347.6
Ukraine	2,927.0	17,729.8	6,498.8	1,121.4	173.7	39,782.0

Source: *United Nations, UN Trade Statistics*
Notes: *US$ totals in this table may differ from the totals given for Exports (fob) by Destination and Total Exports (fob)*

External Trade Statistics

Table 12.10

Exports (fob) by Commodity: SITC Classification 2009 (% Analysis)

% of total exports

	Food and live animals	Beverages and tobacco	Crude materials excluding fuels	Mineral fuels etc	Oils and fats
Western Europe					
Austria	5.46	1.61	2.54	3.44	0.14
Belgium	8.33	0.91	2.30	7.03	0.36
Cyprus	16.91	6.66	5.01	14.02	0.13
Denmark	17.16	1.16	3.39	7.74	0.55
Finland	2.22	0.31	4.84	6.41	0.19
France	9.00	2.92	1.89	3.53	0.29
Germany	4.53	0.86	1.53	2.05	0.19
Gibraltar					
Greece	15.78	3.23	4.40	11.24	1.76
Iceland	41.36	0.14	1.17	0.99	1.96
Ireland	7.51	1.28	1.10	0.71	0.02
Italy	5.87	1.66	1.10	3.62	0.47
Liechtenstein					
Luxembourg	6.39	2.01	1.48	1.23	0.01
Malta	4.26	0.42	0.59	1.54	0.00
Monaco					
Netherlands	10.06	1.50	4.03	11.24	1.22
Norway	6.11	0.06	0.98	64.83	0.14
Portugal	6.72	3.87	4.06	5.07	0.68
Spain	11.25	1.47	2.04	6.90	1.46
Sweden	4.00	0.69	5.99	6.15	0.23
Switzerland	2.73	1.18	0.83	2.75	0.02
Turkey	8.94	0.91	2.18	3.82	0.42
United Kingdom	4.03	2.37	1.97	11.13	0.17
Eastern Europe					
Albania	5.20	0.43	11.51	11.60	0.04
Belarus	10.00	0.12	2.18	37.45	0.30
Bosnia-Herzegovina	5.95	0.95	10.72	13.19	0.77
Bulgaria	10.21	2.94	7.33	12.58	0.67
Croatia	9.86	2.18	6.15	12.88	0.24
Czech Republic	3.41	0.74	2.57	3.58	0.13
Estonia	7.94	1.55	6.24	16.50	0.39
Georgia	5.55	7.59	22.44	2.90	0.15
Hungary	6.06	0.33	1.86	3.17	0.30
Latvia	12.60	3.39	13.15	4.86	0.13
Lithuania	15.91	1.90	3.72	21.31	0.34
Macedonia	10.53	7.32	3.36	1.12	0.30
Moldova	24.62	13.53	6.81	0.42	3.95
Montenegro	4.13	5.30	6.53	7.55	0.06
Poland	8.21	0.96	2.16	4.10	0.22
Romania	4.40	1.45	5.50	5.89	0.27
Russia	2.64	0.28	3.24	66.71	0.27
Serbia	18.09	2.98	3.49	4.67	1.49
Slovakia	2.99	0.13	2.25	4.90	0.07
Slovenia	3.70	0.45	3.01	3.46	0.06
Ukraine	10.18	1.06	8.65	5.53	3.06

Source: *United Nations, UN Trade Statistics*

External Trade Statistics

Exports (fob) by Commodity: SITC Classification 2009 (% Analysis) *(Continued)*

% of total exports

	Chemicals	Basic manufactures	Machinery and transport equipment	Miscellaneous manufactured goods	Others	Total
Western Europe						
Austria	11.63	21.44	37.49	12.02	4.23	100.00
Belgium	31.35	16.00	21.56	9.65	2.51	100.00
Cyprus	19.61	3.42	19.74	14.31	0.18	100.00
Denmark	14.63	10.09	25.16	15.16	4.94	100.00
Finland	10.10	28.14	40.49	5.92	1.40	100.00
France	18.64	12.06	37.70	11.33	2.64	100.00
Germany	15.26	12.81	44.51	10.55	7.71	100.00
Gibraltar						
Greece	13.09	23.02	14.32	10.53	2.64	100.00
Iceland	2.73	39.16	10.01	1.95	0.52	100.00
Ireland	56.48	1.48	16.46	11.03	3.93	100.00
Italy	11.07	18.55	36.62	17.59	3.46	100.00
Liechtenstein						
Luxembourg	7.53	42.29	25.46	10.18	3.42	100.00
Malta	11.91	5.44	57.43	17.18	1.24	100.00
Monaco						
Netherlands	13.11	8.25	26.52	7.36	16.69	100.00
Norway	3.20	7.78	11.27	2.68	2.96	100.00
Portugal	7.13	21.82	26.81	16.40	7.44	100.00
Spain	12.60	18.38	34.92	8.53	2.44	100.00
Sweden	12.68	18.48	36.48	9.75	5.56	100.00
Switzerland	39.19	9.50	21.79	21.81	0.22	100.00
Turkey	4.74	28.00	28.20	17.01	5.79	100.00
United Kingdom	19.45	10.80	31.55	12.12	6.40	100.00
Eastern Europe						
Albania	0.65	16.17	4.76	49.54	0.10	100.00
Belarus	13.86	13.48	14.50	6.01	2.09	100.00
Bosnia-Herzegovina	5.17	24.08	13.42	22.92	2.82	100.00
Bulgaria	7.59	22.78	16.87	16.94	2.09	100.00
Croatia	9.68	15.09	29.59	14.29	0.04	100.00
Czech Republic	6.09	17.26	52.73	11.39	2.09	100.00
Estonia	5.87	15.34	26.74	14.67	4.78	100.00
Georgia	11.17	28.34	12.25	2.28	7.33	100.00
Hungary	7.55	9.31	56.41	7.05	7.96	100.00
Latvia	8.89	21.10	19.69	9.92	6.28	100.00
Lithuania	13.44	9.93	16.72	14.85	1.87	100.00
Macedonia	4.48	13.81	5.30	27.53	26.24	100.00
Moldova	4.92	7.69	11.98	26.06	0.02	100.00
Montenegro	1.81	63.56	5.44	1.47	4.15	100.00
Poland	7.93	21.25	41.59	11.97	1.62	100.00
Romania	5.00	15.13	42.61	17.51	2.23	100.00
Russia	4.38	13.02	3.81	0.80	4.84	100.00
Serbia	7.89	26.15	17.80	15.92	1.50	100.00
Slovakia	4.20	18.93	55.58	8.64	2.31	100.00
Slovenia	16.23	20.79	40.23	11.79	0.28	100.00
Ukraine	7.36	44.57	16.34	2.82	0.44	100.00

Source: United Nations, UN Trade Statistics

External Trade Statistics

Table 12.11

Trade Balance 1980-2009

US$ million

	1980	1985	1990	1995	1996	1997	1998	1999	2000	2001
Western Europe										
Austria	-6,955	-3,747	-7,953	-8,743	-9,513	-6,186	-5,440	-5,431	-4,817	-3,999
Belgium			-1,772	16,166	11,752	14,621	14,409	14,365	10,882	11,635
Cyprus	-671	-771	-1,611	-2,465	-2,587	-2,597	-2,624	-2,623	-2,895	-2,947
Denmark	-2,591	-1,155	3,789	5,750	6,476	4,712	2,509	5,880	6,021	6,946
Finland	-1,484	385	-430	11,459	9,170	9,532	10,662	10,224	11,582	10,688
France	-18,859	-6,666	-17,856	5,298	5,917	17,822	15,400	7,572	-3,722	168
Germany	4,858	25,445	63,951	59,531	65,415	66,811	71,979	69,331	54,761	85,389
Gibraltar		-24	-33	8	-158	-777	-596	-738	-835	-370
Greece	-5,395	-5,596	-11,672	-15,834	-17,724	-16,771	-18,656	-18,244	-17,359	-18,420
Iceland	-81	-90	-89	48	-393	-142	-443	-499	-699	-231
Ireland	-2,755	342	3,065	11,571	12,771	14,287	19,846	24,025	25,623	31,541
Italy	-22,637	-10,976	-11,482	27,958	43,947	30,136	27,255	14,852	9,661	15,438
Liechtenstein										
Luxembourg	-607	-314	-1,291	-1,998	-2,456	-2,379	-2,315	-3,150	-2,769	-2,913
Malta	-455	-359	-831	-1,029	-1,064	-922	-834	-863	-957	-768
Monaco										
Netherlands	-3,472	4,750	5,300	19,402	16,778	16,775	13,627	10,499	14,499	20,612
Norway	1,616	4,430	6,828	9,024	14,030	12,833	2,926	11,289	25,666	26,264
Portugal	-4,670	-1,967	-8,843	-10,100	-10,572	-11,091	-13,722	-14,598	-17,040	-16,735
Spain	-13,358	-5,716	-32,033	-22,273	-19,786	-18,352	-23,921	-34,472	-39,545	-38,452
Sweden	-2,533	1,913	3,293	15,061	17,972	17,271	16,379	16,057	14,407	13,882
Switzerland	-6,709	-3,264	-5,897	1,055	1,735	1,429	1,554	684	-1,237	996
Turkey	-4,999	-3,386	-9,344	-14,111	-20,383	-22,300	-19,040	-13,639	-26,728	-10,065
United Kingdom	-5,415	-8,344	-39,309	-23,200	-25,505	-25,450	-42,222	-49,792	-49,847	-59,278
Eastern Europe										
Albania		-63	-199	-511	-726	-507	-634	-803	-832	-1,020
Belarus				-760	-1,288	-1,388	-1,480	-765	-1,320	-836
Bosnia-Herzegovina				-898	-1,760	-2,020	-2,317	-2,545	-2,034	-2,322
Bulgaria		-1,464	-1,389	-302	-259	100	-755	-1,490	-1,683	-2,148
Croatia			-1,168	-2,834	-3,140	-5,120	-3,758	-3,496	-3,500	-4,395
Czech Republic				-4,699	-7,451	-6,091	-3,919	-3,241	-3,109	-3,095
Estonia				-706	-1,133	-1,506	-1,543	-1,092	-1,070	-988
Georgia				-334	-548	-751	-691	-452	-387	-436
Hungary	-573	314	927	-2,578	-2,427	-2,126	-2,687	-2,973	-3,939	-3,194
Latvia				-513	-876	-1,049	-1,380	-1,222	-1,318	-1,504
Lithuania				-974	-1,228	-1,824	-2,129	-1,873	-1,671	-1,781
Macedonia				-515	-479	-542	-604	-585	-771	-536
Moldova				-102	-249	-282	-380	-112	-305	-325
Montenegro									-94	-205
Poland	-2,499	-366	5,214	-6,155	-12,697	-16,556	-19,303	-18,506	-12,302	-7,663
Romania	-2,634	900	-4,068	-2,368	-3,351	-2,849	-3,521	-1,887	-2,688	-4,167
Russia				14,050	15,684	9,932	11,068	32,078	56,440	42,744
Serbia									-1,772	-2,540
Slovakia				-1,068	-3,199	-3,247	-3,660	-2,220	-413	-1,947
Slovenia			-609	-1,175	-1,111	-985	-1,062	-1,537	-1,379	-891
Ukraine				-2,356	-3,202	-2,896	-2,039	-264	779	198

Source: Euromonitor International from International Monetary Fund (IMF), International Financial Statistics

External Trade Statistics

Trade Balance 1980-2009 *(Continued)*

US$ million

	2002	2003	2004	2005	2006	2007	2008	2009
Western Europe								
Austria	317	-2,336	-1,621	-2,226	-570	556	-2,760	-5,291
Belgium	17,747	20,669	21,196	17,079	15,189	19,108	5,969	17,726
Cyprus	-3,094	-3,455	-4,577	-4,979	-5,798	-7,432	-9,047	-6,517
Denmark	7,429	9,066	8,738	9,305	6,292	4,632	5,933	10,917
Finland	11,041	10,915	10,240	6,760	7,839	8,334	4,730	2,004
France	5,056	2,286	-6,697	-29,643	-37,029	-56,129	-79,702	-59,392
Germany	125,412	147,060	193,557	197,439	199,724	267,820	264,556	191,105
Gibraltar	-103	-237	-653	-510	-507			
Greece	-20,990	-31,229	-37,321	-37,217	-42,866	-52,647	-64,452	-39,687
Iceland	-47	-404	-657	-1,614	-1,845	-1,757	-433	428
Ireland	35,957	38,755	41,358	36,393	32,573	35,204	42,083	54,371
Italy	13,436	11,445	10,796	481	-12,513	-11,630	-18,796	-6,847
Liechtenstein								
Luxembourg	-3,102	-3,712	-4,651	-4,868	-5,259	-6,044	-7,477	-11,529
Malta	-614	-928	-1,510	-1,440	-1,544	-1,768	-2,033	-1,614
Monaco								
Netherlands	25,739	30,837	34,047	39,217	42,157	51,565	50,813	49,422
Norway	24,788	28,267	33,991	48,271	57,842	56,002	82,340	51,574
Portugal	-15,730	-17,225	-22,835	-25,159	-25,930	-29,764	-37,132	-27,330
Spain	-39,994	-52,517	-75,487	-96,517	-112,692	-136,038	-139,212	-69,907
Sweden	15,274	18,221	22,448	19,332	20,238	15,516	14,916	11,265
Switzerland	4,982	5,142	7,496	6,313	9,648	11,626	18,093	18,907
Turkey	-15,495	-22,087	-34,373	-43,298	-54,041	-62,791	-69,936	-38,784
United Kingdom	-71,776	-79,679	-111,517	-124,662	-140,938	-179,807	-173,918	-127,606
Eastern Europe								
Albania	-1,164	-1,416	-1,703	-1,960	-2,261	-3,110	-3,896	-3,460
Belarus	-1,071	-1,612	-2,717	-729	-2,618	-4,418	-6,581	-7,281
Bosnia-Herzegovina	-2,867	-3,382	-4,118	-4,702	-3,992	-5,572	-7,171	-6,186
Bulgaria	-2,238	-3,361	-4,536	-6,423	-8,168	-11,511	-14,531	-7,175
Croatia	-5,819	-8,022	-8,565	-9,754	-11,112	-13,475	-16,617	-10,739
Czech Republic	-2,231	-2,530	-1,051	1,645	1,713	4,293	4,234	7,919
Estonia	-1,366	-1,942	-2,400	-2,514	-3,767	-4,668	-3,590	-1,084
Georgia	-450	-680	-1,199	-1,624	-2,685	-3,977	-4,559	-3,246
Hungary	-3,276	-5,070	-4,744	-3,605	-2,990	-143	-465	5,293
Latvia	-1,769	-2,350	-3,066	-3,483	-5,538	-7,290	-6,497	-2,177
Lithuania	-2,294	-2,698	-3,079	-3,729	-5,259	-7,283	-7,525	-1,844
Macedonia	-880	-939	-1,256	-1,187	-1,355	-1,875	-2,923	-2,341
Moldova	-395	-614	-793	-1,202	-1,642	-2,348	-2,746	-1,991
Montenegro	-282	-198	-461	-518	-644	-1,172	-1,404	-1,234
Poland	-7,255	-5,735	-5,610	-2,768	-7,032	-17,101	-26,033	-4,494
Romania	-3,986	-6,385	-9,179	-12,733	-18,780	-29,552	-33,310	-13,635
Russia	40,238	52,252	76,087	105,822	122,765	108,566	150,595	92,404
Serbia	-3,539	-4,721	-7,230	-5,980	-6,744	-9,729	-10,562	-9,062
Slovakia	-1,875	467	-2,069	-3,027	-3,463	-1,058	-1,076	1,708
Slovenia	-580	-1,090	-1,693	-1,728	-2,011	-2,916	-4,758	-1,540
Ukraine	980	47	3,669	-1,905	-6,672	-11,323	-18,579	-5,705

Source: *Euromonitor International from International Monetary Fund (IMF), International Financial Statistics*

Health

Health Statistics

Table 13.1

Hospitals and Hospital Beds 2009

As stated

	In-patient Beds ('000)	Hospitals and Clinics	Beds per '000 inhabitants
Western Europe			
Austria	65	273	7.8
Belgium	55	207	5.1
Cyprus	3	94	3.2
Denmark	19	48	3.4
Finland	36	326	6.7
France	440	2,612	7.0
Germany	671	3,211	8.2
Gibraltar			
Greece	55	310	4.9
Iceland	4	20	13.6
Ireland	22	175	5.0
Italy	223	1,282	3.7
Liechtenstein			
Luxembourg	3		5.6
Malta	3	9	8.0
Monaco			
Netherlands	73	186	4.4
Norway	16		3.3
Portugal	36	197	3.4
Spain	146	751	3.2
Sweden			
Switzerland	22	301	2.9
Turkey	204	1,369	2.9
United Kingdom	201		3.3
Eastern Europe			
Albania	9	44	3.0
Belarus	109	701	11.3
Bosnia-Herzegovina	12	41	3.1
Bulgaria	49	358	6.5
Croatia	24	80	5.5
Czech Republic	83	333	7.9
Estonia	7	59	5.6
Georgia	13	260	3.1
Hungary	68	176	6.7
Latvia	17	82	7.6
Lithuania	27	157	8.2
Macedonia	9	55	4.6
Moldova	21	66	6.0
Montenegro	2	11	3.9
Poland	257	787	6.7
Romania	140	417	6.5
Russia	1,355	3,783	9.6
Serbia	38	104	5.1
Slovakia	36	143	6.8
Slovenia	9	30	4.6
Ukraine	397	2,554	8.6

Source: *Euromonitor International from OECD/World Health Organisation/National Statistics*

Medical Services

Table 13.2

Doctors, Nurses and Dentists 2009

Number

	Doctors	Dentists	Nurses	Active Pharmacists
Western Europe				
Austria	32,722	4,658	54,861	4,935
Belgium	43,397	8,669	192,629	12,766
Cyprus	1,975	751	3,544	201
Denmark	17,654	4,294	52,676	3,898
Finland	15,054	4,411	50,025	9,043
France	209,734	41,143	503,123	73,626
Germany	293,062	63,562	851,267	50,510
Gibraltar				
Greece	67,549	15,391	36,059	9,998
Iceland	1,156	290	4,478	358
Ireland	13,928	2,774	69,104	4,490
Italy	211,835	32,442	422,475	54,787
Liechtenstein				
Luxembourg	450	394	5,697	334
Malta	1,383	172	2,559	524
Monaco				
Netherlands	67,330	8,190	253,786	2,938
Norway	19,254	4,316	76,779	3,486
Portugal	37,884	6,961	56,689	10,728
Spain	170,283	25,582	340,493	51,183
Sweden	34,850	7,663	103,635	6,743
Switzerland	29,735	4,031	107,660	4,000
Turkey	114,267	18,166	150,373	24,798
United Kingdom	154,070	31,574	610,996	43,154
Eastern Europe				
Albania	3,590	788	13,376	1,296
Belarus	47,913	4,967	116,658	3,049
Bosnia-Herzegovina	5,591	558	17,153	220
Bulgaria	28,167	6,398	33,582	734
Croatia	12,255	3,309	24,524	2,732
Czech Republic	37,218	6,993	86,987	5,832
Estonia	4,495	1,211	8,827	920
Georgia	19,143	1,150	15,169	237
Hungary	25,666	3,886	93,359	5,664
Latvia	6,843	1,610	12,547	5,608
Lithuania	13,899	2,457	24,415	2,962
Macedonia	5,778	1,208	7,781	958
Moldova	11,218	1,631	27,856	3,056
Montenegro	1,243	246	3,220	106
Poland	84,713	13,647	203,328	23,750
Romania	41,358	3,822	84,405	725
Russia	619,715	45,352	1,146,999	11,693
Serbia	20,093	2,363	41,174	1,952
Slovakia	16,187	2,511	28,719	2,585
Slovenia	4,972	1,212	16,036	1,069
Ukraine	145,072	19,090	362,875	21,156

Source: *Euromonitor International from OECD/World Health Organisation*

Health Statistics

Table 13.3

Causes of Death: Male 2009

Per 100,000 inhabitants

	Tuberculosis	HIV	Cancer	Diabetes	Mental and Behaviour Disorders	Diseases of Circulatory System	Diseases of Respiratory System	Diseases of Digestive System
Western Europe								
Austria	0.4	1.6	243.8	29.3	12.3	328.6	60.4	45.4
Belgium	1.5	0.7	286.0	31.1	35.1	306.3	137.3	37.1
Cyprus								
Denmark	0.3	0.5	309.8	26.7	49.8	275.7	84.1	58.5
Finland	0.7	0.5	220.2	11.1	28.8	379.0	49.1	66.3
France	0.6	1.9	293.7	16.9	21.7	160.9	48.9	40.4
Germany	0.7	0.8	283.8	21.6	18.3	371.0	78.4	52.0
Gibraltar								
Greece	1.2	0.3	304.5	13.4	1.2	416.6	104.1	27.2
Iceland								
Ireland	0.8	0.1	188.2	13.2	11.5	101.2	84.5	27.4
Italy	0.7	2.4	320.2	28.4	10.3	324.2	69.0	39.5
Liechtenstein								
Luxembourg								
Malta								
Monaco								
Netherlands	0.2	0.6	271.6	16.9	22.2	227.8	87.6	29.4
Norway	0.4	0.1	245.0	16.5	28.3	279.0	90.1	24.1
Portugal	2.3	8.9	257.9	37.0	4.9	278.3	132.1	46.0
Spain	1.1	4.6	281.3	19.8	18.7	254.9	119.9	47.7
Sweden	0.8	0.3	253.2	24.2	37.6	384.3	55.6	34.0
Switzerland	0.5	1.2	240.9	17.2	29.4	268.0	53.8	29.4
Turkey	11.1		100.7	8.5	3.1	376.9	45.1	31.4
United Kingdom	0.6	0.6	270.0	9.7	23.5	260.0	118.4	46.1
Eastern Europe								
Albania	0.2	0.2	111.7	5.8	3.9	314.6	33.6	12.2
Belarus	20.8		235.8	3.2	11.8	883.9	62.0	52.9
Bosnia-Herzegovina	6.6		237.4	15.8	8.9	432.4	54.5	36.4
Bulgaria	5.7		285.5	30.9	1.5	1,024.0	70.1	55.8
Croatia	2.1		356.9	28.7	21.3	534.1	76.5	70.4
Czech Republic	0.8	0.1	293.5	26.1	2.4	453.2	63.8	53.9
Estonia	7.0	4.7	319.4	20.7	32.8	649.6	50.7	73.2
Georgia	18.7		162.9	2.7	6.3	589.5	48.5	46.3
Hungary	3.7	0.3	371.6	26.2	11.4	642.0	85.3	116.3
Latvia	8.8	2.7	299.5	17.1	13.2	777.2	59.8	66.3
Lithuania	17.8	0.9	312.5	6.7	4.3	721.7	99.4	120.2
Macedonia	2.6		253.3	17.0	1.1	548.7	77.8	32.3
Moldova								
Montenegro	2.1		100.9	7.9	2.7	225.6	23.6	22.6
Poland	3.3	0.7	288.0	16.3	10.7	442.7	67.7	55.8
Romania	11.6	0.6	256.0	10.3	4.2	675.5	74.4	82.1
Russia	31.9	4.1	228.8	4.4	6.3	798.2	75.8	78.5
Serbia	3.3		160.0	12.6	4.3	357.7	37.4	35.9
Slovakia	0.3	0.0	262.6	10.3	0.1	515.8	74.4	71.9
Slovenia	2.1	0.3	331.6	12.6	3.9	328.2	48.4	73.2
Ukraine	51.3		241.2	5.9	12.9	1,084.0	91.1	113.5

Source: *World Health Organisation/Euromonitor International*

Health Statistics

Table 13.4

Causes of Death: Female 2009

Per 100,000 inhabitants

	Tuberculosis	HIV	Cancer	Diabetes	Mental and Behaviour Disorders	Diseases of Circulatory System	Diseases of Respiratory System	Diseases of Digestive System
Western Europe								
Austria	0.4	0.1	209.6	40.1	5.3	447.1	50.8	35.3
Belgium	0.3	0.2	209.9	44.6	43.7	374.4	100.1	38.5
Cyprus								
Denmark	0.2	0.1	275.0	19.4	60.8	295.3	105.0	51.3
Finland	0.3		193.2	10.2	59.4	388.6	28.9	41.9
France	0.4	0.6	192.8	17.5	28.0	190.6	37.8	32.0
Germany	0.4	0.2	233.8	30.2	20.1	486.2	68.1	49.5
Gibraltar								
Greece	0.6	0.1	191.7	13.7	1.3	459.8	98.5	17.8
Iceland								
Ireland	0.3	0.3	165.9	10.7	15.1	143.2	98.7	25.3
Italy	0.6	0.7	226.4	36.9	18.4	392.1	49.2	36.9
Liechtenstein								
Luxembourg								
Malta								
Monaco								
Netherlands	0.2	0.3	218.4	19.9	52.5	250.6	75.3	35.5
Norway	0.9	0.2	211.2	18.9	45.1	316.2	94.0	26.0
Portugal	0.6	1.2	153.4	47.8	5.0	316.0	98.1	29.1
Spain	0.6	1.0	163.9	25.9	35.2	292.1	85.3	39.2
Sweden	0.6	0.0	232.1	20.3	66.0	431.2	55.7	34.5
Switzerland	0.3	0.4	188.4	19.9	57.9	322.1	43.3	37.3
Turkey	3.0		68.9	9.6	1.6	361.4	28.2	20.1
United Kingdom	0.2	0.3	241.1	10.5	43.0	265.4	136.2	49.7
Eastern Europe								
Albania	0.3	0.1	69.6	6.3	5.1	285.0	20.6	7.2
Belarus	2.2		134.3	6.2	3.6	782.0	21.8	27.8
Bosnia-Herzegovina	2.1		143.3	18.1	9.2	433.5	28.6	25.4
Bulgaria	1.3		187.4	31.7	1.0	964.6	40.0	29.2
Croatia	1.0		226.0	38.4	19.2	674.4	49.0	37.6
Czech Republic	0.6	0.1	224.0	34.2	0.6	539.0	49.2	38.7
Estonia	1.5	2.1	217.7	20.8	10.5	670.9	19.0	43.8
Georgia	2.8		106.9	5.4	2.2	573.4	17.3	27.2
Hungary	0.9		265.5	34.2	4.2	677.3	61.6	62.7
Latvia	1.7	0.9	226.3	20.7	11.2	828.4	19.9	49.8
Lithuania	3.7		197.6	10.2	2.9	743.5	32.8	68.9
Macedonia	0.9		160.0	17.4	1.0	551.3	63.9	18.7
Moldova								
Montenegro	0.5		65.8	9.1	2.0	221.7	14.2	12.8
Poland	0.9	0.1	210.4	18.9	1.8	465.5	40.5	35.8
Romania	2.2	0.6	167.7	12.3	0.7	714.2	41.1	54.3
Russia	6.3	1.2	171.8	9.2	2.6	850.7	27.7	50.9
Serbia	0.8		104.3	14.4	3.2	351.6	22.5	20.4
Slovakia	0.5	0.0	185.7	11.1	0.1	573.0	48.2	43.2
Slovenia	1.5	0.2	238.4	15.8	0.9	446.8	40.1	52.5
Ukraine	9.0		160.5	7.2	4.1	1,119.0	24.6	53.6

Source: World Health Organisation/Euromonitor International

Health Statistics

Table 13.5

Food Supply: Average Consumption of Calories, Protein and Fat 2009

Daily averages, calories / grams per inhabitant

	Calories (number)	Protein (grams)	Fat (grams)
Western Europe			
Austria	3,845	108.6	172.6
Belgium	3,696	95.9	165.0
Cyprus	3,164	95.9	141.6
Denmark	3,419	109.0	136.5
Finland	3,237	109.2	131.2
France	3,512	111.9	166.0
Germany	3,571	102.4	146.2
Gibraltar			
Greece	3,737	120.5	155.4
Iceland	3,395	141.9	147.6
Ireland	3,631	104.2	142.9
Italy	3,633	110.6	159.2
Liechtenstein			
Luxembourg			
Malta	3,632	123.4	118.6
Monaco			
Netherlands	3,288	104.8	138.0
Norway	3,462	111.9	136.2
Portugal	3,577	115.8	145.1
Spain	3,236	110.1	154.7
Sweden	3,108	106.3	123.5
Switzerland	3,478	94.1	157.8
Turkey	3,536	101.1	111.5
United Kingdom	3,469	105.0	150.1
Eastern Europe			
Albania	2,889	97.9	93.9
Belarus	3,287	91.2	122.0
Bosnia-Herzegovina	3,075	88.1	70.3
Bulgaria	2,765	74.9	93.9
Croatia	2,996	83.0	116.1
Czech Republic	3,225	93.6	136.7
Estonia	3,200	95.5	88.4
Georgia	2,872	74.0	64.9
Hungary	3,489	87.3	155.4
Latvia	2,937	90.6	119.6
Lithuania	3,442	119.4	103.3
Macedonia	3,219	81.4	130.5
Moldova	2,743	69.2	70.1
Montenegro	2,456		
Poland	3,457	104.8	114.8
Romania	3,452	110.1	111.2
Russia	3,529	104.3	98.8
Serbia	2,776	73.7	117.6
Slovakia	2,930	71.9	114.0
Slovenia	3,237	102.1	121.3
Ukraine	3,238	88.3	97.6

Source: *Euromonitor International from FAO/National Statistics*

Government Health Expenditure 2009

As stated

	Government Health Spend as a % of Total Central Government Spend	Per Capita Health Spend (US$)	Government Spend on Drugs (US$ million)
Western Europe			
Austria	10.1	4,669	3,661.0
Belgium	10.5	4,730	4,535.1
Cyprus	6.6	1,834	
Denmark	10.0	5,648	1,614.6
Finland	8.2	3,876	1,700.0
France	10.9	4,789	33,823.3
Germany	10.2	4,193	44,837.1
Gibraltar			
Greece	9.8	3,066	7,487.9
Iceland	9.5	3,434	62.5
Ireland	7.7	4,077	1,894.3
Italy	9.0	3,326	16,836.2
Liechtenstein			
Luxembourg	6.8	6,933	239.5
Malta	8.0	1,556	
Monaco	5.1	2,268	
Netherlands	9.8	4,915	4,657.4
Norway	9.3	7,073	1,432.7
Portugal	10.4	2,233	2,681.7
Spain	8.7	2,860	20,441.3
Sweden	9.3	4,016	2,951.5
Switzerland	10.8	6,974	3,676.3
Turkey	5.7	444	
United Kingdom	8.6	3,267	
Eastern Europe			
Albania	5.4	200	
Belarus	6.4	324	
Bosnia-Herzegovina	7.6	343	
Bulgaria	4.7	283	
Croatia	7.2	1,005	
Czech Republic	6.9	1,262	1,631.5
Estonia	4.7	685	
Georgia	8.5	209	
Hungary	7.5	958	1,752.3
Latvia	5.8	668	
Lithuania	6.3	682	
Macedonia	8.3	359	
Moldova	8.4	125	
Montenegro	5.3	361	
Poland	6.6	720	2,287.3
Romania	6.0	452	
Russia	5.2	463	
Serbia	7.0	294	
Slovakia	8.1	1,382	1,546.5
Slovenia	8.0	2,048	
Ukraine	7.2	181	

Source: *Euromonitor International from IMF*

Health Statistics

Table 13.7

Obese Population (BMI 30kg/Sq M or More) 1985-2009

% of population aged 15+

	1985	1990	1995	2000	2004	2005	2006	2007	2008	2009
Western Europe										
Austria	7	8	9	10	11	12	12	13	13	14
Belgium	9	10	11	11	13	13	13	14	14	14
Cyprus										
Denmark	5	7	8	10	11	11	11	11	12	12
Finland	7	8	10	11	14	14	14	15	15	16
France	5	6	7	9	10	10	11	11	11	11
Germany	8	9	10	12	13	14	14	14	15	15
Gibraltar										
Greece	7	8	9	10	11	11	11	11	11	11
Iceland		8	11	12	13	14	14	14	15	15
Ireland	5	6	7	9	9	10	10	10	11	11
Italy	4	5	8	9	9	10	10	11	11	11
Liechtenstein										
Luxembourg		11	14	16	19	19	19	20	20	20
Malta										
Monaco										
Netherlands	5	6	7	9	11	11	11	11	12	12
Norway	2	3	5	7	9	9	9	10	10	10
Portugal	4	6	8	11	14	15	15	16	16	16
Spain	6	7	10	12	14	14	15	15	15	15
Sweden	4	6	7	9	10	10	10	10	11	11
Switzerland	4	5	6	7	9	9	10	10	10	10
Turkey	15	19	22	22	21	22	22	22	22	23
United Kingdom	9	13	16	21	23	23	24	24	24	25
Eastern Europe										
Albania										
Belarus	19	20	22	23	24	24	24	25	25	25
Bosnia-Herzegovina	16	17	17	18	18	18	18	18	18	18
Bulgaria	10	11	11	12	16	17	18	18	19	19
Croatia	9	10	10	14	17	17	18	18	18	18
Czech Republic	10	11	11	15	15	16	16	16	17	17
Estonia	10	11	11	14	14	15	15	16	16	16
Georgia	6	6	7	8	10	10	10	11	11	11
Hungary	15	16	17	18	19	19	19	20	20	20
Latvia	15	15	14	12	16	17	17	18	18	18
Lithuania	10	13	16	20	16	17	20	20	20	20
Macedonia	5	6	8	11	14	15	16	17	17	18
Moldova										
Montenegro										
Poland	6	8	11	14	17	17	18	19	19	20
Romania	8	8	8	9	9	9	9	9	9	9
Russia	15	17	18	20	21	21	21	22	22	22
Serbia										
Slovakia	11	11	11	13	17	18	19	20	21	22
Slovenia	11	11	12	14	17	17	17	18	18	18
Ukraine	12	12	12	13	13	13	13	14	14	14

Source: OECD/International Obesity Taskforce/Euromonitor International

Home Ownership

Home Ownership Statistics

Table 14.1

Housing Stock 1980-2009

'000 units

	1980	1985	1990	1995	1996	1997	1998	1999	2000	2001
Western Europe										
Austria	3,038	3,141	3,347	3,590	3,638	3,686	3,734	3,783	3,827	3,858
Belgium	3,811	3,997	3,882	3,931	3,974	4,025	4,076	4,127	4,186	4,249
Cyprus	151	187	222	251	257	262	266	268		
Denmark	2,152	2,239	2,366	2,442	2,455	2,465	2,480	2,496	2,510	2,527
Finland	1,838	2,015	2,210	2,374	2,391	2,416	2,449	2,478	2,512	2,544
France	23,432	25,132	26,792	28,283	28,565	28,844	29,121	29,391	29,699	30,005
Germany	30,956	32,645	33,856	35,954	36,492	37,050	37,532	37,958	38,384	38,682
Gibraltar										
Greece	3,940	4,262	4,588	4,946	5,029	5,107	5,204	5,293	5,387	5,476
Iceland										
Ireland	879	961	1,026	1,115	1,145	1,177	1,212	1,251	1,293	1,337
Italy	21,585	23,282	24,768	26,039	26,267	26,487	26,713	26,907	27,107	27,292
Liechtenstein										
Luxembourg										
Malta										
Monaco										
Netherlands	4,918	5,415	5,802	6,192	6,276	6,358	6,441	6,522	6,590	6,651
Norway	1,544	1,651	1,751	1,844	1,862	1,880	1,901	1,921	1,940	1,964
Portugal	3,756	3,906	4,130	4,508	4,600	4,682	4,771	4,885	5,002	5,106
Spain	13,356	15,062	16,854	18,707	19,080	19,449	19,827	20,197	20,572	21,034
Sweden	3,627	3,835	4,045	4,234	4,249	4,260	4,271	4,282	4,294	4,308
Switzerland	2,703	2,925	3,140	3,390	3,434	3,472	3,508	3,542	3,575	3,604
Turkey	10,359	11,306	12,331	13,651	13,974	14,301	14,664	15,029	15,405	15,784
United Kingdom	21,448	22,383	23,510	24,341	24,529	24,720	24,913	25,097	25,283	25,456
Eastern Europe										
Albania										
Belarus	2,665	2,936	3,285	3,621	3,666	3,709	3,752	3,800	3,819	3,847
Bosnia-Herzegovina										
Bulgaria	2,839	3,162	3,387	3,474	3,512	3,558	3,602	3,642	3,669	3,686
Croatia	1,356	1,502	1,589	1,607	1,615	1,624	1,633	1,645	1,653	1,661
Czech Republic	3,987	4,127	4,217	4,230	4,235	4,244	4,256	4,281	4,321	4,366
Estonia	465	533	596	617	618	619	619	620	621	622
Georgia										
Hungary	3,542	3,826	3,853	3,989	4,010	4,032	4,047	4,061	4,065	4,076
Latvia	854	902	953	952	950	954	955	943	941	942
Lithuania	999	1,077	1,159	1,247	1,270	1,278	1,306	1,324	1,309	1,292
Macedonia										
Moldova										
Montenegro										
Poland	9,794	10,666	11,022	11,491	11,547	11,613	11,688	11,763	11,845	11,946
Romania	6,999	7,645	7,896	7,782	7,811	7,837	7,860	7,885	7,908	8,107
Russia	23,731	29,922	38,679	45,245	46,181	46,949	47,603	48,142	48,561	48,857
Serbia										
Slovakia	1,635	1,702	1,759	1,810	1,821	1,834	1,847	1,859	1,872	1,885
Slovenia	578	632	690	737	744	751	757	765	771	778
Ukraine	16,557	17,146	17,656	18,303	18,565	18,784	18,858	18,866	18,921	18,960

Source: National statistical offices/Euromonitor International

Home Ownership Statistics

Housing Stock 1980-2009 *(Continued)*
'000 units

	2002	2003	2004	2005	2006	2007	2008	2009
Western Europe								
Austria	3,896	3,921	3,940	3,956	3,988	4,016	4,042	4,071
Belgium	4,320	4,387	4,454	4,510	4,563	4,611	4,663	4,714
Cyprus								
Denmark	2,540	2,558	2,578	2,619	2,643	2,669	2,694	2,718
Finland	2,574	2,604	2,632	2,667	2,687	2,732	2,775	2,822
France	30,337	30,669	30,984	31,306	31,622	31,921	32,229	32,514
Germany	38,925	39,142	39,362	39,551	39,754	39,918	40,057	40,181
Gibraltar								
Greece	5,584	5,712	5,839	5,938	6,044	6,143	6,225	6,311
Iceland								
Ireland	1,387	1,390	1,416	1,460	1,509	1,558	1,607	1,651
Italy	27,487	27,664	27,843	28,011	28,188	28,348	28,507	28,644
Liechtenstein								
Luxembourg								
Malta								
Monaco								
Netherlands	6,710	6,764	6,810	6,859	6,912	6,967	7,028	7,083
Norway	1,985	2,047	2,112	2,184	2,215	2,243	2,274	2,307
Portugal	5,232	5,323	5,395	5,470	5,533	5,590	5,647	5,692
Spain	21,551	22,059	22,623	23,210	23,859	24,496	25,151	25,810
Sweden	4,329	4,351	4,380	4,404	4,436	4,470	4,510	4,543
Switzerland	3,638	3,672	3,710	3,749	3,792	3,821	3,851	3,878
Turkey	16,176	16,565	16,941	17,326	17,702	18,071	18,426	18,761
United Kingdom	25,617	25,787	25,964	26,153	26,348	26,546	26,737	26,923
Eastern Europe								
Albania								
Belarus	3,871	3,894	3,907	3,921	3,934	3,965	3,974	3,981
Bosnia-Herzegovina								
Bulgaria	3,692	3,697	3,705	3,716	3,729	3,747	3,772	3,803
Croatia	1,671	1,683	1,693	1,704	1,715	1,728	1,740	1,754
Czech Republic	4,419	4,480	4,556	4,640	4,730	4,842	4,981	5,058
Estonia	623	624	626	629	633	638	645	648
Georgia								
Hungary	4,104	4,119	4,134	4,173	4,209	4,238	4,270	4,307
Latvia	958	967	987	998	1,018	1,036	1,061	1,063
Lithuania	1,295	1,292	1,300	1,300	1,299	1,305	1,316	1,319
Macedonia								
Moldova								
Montenegro								
Poland	12,438	12,596	12,683	12,776	12,877	12,994	13,109	13,258
Romania	8,129	8,152	8,176	8,201	8,231	8,267	8,311	8,366
Russia	49,073	49,265	49,462	49,669	49,796	49,988	50,178	50,318
Serbia								
Slovakia	1,898	1,911	1,925	1,941	1,956	1,970	1,986	2,002
Slovenia	785	791	798	805	812	820	828	836
Ukraine	19,023	19,049	19,075	19,132	19,107	19,183	19,257	19,344

Source: *National statistical offices/Euromonitor International*

Home Ownership Statistics

Table 14.2

New Dwellings Completed 1980-2009

'000 units

	1980	1985	1990	1995	1996	1997	1998	1999	2000	2001
Western Europe										
Austria	51.0	41.2	36.6	53.4	58.0	58.0	57.5	59.5	53.8	45.9
Belgium	48.6	30.3	43.1	41.6	46.3	44.5	43.0	41.4	39.7	38.0
Cyprus	9.0	7.5	8.1	8.8	9.0	9.6	9.9	10.2		
Denmark	30.3	22.7	27.2	13.5	14.2	17.7	18.4	17.5	16.5	17.3
Finland	49.6	50.3	65.4	25.0	20.8	26.9	29.8	28.9	32.7	30.6
France	341.6	327.7	317.7	288.1	281.4	280.1	271.3	297.6	316.7	310.0
Germany	379.3	280.9	256.5	602.8	559.5	578.2	500.7	473.0	423.1	326.2
Gibraltar										
Greece	136.0	88.5	120.2	70.9	86.7	89.6	97.3	88.5	89.3	108.0
Iceland										
Ireland	27.8	23.9	19.5	30.6	33.7	38.8	42.3	46.5	49.8	52.6
Italy	287.0	180.7	194.9	145.3	172.0	156.0	150.0	129.4	142.4	148.4
Liechtenstein										
Luxembourg										
Malta										
Monaco										
Netherlands	116.4	98.1	97.4	93.8	88.9	92.3	90.5	78.6	70.7	73.0
Norway	38.1	26.1	27.1	19.2	17.9	18.7	20.7	19.9	19.5	23.4
Portugal	40.9	39.1	46.8	68.8	69.7	74.2	90.8	108.1	112.4	114.8
Spain	262.9	188.7	281.2	221.3	274.3	299.1	298.8	356.8	416.2	505.3
Sweden	51.4	32.9	58.4	12.7	13.1	13.0	11.5	11.7	13.0	15.4
Switzerland	40.9	44.2	40.0	46.2	42.0	36.0	33.7	33.1	32.2	28.9
Turkey	139.2	121.0	232.0	248.9	267.3	277.1	239.0	215.6	245.2	243.5
United Kingdom	242.0	207.5	203.4	199.7	188.9	191.1	179.7	182.1	178.9	175.5
Eastern Europe										
Albania										
Belarus	80.4	88.5	86.1	52.8	38.2	46.1	47.7	46.1	39.4	32.5
Bosnia-Herzegovina										
Bulgaria	74.3	64.9	26.0	6.8	8.1	7.5	4.9	9.8	8.8	5.9
Croatia	31.0	22.8	18.6	7.4	12.6	12.5	12.6	12.2	16.0	12.9
Czech Republic	80.7	66.7	44.6	12.7	14.5	16.8	22.2	23.7	25.2	24.8
Estonia	14.4	13.5	7.6	1.1	0.9	1.0	0.9	0.8	0.7	0.6
Georgia										
Hungary	89.1	72.5	43.8	24.7	28.3	28.1	20.3	19.3	21.6	28.1
Latvia	19.9	19.9	13.3	1.8	1.5	1.5	1.4	1.1	0.9	0.8
Lithuania	28.3	28.8	22.1	5.6	5.6	5.6	4.2	4.4	4.5	3.8
Macedonia										
Moldova										
Montenegro										
Poland	217.1	189.6	134.2	67.1	62.1	73.7	80.6	82.0	87.8	106.0
Romania	197.8	105.6	48.6	35.8	29.5	29.9	29.7	29.5	26.4	27.0
Russia	436.8	671.8	800.0	602.0	482.0	426.0	388.0	371.0	373.0	382.0
Serbia										
Slovakia	48.2	38.0	24.7	6.2	6.3	7.2	8.2	10.7	12.9	10.3
Slovenia	13.6	10.8	8.1	6.1	6.7	6.6	7.0	5.4	6.8	6.4
Ukraine	329.0	341.0	289.0	119.0	88.8	80.4	70.2	73.5	62.9	65.6

Source: National statistical offices/Euromonitor International

Home Ownership Statistics

New Dwellings Completed 1980-2009 *(Continued)*

'000 units

	2002	2003	2004	2005	2006	2007	2008	2009
Western Europe								
Austria	41.9	40.2	36.2	34.0	33.2	32.6	29.7	22.5
Belgium	36.5	34.9	33.5	32.4	31.2	30.5	29.3	26.6
Cyprus								
Denmark	18.9	24.5	27.3	28.3	28.6	30.4	33.7	32.5
Finland	27.2	28.1	29.3	31.2	33.7	35.9	32.9	32.1
France	334.0	320.0	317.4	305.2	303.0	299.0	300.9	287.1
Germany	289.6	268.1	278.0	242.3	249.4	210.7	189.3	156.3
Gibraltar								
Greece	128.2	127.0	122.2	195.2	125.4	103.9	130.2	115.9
Iceland								
Ireland	57.7	68.8	77.0	81.0	93.4	78.0	81.0	81.0
Italy	145.8	142.3	138.9	134.2	130.2	126.2	120.8	108.4
Liechtenstein								
Luxembourg								
Malta								
Monaco								
Netherlands	66.7	59.6	65.3	67.0	72.4	80.2	89.0	86.0
Norway	21.7	21.4	23.6	29.5	28.5	31.0	32.3	30.7
Portugal	125.1	91.2	73.3	74.6	65.6	59.8	57.3	48.2
Spain	519.3	508.3	565.3	590.6	658.0	694.2	709.9	640.6
Sweden	19.9	20.0	25.3	23.1	29.8	30.5	40.8	40.0
Switzerland	28.6	32.1	36.9	38.0	42.0	35.2	31.4	29.3
Turkey	161.5	183.5	205.2	249.8	295.4	326.5	325.1	307.0
United Kingdom	183.1	190.4	206.1	215.2	218.9	214.4	207.0	155.8
Eastern Europe								
Albania								
Belarus	28.8	32.0	40.4	43.3	45.6	53.1	47.9	44.4
Bosnia-Herzegovina								
Bulgaria	6.2	6.3	9.8	13.9	15.3	21.6	26.9	24.2
Croatia	18.0	18.5	18.8	20.0	22.1	22.8	23.2	19.8
Czech Republic	27.3	27.1	32.3	32.9	30.2	41.6	38.4	33.5
Estonia	1.1	2.4	3.1	3.9	5.1	7.1	7.2	3.7
Georgia								
Hungary	31.5	35.5	43.9	41.1	33.9	36.2	42.6	38.3
Latvia	0.8	0.8	2.8	3.8	5.9	9.3	12.9	9.4
Lithuania	4.6	4.6	6.8	5.9	7.3	9.3	9.2	8.2
Macedonia								
Moldova								
Montenegro								
Poland	97.6	162.7	108.1	114.1	115.4	133.7	165.2	121.9
Romania	27.7	29.1	30.1	32.9	39.6	44.8	56.5	51.2
Russia	396.0	427.0	477.0	515.0	609.0	721.0	786.0	750.9
Serbia								
Slovakia	14.2	14.0	12.6	14.9	14.4	16.5	17.5	15.8
Slovenia	7.3	6.6	7.0	7.5	7.5	8.4	9.2	9.1
Ukraine	64.4	63.2	71.2	76.0	82.0	95.0	96.9	78.4

Source: National statistical offices/Euromonitor International

Home Ownership Statistics

Table 14.3

Households by Tenure 2009

'000 / as stated

	Home Owner with mortgage	Home Owner without mortgage	Rented	Other	Home Owner with mortgage (% of total)	Home Owner without mortgage (% of total)	Rented (% of total)	Other (% of total)
Western Europe								
Austria	674	1,296	1,472	166	18.7	35.9	40.8	4.6
Belgium	1,282	1,759	1,448	121	27.8	38.1	31.4	2.6
Cyprus								
Denmark	837	468	1,182	74	32.7	18.3	46.1	2.9
Finland	582	808	856	285	23.0	31.9	33.8	11.3
France	5,471	9,931	10,591	890	20.4	36.9	39.4	3.3
Germany	9,592	6,064	24,286		24.0	15.2	60.8	
Gibraltar								
Greece	584	2,379	789	249	14.6	59.5	19.7	6.2
Iceland								
Ireland	658	552	384	22	40.7	34.1	23.8	1.4
Italy	5,154	12,562	4,230	2,399	21.2	51.6	17.4	9.9
Liechtenstein								
Luxembourg								
Malta								
Monaco								
Netherlands	3,625	510	2,933	211	49.8	7.0	40.3	2.9
Norway	1,092	521	510		51.4	24.5	24.0	
Portugal	924	2,150	714	342	22.4	52.0	17.3	8.3
Spain	7,433	7,166	1,674	1,103	42.8	41.2	9.6	6.3
Sweden	1,107	1,681	1,360	399	24.4	37.0	29.9	8.8
Switzerland	779	1,394	1,079	155	22.9	40.9	31.7	4.6
Turkey	1,519	12,868	2,603	1,209	8.3	70.7	14.3	6.6
United Kingdom	8,520	10,350	8,296		31.3	38.1	30.5	
Eastern Europe								
Albania								
Belarus	281	3,109	345	359	6.9	75.9	8.4	8.8
Bosnia-Herzegovina								
Bulgaria	186	2,499	221	21	6.4	85.4	7.6	0.7
Croatia	110	1,258	105	36	7.3	83.4	6.9	2.4
Czech Republic	377	1,798	1,161	1,160	8.4	40.0	25.8	25.8
Estonia	88	417	70	14	14.9	70.9	11.9	2.3
Georgia								
Hungary	650	3,223	257	42	15.6	77.3	6.2	1.0
Latvia	124	448	236	2	15.3	55.3	29.1	0.3
Lithuania	116	1,078	77	121	8.4	77.4	5.5	8.7
Macedonia								
Moldova								
Montenegro								
Poland	825	8,414	2,884	2,312	5.7	58.3	20.0	16.0
Romania	379	6,818	234	26	5.1	91.4	3.1	0.4
Russia	2,776	30,448	19,557		5.3	57.7	37.1	
Serbia								
Slovakia	143	1,645	174	297	6.3	72.8	7.7	13.1
Slovenia	34	602	37	62	4.6	81.9	5.0	8.4
Ukraine	531	15,974	3,137	378	2.7	79.8	15.7	1.9

Source: National statistical offices/Euromonitor International

Table 14.4

Households by Type of Dwelling 2009

'000

	Detached House	Semi-Detached & Terraced House	Apartment	Other	Detached House (% of total)	Semi-Detached & Terraced House (% of total)	Apartment (% of total)	Other (% of total)
Western Europe								
Austria	1,148	651	1,736	74	31.8	18.0	48.1	2.0
Belgium	1,024	787	2,533	266	22.2	17.1	54.9	5.8
Cyprus								
Denmark	1,005	321	1,222	14	39.2	12.5	47.7	0.5
Finland	957	387	1,079	109	37.8	15.3	42.6	4.3
France	10,991	3,725	10,943	1,224	40.9	13.9	40.7	4.6
Germany	9,822	7,745	21,381	995	24.6	19.4	53.5	2.5
Gibraltar								
Greece	1,575	1,163	1,233	30	39.4	29.1	30.8	0.7
Iceland								
Ireland	653	775	106	82	40.4	48.0	6.6	5.1
Italy	3,396	2,921	18,029	0	13.9	12.0	74.1	0.0
Liechtenstein								
Luxembourg								
Malta								
Monaco								
Netherlands	1,247	3,852	2,014	166	17.1	52.9	27.7	2.3
Norway	1,303	347	473		61.4	16.4	22.3	
Portugal	1,953	1,118	1,007	53	47.3	27.1	24.4	1.3
Spain	3,997	3,688	9,691		23.0	21.2	55.8	
Sweden	1,843	1,247	1,204	254	40.5	27.4	26.5	5.6
Switzerland	783	734	1,440	450	23.0	21.5	42.3	13.2
Turkey			9,462	381			52.0	2.1
United Kingdom	6,402	16,229	3,792	757	23.6	59.7	14.0	2.8
Eastern Europe								
Albania								
Belarus			2,657	135			64.9	3.3
Bosnia-Herzegovina								
Bulgaria			1,328	15			45.4	0.5
Croatia			1,088	19			72.1	1.3
Czech Republic			2,446	121			54.4	2.7
Estonia	154	33	387	14	26.2	5.6	65.7	2.4
Georgia								
Hungary			2,376	19			56.9	0.5
Latvia	164	53	575	19	20.2	6.5	71.0	2.3
Lithuania	314	130	867	82	22.5	9.3	62.2	5.9
Macedonia								
Moldova								
Montenegro								
Poland			6,916	364			47.9	2.5
Romania			2,766	131			37.1	1.8
Russia	7,441	3,202	40,556	1,582	14.1	6.1	76.8	3.0
Serbia								
Slovakia			1,295	45			57.3	2.0
Slovenia			356				48.5	
Ukraine	9,519	1,947	8,281	273	47.5	9.7	41.4	1.4

Source: National statistical offices/Euromonitor International

Household Profiles

Household Statistics

Table 15.1

Households 1985-2009

'000

	1985	1990	1995	2000	2004	2005	2006	2007	2008	2009
Western Europe										
Austria	2,887.0	2,996.1	3,131.0	3,303.0	3,429.5	3,475.3	3,512.0	3,545.8	3,577.6	3,607.8
Belgium	3,765.7	3,958.8	4,094.6	4,237.8	4,402.3	4,439.7	4,488.2	4,533.2	4,572.3	4,609.7
Cyprus	212.0	229.0	248.7	264.2	266.6	267.4	268.2	269.1	270.1	271.1
Denmark	2,159.5	2,265.0	2,357.6	2,434.1	2,480.9	2,498.6	2,516.3	2,532.0	2,547.4	2,562.1
Finland	1,910.1	2,036.7	2,180.9	2,295.4	2,403.0	2,429.5	2,453.8	2,481.6	2,507.5	2,530.9
France	20,283.0	21,542.0	22,830.0	24,107.7	25,373.9	25,689.0	25,991.7	26,296.0	26,592.9	26,883.1
Germany	32,967.0	34,775.0	36,938.0	38,124.0	39,122.0	39,178.0	39,767.0	39,824.7	39,886.5	39,942.6
Gibraltar	7.0	7.0	7.6	8.0	8.7	8.8	8.9	9.0	9.0	9.1
Greece	3,062.2	3,168.2	3,402.9	3,627.5	3,784.8	3,827.4	3,870.4	3,914.2	3,957.8	4,000.9
Iceland	101.0	107.0	111.9	120.3	125.7	127.0	128.4	129.6	130.7	132.4
Ireland	966.5	1,011.8	1,104.1	1,220.3	1,365.6	1,413.4	1,469.5	1,522.0	1,571.3	1,616.5
Italy	18,916.0	19,687.6	20,822.0	21,645.0	22,813.2	23,267.7	23,611.8	23,885.9	24,126.2	24,345.7
Liechtenstein				12.9	14.0	14.2	14.4	14.6	14.8	15.0
Luxembourg	132.7	142.0	155.5	169.3	178.7	180.7	183.2	185.7	188.3	190.8
Malta	107.0	111.0	115.2	120.4	123.4	124.3	125.1	125.7	126.3	126.8
Monaco	12.0	12.0	14.0	15.3	16.0	16.2	16.4	16.5	16.7	16.9
Netherlands	5,613.0	6,061.0	6,516.0	6,819.0	7,049.3	7,091.0	7,146.1	7,190.5	7,233.3	7,278.9
Norway	1,634.9	1,751.4	1,859.3	1,947.6	1,997.9	2,011.0	2,051.4	2,064.8	2,104.5	2,123.1
Portugal	3,038.9	3,129.1	3,294.1	3,577.8	3,875.2	3,938.5	3,992.7	4,043.8	4,089.6	4,130.3
Spain	10,439.0	11,626.9	12,784.9	13,934.1	15,487.4	15,905.8	16,323.2	16,735.4	17,081.0	17,376.5
Sweden	3,670.0	3,830.0	4,234.1	4,363.0	4,426.0	4,445.4	4,465.2	4,499.6	4,523.3	4,547.4
Switzerland	2,602.0	2,859.8	3,098.0	3,181.6	3,291.7	3,319.9	3,345.0	3,367.6	3,387.9	3,406.9
Turkey	8,962.8	11,188.6	13,232.3	15,070.1	16,426.1	16,770.3	17,119.0	17,474.6	17,834.8	18,198.5
United Kingdom	21,960.4	23,206.6	24,281.8	25,193.1	25,991.2	26,245.9	26,488.3	26,721.7	26,951.8	27,179.5
Eastern Europe										
Albania	589.4	709.7	717.4	728.4	759.4	767.9	776.1	784.0	791.7	799.4
Belarus	3,292.0	3,535.4	3,733.7	3,898.7	4,011.1	4,032.8	4,052.0	4,068.3	4,082.5	4,094.4
Bosnia-Herzegovina	1,124.4	1,236.1	1,016.9	1,149.6	1,198.7	1,204.7	1,211.1	1,216.6	1,221.1	1,224.6
Bulgaria	3,030.3	3,000.4	2,913.9	2,914.1	2,935.5	2,937.1	2,936.7	2,934.8	2,931.7	2,927.4
Croatia	1,480.9	1,536.4	1,527.5	1,474.6	1,491.5	1,496.5	1,500.5	1,503.8	1,506.5	1,508.7
Czech Republic	3,962.0	4,032.4	4,147.4	4,250.6	4,342.1	4,366.2	4,401.4	4,437.2	4,468.6	4,495.9
Estonia	479.0	521.0	572.0	582.1	586.8	587.9	588.9	588.9	588.7	588.3
Georgia	1,364.0	1,421.0	1,322.8	1,253.2	1,208.6	1,199.0	1,190.0	1,181.7	1,174.0	1,167.0
Hungary	3,882.4	3,889.5	3,869.2	3,846.6	3,956.6	4,002.0	4,046.6	4,090.6	4,132.9	4,171.9
Latvia	778.8	833.8	809.6	802.2	806.6	808.0	809.5	810.0	810.3	810.6
Lithuania	1,184.0	1,292.3	1,335.8	1,352.7	1,381.3	1,384.7	1,386.8	1,389.5	1,391.2	1,392.3
Macedonia	430.0	470.0	509.9	549.5	578.3	585.0	591.5	597.7	603.8	609.8
Moldova			1,087.6	1,163.0	1,188.3	1,193.1	1,198.1	1,203.6	1,209.7	1,217.0
Montenegro	150.8	161.3	170.4	177.3	181.4	182.1	182.8	183.5	184.2	184.9
Poland	11,683.5	12,112.6	12,501.0	13,031.1	13,669.7	13,827.0	13,982.7	14,135.4	14,288.5	14,435.0
Romania	7,162.9	7,377.5	7,202.2	7,269.1	7,360.3	7,382.1	7,404.7	7,424.3	7,441.7	7,457.5
Russia	33,552.5	42,280.2	48,871.9	52,196.8	52,930.6	52,954.2	52,947.2	52,914.3	52,858.7	52,781.0
Serbia	2,367.7	2,408.6	2,460.0	2,508.1	2,531.9	2,535.6	2,540.1	2,544.6	2,549.2	2,553.9
Slovakia	1,734.9	1,814.9	1,918.9	2,045.3	2,149.9	2,175.4	2,199.0	2,220.4	2,240.3	2,258.6
Slovenia	607.9	636.3	651.5	675.4	700.7	706.3	713.5	720.9	728.0	734.9
Ukraine	14,097.0	14,559.0	15,774.7	17,684.2	19,437.9	19,672.2	19,821.3	19,933.3	19,997.4	20,020.0

Source: *National statistical offices/Euromonitor International*

Household Statistics

Table 15.2

Household Average Number of Occupants at January 1st 1985-2009

Persons

	1985	1990	1995	2000	2004	2005	2006	2007	2008	2009	Number of Children per Household 2009
Western Europe											
Austria	2.62	2.55	2.54	2.42	2.37	2.36	2.35	2.34	2.33	2.32	0.44
Belgium	2.62	2.51	2.47	2.42	2.36	2.35	2.34	2.33	2.33	2.33	0.48
Cyprus	3.05	2.97	2.94	2.98	3.10	3.13	3.15	3.17	3.19	3.21	0.72
Denmark	2.37	2.27	2.21	2.19	2.18	2.17	2.16	2.15	2.15	2.15	0.48
Finland	2.56	2.44	2.34	2.25	2.17	2.16	2.14	2.13	2.11	2.10	0.43
France	2.72	2.63	2.53	2.44	2.38	2.37	2.35	2.34	2.34	2.32	0.51
Germany	2.36	2.27	2.21	2.16	2.11	2.11	2.07	2.07	2.06	2.05	0.34
Gibraltar	3.80	3.83	3.61	3.43	3.32	3.30	3.28	3.26	3.24	3.23	
Greece	3.24	3.19	3.11	3.01	2.92	2.90	2.87	2.85	2.83	2.81	0.49
Iceland	2.39	2.38	2.39	2.34	2.32	2.33	2.35	2.38	2.41	2.44	0.61
Ireland	3.67	3.47	3.26	3.10	2.95	2.91	2.86	2.83	2.80	2.75	0.68
Italy	2.99	2.88	2.73	2.63	2.54	2.51	2.49	2.48	2.47	2.47	0.42
Liechtenstein				2.52	2.46	2.45	2.43	2.41	2.40	2.39	
Luxembourg	2.76	2.69	2.63	2.58	2.57	2.57	2.56	2.56	2.55	2.55	0.55
Malta	3.22	3.24	3.28	3.23	3.24	3.24	3.23	3.23	3.23	3.22	0.63
Monaco	2.36	2.51	2.26	2.10	2.02	2.01	1.99	1.98	1.97	1.95	
Netherlands	2.58	2.46	2.37	2.33	2.31	2.30	2.29	2.27	2.26	2.25	0.48
Norway	2.54	2.42	2.34	2.30	2.29	2.29	2.26	2.27	2.25	2.26	0.52
Portugal	3.30	3.19	3.04	2.85	2.70	2.67	2.65	2.62	2.60	2.58	0.48
Spain	3.67	3.34	3.08	2.87	2.73	2.71	2.68	2.66	2.64	2.62	0.46
Sweden	2.27	2.23	2.08	2.03	2.03	2.03	2.03	2.03	2.02	2.02	0.42
Switzerland	2.48	2.33	2.27	2.25	2.24	2.23	2.23	2.23	2.22	2.22	0.42
Turkey	5.58	4.89	4.48	4.23	4.09	4.06	4.02	3.99	3.96	3.93	1.24
United Kingdom	2.57	2.46	2.39	2.33	2.30	2.29	2.28	2.28	2.27	2.27	0.48
Eastern Europe											
Albania	5.02	4.64	4.37	4.21	4.08	4.05	4.02	4.00	3.97	3.95	1.16
Belarus	3.02	2.88	2.73	2.57	2.46	2.43	2.41	2.39	2.37	2.36	0.44
Bosnia-Herzegovina	3.78	3.64	3.46	3.26	3.20	3.19	3.17	3.16	3.15	3.14	0.60
Bulgaria	2.95	2.92	2.85	2.74	2.65	2.63	2.61	2.60	2.58	2.57	0.42
Croatia	3.17	3.11	3.06	3.01	2.98	2.97	2.96	2.95	2.94	2.94	0.55
Czech Republic	2.60	2.55	2.49	2.41	2.35	2.34	2.33	2.32	2.32	2.33	0.41
Estonia	3.18	3.01	2.53	2.36	2.30	2.29	2.28	2.28	2.27	2.26	0.42
Georgia	3.64	3.62	3.62	3.54	3.57	3.60	3.70	3.72	3.73	3.76	0.81
Hungary	2.75	2.67	2.67	2.66	2.56	2.52	2.49	2.46	2.43	2.40	0.44
Latvia	3.30	3.20	3.09	2.97	2.88	2.85	2.83	2.82	2.80	2.78	0.49
Lithuania	2.98	2.86	2.73	2.60	2.49	2.47	2.45	2.44	2.42	2.40	0.47
Macedonia	4.25	4.06	3.85	3.66	3.51	3.48	3.44	3.41	3.38	3.35	0.75
Moldova			3.99	3.53	3.21	3.15	3.10	3.05	3.00	2.96	0.65
Montenegro	3.89	3.66	3.52	3.46	3.43	3.42	3.42	3.41	3.40	3.40	0.79
Poland	3.17	3.14	3.06	2.94	2.79	2.76	2.73	2.70	2.67	2.64	0.51
Romania	3.17	3.15	3.09	3.02	2.95	2.93	2.92	2.90	2.89	2.87	0.54
Russia	4.25	3.49	3.04	2.81	2.72	2.71	2.70	2.69	2.69	2.69	0.49
Serbia	3.23	3.15	3.07	3.00	2.95	2.93	2.92	2.91	2.90	2.88	0.64
Slovakia	2.96	2.90	2.79	2.63	2.50	2.48	2.45	2.43	2.41	2.39	0.47
Slovenia	3.21	3.14	3.05	2.94	2.85	2.83	2.81	2.79	2.77	2.75	0.47
Ukraine	3.59	3.54	3.25	2.78	2.44	2.39	2.36	2.33	2.31	2.30	0.41

Source: *National statistics/UN//Euromonitor International*

Households by Urban/Rural Split 2009

% of total

	Urban	Rural	Total
Western Europe			
Austria	72.6	27.4	100.0
Belgium	97.7	2.3	100.0
Cyprus			100.0
Denmark	85.4	14.6	100.0
Finland	65.4	34.6	100.0
France	79.1	20.9	100.0
Germany	85.3	14.7	100.0
Gibraltar			100.0
Greece	77.5	22.5	100.0
Iceland			100.0
Ireland	63.3	36.7	100.0
Italy	73.2	26.8	100.0
Liechtenstein			100.0
Luxembourg			100.0
Malta			100.0
Monaco			100.0
Netherlands	84.5	15.5	100.0
Norway	79.5	20.5	100.0
Portugal	72.7	27.3	100.0
Spain	83.5	16.5	100.0
Sweden	86.4	13.6	100.0
Switzerland	77.9	22.1	100.0
Turkey	63.8	36.2	100.0
United Kingdom	90.0	10.0	100.0
Eastern Europe			
Albania			100.0
Belarus	72.2	27.8	100.0
Bosnia-Herzegovina	50.2	49.8	100.0
Bulgaria	70.4	29.6	100.0
Croatia	61.2	38.8	100.0
Czech Republic	76.4	23.6	100.0
Estonia	70.2	29.8	100.0
Georgia			100.0
Hungary	69.8	30.2	100.0
Latvia	70.5	29.5	100.0
Lithuania	69.2	30.8	100.0
Macedonia	77.0	23.0	100.0
Moldova			100.0
Montenegro	60.8	39.2	100.0
Poland	67.7	32.3	100.0
Romania	54.1	45.9	100.0
Russia	75.1	24.9	100.0
Serbia	59.0	41.0	100.0
Slovakia	55.1	44.9	100.0
Slovenia	54.3	45.7	100.0
Ukraine	69.6	30.4	100.0

Source: National statistical offices/Euromonitor International

Household Statistics

Table 15.4

Households by Number of Persons 2009

% of total households

	One Person	Two Persons	Three Persons	Four Persons	Five Persons	Six or More Persons
Western Europe						
Austria	35.7	28.5	15.9	13.2	4.6	2.1
Belgium	32.9	32.5	15.1	12.6	5.2	1.7
Cyprus						
Denmark	39.1	33.0	11.2	11.4	3.9	1.4
Finland	39.1	34.8	11.6	9.4	3.7	1.5
France	33.9	32.4	14.9	12.3	4.7	1.8
Germany	38.5	35.2	12.8	9.8	3.4	0.3
Gibraltar						
Greece	22.4	30.0	20.5	18.0	5.6	3.5
Iceland						
Ireland	23.4	30.2	17.7	15.7	8.5	4.5
Italy	28.6	29.5	19.8	16.8	4.3	1.0
Liechtenstein						
Luxembourg						
Malta						
Monaco						
Netherlands	35.9	32.6	12.3	13.4	4.2	1.6
Norway	39.7	28.6	12.3	11.6	5.8	2.0
Portugal	20.5	32.6	23.3	17.3	4.9	1.5
Spain	24.5	27.9	19.9	19.4	5.8	2.5
Sweden	47.0	26.0	11.2	11.1	3.4	1.4
Switzerland	37.6	31.6	11.9	12.5	4.6	2.0
Turkey	5.9	15.7	19.0	25.5	14.9	19.0
United Kingdom	34.0	32.1	16.1	13.0	3.7	1.0
Eastern Europe						
Albania						
Belarus	27.4	32.3	26.4	9.2	3.4	1.3
Bosnia-Herzegovina						
Bulgaria	25.2	30.1	20.7	15.9	5.2	2.9
Croatia	22.6	24.5	18.3	18.7	9.2	6.8
Czech Republic	33.0	29.6	17.7	15.3	3.5	0.9
Estonia	35.1	29.5	17.4	12.3	4.0	1.6
Georgia						
Hungary	31.8	30.7	17.5	13.0	4.7	2.2
Latvia	22.5	32.6	19.1	14.4	5.8	5.6
Lithuania	32.3	28.0	18.0	14.4	4.6	2.7
Macedonia						
Moldova						
Montenegro						
Poland	29.0	25.8	17.1	15.4	7.0	5.6
Romania	20.2	27.6	23.1	16.8	7.0	5.3
Russia	24.6	26.7	23.1	16.5	6.2	2.9
Serbia	21.6	25.9	18.4	20.1	7.5	6.5
Slovakia	35.9	23.6	16.7	16.7	4.7	2.3
Slovenia	24.2	24.7	19.8	21.5	6.5	3.3
Ukraine	32.9	33.3	16.5	10.6	3.7	2.9

Source: National statistical offices/Euromonitor International

Household Statistics

Table 15.5

Households by Number of Rooms 2009

% of total

	1	2	3	4	5+	Total
Western Europe						
Austria	8.8	19.4	32.2	20.1	19.4	100.0
Belgium	6.2	14.5	19.2	22.1	38.0	100.0
Cyprus						100.0
Denmark	6.9	21.6	23.3	18.8	29.5	100.0
Finland	13.9	32.2	20.4	19.8	13.8	100.0
France	6.7	12.5	21.2	26.2	33.4	100.0
Germany	2.2	6.3	21.8	29.4	40.4	100.0
Gibraltar						100.0
Greece	3.4	15.9	28.0	38.5	14.4	100.0
Iceland						100.0
Ireland	0.4	2.5	6.3	15.5	75.3	100.0
Italy	0.7	9.1	25.7	34.9	29.6	100.0
Liechtenstein						100.0
Luxembourg						100.0
Malta						100.0
Monaco						100.0
Netherlands	2.9	7.1	21.8	33.6	34.7	100.0
Norway	4.4	11.2	18.9	16.1	49.4	100.0
Portugal	0.7	1.8	12.1	29.5	55.8	100.0
Spain	0.6	2.4	8.7	17.1	71.1	100.0
Sweden	7.9	22.4	25.5	21.5	22.7	100.0
Switzerland	3.7	11.1	26.1	29.5	29.5	100.0
Turkey	4.2	15.3	27.0	37.8	15.7	100.0
United Kingdom	0.2	2.1	7.5	18.1	72.1	100.0
Eastern Europe						
Albania						100.0
Belarus	17.5	38.6	32.9	8.8	2.2	100.0
Bosnia-Herzegovina						100.0
Bulgaria	9.2	37.8	38.9	10.1	4.0	100.0
Croatia	24.5	49.7	19.7	3.8	2.3	100.0
Czech Republic	13.3	39.0	26.5	10.0	11.2	100.0
Estonia	17.9	49.7	29.8	1.5	1.1	100.0
Georgia						100.0
Hungary	17.5	40.7	29.8	6.8	5.2	100.0
Latvia	17.3	49.3	22.8	6.0	4.6	100.0
Lithuania	14.1	45.9	31.7	6.0	2.3	100.0
Macedonia						100.0
Moldova						100.0
Montenegro						100.0
Poland	2.0	14.1	32.4	40.8	10.6	100.0
Romania	9.9	36.0	38.2	11.0	4.9	100.0
Russia	14.1	39.5	26.0	13.7	6.7	100.0
Serbia						100.0
Slovakia	16.3	40.9	29.8	8.0	5.0	100.0
Slovenia	14.2	29.2	26.1	15.8	14.6	100.0
Ukraine	10.8	29.1	31.1	20.0	9.1	100.0

Source: *National statistical offices/Euromonitor International*

Household Statistics

Table 15.6

Households by Sex of Head of Household 2009

% of total

	Male	Female	Total
Western Europe			
Austria	61.1	38.9	100.0
Belgium	68.7	31.3	100.0
Cyprus			100.0
Denmark	55.8	44.2	100.0
Finland	61.4	38.6	100.0
France	72.1	27.9	100.0
Germany	67.5	32.5	100.0
Gibraltar			100.0
Greece	74.9	25.1	100.0
Iceland			100.0
Ireland	57.3	42.7	100.0
Italy	71.7	28.3	100.0
Liechtenstein			100.0
Luxembourg			100.0
Malta			100.0
Monaco			100.0
Netherlands	67.9	32.1	100.0
Norway	61.0	39.0	100.0
Portugal	75.4	24.6	100.0
Spain	76.5	23.5	100.0
Sweden	61.7	38.3	100.0
Switzerland	58.3	41.7	100.0
Turkey	87.1	12.9	100.0
United Kingdom	58.7	41.3	100.0
Eastern Europe			
Albania			100.0
Belarus	49.5	50.5	100.0
Bosnia-Herzegovina			100.0
Bulgaria	70.1	29.9	100.0
Croatia	58.6	41.4	100.0
Czech Republic	63.3	36.7	100.0
Estonia	48.7	51.3	100.0
Georgia			100.0
Hungary	64.8	35.2	100.0
Latvia	52.1	47.9	100.0
Lithuania	49.9	50.1	100.0
Macedonia			100.0
Moldova			100.0
Montenegro			100.0
Poland	60.6	39.4	100.0
Romania	71.0	29.0	100.0
Russia	51.1	48.9	100.0
Serbia			100.0
Slovakia	67.6	32.4	100.0
Slovenia	50.0	50.0	100.0
Ukraine	49.9	50.1	100.0

Source: National statistical offices/Euromonitor International

Household Statistics   **Table 15.7**

Households by Age of Head of Household: 2009
%

	< 29	30-39	40-49	50-59	60+	Total
Western Europe						
Austria	9.19	24.13	18.21	18.90	29.56	100.00
Belgium	9.64	21.43	23.97	13.04	31.92	100.00
Cyprus						
Denmark	9.93	20.81	20.43	19.33	29.50	100.00
Finland	10.84	16.70	19.55	20.03	32.88	100.00
France	11.68	18.18	19.94	18.20	31.99	100.00
Germany	12.73	17.99	17.97	16.73	34.58	100.00
Gibraltar						
Greece	12.75	23.43	22.74	17.11	23.97	100.00
Iceland						
Ireland	15.25	20.88	19.84	19.75	24.28	100.00
Italy	6.64	14.33	17.81	17.66	43.55	100.00
Liechtenstein						
Luxembourg						
Malta						
Monaco						
Netherlands	10.22	20.06	21.11	19.64	28.96	100.00
Norway	16.10	21.05	20.37	17.88	24.59	100.00
Portugal	14.07	20.91	21.46	16.37	27.19	100.00
Spain	4.63	14.75	21.37	20.43	38.81	100.00
Sweden	13.29	15.14	17.62	16.54	37.41	100.00
Switzerland	8.60	18.04	23.23	20.58	29.55	100.00
Turkey	20.65	14.24	21.14	21.19	22.78	100.00
United Kingdom	11.66	19.63	18.14	20.39	30.17	100.00
Eastern Europe						
Albania						
Belarus	8.48	19.17	19.34	19.47	33.54	100.00
Bosnia-Herzegovina						
Bulgaria	1.37	14.03	32.08	25.86	26.66	100.00
Croatia	7.13	14.40	14.24	22.17	42.06	100.00
Czech Republic	12.08	20.70	25.73	19.54	21.96	100.00
Estonia	7.63	23.22	20.13	23.95	25.07	100.00
Georgia						
Hungary	6.57	15.47	15.20	20.41	42.34	100.00
Latvia	9.94	18.51	18.51	17.89	35.15	100.00
Lithuania	7.56	18.69	16.81	18.99	37.96	100.00
Macedonia						
Moldova						
Montenegro						
Poland	10.82	15.07	24.49	18.38	31.24	100.00
Romania	3.86	11.36	17.62	19.67	47.48	100.00
Russia	12.59	14.98	18.45	18.49	35.50	100.00
Serbia						
Slovakia	8.71	29.04	21.90	18.98	21.37	100.00
Slovenia	10.08	19.05	17.72	19.29	33.86	100.00
Ukraine	13.08	15.84	12.62	20.28	38.17	100.00

Source: National statistical offices/Euromonitor International

Household Statistics

Table 15.8

Households by Education of Head of Household 2009

% of total

	Primary & no education	Secondary	Higher	Total
Western Europe				
Austria	23.5	47.9	28.6	100.0
Belgium	19.4	65.4	15.2	100.0
Cyprus				100.0
Denmark	27.9	46.9	25.2	100.0
Finland	34.4	45.7	19.9	100.0
France	14.0	56.8	23.4	100.0
Germany	12.2	60.3	26.0	100.0
Gibraltar				100.0
Greece	47.3	40.1	12.7	100.0
Iceland				100.0
Ireland	20.8	45.4	33.9	100.0
Italy	19.0	70.6	10.4	100.0
Liechtenstein				100.0
Luxembourg				100.0
Malta				100.0
Monaco				100.0
Netherlands	19.1	54.4	26.5	100.0
Norway	24.4	53.8	21.8	100.0
Portugal	58.3	23.8	17.9	100.0
Spain	47.3	34.7	18.1	100.0
Sweden	29.0	46.3	24.7	100.0
Switzerland	20.2	49.6	30.3	100.0
Turkey	66.3	18.6	15.2	100.0
United Kingdom	13.6	56.5	29.9	100.0
Eastern Europe				
Albania				100.0
Belarus	22.2	58.8	18.9	100.0
Bosnia-Herzegovina				100.0
Bulgaria	43.3	39.4	17.3	100.0
Croatia	39.5	47.3	13.3	100.0
Czech Republic	26.2	57.7	16.2	100.0
Estonia	21.9	60.0	18.0	100.0
Georgia				100.0
Hungary	39.9	48.9	11.2	100.0
Latvia	38.5	40.9	20.6	100.0
Lithuania	16.5	67.5	16.0	100.0
Macedonia				100.0
Moldova				100.0
Montenegro				100.0
Poland	25.2	63.9	10.9	100.0
Romania	26.9	63.8	9.3	100.0
Russia	21.3	62.9	15.8	100.0
Serbia				100.0
Slovakia	18.2	65.9	15.9	100.0
Slovenia	24.7	58.6	16.8	100.0
Ukraine	26.6	51.6	21.8	100.0

Source: National statistical offices/Euromonitor International

Household Statistics

Table 15.9

Households by Status of Head of Household 2009

'000 / % of total

	Employee (%)	Employer/ Self- employed (%)	Un- employed (%)	Other (%)	Total (%)
Western Europe					
Austria	56.1	10.1	1.8	31.9	100.0
Belgium	51.1	9.2	5.4	34.3	100.0
Cyprus					
Denmark	49.8	3.5	0.8	45.9	100.0
Finland	58.5	9.6	3.1	28.8	100.0
France	54.0	4.9	10.3	30.7	100.0
Germany	43.6	7.6	9.2	39.6	100.0
Gibraltar					
Greece	43.0	14.8	5.2	36.9	100.0
Iceland					
Ireland	58.4	7.8	2.0	31.8	100.0
Italy	68.1	18.1	7.6	6.3	100.0
Liechtenstein					
Luxembourg					
Malta					
Monaco					
Netherlands	66.7	8.1	2.5	22.8	100.0
Norway	62.2	4.5	2.5	30.8	100.0
Portugal	46.4	17.0	3.0	33.5	100.0
Spain	46.1	9.6	2.7	41.6	100.0
Sweden	62.6	7.7	3.0	26.6	100.0
Switzerland	55.7	13.2	3.7	27.4	100.0
Turkey	37.2	36.2	4.0	22.6	100.0
United Kingdom	54.0	6.3	1.1	38.6	100.0
Eastern Europe					
Albania					
Belarus					
Bosnia-Herzegovina					
Bulgaria	37.8	13.0	12.8	36.3	100.0
Croatia	50.4	2.5	12.1	35.0	100.0
Czech Republic	56.8	13.9	7.4	21.9	100.0
Estonia	59.2	5.5	4.7	30.6	100.0
Georgia					
Hungary	54.7	2.6	1.8	40.9	100.0
Latvia	53.0	5.0	7.7	34.3	100.0
Lithuania	53.5	7.6	7.3	31.6	100.0
Macedonia					
Moldova					
Montenegro					
Poland	47.9	10.9	8.9	32.3	100.0
Romania	25.6	3.5	7.8	63.2	100.0
Russia	56.2	10.5	4.5	28.8	100.0
Serbia					
Slovakia	47.7	4.8	7.1	40.4	100.0
Slovenia	54.0	12.1	4.3	29.6	100.0
Ukraine	37.7	12.9	7.6	41.8	100.0

Source: *National statistical offices/Euromonitor International*

Table 15.10

Households by Type 2009

% of total

	Single Person	Couple Without Children	Couple With Children	Single Parent Family	Other
Western Europe					
Austria	35.7	25.0	30.4	6.2	2.6
Belgium	32.9	23.3	26.7	11.7	5.5
Cyprus					
Denmark	39.1	32.1	17.5	4.4	6.9
Finland	39.1	30.6	21.0	6.2	3.1
France	33.9	26.1	26.4	7.4	6.2
Germany	38.5	31.1	23.1	5.0	2.3
Gibraltar					
Greece	22.4	31.2	21.5	16.2	8.7
Iceland					
Ireland	23.4	16.2	36.8	10.6	13.0
Italy	28.6	21.3	37.8	9.0	3.4
Liechtenstein					
Luxembourg					
Malta					
Monaco					
Netherlands	35.9	28.4	28.1	7.0	0.7
Norway	39.7	22.6	22.7	5.7	9.4
Portugal	20.5	25.3	36.5	13.7	4.0
Spain	24.5	17.4	32.9	8.9	16.2
Sweden	47.0	29.3	16.6	5.1	2.0
Switzerland	37.6	28.5	27.0	5.7	1.2
Turkey	5.9	15.1	63.9	3.5	11.7
United Kingdom	34.0	28.9	18.9	7.5	10.7
Eastern Europe					
Albania					
Belarus	27.4	25.0	25.1	5.9	16.6
Bosnia-Herzegovina					
Bulgaria	25.2	30.2	21.7	2.3	20.7
Croatia	22.6	15.1	26.3	3.7	32.3
Czech Republic	33.0	33.6	25.8	7.2	0.4
Estonia	35.1	21.6	10.8	6.5	25.9
Georgia					
Hungary	31.8	39.1	15.4	7.4	6.3
Latvia	22.5	25.8	15.5	5.6	30.6
Lithuania	32.3	21.3	18.2	3.6	24.5
Macedonia					
Moldova					
Montenegro					
Poland	29.0	24.3	39.5	3.1	4.1
Romania	20.2	32.8	20.1	3.4	23.5
Russia	24.6	25.1	30.3	11.8	8.3
Serbia	21.6	15.9	31.3	9.9	21.3
Slovakia	35.9	30.9	26.9	2.4	3.9
Slovenia	24.2	18.8	18.6	1.6	36.8
Ukraine	32.9	13.5	9.8	2.2	41.5

Source: National statistical offices/Euromonitor International

Household Statistics

Table 15.11

Households by Annual Disposable Income Band 2009
% of total

	Over $500	Over $750	Over $1,000	Over $1,750	Over $2,500	Over $5,000	Over $7,500	Over $10,000	Over $15,000	Over $25,000
Western Europe										
Austria	100.0	100.0	100.0	100.0	100.0	100.0	99.9	99.8	99.2	94.8
Belgium	100.0	100.0	100.0	100.0	99.9	99.7	99.3	98.7	96.6	89.7
Cyprus										
Denmark	100.0	100.0	100.0	99.9	99.7	99.0	97.8	96.3	92.0	80.2
Finland	100.0	100.0	100.0	100.0	100.0	99.9	99.7	99.4	97.6	88.7
France	100.0	100.0	100.0	100.0	100.0	99.8	99.5	99.0	97.4	91.7
Germany	100.0	100.0	100.0	99.9	99.9	99.4	98.6	97.4	93.9	83.0
Gibraltar										
Greece	100.0	100.0	100.0	99.9	99.9	99.4	98.5	97.3	93.5	82.2
Iceland										
Ireland	100.0	100.0	100.0	99.9	99.7	99.1	98.2	97.0	94.0	85.8
Italy	100.0	100.0	100.0	100.0	100.0	99.8	99.3	98.6	95.9	85.8
Liechtenstein										
Luxembourg										
Malta										
Monaco										
Netherlands	100.0	100.0	100.0	100.0	99.9	99.5	98.7	97.5	93.8	81.7
Norway	100.0	100.0	100.0	100.0	100.0	100.0	100.0	99.9	99.7	97.9
Portugal	100.0	100.0	100.0	100.0	99.9	99.3	97.8	95.2	86.7	61.8
Spain	100.0	100.0	100.0	100.0	100.0	99.8	99.3	98.5	95.9	85.5
Sweden	100.0	100.0	100.0	100.0	100.0	100.0	99.9	99.6	97.7	83.3
Switzerland	100.0	100.0	100.0	100.0	100.0	99.9	99.7	99.4	98.5	95.1
Turkey	100.0	100.0	99.9	99.7	99.3	96.4	90.9	83.2	64.6	34.0
United Kingdom	100.0	100.0	100.0	99.9	99.8	99.1	97.8	96.0	91.0	76.7
Eastern Europe										
Albania										
Belarus	100.0	99.9	99.8	98.3	94.3	60.3	30.2	16.2	6.7	2.7
Bosnia-Herzegovina	99.9	99.6	99.3	97.4	94.1	75.2	52.6	34.9	15.8	5.1
Bulgaria	99.8	99.6	99.1	96.7	92.4	68.5	43.5	26.5	11.0	3.7
Croatia	99.8	99.7	99.5	98.7	97.7	92.9	86.5	79.2	63.8	36.9
Czech Republic	100.0	100.0	100.0	100.0	100.0	99.9	99.1	96.5	79.3	30.8
Estonia	100.0	100.0	100.0	99.8	99.5	96.1	87.9	75.2	47.6	17.3
Georgia	98.0	96.3	94.2	86.8	78.5	52.3	33.8	22.2	10.6	3.7
Hungary	100.0	100.0	100.0	100.0	99.8	98.1	91.9	79.8	48.2	15.0
Latvia	99.8	99.6	99.4	98.4	97.0	90.5	82.1	72.7	54.2	27.0
Lithuania	99.9	99.7	99.5	98.7	97.4	91.0	82.0	71.7	51.4	23.0
Macedonia	99.8	99.6	99.3	97.9	95.8	84.2	68.8	53.4	29.9	9.9
Moldova										
Montenegro										
Poland	100.0	99.9	99.9	99.5	98.8	94.2	86.0	75.3	52.5	22.5
Romania	100.0	100.0	100.0	99.9	99.7	94.0	74.7	50.2	21.8	7.1
Russia	99.8	99.5	99.2	97.6	95.2	83.0	67.9	53.5	32.1	12.7
Serbia	100.0	99.9	99.7	99.0	97.6	88.1	72.6	55.8	30.0	9.7
Slovakia	100.0	100.0	100.0	100.0	100.0	99.7	98.5	95.5	81.2	38.2
Slovenia	100.0	100.0	100.0	99.9	99.8	99.0	97.6	95.7	90.2	74.3
Ukraine	99.2	97.8	95.6	84.2	68.2	25.0	9.8	5.0	2.5	1.3

Source: National statistical offices/OECD/Eurostat/Euromonitor International

Household Statistics

Households by Annual Disposable Income Band 2009 *(continued)*

% of total

	Over $35,000	Over $45,000	Over $55,000	Over $65,000	Over $75,000	Over $100,000	Over $125,000	Over $150,000	Over $200,000	Over $250,000	Over $300,000
Western Europe											
Austria	84.2	68.2	51.2	37.0	26.5	12.7	7.3	5.0	3.2	2.4	1.9
Belgium	79.4	67.3	54.9	43.5	33.7	17.5	9.5	5.9	3.3	2.5	2.0
Cyprus											
Denmark	66.5	53.2	41.5	32.0	24.6	13.1	7.6	4.9	2.7	2.1	1.6
Finland	72.2	53.1	36.8	25.2	17.5	8.3	5.0	3.7	2.5	1.9	1.5
France	82.9	71.8	59.7	47.9	37.2	18.3	9.2	5.4	3.4	2.6	2.0
Germany	69.1	54.8	42.1	31.8	23.9	12.1	6.8	4.4	2.7	2.1	1.6
Gibraltar											
Greece	68.0	54.0	41.8	32.1	24.7	13.4	8.0	5.3	3.0	2.2	1.7
Iceland											
Ireland	76.1	66.0	56.2	47.2	39.3	24.5	15.3	9.9	4.9	3.0	2.3
Italy	71.1	55.7	42.4	32.0	24.3	13.2	8.0	5.4	3.1	2.3	1.8
Liechtenstein											
Luxembourg											
Malta											
Monaco											
Netherlands	66.0	50.6	37.6	27.7	20.4	10.3	6.0	4.1	2.6	1.9	1.5
Norway	92.5	82.3	68.2	53.2	40.1	19.6	10.7	6.9	4.0	3.0	2.4
Portugal	39.7	25.5	17.1	12.0	8.8	4.9	3.2	2.4	1.7	1.3	1.0
Spain	70.2	53.7	39.2	28.0	20.0	9.5	5.4	3.7	2.6	1.9	1.5
Sweden	56.9	35.1	22.1	14.8	10.5	5.6	3.8	3.0	2.1	1.5	1.2
Switzerland	89.5	82.2	73.7	64.6	55.6	36.2	22.9	14.6	6.9	4.2	3.1
Turkey	18.4	11.0	7.2	5.1	3.8	2.4	1.7	1.4	1.0	0.7	0.6
United Kingdom	60.4	45.5	33.6	24.7	18.3	9.3	5.5	3.7	2.3	1.8	1.4
Eastern Europe											
Albania											
Belarus	1.8	1.3	1.0	0.8	0.7	0.5	0.4	0.3	0.2	0.1	0.1
Bosnia-Herzegovina	2.7	1.9	1.5	1.2	1.0	0.7	0.5	0.4	0.3	0.2	0.2
Bulgaria	2.2	1.6	1.2	1.0	0.8	0.6	0.4	0.4	0.2	0.2	0.1
Croatia	19.9	10.7	6.2	4.0	3.0	2.1	1.6	1.3	0.9	0.7	0.5
Czech Republic	12.7	7.0	4.8	3.8	3.1	2.2	1.6	1.3	0.9	0.7	0.5
Estonia	8.0	4.7	3.3	2.6	2.2	1.5	1.1	0.9	0.6	0.5	0.4
Georgia	1.9	1.3	1.1	0.9	0.7	0.5	0.4	0.3	0.2	0.2	0.1
Hungary	6.7	4.1	3.1	2.5	2.1	1.4	1.1	0.9	0.6	0.4	0.4
Latvia	13.1	6.9	4.2	3.0	2.4	1.7	1.3	1.0	0.7	0.5	0.4
Lithuania	10.4	5.5	3.5	2.7	2.2	1.5	1.2	0.9	0.6	0.5	0.4
Macedonia	4.5	2.8	2.1	1.7	1.4	1.0	0.8	0.6	0.4	0.3	0.3
Moldova											
Montenegro											
Poland	10.5	5.9	3.9	2.9	2.4	1.6	1.2	1.0	0.7	0.5	0.4
Romania	3.8	2.7	2.1	1.7	1.4	1.0	0.7	0.6	0.4	0.3	0.2
Russia	6.3	3.7	2.6	2.0	1.6	1.1	0.9	0.7	0.5	0.4	0.3
Serbia	4.5	2.9	2.2	1.8	1.5	1.0	0.8	0.6	0.4	0.3	0.3
Slovakia	16.0	8.2	5.3	4.0	3.4	2.3	1.7	1.4	0.9	0.7	0.6
Slovenia	56.0	39.4	26.6	17.6	11.8	5.3	3.4	2.7	1.9	1.4	1.1
Ukraine	0.9	0.6	0.5	0.4	0.3	0.2	0.2	0.1	0.1	0.1	0.1

Source: *National statistical offices/OECD/Eurostat/Euromonitor International*

Household Statistics

Table 15.12

Household Durable Ownership 2009

% of total households

	Air Cond-itioner	Bicycle	Black/White TV	Internet Enabled Computer	Cable TV	Camera	Cassette/Radio Player	CD Player
Western Europe								
Austria	6.0	68.5	0.8	63.4	34.9	98.0	66.8	67.8
Belgium	7.1	69.7	1.7	65.0	91.9	81.9	64.6	63.7
Cyprus								
Denmark	4.8	62.3	1.2	78.0	63.8	99.1	57.3	85.6
Finland	3.1	85.0	1.1	72.0	56.7	86.1	51.9	61.7
France	7.6	74.4	0.7	64.2	12.3	77.4	66.3	23.0
Germany	6.5	79.4	0.6	57.9	57.7	81.7	74.7	81.1
Gibraltar								
Greece	16.7	43.7	1.6	29.8	0.7	90.2	68.9	18.6
Iceland								
Ireland	7.6	61.8	0.0	53.1	37.6	87.1	48.4	39.5
Italy	32.3	51.2	1.6	39.4	0.9	64.0	53.8	11.9
Liechtenstein								
Luxembourg								
Malta								
Monaco								
Netherlands	6.6	92.0	3.0	81.5	80.8	90.7	65.3	85.6
Norway	3.0	81.0	1.5	80.5	46.1	89.6	59.7	86.0
Portugal	10.0	24.4	2.9	46.0	49.6	41.3	66.0	42.1
Spain	18.6	38.3	1.5	52.0	14.1	69.5	87.7	41.2
Sweden	3.3	84.8	1.1	77.6	59.4	90.4	60.5	80.7
Switzerland	9.7	62.3	1.7	74.2	88.7	98.9	59.6	57.7
Turkey	10.2	26.5	6.8	24.6	12.5	30.3	90.9	7.7
United Kingdom	8.1	64.1	0.2	62.7	13.7	83.1	51.8	86.1
Eastern Europe								
Albania								
Belarus	1.7	30.7	5.1	9.3	52.4	28.4	15.0	6.0
Bosnia-Herzegovina	5.8	24.2	2.0	10.0	11.8		26.6	
Bulgaria	2.3	41.0	6.9	26.7	42.1	43.2	33.6	7.0
Croatia	26.4	41.1	2.3	32.4	18.4	61.5	30.9	22.1
Czech Republic	5.0	47.5	2.4	41.2	24.3	58.3	67.8	24.4
Estonia	4.0	77.0	1.8	58.7	57.0	51.0	37.0	13.4
Georgia	5.4	13.8	6.7	2.6	10.9		7.7	
Hungary	3.4	77.1	1.4	51.5	60.8	72.7	71.5	27.7
Latvia	3.9	57.3	3.0	47.0	43.8	31.4	51.7	8.3
Lithuania	3.8	44.5	2.2	51.2	44.8	34.8	56.0	7.6
Macedonia	15.5	40.6	2.8	27.5	37.4		46.1	
Moldova								
Montenegro	35.1		4.5		32.6		31.6	
Poland	4.4	64.1	0.4	44.3	36.0	60.2	50.8	16.8
Romania	2.5	26.5	0.6	20.4	54.7	41.9	27.7	3.0
Russia	3.6	36.8	7.3	31.8	36.4	44.1	48.1	11.1
Serbia	18.1	37.6	4.5	23.3	39.8		31.6	
Slovakia	4.2	67.4	2.1	52.6	39.6	46.6	50.4	10.7
Slovenia	14.9	64.6	5.2	57.5	64.9	68.1	88.4	26.6
Ukraine	4.2	36.0	5.0	8.0	19.5	22.5	15.9	9.2

Source: National statistical offices/Euromonitor International

Household Durable Ownership 2009 *(continued)*

% of total households

	Colour TV Set	Cooker	Dish-Washer	DVD Player/Recorder	Freezer
Western Europe					
Austria	98.9	95.5	79.7	81.4	87.3
Belgium	96.2	96.2	50.1	77.0	64.5
Cyprus					
Denmark	98.2	97.5	59.0	86.0	98.5
Finland	95.2	99.0	55.0	77.8	89.7
France	97.7	97.3	48.5	86.8	54.0
Germany	98.1	96.0	63.4	75.9	76.5
Gibraltar					
Greece	99.8	95.4	34.1	56.8	24.5
Iceland					
Ireland	99.7	98.2	59.3	84.7	38.2
Italy	96.8	95.3	43.4	87.3	48.4
Liechtenstein					
Luxembourg					
Malta					
Monaco					
Netherlands	99.1	95.8	58.9	90.0	85.6
Norway	98.4	98.8	76.6	86.7	91.2
Portugal	99.2	99.9	52.8	84.0	70.2
Spain	99.7	97.5	43.3	75.6	39.8
Sweden	97.9	98.2	71.2	83.2	99.2
Switzerland	94.6	95.6	70.3	86.7	69.5
Turkey	93.2	61.4	27.4	24.0	2.4
United Kingdom	99.1	95.4	37.5	89.4	97.8
Eastern Europe					
Albania					
Belarus	96.0	91.0	4.5	21.3	17.7
Bosnia-Herzegovina	92.2	91.8	11.7	51.8	66.6
Bulgaria	90.9	79.2	4.0	23.4	27.3
Croatia	98.1	95.9	26.3	47.0	76.8
Czech Republic	98.4	98.1	23.2	60.6	32.8
Estonia	97.4	98.1	8.2	44.3	41.4
Georgia	91.5	64.8	0.4	19.6	10.7
Hungary	97.4	97.8	8.3	57.9	51.9
Latvia	96.2	97.6	2.3	33.7	16.4
Lithuania	98.3	97.6	3.2	33.7	18.2
Macedonia	96.6	85.5	8.1	38.5	25.9
Moldova					
Montenegro	98.7	95.8	19.5	33.4	83.4
Poland	97.6	97.5	11.1	52.9	30.6
Romania	93.9	93.5	5.2	22.9	25.1
Russia	96.8	93.5	5.8	47.3	27.6
Serbia	96.5	87.7	6.4	22.5	29.2
Slovakia	99.2	98.0	9.9	37.1	40.9
Slovenia	96.7	96.4	50.7	59.8	81.6
Ukraine	94.9	88.8	0.5	21.6	7.3

Source: National statistical offices/Euromonitor International

Household Statistics

Household Durable Ownership 2009 *(continued)*

% of total households

	Hi-Fi Stereo	Internet Enabled Comp- uter	Microwave Oven	Mobile Phone	Motor- cycle	Passenger Car	Personal Computer	Refrig- erator
Western Europe								
Austria	86.1	69.8	73.6	93.1	30.8	81.5	74.5	99.0
Belgium	72.0	67.4	85.2	93.7	14.9	89.5	77.9	99.2
Cyprus								
Denmark	91.0	83.0	72.0	98.0	22.6	73.4	86.0	99.2
Finland	90.9	77.8	92.2	92.3	13.3	73.9	76.6	97.5
France	65.4	63.0	85.0	80.4	18.7	83.6	69.2	99.8
Germany	75.0	72.3	70.7	90.3	24.6	77.5	78.0	98.8
Gibraltar								
Greece	62.6	38.1	42.7	85.2	11.9	75.2	47.3	95.8
Iceland								
Ireland	72.3	66.7	91.1	93.4	6.0	81.3	72.8	99.7
Italy	57.5	53.5	36.5	88.8	17.3	60.5	61.3	99.0
Liechtenstein								
Luxembourg								
Malta								
Monaco								
Netherlands	92.2	89.7	93.1	94.3	12.4	78.1	90.8	99.4
Norway	91.8	86.0	83.9	98.6	12.1	79.1	88.0	99.1
Portugal	48.9	47.9	85.2	87.4	19.6	68.0	56.0	99.7
Spain	67.3	54.0	84.1	90.9	22.0	77.8	60.4	100.0
Sweden	88.7	86.0	80.2	98.0	4.2	85.8	87.5	99.2
Switzerland	78.5	80.2	65.7	91.1	33.0	89.0	82.7	100.0
Turkey	43.8	30.0	7.4	87.6	12.2	28.9	41.9	98.3
United Kingdom	76.5	69.4	92.4	82.6	9.5	74.5	74.2	99.5
Eastern Europe								
Albania								
Belarus	29.8	19.6	23.0	74.0	4.3	57.5	33.1	97.9
Bosnia-Herzegovina	68.8	14.4	41.8	76.4		54.4	30.7	97.2
Bulgaria	29.5	29.6	34.4	73.5	5.6	48.4	31.7	87.5
Croatia	40.8	40.7	37.5	94.7	21.7	59.2	39.9	98.2
Czech Republic	47.4	50.3	78.6	99.4	26.1	74.8	70.0	78.5
Estonia	56.3	63.0	63.3	92.3	2.5	51.2	65.2	95.5
Georgia	13.5	4.2	14.0	84.4		30.5	17.6	94.1
Hungary	34.5	55.1	87.5	90.4	14.9	52.7	56.8	67.5
Latvia	53.5	56.1	39.2	95.6	0.9	51.9	60.1	99.2
Lithuania	43.7	54.7	67.7	87.0	2.6	58.8	60.0	96.3
Macedonia	28.3	31.7	37.8	80.1		51.0	31.7	98.2
Moldova								
Montenegro	32.7	22.2	34.0	92.2		50.0	28.9	98.5
Poland	43.2	56.5	48.9	86.7	3.3	56.5	62.0	98.8
Romania	16.8	37.9	32.1	90.2	1.3	28.6	45.7	88.1
Russia	48.8	34.6	40.9	90.9	17.2	38.7	45.2	96.5
Serbia	23.6	31.9	17.2	76.0		47.3	35.2	96.7
Slovakia	19.8	62.2	74.1	87.2	6.8	57.7	64.0	83.4
Slovenia	53.9	63.9	54.5	93.8	3.0	80.5	71.2	98.1
Ukraine	18.5	14.7	35.2	81.4	2.1	33.4	24.1	97.1

Source: *National statistical offices/Euromonitor International*

Household Statistics

Household Durable Ownership 2009 *(continued)*

% of total households

	Satell-ite TV	Telephone	Tumble Drier	Vacuum Cleaner	Video Camera	Game Console	Video Recorder	Washing Machine
Western Europe								
Austria	48.1	55.3	23.9	98.2	22.1	17.1	64.5	96.7
Belgium	10.9	73.2	51.0	97.0	31.1	17.1	75.3	89.4
Cyprus								
Denmark	35.0	68.0	52.9	96.6	22.7	16.7	84.1	79.0
Finland	24.4	33.6	57.6	97.2	23.8	18.5	74.9	88.9
France	26.9	86.6	44.4	90.3	8.7	19.8	60.7	94.2
Germany	40.9	90.9	46.2	95.7	11.8	18.6	46.0	96.0
Gibraltar								
Greece	15.6	93.3	13.1	84.7	6.1	10.2	46.3	93.3
Iceland								
Ireland	47.3	82.2	27.1	95.9	12.7	14.0	81.2	97.7
Italy	31.1	72.0	17.9	80.4	26.4	15.7	70.5	97.3
Liechtenstein								
Luxembourg								
Malta								
Monaco								
Netherlands	15.0	99.7	61.5	97.3	28.2	13.0	78.1	97.5
Norway	31.2	88.4	43.0	96.0	22.5	19.7	40.5	88.2
Portugal	18.5	66.4	13.4	85.9	15.1	15.4	47.3	92.8
Spain	20.9	81.2	16.7	83.9	10.0	10.8	66.5	99.1
Sweden	36.5	91.4	45.5	96.8	26.1	15.7	78.3	76.1
Switzerland	16.4	99.0	41.6	99.1	51.4	16.9	64.1	99.6
Turkey	41.5	69.1	1.5	83.5	3.6	16.2	15.1	92.4
United Kingdom	37.8	90.2	58.7	95.9	12.0	17.1	84.0	96.2
Eastern Europe								
Albania								
Belarus	10.8	85.4	1.5	58.9	0.8	5.4	24.7	77.2
Bosnia-Herzegovina	15.4	73.1		80.2				87.4
Bulgaria	8.4	70.7	4.0	83.1	0.3	4.0	38.7	80.0
Croatia	36.0	89.3	8.9	82.7	7.2	9.6	38.9	94.8
Czech Republic	21.7	28.9	2.7	89.8	6.9	10.3	59.9	95.5
Estonia	23.4	45.0	6.0	84.6	9.2	6.4	34.7	87.7
Georgia	0.6	40.3		63.5				49.6
Hungary	21.4	45.2	2.6	93.4	14.0	10.5	62.6	90.5
Latvia	14.6	37.6	3.5	81.3	6.8	6.9	34.5	88.5
Lithuania	11.0	46.7	3.8	81.7	8.6	7.0	24.1	90.6
Macedonia	8.5	67.6		85.4				88.3
Moldova								
Montenegro	31.8	65.8		85.5				80.0
Poland	29.6	62.5	1.5	95.3	6.3	8.3	77.5	88.7
Romania	32.7	44.4	0.5	61.7	0.8	3.2	5.1	71.5
Russia	7.4	59.6	1.2	85.3	7.9	3.9	16.8	96.6
Serbia	7.0	85.2		82.3				86.8
Slovakia	43.3	46.5	1.8	89.0	6.3	8.6	50.4	77.9
Slovenia	16.3	80.0	9.7	93.3	5.9	10.6	49.9	96.9
Ukraine	9.7	55.3	1.5	76.5	4.1	3.8	9.6	84.3

Source: National statistical offices/Euromonitor International

Income and Deductions

Income Statistics

Table 16.1

Gross Income (Annual) 1990-2009

National currency billion / US$ per capita

	1990	1995	2000	2004	2005	2006	2007	2008	2009	US$ per capita 2009
Western Europe										
Austria	122.7	155.9	179.4	200.5	209.2	220.1	230.6	242.0	245.6	40,711
Belgium	130.8	168.0	196.3	215.2	222.3	233.3	245.9	259.0	271.5	35,096
Cyprus										
Denmark	644.4	757.8	901.9	1,033.0	1,088.5	1,153.2	1,203.3	1,235.6	1,194.9	40,442
Finland	76.1	84.3	105.8	124.7	129.0	134.4	142.2	149.8	148.3	38,700
France	992.3	1,176.3	1,391.8	1,625.5	1,684.0	1,760.1	1,838.4	1,899.1	1,910.5	42,511
Germany	1,239.8	1,653.1	1,846.2	2,002.8	2,033.0	2,087.4	2,117.6	2,167.9	2,173.3	36,829
Gibraltar										
Greece	41.1	85.6	127.7	165.8	176.9	189.0	210.8	218.9	217.6	26,879
Iceland										
Ireland	31.1	41.5	68.9	91.3	99.1	108.5	118.7	119.6	107.1	33,429
Italy	612.4	796.9	926.2	1,065.0	1,101.0	1,146.0	1,189.9	1,225.5	1,198.1	27,722
Liechtenstein										
Luxembourg										
Malta										
Monaco										
Netherlands	239.1	288.4	363.3	438.9	450.4	463.0	487.6	508.5	491.7	41,639
Norway	562.1	723.3	1,022.3	1,269.8	1,364.5	1,353.4	1,452.3	1,526.3	1,565.3	51,856
Portugal	49.9	80.1	110.3	131.3	137.7	143.0	149.4	155.9	152.3	19,828
Spain	305.0	425.9	586.3	759.1	820.7	886.7	953.1	1,001.2	948.5	28,956
Sweden	1,225.0	1,564.9	1,943.0	2,276.2	2,370.1	2,453.3	2,553.3	2,625.2	2,658.0	37,744
Switzerland	259.3	304.5	342.4	351.2	363.0	375.0	389.1	404.3	407.5	49,615
Turkey	0.4	7.2	148.9	488.6	570.9	658.3	736.0	818.5	846.0	7,606
United Kingdom	515.2	700.0	917.4	1,099.2	1,162.4	1,216.5	1,257.1	1,307.0	1,291.2	32,682
Eastern Europe										
Albania										
Belarus	0.0	88.7	6,650.4	36,219.7	47,335.6	57,511.2	71,256.8	94,456.9	104,105.2	3,859
Bosnia-Herzegovina		9.5	15.1	16.5	18.5	20.4	21.7	20.4		3,775
Bulgaria	0.0	0.8	19.4	28.7	29.7	32.5	37.7	44.9	43.9	4,149
Croatia	0.2	69.5	136.8	180.7	195.7	211.1	232.7	251.3	242.0	10,343
Czech Republic	595.1	1,189.4	1,732.1	2,185.4	2,307.9	2,495.9	2,733.9	2,914.3	2,862.0	14,341
Estonia		34.9	71.3	106.6	121.6	145.5	175.8	190.7	160.5	10,717
Georgia		3.4	5.6	7.9	8.8	12.3	13.7	15.9	14.8	2,023
Hungary	1,874.2	5,141.6	11,079.0	16,968.0	18,130.3	19,491.2	20,764.3	21,602.8	20,934.7	10,326
Latvia	0.0	2.1	4.0	6.3	7.3	9.0	11.4	12.9	10.2	8,975
Lithuania		21.7	39.5	51.1	58.5	67.5	76.6	90.0	79.2	9,524
Macedonia		145.7	215.0	248.8	263.2	285.2	319.6	372.8	373.5	4,149
Moldova										
Montenegro										
Poland	42.0	315.8	680.5	808.9	859.9	912.9	994.3	1,063.2	1,115.0	9,368
Romania	0.1	6.2	71.4	194.4	222.9	252.7	304.9	374.0	351.1	5,371
Russia	0.5	1,084.9	4,384.5	11,875.6	14,479.0	17,819.9	21,821.6	27,314.3	28,912.0	6,415
Serbia		48.3	365.9	1,356.4	1,661.1	1,935.7	2,227.3	2,720.0	2,795.9	5,616
Slovakia		15.2	26.0	35.7	39.3	43.3	48.4	53.6	53.9	13,880
Slovenia	0.7	9.2	16.6	23.8	25.3	26.9	29.2	32.1	31.1	21,397
Ukraine	0.0	37.2	121.7	273.0	382.1	464.0	604.8	826.6	800.7	2,236

Source: *Euromonitor International from national statistics*

Income Statistics

Table 16.2

Gross Income by Source 2009

% of gross income

	Benefits	Employment	Investments	Other Sources	Total
Western Europe					
Austria	10.95	82.70	5.63	0.72	100.00
Belgium	25.98	57.82	15.56	0.63	100.00
Cyprus					
Denmark	19.28	66.78	7.51	6.43	100.00
Finland	16.41	68.49	12.95	2.15	100.00
France	29.38	61.82	8.43	0.37	100.00
Germany	20.34	62.66	13.79	3.20	100.00
Gibraltar					
Greece	20.84	55.29	20.07	3.80	100.00
Iceland					
Ireland	11.88	69.63	13.68	4.81	100.00
Italy	19.11	60.28	18.19	2.43	100.00
Liechtenstein					
Luxembourg					
Malta					
Monaco					
Netherlands	23.20	63.18	12.95	0.67	100.00
Norway	22.57	71.28	5.89	0.26	100.00
Portugal	15.90	73.78	4.19	6.12	100.00
Spain	10.90	76.72	8.27	4.10	100.00
Sweden	19.56	70.73	6.38	3.33	100.00
Switzerland	23.09	72.85	2.59	1.48	100.00
Turkey	7.39	70.70	18.87	3.04	100.00
United Kingdom	18.91	69.13	7.25	4.71	100.00
Eastern Europe					
Albania					
Belarus	26.23	67.50	0.85	5.42	100.00
Bosnia-Herzegovina					100.00
Bulgaria	19.18	44.63	23.95	12.24	100.00
Croatia	23.61	66.65	5.85	3.89	100.00
Czech Republic	11.94	65.18	17.80	5.08	100.00
Estonia	29.73	63.08	1.41	5.77	100.00
Georgia					100.00
Hungary	19.13	57.60	12.63	10.64	100.00
Latvia	16.75	65.57	16.86	0.81	100.00
Lithuania	20.71	64.11	6.29	8.89	100.00
Macedonia					100.00
Moldova					
Montenegro					
Poland	27.12	58.53	2.10	12.26	100.00
Romania	12.08	73.05	10.68	4.19	100.00
Russia	15.37	77.15	5.94	1.54	100.00
Serbia	18.50	69.41	5.93	6.15	100.00
Slovakia	17.30	79.04	0.88	2.78	100.00
Slovenia	23.33	63.07	3.81	9.78	100.00
Ukraine	13.21	83.39	0.94	2.46	100.00

Source: *Euromonitor International from national statistics*

Income Statistics

Table 16.3

Tax and Social Security Contributions 1990-2009

National currency billion / US$ per capita

	1990	1995	2000	2004	2005	2006	2007	2008	2009	US$ per capita 2009
Western Europe										
Austria	39.2	50.0	60.9	66.8	68.4	71.9	75.7	80.1	81.5	13,503
Belgium	23.0	30.7	39.4	43.3	44.7	45.1	48.6	51.8	54.1	6,990
Cyprus										
Denmark	216.5	261.2	319.1	359.2	378.1	402.1	421.5	432.6	418.3	14,158
Finland	27.6	30.7	39.5	43.0	45.6	47.6	50.1	52.6	52.4	13,674
France	327.3	389.6	468.8	536.0	557.8	580.6	597.9	618.5	616.7	13,722
Germany	326.8	434.7	462.2	512.6	516.6	540.3	549.1	558.9	562.4	9,531
Gibraltar										
Greece	6.9	14.7	26.4	35.4	38.3	41.5	45.3	49.1	48.7	6,013
Iceland										
Ireland	4.1	6.6	12.3	18.0	19.6	22.2	24.3	23.3	21.1	6,588
Italy	77.0	95.5	106.5	106.7	114.3	124.9	136.0	142.0	135.7	3,141
Liechtenstein										
Luxembourg										
Malta										
Monaco										
Netherlands	99.6	123.2	155.4	187.4	193.7	199.1	208.9	220.3	212.3	17,978
Norway	193.1	240.2	356.8	432.1	453.0	482.0	526.2	550.0	562.2	18,624
Portugal	11.7	18.3	27.1	32.6	35.3	36.4	38.1	39.5	38.7	5,045
Spain	87.7	125.4	170.5	218.7	237.4	261.0	288.0	295.9	279.3	8,525
Sweden	459.6	629.1	861.7	955.1	995.8	1,030.8	1,066.9	1,098.2	1,107.9	15,732
Switzerland	55.2	59.8	66.0	59.0	64.6	60.1	62.5	65.2	65.2	7,943
Turkey	0.1	1.6	28.2	78.3	91.5	106.9	116.1	131.2	135.6	1,219
United Kingdom	163.3	208.3	277.4	341.1	371.8	399.2	411.3	422.9	421.4	10,667
Eastern Europe										
Albania										
Belarus	0.0	18.5	1,465.1	8,499.5	11,270.1	13,971.1	16,566.4	21,498.8	23,926.8	887
Bosnia-Herzegovina			1.5	2.7	2.9	3.5	3.8	3.9	3.8	699
Bulgaria	0.0	0.2	4.7	6.0	6.4	6.7	7.9	10.1	9.8	929
Croatia	0.0	3.7	37.4	45.4	48.2	52.5	57.9	62.5	60.6	2,588
Czech Republic	273.9	327.9	501.1	711.5	756.6	820.8	900.7	927.6	884.5	4,432
Estonia		9.5	17.7	29.0	32.9	38.9	47.6	52.7	44.7	2,987
Georgia		0.1	0.0	0.2	0.3	0.5	0.5	0.6	0.5	73
Hungary	500.4	1,366.9	3,183.3	4,806.2	5,231.0	5,760.1	6,446.9	6,883.5	6,686.0	3,298
Latvia	0.0	0.5	0.9	1.5	1.7	2.1	2.8	3.1	2.4	2,073
Lithuania		3.9	8.0	10.1	11.9	14.2	17.1	19.7	17.4	2,097
Macedonia		13.7	20.6	24.5	25.7	26.5	29.1	33.0	32.4	360
Moldova										
Montenegro										
Poland	6.7	74.4	156.4	181.1	200.8	219.9	251.9	268.7	280.2	2,354
Romania	0.0	1.2	13.8	38.0	46.1	52.2	63.2	77.6	72.2	1,105
Russia	0.1	178.5	854.4	2,260.7	2,511.1	3,007.1	3,754.6	4,928.2	5,285.2	1,173
Serbia		12.8	101.1	298.7	367.6	495.3	478.6	545.2	536.7	1,078
Slovakia		4.2	6.5	8.9	9.9	11.2	12.5	14.0	14.2	3,668
Slovenia	0.2	2.5	4.5	6.7	6.9	7.5	8.2	9.2	9.0	6,154
Ukraine	0.0	9.3	24.7	60.4	83.2	100.0	133.1	190.7	184.7	516

Source: *Euromonitor International from national statistics*

Income Statistics   **Table 16.4**

Disposable Income (Annual) 1990-2009

National currency billion / US$ per capita

	1990	1995	2000	2004	2005	2006	2007	2008	2009	US$ per capita 2009
Western Europe										
Austria	83.5	106.0	118.5	133.7	140.9	148.2	154.9	161.9	164.1	27,209
Belgium	107.8	137.2	156.9	172.0	177.6	188.1	197.3	207.2	217.4	28,107
Cyprus										
Denmark	427.9	496.7	582.8	673.7	710.5	751.1	781.8	803.0	776.6	26,283
Finland	48.6	53.6	66.3	81.7	83.4	86.9	92.1	97.2	95.9	25,025
France	665.0	786.7	923.0	1,089.4	1,126.2	1,179.5	1,240.5	1,280.6	1,293.8	28,789
Germany	913.0	1,218.4	1,384.0	1,490.3	1,516.4	1,547.2	1,568.6	1,609.0	1,610.9	27,298
Gibraltar										
Greece	34.3	70.9	101.3	130.4	138.7	147.5	165.6	169.8	169.0	20,867
Iceland										
Ireland	27.0	34.9	56.6	73.3	79.5	86.3	94.4	96.3	86.0	26,841
Italy	535.4	701.4	819.7	958.3	986.7	1,021.0	1,053.9	1,083.5	1,062.3	24,582
Liechtenstein										
Luxembourg										
Malta										
Monaco										
Netherlands	139.4	165.2	207.9	251.4	256.6	263.9	278.6	288.1	279.4	23,661
Norway	369.0	483.1	665.6	837.6	911.5	871.4	926.0	976.3	1,003.1	33,232
Portugal	38.2	61.7	83.2	98.7	102.4	106.7	111.3	116.4	113.5	14,783
Spain	217.3	300.6	415.9	540.4	583.3	625.8	665.2	705.2	669.3	20,431
Sweden	765.4	935.8	1,081.3	1,321.1	1,374.3	1,422.5	1,486.4	1,527.0	1,550.2	22,012
Switzerland	204.2	244.8	276.4	292.2	298.3	314.9	326.6	339.1	342.3	41,671
Turkey	0.3	5.7	120.8	410.3	479.4	551.3	619.9	687.4	710.5	6,387
United Kingdom	351.9	491.7	640.0	758.1	790.5	817.2	845.8	884.1	869.8	22,016
Eastern Europe										
Albania										
Belarus	0.0	70.2	5,185.3	27,720.2	36,065.5	43,540.1	54,690.4	72,958.1	80,178.4	2,972
Bosnia-Herzegovina			8.0	12.4	13.7	15.0	16.6	17.8	16.6	3,076
Bulgaria	0.0	0.6	14.7	22.7	23.4	25.8	29.7	34.8	34.1	3,221
Croatia	0.2	65.8	99.4	135.2	147.5	158.6	174.9	188.8	181.5	7,755
Czech Republic	321.2	861.5	1,231.1	1,473.9	1,551.3	1,675.1	1,833.2	1,986.6	1,977.5	9,909
Estonia		25.4	53.5	77.5	88.7	106.5	128.2	138.0	115.8	7,730
Georgia		3.4	5.6	7.7	8.5	11.8	13.2	15.3	14.3	1,950
Hungary	1,373.8	3,774.7	7,895.7	12,161.8	12,899.3	13,731.2	14,317.4	14,719.4	14,248.6	7,028
Latvia	0.0	1.6	3.0	4.8	5.6	6.9	8.6	9.8	7.8	6,902
Lithuania		17.8	31.5	41.0	46.6	53.3	59.5	70.2	61.8	7,427
Macedonia		132.0	194.5	224.3	237.5	258.7	290.5	339.8	341.1	3,790
Moldova										
Montenegro										
Poland	35.3	241.3	524.1	627.8	659.0	693.0	742.4	794.5	834.9	7,015
Romania	0.1	5.0	57.6	156.3	176.8	200.5	241.6	296.4	278.8	4,266
Russia	0.4	906.5	3,530.1	9,614.9	11,967.8	14,812.8	18,067.0	22,386.1	23,626.8	5,242
Serbia		35.5	264.8	1,057.7	1,293.5	1,440.4	1,748.7	2,174.7	2,259.2	4,538
Slovakia		11.0	19.5	26.9	29.4	32.1	35.9	39.5	39.7	10,212
Slovenia	0.5	6.6	12.1	17.1	18.4	19.4	21.0	22.9	22.2	15,243
Ukraine	0.0	27.9	97.0	212.6	298.8	364.1	471.7	635.9	616.0	1,720

Source: *Euromonitor International from national statistics*

Income Statistics

Table 16.5

Net Savings 1990-2009

National currency billion / US$ per capita

	1990	1995	2000	2004	2005	2006	2007	2008	2009	US$ per capita 2009
Western Europe										
Austria	8.5	11.7	7.7	9.4	10.6	12.7	14.9	17.7	19.2	3,179
Belgium	16.7	26.8	24.9	24.9	25.1	28.3	30.0	32.0	43.5	5,628
Cyprus										
Denmark	11.1	-16.9	-24.0	-22.7	-23.2	-23.2	-26.5	-27.9	-26.5	-898
Finland	4.7	5.6	3.7	7.0	5.9	4.8	5.3	6.0	6.0	1,559
France	85.7	125.3	139.1	171.7	167.6	177.6	192.2	197.0	208.5	4,638
Germany	113.8	180.8	203.7	225.0	227.7	225.8	226.4	233.2	236.4	4,006
Gibraltar										
Greece	1.6	2.6	3.1	1.0	-1.1	-4.6	3.7	-2.6	-2.5	-304
Iceland										
Ireland	6.2	7.6	7.8	7.8	8.4	8.8	9.5	10.0	8.8	2,735
Italy	135.9	151.3	109.9	147.5	148.1	149.3	152.2	160.4	156.9	3,632
Liechtenstein										
Luxembourg										
Malta										
Monaco										
Netherlands	19.7	15.9	0.6	12.9	10.6	13.7	19.4	22.3	21.6	1,833
Norway	21.9	33.4	51.3	82.6	118.0	23.5	22.0	26.4	29.7	984
Portugal	3.6	6.1	4.7	6.1	5.7	5.2	4.1	4.3	5.1	661
Spain	31.6	35.5	45.3	60.6	66.9	70.8	71.4	94.7	84.1	2,568
Sweden	75.0	64.5	3.6	78.8	84.3	80.3	72.7	76.2	85.6	1,215
Switzerland	21.8	29.0	31.4	29.1	29.4	38.3	39.9	41.0	42.5	5,169
Turkey	0.0	0.2	3.3	11.7	14.0	16.5	18.7	23.4	27.2	244
United Kingdom	8.9	43.0	23.4	8.2	6.4	-2.3	-16.4	-7.1	-2.4	-62
Eastern Europe										
Albania										
Belarus	0.0	2.2	173.4	1,590.0	3,187.1	3,949.4	5,788.7	7,383.8	5,981.4	222
Bosnia-Herzegovina			-1.9	-2.6	-2.9	-3.1	-3.2	-3.4	-3.3	-615
Bulgaria	0.0	0.0	-3.7	-4.0	-6.5	-8.7	-9.1	-10.4	-9.0	-851
Croatia	0.0	-10.3	-9.2	-14.9	-14.3	-13.8	-13.8	-13.3	-8.3	-354
Czech Republic	15.1	125.4	96.4	74.7	108.6	137.8	174.4	183.0	172.2	863
Estonia		2.2	1.1	-5.7	-5.7	-5.6	-2.9	1.8	5.8	385
Georgia		0.1	0.2	0.5	0.8	1.0	1.2	1.4	-0.5	-66
Hungary	251.1	708.2	990.9	1,103.6	1,054.9	1,281.9	1,058.7	798.8	806.7	398
Latvia	0.0	0.0	0.1	0.2	0.0	-0.3	-0.4	-0.2	0.0	-30
Lithuania		0.7	2.1	0.4	0.3	0.0	-4.0	-1.9	-1.0	-116
Macedonia		12.6	19.9	16.9	15.8	16.2	19.3	21.3	19.8	220
Moldova										
Montenegro										
Poland	8.5	40.6	54.3	30.4	44.8	40.1	40.5	20.2	21.3	179
Romania	0.0	0.1	3.1	-11.3	-20.2	-32.3	-31.1	-30.4	-23.0	-352
Russia	0.1	186.7	234.9	1,209.3	1,377.8	1,924.9	2,058.6	2,374.5	2,522.4	560
Serbia		-1.4	-27.8	5.0	12.5	-52.3	34.7	151.1	137.6	276
Slovakia		1.1	2.2	1.5	1.7	1.2	2.0	1.9	1.9	494
Slovenia	0.1	0.6	1.7	2.5	3.0	3.2	3.1	3.4	2.8	1,957
Ukraine	0.0	0.8	4.6	31.9	47.3	46.9	50.8	62.5	27.9	78

Source: *Euromonitor International from national statistics*

Income Statistics

Table 16.6

Savings Ratio 1990-2009

% of personal disposable income

	1990	1995	2000	2004	2005	2006	2007	2008	2009
Western Europe									
Austria	10.2	11.0	6.5	7.0	7.5	8.5	9.6	10.9	11.7
Belgium	15.5	19.6	15.9	14.5	14.1	15.0	15.2	15.4	20.0
Cyprus									
Denmark	2.6	-3.4	-4.1	-3.4	-3.3	-3.1	-3.4	-3.5	-3.4
Finland	9.7	10.4	5.5	8.6	7.0	5.6	5.7	6.1	6.2
France	12.9	15.9	15.1	15.8	14.9	15.1	15.5	15.4	16.1
Germany	12.5	14.8	14.7	15.1	15.0	14.6	14.4	14.5	14.7
Gibraltar									
Greece	4.5	3.7	3.1	0.8	-0.8	-3.1	2.2	-1.5	-1.5
Iceland									
Ireland	22.9	21.7	13.7	10.7	10.6	10.2	10.1	10.4	10.2
Italy	25.4	21.6	13.4	15.4	15.0	14.6	14.4	14.8	14.8
Liechtenstein									
Luxembourg									
Malta									
Monaco									
Netherlands	14.1	9.6	0.3	5.1	4.1	5.2	7.0	7.7	7.7
Norway	5.9	6.9	7.7	9.9	12.9	2.7	2.4	2.7	3.0
Portugal	9.4	9.9	5.6	6.2	5.5	4.8	3.7	3.7	4.5
Spain	14.5	11.8	10.9	11.2	11.5	11.3	10.7	13.4	12.6
Sweden	9.8	6.9	0.3	6.0	6.1	5.6	4.9	5.0	5.5
Switzerland	10.7	11.8	11.4	10.0	9.9	12.1	12.2	12.1	12.4
Turkey	3.2	3.5	2.7	2.9	2.9	3.0	3.0	3.4	3.8
United Kingdom	2.5	8.7	3.7	1.1	0.8	-0.3	-1.9	-0.8	-0.3
Eastern Europe									
Albania									
Belarus	16.8	3.2	3.3	5.7	8.8	9.1	10.6	10.1	7.5
Bosnia-Herzegovina			-23.7	-20.7	-20.9	-20.5	-19.4	-18.9	-20.0
Bulgaria	0.3	-2.7	-25.1	-17.8	-27.6	-33.9	-30.5	-29.8	-26.4
Croatia	-17.5	-15.7	-9.3	-11.0	-9.7	-8.7	-7.9	-7.0	-4.6
Czech Republic	4.7	14.6	7.8	5.1	7.0	8.2	9.5	9.2	8.7
Estonia		8.8	2.1	-7.3	-6.5	-5.2	-2.3	1.3	5.0
Georgia		1.5	3.1	7.0	9.0	8.3	9.4	9.1	-3.4
Hungary	18.3	18.8	12.6	9.1	8.2	9.3	7.4	5.4	5.7
Latvia	-46.2	-0.9	2.4	3.7	-0.2	-4.1	-5.2	-2.3	-0.4
Lithuania		4.0	6.6	1.1	0.5	0.0	-6.7	-2.7	-1.6
Macedonia		9.5	10.3	7.5	6.7	6.2	6.7	6.3	5.8
Moldova									
Montenegro									
Poland	24.2	16.8	10.4	6.1	6.8	5.8	5.5	2.5	2.5
Romania	2.1	3.0	5.4	-7.2	-11.4	-16.1	-12.9	-10.3	-8.3
Russia	27.3	20.6	6.7	12.6	11.5	13.0	11.4	10.6	10.7
Serbia		-4.1	-10.5	0.5	1.0	-3.6	2.0	6.9	6.1
Slovakia		10.2	11.5	5.6	5.6	3.8	5.7	4.9	4.8
Slovenia	10.5	9.6	14.1	14.8	16.5	16.6	14.7	15.0	12.8
Ukraine	15.6	3.0	4.7	15.0	15.8	12.9	10.8	9.8	4.5

Source: *Euromonitor International from national statistics*

Industry

Industry Statistics

Table 17.1

General Industrial Production Indices 1980-2009

1995 = 100

	1980	1985	1990	1995	1996	1997	1998	1999	2000	2001
Western Europe										
Austria	68.1	74.2	89.0	100.0	101.0	107.4	116.2	123.2	134.1	138.3
Belgium	80.9	84.1	99.4	100.0	100.8	105.4	108.9	110.1	115.5	115.1
Cyprus	63.0	73.3	97.2	100.0	96.8	96.7	99.4	100.9	105.4	105.1
Denmark	66.3	80.2	86.2	100.0	101.7	106.2	109.4	109.6	115.5	117.2
Finland	65.7	76.2	87.3	100.0	102.9	111.8	122.3	129.3	144.5	144.6
France	87.9	86.1	100.4	100.0	100.9	104.0	107.7	110.2	114.4	115.4
Germany			100.0	100.0	100.7	103.4	107.2	108.4	114.5	114.4
Gibraltar										
Greece	91.9	98.4	101.8	100.0	100.9	102.8	112.0	114.2	122.5	117.5
Iceland										
Ireland	34.4	44.0	63.1	100.0	108.0	126.9	152.3	174.7	199.7	221.7
Italy	82.0	79.5	93.5	100.0	99.1	102.4	104.3	104.4	107.7	106.6
Liechtenstein										
Luxembourg	68.1	82.4	98.0	100.0	100.1	105.3	114.5	116.3	122.1	126.4
Malta										
Monaco										
Netherlands	79.1	83.9	92.2	100.0	102.4	102.6	104.8	106.5	110.0	110.1
Norway	49.7	60.1	78.6	100.0	105.4	109.0	107.8	107.5	110.7	109.9
Portugal	62.3	73.5	100.6	100.0	107.0	109.6	114.0	117.6	118.1	120.4
Spain	81.0	83.4	97.2	100.0	99.3	106.1	111.9	114.8	119.3	117.9
Sweden	73.6	81.0	89.2	100.0	100.9	104.6	110.3	113.4	119.9	118.7
Switzerland	79.9	82.3	97.0	100.0	100.0	104.6	108.4	112.2	121.7	120.9
Turkey		60.0	85.5	100.0	105.9	117.2	118.6	114.3	121.2	109.0
United Kingdom	76.5	82.6	94.1	100.0	101.3	102.8	103.9	105.3	107.2	105.7
Eastern Europe										
Albania				100.0	82.8	53.6	82.5	59.7	121.3	91.3
Belarus			169.2	100.0	103.5	123.0	138.2	152.4	164.3	174.0
Bosnia-Herzegovina										
Bulgaria	143.4	177.8	166.1	100.0	105.1	85.8	78.5	72.2	78.2	79.6
Croatia			178.3	100.0	103.1	110.2	114.2	112.6	114.5	121.3
Czech Republic			131.8	100.0	102.0	106.5	108.2	104.7	105.7	113.6
Estonia			207.0	100.0	102.9	117.9	122.7	118.6	135.9	147.8
Georgia										
Hungary	111.7	122.9	113.8	100.0	103.4	114.8	129.0	142.4	168.4	174.5
Latvia			260.4	100.0	105.5	120.1	123.8	101.7	104.9	115.9
Lithuania			197.2	100.0	104.1	108.9	117.8	104.6	110.1	123.4
Macedonia			207.5	100.0	103.2	104.7	109.5	106.7	110.4	99.3
Moldova										
Montenegro										
Poland	99.9	98.9	80.8	100.0	109.4	121.7	127.4	133.5	143.2	144.5
Romania	148.6	183.5	152.7	100.0	105.7	98.7	81.9	77.7	83.2	90.3
Russia			202.4	100.0	92.4	93.3	88.8	96.7	105.2	108.3
Serbia				100.0	107.3	117.2	121.2	91.7	102.1	102.2
Slovakia			125.3	100.0	102.5	103.8	108.6	106.3	112.6	116.8
Slovenia			124.7	100.0	101.0	102.0	105.8	105.2	111.8	115.1
Ukraine			190.8	100.0	94.9	93.1	91.6	95.9	109.0	123.1

Source: *United Nations/Euromonitor International*
Notes: *Indices based on value of production (or contribution to GDP) at constant prices*

Industry Statistics

General Industrial Production Indices 1980-2009 *(continued)*

1995 = 100

	2002	2003	2004	2005	2006	2007	2008	2009
Western Europe								
Austria	139.7	142.2	152.2	158.2	169.4	179.2	183.4	160.5
Belgium	116.5	117.3	121.6	120.6	126.6	130.2	129.4	111.4
Cyprus	105.2	113.6	115.7	116.8	117.8	121.5	124.7	116.9
Denmark	118.3	118.6	116.9	119.7	124.6	122.2	120.9	102.7
Finland	146.6	146.5	154.3	152.8	168.3	176.1	178.1	140.6
France	113.3	111.9	114.2	114.2	115.1	116.6	113.8	99.8
Germany	113.1	113.7	118.6	122.2	128.7	136.1	136.9	114.4
Gibraltar								
Greece	117.9	118.4	119.2	117.3	118.3	121.0	116.2	105.2
Iceland								
Ireland	239.8	253.4	256.5	266.7	274.4	288.1	283.9	272.1
Italy	105.1	104.5	104.2	103.3	105.8	106.3	103.1	86.4
Liechtenstein								
Luxembourg	129.4	134.1	139.3	140.2	143.1	143.5	137.5	112.6
Malta								
Monaco								
Netherlands	110.1	109.1	113.2	115.7	119.1	123.0	122.0	111.1
Norway	108.9	106.2	105.9	105.9	103.6	102.4	102.9	98.8
Portugal	121.0	119.6	114.8	110.4	113.8	114.2	109.5	100.1
Spain	117.8	119.6	121.9	122.1	126.6	129.6	120.4	100.9
Sweden	118.7	120.5	127.3	130.4	134.4	139.1	135.4	111.0
Switzerland	114.6	114.7	119.7	122.9	132.5	145.1	147.0	135.6
Turkey	119.3	129.7	142.4	162.7	175.4	187.5	185.9	168.0
United Kingdom	103.9	103.2	104.6	102.8	103.0	103.4	100.3	89.9
Eastern Europe								
Albania	75.6	70.5	67.2	60.2	55.1	53.4	51.8	49.0
Belarus	181.9	194.8	225.8	249.7	278.3	301.7	336.7	326.1
Bosnia-Herzegovina								
Bulgaria	83.3	94.2	106.3	113.6	120.5	132.0	132.9	109.7
Croatia	127.3	131.5	135.7	141.9	147.7	155.0	156.9	142.4
Czech Republic	118.2	120.1	132.7	137.8	149.3	165.2	162.2	140.0
Estonia	160.3	177.9	196.4	218.0	239.6	254.9	241.9	178.8
Georgia								
Hungary	180.1	192.5	207.5	221.6	243.5	262.7	262.5	216.2
Latvia	123.9	133.6	143.2	153.4	163.4	165.2	159.0	133.1
Lithuania	131.6	149.3	166.3	178.0	189.6	194.1	204.8	174.9
Macedonia	94.0	98.4	96.2	103.0	106.8	110.7	116.6	107.7
Moldova								
Montenegro								
Poland	146.7	159.6	179.9	186.5	208.9	228.4	234.5	225.6
Romania	94.3	97.5	101.9	104.3	112.3	117.9	119.1	122.0
Russia	111.7	122.3	132.1	138.9	147.8	158.0	159.0	144.2
Serbia	104.1	101.3	109.1	109.6	114.8	119.0	120.4	105.8
Slovakia	125.5	144.6	150.3	151.2	173.8	202.7	209.7	179.8
Slovenia	117.9	119.5	125.3	129.7	137.1	146.9	150.6	124.5
Ukraine	131.2	150.3	168.0	172.8	186.8	201.0	190.6	148.9

Source: *United Nations/Euromonitor International*
Notes: *Indices based on value of production (or contribution to GDP) at constant prices*

Industry Statistics

Table 17.2

Manufacturing Production Indices 1980-2009

1995 = 100

	1980	1985	1990	1995	1996	1997	1998	1999	2000	2001
Western Europe										
Austria	66.5	72.5	88.7	100.0	100.7	108.0	117.8	124.9	137.3	139.9
Belgium	74.4	77.4	94.0	100.0	100.5	105.4	108.4	109.7	116.2	116.1
Cyprus		79.7	103.3	100.0	94.9	94.3	95.4	96.3	100.1	98.2
Denmark	64.8	79.1	86.2	100.0	101.7	106.4	109.5	109.7	115.6	117.9
Finland	66.1	76.7	87.0	100.0	102.5	111.8	123.5	130.9	147.9	147.2
France	93.7	91.9	102.2	100.0	100.6	104.4	108.4	111.5	116.3	117.6
Germany			100.0	100.0	100.5	103.6	108.0	109.4	116.3	116.8
Gibraltar										
Greece	99.4	100.3	102.2	100.0	99.6	101.9	110.2	109.2	114.8	111.9
Iceland										
Ireland	31.6	41.4	61.6	100.0	108.0	129.5	156.8	180.4	208.8	230.5
Italy	83.1	79.8	93.9	100.0	98.9	102.2	103.9	103.6	106.7	105.8
Liechtenstein										
Luxembourg	69.4	84.7	99.0	100.0	100.3	106.1	115.7	117.7	123.6	126.7
Malta										
Monaco										
Netherlands	73.3	79.9	92.9	100.0	100.6	103.2	106.7	109.2	113.8	113.6
Norway	80.8	88.9	89.7	100.0	102.8	106.2	108.8	106.2	103.0	101.9
Portugal	69.5	81.3	104.3	100.0	105.3	110.0	112.8	114.4	114.8	117.4
Spain	81.3	82.2	96.8	100.0	99.3	106.6	113.2	115.8	119.7	117.3
Sweden	73.7	81.0	89.1	100.0	101.0	105.0	111.2	114.6	121.8	120.6
Switzerland	79.2	81.6	97.0	100.0	100.3	104.9	109.1	112.8	123.2	121.8
Turkey		65.2	90.5	100.0	106.5	118.8	118.9	113.9	121.3	109.8
United Kingdom	80.7	83.9	97.7	100.0	100.6	102.7	103.3	104.1	106.6	105.2
Eastern Europe										
Albania				100.0	81.1	74.8	68.5	77.7	116.0	77.6
Belarus			170.9	100.0	103.8	123.6	139.3	154.2	167.0	176.4
Bosnia-Herzegovina										
Bulgaria				100.0	104.8	84.2	74.8	69.7	74.7	75.7
Croatia			188.0	100.0	101.2	105.2	108.6	105.4	108.5	115.4
Czech Republic			162.9	100.0	101.6	108.1	110.9	107.9	108.2	116.2
Estonia			215.5	100.0	102.2	121.1	127.9	124.7	145.3	160.1
Georgia										
Hungary	115.4	126.9	116.4	100.0	103.4	118.5	137.7	154.7	186.8	194.6
Latvia			261.8	100.0	107.3	125.6	130.2	103.6	108.4	116.5
Lithuania			216.0	100.0	100.9	106.6	115.4	102.8	111.9	129.6
Macedonia										
Moldova										
Montenegro										
Poland	93.8	90.9	75.7	100.0	111.5	126.6	134.9	142.4	153.7	153.5
Romania			159.7	100.0	107.2	100.8	82.5	78.5	85.1	93.7
Russia			230.4	100.0	89.7	91.6	85.9	96.9	107.5	109.7
Serbia				100.0	111.1	127.8	133.4	94.7	108.4	109.3
Slovakia			127.9	100.0	102.3	104.0	110.4	106.7	116.6	128.1
Slovenia			126.1	100.0	101.2	101.4	105.4	105.3	112.7	115.9
Ukraine			201.2	100.0	94.9	94.5	93.7	97.1	113.2	132.7

Source: *United Nations/Euromonitor International*
Notes: *Indices based on value of production (or contribution to GDP) at constant prices*

Industry Statistics

Manufacturing Production Indices 1980-2009 *(continued)*
1995 = 100

	2002	2003	2004	2005	2006	2007	2008	2009
Western Europe								
Austria	139.9	143.2	153.6	159.9	172.3	182.9	184.9	159.9
Belgium	117.1	117.7	122.7	120.3	126.0	129.8	129.2	109.0
Cyprus	95.8	103.8	105.5	104.9	104.6	107.8	111.2	100.6
Denmark	119.1	118.2	117.9	120.0	125.0	137.2	130.4	105.6
Finland	150.1	150.1	150.7	161.7	175.7	185.2	184.7	145.3
France	116.0	115.0	117.9	118.3	119.1	121.1	117.5	102.7
Germany	115.5	115.7	119.3	123.7	131.8	140.8	141.1	115.6
Gibraltar								
Greece	111.8	111.3	112.6	111.8	112.7	114.7	110.1	85.3
Iceland								
Ireland	247.8	259.1	259.5	267.7	281.9	302.9	299.2	274.4
Italy	103.8	102.0	102.8	100.2	102.2	102.9	98.1	83.5
Liechtenstein								
Luxembourg	128.9	134.2	140.3	142.8	145.5	146.8	139.2	112.9
Malta								
Monaco								
Netherlands	113.7	112.4	116.3	118.6	121.9	125.7	124.4	113.8
Norway	96.7	92.6	93.9	96.8	101.1	105.2	108.1	104.3
Portugal	117.9	117.3	116.4	114.5	117.2	121.0	117.3	97.0
Spain	117.8	119.6	121.0	120.7	125.6	128.6	119.1	98.3
Sweden	121.8	125.0	130.8	133.9	140.1	144.6	139.5	112.8
Switzerland	115.4	115.3	120.9	124.7	135.2	148.6	158.7	137.9
Turkey	121.8	133.1	146.9	153.9	165.8	176.7	173.5	154.5
United Kingdom	102.4	102.2	104.8	104.0	106.1	106.9	104.2	92.1
Eastern Europe								
Albania	53.6	54.7	51.4	44.5	42.1	38.7	35.3	31.2
Belarus	184.3	197.2	229.4	253.5	282.9	307.5	342.8	331.1
Bosnia-Herzegovina								
Bulgaria	81.3	96.5	117.0	126.5	135.7	146.9	148.9	133.9
Croatia	120.5	126.7	131.8	140.5	151.0	156.4	158.8	139.6
Czech Republic	118.6	125.0	138.4	148.9	166.8	183.2	184.5	152.9
Estonia	174.1	192.8	216.2	241.8	268.1	281.7	266.5	195.4
Georgia								
Hungary	201.6	215.8	234.1	252.6	279.3	303.7	298.1	246.5
Latvia	123.8	133.5	141.8	151.0	158.2	156.6	143.6	125.8
Lithuania	133.3	152.1	170.1	184.7	200.7	209.4	216.3	183.3
Macedonia								
Moldova								
Montenegro								
Poland	156.3	172.8	198.0	207.0	235.3	260.7	271.3	261.3
Romania	99.7	103.7	109.4	112.6	122.3	129.4	130.4	136.9
Russia	110.8	122.2	135.0	142.6	148.9	172.7	179.1	109.3
Serbia	112.5	107.5	118.3	117.3	123.6	128.9	130.0	109.3
Slovakia	138.8	149.0	156.1	163.1	183.8	211.7	216.9	204.1
Slovenia	118.1	120.0	125.8	130.4	139.3	149.2	146.7	125.6
Ukraine	144.5	171.2	194.5	199.6	211.1	235.8	237.1	160.3

Source: *United Nations/Euromonitor International*
Notes: *Indices based on value of production (or contribution to GDP) at constant prices*

Industry Statistics

Table 17.3

Mining Production Indices 1980-2009

1995 = 100

	1980	1985	1990	1995	1996	1997	1998	1999	2000	2001
Western Europe										
Austria	107.0	117.7	111.5	100.0	100.2	96.7	103.9	107.4	112.3	109.6
Belgium			69.0	100.0	106.7	113.4	116.6	125.2	138.1	139.5
Cyprus			82.2	100.0	97.6	101.4	121.1	130.2	135.3	128.9
Denmark			103.1	100.0	103.4	87.8	93.0	93.5	93.8	92.3
Finland			94.9	100.0	100.6	127.0	92.7	128.1	99.4	120.0
France			116.0	100.0	91.7	88.0	86.9	86.8	88.4	87.4
Germany	57.2	104.7	100.0	100.0	94.4	92.2	85.8	85.5	79.6	74.3
Gibraltar										
Greece	155.3	153.7	120.9	100.0	103.6	103.9	102.6	96.4	109.3	111.9
Iceland										
Ireland	65.6	65.6	85.7	100.0	98.4	84.2	78.0	92.9	114.7	114.6
Italy			87.6	100.0	102.4	108.5	107.9	107.8	98.4	90.8
Liechtenstein										
Luxembourg			103.4	100.0	89.9	89.4	100.2	107.8	108.8	109.9
Malta										
Monaco										
Netherlands			89.1	100.0	113.5	104.2	103.1	99.5	97.2	104.1
Norway			94.1	100.0	99.5	103.3	109.2	109.8	115.7	119.2
Portugal			114.3	100.0	103.3	103.3	105.2	102.2	103.8	105.8
Spain			101.9	100.0	94.3	91.9	92.0	90.1	91.1	88.2
Sweden			95.0	100.0	98.3	94.9	94.5	96.4	97.8	95.5
Switzerland				100.0	98.3	100.5	87.9	93.5	94.2	94.7
Turkey			95.5	100.0	103.3	109.4	121.7	109.6	106.6	98.0
United Kingdom			73.3	100.0	103.2	102.1	104.2	108.6	105.1	99.3
Eastern Europe										
Albania				100.0	87.7	54.5	56.2	41.4	36.4	32.1
Belarus				100.0	99.0	111.7	118.6	123.9	117.5	130.6
Bosnia-Herzegovina										
Bulgaria				100.0	115.5	93.3	90.9	78.6	80.7	73.7
Croatia			132.1	100.0	97.0	96.6	94.2	96.1	97.8	99.8
Czech Republic	125.0	137.5	144.7	100.0	101.4	98.5	92.8	81.6	88.2	88.9
Estonia	268.8	236.5	195.7	100.0	105.7	105.3	100.7	87.0	91.7	95.0
Georgia										
Hungary			192.3	100.0	102.5	93.9	74.7	75.3	68.2	79.4
Latvia	579.9	168.2	257.7	100.0	102.4	110.4	117.2	123.9	134.9	141.4
Lithuania				100.0	122.0	136.3	185.7	177.1	198.1	263.1
Macedonia										
Moldova										
Montenegro										
Poland			108.8	100.0	101.3	99.7	86.6	83.2	82.1	77.9
Romania			120.5	100.0	100.7	95.0	81.6	76.1	79.8	84.4
Russia			141.2	100.0	97.0	97.2	94.9	98.7	105.0	111.3
Serbia				100.0	99.2	106.0	105.4	86.0	93.8	81.9
Slovakia			233.6	100.0	105.6	118.0	104.7	103.8	101.4	88.1
Slovenia			132.3	100.0	100.5	102.3	102.0	97.8	95.2	87.7
Ukraine			201.2	100.0	94.8	97.9	95.3	98.3	104.6	108.0

Source: *United Nations/Euromonitor International*
Notes: *Indices based on value of production (or contribution to GDP) at constant prices*

Industry Statistics

Mining Production Indices 1980-2009 *(continued)*

1995 = 100

	2002	2003	2004	2005	2006	2007	2008	2009
Western Europe								
Austria	113.1	112.5	106.2	104.4	115.0	114.9	116.6	113.0
Belgium	182.2	190.1	186.3	195.3	201.0	258.5	277.3	186.9
Cyprus	143.6	149.0	156.0	162.1	160.2	159.7	179.7	149.1
Denmark	88.2	95.8	100.6	105.0	99.2	89.3	89.3	78.6
Finland	131.1	131.7	115.5	151.1	190.7	149.8	149.7	182.4
France	83.0	81.9	81.2	79.1	81.2	81.8	78.9	71.3
Germany	73.2	72.6	70.3	69.2	67.0	66.6	60.7	63.6
Gibraltar								
Greece	122.7	116.4	116.5	110.3	107.1	106.1	101.5	77.1
Iceland								
Ireland	109.0	132.7	129.8	129.4	141.1	147.0	133.6	106.9
Italy	106.2	108.2	106.0	114.1	110.7	111.6	101.3	84.9
Liechtenstein								
Luxembourg	100.0	88.7	87.0	85.6	67.1	68.2	66.9	60.6
Malta								
Monaco								
Netherlands	104.5	101.3	112.3	92.4	88.5	89.4	98.4	91.0
Norway	117.2	123.7	117.6	114.6	126.1	146.4	145.3	100.8
Portugal	100.2	90.7	94.6	92.5	83.4	92.0	94.0	83.1
Spain	87.7	87.7	83.5	80.2	82.2	81.1	70.7	54.4
Sweden	96.9	95.9	104.4	110.5	111.6	118.3	119.6	100.8
Switzerland	93.3	92.6	96.5	91.5	100.4	106.6	98.0	101.8
Turkey	90.0	86.9	90.4	102.9	111.4	120.7	129.6	126.1
United Kingdom	99.7	94.6	87.3	80.0	74.0	72.6	67.9	61.2
Eastern Europe								
Albania	31.8	28.7	26.4	24.3	23.1	22.1	20.2	19.0
Belarus	134.7	147.4	160.8	173.5	178.0	189.2	197.3	207.2
Bosnia-Herzegovina								
Bulgaria	73.3	78.4	94.7	95.1	96.7	89.3	86.3	76.7
Croatia	116.8	119.4	115.5	112.1	122.7	127.0	124.8	111.4
Czech Republic	89.7	90.0	89.4	89.9	92.2	90.6	88.3	85.4
Estonia	109.7	115.3	105.1	116.9	127.5	141.2	123.2	116.4
Georgia								
Hungary	71.9	69.4	76.3	73.7	85.7	71.1	98.1	84.1
Latvia	154.2	162.4	180.3	226.3	247.3	281.0	287.9	285.1
Lithuania	250.8	271.8	251.2	231.4	228.8	231.2	214.5	135.1
Macedonia								
Moldova								
Montenegro								
Poland	75.5	74.1	76.4	74.2	75.3	73.2	73.6	63.6
Romania	80.0	79.4	81.2	80.6	82.8	82.5	82.3	71.5
Russia	118.8	129.2	137.9	139.8	142.8	145.6	145.8	87.0
Serbia	83.6	84.6	83.6	85.3	88.3	87.7	90.9	87.0
Slovakia	113.3	107.0	95.3	91.9	83.1	84.4	83.8	93.1
Slovenia	94.4	99.9	92.9	99.2	109.5	113.5	111.7	115.4
Ukraine	110.5	116.5	121.3	125.5	132.9	136.4	139.8	116.6

Source: *United Nations/Euromonitor International*
Notes: *Indices based on value of production (or contribution to GDP) at constant prices*

IT and Telecommunications

IT and Telecommunications Statistics

Table 18.1

Internet Users 1990-2009
'000

	1990	1995	2000	2004	2005	2006	2007	2008	2009
Western Europe									
Austria	10	150	2,700	4,249	4,504	5,005	5,602	4,950	5,308
Belgium	0	100	3,000	5,581	6,043	6,471	7,006	7,436	7,833
Cyprus		3	120	264	259	287	325	339	378
Denmark	5	200	2,090	4,115	4,182	4,520	4,408	4,630	4,783
Finland	20	710	1,927	3,665	3,832	4,052	4,169	4,357	4,509
France	30	950	8,460	23,732	26,154	30,100	31,571	33,848	36,899
Germany	100	1,500	24,800	50,414	53,748	57,074	59,472	62,500	64,400
Gibraltar			6	6	6	6	6	7	7
Greece	0	80	1,000	2,220	2,446	3,231	3,678	3,631	4,035
Iceland		30	125	168	183	194	202	211	218
Ireland	0	40	679	1,387	1,535	2,147	2,452	2,830	3,128
Italy	10	300	13,200	27,170	28,000	30,764	32,000	29,118	31,124
Liechtenstein			12	22	22	23	23	23	24
Luxembourg		7	100	298	321	334	364	389	410
Malta		1	51	139	153	167	183	200	217
Monaco									
Netherlands	50	1,000	7,000	11,602	12,876	13,231	13,792	14,273	14,625
Norway	30	280	1,200	3,448	3,696	3,760	3,993	4,088	4,171
Portugal	0	150	1,680	3,028	3,358	3,796	4,249	4,451	4,734
Spain	5	150	5,486	17,059	18,948	20,822	23,025	26,171	28,556
Sweden	50	450	4,048	7,386	7,323	7,800	7,295	7,524	7,716
Switzerland	40	250	3,440	4,923	5,077	5,301	5,433	5,739	6,015
Turkey	0	50	2,500	9,389	10,247	13,150	21,141	24,483	27,775
United Kingdom	50	1,100	15,800	37,472	39,381	39,499	43,754	48,755	51,531
Eastern Europe									
Albania		0	4	75	188	471	591	653	700
Belarus	0	0	187	2,461	2,577	2,694	2,810	2,934	3,061
Bosnia-Herzegovina	0	0	40	585	806	950	1,055	1,308	1,472
Bulgaria	0	10	430	1,245	1,545	1,841	2,368	2,246	2,535
Croatia	0	24	299	1,375	1,472	1,685	1,985	2,244	2,468
Czech Republic	0	150	1,000	3,273	3,270	4,492	4,991	5,433	5,970
Estonia	0	40	392	668	785	808	855	927	963
Georgia	0	1	23	176	271	332	360	388	418
Hungary	0	70	715	2,835	3,736	4,532	5,215	5,500	5,933
Latvia	0	0	150	765	969	1,148	1,252	1,358	1,445
Lithuania	0	0	225	999	1,167	1,435	1,661	1,777	1,905
Macedonia	0	0	30	428	482	513	605	847	922
Moldova		0	53	406	550	728	954	1,204	1,410
Montenegro				160	243	266	280	312	331
Poland	0	250	2,800	11,182	13,485	15,399	16,756	18,900	20,875
Romania	0	17	800	2,615	3,582	4,542	5,145	5,939	6,685
Russia		220	2,900	18,500	21,800	25,689	30,000	35,019	40,480
Serbia				1,517	777	1,400	1,500	2,360	2,733
Slovakia	0	28	507	1,450	1,700	1,931	2,312	2,771	3,016
Slovenia	0	57	300	728	924	1,003	1,061	992	1,059
Ukraine	0	22	350	5,000	8,000	9,000	10,000	10,354	10,663

Source: *International Telecommunications Union/World Bank/Trade Sources/Euromonitor International*

Table 18.2

Dial-Up Internet Subscribers 1998-2009
'000

	1998	1999	2000	2001	2002	2003	2004	2005	2006	2007	2008	2009
Western Europe												
Austria	215	574	860	779	749	908	714	598	948	899	798	675
Belgium	196	536	1,006	965	879	666	416	273	203	146	93	54
Cyprus	25	40	52	63	73	66	64	59	43	33	20	13
Denmark	580	1,125	1,221	1,218	1,120	964	744	465	164	143	137	94
Finland	290	457	581	816	784	827	600	403	291	217	159	109
France	1,267	2,975	5,263	6,385	7,469	7,048	5,378	3,746	2,557	1,508	975	651
Germany	3,750	7,980	12,735	11,900	11,795	12,530	12,000	9,200	7,330	5,940	4,776	3,778
Gibraltar												
Greece	100	193	271	288	392	520	649	722	467	244	237	208
Iceland	9	13	45	40	27	10	10	9	11	8	7	6
Ireland	120	240	550	600	648	683	664	603	444	290	232	186
Italy	1,140	2,870	5,685	11,610	12,150	14,550	12,426	10,878	9,602	8,469	7,427	6,335
Liechtenstein												
Luxembourg	6	11	25	41	64	92	77	49	32	10	9	7
Malta												
Monaco												
Netherlands	992	2,667	3,408	4,034	3,329	3,012	2,094	1,500	778	629	515	426
Norway	370	702	1,153	1,147	1,198	889	747	429	268	166	105	66
Portugal	173	255	313	370	406	403	395	271	190	124	41	14
Spain	667	2,240	3,146	3,244	2,677	2,559	1,852	1,199	847	536	155	79
Sweden	1,450	1,873	1,993	2,232	2,192	2,148	1,883	767	665	774	805	749
Switzerland	425	992	1,609	2,060	1,882	1,947	1,023	961	839	434	316	235
Turkey	194	312	460	669	919	996	933	663	406	131	93	59
United Kingdom	3,750	7,400	8,368	11,029	10,929	11,328	9,377	6,422	4,320	2,672	2,104	1,507
Eastern Europe												
Albania												
Belarus	2	4	5	8	18	23	30	36	40	41	41	38
Bosnia-Herzegovina	4	4	18	22	87	137	162	176	198	189	148	109
Bulgaria	1	2	6	7	9	32	39	41	82	18	15	1
Croatia	30	75	187	331	538	567	832	838	964	937	836	655
Czech Republic	18	200	416	1,250	1,629	2,114	1,893	1,643	1,413	1,191	969	740
Estonia	35	60	80	79	75	47	33	18	12	6	7	6
Georgia	2	2	3	3	3	3	89	176	135	235	308	323
Hungary	73	136	217	298	334	391	370	325	93	63	44	30
Latvia	2	21	33	40	28	27	18	12	6	3	1	1
Lithuania	16	31	53	56	59	47	45	23	11	6	5	5
Macedonia	8	13	30	45	59	73	89	95	94	173	107	66
Moldova												
Montenegro	2	4	8	14	23	34	53	73	63	52	41	30
Poland	421	750	930	1,128	1,484	2,532	1,699	1,741	333	560	522	326
Romania	27	50	100	300	350	449	824	413	337	205	98	37
Russia	260	400	492	1,027	1,880	3,022	4,352	5,827	7,272	8,480	9,303	9,404
Serbia	11	31	74	150	262	426	584	708	883	686	393	249
Slovakia	35	47	68	100	130	160	152	113	78	61	65	69
Slovenia	43	72	139	172	184	186	232	201	127	73	30	16
Ukraine	28	45	67	120	229	457	904	1,614	2,288	2,860	2,822	2,243

Source: *Euromonitor International from trade sources/national statistics*

IT and Telecommunications Statistics

Table 18.3

Broadband Internet Subscribers 1998-2009

'000

	1998	1999	2000	2001	2002	2003	2004	2005	2006	2007	2008	2009
Western Europe												
Austria	0.0	50.9	190.5	320.6	451.0	589.0	870.0	1,174.0	1,432.0	1,622.0	1,792.4	1,959.1
Belgium	10.9	23.0	144.0	460.0	815.4	1,242.9	1,619.9	2,010.6	2,356.5	2,715.3	2,962.5	3,175.7
Cyprus	0.0	0.0	0.0	2.5	5.9	10.0	17.1	31.9	62.8	97.0	104.0	116.5
Denmark	0.0	10.0	67.0	238.0	451.3	718.3	1,017.6	1,343.9	1,735.3	1,958.8	2,021.4	2,117.8
Finland	0.0	8.5	35.0	134.0	273.5	491.1	800.0	1,174.2	1,428.0	1,617.0	1,762.5	1,873.6
France	13.5	55.0	196.0	601.5	1,591.0	3,569.4	6,561.0	9,471.0	12,711.0	15,550.0	17,725.0	19,355.7
Germany	0.0	20.0	265.0	2,100.0	3,205.0	4,470.0	7,000.0	10,800.0	15,000.0	19,600.0	22,532.0	25,190.8
Gibraltar												
Greece	0.0	0.0	0.0	0.0	2.0	10.5	51.5	160.1	488.2	1,017.5	1,506.6	1,972.2
Iceland	0.0	0.1	2.4	10.4	24.3	41.6	55.8	78.0	87.7	97.9	99.9	101.8
Ireland	0.0	0.0	0.0	0.0	10.6	41.8	152.1	322.5	601.9	805.9	896.3	986.0
Italy	0.0	30.0	115.0	390.0	850.0	2,250.0	4,724.5	6,821.9	8,638.9	10,122.1	11,283.0	12,471.1
Liechtenstein												
Luxembourg	0.0	0.0	0.0	1.2	5.7	15.4	36.5	70.1	98.8	128.5	141.6	152.3
Malta												
Monaco												
Netherlands	75.5	167.8	260.0	466.2	1,171.0	1,988.0	3,206.0	4,100.0	5,192.2	5,507.0	5,855.0	6,134.3
Norway	0.0	2.3	22.4	88.4	205.3	398.8	671.7	991.3	1,244.5	1,439.7	1,607.8	1,723.5
Portugal	0.0	0.3	25.2	99.3	260.6	502.0	838.4	1,165.4	1,425.7	1,524.6	1,692.3	1,808.2
Spain	0.0	1.0	76.4	430.1	1,247.5	2,121.9	3,401.4	5,035.2	6,690.7	8,070.3	9,157.0	10,002.1
Sweden	0.0	7.0	249.0	587.0	840.0	1,095.0	1,410.0	2,522.0	2,930.0	3,280.0	3,421.0	3,580.4
Switzerland	0.0	0.0	56.4	140.0	455.2	783.9	1,227.4	1,624.2	1,988.1	2,379.5	2,533.6	2,667.9
Turkey	0.0	0.0	0.0	10.9	21.2	199.3	577.9	1,589.8	2,773.7	4,554.0	5,736.6	6,729.1
United Kingdom	0.0	0.0	52.9	331.0	1,356.5	3,113.7	6,123.9	9,898.7	13,013.2	15,605.2	17,275.7	18,605.9
Eastern Europe												
Albania												
Belarus	0.0	0.0	0.0	0.0	0.0	0.1	0.8	1.6	11.4	22.8	34.0	45.6
Bosnia-Herzegovina	0.0	0.0	0.0	0.0	0.2	1.5	6.6	13.7	40.0	84.7	188.5	299.5
Bulgaria	0.0	0.0	0.0	0.0	0.0	0.0	74.1	165.5	384.7	629.1	853.1	1,060.4
Croatia	0.0	0.0	0.0	0.0	0.0	3.4	23.0	116.0	251.8	387.1	524.7	737.9
Czech Republic	0.0	0.0	2.5	6.2	15.3	34.7	236.0	709.1	1,112.5	1,496.7	1,769.7	2,040.4
Estonia	0.0	0.0	3.0	17.3	45.7	90.3	138.7	179.2	246.8	277.8	317.9	340.2
Georgia	0.0	0.0	0.0	0.4	0.9	1.4	1.9	2.4	27.0	46.7	107.8	208.4
Hungary	0.0	1.2	3.4	24.0	111.5	264.3	411.1	651.7	1,198.8	1,428.7	1,696.7	1,891.8
Latvia	0.0	0.0	0.3	3.2	10.0	19.5	49.1	60.8	109.7	146.1	179.9	210.9
Lithuania	0.0	0.1	0.1	2.8	40.3	114.1	129.1	234.1	368.7	507.6	590.1	660.9
Macedonia	0.0	0.0	0.0	0.0	0.0	0.0	0.0	12.4	36.5	100.5	179.0	261.5
Moldova												
Montenegro	0.0	0.0	0.0	0.0	0.0	0.0	0.0	7.7	25.8	43.6	63.2	80.5
Poland	0.0	0.0	0.0	12.0	121.7	195.8	811.8	945.2	2,911.2	3,427.6	3,995.5	4,582.8
Romania	0.0	0.0	1.0	6.0	15.8	196.1	104.3	377.1	1,088.2	1,949.1	2,510.0	2,886.5
Russia	0.0	0.0	0.0	0.0	11.0	343.0	675.0	1,589.0	2,900.0	4,000.0	6,398.0	9,235.5
Serbia	0.0	0.0	0.0	0.0	0.0	0.0	16.0	48.4	121.7	325.7	451.2	579.8
Slovakia	0.0	0.0	0.0	0.0	4.1	22.5	78.8	181.5	317.0	472.0	618.9	750.0
Slovenia	0.0	0.0	1.5	5.5	24.0	58.0	115.1	196.7	274.5	344.8	426.6	503.0
Ukraine	0.0	0.0	0.0	0.0	0.5	20.5	63.6	130.0	520.0	800.0	1,600.0	2,644.8

Source: Euromonitor International from trade sources/national statistics

Table 18.4

Personal Computers in Use 1990-2009

'000

	1990	1995	2000	2004	2005	2006	2007	2008	2009
Western Europe									
Austria		1,300	2,900	4,729	4,996	5,209	5,405	5,583	5,738
Belgium		1,800	2,300	3,627	3,954	4,400	4,706	5,001	5,283
Cyprus		35	150	249	279	324	354	383	413
Denmark		1,400	2,700	3,543	3,772	3,962	4,142	4,305	4,449
Finland		1,200	2,050	2,515	2,625	2,717	2,805	2,888	2,963
France		8,500	17,920	30,000	35,000	40,000	44,140	48,047	51,655
Germany		14,600	27,640	45,000	50,000	54,000	57,658	60,994	63,903
Gibraltar									
Greece		350	750	986	1,020	1,045	1,077	1,106	1,132
Iceland		55	110	138	142	160	176	191	203
Ireland		660	1,360	2,011	2,198	2,480	2,720	2,922	3,092
Italy		4,800	10,300	18,150	21,486	23,770	25,937	27,972	29,690
Liechtenstein									
Luxembourg			200	285	290	318	342	362	379
Malta		30	80	118	126	132	138	144	149
Monaco									
Netherlands		3,100	6,300	11,110	13,943	14,900	15,734	16,465	17,108
Norway		1,193	2,200	2,630	2,745	2,931	3,084	3,212	3,342
Portugal		550	1,050	1,402	1,607	1,719	1,829	1,922	2,010
Spain		2,400	5,800	10,957	12,000	16,000	17,640	18,981	20,076
Sweden		2,200	4,500	6,861	7,548	8,000	8,529	8,988	9,385
Switzerland		2,000	4,700	6,105	6,430	6,630	6,930	7,133	7,322
Turkey		920	2,500	3,703	4,073	4,400	4,743	5,077	5,398
United Kingdom		11,800	20,190	35,890	45,659	48,600	51,294	53,665	55,842
Eastern Europe									
Albania			25	48	54	120	144	158	171
Belarus									
Bosnia-Herzegovina									
Bulgaria		140	361	461	525	604	681	744	800
Croatia		100	499	837	870	900	927	954	978
Czech Republic		550	1,250	2,450	2,800	3,075	3,344	3,588	3,799
Estonia			220	620	650	680	700	720	738
Georgia									
Hungary		400	870	1,476	1,456	1,845	2,572	3,150	3,597
Latvia		20	340	501	566	748	890	1,002	1,089
Lithuania		24	240	533	616	620	623	626	628
Macedonia									
Moldova		9	64	112	348	424	489	544	591
Montenegro									
Poland		1,100	2,670	4,520	5,346	6,456	7,372	8,131	8,760
Romania		300	713	2,450	2,800	3,200	4,144	4,892	5,484
Russia		2,600	9,300	15,000	17,400	19,000	20,644	22,235	23,610
Serbia									
Slovakia		220	740	1,593	1,929	2,320	2,776	3,115	3,433
Slovenia		200	548	704	808	816	858	892	920
Ukraine		430	890	1,327	1,810	2,121	2,402	2,653	2,877

Source: International Telecommunications Union/World Bank/Trade Sources/Euromonitor International

IT and Telecommunications Statistics

Table 18.5

Capital Investment in Telecommunications 1985-2009

National currency million / US$ million

	1985	1990	1995	2000	2004	2005	2006	2007	2008	2009	US$ million 2009
Western Europe											
Austria	756	1,163	1,170	918	684	759	750	724	700	684	949.9
Belgium		629	993	1,574	1,328	1,063	1,051	1,022	1,019	997	1,384.7
Cyprus		17	23	68	44	41	38	63	68	69	96.4
Denmark		3,254	3,078	9,015	5,722	6,874	7,357	6,661	6,784	6,824	1,273.0
Finland	384	499	616	888	726	675	658	639	605	582	808.5
France		3,987	4,772	7,841	5,495	6,342	7,015	5,961	6,732	6,871	9,548.1
Germany	0	9,832	7,921	9,650	5,700	5,800	6,500	6,833	7,225	7,464	10,372.1
Gibraltar		2	2	3	2	3	3	3	3	3	5.0
Greece		175	458	2,114	1,088	721	805	1,294	1,363	1,573	2,186.5
Iceland	400	838	1,958	5,459	5,612	5,689	5,494	8,483	8,817	9,180	74.2
Ireland	178	223	246	410	242	243	256	262	250	238	330.8
Italy	2,761	5,113	3,966	7,113	7,084	8,000	6,837	6,791	6,728	6,657	9,251.1
Liechtenstein	11	12	16	18	19	19	20	21	21	21	19.7
Luxembourg		51	57	63	92	82	81	90	92	95	131.4
Malta	2	9	6	11	22	20	18	16	15	13	18.7
Monaco		1	1	1	1	1	1	1	1	1	1.7
Netherlands	637	1,108	1,250	3,353	3,312	3,445	3,361	3,412	3,475	3,524	4,896.4
Norway		2,747	5,129	18,718	21,869	22,738	24,182	25,081	26,130	27,074	4,304.4
Portugal	108	371	678	1,249	679	733	763	1,193	718	769	1,068.4
Spain		4,335	2,334	7,332	4,715	5,515	5,686	5,788	5,767	5,733	7,967.0
Sweden		6,286	7,783	22,621	11,592	8,832	10,198	10,698	11,610	11,968	1,563.8
Switzerland		3,077	2,156	3,794	2,060	2,030	6,487	2,414	3,010	3,210	2,954.7
Turkey		2	20	393	1,447	1,862	1,650	2,479	2,687	2,823	1,815.0
United Kingdom		2,758	4,557	10,971	7,630	7,442	7,408	7,248	6,716	6,596	10,286.5
Eastern Europe											
Albania		30	476	2,640	6,277	5,733	5,402	6,106	6,300	6,599	69.5
Belarus			482	39,390	288,841	343,441	382,535	418,380	452,441	475,354	170.4
Bosnia-Herzegovina			20	111	404	474	524	571	652	685	486.4
Bulgaria			3	115	580	946	815	1,053	1,230	1,386	985.2
Croatia		2	2,079	2,718	1,718	1,884	2,056	1,781	1,926	1,989	376.4
Czech Republic			20,000	46,430	12,206	13,736	14,171	16,153	16,682	17,238	904.2
Estonia			477	863	699	782	1,261	1,481	1,575	1,657	147.2
Georgia		0	5	163	149	156	168	181	186	191	114.6
Hungary	4,715	13,334	85,651	152,784	91,405	93,107	86,801	89,747	82,218	74,520	368.3
Latvia			62	44	15	29	29	35	34	33	66.0
Lithuania		0	120	517	273	394	526	547	575	595	239.5
Macedonia			1,604	3,033	1,878	2,038	2,199	2,060	1,912	1,781	40.4
Moldova			52	425	847	1,141	1,184	1,926	2,212	2,395	215.5
Montenegro											
Poland		160	2,149	5,953	5,959	5,966	7,586	7,858	8,131	8,407	2,693.6
Romania		0	48	1,273	2,408	2,525	2,794	3,038	3,331	3,614	1,185.1
Russia			3,525	16,698	50,276	59,411	68,273	74,703	78,670	79,299	2,496.7
Serbia					21,662	18,336	15,010	36,633	39,428	43,365	641.7
Slovakia			144	193	342	338	353	387	432	463	642.9
Slovenia		66	112	408	216	249	325	243	237	228	316.3
Ukraine			270	1,458	5,609	8,486	9,808	11,200	12,591	13,831	1,775.2

Source: *Euromonitor International from International Telecommunications Union/national statistics*

IT and Telecommunications Statistics

Table 18.6

Mobile Telephone Subscriptions 1990-2009
'000

	1990	1995	2000	2004	2005	2006	2007	2008	2009
Western Europe									
Austria	73.7	383.5	6,117.0	7,992.0	8,665.0	9,281.0	9,912.0	10,816.0	11,225.7
Belgium	42.9	235.3	5,629.0	9,131.7	9,604.7	9,847.4	10,738.1	11,822.2	12,398.8
Cyprus	3.2	44.5	218.3	658.2	782.5	867.8	988.3	1,016.7	1,048.1
Denmark	148.2	822.3	3,363.6	5,166.9	5,449.2	5,828.2	6,310.0	6,550.7	6,738.1
Finland	257.9	1,039.1	3,728.6	4,988.0	5,270.0	5,670.0	6,080.0	6,830.0	7,136.2
France	283.2	1,302.5	29,052.4	44,544.0	48,088.0	51,662.0	55,358.1	57,972.0	60,109.7
Germany	272.6	3,725.0	48,202.0	71,322.0	79,271.0	85,652.0	97,151.0	107,245.0	109,537.4
Gibraltar		0.7	5.6	18.4	20.7	22.4	23.8	24.8	25.6
Greece		273.0	5,932.4	9,324.3	10,260.4	10,979.8	12,294.9	13,799.3	14,624.6
Iceland	10.0	30.9	214.9	290.1	283.1	301.9	327.6	346.6	367.2
Ireland	25.0	158.0	2,461.0	3,860.0	4,270.0	4,740.7	4,982.7	5,048.1	5,224.6
Italy	266.0	3,923.0	42,246.0	62,750.0	71,500.0	80,418.0	89,801.0	88,580.0	91,532.4
Liechtenstein	0.6	9.5	10.0	25.5	27.5	28.8	32.0	34.1	36.0
Luxembourg	0.8	26.8	303.3	470.0	510.0	713.0	684.5	707.0	726.5
Malta	1.1	10.8	114.4	306.1	324.0	346.8	371.5	385.6	396.6
Monaco	0.4	3.0	18.7	24.8	24.9	24.8	24.6	24.3	24.8
Netherlands	79.0	539.0	10,755.0	14,800.0	15,834.0	17,296.0	19,285.0	19,927.0	20,528.7
Norway	196.8	981.3	3,224.0	4,524.8	4,754.5	5,007.7	5,191.6	5,353.7	5,495.2
Portugal	6.5	340.8	6,665.0	10,571.1	11,447.3	12,226.4	13,450.9	14,909.6	15,745.0
Spain	54.7	945.0	24,265.1	38,622.6	42,694.1	46,152.0	48,422.5	49,681.6	50,901.3
Sweden	461.2	2,008.0	6,372.3	8,785.0	9,104.0	9,607.0	10,371.0	10,854.3	11,173.0
Switzerland	125.0	447.2	4,638.5	6,274.8	6,834.2	7,436.2	8,208.9	8,780.0	9,263.4
Turkey	31.8	437.1	16,133.4	34,707.5	43,609.0	52,662.7	61,975.8	65,824.1	70,291.4
United Kingdom	1,114.0	5,735.8	43,452.0	59,687.9	65,471.7	69,764.9	73,224.2	75,565.4	77,308.9
Eastern Europe									
Albania		1.8	29.8	1,259.6	1,530.2	1,900.0	2,300.0	3,141.2	3,372.3
Belarus		5.9	49.4	2,239.3	4,099.5	5,960.0	6,960.0	7,517.7	7,841.0
Bosnia-Herzegovina			93.4	1,407.4	1,594.4	1,887.8	2,450.4	3,179.0	3,595.3
Bulgaria		20.9	738.0	4,729.7	6,244.9	8,253.4	9,897.5	10,633.3	10,982.4
Croatia	0.2	33.7	1,033.0	2,835.5	3,649.7	4,395.2	5,034.6	5,924.0	6,157.9
Czech Republic		48.9	4,346.0	10,782.6	11,775.9	12,406.2	13,228.6	13,780.2	14,136.1
Estonia		30.5	557.0	1,255.7	1,445.3	1,658.7	1,981.8	2,524.5	2,749.9
Georgia		0.2	194.7	840.6	1,174.3	1,703.9	2,599.7	3,239.5	3,721.0
Hungary	2.6	265.0	3,076.3	8,727.2	9,320.0	9,965.7	11,029.9	12,224.2	12,791.7
Latvia		15.0	401.3	1,536.7	1,871.6	2,183.7	2,217.0	2,325.6	2,394.3
Lithuania		14.8	524.0	3,051.2	4,353.4	4,718.2	4,921.1	5,022.6	5,077.1
Macedonia			401.9	1,106.5	1,207.7	1,293.1	1,380.1	1,605.5	1,727.5
Moldova		0.0	139.0	787.0	1,089.8	1,358.2	1,882.8	2,420.0	2,937.8
Montenegro									
Poland		75.0	6,747.0	23,096.1	29,166.4	36,745.5	41,388.8	45,634.3	48,682.4
Romania		9.1	2,499.0	10,215.4	13,354.1	15,991.0	20,417.0	24,467.0	27,056.4
Russia		88.5	3,263.2	73,722.2	120,000.0	150,674.0	163,300.0	187,500.0	203,513.3
Serbia									
Slovakia		12.3	1,243.7	4,275.2	4,540.4	4,893.2	6,068.1	5,520.0	5,892.7
Slovenia		27.3	1,215.6	1,848.6	1,759.2	1,819.6	1,928.4	2,054.9	2,129.8
Ukraine		14.0	818.5	13,735.0	30,013.5	48,987.3	55,240.4	55,694.5	56,140.0

Source: International Telecommunications Union/World Bank/Trade Sources/Euromonitor International

IT and Telecommunications Statistics

Table 18.7

Mobile Telecommunications Revenues 1990-2009

% of telecom revenue

	1990	1995	2000	2004	2005	2006	2007	2008	2009
Western Europe									
Austria			47	64	59	59	60	59	60
Belgium	2	10	48	44	45	43	42	40	39
Cyprus			32	49	47	45	51	53	54
Denmark		14	24	34	36	39	39	41	41
Finland	9	20	36	50	50	50	51	53	53
France	3	7	26	38	40	41	42	43	44
Germany		10	32	34	34	35	32	32	33
Gibraltar									
Greece		11	34	52	51	54	54	56	57
Iceland		10	27	42	43	47	49	51	52
Ireland			42	46	46	45	45	45	46
Italy			38	44	38	36	36	36	36
Liechtenstein									
Luxembourg	1	5	18	47	51	52	51	51	52
Malta		5	44	42	44	47	47	48	48
Monaco									
Netherlands	3	10	26	41	43	44	47	49	51
Norway		15	35	41	44	46	48	50	51
Portugal		14	42	36	36	37	40	42	44
Spain	1	5	41	28	30	32	34	36	37
Sweden	14	25	21	22	22	21	22	22	23
Switzerland		6	23	30	30	29	30	30	30
Turkey	2	7	43	44	53	56	61	63	66
United Kingdom		13	18	28	28	29	31	32	33
Eastern Europe									
Albania			28	77	74	77	82	85	88
Belarus			0	0	0	0	0	0	0
Bosnia-Herzegovina			22	40	45	42	43	45	46
Bulgaria				49	55	59	61	65	68
Croatia		4	28	53	53	56	56	57	58
Czech Republic		7	45	67	67	73	58	60	60
Estonia		29	47	48	61	62	60	61	61
Georgia			51	60	59	65	64	66	67
Hungary		33	30	34	34	37	40	42	44
Latvia		6	53	60	62	64	66	68	69
Lithuania		0		51	47	46	47	46	46
Macedonia			32	35	34	54	56	58	60
Moldova				37	37	42	44	47	49
Montenegro				58	61	65	70	73	77
Poland		8	24	44	46	48	50	52	54
Romania				46	50	56	58	60	62
Russia			26	44	45	47	49	51	52
Serbia				23	42	47	57	66	73
Slovakia		12	35	59	60	65	65	66	66
Slovenia			63	49	48	48	43	40	37
Ukraine			20	47	56	64	68	72	76

Source: Euromonitor International from International Telecommunications Union

Table 18.8

Mobile Telephone Calls 1990-2009
Million minutes

	1990	1995	2000	2004	2005	2006	2007	2008	2009
Western Europe									
Austria			6,000	9,261	9,367	9,475	9,585	9,692	9,796
Belgium									
Cyprus									
Denmark		564	2,695	3,996	4,192	4,345	4,463	4,551	4,611
Finland		316	5,294	7,945	8,162	8,327	8,455	8,559	8,647
France			35,524	56,283	57,191	57,913	58,560	59,175	59,773
Germany			24,347	34,678	35,269	35,643	35,921	36,157	36,371
Gibraltar			5	8	9	9	10	11	11
Greece			5,700	9,327	9,476	9,571	9,644	9,708	9,767
Iceland			194	248	252	255	259	262	264
Ireland									
Italy			58,000	76,661	77,279	77,821	78,320	78,793	79,239
Liechtenstein									
Luxembourg			170	275	279	284	288	292	296
Malta			33	68	69	70	71	72	72
Monaco									
Netherlands			6,200	9,438	9,606	9,731	9,838	9,936	10,030
Norway			2,994	4,773	4,957	5,105	5,220	5,309	5,373
Portugal		436	6,187	10,155	10,317	10,439	10,540	10,630	10,714
Spain			17,026	40,388	52,193	62,682	73,903	78,302	82,997
Sweden			4,742	6,771	7,026	7,222	7,367	7,468	7,525
Switzerland			4,148	5,364	5,450	5,511	5,562	5,606	5,649
Turkey				9,606	10,231	10,682	11,046	11,369	11,674
United Kingdom		5,059	38,206	58,791	59,616	60,261	60,835	61,384	61,927
Eastern Europe									
Albania									
Belarus		6		1,713	2,403	2,735	2,860	2,912	2,931
Bosnia-Herzegovina									
Bulgaria									
Croatia				1,867	1,973	2,027	2,058	2,076	2,090
Czech Republic				2,344	2,389	2,412	2,428	2,440	2,451
Estonia									
Georgia									
Hungary									
Latvia									
Lithuania			284	1,227	1,288	1,319	1,337	1,347	1,352
Macedonia									
Moldova									
Montenegro				347	349	489	728	1,028	1,180
Poland									
Romania				2,522	2,856	3,073	3,205	3,285	3,332
Russia									
Serbia									
Slovakia			1,133	3,802	3,957	4,050	4,115	4,166	4,211
Slovenia				1,894	1,913	1,929	1,944	1,957	1,969
Ukraine									

Source: Euromonitor International from International Telecommunications Union

IT and Telecommunications Statistics

Table 18.9

Mobile Telephone Calls per Mobile Telephone Subscriber 1990-2009
Minutes

	1990	1995	2000	2004	2005	2006	2007	2008	2009
Western Europe									
Austria			980.9	1,158.8	1,081.1	1,020.9	967.0	896.1	872.6
Belgium									
Cyprus									
Denmark		685.9	801.2	773.4	769.3	745.6	707.3	694.8	684.3
Finland		304.1	1,419.8	1,592.8	1,548.8	1,468.6	1,390.6	1,253.1	1,211.7
France			1,222.8	1,263.5	1,189.3	1,121.0	1,057.8	1,020.7	994.4
Germany			505.1	486.2	444.9	416.1	369.7	337.1	332.0
Gibraltar			898.9	435.6	419.7	417.2	420.5	428.5	439.2
Greece			960.8	1,000.3	923.5	871.7	784.4	703.5	667.9
Iceland			902.2	855.0	890.5	845.7	789.2	755.5	719.4
Ireland									
Italy			1,372.9	1,221.7	1,080.8	967.7	872.1	889.5	865.7
Liechtenstein									
Luxembourg			560.6	585.9	547.9	397.7	420.3	412.8	407.5
Malta			288.4	222.4	213.2	201.7	190.5	185.6	182.4
Monaco									
Netherlands			576.5	637.7	606.6	562.6	510.1	498.6	488.6
Norway			928.7	1,054.8	1,042.5	1,019.3	1,005.6	991.7	977.7
Portugal		1,279.2	928.3	960.6	901.3	853.8	783.6	713.0	680.4
Spain			701.7	1,045.7	1,222.5	1,358.2	1,526.2	1,576.1	1,630.5
Sweden			744.2	770.8	771.7	751.7	710.4	688.0	673.5
Switzerland			894.3	854.9	797.4	741.2	677.5	638.5	609.8
Turkey				276.8	234.6	202.8	178.2	172.7	166.1
United Kingdom		882.0	879.3	985.0	910.6	863.8	830.8	812.3	801.0
Eastern Europe									
Albania									
Belarus		1,017.5		765.0	586.2	458.8	411.0	387.3	373.8
Bosnia-Herzegovina									
Bulgaria									
Croatia				658.3	540.5	461.3	408.7	350.5	339.5
Czech Republic				217.4	202.8	194.4	183.5	177.1	173.4
Estonia									
Georgia									
Hungary									
Latvia									
Lithuania			542.2	402.1	295.9	279.7	271.6	268.2	266.3
Macedonia									
Moldova									
Montenegro									
Poland									
Romania				246.9	213.8	192.1	157.0	134.3	123.2
Russia									
Serbia									
Slovakia			910.9	889.4	871.6	827.8	678.1	754.7	714.5
Slovenia				1,024.5	1,087.5	1,060.1	1,008.2	952.4	924.7
Ukraine									

Source: *Euromonitor International from national statistics*

IT and Telecommunications Statistics

Table 18.10

Telephone Lines in Use 1990-2009

'000

	1990	1995	2000	2004	2005	2006	2007	2008	2009
Western Europe									
Austria	3,223	3,797	3,997	3,821	3,739	3,605	3,407	3,342	3,215
Belgium	3,913	4,682	5,036	4,801	4,795	4,728	4,668	4,457	4,322
Cyprus	246	347	440	418	420	408	384	413	416
Denmark	2,911	3,193	3,835	3,491	3,348	3,099	2,825	2,487	2,340
Finland	2,670	2,810	2,849	2,368	2,120	1,910	1,740	1,650	1,550
France	28,085	32,400	33,987	33,703	33,707	34,125	34,800	35,000	35,808
Germany	31,887	42,000	50,220	54,526	54,791	54,500	53,400	51,500	49,815
Gibraltar	11	17	24	25	25	24	24	24	24
Greece	3,949	5,163	5,659	6,352	6,312	6,170	6,010	5,975	5,851
Iceland	130	149	196	190	194	189	187	185	183
Ireland	983	1,310	1,832	2,015	2,052	2,196	2,237	2,202	2,194
Italy	22,350	24,845	27,153	25,957	25,049	26,890	25,087	20,031	18,746
Liechtenstein	17	20	20	20	20	20	20	20	20
Luxembourg	184	229	249	245	245	248	248	261	266
Malta	128	171	204	206	202	208	230	241	246
Monaco	24	31	30	31	31	31	31	32	32
Netherlands	6,940	8,124	9,889	7,861	7,600	7,450	7,404	7,324	7,231
Norway	2,132	2,444	2,401	2,180	2,109	2,055	1,990	1,929	1,865
Portugal	2,379	3,643	4,321	4,238	4,234	4,236	4,195	4,121	4,048
Spain	12,603	15,095	17,104	17,934	19,461	19,865	20,192	20,200	20,302
Sweden	5,849	6,013	5,751	5,688	5,635	5,551	5,506	5,281	5,140
Switzerland	3,943	4,480	5,236	5,254	5,150	5,022	4,927	4,820	4,711
Turkey	6,861	13,127	18,395	19,125	18,978	18,832	18,201	17,502	16,822
United Kingdom	25,368	29,411	35,228	34,576	34,068	33,849	33,815	33,209	32,862
Eastern Europe									
Albania	40	42	153	275	279	283	300	316	323
Belarus	1,574	1,968	2,752	3,176	3,284	3,368	3,672	3,750	3,920
Bosnia-Herzegovina		238	780	952	969	989	1,064	1,031	1,052
Bulgaria	2,175	2,563	2,882	2,727	2,490	2,399	2,300	2,258	2,236
Croatia	823	1,287	1,721	1,888	1,883	1,831	1,847	1,851	1,857
Czech Republic	1,624	2,444	3,872	3,428	3,217	2,888	2,403	2,278	2,130
Estonia	320	412	523	444	442	452	495	498	511
Georgia	540	554	509	683	570	553	556	568	573
Hungary	996	2,157	3,798	3,564	3,416	3,360	3,251	3,094	2,954
Latvia	620	705	735	650	731	657	644	631	618
Lithuania	781	941	1,188	820	801	792	799	785	780
Macedonia	286	351	507	537	534	491	464	457	459
Moldova	462	566	584	863	929	1,018	1,080	1,151	1,205
Montenegro				290	349	353	383	400	422
Poland	3,293	5,728	10,946	12,554	11,836	11,476	10,336	10,249	10,103
Romania	2,366	2,968	3,899	4,388	4,383	4,198	4,257	5,036	5,217
Russia	20,700	25,019	32,070	38,500	40,100	43,900	44,200	45,516	45,871
Serbia				2,685	2,527	2,719	2,993	3,085	3,259
Slovakia	711	1,118	1,698	1,250	1,197	1,167	1,151	1,098	1,063
Slovenia	422	615	785	811	816	837	857	1,010	1,075
Ukraine	7,028	8,311	10,417	12,142	11,667	12,341	12,858	13,177	13,584

Source: *Euromonitor International from International Telecommunications Union/national statistics*

IT and Telecommunications Statistics

Table 18.11

National Telephone Calls 1990-2009

Million minutes

	1990	1995	2000	2004	2005	2006	2007	2008	2009
Western Europe									
Austria		13,760	9,758	11,800	7,315	6,732	5,732	5,853	5,536
Belgium			22,067	15,901	14,421	13,451	12,795	12,334	11,750
Cyprus	1,393	1,783	1,658	1,606	1,844	2,083	2,905	3,318	3,492
Denmark	10,920	12,657	22,438	32,322	26,466	27,374	28,197	29,020	29,871
Finland		13,982	17,983	11,443	7,789	5,344	4,025	3,068	2,290
France	104,664	104,400	104,838	86,879	86,155	85,432	84,683	82,624	81,447
Germany		167,762	187,121	183,000	173,000	163,000	155,000	124,104	109,833
Gibraltar	91	144	151	178	186	183	195	201	209
Greece				18,804	18,408	17,649	16,892	14,685	13,552
Iceland			1,923	1,398	965	850	712	635	568
Ireland		6,779	9,480	5,798	5,995	5,613	5,240	5,518	5,967
Italy		99,464	130,730	95,850	96,367	54,400	48,474	42,972	37,622
Liechtenstein		57	71	58	56	51	48	45	42
Luxembourg				988	854	765	727	681	653
Malta	374	812	998	657	571	524	487	460	474
Monaco	1,045	1,256	1,214	1,243	1,251	1,259	1,267	1,276	1,281
Netherlands			34,400	30,143	29,752	29,099	29,015	28,468	28,101
Norway		11,625	15,135	11,086	9,637	8,112	6,939	6,242	5,929
Portugal			15,801	19,950	21,572	21,538	22,351	23,458	23,993
Spain	46,025	45,587	51,345	53,787	52,790	50,433	51,276	49,334	47,521
Sweden	39,726	50,386	85,657	70,739	67,496	62,384	52,596	47,907	45,406
Switzerland	14,076	14,831	17,213	13,968	13,266	12,799	12,226	11,324	10,732
Turkey		37,384	26,859	54,884	52,897	39,880	27,860	20,451	14,807
United Kingdom		116,632	134,438	116,422	110,359	105,560	96,721	91,875	86,835
Eastern Europe									
Albania		123	235	436	567	636	580	588	579
Belarus	1,064	1,287	2,046	5,837	6,129	6,435	6,757	6,919	7,139
Bosnia-Herzegovina									
Bulgaria			12,798	5,204	2,599	3,135	2,991	2,158	1,789
Croatia				4,854	4,670	3,982	3,514	3,292	3,254
Czech Republic			10,629	4,591	3,762	3,156	1,855	1,303	828
Estonia		114	2,304	1,001	972	1,163	974	878	818
Georgia			2,440	2,829	2,891	2,989	3,523	3,626	3,742
Hungary		6,450	11,650	7,158	7,342	7,127	6,253	5,847	5,298
Latvia			1,719	1,355	1,205	1,121	1,060	1,008	970
Lithuania			4,138	1,557	1,574	1,547	1,478	1,555	1,584
Macedonia		2,274	2,277	1,140	744	1,390	1,287	1,164	1,062
Moldova		229	2,050	2,816	3,261	3,534	3,617	3,854	4,104
Montenegro									
Poland		23,110	36,352	25,474	26,162	22,273	19,141	16,887	15,317
Romania		7,173	5,460	7,736	7,162	7,069	6,626	7,348	7,503
Russia									
Serbia					11,071	10,872	10,673	13,464	14,262
Slovakia		2,295	3,193	1,588	1,543	1,464	1,469	1,588	1,726
Slovenia	3,155	3,392	3,690	4,422	4,495	4,563	4,655	4,793	4,905
Ukraine		20,670	25,908	33,095	35,645	36,702	38,172	39,923	41,059

Source: Euromonitor International from International Telecommunications Union/national statistics

Table 18.12

International Outgoing Telephone Calls 1990-2009

Million minutes

	1990	1995	2000	2004	2005	2006	2007	2008	2009
Western Europe									
Austria	559	901	1,087	1,181	1,233	1,236	1,192	1,072	1,030
Belgium	731	1,106	1,543	1,728	1,776	1,599	1,531	1,453	1,415
Cyprus	57	117	193	406	467	253	291	326	362
Denmark	368	529	707	663	637	596	577	559	540
Finland	186	314	468	215	187	155	126	99	78
France	2,126	2,850	4,952	4,281	4,116	4,823	6,481	7,200	7,749
Germany	3,146	5,238	9,223	10,000	11,000	12,000	14,000	15,490	16,895
Gibraltar		12	18	18	19	20	20	21	21
Greece	213	463	793	883	968	1,018	1,033	1,063	1,082
Iceland	19	29	60	33	32	40	43	47	51
Ireland	261	407	1,250	1,176	1,143	1,278	1,285	1,351	1,375
Italy	1,043	1,839	4,138	3,633	3,596	3,739	3,812	3,766	3,741
Liechtenstein	11	16	55	38	35	33	31	28	26
Luxembourg	151	232	326	435	427	423	419	433	436
Malta	13	29	43	33	43	48	44	44	44
Monaco									
Netherlands	905	1,459	2,550	1,769	1,570	1,385	1,191	956	792
Norway	281	437	559	516	562	622	629	643	650
Portugal	156	300	505	508	591	550	566	571	581
Spain	611	1,063	2,956	3,688	4,705	5,441	5,993	6,544	6,954
Sweden	631	875	1,086	1,188	1,189	1,081	1,080	1,079	1,090
Switzerland	1,332	1,733	2,624	2,685	2,348	2,256	2,409	2,519	2,690
Turkey	159	374	732	715	721	515	490	443	410
United Kingdom	2,530	4,068	7,981	6,210	5,747	5,715	6,109	6,283	6,569
Eastern Europe									
Albania	20	23	72	60	61	61	62	62	62
Belarus		132	178	299	314	330	352	364	381
Bosnia-Herzegovina		10	93	204	247	276	303	336	359
Bulgaria	62	84	110	110	116	85	126	136	145
Croatia	69	211	222	320	377	310	313	316	318
Czech Republic	83	259	360	289	274	260	243	230	216
Estonia		53	78	76	73	69	67	66	64
Georgia	5	13	60	70	63	106	195	227	252
Hungary	122	247	211	161	212	169	154	160	164
Latvia		44	58	44	40	49	48	47	45
Lithuania	2	55	39	45	54	53	51	50	48
Macedonia		45	73	21	16	28	26	25	24
Moldova		66	43	81	89	109	140	160	179
Montenegro				39	44	47	51	54	56
Poland	81	381	676	445	449	399	430	436	457
Romania	25	88	168	250	246	318	339	361	384
Russia	72	898	944	1,258	1,171	1,127	1,083	1,057	1,039
Serbia									
Slovakia	4	59	162	133	168	250	293	319	343
Slovenia		101	102	103	106	108	114	117	121
Ukraine		422	383	478	550	692	744	795	827

Source: *Euromonitor International from International Telecommunications Union/national statistics*

Labour

Labour Statistics

Table 19.1

Employed Population 1980-2009
'000

	1980	1985	1990	1995	2000	2004	2005	2006	2007	2008	2009
Western Europe											
Austria		3,228	3,421	3,732	3,777	3,744	3,824	3,928	4,028	4,062	4,048
Belgium	3,699	3,505	3,623	3,794	4,098	4,081	4,161	4,264	4,381	4,454	4,462
Cyprus	229	243	266	289	296	339	348	358	378	382	384
Denmark	2,364	2,569	2,670	2,614	2,733	2,729	2,744	2,797	2,790	2,795	2,727
Finland	2,232	2,466	2,494	2,137	2,355	2,385	2,420	2,466	2,511	2,540	2,508
France	21,599	22,039	22,504	23,124	23,862	24,906	25,077	25,060	25,513	25,760	25,274
Germany		32,687	36,070	35,782	36,324	36,077	37,454	38,248	38,329	39,034	39,093
Gibraltar	12	12	14	11	12	13	13	13	13	13	13
Greece	3,504	3,588	3,453	3,827	3,980	4,208	4,371	4,446	4,510	4,551	4,482
Iceland				142	156	157	160	170	177	179	174
Ireland			1,133	1,265	1,663	1,834	1,926	2,015	2,102	2,090	2,010
Italy	20,626	20,740	21,275	20,099	21,314	22,381	22,561	22,992	23,222	23,059	22,882
Liechtenstein			20	22	27	30	30	31	32	33	35
Luxembourg				164	181	186	193	196	204	207	209
Malta	120	113	127	133	141	146	148	150	150	154	154
Monaco											
Netherlands	5,373	5,593	6,395	6,889	7,810	7,923	7,885	8,105	8,311	8,391	8,443
Norway	1,904	2,014	2,031	2,079	2,268	2,274	2,288	2,363	2,443	2,497	2,539
Portugal	3,995	4,314	4,720	4,437	4,926	5,230	5,124	5,157	5,169	5,200	5,100
Spain	11,557	10,641	12,579	12,512	15,505	17,971	18,973	19,748	20,356	20,014	18,804
Sweden	3,933	4,298	4,575	4,111	4,242	4,233	4,348	4,429	4,539	4,609	4,551
Switzerland				3,687	3,882	3,959	3,974	4,053	4,124	4,152	4,153
Turkey			19,309	20,840	21,725	21,593	21,711	22,069	21,093	20,623	19,433
United Kingdom				26,062	27,833	27,987	28,619	28,926	29,100	29,203	28,829
Eastern Europe											
Albania				1,140	1,068	1,135	1,136	1,140	1,147	1,153	1,150
Belarus				4,393	4,443	4,344	4,359	4,374	4,482	4,601	4,578
Bosnia-Herzegovina						836	812	811	849	890	877
Bulgaria				3,216	2,919	2,922	2,980	3,110	3,239	3,316	3,306
Croatia					1,574	1,563	1,573	1,586	1,613	1,623	1,600
Czech Republic			5,225	5,001	4,723	4,706	4,766	4,828	4,922	4,992	4,873
Estonia			790	662	615	596	608	646	655	647	595
Georgia					1,749	1,783	1,745	1,747	1,704	1,602	1,573
Hungary				3,679	3,849	3,900	3,902	3,930	3,926	3,877	3,766
Latvia					969	1,018	1,036	1,088	1,120	1,109	1,005
Lithuania			1,622	1,529	1,398	1,436	1,473	1,499	1,534	1,520	1,395
Macedonia		493	518	555	553	523	545	571	590	611	635
Moldova					1,514	1,317	1,318	1,257	1,247	1,251	1,182
Montenegro				241	205	184	179	182	212	219	215
Poland				14,727	14,526	13,795	14,115	14,590	15,240	15,610	15,303
Rumania				9,902	9,938	9,275	9,133	9,306	9,356	9,364	9,269
Russia				62,870	63,125	67,222	68,145	68,807	70,574	70,167	68,989
Serbia				2,954	3,015	2,881	2,719	2,624	2,656	2,754	2,609
Slovakia			2,430	2,156	2,112	2,177	2,215	2,302	2,358	2,406	2,360
Slovenia				888	899	945	948	969	996	987	968
Ukraine				24,563	20,191	20,925	21,445	21,502	21,545	21,521	20,816

Source: *International Labour Organisation/Euromonitor International*

Labour Statistics   **Table 19.2**

Employment by Activity 2009

% of total employed population

	Agriculture, Forestry & Fishing	Community, Social & Personal Services	Construction	Electricity, Gas & Water	Finance, Insurance, Real Estate & Business	Manufact-uring
Western Europe						
Austria	5.6	27.1	8.1	0.6	13.5	16.6
Belgium	2.0	35.1	7.4	0.9	13.4	15.9
Cyprus	3.7	28.0	10.9	0.9	13.6	9.3
Denmark	2.8	36.8	6.8	0.6	12.7	15.4
Finland	4.4	32.2	7.1	0.6	14.7	17.6
France	3.3	34.0	7.0	0.7	13.8	15.2
Germany	2.2	30.2	6.7	0.9	13.8	22.0
Gibraltar						
Greece	11.2	25.3	9.0	0.9	9.0	12.2
Iceland	1.8	35.8	9.7	1.0	16.0	10.2
Ireland	5.2	26.7	13.7	0.7	13.8	12.4
Italy	3.8	24.7	8.4	0.5	14.0	20.8
Liechtenstein						
Luxembourg	1.5	22.6	11.3	0.4	25.2	10.4
Malta	2.1	29.5	7.7	2.3	11.1	14.5
Monaco						
Netherlands	3.0	33.4	6.0	0.5	15.2	12.2
Norway	2.6	39.1	7.6	0.7	13.6	11.2
Portugal	11.6	22.0	11.2	0.7	8.6	17.9
Spain	4.3	21.6	13.6	0.5	12.9	14.7
Sweden	2.4	37.4	6.6	0.5	17.1	14.1
Switzerland	4.0	26.8	6.8	0.6	17.8	15.8
Turkey	24.3	12.2	6.2	0.4	5.1	19.3
United Kingdom	1.4	33.6	8.3	0.8	16.6	12.7
Eastern Europe						
Albania	57.7	18.5	5.5	0.8		7.1
Belarus	15.8	23.7	4.0	2.4	2.7	22.4
Bosnia-Herzegovina						
Bulgaria	23.4	19.3	6.3	1.0	3.1	21.2
Croatia	11.2	20.4	9.3	1.9	7.8	20.2
Czech Republic	3.4	23.0	8.9	1.4	9.8	29.1
Estonia	4.5	24.8	14.3	1.1	9.2	19.7
Georgia	52.7	16.9	5.0	1.0	3.5	4.8
Hungary	4.4	26.8	7.9	1.4	10.6	22.6
Latvia	7.2	25.8	11.6	1.8	8.9	15.1
Lithuania	8.7	23.3	13.9	1.7	7.3	17.2
Macedonia	18.0	22.5	7.0	2.7	4.0	21.2
Moldova	30.4	22.4	6.9	1.9	3.8	10.9
Montenegro						
Poland	13.7	22.2	7.4	1.3	9.6	21.0
Romania	28.4	15.6	8.1	1.8	4.3	21.0
Russia	8.3	28.0	7.9	3.0	8.3	16.0
Serbia						
Slovakia	4.0	23.1	10.3	1.6	8.3	27.1
Slovenia	10.7	24.3	6.2	0.8	9.0	25.8
Ukraine	15.0	23.6	5.0		7.8	15.1

Source: International Labour Organisation/Euromonitor International

Labour Statistics

Employment by Activity 2009 *(continued)*

% of total employed population

	Mining & Quarrying	Transport, Storage & Commun- ications	Wholesale & Retail Trade, Restaurants & Hotels	Undefined Sectors	Total
Western Europe					
Austria	0.3	5.9	22.5		100.0
Belgium	0.3	7.4	15.7	1.7	100.0
Cyprus	0.2	6.2	23.0	4.3	100.0
Denmark	0.2	6.1	18.2	0.2	100.0
Finland	0.2	6.8	15.8	0.6	100.0
France	0.1	6.3	17.5	2.2	100.0
Germany	0.3	5.7	17.5	0.6	100.0
Gibraltar					
Greece	0.4	5.8	24.8	1.5	100.0
Iceland	0.1	6.1	18.8	0.5	100.0
Ireland	0.5	5.7	20.5	0.8	100.0
Italy	0.2	5.4	20.3	1.7	100.0
Liechtenstein					
Luxembourg	0.1	8.2	17.9	2.4	100.0
Malta	0.3	8.4	23.9	0.2	100.0
Monaco					
Netherlands	0.1	6.1	18.7	4.7	100.0
Norway	1.6	6.4	17.0	0.2	100.0
Portugal	0.4	4.3	20.0	3.5	100.0
Spain	0.3	5.7	22.7	3.8	100.0
Sweden	0.2	6.1	15.5	0.1	100.0
Switzerland	0.1	6.2	20.6	1.4	100.0
Turkey	0.6	5.3	22.1	4.4	100.0
United Kingdom	0.5	6.7	18.4	0.9	100.0
Eastern Europe					
Albania	0.5	1.1	8.8		100.0
Belarus	1.3	6.8	17.5	3.2	100.0
Bosnia-Herzegovina					
Bulgaria	1.2	6.3	18.2		100.0
Croatia	0.7	7.5	20.7	0.3	100.0
Czech Republic	1.1	7.3	15.8	0.1	100.0
Estonia	0.8	8.7	16.9		100.0
Georgia	0.3	4.2	10.8	0.9	100.0
Hungary	0.2	7.3	18.7	0.1	100.0
Latvia	0.2	9.4	19.5	0.4	100.0
Lithuania	0.4	7.7	19.6	0.2	100.0
Macedonia	0.8	7.6	15.7	0.5	100.0
Moldova	0.3	5.9	17.0	0.4	100.0
Montenegro					
Poland	1.1	6.5	17.2	0.1	100.0
Romania	1.1	5.3	14.5		100.0
Russia	1.9	9.3	17.2	0.1	100.0
Serbia					
Slovakia	0.7	7.2	17.3	0.4	100.0
Slovenia	0.3	6.3	15.4	1.3	100.0
Ukraine	3.2	7.0	23.2		100.0

Source: *International Labour Organisation/Euromonitor International*

Labour Statistics

Table 19.3

Paid Employment in Manufacturing 1980-2009
'000

	1980	1985	1990	1995	2000	2004	2005	2006	2007	2008	2009
Western Europe											
Austria	1,259	1,153	1,098	862	726	656	668	701	689	660	657
Belgium	1,008	873	856	747	714	677	682	667	683	697	691
Cyprus	30	34	37	34	27	29	31	30	30	30	30
Denmark	374	398	401	496	488	419	424	411	417	418	414
Finland	567	528	495	403	437	411	414	417	421	425	423
France	5,182	4,584	4,410	3,909	3,900	3,618	3,524	3,495	3,459	3,478	3,438
Germany	8,717	8,064	8,876	8,499	8,141	7,723	7,613	7,741	7,995	8,168	8,096
Gibraltar	3	3	1	1	1	1	0	1	1	1	1
Greece	496	462	457	398	409	419	413	409	408	411	419
Iceland	25	27	23	21	21	20	19	18	17	17	17
Ireland	243	201	210	229	270	258	252	247	247	245	241
Italy	4,745	4,101	4,081	4,027	4,060	4,067	4,086	4,075	4,114	4,084	3,997
Liechtenstein											
Luxembourg	38	35	34	32	33	32	32	33	35	35	35
Malta	40	34	36	31	31	27	26	25	24	24	23
Monaco											
Netherlands	1,121	1,042	1,143	1,029	1,043	970	968	955	972	984	983
Norway	371	337	301	300	284	255	256	262	268	274	272
Portugal	921	926	1,037	858	961	872	853	867	842	846	837
Spain	2,723	2,199	2,557	2,045	2,578	2,709	2,720	2,716	2,712	2,666	2,547
Sweden	1,002	935	903	716	721	641	616	614	618	628	617
Switzerland	692	665	728	738	698	654	656	668	680	690	684
Turkey	1,986	2,129	2,582	2,525	2,845	3,121	3,366	3,478	3,344	3,234	3,185
United Kingdom	6,935	5,567	4,756	4,072	3,941	3,253	3,131	3,160	3,178	3,190	3,135
Eastern Europe											
Albania					32	38	38	39	40	41	43
Belarus		1,430	1,437	1,216	1,208	1,121	1,111	1,101	1,095	1,088	1,072
Bosnia-Herzegovina						89	83	82	82	80	80
Bulgaria	1,308	1,512	1,588	787	562	607	607	627	628	631	625
Croatia		537	546	338	278	277	274	280	289	291	287
Czech Republic	1,540	1,646	1,543	1,332	1,192	1,175	1,197	1,254	1,295	1,313	1,291
Estonia		215	206	158	133	134	133	131	129	127	123
Georgia					86	65	65	65	63	63	62
Hungary	1,386	1,278	1,118	652	753	715	689	753	750	696	684
Latvia			236	165	149	163	158	160	160	151	139
Lithuania			670	652	318	243	246	255	255	255	249	238
Macedonia			178	187	120	99	84	82	78	75	73	72
Moldova			387	365	156	98	108	106	104	97	93	92
Montenegro											
Poland	4,126	3,702	3,014	2,616	2,467	2,244	2,259	2,311	2,413	2,471	2,397
Romania	3,031	3,266	3,452	2,192	1,560	1,492	1,425	1,409	1,415	1,411	1,361
Russia	23,812	23,490	18,884	13,181	12,335	12,448	12,278	12,233	12,089	11,358	10,924
Serbia											
Slovakia				556	516	547	557	574	597	610	594
Slovenia		383	373	297	253	254	261	248	251	253	249
Ukraine			5,975	4,159	2,916	2,351	2,371	2,329	2,268	2,192	2,122

Source: International Labour Organisation/Euromonitor International

Labour Statistics

Table 19.4

Unemployed Population 1980-2009

'000

	1980	1985	1990	1995	2000	2004	2005	2006	2007	2008	2009
Western Europe											
Austria		121	115	144	139	194	208	196	186	161	203
Belgium	453	455	285	390	303	374	383	383	354	334	383
Cyprus	6	11	7	11	15	17	20	17	15	15	21
Denmark	245	184	242	196	130	163	143	118	113	97	174
Finland	106	130	82	383	254	229	220	204	184	173	225
France	1,381	1,996	2,049	2,899	2,365	2,541	2,559	2,547	2,330	2,177	2,648
Germany		2,602	2,005	3,179	3,123	3,647	3,772	3,380	3,483	3,070	3,159
Gibraltar	0	1	0	2	0	0	1	1	1	1	1
Greece	215	304	281	424	503	493	478	434	408	378	469
Iceland				7	4	5	4	5	4	6	14
Ireland			172	178	72	86	89	93	100	141	270
Italy	1,645	2,388	2,618	2,633	2,408	1,959	1,890	1,670	1,506	1,669	1,936
Liechtenstein			0	0	0	1	1	1	1	1	1
Luxembourg				5	4	10	9	10	9	11	13
Malta	4	10	5	5	10	11	12	12	10	10	12
Monaco											
Netherlands	382	621	518	524	250	417	424	355	301	260	299
Norway	33	53	111	107	81	107	111	83	63	65	82
Portugal	324	382	229	343	200	376	421	430	449	428	537
Spain	1,488	2,939	2,441	3,716	2,497	2,214	1,912	1,837	1,834	2,558	4,135
Sweden	80	124	74	343	252	353	365	336	297	306	412
Switzerland				129	106	178	185	166	153	146	178
Turkey			1,566	1,689	1,510	2,477	2,493	2,426	2,423	2,549	3,137
United Kingdom				2,351	1,579	1,383	1,443	1,649	1,621	1,749	2,360
Eastern Europe											
Albania				169	216	191	186	183	174	168	172
Belarus				131	94	84	68	52	44	37	42
Bosnia-Herzegovina						339	363	366	347	272	279
Bulgaria				565	574	400	334	306	239	197	243
Croatia					297	250	229	199	172	149	160
Czech Republic			227	207	457	427	409	372	276	230	348
Estonia			5	68	90	64	52	41	32	38	95
Georgia					212	258	279	275	261	316	319
Hungary				417	263	253	304	317	312	328	419
Latvia					163	119	99	80	71	90	208
Lithuania			273	266	274	184	133	89	69	94	222
Macedonia		136	159	229	260	310	324	321	317	311	301
Moldova					141	116	104	100	67	52	81
Montenegro				82	65	76	77	77	51	44	51
Poland				2,277	2,785	3,230	3,047	2,350	1,620	1,195	1,367
Romania				859	759	807	709	733	640	577	639
Russia				6,600	6,858	5,687	5,287	5,339	4,585	4,718	6,306
Serbia				530	583	655	714	692	585	433	501
Slovakia			202	325	483	481	428	353	291	256	305
Slovenia				71	70	61	58	61	48	43	59
Ukraine				1,457	2,650	1,969	1,664	1,569	1,473	1,471	2,109

Source: *International Labour Organisation/Euromonitor International*

Table 19.5

Unemployment Rate 1980-2009
% of economically active population

	1980	1985	1990	1995	2000	2004	2005	2006	2007	2008	2009
Western Europe											
Austria		3.6	3.2	3.7	3.5	4.9	5.2	4.7	4.4	3.8	4.8
Belgium	10.9	11.5	7.3	9.3	6.9	8.4	8.4	8.3	7.5	7.0	7.9
Cyprus	2.5	4.4	2.6	3.7	4.9	4.7	5.3	4.5	3.9	3.7	5.3
Denmark	9.4	6.7	8.3	7.0	4.5	5.6	5.0	4.0	3.9	3.4	6.0
Finland	4.6	5.0	3.2	15.2	9.7	8.8	8.3	7.6	6.8	6.4	8.2
France	6.0	8.3	8.3	11.1	9.0	9.3	9.3	9.2	8.4	7.8	9.5
Germany		7.4	5.3	8.2	7.9	9.2	9.2	8.1	8.3	7.3	7.5
Gibraltar	1.7	3.7	2.7	16.6	3.2	3.4	3.7	3.8	3.9	4.0	4.0
Greece	5.8	7.8	7.5	10.0	11.2	10.5	9.9	8.9	8.3	7.7	9.5
Iceland				4.9	2.3	3.1	2.6	2.9	2.3	3.0	7.2
Ireland			13.2	12.3	4.2	4.5	4.4	4.4	4.6	6.3	11.8
Italy	7.4	10.3	11.0	11.6	10.1	8.0	7.7	6.8	6.1	6.7	7.8
Liechtenstein			0.1	0.9	1.3	2.4	2.7	2.5	2.0	1.9	1.7
Luxembourg				2.9	2.2	5.0	4.6	4.6	4.2	4.9	5.7
Malta	3.3	8.1	3.9	3.7	6.7	7.2	7.3	7.3	6.5	6.1	7.0
Monaco											
Netherlands	6.6	10.0	7.5	7.1	3.1	5.0	5.1	4.2	3.5	3.0	3.4
Norway	1.7	2.6	5.2	4.9	3.4	4.5	4.6	3.4	2.5	2.6	3.1
Portugal	7.5	8.1	4.6	7.2	3.9	6.7	7.6	7.7	8.0	7.6	9.5
Spain	11.4	21.6	16.3	22.9	13.9	11.0	9.2	8.5	8.3	11.3	18.0
Sweden	2.0	2.8	1.6	7.7	5.6	7.7	7.7	7.1	6.2	6.2	8.3
Switzerland				3.4	2.7	4.3	4.4	3.9	3.6	3.4	4.1
Turkey			7.5	7.5	6.5	10.3	10.3	9.9	10.3	11.0	13.9
United Kingdom				8.3	5.4	4.7	4.8	5.4	5.3	5.7	7.6
Eastern Europe											
Albania				12.9	16.8	14.4	14.1	13.8	13.2	12.7	13.0
Belarus				2.9	2.1	1.9	1.5	1.2	1.0	0.8	0.9
Bosnia-Herzegovina						28.8	30.9	31.1	29.0	23.4	24.1
Bulgaria				14.9	16.4	12.0	10.1	8.9	6.9	5.6	6.9
Croatia					15.9	13.8	12.7	11.1	9.6	8.4	9.1
Czech Republic			4.2	4.0	8.8	8.3	7.9	7.2	5.3	4.4	6.7
Estonia			0.7	9.3	12.7	9.6	7.9	5.9	4.7	5.5	13.8
Georgia					10.8	12.6	13.8	13.6	13.3	16.5	16.9
Hungary				10.2	6.4	6.1	7.2	7.5	7.4	7.8	10.0
Latvia					14.4	10.4	8.7	6.8	6.0	7.5	17.2
Lithuania			14.4	14.8	16.4	11.4	8.3	5.6	4.3	5.8	13.7
Macedonia		21.6	23.5	29.2	31.9	37.2	37.3	36.0	34.9	33.7	32.2
Moldova					8.5	8.1	7.3	7.4	5.1	4.0	6.4
Montenegro				25.3	24.0	29.1	30.3	29.6	19.3	16.8	19.1
Poland				13.4	16.1	19.0	17.8	13.9	9.6	7.1	8.2
Romania				8.0	7.1	8.0	7.2	7.3	6.4	5.8	6.5
Russia				9.5	9.8	7.8	7.2	7.2	6.1	6.3	8.4
Serbia				15.2	16.2	18.5	20.8	20.9	18.1	13.6	16.1
Slovakia			7.7	13.1	18.6	18.1	16.2	13.3	11.0	9.6	11.4
Slovenia				7.4	7.2	6.1	5.8	5.9	4.6	4.2	5.7
Ukraine				5.6	11.6	8.6	7.2	6.8	6.4	6.4	9.2

Source: International Labour Organisation/Euromonitor International

Labour Statistics

Table 19.6

Average Working Week in Non-Agricultural Activities 1980-2009
Hours

	1980	1985	1990	1995	2000	2004	2005	2006	2007	2008	2009
Western Europe											
Austria			34.6	35.4	35.4	34.9	34.1	34.1	34.0	33.8	33.7
Belgium	33.8	33.3	33.7	36.2	33.0	32.8	32.7	32.7	32.6	32.6	32.5
Cyprus	42.0	41.0	42.0	40.0	40.0	39.8	39.9	39.9	40.0	40.0	40.1
Denmark	32.6	32.1	31.5	31.5	31.6	31.7	31.7	31.8	31.8	31.8	31.8
Finland		36.4	35.5	36.5	36.3	36.0	35.9	35.8	36.0	36.2	36.3
France	40.8	38.9	39.0	35.4	35.6	34.5	34.7	34.6	34.9	35.0	35.1
Germany	41.6	40.7	39.7	38.5	38.2	38.0	37.9	37.9	37.8	37.8	37.7
Gibraltar	43.2	44.5	45.1	43.6	43.0	41.7	41.6	41.9	41.7	41.7	41.7
Greece				41.0	41.0	41.0	41.1	40.5	40.1	39.9	39.5
Iceland	49.3	48.6	46.4	46.0	42.8	40.4	39.8	39.2	38.7	38.3	37.8
Ireland			35.4	38.6	37.1	36.3	36.2	36.0	35.9	35.6	35.4
Italy	39.0	38.7	38.8	39.4	39.1	39.1	39.3	39.2	39.2	38.9	38.8
Liechtenstein											
Luxembourg	40.2	40.6	40.3	40.8	40.7	40.6	40.6	40.5	40.5	40.5	40.4
Malta	40.0	40.0	39.3	38.8	38.0	38.4	38.3	38.1	38.7	37.9	37.9
Monaco											
Netherlands	40.6	40.3	40.1	39.3	38.4	38.4	38.4	38.4	38.4	38.4	38.5
Norway	35.5	35.5	35.3	34.9	34.7	34.3	34.6	34.3	34.1	34.2	34.1
Portugal	38.4	41.0	41.1	38.1	37.3	35.4	35.7	35.7	35.2	35.1	34.9
Spain	40.1	37.2	36.7	36.1	35.4	34.9	34.6	34.8	34.5	34.5	34.4
Sweden	35.6	36.3	37.5	36.6	36.9	35.9	36.4	36.3	35.9	35.9	35.7
Switzerland	44.3	43.4	42.2	41.9	36.4	36.1	36.0	36.1	36.3	36.4	36.5
Turkey			50.1	51.3	51.6	52.5	54.0	54.1	51.8	52.4	51.9
United Kingdom			40.5	40.3	39.8	39.6	39.5	39.5	39.4	39.4	39.4
Eastern Europe											
Albania											
Belarus				35.5	38.3	39.0	38.8	38.8	38.8	38.8	38.8
Bosnia-Herzegovina											
Bulgaria					33.3	34.0	34.0	34.0	34.0	34.0	34.0
Croatia		45.5	44.5	44.5	41.8	41.5	41.3	41.2	41.1	41.0	40.9
Czech Republic				40.4	40.5	40.5	40.5	40.5	40.5	40.5	40.5
Estonia				34.0	34.7	34.7	34.8	34.7	34.7	34.2	34.0
Georgia					38.6	39.4	39.7	39.9	40.1	40.2	40.4
Hungary				36.6	37.3	37.6	37.7	37.9	38.1	38.3	38.5
Latvia				40.8	41.3	39.4	39.8	39.5	39.0	37.2	36.6
Lithuania				37.2	38.0	38.2	37.8	37.2	37.5	37.3	37.2
Macedonia											
Moldova				28.8	29.7	32.4	32.2	31.5	32.2	32.2	32.2
Montenegro											
Poland	37.5	39.8	37.0	40.4	40.0	39.8	39.6	41.0	40.5	40.7	41.1
Romania				39.0	37.4	37.0	37.0	37.0	37.0	37.0	37.0
Russia				32.6	32.9	33.5	33.6	33.7	33.8	33.9	34.1
Serbia											
Slovakia				37.0	36.5	35.3	35.0	34.8	35.0	34.8	34.8
Slovenia		37.4	37.7	40.7	40.5	36.0	36.3	39.8	34.9	34.5	33.9
Ukraine				32.0	34.8	34.8	35.1	35.4	35.6	35.8

Source: *International Labour Organisation/Euromonitor International*
Notes: *Hours actually worked by wage earners, unless otherwise stated*

Labour Statistics

Table 19.7

Average Working Week in Manufacturing 1980-2009
Hours

	1980	1985	1990	1995	2000	2004	2005	2006	2007	2008	2009
Western Europe											
Austria	36.5	36.2	34.9	36.1	36.6	36.0	35.2	35.6	35.6	35.5	35.5
Belgium	33.4	33.1	33.4	32.9	32.9	32.9	32.9	32.8	32.8	32.8	32.8
Cyprus	41.0	41.0	41.0	40.0	40.2	40.0	39.9	40.4	40.5	40.6	40.8
Denmark	32.6	32.1	31.5	31.5	31.6	31.7	31.7	31.8	31.8	31.8	31.8
Finland	33.2	32.3	38.2	38.0	38.0	37.5	37.8	37.8	37.7	38.2	38.3
France	40.6	38.6	38.7	37.1	36.3	36.0	36.3	36.4	36.5	36.7	36.8
Germany	41.6	40.7	37.8	38.6	37.9	37.6	37.6	37.9	38.0	38.0	38.2
Gibraltar	45.8	48.7	46.9	46.8	45.1	50.0	49.1	47.7	47.2	46.6	46.1
Greece	40.7	39.3	41.1	42.0	43.0	42.3	42.3	42.1	42.0	41.9	41.8
Iceland				42.9	43.5	41.1	42.2	42.7	42.2	43.0	43.3
Ireland	41.1	41.1	38.8	40.4	39.5	39.1	39.0	38.8	39.1	38.9	38.9
Italy	38.5	39.0	39.0	40.7	40.5	39.4	39.7	39.7	39.9	39.5	39.4
Liechtenstein											
Luxembourg	40.0	40.2	39.8	40.2	40.0	39.6	39.5	39.4	39.3	39.2	39.1
Malta	40.0	40.0	39.9	39.9	41.0	39.4	40.2	39.2	40.3	39.4	39.2
Monaco											
Netherlands	40.8	40.3	39.9	39.0	38.6	38.5	38.5	38.5	38.5	38.5	38.5
Norway	38.1	38.2	37.0	36.7	36.5	36.3	36.9	36.8	36.7	36.6	36.5
Portugal	39.0	40.8	40.7	38.2	37.0	36.1	36.6	36.8	35.9	36.1	35.9
Spain	38.8	36.3	36.7	36.7	36.1	35.8	36.2	36.5	36.1	36.0	35.9
Sweden	37.7	38.4	38.5	37.6	38.2	37.5	37.9	37.7	37.6	37.5	37.4
Switzerland	43.8	43.0	41.6	41.4	41.1	39.9	40.3	40.6	40.9	41.3	41.6
Turkey			48.8	50.9	51.3	52.1	53.7	54.0	51.8	52.8	52.5
United Kingdom		41.8	42.4	42.2	41.4	40.9	40.8	40.7	40.6	40.5	40.4
Eastern Europe											
Albania											
Belarus											
Bosnia-Herzegovina											
Bulgaria					32.9	34.0	34.0	34.0	34.0	34.0	34.0
Croatia		46.2	45.1	44.3	41.5	41.4	41.0	40.9	40.8	40.6	40.4
Czech Republic	43.5	43.1	40.1	40.4	40.7	40.6	40.5	40.5	40.4	40.3	40.3
Estonia				33.3	34.2	34.3	34.2	34.2	34.0	33.6	33.4
Georgia					38.0	40.7	41.4	42.1	42.6	43.1	43.7
Hungary	40.2	36.3	35.9	36.8	37.4	37.6	37.7	38.0	38.3	38.4	38.6
Latvia				38.8	40.8	40.4	40.8	40.4	38.8	37.1	36.2
Lithuania					38.6	39.0	38.5	37.8	37.9	37.7	37.6
Macedonia											
Moldova		34.9	34.5	22.3	24.4	30.3	30.4	29.5	31.3	31.4	31.7
Montenegro											
Poland	39.8	38.3	35.8	41.7	41.3	41.2	41.2	42.0	41.4	41.5	41.6
Romania		39.5	39.0	38.2	39.5	40.8	40.6	41.0	41.0	41.1	41.2
Russia				28.9	29.1	28.6	28.5	28.4	28.3	28.2	28.1
Serbia											
Slovakia				35.3	35.5	35.5	35.5	35.8	36.4	36.6	37.0
Slovenia		37.1	37.5	40.7	40.3	36.1	37.1	39.9	35.1	34.8	34.0
Ukraine					29.5	35.5	35.5	36.3	37.1	37.6	38.4

Source: *International Labour Organisation/Euromonitor International*
Notes: *Hours actually worked by wage earners, unless otherwise stated*

Labour Statistics **Table 19.8**

Economically Active Population by Age Group 2009
'000

	Under 15	15-19	20-24	25-29	30-34	35-39	40-44
Western Europe							
Austria		215.4	385.6	453.4	493.7	594.1	649.5
Belgium		67.5	400.2	579.8	597.8	652.5	720.0
Cyprus		11.7	33.8	58.7	55.1	47.0	49.1
Denmark		214.1	236.9	277.6	337.3	359.2	370.5
Finland		122.1	246.7	285.7	287.7	288.5	341.1
France		627.0	2,263.7	3,419.2	3,502.3	3,824.7	3,937.2
Germany		1,487.8	3,447.1	4,161.9	4,134.6	4,858.2	6,414.7
Gibraltar							
Greece		55.4	313.7	670.1	709.2	709.5	705.7
Iceland		16.3	18.1	20.0	19.5	19.7	20.7
Ireland		82.6	271.7	356.4	316.9	279.5	254.3
Italy		307.4	1,535.3	2,606.6	3,568.6	3,892.7	3,856.4
Liechtenstein							
Luxembourg		2.6	13.1	27.8	32.3	34.6	35.3
Malta		9.4	23.1	22.6	25.2	17.5	17.6
Monaco							
Netherlands		666.5	818.2	876.1	880.3	1,080.6	1,132.4
Norway		144.8	225.4	265.1	301.4	335.5	323.6
Portugal		97.4	424.8	691.2	781.1	718.5	713.9
Spain		556.8	1,797.4	2,980.5	3,575.2	3,364.5	3,115.4
Sweden		199.9	418.6	488.6	556.3	597.4	615.0
Switzerland		240.1	371.2	427.6	445.5	501.7	569.0
Turkey	509.9	1,520.8	2,556.6	3,576.8	3,632.4	3,145.6	2,566.7
United Kingdom		1,617.3	3,187.9	3,494.5	3,181.9	3,677.8	3,828.9
Eastern Europe							
Albania							
Belarus		53.3	513.0	634.3	592.5	573.2	561.7
Bosnia-Herzegovina		31.5	123.1	141.4	150.8	154.7	155.2
Bulgaria		35.9	267.8	332.8	453.1	504.9	491.9
Croatia		32.2	138.9	198.5	171.0	200.4	243.6
Czech Republic		43.0	381.5	631.5	755.5	685.8	654.0
Estonia		12.5	65.3	84.6	84.3	82.7	85.4
Georgia		41.7	160.8	182.5	187.9	181.3	179.3
Hungary		25.6	285.9	576.7	637.6	613.2	512.9
Latvia		27.0	122.8	141.8	143.8	144.5	152.6
Lithuania		14.2	155.4	193.5	186.7	211.1	215.3
Macedonia		30.8	90.8	124.4	130.2	120.4	120.9
Moldova		28.7	107.3	127.3	136.3	145.2	155.5
Montenegro		7.4	27.2	33.7	35.3	32.0	35.4
Poland		216.1	1,556.4	2,484.9	2,504.0	2,135.7	1,949.1
Romania		165.0	756.8	1,194.6	1,435.4	1,368.9	1,329.4
Russia		1,620.6	7,754.8	10,117.5	9,579.4	8,744.2	8,889.6
Serbia		52.5	198.0	285.7	394.1	405.3	379.0
Slovakia		26.6	231.4	381.3	390.5	347.6	340.9
Slovenia		17.8	76.0	130.6	143.4	138.7	145.0
Ukraine		486.5	2,359.1	2,934.1	2,744.7	2,715.3	2,630.6

Source: *International Labour Organisation/Euromonitor International*

Labour Statistics

Economically Active Population by Age Group 2009 *(continued)*
'000

	45-49	50-54	55-59	60-64	Over 65	Total
Western Europe						
Austria	577.8	450.8	286.7	85.8	58.7	4,251.4
Belgium	702.7	571.1	399.8	104.9	48.4	4,844.8
Cyprus	47.9	41.9	32.2	17.6	10.2	405.2
Denmark	339.9	308.6	299.1	127.7	29.6	2,900.7
Finland	344.6	336.2	296.3	147.9	36.2	2,733.0
France	3,771.3	3,520.8	2,361.7	552.3	142.0	27,922.0
Germany	5,904.1	5,008.6	4,449.0	1,709.8	677.2	42,253.0
Gibraltar						
Greece	622.4	512.1	367.5	193.8	92.0	4,951.3
Iceland	20.7	19.1	16.3	11.9	5.7	188.0
Ireland	233.6	197.3	151.7	89.9	45.4	2,279.3
Italy	3,375.1	2,807.2	1,798.1	686.1	384.7	24,818.3
Liechtenstein						
Luxembourg	31.7	26.0	14.5	2.8	0.4	221.1
Malta	18.5	19.5	9.0	2.8		165.2
Monaco						
Netherlands	1,103.6	951.9	740.2	367.8	124.8	8,742.4
Norway	297.1	273.6	244.0	159.7	51.4	2,621.6
Portugal	649.1	563.2	397.8	261.0	338.7	5,636.7
Spain	2,763.9	2,238.5	1,540.7	848.6	157.3	22,938.8
Sweden	552.0	528.4	519.6	394.5	92.9	4,963.0
Switzerland	547.6	465.7	393.4	254.3	114.5	4,330.8
Turkey	1,996.8	1,316.1	791.2	485.2	472.6	22,570.5
United Kingdom	3,969.2	3,538.9	2,497.5	1,560.3	635.1	31,189.3
Eastern Europe						
Albania						
Belarus	663.7	615.2	313.7	77.0	22.5	4,620.0
Bosnia-Herzegovina	152.1	108.8	76.2	34.4	27.7	1,155.9
Bulgaria	521.4	369.0	348.1	159.6	64.7	3,549.2
Croatia	262.0	245.8	167.3	58.0	42.7	1,760.4
Czech Republic	627.3	666.6	519.7	185.4	71.1	5,221.4
Estonia	71.9	82.3	58.7	38.2	24.1	689.9
Georgia	207.0	207.0	188.5	118.9	237.5	1,892.5
Hungary	506.1	574.2	348.8	73.0	30.6	4,184.7
Latvia	151.3	134.1	99.0	53.8	42.3	1,212.8
Lithuania	231.0	180.6	132.0	63.5	33.4	1,616.9
Macedonia	116.7	105.0	66.3	23.4	7.9	936.8
Moldova	205.7	146.7	138.9	37.5	34.2	1,263.1
Montenegro	33.8	35.8	17.1	5.9	2.0	265.5
Poland	2,079.1	2,092.7	1,094.1	355.8	201.5	16,669.5
Romania	998.0	1,080.7	763.5	348.1	467.9	9,908.4
Russia	10,762.4	9,254.9	5,774.2	1,579.0	1,218.2	75,294.7
Serbia	422.1	417.1	312.9	105.4	137.3	3,109.5
Slovakia	347.4	343.2	203.7	47.0	5.2	2,664.8
Slovenia	140.0	125.0	70.8	18.6	20.8	1,026.8
Ukraine	2,936.1	2,527.9	1,589.4	603.1	1,397.7	22,924.6

Source: International Labour Organisation/Euromonitor International

Labour Statistics   **Table 19.9**

Economically Active Population by Age Group 2009 (% Analysis)
% of total EAP

	Under 15	15-19	20-24	25-29	30-34	35-39	40-44
Western Europe							
Austria		5.1	9.1	10.7	11.6	14.0	15.3
Belgium		1.4	8.3	12.0	12.3	13.5	14.9
Cyprus		2.9	8.3	14.5	13.6	11.6	12.1
Denmark		7.4	8.2	9.6	11.6	12.4	12.8
Finland		4.5	9.0	10.5	10.5	10.6	12.5
France		2.2	8.1	12.2	12.5	13.7	14.1
Germany		3.5	8.2	9.8	9.8	11.5	15.2
Gibraltar							
Greece		1.1	6.3	13.5	14.3	14.3	14.3
Iceland		8.7	9.6	10.6	10.4	10.5	11.0
Ireland		3.6	11.9	15.6	13.9	12.3	11.2
Italy		1.2	6.2	10.5	14.4	15.7	15.5
Liechtenstein							
Luxembourg		1.2	5.9	12.6	14.6	15.6	16.0
Malta		5.7	14.0	13.7	15.3	10.6	10.7
Monaco							
Netherlands		7.6	9.4	10.0	10.1	12.4	13.0
Norway		5.5	8.6	10.1	11.5	12.8	12.3
Portugal		1.7	7.5	12.3	13.9	12.7	12.7
Spain		2.4	7.8	13.0	15.6	14.7	13.6
Sweden		4.0	8.4	9.8	11.2	12.0	12.4
Switzerland		5.5	8.6	9.9	10.3	11.6	13.1
Turkey	2.3	6.7	11.3	15.8	16.1	13.9	11.4
United Kingdom		5.2	10.2	11.2	10.2	11.8	12.3
Eastern Europe							
Albania							
Belarus		1.2	11.1	13.7	12.8	12.4	12.2
Bosnia-Herzegovina		2.7	10.6	12.2	13.0	13.4	13.4
Bulgaria		1.0	7.5	9.4	12.8	14.2	13.9
Croatia		1.8	7.9	11.3	9.7	11.4	13.8
Czech Republic		0.8	7.3	12.1	14.5	13.1	12.5
Estonia		1.8	9.5	12.3	12.2	12.0	12.4
Georgia		2.2	8.5	9.6	9.9	9.6	9.5
Hungary		0.6	6.8	13.8	15.2	14.7	12.3
Latvia		2.2	10.1	11.7	11.9	11.9	12.6
Lithuania		0.9	9.6	12.0	11.5	13.1	13.3
Macedonia		3.3	9.7	13.3	13.9	12.9	12.9
Moldova		2.3	8.5	10.1	10.8	11.5	12.3
Montenegro		2.8	10.3	12.7	13.3	12.1	13.3
Poland		1.3	9.3	14.9	15.0	12.8	11.7
Romania		1.7	7.6	12.1	14.5	13.8	13.4
Russia		2.2	10.3	13.4	12.7	11.6	11.8
Serbia		1.7	6.4	9.2	12.7	13.0	12.2
Slovakia		1.0	8.7	14.3	14.7	13.0	12.8
Slovenia		1.7	7.4	12.7	14.0	13.5	14.1
Ukraine		2.1	10.3	12.8	12.0	11.8	11.5

Source: *International Labour Organisation/Euromonitor International*

Labour Statistics

Economically Active Population by Age Group 2009 (% Analysis) *(continued)*
% of total EAP

	45-49	50-54	55-59	60-64	Over 65	Total
Western Europe						
Austria	13.6	10.6	6.7	2.0	1.4	100.0
Belgium	14.5	11.8	8.3	2.2	1.0	100.0
Cyprus	11.8	10.3	7.9	4.3	2.5	100.0
Denmark	11.7	10.6	10.3	4.4	1.0	100.0
Finland	12.6	12.3	10.8	5.4	1.3	100.0
France	13.5	12.6	8.5	2.0	0.5	100.0
Germany	14.0	11.9	10.5	4.0	1.6	100.0
Gibraltar						
Greece	12.6	10.3	7.4	3.9	1.9	100.0
Iceland	11.0	10.2	8.7	6.3	3.0	100.0
Ireland	10.2	8.7	6.7	3.9	2.0	100.0
Italy	13.6	11.3	7.2	2.8	1.6	100.0
Liechtenstein						
Luxembourg	14.3	11.8	6.6	1.3	0.2	100.0
Malta	11.2	11.8	5.4	1.7		100.0
Monaco						
Netherlands	12.6	10.9	8.5	4.2	1.4	100.0
Norway	11.3	10.4	9.3	6.1	2.0	100.0
Portugal	11.5	10.0	7.1	4.6	6.0	100.0
Spain	12.0	9.8	6.7	3.7	0.7	100.0
Sweden	11.1	10.6	10.5	7.9	1.9	100.0
Switzerland	12.6	10.8	9.1	5.9	2.6	100.0
Turkey	8.8	5.8	3.5	2.1	2.1	100.0
United Kingdom	12.7	11.3	8.0	5.0	2.0	100.0
Eastern Europe						
Albania						
Belarus	14.4	13.3	6.8	1.7	0.5	100.0
Bosnia-Herzegovina	13.2	9.4	6.6	3.0	2.4	100.0
Bulgaria	14.7	10.4	9.8	4.5	1.8	100.0
Croatia	14.9	14.0	9.5	3.3	2.4	100.0
Czech Republic	12.0	12.8	10.0	3.6	1.4	100.0
Estonia	10.4	11.9	8.5	5.5	3.5	100.0
Georgia	10.9	10.9	10.0	6.3	12.5	100.0
Hungary	12.1	13.7	8.3	1.7	0.7	100.0
Latvia	12.5	11.1	8.2	4.4	3.5	100.0
Lithuania	14.3	11.2	8.2	3.9	2.1	100.0
Macedonia	12.5	11.2	7.1	2.5	0.8	100.0
Moldova	16.3	11.6	11.0	3.0	2.7	100.0
Montenegro	12.7	13.5	6.4	2.2	0.7	100.0
Poland	12.5	12.6	6.6	2.1	1.2	100.0
Romania	10.1	10.9	7.7	3.5	4.7	100.0
Russia	14.3	12.3	7.7	2.1	1.6	100.0
Serbia	13.6	13.4	10.1	3.4	4.4	100.0
Slovakia	13.0	12.9	7.6	1.8	0.2	100.0
Slovenia	13.6	12.2	6.9	1.8	2.0	100.0
Ukraine	12.8	11.0	6.9	2.6	6.1	100.0

Source: International Labour Organisation/Euromonitor International

Labour Statistics | **Table 19.10**

Economically Active Population by Sex 2009

As stated

	Total ('000)	EAP as % Total Population	Males ('000)	Males as % Total EAP	Females ('000)	Females as % Total EAP
Western Europe						
Austria	4,251	50.7	2,296	54.0	1,955	46.0
Belgium	4,845	45.1	2,620	54.1	2,225	45.9
Cyprus	405	46.5	223	55.0	183	45.0
Denmark	2,901	52.6	1,531	52.8	1,369	47.2
Finland	2,733	51.3	1,415	51.8	1,318	48.2
France	27,922	44.7	14,687	52.6	13,235	47.4
Germany	42,253	51.5	22,793	53.9	19,460	46.1
Gibraltar	13	45.5	8	57.9	6	42.1
Greece	4,951	44.0	2,937	59.3	2,014	40.7
Iceland	188	58.3	103	54.7	85	45.3
Ireland	2,279	51.2	1,293	56.7	986	43.3
Italy	24,818	41.3	14,824	59.7	9,994	40.3
Liechtenstein	35	98.1				
Luxembourg	221	45.5	120	54.3	101	45.7
Malta	165	40.4	107	65.0	58	35.0
Monaco						
Netherlands	8,742	53.3	4,727	54.1	4,015	45.9
Norway	2,622	54.6	1,379	52.6	1,242	47.4
Portugal	5,637	52.8	2,998	53.2	2,639	46.8
Spain	22,939	50.4	13,116	57.2	9,822	42.8
Sweden	4,963	53.9	2,607	52.5	2,356	47.5
Switzerland	4,331	57.3	2,351	54.3	1,980	45.7
Turkey	22,570	31.6	16,823	74.5	5,748	25.5
United Kingdom	31,189	50.6	17,004	54.5	14,186	45.5
Eastern Europe						
Albania	1,322	41.9	648	49.0	673	51.0
Belarus	4,620	47.8	2,183	47.3	2,437	52.7
Bosnia-Herzegovina	1,156	30.1	723	62.6	433	37.4
Bulgaria	3,549	47.2	1,890	53.3	1,659	46.7
Croatia	1,760	39.8	965	54.8	796	45.2
Czech Republic	5,221	49.9	2,968	56.8	2,254	43.2
Estonia	690	51.8	338	49.0	352	51.0
Georgia	1,893	43.2	1,018	53.8	875	46.2
Hungary	4,185	41.8	2,278	54.4	1,907	45.6
Latvia	1,213	53.8	624	51.4	589	48.6
Lithuania	1,617	48.3	819	50.6	798	49.4
Macedonia	937	45.9	567	60.5	370	39.5
Moldova	1,263	35.1	649	51.3	615	48.7
Montenegro	266	42.3	149	56.1	117	43.9
Poland	16,670	43.7	9,177	55.1	7,492	44.9
Romania	9,908	46.2	5,530	55.8	4,378	44.2
Russia	75,295	53.1	38,095	50.6	37,200	49.4
Serbia	3,109	42.2	1,759	56.6	1,351	43.4
Slovakia	2,665	49.4	1,470	55.2	1,195	44.8
Slovenia	1,027	50.8	556	54.1	471	45.9
Ukraine	22,925	49.9	11,676	50.9	11,249	49.1

Source: *International Labour Organisation/Euromonitor International*

Media and Leisure

Media and Leisure Statistics

Table 20.1

Cinemas 2009

As stated

	Seating Capacity of Fixed Cinemas ('000)	Number of Cinema Screens	Box Office Revenues (US$ million)	Annual cinema trips per capita
Western Europe				
Austria	104.4	580	144.9	1.9
Belgium	106.8	490	177.6	2.0
Cyprus		31	7.9	1.0
Denmark	58.5	398	168.2	2.4
Finland	53.8	311	73.5	1.3
France	1,066.6	5,414	1,573.3	3.0
Germany	826.1	4,803	1,098.6	1.6
Gibraltar				
Greece		542		1.1
Iceland				4.5
Ireland	76.7	431	172.3	6.5
Italy		3,381	891.7	1.9
Liechtenstein				
Luxembourg	6.1	32	14.0	2.3
Malta		37	2.9	2.4
Monaco				
Netherlands	108.7	647	226.6	1.5
Norway	78.7	423	144.4	2.5
Portugal	112.7	569	96.9	1.5
Spain	929.0	4,129	859.3	2.4
Sweden	163.2	837	163.1	1.7
Switzerland	113.2	563	190.9	1.9
Turkey	239.3	1,544	189.7	0.6
United Kingdom	760.9	3,589	1,317.3	2.7
Eastern Europe				
Albania				
Belarus				0.0
Bosnia-Herzegovina				
Bulgaria	21.3	94	12.7	0.4
Croatia	34.2	113	14.2	0.7
Czech Republic	151.8	687	62.9	1.2
Estonia		65		1.2
Georgia				
Hungary	77.0	401	49.2	1.1
Latvia	11.3	48	13.5	1.1
Lithuania	19.7	78	15.9	1.0
Macedonia	5.5	25		0.1
Moldova				
Montenegro				0.0
Poland	247.8	1,037	170.8	0.9
Romania	46.3	135	16.8	0.2
Russia		1,848	729.6	0.9
Serbia				
Slovakia	89.9	234	16.4	0.6
Slovenia	22.8	109	13.2	1.3
Ukraine		2,356		0.1

Source: *Euromonitor International from EAO/national statistics*

Media and Leisure Statistics

Table 20.2

Cinema Attendances 1990-2009

Million

	1990	1995	2000	2003	2004	2005	2006	2007	2008	2009
Western Europe										
Austria	10.2	11.5	16.3	17.7	19.4	15.7	17.3	15.7	15.6	15.6
Belgium	17.1	19.2	23.5	22.7	24.1	22.1	23.9	22.7	21.9	21.9
Cyprus			0.9	1.0	1.0	0.8	0.8	0.9	0.9	0.9
Denmark	9.6	8.8	10.7	12.3	12.8	12.2	12.6	12.1	13.1	13.0
Finland	6.2	5.3	7.1	7.7	6.9	6.1	6.7	6.5	6.9	6.8
France	121.8	130.2	165.8	173.5	195.5	175.5	188.8	177.9	189.7	188.1
Germany	91.0	123.9	152.5	149.0	156.7	127.3	136.7	125.4	129.4	129.2
Gibraltar										
Greece	13.0	8.2	13.5	15.0	12.0	12.7	12.8	13.8	11.8	11.9
Iceland		1.6	1.5	1.5	1.4	1.5	1.5	1.5	1.5	1.5
Ireland	7.5	9.8	14.9	10.0	13.0	17.0	26.0	23.0	39.0	28.8
Italy	90.7	90.7	104.2	110.5	116.3	105.6	106.1	116.4	111.6	112.3
Liechtenstein										
Luxembourg	0.6	0.7	1.4	1.3	1.4	1.2	1.3	1.2	1.1	1.1
Malta			1.0	1.1	1.0	1.0	0.9	1.0	1.0	1.0
Monaco										
Netherlands	14.6	17.2	21.5	25.0	23.0	20.6	23.4	23.1	23.5	23.8
Norway	10.8	11.0	11.6	13.0	12.0	11.3	12.0	10.8	11.9	11.9
Portugal	9.6	12.0	17.9	18.7	17.1	15.8	16.4	16.3	16.0	16.0
Spain	78.5	96.7	135.4	137.5	143.9	127.7	121.7	116.9	107.8	110.0
Sweden	15.7	15.2	17.0	18.2	16.6	14.6	15.3	14.9	15.2	15.3
Switzerland	13.6	15.0	15.6	16.5	17.2	15.0	16.4	13.8	14.3	14.4
Turkey	9.5	12.6	25.3	24.6	29.7	27.3	34.9	31.2	38.5	39.7
United Kingdom	97.4	114.9	142.5	167.3	171.3	164.7	156.6	162.4	164.2	164.3
Eastern Europe										
Albania										
Belarus										
Bosnia-Herzegovina										
Bulgaria		3.4	2.2	3.0	3.1	2.4	2.4	2.5	2.8	2.8
Croatia		3.7	2.7	2.3	3.0	2.2	2.7	2.5	3.3	3.2
Czech Republic		9.3	8.7	12.1	12.0	9.5	11.5	12.8	12.9	12.5
Estonia	1.1	1.0	1.1	1.3	1.2	1.1	1.6	1.6	1.5	1.6
Georgia										
Hungary	14.1	14.0	14.3	13.7	13.7	12.1	11.7	11.1	10.4	10.6
Latvia	0.4	1.0	1.5	1.1	1.7	1.7	2.1	2.4	2.4	2.4
Lithuania		0.7	2.1	1.4	1.5	1.2	2.5	3.3	3.4	3.5
Macedonia			0.6	0.3	0.3	0.1	0.1	0.1	0.1	0.1
Moldova										
Montenegro				0.1	0.1	0.1	0.0	0.0	0.0	0.0
Poland	16.0	22.0	18.7	23.8	33.4	23.6	32.0	32.6	33.8	34.9
Romania	32.7	17.0	5.1	4.5	4.0	2.8	2.8	2.9	3.8	3.9
Russia	10.3	13.3	42.8	68.0	67.4	83.6	91.8	106.6	123.9	128.4
Serbia										
Slovakia	8.4	5.6	2.6	3.0	2.9	2.2	3.4	2.8	3.4	3.5
Slovenia	4.0	2.9	2.2	3.0	3.0	2.4	2.7	2.7	2.6	2.7
Ukraine										

Source: *Euromonitor International from European Audiovisual Observatory/national statistics*

Media and Leisure Statistics

Table 20.3

DVD Rentals 2009

Number / as stated

	DVD rental transactions (million)	DVD rental turnover (US$ million)	New DVD rental releases	Video and DVD rental outlets
Western Europe				
Austria	5.0	19.04	415	350
Belgium	20.3	87.41	900	750
Cyprus				
Denmark	9.0	58.61	637	1,725
Finland	5.7	30.02	631	780
France	19.8	69.90	493	1,700
Germany	101.3	338.09	400	4,137
Gibraltar				
Greece	4.1	8.48	525	530
Iceland	2.0	7.49	361	190
Ireland	14.0	91.57	450	950
Italy	53.4	203.58	325	2,200
Liechtenstein				
Luxembourg				
Malta				
Monaco				
Netherlands	18.8	76.71	750	700
Norway	7.6	69.14	626	1,256
Portugal	10.3	39.46	570	600
Spain	64.0	202.74	597	1,900
Sweden	26.2	144.10	623	565
Switzerland	1.8	10.77	425	290
Turkey				
United Kingdom	72.4	327.19	454	1,850
Eastern Europe				
Albania				
Belarus				
Bosnia-Herzegovina				
Bulgaria				
Croatia	2.1	4.84	385	800
Czech Republic		15.69	370	775
Estonia				
Georgia				
Hungary	2.4	7.55	330	1,000
Latvia				
Lithuania				
Macedonia				
Moldova				
Montenegro				
Poland	1.9	3.30	486	1,100
Romania				
Russia				
Serbia				
Slovakia				
Slovenia				
Ukraine				

Source: Euromonitor International from EAO/national statistics

Table 20.4

Newspapers 2009

Number / as stated

	Total Number	Dailies	Non-Dailies	Total Circulation ('000)	Daily Circulation ('000)	Non-daily Circulation ('000)
Western Europe						
Austria	239	19	220	2,932	2,932	
Belgium	29	23	6	2,460	1,670	790
Cyprus	33	22	11	151	104	47
Denmark	306	36	270	11,714	2,933	8,781
Finland	331	53	278	3,311	2,404	907
France	140	95	45	14,646	10,299	4,347
Germany	1,793	357	1,436	112,120	19,642	92,478
Gibraltar	6	2	4	8	8	
Greece	55	44	11	1,604	1,388	216
Iceland	29	5	24	272	186	86
Ireland	158	11	147	3,061	981	2,080
Italy	510	92	418	10,238	9,730	508
Liechtenstein	2	2		20	20	
Luxembourg	23	8	15	418	251	167
Malta	11	4	7	102	102	
Monaco	2		2			
Netherlands	514	34	480	20,426	5,211	15,215
Norway	223	73	150	2,795	2,130	665
Portugal	59	24	35	6,155	1,220	4,935
Spain	349	160	189	14,580	7,960	6,620
Sweden	227	90	137	6,560	4,250	2,310
Switzerland	517	94	423	4,570	4,140	430
Turkey	5,329	80	5,249	5,701	5,701	
United Kingdom	1,236	111	1,125	43,494	17,400	26,094
Eastern Europe						
Albania	112	28	84	78	78	
Belarus	645	14	631	16,200	700	15,500
Bosnia-Herzegovina	53	7	46	75	75	
Bulgaria	451	64	387	4,307	481	3,826
Croatia	224	17	207	3,755	630	3,125
Czech Republic	577	84	493	14,640	2,011	12,629
Estonia	160	17	143	547	314	233
Georgia	83	10	73	45	45	
Hungary	241	28	213	2,727	1,590	1,137
Latvia	131	18	113	2,116	340	1,776
Lithuania	325	25	300	2,575	745	1,830
Macedonia	23	12	11	334	300	34
Moldova	237	7	230	1,503	430	1,073
Montenegro	50	4	46			
Poland	68	49	19	4,489	4,013	476
Romania		82		1,992	1,712	280
Russia	28,551	521	28,030	9,305,331		
Serbia	19	10				
Slovakia	11	10	1	504	498	6
Slovenia	259	8	251	1,484	385	1,099
Ukraine	2,369	57	2,312		4,471	

Source: *Euromonitor International from World Association of Newspapers*

Media and Leisure Statistics

Table 20.5

Colour TV Households 2004-2009
'000

	2004	2005	2006	2007	2008	2009
Western Europe						
Austria	3,377.0	3,426.6	3,466.9	3,503.1	3,536.7	3,568.6
Belgium	4,226.2	4,262.1	4,308.7	4,354.7	4,395.4	4,434.3
Cyprus						
Denmark	2,427.7	2,446.9	2,465.9	2,482.8	2,499.3	2,515.0
Finland	2,299.2	2,317.6	2,331.1	2,359.4	2,385.2	2,408.3
France	24,054.5	24,455.9	25,212.0	25,586.0	25,937.0	26,256.6
Germany	38,050.7	38,198.6	38,855.9	38,978.9	39,094.5	39,195.0
Gibraltar						
Greece	3,737.7	3,793.0	3,846.4	3,897.2	3,946.3	3,993.3
Iceland						
Ireland	1,355.1	1,405.3	1,462.9	1,516.2	1,566.4	1,612.2
Italy	21,965.2	22,290.5	22,714.6	23,032.0	23,310.7	23,561.8
Liechtenstein						
Luxembourg						
Malta						
Monaco						
Netherlands	6,928.1	6,982.5	7,049.7	7,106.2	7,160.5	7,216.6
Norway	1,959.1	1,973.3	2,014.5	2,028.9	2,069.0	2,088.4
Portugal	3,805.9	3,878.7	3,940.4	3,999.3	4,051.6	4,098.4
Spain	15,348.0	15,794.5	16,241.6	16,635.0	17,012.7	17,326.7
Sweden	4,282.6	4,311.0	4,344.6	4,387.7	4,419.1	4,449.9
Switzerland	3,101.8	3,132.0	3,158.5	3,182.4	3,203.9	3,224.3
Turkey	14,914.9	15,326.3	15,742.7	16,139.5	16,550.7	16,961.0
United Kingdom	25,731.3	25,983.4	26,223.4	26,454.5	26,695.7	26,935.9
Eastern Europe						
Albania						
Belarus	3,653.3	3,750.5	3,808.9	3,856.8	3,896.7	3,929.8
Bosnia-Herzegovina	1,089.5	1,102.1	1,103.3	1,111.8	1,122.0	1,129.5
Bulgaria	2,473.2	2,527.2	2,571.9	2,609.3	2,639.2	2,662.4
Croatia	1,397.6	1,426.2	1,424.0	1,446.7	1,467.3	1,480.8
Czech Republic	4,183.8	4,235.2	4,290.5	4,344.0	4,386.3	4,425.3
Estonia	555.2	560.2	559.4	565.3	570.2	573.0
Georgia	1,029.3	1,041.0	1,053.5	1,062.9	1,067.1	1,068.3
Hungary	3,818.1	3,872.6	3,924.9	3,975.4	4,022.8	4,065.4
Latvia	748.5	759.5	767.5	772.2	776.6	779.8
Lithuania	1,270.8	1,301.6	1,331.3	1,347.8	1,363.4	1,368.5
Macedonia	546.6	559.0	569.6	576.8	582.7	589.0
Moldova						
Montenegro	176.6	180.3	182.1	179.3	180.1	182.6
Poland	13,169.9	13,273.9	13,549.2	13,752.7	13,932.2	14,089.9
Romania	5,763.1	6,208.4	6,515.6	6,730.8	6,892.4	7,002.2
Russia	48,008.1	48,717.9	49,717.4	50,337.3	50,781.4	51,102.6
Serbia	2,397.7	2,406.3	2,438.5	2,442.8	2,449.8	2,463.7
Slovakia	1,973.6	2,060.1	2,153.8	2,192.6	2,218.5	2,240.8
Slovenia	674.7	680.2	689.2	695.7	702.8	710.6
Ukraine	16,133.5	16,878.8	17,581.5	18,199.1	18,777.5	19,005.6

Source: *Euromonitor International from Council of Europe*

Table 20.6

Cable TV Households 2004-2009
'000

	2004	2005	2006	2007	2008	2009	Cable TV households as % of colour TV households 2009
Western Europe							
Austria	1,258.2	1,277.3	1,351.3	1,306.6	1,279.2	1,259.1	35.3
Belgium	3,999.3	4,003.7	4,098.3	4,155.1	4,198.5	4,237.2	95.6
Cyprus							
Denmark	1,504.8	1,542.7	1,562.6	1,587.8	1,613.0	1,635.6	65.0
Finland	1,185.8	1,246.3	1,317.7	1,372.3	1,409.2	1,435.8	59.6
France	3,842.9	3,622.1	3,378.9	3,302.8	3,294.9	3,306.6	12.6
Germany	20,720.0	20,865.1	20,656.9	20,533.5	21,789.3	23,028.8	58.8
Gibraltar							
Greece	5.4	9.1	14.7	20.8	25.6	29.6	0.7
Iceland							
Ireland	603.5	665.3	691.7	682.9	641.0	607.7	37.7
Italy	200.1	204.2	207.1	208.3	218.5	229.0	1.0
Liechtenstein							
Luxembourg							
Malta							
Monaco							
Netherlands	6,392.1	6,329.4	6,108.6	5,956.0	5,897.8	5,882.8	81.5
Norway	871.1	895.6	923.3	938.0	963.8	979.3	46.9
Portugal	1,456.9	1,545.6	1,584.9	1,713.0	1,916.4	2,049.6	50.0
Spain	1,678.8	1,838.7	1,989.8	2,426.6	2,664.6	2,450.1	14.1
Sweden	2,494.2	2,549.4	2,589.3	2,634.2	2,669.3	2,701.3	60.7
Switzerland	2,812.1	2,903.0	2,945.4	2,975.0	3,000.2	3,023.0	93.8
Turkey	1,957.6	2,012.4	1,951.6	2,027.0	2,140.2	2,271.2	13.4
United Kingdom	3,428.1	3,450.1	3,541.5	3,618.0	3,679.6	3,727.6	13.8
Eastern Europe							
Albania							
Belarus	1,402.8	1,554.5	1,809.4	1,969.3	2,071.0	2,143.5	54.5
Bosnia-Herzegovina	102.6	111.9	118.8	127.9	136.6	144.4	12.8
Bulgaria	636.3	1,069.8	1,195.0	1,234.1	1,198.2	1,233.5	46.3
Croatia	174.4	225.9	229.6	246.6	262.9	277.6	18.7
Czech Republic	1,072.5	1,039.2	937.5	958.4	1,027.8	1,094.3	24.7
Estonia	279.9	286.3	308.0	319.8	328.5	335.3	58.5
Georgia	88.2	95.5	104.3	112.6	120.3	127.2	11.9
Hungary	2,213.1	2,283.4	2,361.1	2,427.3	2,484.3	2,536.5	62.4
Latvia	381.9	379.4	360.2	358.0	356.6	355.4	45.6
Lithuania	377.0	415.9	477.1	530.8	584.3	624.2	45.6
Macedonia	29.4	50.0	87.2	168.6	205.2	228.1	38.7
Moldova							
Montenegro	43.9	48.3	51.7	54.5	57.3	60.2	33.0
Poland	3,654.1	4,480.9	4,704.3	4,888.8	5,060.9	5,203.0	36.9
Romania	3,128.9	3,666.7	3,824.5	3,908.6	4,004.2	4,078.3	58.2
Russia	18,628.9	18,847.2	19,003.7	19,112.4	19,183.3	19,224.0	37.6
Serbia	820.3	867.2	904.0	932.6	979.0	1,015.5	41.2
Slovakia	766.3	704.0	733.7	790.0	850.6	894.6	39.9
Slovenia	385.4	381.4	378.1	389.3	444.1	477.2	67.1
Ukraine	2,507.5	2,695.1	2,893.7	3,337.6	3,633.3	3,897.1	20.5

Source: *Euromonitor International from Council of Europe*

Media and Leisure Statistics

Table 20.7

Satellite TV Households 2004-2009
'000

	2004	2005	2006	2007	2008	2009	Satellite TV households as % of colour TV households 2009
Western Europe							
Austria	1,609.2	1,696.3	1,723.6	1,730.7	1,727.7	1,734.9	48.6
Belgium	316.3	350.5	399.5	438.5	471.4	500.6	11.3
Cyprus							
Denmark	806.3	834.5	855.5	872.3	885.0	896.0	35.6
Finland	445.0	489.8	532.5	567.5	596.0	618.5	25.7
France	6,310.0	6,504.2	6,698.1	6,900.1	7,075.5	7,229.5	27.5
Germany	15,470.0	16,288.1	16,880.9	16,908.8	16,440.9	16,325.8	41.7
Gibraltar							
Greece	444.9	457.9	495.0	537.4	580.6	622.1	15.6
Iceland							
Ireland	388.1	475.0	556.0	648.3	703.9	763.9	47.4
Italy	5,589.2	6,165.9	6,587.7	6,950.8	7,286.1	7,571.5	32.1
Liechtenstein							
Luxembourg							
Malta							
Monaco							
Netherlands	790.0	882.8	953.4	1,006.6	1,052.2	1,091.3	15.1
Norway	549.4	581.2	613.4	629.6	650.3	662.3	31.7
Portugal	546.8	601.8	654.8	695.5	732.0	763.7	18.6
Spain	2,561.6	2,837.6	2,874.5	3,330.3	3,399.1	3,631.7	21.0
Sweden	1,361.8	1,451.2	1,515.9	1,571.9	1,616.5	1,657.7	37.3
Switzerland	411.5	461.5	417.1	498.4	536.5	560.0	17.4
Turkey	4,352.9	4,997.5	5,820.5	6,488.0	7,077.3	7,545.1	44.5
United Kingdom	8,126.1	8,677.5	9,260.3	9,621.5	9,986.4	10,286.3	38.2
Eastern Europe							
Albania							
Belarus	211.8	270.2	324.2	367.8	406.6	443.4	11.3
Bosnia-Herzegovina	174.4	178.8	182.3	184.9	186.8	188.1	16.7
Bulgaria	211.4	220.9	225.5	235.7	239.8	245.6	9.2
Croatia	509.5	519.8	527.9	534.4	539.4	543.5	36.7
Czech Republic	434.2	436.6	506.2	585.7	804.3	973.5	22.0
Estonia	112.4	119.4	125.2	130.0	134.0	137.7	24.0
Georgia	1.2	2.2	3.6	5.4	6.6	7.5	0.7
Hungary	846.2	856.3	866.1	875.7	884.8	893.2	22.0
Latvia	104.6	107.0	110.0	113.1	115.9	118.4	15.2
Lithuania	121.6	131.5	127.6	140.3	148.0	153.7	11.2
Macedonia	41.3	43.6	45.9	47.9	49.7	52.0	8.8
Moldova							
Montenegro	34.8	35.9	35.9	37.2	54.3	58.9	32.2
Poland	3,380.2	3,604.7	3,859.2	4,035.6	4,165.8	4,265.9	30.3
Romania	268.7	387.6	619.2	1,736.8	2,215.2	2,441.9	34.9
Russia	2,672.9	3,009.9	3,278.0	3,526.1	3,717.4	3,894.5	7.6
Serbia	260.8	294.1	157.5	147.6	170.8	179.1	7.3
Slovakia	890.9	912.1	931.9	948.9	964.2	978.8	43.7
Slovenia	114.0	115.1	116.3	117.5	118.7	119.8	16.9
Ukraine	174.9	236.1	555.0	1,186.0	1,819.8	1,951.2	10.3

Source: *Euromonitor International from Council of Europe*

Table 20.8

Number of Digital Satellite Pay TV Subscribers 2004-2009
'000

	2004	2005	2006	2007	2008	2009	Digital pay TV house-holds as % of colour TV house-holds 2009
Western Europe							
Austria	1,705.0	1,971.3	1,929.6	1,987.8	2,019.3	2,024.6	56.7
Belgium	38.0	44.0	50.0	51.7	53.2	54.2	1.2
Cyprus	58.3						
Denmark	332.0	347.5	392.6	383.4	377.7	374.4	14.9
Finland	45.0	27.8	17.7	22.2	24.7	25.0	1.0
France	4,255.0	4,520.0	4,544.0	5,225.0	5,117.2	5,050.9	19.2
Germany	1,532.0	1,594.7	1,480.5	1,485.2	1,481.5	1,494.1	3.8
Gibraltar							
Greece	185.3	221.0	209.8	204.8	202.6	204.6	5.1
Iceland							
Ireland	364.0	393.0	421.0	497.0	530.3	564.6	35.0
Italy	2,800.0	3,596.0	3,820.0	4,240.0	4,080.0	4,026.2	17.1
Liechtenstein							
Luxembourg							
Malta							
Monaco							
Netherlands	56.0	600.0	700.0	726.9	754.9	761.3	10.5
Norway	489.0	525.7	593.4	599.1	603.7	606.9	29.1
Portugal	367.0	389.0	373.0	427.0	429.5	431.2	10.5
Spain	1,822.0	1,960.0	1,990.0	2,056.0	2,082.0	2,095.6	12.1
Sweden	584.0	608.0	676.3	680.9	685.0	688.2	15.5
Switzerland							
Turkey	1,015.0						
United Kingdom	7,240.0	7,666.0	7,720.0	8,085.0	8,178.9	8,235.9	30.6
Eastern Europe							
Albania							
Belarus							
Bosnia-Herzegovina							
Bulgaria		29.0					
Croatia							
Czech Republic	81.7	112.5	134.5	128.1	122.9	121.8	2.8
Estonia							
Georgia							
Hungary	127.0	171.0	176.8	158.9	166.9	167.3	4.1
Latvia							
Lithuania							
Macedonia							
Moldova							
Montenegro							
Poland	1,265.0	1,200.0	1,500.0	1,602.9	1,745.7	1,768.4	12.6
Romania		185.0					
Russia	283.0	360.0	450.0	560.0	571.5	580.4	1.1
Serbia							
Slovakia	14.2	17.3	17.1	22.3	21.4	20.9	0.9
Slovenia							
Ukraine							

Source: *Euromonitor International from Council of Europe*

Population

Population Statistics

Table 21.1

Total Population 1980-2009: National Estimates at Mid-Year
'000 / % growth

	1980	1985	1990	1995	1996	1997	1998	1999	2000	2001
Western Europe										
Austria	7,549	7,565	7,678	7,948	7,959	7,968	7,977	7,992	8,012	8,043
Belgium	9,859	9,858	9,967	10,137	10,157	10,181	10,203	10,226	10,251	10,287
Cyprus	614	651	685	737	748	759	770	781	792	802
Denmark	5,123	5,114	5,141	5,233	5,263	5,285	5,304	5,322	5,340	5,359
Finland	4,780	4,902	4,986	5,108	5,125	5,140	5,153	5,165	5,176	5,188
France	53,880	55,284	56,709	57,844	58,026	58,207	58,398	58,673	59,049	59,454
Germany	78,289	77,685	79,433	81,678	81,915	82,035	82,047	82,100	82,212	82,350
Gibraltar	27	27	27	27	27	27	27	27	28	28
Greece	9,643	9,934	10,157	10,634	10,709	10,777	10,835	10,883	10,917	10,950
Iceland	229	243	256	269	272	274	277	280	282	285
Ireland	3,413	3,546	3,514	3,609	3,638	3,674	3,713	3,755	3,805	3,866
Italy	56,434	56,593	56,719	56,844	56,860	56,890	56,907	56,916	56,942	56,977
Liechtenstein	26	27	29	31	31	31	32	32	33	33
Luxembourg	364	368	384	411	417	423	429	434	440	445
Malta	326	346	362	379	381	384	386	388	390	393
Monaco	26	29	30	32	32	32	32	32	32	32
Netherlands	14,150	14,492	14,952	15,459	15,530	15,611	15,707	15,812	15,926	16,046
Norway	4,086	4,153	4,241	4,359	4,381	4,405	4,431	4,462	4,491	4,514
Portugal	9,766	10,024	9,983	10,030	10,058	10,091	10,129	10,172	10,226	10,293
Spain	37,439	38,419	38,850	39,387	39,478	39,582	39,721	39,926	40,263	40,720
Sweden	8,310	8,350	8,559	8,827	8,841	8,846	8,851	8,858	8,872	8,896
Switzerland	6,319	6,470	6,716	7,041	7,072	7,089	7,110	7,144	7,184	7,230
Turkey	45,530	50,510	55,139	59,728	60,633	61,523	62,407	63,298	64,175	65,043
United Kingdom	56,314	56,550	57,248	58,019	58,167	58,317	58,487	58,682	58,893	59,109
Eastern Europe										
Albania	2,698	2,995	3,290	3,120	3,096	3,081	3,073	3,069	3,068	3,073
Belarus	9,627	9,958	10,189	10,194	10,160	10,117	10,072	10,035	10,005	9,971
Bosnia-Herzegovina	4,059	4,279	4,444	3,482	3,451	3,504	3,619	3,721	3,771	3,801
Bulgaria	8,851	8,952	8,718	8,264	8,189	8,122	8,062	8,006	7,954	7,903
Croatia	4,600	4,712	4,781	4,581	4,533	4,537	4,527	4,498	4,440	4,441
Czech Republic	10,285	10,302	10,303	10,308	10,291	10,275	10,260	10,245	10,228	10,213
Estonia	1,477	1,529	1,569	1,437	1,416	1,400	1,386	1,376	1,370	1,364
Georgia	4,787	4,984	5,159	4,734	4,616	4,532	4,487	4,453	4,418	4,386
Hungary	10,713	10,628	10,374	10,329	10,311	10,290	10,267	10,238	10,211	10,188
Latvia	2,512	2,579	2,663	2,485	2,457	2,433	2,410	2,390	2,373	2,355
Lithuania	3,413	3,545	3,698	3,629	3,602	3,575	3,549	3,524	3,500	3,481
Macedonia	1,801	1,834	1,916	1,968	1,978	1,988	1,997	2,005	2,013	2,019
Moldova	4,029	4,234	4,370	4,323	4,286	4,242	4,190	4,131	4,067	3,997
Montenegro	586	587	591	601	604	607	609	612	614	617
Poland	35,574	37,202	38,031	38,275	30,209	38,292	38,284	38,270	38,258	38,248
Romania	22,207	22,733	23,202	22,239	22,146	22,062	22,001	21,953	21,908	21,860
Russia	138,483	143,033	147,969	148,376	148,160	147,915	147,671	147,215	146,597	145,976
Serbia	7,739	7,647	7,581	7,558	7,554	7,550	7,543	7,535	7,523	7,508
Slovakia	4,980	5,156	5,278	5,353	5,362	5,370	5,374	5,377	5,379	5,379
Slovenia	1,901	1,962	1,998	1,990	1,989	1,986	1,982	1,983	1,989	1,992
Ukraine	49,866	50,752	51,590	51,087	50,637	50,187	49,759	49,330	48,889	48,452

Source: National statistical offices/UN/Euromonitor International

Population Statistics

Total Population 1980-2009: National Estimates at Mid-Year *(continued)*

'000 / % growth

	2002	2003	2004	2005	2006	2007	2008	2009	% Growth 1980-2009
Western Europe									
Austria	8,084	8,121	8,173	8,236	8,290	8,333	8,367	8,396	11.2
Belgium	10,333	10,376	10,421	10,479	10,548	10,626	10,708	10,789	9.4
Cyprus	812	822	831	841	849	858	867	875	42.7
Denmark	5,376	5,391	5,405	5,419	5,437	5,461	5,494	5,519	7.7
Finland	5,201	5,213	5,228	5,246	5,266	5,289	5,313	5,336	11.7
France	59,863	60,264	60,643	60,996	61,353	61,822	62,277	62,610	16.2
Germany	82,488	82,534	82,516	82,469	82,376	82,266	82,110	81,862	4.6
Gibraltar	28	29	29	29	29	29	29	29	9.9
Greece	10,988	11,024	11,062	11,104	11,147	11,190	11,232	11,271	16.9
Iceland	287	290	294	299	305	312	319	326	42.1
Ireland	3,932	3,996	4,068	4,159	4,261	4,357	4,426	4,453	30.5
Italy	57,157	57,605	58,175	58,607	58,941	59,375	59,836	60,227	6.7
Liechtenstein	34	34	34	35	35	35	36	36	40.9
Luxembourg	451	456	461	467	472	478	483	489	34.2
Malta	396	399	401	404	405	407	408	409	25.5
Monaco	32	32	32	33	33	33	33	33	25.6
Netherlands	16,149	16,225	16,282	16,320	16,346	16,371	16,397	16,425	16.1
Norway	4,538	4,565	4,592	4,623	4,661	4,709	4,768	4,829	18.2
Portugal	10,368	10,441	10,502	10,549	10,589	10,626	10,656	10,682	9.4
Spain	41,314	42,005	42,692	43,398	44,121	44,770	45,289	45,724	22.1
Sweden	8,925	8,958	8,994	9,030	9,081	9,135	9,179	9,223	11.0
Switzerland	7,285	7,339	7,390	7,437	7,478	7,514	7,545	7,575	19.9
Turkey	65,905	66,761	67,608	68,445	69,275	70,138	71,052	71,995	58.1
United Kingdom	59,328	59,569	59,880	60,227	60,605	61,001	61,399	61,789	9.7
Eastern Europe									
Albania	3,082	3,093	3,105	3,116	3,127	3,138	3,149	3,162	17.2
Belarus	9,925	9,874	9,825	9,775	9,733	9,702	9,681	9,662	0.4
Bosnia-Herzegovina	3,822	3,834	3,840	3,843	3,843	3,844	3,844	3,844	-5.3
Bulgaria	7,852	7,803	7,753	7,702	7,650	7,598	7,545	7,493	-15.3
Croatia	4,443	4,442	4,443	4,443	4,441	4,437	4,432	4,425	-3.8
Czech Republic	10,205	10,207	10,216	10,236	10,269	10,334	10,424	10,490	2.0
Estonia	1,359	1,354	1,349	1,346	1,342	1,337	1,333	1,328	-10.1
Georgia	4,357	4,329	4,318	4,361	4,398	4,388	4,384	4,387	-8.4
Hungary	10,159	10,130	10,107	10,087	10,067	10,048	10,029	10,010	-6.6
Latvia	2,339	2,325	2,313	2,301	2,288	2,274	2,260	2,247	-10.5
Lithuania	3,469	3,454	3,436	3,414	3,394	3,376	3,357	3,339	-2.2
Macedonia	2,024	2,028	2,032	2,035	2,037	2,039	2,040	2,041	13.4
Moldova	3,924	3,854	3,789	3,734	3,688	3,650	3,618	3,590	-10.9
Montenegro	619	621	623	624	625	626	627	629	7.3
Poland	38,230	38,205	38,182	38,165	38,141	38,121	38,126	38,152	7.2
Romania	21,803	21,742	21,685	21,634	21,583	21,526	21,466	21,402	-3.6
Russia	145,306	144,566	143,821	143,114	142,487	142,115	141,956	141,845	2.4
Serbia	7,490	7,472	7,452	7,431	7,412	7,393	7,376	7,359	-4.9
Slovakia	5,379	5,380	5,382	5,387	5,390	5,393	5,394	5,396	8.4
Slovenia	1,995	1,996	1,997	2,000	2,007	2,013	2,020	2,026	6.5
Ukraine	48,032	47,633	47,272	46,925	46,607	46,329	46,078	45,873	-8.0

Source: National statistical offices/UN/Euromonitor International

Population Statistics

Table 21.2

Total Population 1980-2009: National Estimates at January 1st
'000

	1980	1985	1990	1995	1996	1997	1998	1999	2000	2001
Western Europe										
Austria	7,546	7,563	7,645	7,943	7,953	7,965	7,971	7,982	8,002	8,021
Belgium	9,855	9,858	9,948	10,131	10,143	10,170	10,192	10,214	10,239	10,263
Cyprus	611	647	681	731	743	754	765	776	787	797
Denmark	5,122	5,111	5,135	5,216	5,251	5,275	5,295	5,314	5,330	5,349
Finland	4,771	4,894	4,974	5,099	5,117	5,132	5,147	5,160	5,171	5,181
France	53,731	55,157	56,577	57,753	57,936	58,116	58,299	58,497	58,850	59,249
Germany	78,180	77,709	79,113	81,539	81,817	82,012	82,057	82,037	82,163	82,260
Gibraltar	27	27	27	27	27	27	27	27	27	28
Greece	9,584	9,919	10,121	10,595	10,674	10,745	10,808	10,861	10,904	10,931
Iceland	228	241	255	267	270	273	276	278	281	283
Ireland	3,393	3,544	3,507	3,598	3,620	3,655	3,694	3,732	3,778	3,833
Italy	56,388	56,588	56,694	56,844	56,844	56,876	56,904	56,909	56,924	56,961
Liechtenstein	26	27	28	31	31	31	31	32	32	33
Luxembourg	364	367	382	409	414	420	426	431	437	442
Malta	324	344	360	378	380	383	385	387	389	392
Monaco	26	28	30	32	32	32	32	32	32	32
Netherlands	14,091	14,454	14,893	15,424	15,494	15,567	15,654	15,760	15,864	15,987
Norway	4,079	4,146	4,233	4,348	4,370	4,393	4,418	4,445	4,478	4,503
Portugal	9,714	10,017	9,996	10,018	10,043	10,073	10,110	10,149	10,195	10,257
Spain	37,242	38,353	38,826	39,343	39,431	39,525	39,639	39,803	40,050	40,477
Sweden	8,303	8,343	8,527	8,816	8,837	8,844	8,848	8,854	8,861	8,883
Switzerland	6,304	6,456	6,674	7,019	7,062	7,081	7,096	7,124	7,164	7,204
Turkey	45,032	50,034	54,675	59,274	60,182	61,085	61,960	62,855	63,741	64,610
United Kingdom	56,285	56,482	57,157	57,943	58,095	58,239	58,395	58,580	58,785	59,000
Eastern Europe										
Albania	2,671	2,957	3,289	3,134	3,106	3,087	3,076	3,070	3,068	3,069
Belarus	9,592	9,929	10,189	10,210	10,177	10,142	10,093	10,051	10,019	9,990
Bosnia-Herzegovina	4,040	4,246	4,498	3,523	3,442	3,459	3,550	3,689	3,753	3,790
Bulgaria	8,835	8,954	8,767	8,303	8,224	8,154	8,091	8,033	7,978	7,929
Croatia	4,598	4,702	4,778	4,669	4,494	4,572	4,501	4,554	4,442	4,437
Czech Republic	10,277	10,302	10,301	10,317	10,300	10,283	10,268	10,253	10,236	10,220
Estonia	1,472	1,523	1,571	1,448	1,425	1,406	1,393	1,379	1,372	1,367
Georgia	4,770	4,961	5,145	4,794	4,675	4,558	4,505	4,470	4,435	4,401
Hungary	10,709	10,657	10,375	10,337	10,321	10,301	10,280	10,253	10,222	10,200
Latvia	2,509	2,570	2,668	2,501	2,470	2,445	2,421	2,399	2,382	2,364
Lithuania	3,404	3,529	3,694	3,643	3,615	3,588	3,562	3,536	3,512	3,487
Macedonia	1,795	1,828	1,909	1,963	1,973	1,983	1,993	2,002	2,009	2,016
Moldova	4,010	4,215	4,364	4,339	4,307	4,266	4,218	4,162	4,100	4,033
Montenegro	586	586	590	600	603	605	608	610	613	616
Poland	35,413	37,063	37,988	38,265	38,284	38,294	38,290	38,277	38,263	38,254
Romania	22,133	22,687	23,211	22,285	22,193	22,099	22,026	21,976	21,929	21,887
Russia	138,127	142,539	147,665	148,460	148,292	148,029	147,802	147,539	146,890	146,304
Serbia	7,748	7,655	7,585	7,559	7,556	7,552	7,547	7,540	7,530	7,517
Slovakia	4,963	5,140	5,270	5,349	5,358	5,366	5,373	5,376	5,379	5,379
Slovenia	1,893	1,949	1,996	1,989	1,990	1,987	1,985	1,978	1,988	1,990
Ukraine	49,781	50,648	51,557	51,301	50,874	50,400	49,974	49,545	49,115	48,663

Source: *Euromonitor International from national statistics/UN*

Population Statistics

Total Population 1980-2009: National Estimates at January 1st *(continued)*
'000

	2002	2003	2004	2005	2006	2007	2008	2009	% Growth 1980-2009
Western Europe									
Austria	8,065	8,102	8,140	8,207	8,266	8,314	8,352	8,383	11.1
Belgium	10,310	10,356	10,396	10,446	10,511	10,585	10,667	10,750	9.1
Cyprus	807	817	827	836	845	854	862	871	42.6
Denmark	5,368	5,384	5,398	5,411	5,427	5,447	5,476	5,511	7.6
Finland	5,195	5,206	5,220	5,237	5,256	5,277	5,300	5,325	11.6
France	59,660	60,067	60,462	60,825	61,167	61,538	62,106	62,449	16.2
Germany	82,440	82,537	82,532	82,501	82,438	82,315	82,218	82,002	4.9
Gibraltar	28	28	29	29	29	29	29	29	10.2
Greece	10,969	11,006	11,041	11,083	11,125	11,169	11,211	11,252	17.4
Iceland	286	288	291	296	301	308	315	323	41.4
Ireland	3,900	3,964	4,028	4,109	4,209	4,313	4,401	4,450	31.2
Italy	56,994	57,321	57,888	58,462	58,752	59,131	59,619	60,053	6.5
Liechtenstein	34	34	34	35	35	35	35	36	38.7
Luxembourg	448	453	459	464	470	475	481	486	33.5
Malta	394	397	400	403	405	406	407	409	26.1
Monaco	32	32	32	33	33	33	33	33	26.3
Netherlands	16,105	16,193	16,258	16,306	16,334	16,358	16,383	16,410	16.5
Norway	4,524	4,552	4,577	4,606	4,640	4,681	4,737	4,799	17.7
Portugal	10,329	10,407	10,475	10,529	10,570	10,609	10,643	10,670	9.8
Spain	40,964	41,664	42,345	43,038	43,758	44,484	45,056	45,521	22.2
Sweden	8,909	8,941	8,976	9,011	9,048	9,113	9,157	9,201	10.8
Switzerland	7,256	7,314	7,364	7,415	7,459	7,497	7,530	7,560	19.9
Turkey	65,477	66,334	67,188	68,029	68,861	69,689	70,586	71,517	58.8
United Kingdom	59,218	59,438	59,700	60,060	60,393	60,817	61,186	61,612	9.5
Eastern Europe									
Albania	3,076	3,087	3,099	3,111	3,122	3,132	3,143	3,155	18.1
Belarus	9,951	9,899	9,849	9,800	9,751	9,714	9,690	9,672	0.8
Bosnia-Herzegovina	3,813	3,830	3,837	3,843	3,843	3,844	3,844	3,844	-4.8
Bulgaria	7,877	7,827	7,778	7,728	7,676	7,624	7,571	7,519	-14.9
Croatia	4,444	4,442	4,442	4,444	4,443	4,440	4,435	4,429	-3.7
Czech Republic	10,206	10,203	10,211	10,221	10,251	10,287	10,381	10,468	1.9
Estonia	1,361	1,356	1,351	1,348	1,345	1,340	1,335	1,331	-9.6
Georgia	4,372	4,343	4,315	4,322	4,401	4,395	4,382	4,385	-8.1
Hungary	10,175	10,142	10,117	10,098	10,077	10,058	10,039	10,020	-6.4
Latvia	2,346	2,331	2,319	2,306	2,295	2,280	2,267	2,253	-10.2
Lithuania	3,476	3,463	3,446	3,425	3,403	3,385	3,366	3,348	-1.7
Macedonia	2,022	2,026	2,030	2,034	2,036	2,038	2,040	2,041	13.7
Moldova	3,961	3,888	3,820	3,759	3,709	3,667	3,633	3,604	-10.1
Montenegro	618	620	622	623	624	626	627	628	7.3
Poland	38,242	38,219	38,191	38,174	38,157	38,125	38,116	38,136	7.7
Romania	21,833	21,773	21,711	21,659	21,610	21,556	21,497	21,435	-3.2
Russia	145,649	144,964	144,168	143,474	142,754	142,221	142,009	141,904	2.7
Serbia	7,500	7,481	7,463	7,441	7,421	7,402	7,384	7,367	-4.9
Slovakia	5,379	5,379	5,380	5,385	5,389	5,392	5,394	5,395	8.7
Slovenia	1,994	1,995	1,996	1,998	2,003	2,010	2,016	2,023	6.9
Ukraine	48,241	47,824	47,443	47,101	46,749	46,466	46,192	45,963	-7.7

Source: *Euromonitor International from national statistics/UN*

Population Statistics

Table 21.3

Population by Sex and Age at January 1st 2009
'000

	Total	Male	Female	0-14	15-64	65+
Western Europe						
Austria	8,383	4,082	4,301	1,272	5,655	1,456
Belgium	10,750	5,268	5,482	1,810	7,100	1,840
Cyprus	871	424	447	155	603	113
Denmark	5,511	2,732	2,779	1,008	3,628	875
Finland	5,325	2,610	2,716	891	3,542	893
France	62,449	30,234	32,215	11,472	40,595	10,382
Germany	82,002	40,198	41,804	11,133	54,171	16,699
Gibraltar	29	15	15	5	19	5
Greece	11,252	5,568	5,684	1,602	7,557	2,093
Iceland	323	165	157	66	219	38
Ireland	4,450	2,215	2,235	931	3,027	492
Italy	60,053	29,158	30,896	8,421	39,521	12,111
Liechtenstein	36	18	18	6	25	4
Luxembourg	486	241	245	87	331	68
Malta	409	204	205	64	286	59
Monaco	33	16	17	5	21	7
Netherlands	16,410	8,117	8,293	2,911	11,043	2,456
Norway	4,799	2,395	2,404	912	3,182	705
Portugal	10,670	5,168	5,502	1,645	7,154	1,871
Spain	45,521	22,460	23,061	6,731	31,081	7,709
Sweden	9,201	4,568	4,633	1,519	6,036	1,646
Switzerland	7,560	3,695	3,865	1,156	5,139	1,265
Turkey	71,517	35,901	35,616	18,789	47,835	4,893
United Kingdom	61,612	30,240	31,372	10,781	40,844	9,987
Eastern Europe						
Albania	3,155	1,557	1,598	743	2,112	301
Belarus	9,672	4,512	5,160	1,418	6,898	1,356
Bosnia-Herzegovina	3,844	1,850	1,995	591	2,722	532
Bulgaria	7,519	3,642	3,877	986	5,215	1,319
Croatia	4,429	2,133	2,296	680	2,980	769
Czech Republic	10,468	5,136	5,331	1,480	7,431	1,556
Estonia	1,331	612	718	198	907	226
Georgia	4,385	2,081	2,305	742	3,014	630
Hungary	10,020	4,754	5,265	1,494	6,896	1,629
Latvia	2,253	1,038	1,215	307	1,557	390
Lithuania	3,348	1,558	1,790	501	2,311	537
Macedonia	2,041	1,018	1,023	364	1,437	240
Moldova	3,604	1,712	1,892	607	2,596	400
Montenegro	628	301	327	121	416	90
Poland	38,136	18,415	19,721	5,829	27,160	5,146
Romania	21,435	10,434	11,001	3,267	15,005	3,163
Russia	141,904	65,642	76,262	21,143	101,928	18,832
Serbia	7,367	3,570	3,798	1,338	4,970	1,059
Slovakia	5,395	2,621	2,775	832	3,912	651
Slovenia	2,023	994	1,029	280	1,411	332
Ukraine	45,963	21,185	24,778	6,476	32,170	7,317

Source: Euromonitor International from national statistics/UN

Population Statistics

Table 21.4

Population by Sex and Age (%) at January 1st 2009

% of total population

	Total	Male	Female	0-14	15-64	65+
Western Europe						
Austria	100.00	48.70	51.30	15.18	67.45	17.37
Belgium	100.00	49.00	51.00	16.84	66.05	17.12
Cyprus	100.00	48.69	51.31	17.80	69.22	12.97
Denmark	100.00	49.57	50.43	18.29	65.82	15.89
Finland	100.00	49.01	50.99	16.73	66.51	16.77
France	100.00	48.41	51.59	18.37	65.00	16.62
Germany	100.00	49.02	50.98	13.58	66.06	20.36
Gibraltar	100.00	50.15	49.85	17.73	65.39	16.88
Greece	100.00	49.48	50.52	14.23	67.16	18.60
Iceland	100.00	51.21	48.79	20.56	67.73	11.71
Ireland	100.00	49.77	50.23	20.93	68.02	11.05
Italy	100.00	48.55	51.45	14.02	65.81	20.17
Liechtenstein	100.00	49.33	50.67	16.68	71.01	12.31
Luxembourg	100.00	49.60	50.40	17.79	68.18	14.03
Malta	100.00	49.80	50.20	15.58	70.04	14.38
Monaco	100.00	47.54	52.46	13.77	63.67	22.56
Netherlands	100.00	49.47	50.53	17.74	67.29	14.97
Norway	100.00	49.90	50.10	19.01	66.31	14.69
Portugal	100.00	48.44	51.56	15.42	67.05	17.53
Spain	100.00	49.34	50.66	14.79	68.28	16.93
Sweden	100.00	49.65	50.35	16.51	65.60	17.89
Switzerland	100.00	48.87	51.13	15.29	67.97	16.74
Turkey	100.00	50.20	49.80	26.27	66.89	6.84
United Kingdom	100.00	49.08	50.92	17.50	66.29	16.21
Eastern Europe						
Albania	100.00	49.36	50.64	23.55	66.92	9.53
Belarus	100.00	46.65	53.35	14.66	71.32	14.02
Bosnia-Herzegovina	100.00	48.12	51.88	15.37	70.79	13.84
Bulgaria	100.00	48.44	51.56	13.11	69.35	17.54
Croatia	100.00	48.16	51.84	15.36	67.28	17.36
Czech Republic	100.00	49.07	50.93	14.14	70.99	14.87
Estonia	100.00	46.00	54.00	14.86	68.13	17.01
Georgia	100.00	47.45	52.55	16.92	68.72	14.36
Hungary	100.00	47.45	52.55	14.91	68.83	16.26
Latvia	100.00	46.07	53.93	13.60	69.09	17.31
Lithuania	100.00	46.53	53.47	14.95	69.01	16.03
Macedonia	100.00	49.86	50.14	17.83	70.41	11.76
Moldova	100.00	47.50	52.50	16.85	72.04	11.11
Montenegro	100.00	47.88	52.12	19.31	66.32	14.38
Poland	100.00	48.29	51.71	15.29	71.22	13.49
Romania	100.00	48.68	51.32	15.24	70.00	14.76
Russia	100.00	46.26	53.74	14.90	71.83	13.27
Serbia	100.00	48.45	51.55	18.16	67.46	14.37
Slovakia	100.00	48.57	51.43	15.43	72.50	12.07
Slovenia	100.00	49.15	50.85	13.84	69.77	16.39
Ukraine	100.00	46.09	53.91	14.09	69.99	15.92

Source: Euromonitor International from national statistics/UN

Population Statistics

Table 21.5

Live Births 1985-2009
'000

	1985	1990	1995	2000	2004	2005	2006	2007	2008	2009
Western Europe										
Austria	87.4	90.5	88.7	78.3	79.0	78.2	77.6	77.2	77.0	76.8
Belgium	114.3	123.6	114.2	114.9	115.6	118.0	121.4	120.7	125.0	126.0
Cyprus	13.2	12.8	11.5	10.0	9.6	9.7	9.7	9.8	9.9	10.1
Denmark	53.7	63.4	69.8	67.1	64.6	64.3	65.0	64.1	65.0	63.8
Finland	62.8	65.5	63.1	56.7	57.8	57.7	58.8	58.7	59.3	59.5
France	768.4	762.4	729.6	774.8	767.8	774.4	796.9	786.0	801.0	803.0
Germany	813.8	905.7	765.2	767.0	705.6	685.8	672.7	684.9	682.5	665.6
Gibraltar	0.5	0.5	0.4	0.4	0.4	0.4	0.4	0.4	0.4	0.4
Greece	116.5	102.2	101.5	101.0	97.5	97.0	96.7	96.4	96.1	95.8
Iceland	4.3	4.5	4.4	4.2	4.3	4.4	4.4	4.5	4.6	4.7
Ireland	62.4	53.0	48.8	54.8	62.0	61.4	65.4	70.6	75.1	74.8
Italy	577.3	569.3	525.6	543.1	562.6	554.0	560.0	563.9	575.8	576.2
Liechtenstein	0.4	0.4	0.4	0.4	0.4	0.4	0.4	0.4	0.4	0.3
Luxembourg	4.3	4.8	5.4	5.5	5.4	5.4	5.4	5.4	5.5	5.5
Malta	5.6	5.4	5.0	4.3	3.8	3.7	3.7	3.7	3.7	3.7
Monaco		0.8	0.8	0.8	0.8	0.9	0.9	0.9	1.0	1.0
Netherlands	178.1	198.0	190.5	206.6	194.0	187.9	185.1	182.4	180.4	178.9
Norway	51.1	60.9	60.3	59.2	57.0	56.8	58.5	58.5	60.5	60.8
Portugal	130.5	116.4	107.1	120.0	118.3	118.9	119.4	119.5	119.0	118.1
Spain	456.3	401.4	363.5	397.6	454.6	465.6	471.1	476.6	480.4	484.3
Sweden	98.5	123.9	103.4	90.4	100.9	101.3	105.9	106.4	107.0	107.6
Switzerland	74.7	83.9	82.2	78.5	73.1	72.9	72.4	72.1	72.0	72.1
Turkey	1,437.4	1,395.0	1,468.0	1,494.0	1,360.0	1,361.0	1,362.0	1,361.0	1,272.0	1,238.3
United Kingdom	750.7	798.6	732.0	679.3	716.0	722.5	748.6	772.2	796.1	804.3
Eastern Europe										
Albania	78.1	77.8	67.1	51.9	45.3	45.0	45.1	45.5	46.1	46.7
Belarus	165.0	142.2	101.1	93.7	88.9	90.5	96.7	103.6	107.9	108.9
Bosnia-Herzegovina	72.7	67.0	47.9	39.6	35.2	34.6	34.0	33.8	34.6	34.7
Bulgaria	119.0	105.2	72.0	73.7	69.9	71.1	72.4	71.9	71.3	70.6
Croatia	62.7	55.4	50.2	43.7	40.3	42.5	42.4	42.6	42.8	43.0
Czech Republic	135.9	130.6	96.1	90.9	97.7	102.2	105.8	114.6	119.6	115.9
Estonia	23.6	22.3	13.5	13.1	14.0	14.4	14.7	14.8	15.0	15.1
Georgia	97.7	92.8	56.3	48.8	49.6	46.5	47.8	49.3	56.6	56.7
Hungary	130.2	125.7	112.1	97.6	95.1	97.5	99.4	99.0	98.5	98.0
Latvia	39.8	37.9	21.6	20.2	20.3	21.5	21.7	22.1	22.5	22.9
Lithuania	58.5	56.9	41.2	34.1	30.4	30.5	31.1	31.2	31.4	31.6
Macedonia	35.3	33.0	29.2	25.2	23.5	23.1	22.7	22.4	22.0	21.7
Moldova	92.6	80.4	59.3	48.3	44.7	44.6	44.6	44.8	44.9	45.1
Montenegro	9.9	9.6	9.9	9.2	7.8	7.4	7.5	7.5	7.5	7.4
Poland	680.1	547.7	433.1	378.3	356.1	364.4	374.2	387.9	414.5	417.6
Romania	358.8	314.7	236.6	234.5	216.3	221.0	221.7	221.7	221.0	219.5
Russia	2,375.1	1,988.9	1,363.8	1,266.8	1,502.5	1,457.4	1,479.6	1,610.1	1,713.9	1,757.3
Serbia	115.7	103.2	88.6	83.4	85.1	85.7	86.2	86.7	87.1	87.4
Slovakia	90.2	80.0	61.4	55.2	53.7	54.4	52.6	52.4	52.3	52.3
Slovenia	25.9	22.4	19.0	18.2	18.0	18.2	18.2	18.4	18.6	18.9
Ukraine	762.8	657.2	492.9	385.1	427.3	426.1	460.4	472.7	510.6	512.5

Source: National statistical offices/UN/Euromonitor International

Population Statistics

Table 21.6

Deaths 1985-2009

'000

	1985	1990	1995	2000	2004	2005	2006	2007	2008	2009
Western Europe										
Austria	89.6	83.0	81.2	76.8	74.3	75.2	75.3	75.4	75.7	76.1
Belgium	112.7	104.5	104.6	104.9	101.9	103.3	101.6	100.7	101.6	104.0
Cyprus	5.7	5.7	5.3	5.5	5.8	5.9	6.0	6.1	6.2	6.3
Denmark	58.4	60.9	63.1	58.0	55.8	55.0	55.5	55.6	54.6	54.1
Finland	48.2	50.1	49.3	49.3	47.6	47.9	48.1	49.1	49.0	49.7
France	552.5	526.2	531.6	530.9	509.4	527.5	516.4	521.0	533.0	549.7
Germany	929.6	921.4	884.6	838.8	818.3	830.2	821.6	827.2	844.4	864.6
Gibraltar	0.3	0.3	0.2	0.3	0.2	0.2	0.2	0.2	0.2	0.2
Greece	92.9	94.2	100.2	103.0	97.3	96.6	96.2	95.9	95.7	95.6
Iceland	1.7	1.7	1.8	1.8	1.8	1.8	1.8	1.9	1.9	1.9
Ireland	33.2	31.4	32.3	31.4	28.2	27.4	27.5	28.1	28.2	29.2
Italy	547.4	541.8	554.3	555.5	545.1	588.9	557.9	573.0	579.5	593.0
Liechtenstein		0.2	0.2	0.2	0.2	0.2	0.2	0.2	0.2	0.2
Luxembourg	4.0	4.0	4.0	4.0	3.9	3.9	3.9	3.9	3.9	3.9
Malta	3.0	2.7	2.9	3.0	3.0	3.1	3.1	3.2	3.2	3.3
Monaco		0.6	0.6	0.5	0.5	0.6	0.5	0.5	0.5	0.5
Netherlands	122.7	128.8	135.7	140.5	136.6	136.4	135.8	137.4	139.2	141.1
Norway	44.4	46.0	45.2	44.0	41.2	41.2	41.3	42.0	41.7	41.9
Portugal	97.3	103.1	103.5	105.4	112.7	113.9	114.9	115.5	115.5	115.2
Spain	312.5	333.1	346.2	360.4	371.9	387.0	381.0	385.8	390.7	395.6
Sweden	94.0	95.2	94.0	93.5	90.5	91.7	91.2	91.1	91.0	90.8
Switzerland	59.6	63.7	63.4	62.5	60.2	61.1	61.4	61.8	62.3	62.9
Turkey	422.5	404.0	436.0	477.0	443.0	450.0	456.0	464.0	454.0	461.8
United Kingdom	670.7	641.8	645.5	608.4	583.1	582.7	572.2	574.7	573.7	578.6
Eastern Europe										
Albania	17.2	18.8	19.9	18.4	18.0	18.3	18.7	19.1	19.5	19.9
Belarus	105.7	109.6	133.8	134.9	140.1	141.9	138.4	133.0	133.9	135.8
Bosnia-Herzegovina	29.0	29.1	26.8	30.5	32.6	34.4	33.2	35.0	34.0	34.8
Bulgaria	107.5	108.6	114.7	115.1	110.1	113.4	113.2	112.6	111.9	111.2
Croatia	52.1	52.2	50.5	50.2	49.8	51.8	51.2	51.7	52.2	52.7
Czech Republic	131.6	129.2	117.9	109.0	107.2	107.9	104.4	104.6	104.9	106.0
Estonia	19.3	19.5	20.8	18.4	17.7	17.3	17.6	17.6	17.6	17.6
Georgia	46.2	50.7	49.1	47.4	48.8	40.7	42.3	41.2	43.0	43.8
Hungary	147.6	145.7	145.4	135.6	132.5	135.7	132.3	132.2	131.9	131.3
Latvia	34.2	34.8	38.9	32.2	32.0	32.8	33.4	33.4	33.4	33.3
Lithuania	39.2	39.8	45.3	38.9	41.3	43.8	44.7	44.9	45.0	45.2
Macedonia	13.7	15.1	15.9	16.8	17.7	18.0	18.3	18.5	18.8	19.0
Moldova	45.6	45.3	49.9	50.4	48.9	48.5	48.1	47.7	47.4	47.2
Montenegro	3.5	3.8	4.8	5.4	5.7	5.8	6.0	6.1	6.2	6.2
Poland	384.0	390.3	386.1	368.0	363.5	368.3	369.7	377.2	379.4	384.9
Romania	246.7	247.1	271.7	255.8	258.9	262.1	264.6	267.0	268.7	270.2
Russia	1,625.3	1,656.0	2,203.8	2,225.3	2,295.4	2,303.9	2,166.7	2,080.4	2,076.0	2,097.3
Serbia	94.7	98.4	103.9	109.3	111.6	112.4	113.2	114.0	114.9	115.7
Slovakia	52.5	54.6	52.7	52.7	51.9	53.5	52.8	53.0	53.2	53.4
Slovenia	19.9	18.6	19.0	18.6	18.5	18.8	18.5	18.7	18.9	19.1
Ukraine	617.5	629.6	792.6	758.1	761.3	782.0	758.1	762.9	754.5	706.7

Source: *National statistical offices/UN/Euromonitor International*

Population Statistics

Table 21.7

Birth Rates 1985-2009

Per '000 inhabitants

	1985	1990	1995	2000	2004	2005	2006	2007	2008	2009
Western Europe										
Austria	11.6	11.8	11.2	9.8	9.7	9.5	9.4	9.3	9.2	9.2
Belgium	11.6	12.4	11.3	11.2	11.1	11.3	11.5	11.4	11.7	11.7
Cyprus	20.4	18.8	15.8	12.7	11.7	11.6	11.5	11.5	11.5	11.5
Denmark	10.5	12.3	13.3	12.6	12.0	11.9	12.0	11.7	11.8	11.6
Finland	12.8	13.2	12.4	11.0	11.1	11.0	11.2	11.1	11.2	11.2
France	13.9	13.4	12.6	13.1	12.7	12.7	13.0	12.7	12.9	12.8
Germany	10.5	11.4	9.4	9.3	8.6	8.3	8.2	8.3	8.3	8.1
Gibraltar	18.7	19.8	15.9	14.9	14.6	14.4	12.8	13.6	13.5	13.4
Greece	11.7	10.1	9.6	9.3	8.8	8.8	8.7	8.6	8.6	8.5
Iceland	17.7	17.5	16.5	14.8	14.7	14.7	14.8	14.7	14.7	14.5
Ireland	17.6	15.1	13.5	14.4	15.2	14.8	15.4	16.2	17.0	16.8
Italy	10.2	10.0	9.2	9.5	9.7	9.5	9.5	9.5	9.6	9.6
Liechtenstein	14.0	13.4	13.9	13.0	10.8	11.0	10.3	10.0	9.9	9.8
Luxembourg	11.8	12.7	13.3	12.5	11.7	11.6	11.5	11.4	11.3	11.3
Malta	16.3	15.0	13.3	11.1	9.5	9.3	9.1	9.1	9.0	9.0
Monaco		26.3	26.3	23.7	25.5	27.5	27.0	28.7	29.0	29.2
Netherlands	12.3	13.3	12.4	13.0	11.9	11.5	11.3	11.1	11.0	10.9
Norway	12.3	14.4	13.8	13.2	12.4	12.3	12.6	12.4	12.7	12.6
Portugal	13.0	11.6	10.7	11.8	11.3	11.3	11.3	11.3	11.2	11.1
Spain	11.9	10.3	9.2	9.9	10.7	10.8	10.8	10.7	10.7	10.6
Sweden	11.8	14.5	11.7	10.2	11.2	11.2	11.7	11.7	11.7	11.7
Switzerland	11.6	12.6	11.7	11.0	9.9	9.8	9.7	9.6	9.6	9.5
Turkey	28.5	25.3	24.6	23.3	20.1	19.9	19.7	19.4	17.9	17.2
United Kingdom	13.3	14.0	12.6	11.5	12.0	12.0	12.4	12.7	13.0	13.0
Eastern Europe										
Albania	26.4	23.7	21.4	16.9	14.6	14.5	14.5	14.5	14.7	14.8
Belarus	16.6	14.0	9.9	9.4	9.1	9.3	9.9	10.7	11.1	11.3
Bosnia-Herzegovina	17.0	15.1	13.8	10.5	9.2	9.0	8.9	8.8	9.0	9.0
Bulgaria	13.3	12.0	8.7	9.2	9.0	9.2	9.4	9.4	9.4	9.4
Croatia	13.3	11.6	10.7	9.8	9.1	9.6	9.5	9.6	9.6	9.7
Czech Republic	13.2	12.7	9.3	8.9	9.6	10.0	10.3	11.1	11.5	11.0
Estonia	15.5	14.2	9.3	9.5	10.4	10.6	10.9	11.1	11.2	11.4
Georgia	19.6	18.0	11.9	11.0	11.5	10.7	10.9	11.2	12.9	12.9
Hungary	12.2	12.1	10.8	9.5	9.4	9.7	9.9	9.8	9.8	9.8
Latvia	15.5	14.2	8.6	8.5	8.8	9.3	9.5	9.7	9.9	10.1
Lithuania	16.6	15.4	11.3	9.7	8.8	8.9	9.1	9.2	9.3	9.5
Macedonia	19.3	17.3	14.9	12.5	11.6	11.4	11.2	11.0	10.8	10.7
Moldova	22.0	18.4	13.7	11.8	11.7	11.9	12.0	12.2	12.4	12.5
Montenegro	16.9	16.2	16.4	15.0	12.6	11.8	12.1	12.0	11.9	11.9
Poland	18.3	14.4	11.3	9.9	9.3	9.5	9.8	10.2	10.9	10.9
Romania	15.8	13.6	10.6	10.7	10.0	10.2	10.3	10.3	10.3	10.2
Russia	16.6	13.4	9.2	8.6	10.4	10.2	10.4	11.3	12.1	12.4
Serbia	15.1	13.6	11.7	11.1	11.4	11.5	11.6	11.7	11.8	11.9
Slovakia	17.5	15.2	11.5	10.3	10.0	10.1	9.8	9.7	9.7	9.7
Slovenia	13.3	11.2	9.5	9.1	9.0	9.1	9.1	9.1	9.2	9.3
Ukraine	15.0	12.7	9.6	7.9	9.0	9.1	9.9	10.2	11.1	11.2

Source: National statistical offices/UN/Euromonitor International

Population Statistics

Table 21.8

Death Rates 1985-2009

Per '000 inhabitants

	1985	1990	1995	2000	2004	2005	2006	2007	2008	2009
Western Europe										
Austria	11.8	10.9	10.2	9.6	9.1	9.2	9.1	9.1	9.1	9.1
Belgium	11.4	10.5	10.3	10.2	9.8	9.9	9.6	9.5	9.5	9.6
Cyprus	8.8	8.3	7.3	7.0	7.0	7.0	7.0	7.1	7.2	7.2
Denmark	11.4	11.9	12.1	10.9	10.3	10.1	10.2	10.2	9.9	9.8
Finland	9.8	10.1	9.7	9.5	9.1	9.2	9.1	9.3	9.2	9.3
France	10.0	9.3	9.2	9.0	8.4	8.6	8.4	8.4	8.6	8.8
Germany	12.0	11.6	10.8	10.2	9.9	10.1	10.0	10.1	10.3	10.6
Gibraltar	10.4	10.4	7.5	9.6	8.4	8.6	7.9	7.8	7.8	7.7
Greece	9.4	9.3	9.5	9.4	8.8	8.7	8.6	8.6	8.5	8.5
Iceland	6.9	6.8	6.8	6.4	6.1	6.1	6.1	6.1	6.0	6.0
Ireland	9.4	8.9	8.9	8.2	6.9	6.6	6.4	6.4	6.4	6.6
Italy	9.7	9.6	9.8	9.8	9.4	10.0	9.5	9.7	9.7	9.8
Liechtenstein		6.9	7.3	7.4	5.8	6.2	6.3	6.5	6.5	6.5
Luxembourg	11.0	10.5	9.8	9.1	8.6	8.5	8.3	8.2	8.1	8.1
Malta	8.6	7.6	7.6	7.7	7.6	7.6	7.7	7.8	7.9	8.0
Monaco		19.5	17.7	17.1	16.2	18.5	16.4	16.1	16.1	15.8
Netherlands	8.5	8.7	8.8	8.9	8.4	8.4	8.3	8.4	8.5	8.6
Norway	10.7	10.9	10.4	9.8	9.0	8.9	8.9	8.9	8.7	8.7
Portugal	9.7	10.3	10.3	10.3	10.8	10.8	10.9	10.9	10.9	10.8
Spain	8.1	8.6	8.8	9.0	8.8	9.0	8.7	8.7	8.7	8.7
Sweden	11.3	11.2	10.7	10.5	10.1	10.2	10.1	10.0	9.9	9.9
Switzerland	9.2	9.6	9.0	8.7	8.2	8.2	8.2	8.2	8.3	8.3
Turkey	8.4	7.3	7.3	7.4	6.6	6.6	6.6	6.6	6.4	6.4
United Kingdom	11.9	11.2	11.1	10.3	9.7	9.7	9.4	9.4	9.3	9.4
Eastern Europe										
Albania	5.8	5.7	6.4	6.0	5.8	5.9	6.0	6.1	6.2	6.3
Belarus	10.6	10.8	13.1	13.5	14.3	14.5	14.2	13.7	13.8	14.1
Bosnia-Herzegovina	6.8	6.5	7.7	8.1	8.5	9.0	8.6	9.1	8.8	9.1
Bulgaria	12.0	12.4	13.8	14.4	14.2	14.7	14.7	14.8	14.8	14.8
Croatia	11.1	10.9	10.8	11.3	11.2	11.7	11.5	11.6	11.8	11.9
Czech Republic	12.8	12.5	11.4	10.7	10.5	10.5	10.2	10.1	10.1	10.1
Estonia	12.7	12.4	14.4	13.4	13.1	12.9	13.1	13.1	13.2	13.2
Georgia	9.3	9.8	10.4	10.7	11.3	9.3	9.6	9.4	9.8	10.0
Hungary	13.9	14.0	14.1	13.3	13.1	13.4	13.1	13.1	13.1	13.1
Latvia	13.3	13.0	15.6	13.5	13.8	14.2	14.6	14.6	14.7	14.8
Lithuania	11.1	10.8	12.4	11.1	12.0	12.8	13.1	13.3	13.4	13.5
Macedonia	7.5	7.9	8.1	8.4	8.7	8.8	9.0	9.1	9.2	9.3
Moldova	10.8	10.4	11.5	12.3	12.8	12.9	13.0	13.0	13.1	13.1
Montenegro	6.0	6.5	7.9	8.8	9.2	9.4	9.6	9.7	9.8	9.9
Poland	10.3	10.3	10.1	9.6	9.5	9.6	9.7	9.9	10.0	10.1
Romania	10.9	10.6	12.2	11.7	11.9	12.1	12.2	12.4	12.5	12.6
Russia	11.4	11.2	14.9	15.2	16.0	16.1	15.2	14.6	14.6	14.8
Serbia	12.4	13.0	13.7	14.5	15.0	15.1	15.3	15.4	15.6	15.7
Slovakia	10.2	10.4	9.9	9.8	9.6	9.9	9.8	9.8	9.9	9.9
Slovenia	10.2	9.3	9.5	9.4	9.3	9.4	9.2	9.3	9.3	9.4
Ukraine	12.2	12.2	15.5	15.5	16.1	16.7	16.3	16.5	16.4	15.4

Source: *National statistical offices/UN/Euromonitor International*

Population Statistics

Table 21.9

Infant Mortality Rates 1985-2009

Deaths per '000 live births

	1985	1990	1995	2000	2004	2005	2006	2007	2008	2009
Western Europe										
Austria	11.2	7.8	5.4	4.8	4.0	3.9	3.8	3.7	3.6	3.5
Belgium	9.8	6.5	5.8	4.8	4.1	4.0	3.9	3.8	3.7	3.6
Cyprus	14.4	11.0	8.5	5.6	3.5	3.5	3.3	3.1	3.0	2.8
Denmark	7.9	7.5	5.1	5.3	4.4	4.3	4.2	4.1	4.0	3.9
Finland	6.3	5.6	3.9	3.6	3.0	2.9	2.7	2.7	2.7	2.5
France	8.3	7.3	4.9	4.4	4.0	4.0	3.8	3.7	3.7	3.6
Germany	9.1	7.0	5.3	4.4	4.0	3.9	3.9	3.7	3.7	3.6
Gibraltar										
Greece	14.1	9.7	8.1	6.0	4.6	4.4	4.1	4.0	3.9	3.8
Iceland	6.1	5.5	4.1	3.2	3.0	3.0	3.0	2.9	2.9	2.9
Ireland	8.8	8.2	6.4	6.2	5.0	4.9	4.8	4.7	4.6	4.6
Italy	10.5	8.2	6.2	4.5	4.1	4.0	3.9	3.8	3.7	3.7
Liechtenstein										
Luxembourg	9.1	7.0	6.0	5.0	5.0	4.0	2.5	1.8	1.6	1.3
Malta	10.9	9.1	8.5	7.3	6.8	6.7	6.6	6.5	6.4	6.3
Monaco	7.6	7.0	6.0	5.0	3.0	4.0	3.0	2.8	2.7	2.4
Netherlands	8.0	7.1	5.5	5.1	4.6	4.6	4.5	4.3	4.2	4.1
Norway [a]	8.5	6.9	4.0	3.8	3.3	3.2	3.1	2.9	2.9	2.8
Portugal [b]	17.8	11.0	7.5	5.5	3.7	3.4	3.2	3.1	2.9	2.8
Spain	8.9	7.6	5.5	3.9	3.1	3.0	2.9	2.8	2.7	2.6
Sweden	6.8	6.0	4.1	3.4	2.9	2.8	2.7	2.6	2.4	2.3
Switzerland	6.9	6.8	5.0	4.9	4.2	4.1	4.0	3.9	3.8	3.7
Turkey	93.6	54.0	44.6	40.2	37.5	36.6	36.5	35.6	34.8	34.1
United Kingdom	10.7	8.9	7.0	6.3	5.8	5.6	5.6	5.4	5.3	5.2
Eastern Europe										
Albania	43.8	37.0	29.0	22.0	18.6	18.3	18.1	17.8	17.6	17.4
Belarus	14.6	12.1	13.5	9.3	7.1	6.7	6.4	6.2	6.1	5.9
Bosnia-Herzegovina	24.3	18.0	16.0	15.0	13.0	13.0	12.8	12.2	11.9	11.7
Bulgaria [c]	15.4	14.8	14.8	13.3	12.6	12.2	12.1	11.8	11.6	11.2
Croatia	16.6	10.7	8.9	7.4	6.5	6.3	6.2	6.0	5.9	5.8
Czech Republic	12.5	10.8	7.7	4.1	3.8	3.6	3.5	3.5	3.4	3.2
Estonia	14.1	12.3	14.8	8.4	6.6	6.2	5.9	5.5	5.4	5.2
Georgia	23.9	20.5	28.4	22.5	23.8	19.7	15.8	13.3	12.1	11.3
Hungary	20.4	14.8	10.7	9.2	6.9	6.8	6.3	6.0	5.9	5.7
Latvia	13.0	13.7	18.8	10.4	9.3	9.0	8.7	8.3	8.1	7.8
Lithuania	14.2	10.2	12.5	8.6	6.7	6.5	6.1	5.9	5.6	5.3
Macedonia	44.1	34.0	24.0	22.0	18.3	15.0	11.5	10.3	9.9	9.7
Moldova	30.9	19.0	21.2	18.3	12.2	12.4	11.8	11.3	11.0	11.0
Montenegro	20.9	19.3	20.5	22.5	23.4	23.2	23.0	22.6	22.2	21.8
Poland	22.2	19.4	13.6	8.1	6.6	6.3	5.9	5.8	5.5	5.3
Romania	25.6	26.9	21.2	18.6	15.0	14.5	13.7	13.2	12.7	12.1
Russia	20.8	17.6	18.2	15.2	11.5	11.0	10.6	10.2	9.9	9.6
Serbia										
Slovakia	16.3	12.0	11.0	8.6	7.3	7.1	6.7	6.3	6.2	5.8
Slovenia	13.0	8.4	5.5	4.9	4.0	3.9	3.7	3.7	3.6	3.6
Ukraine	15.9	13.0	14.8	12.0	9.5	9.1	8.7	8.4	8.2	8.0

Source: *Euromonitor International from UN/national statistical offices/Eurostat*
Notes: *Rates refer to deaths of infants under one year*
(a) Rates from 1977 to 1990 are annual averages for five-year periods, (b) NUTS Nomenclature of Territorial Units of Statistics; Note: 1998 data new methodology, (c) The crude death rates are calculated per thousands of the average annual population

Table 21.10

Marriage Rates 1985-2009
Per '000 inhabitants

	1985	1990	1995	2000	2004	2005	2006	2007	2008	2009
Western Europe										
Austria	5.9	5.9	5.4	4.9	4.7	4.8	4.8	4.9	4.9	4.9
Belgium	5.8	6.5	5.1	4.4	4.2	4.2	4.2	4.2	4.2	4.3
Cyprus	8.7	8.2	9.1	11.8	13.3	13.4	13.3	13.3	13.3	13.3
Denmark	5.7	6.1	6.7	7.2	7.0	7.1	7.1	7.1	7.2	7.2
Finland	5.3	5.0	4.7	5.1	5.6	5.7	5.7	5.7	5.8	5.8
France	4.9	5.1	4.4	5.1	4.3	4.2	4.1	4.0	3.9	3.9
Germany	6.4	6.5	5.3	5.1	4.8	4.8	4.8	4.9	4.9	4.9
Gibraltar				5.4	5.5	6.3	5.5	5.4	5.4	5.3
Greece	6.4	5.8	6.0	4.5	5.5	5.4	5.4	5.3	5.3	5.2
Iceland	5.2	4.5	4.6	6.3	5.2	5.6	5.8	5.5	5.6	5.6
Ireland	5.3	5.1	4.3	5.1	5.1	5.0	5.0	4.9	4.8	4.7
Italy	5.3	5.6	5.1	5.0	4.5	4.5	4.4	4.4	4.4	4.3
Liechtenstein	12.7	11.5	13.4	7.3	4.8	5.4	4.3	5.2	5.2	5.2
Luxembourg	5.4	6.1	5.1	4.9	4.4	4.4	4.1	4.1	4.1	4.1
Malta	7.4	6.9	6.1	6.5	6.0	5.9	6.0	6.1	6.1	6.1
Monaco			6.0	5.0	5.3	5.0	4.9	4.9	4.8	4.8
Netherlands	5.7	6.4	5.3	5.6	4.5	4.4	4.3	4.2	4.2	4.1
Norway	4.9	5.2	5.0	5.7	4.9	4.9	4.7	5.0	5.3	5.2
Portugal	6.8	7.2	6.6	6.3	5.0	5.0	5.0	4.9	4.9	4.8
Spain	5.2	5.7	5.1	5.4	5.1	5.0	5.0	4.9	4.8	4.7
Sweden	4.6	4.7	3.8	4.5	4.8	4.8	4.9	4.9	5.0	5.0
Switzerland	6.0	7.0	5.8	5.5	5.4	5.3	5.2	5.2	5.1	5.1
Turkey	7.4	8.3	7.6	6.9	6.7	6.7	6.6	6.5	6.4	6.3
United Kingdom	7.0	6.6	5.6	5.2	5.2	5.2	5.1	5.1	5.1	5.1
Eastern Europe										
Albania	8.5	8.8	8.0	8.4	6.8	7.0	6.8	7.1	7.2	7.2
Belarus	9.9	9.7	7.5	6.2	7.2	7.3	7.4	7.4	7.5	7.5
Bosnia-Herzegovina	7.8	6.7	6.2	5.8	5.8	5.6	5.6	5.6	5.6	5.5
Bulgaria	7.4	6.8	4.4	4.4	4.0	4.0	4.0	4.0	4.0	3.9
Croatia	6.6	5.8	5.2	5.0	5.1	5.1	5.1	5.2	5.2	5.2
Czech Republic	7.8	8.8	5.3	5.4	5.0	5.1	5.1	5.1	5.1	5.1
Estonia	8.4	7.5	4.8	4.0	4.5	4.5	4.6	4.6	4.7	4.7
Georgia	8.9	6.8	4.5	2.9	3.4	4.2	5.0	5.7	6.0	5.9
Hungary	6.9	6.4	5.2	4.7	4.3	4.3	4.3	4.3	4.3	4.3
Latvia	9.4	8.9	4.4	3.9	4.5	4.6	4.7	4.8	4.9	5.0
Lithuania	9.7	9.8	6.1	4.8	5.6	5.8	6.0	6.3	6.4	6.6
Macedonia	8.9	8.2	8.1	7.1	6.9	7.1	7.3	7.6	7.4	7.3
Moldova	9.7	9.4	7.6	5.3	6.6	6.7	6.6	6.7	6.8	6.8
Montenegro	6.9	6.5	6.3	6.3	5.5	5.3	5.5	6.4	6.3	6.3
Poland	7.2	6.7	5.4	5.5	5.1	5.2	5.2	5.2	5.2	5.3
Romania	7.1	8.3	6.9	6.2	6.2	6.3	6.3	6.4	6.4	6.4
Russia	9.7	8.9	7.2	6.1	6.8	7.4	7.6	7.7	7.9	8.0
Serbia	6.4	6.0	5.5	5.7	5.6	5.2	5.4	5.6	5.6	5.6
Slovakia	7.6	7.7	5.1	4.8	4.9	4.9	5.0	5.0	5.1	5.1
Slovenia	5.4	4.3	4.1	3.6	3.3	3.3	3.2	3.2	3.2	3.2
Ukraine	9.7	9.4	8.4	5.6	5.9	5.8	5.8	5.8	5.7	5.7

Source: *National statistical offices/Council of Europe/UN/Euromonitor International*
Notes: *Rates refer to legal marriages (recognised marriages performed and registered)*

Population Statistics

Table 21.11

Divorce Rates 1985-2009

Per '000 inhabitants

	1985	1990	1995	2000	2004	2005	2006	2007	2008	2009
Western Europe										
Austria	2.0	2.1	2.3	2.4	2.3	2.3	2.2	2.2	2.2	2.2
Belgium	1.9	2.0	3.5	2.6	3.0	3.0	3.0	3.0	3.0	3.0
Cyprus	0.4	0.5	1.0	1.5	2.0	1.8	2.1	1.9	1.9	1.9
Denmark	2.8	2.7	2.5	2.7	2.9	3.0	3.0	3.0	3.1	3.1
Finland	1.9	2.6	2.8	2.7	2.5	2.5	2.5	2.5	2.4	2.4
France	1.9	1.9	2.1	1.9	2.1	2.2	2.2	2.2	2.2	2.3
Germany	2.3	2.0	2.1	2.4	2.7	2.7	2.8	2.8	2.9	3.0
Gibraltar				3.5	4.1	3.3	4.1	4.0	3.9	4.0
Greece	0.8	0.6	1.0	1.0	1.1	1.1	1.2	1.2	1.2	1.3
Iceland	2.2	1.9	1.8	1.9	1.9	1.9	1.7	1.7	1.7	1.6
Ireland				0.7	0.7	0.7	0.7	0.7	0.7	0.7
Italy	0.3	0.5	0.5	0.7	0.8	0.8	0.8	0.8	0.8	0.8
Liechtenstein		1.0	1.2	3.9	2.9	2.7	2.3	2.8	2.7	2.7
Luxembourg	1.8	2.0	1.8	2.4	2.3	2.3	2.5	2.3	2.3	2.3
Malta										
Monaco			2.5	2.6	2.5	2.1	2.1	2.2	2.3	2.2
Netherlands	2.4	1.9	2.2	2.2	1.9	1.8	1.8	1.8	1.7	1.7
Norway	2.0	2.4	2.4	2.2	2.4	2.4	2.3	2.2	2.1	2.1
Portugal	0.9	0.9	1.2	1.9	2.2	2.3	2.4	2.4	2.4	2.5
Spain	0.5	0.6	0.8	1.0	1.0	1.1	1.1	1.1	1.1	1.1
Sweden	2.4	2.3	2.6	2.4	2.2	2.2	2.2	2.2	2.1	2.1
Switzerland	1.8	2.0	2.2	1.5	2.4	2.5	2.6	2.6	2.7	2.7
Turkey	0.4	0.5	0.5	0.5	0.8	0.8	0.8	0.8	0.8	0.8
United Kingdom	3.1	2.9	2.9	2.6	2.8	2.9	2.9	2.9	2.9	3.0
Eastern Europe										
Albania	0.8	0.8	0.7	0.7	1.0	1.3	1.3	1.1	1.1	1.0
Belarus	3.1	3.4	4.1	4.3	3.1	2.9	2.8	2.7	2.6	2.6
Bosnia-Herzegovina	0.4	0.4	0.5	0.5	0.4	0.5	0.4	0.4	0.5	0.5
Bulgaria	1.6	1.3	1.3	1.3	1.9	2.0	2.2	2.4	2.5	2.6
Croatia	1.1	1.1	0.9	1.0	1.1	1.2	1.2	1.2	1.3	1.3
Czech Republic	3.0	3.1	3.0	2.9	3.2	3.3	3.3	3.3	3.4	3.4
Estonia	4.0	3.7	5.1	3.1	3.1	3.1	3.1	3.1	3.2	3.2
Georgia	1.3	1.3	0.6	0.4	0.4	0.4	0.5	0.5	0.5	0.5
Hungary	2.8	2.4	2.4	2.3	2.4	2.4	2.4	2.4	2.3	2.3
Latvia	4.5	4.0	3.1	2.6	2.3	2.3	2.3	2.4	2.4	2.4
Lithuania	3.2	3.5	2.8	3.1	3.2	3.2	3.3	3.4	3.5	3.5
Macedonia	0.4	0.4	0.4	0.7	0.8	0.8	0.7	0.7	0.7	0.7
Moldova	2.7	3.0	3.4	2.4	3.9	4.0	4.1	4.2	4.2	4.3
Montenegro	0.6	0.6	0.7	0.7	0.8	0.8	0.8	0.7	0.7	0.7
Poland	1.3	1.1	1.0	1.1	1.5	1.5	1.5	1.6	1.6	1.6
Romania	1.4	1.4	1.6	1.4	1.6	1.7	1.7	1.8	1.8	1.9
Russia	4.0	3.8	4.5	4.3	4.4	4.2	4.1	4.0	3.9	3.8
Serbia	1.2	1.1	1.0	1.0	1.2	1.0	1.1	1.2	1.2	1.2
Slovakia	1.5	1.7	1.7	1.7	2.0	2.1	2.2	2.2	2.3	2.3
Slovenia	1.3	0.9	0.8	1.1	1.2	1.2	1.2	1.2	1.2	1.2
Ukraine	3.6	3.7	3.9	4.0	3.6	3.6	3.6	3.5	3.5	3.5

Source: *National statistical offices/Council of Europe/UN/Euromonitor International*
Notes: *Rates refer to final divorce decrees granted under civil law*

Population Statistics

Table 21.12

Fertility Rates 1985-2009

Children born per female

	1985	1990	1995	2000	2004	2005	2006	2007	2008	2009
Western Europe										
Austria	1.5	1.5	1.4	1.4	1.4	1.4	1.4	1.4	1.4	1.4
Belgium	1.5	1.6	1.6	1.6	1.7	1.7	1.8	1.8	1.8	1.8
Cyprus	2.5	2.4	2.2	1.7	1.6	1.5	1.5	1.5	1.5	1.5
Denmark	1.5	1.7	1.8	1.8	1.8	1.8	1.9	1.8	1.9	1.9
Finland	1.6	1.8	1.8	1.7	1.8	1.8	1.8	1.8	1.8	1.8
France	1.8	1.8	1.7	1.9	1.9	1.9	2.0	2.0	2.1	2.1
Germany	1.4	1.5	1.2	1.4	1.4	1.3	1.3	1.4	1.4	1.4
Gibraltar										
Greece	1.7	1.4	1.3	1.3	1.3	1.2	1.2	1.2	1.2	1.2
Iceland	2.2	2.2	2.1	2.0	2.0	2.0	2.1	2.1	2.1	2.1
Ireland	2.6	2.1	1.9	1.9	2.0	1.9	1.9	1.9	2.0	2.1
Italy	1.4	1.4	1.2	1.3	1.3	1.3	1.4	1.4	1.4	1.4
Liechtenstein										
Luxembourg	1.5	1.6	1.7	1.7	1.7	1.7	1.7	1.7	1.7	1.7
Malta	2.0	2.0	2.0	1.6	1.4	1.3	1.3	1.3	1.3	1.3
Monaco										
Netherlands	1.5	1.6	1.5	1.7	1.7	1.7	1.8	1.8	1.8	1.8
Norway	1.7	1.9	1.9	1.9	1.8	1.8	1.9	1.9	2.0	1.9
Portugal	1.7	1.6	1.4	1.6	1.5	1.5	1.5	1.5	1.5	1.5
Spain	1.6	1.4	1.2	1.3	1.3	1.3	1.3	1.4	1.4	1.4
Sweden	1.7	2.1	1.7	1.6	1.8	1.8	1.8	1.8	1.8	1.8
Switzerland	1.5	1.6	1.5	1.5	1.4	1.4	1.4	1.4	1.4	1.4
Turkey	3.6	3.1	2.8	2.3	2.2	2.2	2.2	2.2	2.1	2.1
United Kingdom	1.8	1.8	1.7	1.6	1.8	1.8	1.9	1.9	1.9	1.9
Eastern Europe										
Albania	3.2	2.9	2.6	2.2	1.9	1.9	1.9	1.9	1.9	1.9
Belarus	2.1	1.9	1.4	1.3	1.2	1.2	1.3	1.4	1.4	1.4
Bosnia-Herzegovina	2.0	1.7	1.6	1.3	1.2	1.2	1.2	1.2	1.2	1.2
Bulgaria	2.0	1.8	1.2	1.3	1.3	1.3	1.3	1.3	1.3	1.3
Croatia	1.8	1.7	1.6	1.4	1.4	1.4	1.4	1.4	1.4	1.5
Czech Republic	2.0	1.9	1.3	1.1	1.2	1.3	1.3	1.4	1.5	1.4
Estonia	2.1	2.0	1.3	1.4	1.5	1.5	1.5	1.5	1.5	1.5
Georgia	2.3	2.2	1.5	1.5	1.5	1.4	1.4	1.5	1.7	1.7
Hungary	1.9	1.9	1.6	1.3	1.3	1.3	1.3	1.3	1.4	1.4
Latvia	2.1	2.0	1.3	1.2	1.2	1.3	1.3	1.3	1.4	1.4
Lithuania	2.1	2.0	1.6	1.4	1.3	1.3	1.3	1.3	1.3	1.3
Macedonia	2.3	2.1	2.0	1.8	1.7	1.6	1.6	1.5	1.5	1.5
Moldova	2.6	2.4	1.9	1.6	1.5	1.5	1.5	1.5	1.5	1.5
Montenegro	2.3	2.0	1.8	1.8	1.8	1.8	1.8	1.8	1.8	1.8
Poland	2.3	2.0	1.6	1.4	1.2	1.2	1.3	1.3	1.4	1.4
Romania	2.3	1.8	1.3	1.3	1.3	1.3	1.3	1.3	1.3	1.4
Russia	2.1	1.9	1.3	1.2	1.3	1.3	1.3	1.4	1.4	1.4
Serbia	2.3	2.1	1.8	1.7	1.8	1.8	1.8	1.8	1.8	1.8
Slovakia	2.3	2.1	1.5	1.3	1.2	1.3	1.3	1.3	1.3	1.3
Slovenia	1.7	1.5	1.3	1.3	1.3	1.3	1.3	1.3	1.3	1.3
Ukraine	2.0	1.8	1.4	1.1	1.2	1.2	1.3	1.3	1.5	1.5

Source: *National statistical offices/UN/Euromonitor International*

Population Statistics

Table 21.13

Life Expectancy at Birth 2009

Years

	Male	Female
Western Europe		
Austria	78.0	83.5
Belgium	77.7	83.2
Cyprus	77.5	82.2
Denmark	76.7	81.2
Finland	76.7	83.5
France	77.7	84.6
Germany	77.8	82.8
Gibraltar	74.5	79.6
Greece	77.9	82.6
Iceland	80.4	83.5
Ireland	77.8	82.5
Italy	78.8	84.4
Liechtenstein	80.2	85.6
Luxembourg	78.4	83.2
Malta	77.2	82.5
Monaco	78.9	85.6
Netherlands	78.6	82.6
Norway	78.6	83.3
Portugal	75.7	81.9
Spain	79.1	85.1
Sweden	79.5	83.4
Switzerland	79.9	84.5
Turkey	69.7	74.5
United Kingdom	77.6	82.1
Eastern Europe		
Albania	73.7	80.0
Belarus	65.0	76.4
Bosnia-Herzegovina	72.7	77.9
Bulgaria	70.0	77.2
Croatia	72.6	79.8
Czech Republic	74.2	80.2
Estonia	69.0	79.7
Georgia	68.3	75.2
Hungary	70.2	78.4
Latvia	67.3	78.0
Lithuania	66.4	77.7
Macedonia	72.0	76.8
Moldova	64.9	72.5
Montenegro	72.0	76.7
Poland	71.5	80.2
Romania	69.4	76.3
Russia	62.2	74.4
Serbia	71.3	76.4
Slovakia	71.0	78.9
Slovenia	75.6	82.5
Ukraine	62.7	74.4

Source: Euromonitor International from World Bank

Table 21.14

Population Density 1985-2009

Persons per sq km

	1985	1990	1995	2000	2004	2005	2006	2007	2008	2009
Western Europe										
Austria	91.7	92.7	96.3	97.1	98.7	99.5	100.3	100.8	101.3	101.7
Belgium	325.6	328.5	334.6	338.1	343.3	345.0	347.1	349.6	352.3	355.0
Cyprus	70.1	73.7	79.2	85.1	89.5	90.5	91.5	92.4	93.3	94.3
Denmark	120.6	121.1	122.9	125.6	127.2	127.5	127.9	128.4	129.1	129.9
Finland	16.1	16.3	16.7	17.0	17.1	17.2	17.3	17.4	17.4	17.5
France	100.7	103.3	105.5	107.5	110.4	111.1	111.7	112.4	113.4	114.0
Germany	222.6	226.6	233.6	235.5	236.6	236.6	236.4	236.1	235.8	235.2
Gibraltar	2,660.1	2,684.4	2,730.6	2,737.9	2,882.2	2,910.0	2,925.4	2,930.6	2,928.6	2,924.5
Greece	77.0	78.5	82.2	84.6	85.7	86.0	86.3	86.6	87.0	87.3
Iceland	2.4	2.5	2.7	2.8	2.9	2.9	3.0	3.1	3.1	3.2
Ireland	51.4	50.9	52.2	54.8	58.5	59.6	61.1	62.6	63.9	64.6
Italy	192.4	192.8	193.3	193.5	196.8	198.8	199.7	201.0	202.7	204.2
Liechtenstein	166.8	177.8	191.4	202.7	214.3	216.3	218.2	219.8	221.8	223.7
Luxembourg	141.9	147.7	158.1	168.7	177.1	179.2	181.3	183.4	185.6	187.7
Malta	1,076.1	1,125.4	1,180.6	1,215.3	1,250.5	1,258.0	1,264.1	1,269.1	1,273.3	1,277.2
Monaco	14,182.0	15,066.0	15,800.0	16,004.5	16,197.0	16,250.0	16,302.0	16,355.5	16,409.5	16,465.5
Netherlands	428.1	441.1	456.9	469.9	481.6	483.0	483.8	484.5	485.3	486.1
Norway	13.6	13.9	14.3	14.7	15.0	15.1	15.2	15.4	15.5	15.7
Portugal	109.5	109.2	109.5	111.4	114.5	115.1	115.6	116.0	116.4	116.7
Spain	76.8	77.7	78.8	80.3	84.8	86.2	87.7	89.1	90.3	91.2
Sweden	20.3	20.8	21.5	21.6	21.9	22.0	22.0	22.2	22.3	22.4
Switzerland	161.4	166.8	175.5	179.1	184.1	185.4	186.5	187.4	188.3	189.0
Turkey	65.0	71.0	77.0	82.8	87.3	88.4	89.5	90.5	91.7	92.9
United Kingdom	233.5	236.3	239.5	243.0	246.8	248.3	249.6	251.4	252.9	254.7
Eastern Europe										
Albania	107.9	120.1	114.4	112.0	113.1	113.5	113.9	114.3	114.7	115.2
Belarus		50.3	49.4	48.6	48.3	48.1	47.9	47.8	47.7	
Bosnia-Herzegovina	83.1	88.0	68.8	73.3	74.9	75.0	75.1	75.1	75.1	75.1
Bulgaria	80.9	79.2	75.1	72.1	71.5	71.1	70.7	70.2	69.7	69.2
Croatia			83.5	79.4	79.4	79.4	79.4	79.3	79.3	79.1
Czech Republic	133.3	133.3	133.5	132.5	132.2	132.3	132.7	133.2	134.4	135.5
Estonia	36.0	37.2	34.2	32.4	31.9	31.8	31.7	31.6	31.5	31.4
Georgia	71.4	74.0	69.0	63.8	62.1	62.2	63.3	63.2	63.1	63.1
Hungary	118.6	115.4	115.0	114.1	112.9	112.7	112.4	112.2	112.0	111.8
Latvia	41.4	43.0	40.2	38.3	37.3	37.1	36.9	36.7	36.4	36.2
Lithuania	54.5	57.0	58.1	56.0	55.0	54.6	54.3	54.0	53.7	53.4
Macedonia	71.9	75.1	77.2	79.0	79.8	80.0	80.1	80.8	80.9	81.0
Moldova		131.8	124.7	116.2	114.3	112.8	111.5	110.5	109.6	
Montenegro	43.1	43.4	44.1	45.1	45.7	45.8	46.4	46.5	46.6	46.7
Poland	121.7	124.8	125.7	125.7	125.5	124.6	125.4	125.3	125.3	125.4
Romania	98.5	101.2	97.1	95.5	94.4	94.2	94.0	93.8	93.5	93.2
Russia	8.4	8.7	9.1	9.0	8.8	8.8	8.7	8.7	8.7	8.7
Serbia	86.6	85.8	85.6	85.2	84.5	84.2	84.0	83.8	83.6	83.4
Slovakia	106.9	109.6	111.2	111.8	111.9	112.0	112.0	112.1	112.1	112.2
Slovenia	96.8	99.2	98.8	98.7	99.1	99.2	99.5	99.8	100.1	100.4
Ukraine	87.4	89.0	88.5	84.8	81.9	81.3	80.7	80.2	79.7	79.3

Source: *National statistical offices/UN/Euromonitor International*

Population Statistics

Table 21.15

Urban Population 1985-2009
% of total population

	1985	1990	1995	2000	2004	2005	2006	2007	2008	2009
Western Europe										
Austria	58.8	63.5	65.7	66.5	66.9	67.0	67.1	67.2	67.3	67.4
Belgium	95.9	96.4	96.8	97.1	97.3	97.3	97.3	97.2	96.9	96.6
Cyprus	64.7	66.8	68.0	68.6	69.2	69.3	69.5	69.7	69.9	70.1
Denmark	84.3	84.8	85.1	85.1	85.4	85.5	85.6	85.7	85.8	85.9
Finland	56.6	56.8	57.8	60.4	62.1	62.2	62.3	62.4	62.6	62.6
France	73.6	74.1	74.9	75.8	76.5	76.7	76.9	77.1	77.3	77.6
Germany	72.7	73.1	73.3	73.1	73.3	73.4	73.4	73.5	73.6	73.7
Gibraltar	100.0	100.0	100.0	100.0	100.0	100.0	100.0	100.0	100.0	100.0
Greece	58.4	58.8	59.3	60.1	61.1	61.5	61.8	62.1	62.4	62.7
Iceland	89.6	90.8	91.6	92.2	92.2	92.2	92.2	92.3	92.3	92.3
Ireland	56.3	56.9	57.9	59.1	60.1	60.4	60.7	60.8	61.0	61.6
Italy	66.8	66.7	66.9	67.2	67.5	67.6	67.7	67.9	68.0	68.2
Liechtenstein	17.6	16.9	16.5	15.1	14.6	14.6	14.5	14.5	14.5	14.4
Luxembourg	80.7	80.9	82.9	83.8	83.0	82.8	82.7	82.5	82.4	82.3
Malta	89.8	90.4	90.9	92.4	93.4	93.6	93.9	94.1	94.3	94.5
Monaco	100.0	100.0	100.0	100.0	100.0	100.0	100.0	100.0	100.0	100.0
Netherlands	59.2	60.0	60.9	63.0	64.8	65.3	65.7	66.2	66.7	67.2
Norway	71.3	72.1	73.4	76.1	79.5	80.4	81.1	81.9	82.6	83.2
Portugal	37.5	46.3	50.3	53.1	55.1	55.7	56.2	56.8	57.3	57.8
Spain	74.2	75.3	75.9	76.3	76.6	76.7	76.8	76.9	77.0	77.2
Sweden	83.1	83.1	83.2	83.3	83.4	83.4	83.5	83.5	83.6	83.7
Switzerland	66.4	68.0	67.7	67.6	67.9	68.0	68.1	68.2	68.3	68.3
Turkey	55.5	60.5	64.1	68.0	70.4	70.9	71.5	72.1	72.5	72.9
United Kingdom	88.6	88.7	89.0	89.4	89.6	89.7	89.8	89.9	90.0	90.1
Eastern Europe										
Albania	35.1	36.4	38.9	41.7	44.2	44.8	45.4	46.1	46.7	47.3
Belarus	62.0	66.0	67.8	69.8	71.8	72.2	72.6	73.0	73.5	73.9
Bosnia-Herzegovina	37.6	39.2	41.1	43.2	45.2	45.7	46.3	46.9	47.4	48.0
Bulgaria	65.8	67.1	67.8	68.4	70.3	70.7	71.1	71.5	71.8	72.1
Croatia	52.2	54.0	55.8	57.7	59.5	59.9	60.3	60.8	61.3	61.7
Czech Republic	75.2	75.0	74.5	74.1	74.3	74.5	74.7	74.8	74.5	74.1
Estonia	71.0	71.5	70.0	69.2	69.3	69.3	69.3	69.4	69.4	69.5
Georgia	53.9	55.2	54.0	52.7	52.2	52.2	52.3	52.3	52.4	52.6
Hungary	62.8	65.4	65.2	64.5	66.0	66.2	66.5	66.8	67.1	67.3
Latvia	68.5	69.0	68.7	68.1	67.9	68.0	68.1	68.2	68.3	68.4
Lithuania	65.1	68.1	67.5	67.1	67.0	67.1	67.1	67.2	67.2	67.3
Macedonia	55.7	57.8	60.7	64.9	68.1	68.9	69.6	70.3	71.0	71.6
Moldova	44.2	46.8	46.3	44.6	43.0	42.6	42.2	41.9	41.7	41.4
Montenegro	42.4	48.0	53.4	58.5	60.8	61.2	61.0	60.6	60.2	59.8
Poland	61.2	61.8	61.8	61.8	61.8	61.8	61.8	61.8	61.8	61.7
Romania	53.0	54.3	54.9	54.6	54.8	54.9	54.9	54.9	55.0	55.0
Russia	72.0	73.6	73.0	73.1	73.4	73.0	72.9	73.0	73.1	73.1
Serbia	48.3	50.4	50.9	51.1	51.4	51.5	51.6	51.8	52.0	52.2
Slovakia	55.6	56.9	56.3	55.5	55.8	55.9	56.2	56.3	56.5	56.7
Slovenia	50.4	50.8	50.8	50.8	50.8	50.8	50.9	51.0	51.1	51.1
Ukraine	66.4	67.5	67.8	67.4	67.5	67.6	67.7	67.8	67.9	68.0

Source: National statistical offices/UN/Euromonitor International

Population Statistics

Table 21.16

Rural Population 1985-2009

% of total population

	1985	1990	1995	2000	2004	2005	2006	2007	2008	2009
Western Europe										
Austria	41.2	36.5	34.3	33.5	33.1	33.0	32.9	32.8	32.7	32.6
Belgium	4.1	3.6	3.2	2.9	2.7	2.7	2.7	2.7	2.6	2.6
Cyprus	35.3	33.2	32.0	31.4	30.8	30.7	30.5	30.3	30.1	29.9
Denmark	15.7	15.2	14.9	14.9	14.6	14.5	14.4	14.3	14.2	14.1
Finland	43.4	43.2	42.2	39.6	37.9	37.8	37.7	37.6	37.4	37.4
France	26.4	25.9	25.1	24.2	23.5	23.3	23.1	22.9	22.7	22.4
Germany	27.3	26.9	26.7	26.9	26.7	26.6	26.6	26.5	26.4	26.3
Gibraltar										
Greece	41.6	41.2	40.7	39.9	38.9	38.5	38.2	37.9	37.6	37.3
Iceland	10.4	9.2	8.4	7.8	7.8	7.8	7.8	7.7	7.7	7.7
Ireland	43.7	43.1	42.1	40.9	39.9	39.6	39.3	38.9	38.5	38.4
Italy	33.2	33.3	33.1	32.8	32.5	32.4	32.3	32.1	32.0	31.8
Liechtenstein	82.4	83.1	83.5	84.9	85.4	85.4	85.5	85.5	85.5	85.6
Luxembourg	19.3	19.1	17.1	16.2	17.0	17.2	17.3	17.5	17.6	17.7
Malta	10.2	9.6	9.1	7.6	6.6	6.4	6.1	5.9	5.7	5.5
Monaco										
Netherlands	40.8	40.0	39.1	37.0	35.2	34.7	34.3	33.8	33.3	32.8
Norway	28.7	27.9	26.6	23.9	20.5	19.6	18.9	18.1	17.4	16.8
Portugal	62.5	53.7	49.7	46.9	44.9	44.3	43.8	43.2	42.7	42.2
Spain	25.8	24.7	24.1	23.7	23.4	23.3	23.2	23.1	23.0	22.8
Sweden	16.9	16.9	16.8	16.7	16.6	16.6	16.5	16.5	16.4	16.3
Switzerland	33.6	32.0	32.3	32.4	32.1	32.0	31.9	31.8	31.7	31.7
Turkey	43.8	41.0	39.1	36.9	34.8	34.3	33.8	33.3	32.8	32.4
United Kingdom	11.4	11.3	11.0	10.6	10.4	10.3	10.2	10.1	10.0	9.9
Eastern Europe										
Albania	64.9	63.6	61.1	58.3	55.8	55.2	54.6	53.9	53.3	52.7
Belarus	38.0	34.0	32.2	30.2	28.2	27.8	27.4	27.0	26.5	26.1
Bosnia-Herzegovina	62.4	60.8	58.9	56.8	54.8	54.3	53.7	53.1	52.6	52.0
Bulgaria	34.2	32.9	32.2	31.6	29.7	29.3	28.9	28.5	28.2	27.9
Croatia	47.8	46.0	44.2	42.3	40.5	40.1	39.7	39.2	38.7	38.3
Czech Republic	24.8	25.0	25.5	25.9	25.7	25.5	25.3	25.2	24.9	24.6
Estonia	29.0	28.5	30.0	30.8	30.7	30.7	30.7	30.6	30.6	30.5
Georgia	46.1	44.8	46.0	47.3	47.8	47.8	47.7	47.7	47.6	47.4
Hungary	37.2	34.6	34.8	35.5	34.0	33.8	33.5	33.2	32.9	32.7
Latvia	31.5	31.0	31.3	31.9	32.1	32.0	31.9	31.8	31.7	31.6
Lithuania	34.9	31.9	32.5	32.9	33.0	32.9	32.9	32.8	32.8	32.7
Macedonia	44.3	42.2	39.3	35.1	31.9	31.1	30.4	29.7	29.0	28.4
Moldova	55.8	53.2	53.7	55.4	57.0	57.4	57.8	58.1	58.3	58.6
Montenegro	57.6	52.0	46.6	41.5	39.2	38.8	39.0	39.4	39.8	40.2
Poland	38.8	38.2	38.2	38.2	38.2	38.2	38.2	38.2	38.0	37.9
Romania	47.0	45.7	45.1	45.4	45.2	45.1	45.1	45.1	45.0	45.0
Russia	28.0	26.4	27.0	26.9	26.6	27.0	27.1	27.0	26.9	26.9
Serbia	51.7	49.6	49.1	48.9	48.6	48.5	48.4	48.2	48.0	47.8
Slovakia	44.4	43.1	43.7	44.5	44.2	44.1	43.8	43.7	43.5	43.3
Slovenia	49.6	49.2	49.2	49.2	49.2	49.2	49.1	49.0	48.9	48.9
Ukraine	33.6	32.5	32.2	32.6	32.5	32.4	32.3	32.2	32.1	31.9

Source: National statistical offices/UN/Euromonitor International

Population Statistics

Table 21.17

Pensioners 1990-2009
'000

	1990	1995	2000	2004	2005	2007	2008	2009
Western Europe								
Austria	1,361	1,393	1,438	1,529	1,567	1,627	1,659	1,689
Belgium	1,649	1,776	1,875	1,884	1,893	1,857	1,873	1,840
Cyprus	74	79	89	99	102	107	110	113
Denmark	800	799	790	805	813	835	853	875
Finland	662	720	767	813	831	869	875	893
France	10,764	11,599	12,132	12,502	12,661	13,137	13,562	13,929
Germany (a)	11,794	12,542	13,351	14,860	15,367	16,299	16,519	16,699
Gibraltar								
Greece	1,675	1,893	2,129	2,267	2,304	2,382	2,415	2,439
Iceland	23	26	29	30	31	32	32	33
Ireland	399	411	424	449	458	469	479	492
Italy	10,073	11,117	12,085	12,886	13,087	13,498	13,724	13,956
Liechtenstein								
Luxembourg	51	57	62	65	66	67	67	68
Malta	38	43	48	52	53	56	57	59
Monaco								
Netherlands	1,906	2,034	2,152	2,251	2,289	2,368	2,406	2,456
Norway	606	622	618	603	604	610	614	617
Portugal	1,322	1,475	1,635	1,761	1,791	1,826	1,847	1,871
Spain (b)	5,215	5,946	6,706	7,144	7,228	7,445	7,583	7,709
Sweden	1,518	1,540	1,533	1,541	1,554	1,583	1,611	1,646
Switzerland	1,007	1,067	1,129	1,193	1,211	1,255	1,281	1,309
Turkey	6,310	6,957	7,168	7,297	7,400	7,485	7,657	7,693
United Kingdom (c)	10,499	10,616	10,767	11,050	11,186	11,437	11,669	11,868
Eastern Europe								
Albania	218	245	282	318	327	344	353	362
Belarus	2,000	2,143	2,145	2,082	2,080	2,074	2,087	2,093
Bosnia-Herzegovina	274	287	415	501	514	528	530	532
Bulgaria (b)	1,806	1,857	1,841	1,791	1,749	1,702	1,682	1,665
Croatia	702	795	840	867	873	879	888	893
Czech Republic (d)	1,973	1,988	2,038	2,103	2,129	2,184	2,204	2,231
Estonia	250	258	270	278	279	275	271	266
Georgia	639	669	698	707	711	728	730	737
Hungary	1,920	1,980	2,028	2,091	2,044	2,007	2,013	1,958
Latvia	408	431	446	469	471	467	456	453
Lithuania	697	738	719	676	676	659	658	659
Macedonia	172	207	238	257	261	269	273	278
Moldova	590	607	612	590	587	590	595	602
Montenegro	33	36	37	34	34	36	37	39
Poland	4,792	5,181	5,564	5,802	5,847	5,983	6,082	6,196
Romania	3,518	3,840	4,053	4,113	4,127	4,136	4,104	4,063
Russia	27,621	29,876	30,138	29,259	29,161	29,351	29,760	30,033
Serbia	1,095	1,249	1,351	1,368	1,367	1,366	1,368	1,332
Slovakia	912	934	965	983	988	976	965	957
Slovenia	365	397	423	447	450	460	460	460
Ukraine	10,957	11,533	11,621	11,248	11,213	11,108	11,106	11,111

Source: Euromonitor International from national statistics/UN
Notes: (a) Data refer to number of pensions paid, (b) Data refer to all kinds of pensions, (c) Data refer to population of retirement age only, (d) Data refer to post-working age economically inactive population

Table 21.18

Population by Marital Status 2009

'000 / % analysis

	Married	Divorced	Widowed	Single	Married (% analysis)	Divorced (% analysis)	Widowed (% analysis)	Single (% analysis)
Western Europe								
Austria	3,615	612	555	3,601	43.13	7.29	6.62	42.95
Belgium	4,516	844	722	4,578	42.36	7.92	6.78	42.95
Cyprus								
Denmark	2,206	422	324	2,560	40.02	7.65	5.88	46.45
Finland	1,992	507	303	2,524	37.40	9.51	5.68	47.40
France	24,824	3,833	3,967	29,825	39.75	6.14	6.35	47.76
Germany	35,550	6,275	5,870	34,307	43.35	7.65	7.16	41.84
Gibraltar								
Greece	5,634	341	835	4,442	50.07	3.03	7.42	39.47
Iceland								
Ireland	1,638	198	198	2,414	36.82	4.45	4.44	54.28
Italy	30,136	930	4,732	23,254	51.03	1.58	8.01	39.38
Liechtenstein								
Luxembourg								
Malta								
Monaco								
Netherlands	6,879	1,047	856	7,627	41.92	6.38	5.22	46.48
Norway	1,707	435	259	2,399	35.56	9.07	5.39	49.98
Portugal	5,832	305	659	3,874	54.66	2.86	6.17	36.31
Spain	23,190	1,532	2,877	17,921	50.94	3.37	6.32	39.37
Sweden	3,066	894	496	4,745	33.32	9.72	5.40	51.57
Switzerland	3,427	409	499	3,225	45.34	5.41	6.60	42.66
Turkey	36,004	790	2,657	35,789	47.85	1.05	3.53	47.57
United Kingdom	24,204	4,892	3,668	28,848	39.28	7.94	5.95	46.82
Eastern Europe								
Albania								
Belarus	4,424	796	888	3,564	45.74	8.23	9.18	36.85
Bosnia-Herzegovina								
Bulgaria	4,002	312	750	2,455	53.22	4.15	9.97	32.66
Croatia	2,070	137	442	1,768	46.87	3.10	10.01	40.02
Czech Republic	4,618	1,002	755	3,963	44.67	9.69	7.30	38.34
Estonia	432	155	125	619	32.47	11.64	9.41	46.48
Georgia	2,600	132	492	1,159	59.33	3.01	11.22	26.44
Hungary	4,030	877	992	4,121	40.22	8.75	9.90	41.13
Latvia	806	287	205	956	35.76	12.73	9.09	42.42
Lithuania	1,376	348	265	1,359	41.11	10.39	7.92	40.58
Macedonia	983	23	107	928	48.15	1.14	5.24	45.47
Moldova								
Montenegro	359	17	58	195	57.09	2.71	9.20	31.01
Poland	17,262	1,611	3,011	16,106	45.44	4.24	7.92	42.40
Romania	9,902	878	2,120	8,535	46.20	4.10	9.89	39.82
Russia	65,463	12,628	14,119	49,693	46.13	8.90	9.95	35.02
Serbia	3,707	269	714	2,677	50.32	3.65	9.69	36.34
Slovakia	2,360	294	404	2,338	43.73	5.45	7.49	43.33
Slovenia	819	101	142	960	40.49	5.00	7.03	47.48
Ukraine	21,975	4,114	5,091	14,695	47.90	8.97	11.10	32.03

Source: *Euromonitor International from national statistics/UN*

Population Statistics

Table 21.19

Population by Educational Attainment 2009

'000 / % analysis

	Primary	Secondary	Higher	No Education	Other/ Unknown	Primary (% analysis)	Secondary (% analysis)	Higher (% analysis)	No Education (% analysis)	Other/ Unknown (% analysis)
Western Europe										
Austria	1,235	4,249	1,627	0	0	17.37	59.75	22.88	0.00	0.00
Belgium	1,421	5,192	2,191	56	0	16.04	58.59	24.73	0.63	0.00
Cyprus										
Denmark	673	2,601	1,070	0	160	14.95	57.75	23.76	0.00	3.54
Finland	717	2,534	1,184	0	0	16.17	57.14	26.69	0.00	0.00
France	7,471	29,233	11,128	273	2,872	14.66	57.35	21.83	0.54	5.63
Germany	8,918	42,927	17,866	0	1,159	12.58	60.57	25.21	0.00	1.64
Gibraltar										
Greece	2,225	5,545	1,747	133	0	23.05	57.46	18.11	1.38	0.00
Iceland										
Ireland	559	2,053	743	14	172	15.80	57.97	20.99	0.39	4.86
Italy	8,926	33,732	5,640	2,521						
Liechtenstein										
Luxembourg										
Malta										
Monaco										
Netherlands	1,494	8,405	3,600	0	0	11.07	62.27	26.67	0.00	0.00
Norway	372	2,506	910	0	99	9.58	64.48	23.41	0.00	2.54
Portugal	2,154	4,753	1,657	460	0	23.87	52.67	18.36	5.10	0.00
Spain	6,928	21,693	7,458	547	2,164	17.86	55.92	19.23	1.41	5.58
Sweden	709	4,533	2,325	0	115	9.23	59.01	30.27	0.00	1.50
Switzerland	828	3,855	1,721	0	0	12.92	60.20	26.88	0.00	0.00
Turkey	26,524	18,758	4,612	4,976	10	48.33	34.18	8.40	9.07	0.02
United Kingdom	6,522	29,175	14,814	319	0	12.83	57.40	29.14	0.63	0.00
Eastern Europe										
Albania										
Belarus	1,530	5,104	1,225	395	0	18.54	61.84	14.84	4.78	0.00
Bosnia-Herzegovina										
Bulgaria	1,492	4,222	750	69	0	22.83	64.63	11.48	1.06	0.00
Croatia	599	2,574	500	56	18	15.99	68.68	13.35	1.49	0.48
Czech Republic	1,330	6,113	1,276	41	121	14.97	68.83	14.37	0.46	1.36
Estonia	136	813	179	5	0	12.00	71.79	15.77	0.44	0.00
Georgia	843	1,555	873		373					
Hungary	1,424	5,848	1,199	56	0	16.70	68.59	14.06	0.65	0.00
Latvia	299	1,332	295	21	0	15.34	68.44	15.15	1.06	0.01
Lithuania	370	2,013	441	24	0	12.98	70.69	15.50	0.84	0.00
Macedonia	590	642	192	252						
Moldova										
Montenegro	149	260	68	19	11	29.37	51.34	13.36	3.68	2.25
Poland	5,346	21,799	4,484	207	410	16.58	67.60	13.91	0.64	1.27
Romania	4,030	11,882	1,860	387	9	22.18	65.40	10.24	2.13	0.05
Russia	21,841	74,645	18,008	6,267	0	18.09	61.81	14.91	5.19	0.00
Serbia	2,305	2,738	732	244	10	38.24	45.42	12.14	4.05	0.16
Slovakia	727	3,144	616	19	57	15.93	68.90	13.50	0.41	1.25
Slovenia	210	1,248	274	11	0	12.02	71.60	15.73	0.65	0.00
Ukraine	9,200	23,359	4,934	2,025	0	23.28	59.11	12.48	5.12	0.00

Source: Euromonitor International from national statistics/UN

Population Statistics

Table 21.20

Male and Female Population by Age at January 1st 2009

'000

	Males			Females		
	0-14	**15-64**	**65+**	**0-14**	**15-64**	**65+**
Western Europe						
Austria	651	2,832	599	621	2,822	857
Belgium	925	3,570	772	885	3,530	1,068
Cyprus	80	294	50	76	309	63
Denmark	516	1,831	385	492	1,797	491
Finland	455	1,789	365	436	1,752	528
France	5,845	20,105	4,284	5,627	20,490	6,098
Germany	5,713	27,416	7,069	5,420	26,755	9,629
Gibraltar						
Greece	825	3,820	923	777	3,737	1,170
Iceland	34	114	17	32	105	20
Ireland	477	1,518	220	454	1,509	272
Italy	4,330	19,744	5,084	4,091	19,777	7,028
Liechtenstein						
Luxembourg	44	168	29	42	164	39
Malta	33	146	25	31	141	34
Monaco						
Netherlands	1,491	5,561	1,065	1,420	5,482	1,391
Norway	467	1,624	304	445	1,558	401
Portugal	847	3,540	782	799	3,614	1,089
Spain	3,460	15,728	3,272	3,271	15,354	4,436
Sweden	779	3,063	727	740	2,973	919
Switzerland	592	2,567	535	563	2,572	730
Turkey	9,647	24,115	2,139	9,142	23,720	2,754
United Kingdom	5,517	20,361	4,362	5,264	20,482	5,626
Eastern Europe						
Albania	384	1,040	133	359	1,071	167
Belarus	729	3,349	434	689	3,549	922
Bosnia-Herzegovina	305	1,317	228	286	1,405	304
Bulgaria	506	2,596	540	480	2,619	779
Croatia	348	1,486	298	332	1,493	471
Czech Republic	760	3,757	620	720	3,675	936
Estonia	102	436	75	96	471	151
Georgia	394	1,438	248	348	1,575	382
Hungary	767	3,392	595	728	3,504	1,034
Latvia	157	753	128	150	803	262
Lithuania	257	1,118	183	244	1,193	353
Macedonia	189	726	103	175	711	137
Moldova	309	1,256	147	299	1,340	253
Montenegro	62	201	38	59	216	52
Poland	2,990	13,485	1,940	2,839	13,675	3,206
Romania	1,676	7,474	1,284	1,591	7,532	1,879
Russia	10,839	48,857	5,945	10,304	53,071	12,887
Serbia	680	2,446	444	658	2,524	615
Slovakia	427	1,951	243	406	1,961	408
Slovenia	144	721	129	136	690	202
Ukraine	3,325	15,410	2,450	3,151	16,760	4,867

Source: *Euromonitor International from national statistics/UN*

Population Statistics

Table 21.21

Male Population at January 1st 1990-2009
'000

	1990	1995	2000	2004	2005	2007	2008	2009
Western Europe								
Austria	3,655	3,831	3,868	3,950	3,986	4,045	4,065	4,082
Belgium	4,860	4,955	5,006	5,087	5,111	5,181	5,224	5,268
Cyprus	339	365	387	403	407	415	420	424
Denmark	2,531	2,573	2,634	2,670	2,677	2,697	2,713	2,732
Finland	2,413	2,482	2,523	2,553	2,562	2,584	2,597	2,610
France	27,544	28,078	28,579	29,379	29,555	29,907	30,064	30,234
Germany	38,110	39,645	40,091	40,356	40,354	40,301	40,274	40,198
Gibraltar	14	14	14	14	15	15	15	15
Greece	4,982	5,243	5,400	5,464	5,487	5,529	5,549	5,568
Iceland	128	134	141	146	148	156	161	165
Ireland	1,743	1,787	1,877	2,003	2,047	2,158	2,196	2,215
Italy	27,528	27,569	27,563	28,069	28,377	28,718	28,950	29,158
Liechtenstein	14	15	16	17	17	17	17	18
Luxembourg	187	200	215	227	230	235	238	241
Malta	178	187	193	199	200	202	203	204
Monaco	14	15	15	15	15	16	16	16
Netherlands	7,358	7,627	7,846	8,046	8,066	8,089	8,103	8,117
Norway	2,093	2,150	2,217	2,269	2,284	2,326	2,360	2,395
Portugal	4,819	4,827	4,918	5,066	5,094	5,136	5,154	5,168
Spain	19,025	19,269	19,607	20,802	21,173	21,930	22,222	22,460
Sweden	4,212	4,356	4,380	4,447	4,466	4,521	4,544	4,568
Switzerland	3,258	3,428	3,501	3,602	3,629	3,669	3,683	3,695
Turkey	27,539	29,816	32,024	33,716	34,128	34,940	35,377	35,901
United Kingdom	27,774	28,156	28,634	29,193	29,395	29,818	30,003	30,240
Eastern Europe								
Albania	1,687	1,579	1,525	1,534	1,539	1,548	1,552	1,557
Belarus	4,777	4,780	4,703	4,610	4,583	4,535	4,522	4,512
Bosnia-Herzegovina	2,223	1,708	1,809	1,847	1,849	1,849	1,849	1,850
Bulgaria	4,324	4,069	3,888	3,780	3,752	3,695	3,669	3,642
Croatia	2,315	2,244	2,138	2,138	2,139	2,138	2,136	2,133
Czech Republic	4,998	5,013	4,981	4,975	4,981	5,026	5,083	5,136
Estonia	735	671	633	622	621	617	614	612
Georgia	2,440	2,268	2,093	2,032	2,037	2,080	2,078	2,081
Hungary	4,985	4,942	4,865	4,804	4,793	4,774	4,764	4,754
Latvia	1,241	1,154	1,097	1,068	1,063	1,051	1,044	1,038
Lithuania	1,747	1,717	1,644	1,609	1,598	1,577	1,567	1,558
Macedonia	958	983	1,004	1,014	1,015	1,017	1,017	1,018
Moldova	2,080	2,073	1,959	1,819	1,789	1,743	1,726	1,712
Montenegro	305	308	308	304	303	301	301	301
Poland	18,516	18,602	18,550	18,486	18,470	18,427	18,412	18,415
Romania	11,451	10,938	10,724	10,592	10,562	10,499	10,467	10,434
Russia	69,115	69,659	68,698	67,024	66,603	65,849	65,717	65,642
Serbia	3,715	3,691	3,666	3,625	3,612	3,590	3,579	3,570
Slovakia	2,578	2,605	2,614	2,611	2,613	2,618	2,619	2,621
Slovenia	968	964	971	977	977	986	990	994
Ukraine	23,826	23,793	22,755	21,928	21,755	21,435	21,298	21,185

Source: *Euromonitor International from national statistics/UN*

Population Statistics   **Table 21.22**

Female Population at January 1st 1990-2009
'000

	1990	1995	2000	2004	2005	2007	2008	2009
Western Europe								
Austria	3,990	4,112	4,134	4,190	4,220	4,269	4,287	4,301
Belgium	5,088	5,176	5,233	5,309	5,335	5,403	5,443	5,482
Cyprus	341	366	399	424	429	439	443	447
Denmark	2,605	2,642	2,696	2,728	2,734	2,750	2,763	2,779
Finland	2,562	2,617	2,648	2,667	2,675	2,693	2,704	2,716
France	29,033	29,674	30,270	31,083	31,270	31,631	32,042	32,215
Germany	41,003	41,894	42,073	42,176	42,147	42,014	41,944	41,804
Gibraltar	13	14	14	14	15	15	15	15
Greece	5,139	5,352	5,504	5,576	5,596	5,640	5,663	5,684
Iceland	127	133	140	145	147	152	155	157
Ireland	1,764	1,810	1,901	2,025	2,062	2,155	2,205	2,235
Italy	29,167	29,275	29,361	29,820	30,086	30,413	30,670	30,896
Liechtenstein	15	16	17	17	18	18	18	18
Luxembourg	195	208	222	232	235	240	242	245
Malta	182	191	196	201	203	204	205	205
Monaco	16	17	17	17	17	17	17	17
Netherlands	7,534	7,797	8,018	8,212	8,240	8,269	8,281	8,293
Norway	2,140	2,198	2,261	2,308	2,322	2,355	2,377	2,404
Portugal	5,177	5,191	5,277	5,408	5,435	5,473	5,489	5,502
Spain	19,802	20,075	20,443	21,543	21,865	22,555	22,835	23,061
Sweden	4,315	4,460	4,481	4,529	4,545	4,592	4,613	4,633
Switzerland	3,416	3,591	3,664	3,763	3,786	3,828	3,848	3,865
Turkey	27,136	29,458	31,717	33,472	33,901	34,749	35,210	35,616
United Kingdom	29,383	29,787	30,151	30,507	30,665	30,999	31,183	31,372
Eastern Europe								
Albania	1,602	1,555	1,543	1,564	1,571	1,584	1,591	1,598
Belarus	5,411	5,431	5,316	5,239	5,217	5,179	5,168	5,160
Bosnia-Herzegovina	2,276	1,815	1,944	1,991	1,994	1,995	1,994	1,995
Bulgaria	4,444	4,234	4,091	3,999	3,976	3,928	3,903	3,877
Croatia	2,463	2,425	2,304	2,304	2,305	2,302	2,299	2,296
Czech Republic	5,302	5,304	5,256	5,237	5,240	5,261	5,298	5,331
Estonia	836	777	739	729	727	723	721	718
Georgia	2,706	2,527	2,342	2,283	2,285	2,315	2,304	2,305
Hungary	5,390	5,395	5,356	5,313	5,304	5,284	5,275	5,265
Latvia	1,428	1,346	1,285	1,251	1,244	1,230	1,222	1,215
Lithuania	1,946	1,926	1,868	1,837	1,827	1,808	1,799	1,790
Macedonia	951	981	1,005	1,017	1,019	1,022	1,023	1,023
Moldova	2,284	2,266	2,142	2,001	1,971	1,924	1,907	1,892
Montenegro	286	292	306	318	320	324	326	327
Poland	19,472	19,663	19,713	19,704	19,704	19,699	19,704	19,721
Romania	11,761	11,347	11,205	11,119	11,097	11,056	11,030	11,001
Russia	78,550	78,801	78,192	77,144	76,871	76,372	76,292	76,262
Serbia	3,870	3,869	3,864	3,838	3,829	3,812	3,805	3,798
Slovakia	2,692	2,743	2,764	2,769	2,771	2,774	2,774	2,775
Slovenia	1,028	1,025	1,017	1,020	1,021	1,024	1,026	1,029
Ukraine	27,730	27,508	26,360	25,515	25,347	25,031	24,895	24,778

Source: Euromonitor International from national statistics/UN

Population Statistics

Table 21.23

Children Aged 0-14 Years at January 1st 1990-2009
'000

	1990	1995	2000	2004	2005	2007	2008	2009
Western Europe								
Austria	1,340	1,417	1,372	1,329	1,323	1,300	1,287	1,272
Belgium	1,801	1,827	1,805	1,797	1,795	1,798	1,800	1,810
Cyprus	176	184	178	168	166	160	157	155
Denmark	881	901	981	1,018	1,018	1,014	1,010	1,008
Finland	962	972	943	920	915	901	895	891
France	11,389	11,330	11,101	11,210	11,223	11,295	11,380	11,472
Germany	12,639	13,294	12,897	12,162	11,925	11,441	11,282	11,133
Gibraltar	5	5	5	5	5	5	5	5
Greece	1,984	1,850	1,682	1,599	1,598	1,594	1,596	1,602
Iceland	64	65	65	65	65	66	66	66
Ireland	959	883	829	841	851	879	905	931
Italy	9,522	8,402	8,150	8,190	8,256	8,322	8,366	8,421
Liechtenstein	6	6	6	6	6	6	6	6
Luxembourg	66	74	82	85	86	86	86	87
Malta	85	83	78	72	70	67	65	64
Monaco	4	4	4	4	4	4	5	5
Netherlands	2,715	2,838	2,946	3,016	3,009	2,959	2,934	2,911
Norway	801	845	895	911	909	906	907	912
Portugal	2,081	1,796	1,655	1,649	1,647	1,643	1,644	1,645
Spain	7,856	6,657	5,965	6,151	6,241	6,481	6,610	6,731
Sweden	1,522	1,663	1,640	1,599	1,584	1,546	1,529	1,519
Switzerland	1,137	1,237	1,249	1,214	1,205	1,181	1,167	1,156
Turkey	18,004	18,588	18,619	18,699	18,653	18,698	18,642	18,789
United Kingdom	10,833	11,292	11,244	10,892	10,848	10,716	10,740	10,781
Eastern Europe								
Albania	1,078	997	932	846	823	781	761	743
Belarus	2,351	2,252	1,898	1,595	1,530	1,444	1,422	1,418
Bosnia-Herzegovina	1,090	777	743	661	639	608	599	591
Bulgaria	1,801	1,506	1,267	1,102	1,069	1,018	1,000	986
Croatia	952	858	760	723	712	693	687	680
Czech Republic	2,239	1,945	1,700	1,554	1,527	1,480	1,477	1,480
Estonia	350	302	251	216	208	199	197	198
Georgia	1,267	1,157	972	826	801	771	753	742
Hungary	2,131	1,892	1,729	1,606	1,580	1,529	1,510	1,494
Latvia	572	522	428	357	341	318	310	307
Lithuania	834	798	710	609	585	538	516	501
Macedonia	499	483	444	410	401	382	373	364
Moldova	1,218	1,154	974	760	715	647	624	607
Montenegro	155	142	134	125	122	121	121	121
Poland	9,600	8,849	7,480	6,580	6,377	6,022	5,901	5,829
Romania	5,508	4,694	4,126	3,566	3,437	3,319	3,285	3,267
Russia	34,031	32,050	27,066	22,613	21,871	20,881	20,824	21,143
Serbia	1,761	1,648	1,499	1,397	1,379	1,352	1,344	1,338
Slovakia	1,341	1,224	1,065	944	919	871	851	832
Slovenia	418	369	320	292	287	281	280	280
Ukraine	11,084	10,529	8,781	7,247	6,990	6,606	6,501	6,476

Source: Euromonitor International from national statistics/UN

Population Statistics

Table 21.24

Persons of Working Age (15-64 Years) at January 1st 1990-2009
'000

	1990	1995	2000	2004	2005	2007	2008	2009
Western Europe								
Austria	5,165	5,330	5,397	5,547	5,572	5,610	5,634	5,655
Belgium	6,673	6,707	6,719	6,819	6,851	6,977	7,047	7,100
Cyprus	431	468	519	559	569	587	595	603
Denmark	3,454	3,516	3,558	3,575	3,581	3,598	3,613	3,628
Finland	3,350	3,407	3,461	3,486	3,491	3,507	3,531	3,542
France	37,317	37,736	38,327	39,380	39,611	40,132	40,470	40,595
Germany	54,680	55,702	55,915	55,510	55,209	54,574	54,417	54,171
Gibraltar	18	18	18	19	19	19	19	19
Greece	6,781	7,197	7,432	7,471	7,478	7,506	7,531	7,557
Iceland	164	172	183	192	196	206	213	219
Ireland	2,148	2,304	2,525	2,738	2,800	2,965	3,017	3,027
Italy	38,820	39,072	38,462	38,569	38,827	39,017	39,300	39,521
Liechtenstein	20	21	23	24	25	25	25	25
Luxembourg	264	277	293	308	313	322	327	331
Malta	238	251	263	276	279	284	285	286
Monaco	20	20	21	21	21	21	21	21
Netherlands	10,272	10,552	10,766	10,991	11,008	11,031	11,042	11,043
Norway	2,741	2,809	2,901	2,993	3,019	3,090	3,136	3,182
Portugal	6,593	6,747	6,905	7,064	7,091	7,140	7,152	7,154
Spain	25,755	26,740	27,379	29,050	29,569	30,558	30,864	31,081
Sweden	5,488	5,614	5,689	5,835	5,873	5,984	6,017	6,036
Switzerland	4,565	4,750	4,821	4,994	5,035	5,103	5,125	5,139
Turkey	32,954	36,263	40,137	43,576	44,388	46,028	46,944	47,835
United Kingdom	37,340	37,477	38,248	39,280	39,595	40,381	40,599	40,844
Eastern Europe								
Albania	2,036	1,938	1,908	1,991	2,017	2,066	2,089	2,112
Belarus	6,764	6,712	6,790	6,846	6,850	6,851	6,867	6,898
Bosnia-Herzegovina	3,135	2,459	2,595	2,675	2,689	2,708	2,715	2,722
Bulgaria	5,830	5,564	5,421	5,346	5,334	5,287	5,253	5,215
Croatia	3,276	3,175	2,984	2,986	2,988	2,988	2,980	2,980
Czech Republic	6,777	7,018	7,124	7,234	7,259	7,325	7,391	7,431
Estonia	1,039	953	916	917	917	912	909	907
Georgia	3,396	3,101	2,907	2,881	2,903	2,990	2,998	3,014
Hungary	6,870	6,987	6,961	6,944	6,940	6,928	6,912	6,896
Latvia	1,781	1,642	1,600	1,587	1,584	1,573	1,566	1,557
Lithuania	2,461	2,402	2,319	2,319	2,323	2,319	2,317	2,311
Macedonia	1,268	1,309	1,363	1,399	1,407	1,423	1,431	1,437
Moldova	2,784	2,794	2,723	2,644	2,629	2,611	2,604	2,596
Montenegro	387	405	419	417	416	416	416	416
Poland	24,607	25,230	26,164	26,659	26,778	26,987	27,083	27,160
Romania	15,319	14,912	14,873	15,012	15,047	15,038	15,025	15,005
Russia	99,056	99,008	101,761	102,264	101,916	101,386	101,596	101,928
Serbia	5,097	5,031	5,005	4,974	4,969	4,969	4,971	4,970
Slovakia	3,387	3,547	3,700	3,815	3,840	3,882	3,897	3,912
Slovenia	1,367	1,381	1,392	1,405	1,404	1,411	1,411	1,411
Ukraine	34,298	33,811	33,515	32,827	32,604	32,256	32,184	32,170

Source: Euromonitor International from national statistics/UN

Population Statistics

Table 21.25

Persons Aged 65 Years and over at January 1st 1990-2009
'000

	1990	1995	2000	2004	2005	2007	2008	2009
Western Europe								
Austria	1,140	1,197	1,234	1,264	1,312	1,404	1,431	1,456
Belgium	1,474	1,597	1,715	1,780	1,800	1,810	1,820	1,840
Cyprus	74	79	89	99	102	107	110	113
Denmark	800	799	790	805	813	835	853	875
Finland	662	720	767	813	831	869	875	893
France	7,872	8,686	9,422	9,871	9,991	10,111	10,256	10,382
Germany	11,794	12,542	13,351	14,860	15,367	16,299	16,519	16,699
Gibraltar	3	4	4	5	5	5	5	5
Greece	1,356	1,548	1,790	1,971	2,007	2,069	2,084	2,093
Iceland	27	30	33	34	35	36	37	38
Ireland	399	411	424	449	458	469	479	492
Italy	8,352	9,371	10,312	11,128	11,379	11,793	11,953	12,111
Liechtenstein	3	3	3	4	4	4	4	4
Luxembourg	51	57	62	65	66	67	67	68
Malta	38	43	48	52	53	56	57	59
Monaco	7	7	7	7	7	7	7	7
Netherlands	1,906	2,034	2,152	2,251	2,289	2,368	2,406	2,456
Norway	691	695	683	674	678	686	693	705
Portugal	1,322	1,475	1,635	1,761	1,791	1,826	1,847	1,871
Spain	5,215	5,946	6,706	7,144	7,228	7,445	7,583	7,709
Sweden	1,518	1,540	1,533	1,541	1,554	1,583	1,611	1,646
Switzerland	972	1,032	1,094	1,157	1,174	1,213	1,239	1,265
Turkey	3,717	4,423	4,985	4,913	4,987	4,964	5,000	4,893
United Kingdom	8,984	9,175	9,293	9,528	9,617	9,720	9,847	9,987
Eastern Europe								
Albania	175	199	228	262	271	286	293	301
Belarus	1,074	1,247	1,332	1,407	1,420	1,420	1,400	1,356
Bosnia-Herzegovina	274	287	415	501	514	528	530	532
Bulgaria	1,136	1,233	1,290	1,330	1,325	1,318	1,318	1,319
Croatia	550	636	697	733	745	759	767	769
Czech Republic	1,285	1,354	1,412	1,423	1,435	1,482	1,513	1,556
Estonia	182	193	205	219	222	228	229	226
Georgia	482	537	557	607	618	634	631	630
Hungary	1,374	1,458	1,531	1,567	1,578	1,601	1,618	1,629
Latvia	315	336	353	375	381	390	391	390
Lithuania	399	443	483	518	517	528	534	537
Macedonia	142	171	202	222	226	233	237	240
Moldova	362	391	403	415	415	409	405	400
Montenegro	49	53	59	80	85	89	90	90
Poland	3,781	4,186	4,619	4,951	5,018	5,117	5,131	5,146
Romania	2,383	2,679	2,930	3,133	3,175	3,198	3,186	3,163
Russia	14,578	17,402	18,063	19,291	19,687	19,954	19,589	18,832
Serbia	727	880	1,026	1,092	1,094	1,081	1,070	1,059
Slovakia	541	578	613	620	626	639	645	651
Slovenia	212	240	275	300	306	319	325	332
Ukraine	6,175	6,961	6,819	7,369	7,508	7,603	7,507	7,317

Source: Euromonitor International from national statistics/UN

Population Statistics   **Table 21.26**

Population by Age Group at January 1st 2009
'000

	0-4	5-9	10-14	15-19	20-24	25-29	30-34	35-39
Western Europe								
Austria	399.9	411.1	461.2	505.9	517.5	551.4	536.9	629.6
Belgium	612.9	591.0	606.1	654.1	649.8	689.4	687.5	756.0
Cyprus	49.2	49.7	56.1	65.7	67.6	68.5	63.7	59.4
Denmark	326.9	331.1	350.1	342.9	315.7	315.1	362.1	386.2
Finland	294.7	286.8	309.3	333.1	324.6	339.3	333.7	311.8
France	3,917.3	3,869.2	3,685.7	3,831.4	3,949.9	4,008.6	3,892.3	4,402.7
Germany	3,441.3	3,717.0	3,974.5	4,475.1	4,920.0	5,010.2	4,718.5	5,618.8
Gibraltar								
Greece	542.7	520.9	538.0	576.0	647.6	804.0	873.0	876.6
Iceland	22.8	21.2	22.3	23.7	23.3	24.5	24.1	23.0
Ireland	338.2	306.9	286.3	279.9	312.1	414.2	370.3	346.5
Italy	2,832.0	2,806.0	2,783.0	2,972.8	3,107.4	3,559.3	4,367.8	4,825.0
Liechtenstein								
Luxembourg	27.5	28.5	30.5	30.1	29.5	31.0	34.3	38.5
Malta	18.5	20.7	24.5	27.1	29.8	31.5	31.5	27.8
Monaco								
Netherlands	923.9	1,008.2	979.0	1,007.7	984.6	979.3	998.0	1,229.9
Norway	298.5	298.9	314.8	319.2	294.7	302.6	319.8	361.8
Portugal	544.8	561.1	539.5	573.6	628.2	760.6	850.5	814.0
Spain	2,414.2	2,236.4	2,080.0	2,237.5	2,622.3	3,452.3	4,019.5	3,869.5
Sweden	518.2	485.7	515.0	638.6	571.6	549.7	578.3	622.7
Switzerland	365.2	375.6	414.9	451.2	453.1	477.6	500.4	564.1
Turkey	5,998.3	6,318.1	6,472.2	6,185.1	6,256.6	6,518.8	5,810.1	5,330.5
United Kingdom	3,746.5	3,397.4	3,637.2	3,974.5	4,288.9	4,156.6	3,817.3	4,379.8
Eastern Europe								
Albania	219.5	229.1	294.4	309.6	294.7	245.7	194.7	190.9
Belarus	485.5	451.5	481.2	665.9	831.9	783.2	697.5	672.6
Bosnia-Herzegovina	172.4	194.8	223.6	244.9	302.1	292.2	275.9	276.0
Bulgaria	333.8	330.4	321.9	440.0	511.8	538.7	580.3	548.4
Croatia	211.7	214.9	253.8	259.9	289.9	314.9	305.1	293.8
Czech Republic	543.2	460.5	476.4	637.2	707.5	784.6	942.5	794.2
Estonia	72.1	63.2	62.4	89.5	106.3	99.4	92.1	92.6
Georgia	255.1	224.9	261.8	358.8	365.1	312.9	291.5	279.4
Hungary	489.2	480.9	524.2	611.4	650.0	729.5	866.1	723.8
Latvia	108.8	98.8	98.9	155.7	184.4	168.2	157.2	159.0
Lithuania	151.8	159.0	189.8	253.7	270.8	236.8	220.2	241.4
Macedonia	110.6	119.9	133.3	155.1	159.4	163.6	157.7	149.0
Moldova	207.9	177.6	221.8	312.9	353.6	287.5	239.9	218.9
Montenegro	41.0	40.0	40.2	43.3	50.6	47.8	44.1	39.8
Poland	1,888.3	1,816.8	2,124.3	2,620.3	3,076.7	3,236.0	2,979.1	2,549.5
Romania	1,083.8	1,068.8	1,114.4	1,371.4	1,708.2	1,643.2	1,771.4	1,694.4
Russia	7,708.9	6,661.1	6,773.2	9,278.5	12,582.2	11,893.4	10,684.8	9,855.8
Serbia	463.6	438.0	436.6	490.8	537.1	551.4	540.1	515.8
Slovakia	269.1	262.2	301.1	381.0	427.0	457.6	466.8	393.0
Slovenia	93.2	90.8	95.9	109.3	131.9	150.1	153.6	146.0
Ukraine	2,272.3	1,925.3	2,278.4	3,028.5	3,801.5	3,626.7	3,348.6	3,198.7

Source: Euromonitor International from national statistics/UN

Population Statistics

Population by Age Group at January 1st 2009 *(continued)*
'000

	40-44	45-49	50-54	55-59	60-64	65-69	70-74	75-79	80+
Western Europe									
Austria	716.6	682.7	572.0	491.8	450.4	484.4	304.4	275.1	392.3
Belgium	801.4	811.2	753.6	681.5	615.5	461.4	453.2	407.6	517.7
Cyprus	62.1	62.1	59.4	50.2	44.4	36.7	28.5	22.4	25.5
Denmark	424.4	388.7	363.1	351.5	378.1	280.1	211.1	157.5	226.9
Finland	368.1	378.0	381.8	394.9	376.3	255.5	217.7	180.9	238.6
France	4,377.7	4,319.8	4,159.2	4,106.1	3,546.9	2,509.8	2,416.4	2,222.3	3,233.6
Germany	7,050.1	6,887.3	5,899.4	5,364.9	4,226.6	5,137.3	4,511.7	2,994.8	4,054.9
Gibraltar									
Greece	867.2	801.3	763.0	686.4	661.7	540.2	582.8	488.3	482.0
Iceland	22.4	23.2	21.5	18.3	14.9	11.0	8.5	7.8	10.5
Ireland	311.9	291.6	260.5	234.5	205.4	153.7	122.6	94.8	120.5
Italy	4,966.3	4,487.5	3,962.3	3,701.6	3,570.9	3,247.7	2,962.3	2,501.7	3,399.6
Liechtenstein									
Luxembourg	41.8	39.5	33.9	28.9	23.9	19.0	17.0	14.4	17.8
Malta	24.5	28.1	29.8	28.1	28.0	18.6	15.0	11.7	13.6
Monaco									
Netherlands	1,292.2	1,270.1	1,157.0	1,080.1	1,044.1	748.8	602.5	488.4	616.5
Norway	359.8	328.4	315.0	293.1	287.7	198.0	152.6	134.6	219.6
Portugal	788.9	769.0	707.7	661.2	600.2	516.5	492.7	405.5	456.1
Spain	3,660.3	3,357.3	2,924.1	2,561.9	2,376.5	1,947.2	1,848.8	1,697.7	2,214.9
Sweden	672.8	599.0	583.1	587.8	632.5	484.1	365.9	305.7	490.6
Switzerland	635.8	604.8	528.1	472.7	450.9	364.9	294.3	248.1	358.2
Turkey	4,740.3	4,284.2	3,643.2	2,878.1	2,188.3	1,701.4	1,274.7	1,064.1	853.3
United Kingdom	4,706.5	4,398.1	3,838.1	3,615.8	3,668.2	2,789.1	2,413.7	1,979.0	2,805.5
Eastern Europe									
Albania	204.5	208.6	194.5	146.4	122.1	103.7	86.0	56.7	54.2
Belarus	685.7	804.0	747.7	609.8	399.4	374.0	398.4	300.2	283.4
Bosnia-Herzegovina	290.0	304.9	292.0	255.6	188.0	158.5	167.6	118.2	87.8
Bulgaria	505.3	522.4	533.0	542.6	492.0	389.0	357.1	293.2	279.4
Croatia	313.0	325.3	333.6	310.4	233.7	226.0	215.1	172.6	154.9
Czech Republic	708.0	654.5	731.0	764.4	707.4	506.0	363.3	325.0	361.9
Estonia	86.1	94.3	92.1	85.6	68.4	66.5	60.9	48.2	50.8
Georgia	293.3	343.4	313.6	262.8	192.9	169.2	203.5	130.3	127.0
Hungary	651.3	611.6	759.8	708.9	584.0	505.0	404.4	338.0	381.5
Latvia	154.0	169.7	157.6	138.0	113.1	121.6	103.8	80.0	84.7
Lithuania	246.6	266.5	223.9	193.7	157.1	162.4	142.5	115.9	116.0
Macedonia	146.5	143.3	139.0	126.2	97.4	80.7	68.1	50.1	41.0
Moldova	228.7	276.2	274.6	240.5	162.8	125.0	122.0	82.2	71.2
Montenegro	39.0	41.8	42.9	38.2	29.0	24.7	26.6	19.4	19.6
Poland	2,348.6	2,638.9	3,023.0	2,755.2	1,932.7	1,412.9	1,375.7	1,157.4	1,200.2
Romania	1,538.0	1,286.2	1,541.0	1,417.9	1,033.7	928.8	921.0	692.7	619.6
Russia	9,401.6	11,677.1	11,187.0	9,593.7	5,774.3	5,473.3	5,709.1	3,853.2	3,796.6
Serbia	486.4	472.5	500.6	507.5	368.0	286.5	300.6	251.6	220.0
Slovakia	366.2	378.6	402.0	368.7	270.8	209.6	162.1	136.3	143.2
Slovenia	155.9	155.2	156.6	146.9	105.9	100.4	85.0	71.2	75.0
Ukraine	3,081.4	3,588.5	3,366.2	3,074.5	2,055.0	2,241.6	2,213.9	1,368.6	1,493.1

Source: Euromonitor International from national statistics/UN

Population Statistics   **Table 21.27**

Population by Age Group (%) at January 1st 2009
% of total

	0-4	5-9	10-14	15-19	20-24	25-29	30-34	35-39
Western Europe								
Austria	4.77	4.90	5.50	6.03	6.17	6.58	6.40	7.51
Belgium	5.70	5.50	5.64	6.08	6.04	6.41	6.40	7.03
Cyprus	5.65	5.71	6.44	7.55	7.76	7.86	7.31	6.81
Denmark	5.93	6.01	6.35	6.22	5.73	5.72	6.57	7.01
Finland	5.53	5.39	5.81	6.26	6.10	6.37	6.27	5.86
France	6.27	6.20	5.90	6.14	6.33	6.42	6.23	7.05
Germany	4.20	4.53	4.85	5.46	6.00	6.11	5.75	6.85
Gibraltar								
Greece	4.82	4.63	4.78	5.12	5.76	7.15	7.76	7.79
Iceland	7.07	6.58	6.91	7.33	7.21	7.58	7.46	7.11
Ireland	7.60	6.90	6.43	6.29	7.01	9.31	8.32	7.79
Italy	4.72	4.67	4.63	4.95	5.17	5.93	7.27	8.03
Liechtenstein								
Luxembourg	5.65	5.87	6.28	6.19	6.06	6.38	7.06	7.92
Malta	4.52	5.07	6.00	6.62	7.29	7.72	7.72	6.80
Monaco								
Netherlands	5.63	6.14	5.97	6.14	6.00	5.97	6.08	7.49
Norway	6.22	6.23	6.56	6.65	6.14	6.30	6.66	7.54
Portugal	5.11	5.26	5.06	5.38	5.89	7.13	7.97	7.63
Spain	5.30	4.91	4.57	4.92	5.76	7.58	8.83	8.50
Sweden	5.63	5.28	5.60	6.94	6.21	5.97	6.28	6.77
Switzerland	4.83	4.97	5.49	5.97	5.99	6.32	6.62	7.46
Turkey	8.39	8.83	9.05	8.65	8.75	9.12	8.12	7.45
United Kingdom	6.08	5.51	5.90	6.45	6.96	6.75	6.20	7.11
Eastern Europe								
Albania	6.96	7.26	9.33	9.81	9.34	7.79	6.17	6.05
Belarus	5.02	4.67	4.98	6.88	8.60	8.10	7.21	6.95
Bosnia-Herzegovina	4.48	5.07	5.82	6.37	7.86	7.60	7.18	7.18
Bulgaria	4.44	4.39	4.28	5.85	6.81	7.16	7.72	7.29
Croatia	4.78	4.85	5.73	5.87	6.55	7.11	6.89	6.63
Czech Republic	5.19	4.40	4.55	6.09	6.76	7.50	9.00	7.59
Estonia	5.42	4.75	4.69	6.73	7.99	7.47	6.92	6.96
Georgia	5.82	5.13	5.97	8.18	8.33	7.14	6.65	6.37
Hungary	4.88	4.80	5.23	6.10	6.49	7.28	8.64	7.22
Latvia	4.83	4.38	4.39	6.91	8.18	7.46	6.98	7.05
Lithuania	4.53	4.75	5.67	7.58	8.09	7.07	6.58	7.21
Macedonia	5.42	5.87	6.53	7.60	7.81	8.02	7.73	7.30
Moldova	5.77	4.93	6.16	8.68	9.81	7.98	6.66	6.07
Montenegro	6.53	6.37	6.40	6.90	8.06	7.61	7.01	6.34
Poland	4.95	4.76	5.57	6.87	8.07	8.49	7.81	6.69
Romania	5.06	4.99	5.20	6.40	7.97	7.67	8.26	7.90
Russia	5.43	4.69	4.77	6.54	8.87	8.38	7.53	6.95
Serbia	6.29	5.95	5.93	6.66	7.29	7.48	7.33	7.00
Slovakia	4.99	4.86	5.58	7.06	7.91	8.48	8.65	7.28
Slovenia	4.61	4.49	4.74	5.40	6.52	7.42	7.60	7.22
Ukraine	4.94	4.19	4.96	6.59	8.27	7.89	7.29	6.96

Source: Euromonitor International from national statistics/UN

Population Statistics

Population by Age Group (%) at January 1st 2009 *(continued)*
% of total

	40-44	45-49	50-54	55-59	60-64	65-69	70-74	75-79	80+
Western Europe									
Austria	8.55	8.14	6.82	5.87	5.37	5.78	3.63	3.28	4.68
Belgium	7.46	7.55	7.01	6.34	5.73	4.29	4.22	3.79	4.82
Cyprus	7.13	7.13	6.82	5.76	5.09	4.21	3.27	2.57	2.93
Denmark	7.70	7.05	6.59	6.38	6.86	5.08	3.83	2.86	4.12
Finland	6.91	7.10	7.17	7.42	7.07	4.80	4.09	3.40	4.48
France	7.01	6.92	6.66	6.58	5.68	4.02	3.87	3.56	5.18
Germany	8.60	8.40	7.19	6.54	5.15	6.26	5.50	3.65	4.94
Gibraltar									
Greece	7.71	7.12	6.78	6.10	5.88	4.80	5.18	4.34	4.28
Iceland	6.93	7.18	6.66	5.66	4.61	3.40	2.64	2.42	3.26
Ireland	7.01	6.55	5.85	5.27	4.62	3.45	2.75	2.13	2.71
Italy	8.27	7.47	6.60	6.16	5.95	5.41	4.93	4.17	5.66
Liechtenstein									
Luxembourg	8.61	8.12	6.98	5.94	4.92	3.90	3.49	2.96	3.67
Malta	6.00	6.88	7.28	6.88	6.85	4.55	3.66	2.85	3.32
Monaco									
Netherlands	7.87	7.74	7.05	6.58	6.36	4.56	3.67	2.98	3.76
Norway	7.50	6.84	6.56	6.11	5.99	4.12	3.18	2.80	4.58
Portugal	7.39	7.21	6.63	6.20	5.62	4.84	4.62	3.80	4.27
Spain	8.04	7.38	6.42	5.63	5.22	4.28	4.06	3.73	4.87
Sweden	7.31	6.51	6.34	6.39	6.87	5.26	3.98	3.32	5.33
Switzerland	8.41	8.00	6.99	6.25	5.96	4.83	3.89	3.28	4.74
Turkey	6.63	5.99	5.09	4.02	3.06	2.38	1.78	1.49	1.19
United Kingdom	7.64	7.14	6.23	5.87	5.95	4.53	3.92	3.21	4.55
Eastern Europe									
Albania	6.48	6.61	6.16	4.64	3.87	3.29	2.73	1.80	1.72
Belarus	7.09	8.31	7.73	6.30	4.13	3.87	4.12	3.10	2.93
Bosnia-Herzegovina	7.54	7.93	7.60	6.65	4.89	4.12	4.36	3.08	2.28
Bulgaria	6.72	6.95	7.09	7.22	6.54	5.17	4.75	3.90	3.72
Croatia	7.07	7.35	7.53	7.01	5.28	5.10	4.86	3.90	3.50
Czech Republic	6.76	6.25	6.98	7.30	6.76	4.83	3.47	3.10	3.46
Estonia	6.47	7.09	6.92	6.44	5.14	5.00	4.58	3.62	3.82
Georgia	6.69	7.83	7.15	5.99	4.40	3.86	4.64	2.97	2.90
Hungary	6.50	6.10	7.58	7.07	5.83	5.04	4.04	3.37	3.81
Latvia	6.83	7.53	6.99	6.12	5.02	5.40	4.61	3.55	3.76
Lithuania	7.37	7.96	6.69	5.79	4.69	4.85	4.26	3.46	3.46
Macedonia	7.18	7.02	6.81	6.18	4.77	3.95	3.34	2.46	2.01
Moldova	6.35	7.67	7.62	6.68	4.52	3.47	3.38	2.28	1.97
Montenegro	6.21	6.66	6.82	6.08	4.62	3.93	4.24	3.08	3.12
Poland	6.16	6.92	7.93	7.22	5.07	3.71	3.61	3.04	3.15
Romania	7.17	6.00	7.19	6.61	4.82	4.33	4.30	3.23	2.89
Russia	6.63	8.23	7.88	6.76	4.07	3.86	4.02	2.72	2.68
Serbia	6.60	6.41	6.80	6.89	4.99	3.89	4.08	3.42	2.99
Slovakia	6.79	7.02	7.45	6.83	5.02	3.89	3.00	2.53	2.65
Slovenia	7.71	7.67	7.74	7.26	5.23	4.96	4.20	3.52	3.71
Ukraine	6.70	7.81	7.32	6.69	4.47	4.88	4.82	2.98	3.25

Source: *Euromonitor International from national statistics/UN*

Population Statistics

Table 21.28

Total Population 2010-2020 at January 1st
'000

	2010	2011	2012	2013	2014	2015	2016	2017	2018	2019	2020
Western Europe											
Austria	8,409	8,434	8,459	8,484	8,507	8,530	8,553	8,574	8,595	8,615	8,634
Belgium	10,827	10,896	10,963	11,029	11,093	11,156	11,217	11,278	11,337	11,396	11,453
Cyprus	880	889	897	906	916	925	934	943	952	961	970
Denmark	5,526	5,541	5,557	5,572	5,587	5,602	5,617	5,633	5,648	5,664	5,681
Finland	5,348	5,369	5,388	5,408	5,426	5,444	5,461	5,477	5,492	5,507	5,520
France	62,772	63,056	63,340	63,618	63,889	64,153	64,411	64,662	64,907	65,146	65,379
Germany	81,722	81,421	81,148	80,884	80,631	80,374	80,110	79,841	79,568	79,288	79,003
Gibraltar	29	29	29	29	29	29	29	29	29	29	29
Greece	11,290	11,325	11,357	11,387	11,414	11,437	11,457	11,473	11,486	11,495	11,501
Iceland	329	335	340	345	349	353	357	361	364	367	370
Ireland	4,456	4,438	4,435	4,442	4,453	4,468	4,484	4,501	4,520	4,538	4,558
Italy	60,401	60,669	60,892	61,081	61,247	61,392	61,523	61,641	61,746	61,842	61,929
Liechtenstein	36	36	37	37	37	38	38	38	38	39	39
Luxembourg	492	497	503	509	514	520	526	532	538	544	550
Malta	410	411	413	414	415	417	418	419	420	421	422
Monaco	33	33	33	33	34	34	34	34	34	34	34
Netherlands	16,439	16,470	16,501	16,531	16,561	16,590	16,619	16,646	16,673	16,700	16,726
Norway	4,858	4,913	4,964	5,013	5,061	5,108	5,156	5,205	5,254	5,303	5,352
Portugal	10,694	10,716	10,736	10,752	10,767	10,779	10,788	10,794	10,798	10,800	10,799
Spain	45,928	46,305	46,673	47,035	47,388	47,732	48,067	48,391	48,700	48,992	49,268
Sweden	9,244	9,288	9,332	9,376	9,421	9,466	9,513	9,561	9,609	9,657	9,706
Switzerland	7,589	7,618	7,647	7,675	7,704	7,732	7,761	7,790	7,819	7,849	7,879
Turkey	72,474	73,312	74,056	74,787	75,505	76,209	76,899	77,573	78,232	78,876	79,503
United Kingdom	61,966	62,260	62,582	62,938	63,325	63,717	64,114	64,514	64,918	65,324	65,730
Eastern Europe											
Albania	3,169	3,185	3,202	3,220	3,238	3,256	3,274	3,291	3,307	3,323	3,338
Belarus	9,653	9,626	9,599	9,572	9,544	9,515	9,486	9,457	9,426	9,395	9,362
Bosnia-Herzegovina	3,844	3,844	3,843	3,841	3,840	3,837	3,833	3,828	3,823	3,816	3,809
Bulgaria	7,467	7,415	7,362	7,306	7,250	7,191	7,131	7,070	7,009	6,947	6,885
Croatia	4,421	4,413	4,404	4,394	4,384	4,374	4,363	4,351	4,340	4,327	4,315
Czech Republic	10,512	10,547	10,582	10,616	10,647	10,674	10,700	10,723	10,743	10,760	10,775
Estonia	1,326	1,322	1,317	1,312	1,307	1,302	1,298	1,293	1,289	1,285	1,282
Georgia	4,389	4,393	4,398	4,403	4,409	4,414	4,418	4,422	4,425	4,428	4,429
Hungary	10,000	9,980	9,954	9,926	9,898	9,871	9,844	9,818	9,793	9,770	9,748
Latvia	2,240	2,228	2,214	2,199	2,185	2,172	2,159	2,146	2,133	2,121	2,110
Lithuania	3,329	3,311	3,292	3,272	3,253	3,234	3,216	3,198	3,181	3,165	3,150
Macedonia	2,041	2,041	2,041	2,040	2,039	2,037	2,035	2,033	2,031	2,028	2,025
Moldova	3,576	3,549	3,525	3,502	3,482	3,462	3,444	3,427	3,411	3,395	3,378
Montenegro	629	630	631	632	633	634	635	636	637	637	638
Poland	38,167	38,189	38,212	38,233	38,253	38,269	38,279	38,284	38,281	38,270	38,248
Romania	21,370	21,302	21,232	21,145	21,056	20,953	20,844	20,733	20,621	20,506	20,389
Russia	141,786	141,467	141,173	140,935	140,724	140,507	140,275	140,026	139,761	139,477	139,170
Serbia	7,351	7,335	7,321	7,307	7,293	7,281	7,268	7,257	7,246	7,235	7,225
Slovakia	5,397	5,398	5,398	5,398	5,398	5,398	5,397	5,396	5,395	5,393	5,390
Slovenia	2,029	2,035	2,039	2,042	2,045	2,048	2,051	2,053	2,056	2,059	2,061
Ukraine	45,783	45,544	45,300	45,063	44,831	44,601	44,377	44,151	43,925	43,698	43,465

Source: Euromonitor International from national statistics/UN

Population Statistics

Table 21.29

Children Aged 0-14 Years Forecasts at January 1st 2010-2020
'000

	2010	2011	2012	2013	2014	2015	2016	2017	2018	2019	2020
Western Europe											
Austria	1,259	1,249	1,238	1,232	1,228	1,228	1,227	1,228	1,227	1,227	1,224
Belgium	1,823	1,837	1,849	1,862	1,877	1,892	1,907	1,923	1,941	1,958	1,972
Cyprus	153	153	152	153	153	154	156	157	159	161	163
Denmark	1,000	992	986	979	974	969	963	960	958	957	956
Finland	887	885	885	887	891	895	900	905	911	915	918
France	11,561	11,616	11,665	11,723	11,769	11,795	11,793	11,794	11,804	11,812	11,819
Germany	10,995	10,833	10,636	10,424	10,239	10,072	9,908	9,778	9,665	9,565	9,466
Gibraltar	5	5	5	5	5	5	5	5	5	5	5
Greece	1,606	1,609	1,615	1,621	1,630	1,637	1,640	1,640	1,638	1,633	1,625
Iceland	67	67	68	68	69	69	70	71	71	72	72
Ireland	942	945	950	956	963	969	975	981	985	989	991
Italy	8,475	8,516	8,546	8,568	8,580	8,582	8,568	8,554	8,535	8,506	8,465
Liechtenstein	6	6	6	6	6	6	6	6	6	6	6
Luxembourg	87	87	87	87	87	87	88	89	90	91	92
Malta	62	61	60	59	58	58	58	57	57	58	58
Monaco	5	5	5	5	5	5	5	5	5	5	5
Netherlands	2,886	2,867	2,847	2,826	2,799	2,771	2,738	2,711	2,686	2,664	2,651
Norway	918	923	926	929	934	939	944	952	962	971	980
Portugal	1,649	1,650	1,650	1,650	1,647	1,636	1,626	1,613	1,596	1,579	1,564
Spain	6,851	6,972	7,091	7,207	7,313	7,401	7,468	7,515	7,550	7,553	7,541
Sweden	1,513	1,516	1,527	1,542	1,559	1,577	1,594	1,611	1,624	1,635	1,645
Switzerland	1,145	1,137	1,128	1,122	1,117	1,115	1,118	1,122	1,128	1,135	1,143
Turkey	18,639	18,542	18,410	18,216	17,999	17,739	17,501	17,301	17,205	17,132	17,032
United Kingdom	10,831	10,867	10,912	10,977	11,071	11,188	11,332	11,491	11,649	11,791	11,919
Eastern Europe											
Albania	726	712	698	688	680	677	677	681	687	693	699
Belarus	1,420	1,428	1,440	1,458	1,470	1,480	1,489	1,498	1,509	1,519	1,526
Bosnia-Herzegovina	582	573	563	552	542	533	526	521	517	514	511
Bulgaria	977	973	970	971	970	961	951	939	927	914	897
Croatia	674	668	659	652	647	644	642	644	646	649	651
Czech Republic	1,493	1,514	1,539	1,563	1,585	1,607	1,626	1,641	1,652	1,661	1,663
Estonia	199	202	204	207	211	214	216	219	221	223	223
Georgia	735	733	735	740	747	754	761	767	771	774	774
Hungary	1,481	1,469	1,462	1,460	1,459	1,461	1,458	1,457	1,455	1,454	1,453
Latvia	306	308	312	317	322	326	329	332	335	336	338
Lithuania	491	482	475	470	465	462	460	461	463	464	465
Macedonia	356	349	343	338	334	329	325	322	318	315	312
Moldova	595	587	584	584	587	591	597	603	609	612	614
Montenegro	122	122	123	123	123	123	123	123	122	122	122
Poland	5,780	5,749	5,730	5,730	5,745	5,766	5,786	5,812	5,840	5,860	5,864
Romania	3,250	3,241	3,234	3,223	3,204	3,183	3,160	3,143	3,128	3,105	3,073
Russia	21,487	21,785	22,175	22,644	23,103	23,598	24,058	24,483	24,788	24,979	25,107
Serbia	1,336	1,336	1,339	1,343	1,347	1,350	1,352	1,352	1,349	1,345	1,339
Slovakia	820	813	807	803	801	799	799	801	804	806	805
Slovenia	280	281	282	283	285	287	289	291	292	294	295
Ukraine	6,482	6,475	6,475	6,508	6,549	6,612	6,677	6,748	6,804	6,836	6,842

Source: *Euromonitor International from national statistics/UN*

Population Statistics

Table 21.30

Persons of Working Age (15-64 Years) Forecasts at January 1st 2010-2020
'000

	2010	2011	2012	2013	2014	2015	2016	2017	2018	2019	2020
Western Europe											
Austria	5,669	5,700	5,718	5,716	5,713	5,711	5,709	5,708	5,706	5,701	5,696
Belgium	7,140	7,174	7,189	7,203	7,215	7,226	7,239	7,250	7,253	7,257	7,260
Cyprus	610	616	622	627	632	636	640	644	648	651	653
Denmark	3,622	3,614	3,601	3,592	3,585	3,582	3,580	3,577	3,573	3,569	3,565
Finland	3,549	3,540	3,521	3,499	3,475	3,453	3,434	3,416	3,397	3,381	3,365
France	40,701	40,808	40,751	40,653	40,560	40,489	40,443	40,424	40,388	40,367	40,336
Germany	53,889	53,843	53,772	53,630	53,429	53,142	52,826	52,491	52,128	51,760	51,367
Gibraltar	19	19	19	19	19	19	19	19	19	19	19
Greece	7,562	7,559	7,541	7,527	7,519	7,518	7,497	7,484	7,471	7,463	7,447
Iceland	224	228	231	234	236	238	240	241	242	243	244
Ireland	3,017	2,991	2,975	2,967	2,962	2,960	2,959	2,959	2,961	2,964	2,968
Italy	39,681	39,807	39,740	39,663	39,567	39,506	39,461	39,437	39,414	39,391	39,345
Liechtenstein	26	26	26	26	26	27	27	27	27	27	28
Luxembourg	336	341	345	349	354	358	361	365	368	372	375
Malta	287	287	287	286	285	284	283	282	282	281	280
Monaco	21	21	21	21	21	21	21	22	22	22	22
Netherlands	11,039	11,040	10,974	10,919	10,882	10,854	10,836	10,816	10,786	10,758	10,720
Norway	3,218	3,250	3,273	3,296	3,318	3,342	3,365	3,388	3,407	3,426	3,446
Portugal	7,148	7,139	7,135	7,125	7,106	7,097	7,081	7,067	7,053	7,040	7,020
Spain	31,234	31,344	31,440	31,530	31,626	31,730	31,841	31,965	32,086	32,212	32,330
Sweden	6,040	6,036	6,023	6,008	5,993	5,981	5,976	5,977	5,980	5,987	6,001
Switzerland	5,149	5,158	5,163	5,167	5,167	5,169	5,167	5,167	5,163	5,157	5,150
Turkey	48,636	49,373	50,132	50,915	51,718	52,402	53,062	53,800	54,378	54,940	55,437
United Kingdom	41,008	41,127	41,180	41,194	41,256	41,339	41,426	41,518	41,618	41,733	41,862
Eastern Europe											
Albania	2,135	2,158	2,180	2,201	2,218	2,231	2,240	2,244	2,245	2,244	2,240
Belarus	6,906	6,916	6,893	6,855	6,809	6,746	6,695	6,643	6,587	6,537	6,478
Bosnia-Herzegovina	2,727	2,731	2,734	2,735	2,733	2,728	2,717	2,702	2,683	2,661	2,638
Bulgaria	5,171	5,115	5,048	4,976	4,903	4,832	4,757	4,696	4,632	4,569	4,510
Croatia	2,982	2,991	2,990	2,983	2,972	2,955	2,935	2,915	2,890	2,863	2,835
Czech Republic	7,418	7,395	7,342	7,285	7,234	7,187	7,139	7,091	7,047	7,006	6,971
Estonia	902	898	890	881	871	860	852	843	835	828	821
Georgia	3,024	3,030	3,031	3,028	3,023	3,014	3,003	2,990	2,975	2,960	2,944
Hungary	6,870	6,858	6,834	6,789	6,736	6,680	6,623	6,569	6,519	6,453	6,375
Latvia	1,547	1,536	1,522	1,505	1,486	1,467	1,451	1,435	1,419	1,407	1,393
Lithuania	2,305	2,294	2,284	2,271	2,256	2,238	2,218	2,197	2,175	2,156	2,137
Macedonia	1,442	1,445	1,446	1,446	1,445	1,442	1,438	1,432	1,426	1,418	1,410
Moldova	2,583	2,566	2,545	2,520	2,492	2,462	2,429	2,395	2,360	2,327	2,296
Montenegro	417	417	417	416	416	415	414	413	412	411	410
Poland	27,221	27,253	27,170	27,035	26,861	26,668	26,454	26,215	25,963	25,709	25,462
Romania	14,963	14,938	14,871	14,797	14,710	14,570	14,429	14,291	14,143	14,006	13,857
Russia	102,144	102,007	101,374	100,546	99,789	98,689	97,684	96,695	95,732	94,975	94,093
Serbia	4,965	4,953	4,936	4,914	4,887	4,858	4,826	4,794	4,762	4,732	4,706
Slovakia	3,916	3,919	3,916	3,903	3,885	3,865	3,837	3,802	3,765	3,730	3,696
Slovenia	1,414	1,419	1,417	1,412	1,405	1,398	1,389	1,380	1,369	1,358	1,349
Ukraine	32,121	32,112	31,920	31,680	31,326	30,858	30,442	30,037	29,692	29,393	29,070

Source: Euromonitor International from national statistics/UN

Population Statistics

Table 21.31

Persons Aged 65 Years and Over Forecasts at January 1st 2010-2020
'000

	2010	2011	2012	2013	2014	2015	2016	2017	2018	2019	2020
Western Europe											
Austria	1,481	1,485	1,502	1,535	1,566	1,592	1,616	1,637	1,662	1,687	1,714
Belgium	1,864	1,885	1,925	1,963	2,001	2,037	2,072	2,105	2,143	2,181	2,221
Cyprus	116	119	123	126	130	134	137	141	145	149	153
Denmark	904	935	970	1,001	1,028	1,051	1,074	1,095	1,117	1,139	1,160
Finland	912	944	982	1,022	1,060	1,095	1,127	1,155	1,185	1,211	1,236
France	10,510	10,631	10,924	11,242	11,560	11,869	12,175	12,444	12,715	12,966	13,224
Germany	16,837	16,745	16,739	16,830	16,963	17,159	17,376	17,572	17,775	17,963	18,169
Gibraltar	5	5	5	5	5	5	5	5	5	5	5
Greece	2,122	2,156	2,201	2,239	2,265	2,282	2,320	2,349	2,377	2,400	2,430
Iceland	39	40	41	43	44	46	47	49	50	52	54
Ireland	497	501	509	518	528	539	550	561	573	586	599
Italy	12,245	12,346	12,606	12,851	13,100	13,304	13,494	13,650	13,797	13,945	14,119
Liechtenstein	5	5	5	5	5	5	5	5	5	5	5
Luxembourg	69	70	71	72	74	75	77	78	80	82	83
Malta	61	63	66	69	72	75	77	79	81	83	85
Monaco	7	7	8	8	8	8	8	8	8	8	8
Netherlands	2,514	2,563	2,679	2,787	2,881	2,965	3,045	3,120	3,201	3,278	3,355
Norway	722	740	765	787	808	827	847	865	885	906	927
Portugal	1,897	1,927	1,950	1,977	2,014	2,046	2,081	2,115	2,150	2,181	2,216
Spain	7,843	7,989	8,142	8,298	8,449	8,601	8,758	8,911	9,065	9,227	9,397
Sweden	1,691	1,736	1,782	1,825	1,868	1,908	1,943	1,973	2,004	2,036	2,061
Switzerland	1,294	1,323	1,355	1,387	1,419	1,448	1,476	1,501	1,529	1,556	1,586
Turkey	5,198	5,397	5,515	5,656	5,788	6,068	6,335	6,472	6,650	6,804	7,034
United Kingdom	10,126	10,267	10,489	10,767	10,999	11,190	11,356	11,505	11,652	11,801	11,949
Eastern Europe											
Albania	308	316	323	331	340	348	357	366	375	386	399
Belarus	1,326	1,282	1,266	1,259	1,265	1,289	1,303	1,315	1,330	1,339	1,358
Bosnia-Herzegovina	535	540	546	554	564	576	590	605	623	641	659
Bulgaria	1,319	1,327	1,345	1,358	1,376	1,398	1,423	1,435	1,449	1,465	1,479
Croatia	765	754	755	760	765	775	785	792	803	816	828
Czech Republic	1,601	1,638	1,702	1,768	1,827	1,880	1,935	1,991	2,044	2,093	2,140
Estonia	224	222	223	224	225	228	230	232	234	235	238
Georgia	629	630	632	635	639	645	654	665	679	694	711
Hungary	1,649	1,653	1,658	1,678	1,703	1,729	1,763	1,792	1,820	1,862	1,919
Latvia	387	383	379	378	378	379	378	379	379	378	379
Lithuania	534	535	533	531	532	535	538	541	544	546	548
Macedonia	244	247	251	255	260	266	272	279	287	295	303
Moldova	397	396	397	399	403	409	418	429	442	456	469
Montenegro	91	91	92	93	95	96	98	100	102	104	106
Poland	5,166	5,188	5,312	5,468	5,648	5,834	6,039	6,257	6,479	6,701	6,922
Romania	3,156	3,123	3,127	3,125	3,142	3,200	3,255	3,299	3,350	3,395	3,459
Russia	18,155	17,674	17,624	17,745	17,832	18,220	18,533	18,847	19,241	19,523	19,969
Serbia	1,050	1,046	1,045	1,050	1,059	1,072	1,090	1,111	1,135	1,158	1,181
Slovakia	660	666	675	692	712	734	761	792	825	857	889
Slovenia	335	335	340	347	355	363	373	383	394	406	417
Ukraine	7,180	6,957	6,905	6,875	6,955	7,132	7,258	7,366	7,429	7,470	7,553

Source: Euromonitor International from national statistics/UN

Retailing

Retailing Statistics

Table 22.1

Retail Sales 2004-2009

US$ billion

	2004	2005	2006	2007	2008	2009
Western Europe						
Austria	62.9	63.7	65.1	72.4	78.4	70.2
Belgium	75.0	77.4	80.7	92.3	103.2	92.0
Denmark	38.4	40.7	43.5	50.2	53.7	46.2
Finland	34.9	36.8	39.0	45.3	50.9	44.5
France	445.2	451.5	469.2	526.6	576.3	515.4
Germany	449.1	450.8	463.3	519.4	563.3	503.5
Greece	57.9	64.3	69.1	79.3	85.0	73.7
Ireland	36.1	37.7	39.7	45.6	49.9	44.3
Italy	317.0	323.7	336.0	376.0	412.4	373.5
Netherlands	98.3	96.7	101.3	114.7	126.9	116.4
Norway	38.7	42.3	44.8	52.1	56.4	47.2
Portugal	43.6	45.0	47.6	54.0	59.9	54.0
Spain	241.4	251.9	264.3	298.2	321.8	283.1
Sweden	59.6	60.4	64.6	73.7	78.5	61.6
Switzerland	73.8	74.2	74.8	80.5	92.8	86.7
Turkey	99.5	109.5	112.7	136.5	140.9	114.4
United Kingdom	485.9	492.5	515.7	575.2	538.3	425.6
Eastern Europe						
Belarus	6.5	8.4	10.5	12.9	17.1	15.0
Bulgaria	7.3	7.8	8.4	9.6	10.8	9.6
Croatia	11.8	12.7	13.4	14.9	16.4	13.0
Czech Republic	21.7	24.2	26.9	31.3	38.8	30.3
Estonia	3.1	3.6	4.3	5.5	5.9	4.5
Hungary	25.2	26.8	27.3	32.3	35.0	26.4
Latvia	3.6	4.3	5.3	6.8	7.6	5.8
Lithuania	4.9	5.6	6.3	8.1	9.3	6.9
Poland	64.6	74.7	79.5	94.8	114.5	82.1
Romania	13.7	17.9	21.5	29.8	33.8	27.5
Russia	129.0	160.1	204.5	265.7	328.5	234.8
Slovakia	9.9	11.2	13.1	16.5	19.3	16.0
Slovenia	4.9	5.6	6.4	8.2	10.2	9.6
Ukraine	21.0	25.9	30.7	37.6	44.1	29.7

Source: Euromonitor International from national sources

Retailing Statistics   **Table 22.2**

Store-Based Retailer Sales by Grocery/Non Grocery Split 2009
US$ billion

	Grocery Retailers	Non-Grocery Retailers	Total
Western Europe			
Austria	28.4	39.4	67.8
Belgium	46.0	43.7	89.7
Denmark	24.7	19.5	44.3
Finland	19.5	22.8	42.3
France	272.0	220.5	492.5
Germany	221.0	243.2	464.2
Greece	35.5	37.1	72.6
Ireland	22.1	21.3	43.4
Italy	158.6	205.2	363.7
Netherlands	46.9	64.4	111.3
Norway	23.8	21.9	45.7
Portugal	26.6	26.1	52.6
Spain	125.7	150.6	276.3
Sweden	29.8	29.6	59.4
Switzerland	42.3	40.8	83.1
Turkey	56.4	55.0	111.4
United Kingdom	196.8	190.3	387.2
Eastern Europe			
Belarus	7.5	7.3	14.8
Bulgaria	4.0	5.5	9.5
Croatia	8.0	4.8	12.8
Czech Republic	14.1	14.7	28.8
Estonia	2.4	2.0	4.4
Hungary	14.6	10.9	25.6
Latvia	3.1	2.6	5.7
Lithuania	4.3	2.5	6.8
Poland	44.4	35.5	79.9
Romania	16.7	10.2	26.9
Russia	143.4	84.1	227.6
Slovakia	8.2	7.4	15.6
Slovenia	5.3	4.0	9.3
Ukraine	15.8	13.0	28.8

Source: *Euromonitor International from national sources*

Retailing Statistics   **Table 22.3**

Store-Based Retailer Outlets by Grocery/Non Grocery Split 2009

No of outlets

	Grocery Retailers	Non-Grocery Retailers	Total
Western Europe			
Austria	15,203	34,517	49,720
Belgium	24,712	48,605	73,317
Denmark	10,114	15,030	25,144
Finland	6,354	21,774	28,128
France	94,102	205,664	299,766
Germany	107,862	192,262	300,124
Greece	82,810	97,273	180,083
Ireland	8,660	13,826	22,486
Italy	263,392	575,146	838,538
Netherlands	33,769	73,162	106,931
Norway	9,734	22,043	31,777
Portugal	46,163	87,623	133,786
Spain	159,225	412,484	571,709
Sweden	13,218	35,673	48,891
Switzerland	16,872	29,192	46,064
Turkey	312,770	267,634	580,404
United Kingdom	92,677	190,457	283,134
Eastern Europe			
Belarus	20,827	16,287	37,114
Bulgaria	36,011	44,757	80,768
Croatia	15,665	18,699	34,364
Czech Republic	20,428	66,239	86,667
Estonia	1,479	2,631	4,110
Hungary	41,204	98,584	139,788
Latvia	5,272	6,898	12,170
Lithuania	8,115	7,337	15,452
Poland	160,897	158,385	319,282
Romania	72,772	61,477	134,249
Russia	315,957	154,387	470,344
Slovakia	25,587	20,489	46,076
Slovenia	2,203	2,973	5,176
Ukraine	61,968	51,099	113,067

Source: *Euromonitor International from national sources*

Retailing Statistics

Table 22.4

Grocery Retailer Sales by Type 2009

% of total

	Hypermarkets	Supermarkets	Discounters	Small grocery retailers	Food/drink tobacco specialists	Other grocery retailers	Total
Western Europe							
Austria	7.36	39.19	23.12	11.56	10.62	8.17	100.00
Belgium	7.93	49.55	10.97	16.28	14.25	1.03	100.00
Denmark	20.98	33.10	25.10	15.47	5.02	0.32	100.00
Finland	29.77	28.01	4.38	29.16	8.33	0.36	100.00
France	42.10	34.75	7.09	7.43	7.73	0.90	100.00
Germany	19.89	23.75	36.33	11.89	6.86	1.29	100.00
Greece	3.06	36.80	6.31	10.51	17.21	26.11	100.00
Ireland	3.02	42.73	4.46	43.57	5.81	0.41	100.00
Italy	18.75	34.20	8.08	21.59	17.06	0.32	100.00
Netherlands	3.18	63.56	12.16	8.80	8.45	3.84	100.00
Norway	8.46	31.29	39.28	11.70	8.29	0.97	100.00
Portugal	19.27	42.75	10.53	8.05	15.56	3.84	100.00
Spain	17.08	46.87	6.45	4.73	22.47	2.40	100.00
Sweden	18.82	38.04	10.85	17.35	14.09	0.85	100.00
Switzerland	12.23	53.61	8.23	10.56	15.23	0.14	100.00
Turkey	5.38	29.56	10.57	35.39	19.07	0.02	100.00
United Kingdom	35.42	32.95	3.42	19.33	7.46	1.41	100.00
Eastern Europe							
Belarus	3.29	12.58	0.71	17.40	10.47	55.56	100.00
Bulgaria	6.84	22.05		48.27	18.57	4.27	100.00
Croatia	25.40	28.40	3.30	36.26	6.17	0.48	100.00
Czech Republic	40.56	13.54	15.62	13.47	9.18	7.62	100.00
Estonia	22.37	28.71	12.28	32.87	2.74	1.02	100.00
Hungary	29.70	8.43	11.58	39.69	10.18	0.41	100.00
Latvia	12.67	25.42	7.34	52.10	2.29	0.18	100.00
Lithuania	21.72	47.03	3.57	22.64	1.67	3.39	100.00
Poland	19.79	15.07	12.80	41.75	5.90	4.68	100.00
Romania	25.29	9.09	8.07	17.13	14.76	25.66	100.00
Russia	8.73	30.44	10.83	29.64	3.01	17.35	100.00
Slovakia	24.52	25.50	3.42	39.60	5.21	1.75	100.00
Slovenia	24.79	32.03	11.51	28.36	1.53	1.78	100.00
Ukraine	12.68	39.54		12.11	3.05	32.62	100.00

Source: *Euromonitor International from national sources*

Retailing Statistics

Table 22.5

Non-Grocery Retailer Sales by Type 2009

% of total

	Department stores	Variety stores	Mass merchandisers	Health & beauty retailers
Western Europe				
Austria		0.81		15.69
Belgium	2.26	1.51		20.60
Denmark	2.92	2.33	0.49	16.24
Finland	7.62	6.10	1.88	15.54
France	2.58	2.37		26.54
Germany	3.30	1.79		32.76
Greece	3.59	0.51		17.20
Ireland	10.46	20.42		14.34
Italy	1.63	1.24		18.58
Netherlands	5.65	3.32		18.80
Norway	0.34	2.81		13.52
Portugal	2.14	4.39		19.87
Spain	8.42	1.70		18.54
Sweden	2.49	3.13	1.41	17.08
Switzerland	11.84	1.40		16.19
Turkey	2.37	0.01		11.02
United Kingdom	11.58	6.26	1.36	10.40
Eastern Europe				
Belarus	32.61			13.67
Bulgaria		0.12		17.56
Croatia	2.46			21.55
Czech Republic	4.21	8.47		17.26
Estonia	3.72			13.69
Hungary	1.39	8.60		15.97
Latvia	2.49			19.24
Lithuania	0.09	1.16		31.79
Poland	5.20	0.98		22.51
Romania	1.51			18.91
Russia	5.08			14.74
Slovakia	2.50	4.75		35.04
Slovenia	1.45	0.07		30.75
Ukraine		1.21		24.66

Source: *Euromonitor International from national sources*

Retailing Statistics

Non-Grocery Retailer Sales by Type 2009 *(continued)*
% of total

	Clothing and footwear retailers	Home and garden retailers	Electronics and appliance retailers	Leisure and personal goods retailers	Other non-grocery retailers	Total
Western Europe						
Austria	16.20	26.25	13.66	13.52	13.87	100.00
Belgium	19.82	21.63	12.04	16.83	5.30	100.00
Denmark	21.29	26.92	12.18	15.68	1.95	100.00
Finland	9.32	27.87	14.45	9.71	7.51	100.00
France	15.89	21.65	10.41	18.07	2.50	100.00
Germany	15.52	23.56	10.61	12.02	0.45	100.00
Greece	18.72	30.41	10.82	14.62	4.14	100.00
Ireland	17.52	18.64	2.67	13.57	2.38	100.00
Italy	27.19	23.18	6.71	13.23	8.23	100.00
Netherlands	15.28	29.05	8.11	15.17	4.62	100.00
Norway	21.97	30.76	12.70	16.67	1.22	100.00
Portugal	16.74	23.17	9.22	18.69	5.79	100.00
Spain	18.03	19.58	5.40	25.48	2.84	100.00
Sweden	17.68	26.17	11.32	15.46	5.26	100.00
Switzerland	19.24	13.19	8.30	13.51	16.32	100.00
Turkey	25.69	18.88	23.49	18.53		100.00
United Kingdom	21.68	16.47	9.55	18.70	4.01	100.00
Eastern Europe						
Belarus	20.35	13.00	4.26	3.36	12.75	100.00
Bulgaria	28.86	22.15	14.30	13.22	3.79	100.00
Croatia	13.08	22.52	12.05	12.56	15.78	100.00
Czech Republic	16.44	19.74	10.60	12.73	10.56	100.00
Estonia	11.03	43.05	6.71	19.02	2.78	100.00
Hungary	12.79	19.50	10.30	21.06	10.39	100.00
Latvia	16.73	39.58	6.78	8.84	6.33	100.00
Lithuania	17.87	25.51	11.54	10.12	1.91	100.00
Poland	14.55	20.02	14.63	16.98	5.13	100.00
Romania	6.65	26.12	17.82	16.04	12.96	100.00
Russia	13.63	17.60	28.45	12.10	8.41	100.00
Slovakia	16.85	19.81	4.06	11.73	5.25	100.00
Slovenia	17.53	31.50	6.01	11.65	1.05	100.00
Ukraine	32.80	13.46	14.32	11.22	2.34	100.00

Source: Euromonitor International from national sources

Retailing Statistics   **Table 22.6**

Non-Store Retailer Sales by Type 2009

US$ billion

	Vending	Home shopping	Internet retailing	Direct selling	Total
Western Europe					
Austria	0.41	0.94	0.83	0.26	2.44
Belgium	0.35	0.24	1.48	0.27	2.33
Denmark	0.09	0.14	1.69	0.07	1.99
Finland	0.07	0.38	1.53	0.23	2.22
France	0.66	4.80	14.20	3.22	22.87
Germany	4.85	13.14	18.83	2.52	39.34
Greece	0.01	0.16	0.77	0.23	1.17
Ireland	0.16	0.14	0.55	0.04	0.89
Italy	2.11	1.12	3.02	3.50	9.75
Netherlands	0.46	0.91	3.49	0.20	5.05
Norway	0.05	0.57	0.77	0.15	1.53
Portugal	0.53	0.30	0.34	0.19	1.35
Spain	2.01	0.79	3.29	0.78	6.87
Sweden	0.12	0.76	1.27	0.08	2.23
Switzerland	0.48	1.23	1.61	0.25	3.57
Turkey			0.92	2.10	3.02
United Kingdom	0.64	8.40	28.10	1.24	38.38
Eastern Europe					
Belarus	0.00		0.06	0.07	0.14
Bulgaria	0.01	0.00	0.02	0.08	0.11
Croatia	0.03	0.03	0.06	0.07	0.19
Czech Republic	0.06	0.27	1.01	0.23	1.56
Estonia	0.02	0.06	0.00	0.02	0.10
Hungary	0.04	0.21	0.34	0.23	0.82
Latvia	0.00	0.01	0.04	0.03	0.08
Lithuania	0.01	0.00	0.07	0.06	0.14
Montenegro	0.00	0.00	0.00	0.00	0.01
Poland	0.06	0.13	1.48	0.63	2.29
Romania	0.00	0.16	0.13	0.32	0.61
Russia	0.35	1.81	2.92	2.17	7.25
Serbia	0.00	0.00	0.01	0.02	0.03
Slovakia	0.04	0.12	0.08	0.13	0.37
Slovenia	0.02	0.07	0.10	0.03	0.22
Ukraine	0.02	0.01	0.26	0.63	0.93

Source: *Euromonitor International from national sources*

Retailing Statistics   **Table 22.7**

Non-Store Retailer Sales by Type (% Analysis) 2009
% of total

	Vending	Home shopping	Internet retailing	Direct selling	Total
Western Europe					
Austria	16.7	38.6	33.9	10.8	100.0
Belgium	14.8	10.1	63.5	11.5	100.0
Denmark	4.5	6.9	84.8	3.7	100.0
Finland	3.3	17.2	69.2	10.4	100.0
France	2.9	21.0	62.1	14.1	100.0
Germany	12.3	33.4	47.9	6.4	100.0
Greece	1.1	13.4	65.5	20.0	100.0
Ireland	17.6	15.6	62.0	4.8	100.0
Italy	21.6	11.5	30.9	35.9	100.0
Netherlands	9.0	18.0	69.1	3.9	100.0
Norway	3.0	37.3	50.2	9.5	100.0
Portugal	39.0	22.0	25.2	13.8	100.0
Spain	29.3	11.5	47.9	11.3	100.0
Sweden	5.2	34.0	57.1	3.7	100.0
Switzerland	13.5	34.4	45.2	6.9	100.0
Turkey			30.4	69.6	100.0
United Kingdom	1.7	21.9	73.2	3.2	100.0
Eastern Europe					
Belarus	2.1		45.7	52.2	100.0
Bulgaria	10.2	1.1	20.9	67.8	100.0
Croatia	16.6	17.3	29.7	36.4	100.0
Czech Republic	3.8	17.0	64.3	14.9	100.0
Estonia	18.1	61.7	3.3	16.8	100.0
Hungary	4.7	26.0	41.4	27.9	100.0
Latvia	1.4	14.1	49.7	34.8	100.0
Lithuania	5.6	1.3	53.3	39.8	100.0
Montenegro	14.6	2.4	1.0	81.9	100.0
Poland	2.5	5.5	64.4	27.6	100.0
Romania	0.1	26.1	21.4	52.3	100.0
Russia	4.9	25.0	40.2	29.9	100.0
Serbia	13.9	4.7	22.9	58.4	100.0
Slovakia	10.2	31.2	22.4	36.2	100.0
Slovenia	7.8	32.4	45.3	14.6	100.0
Ukraine	1.9	1.5	28.2	68.4	100.0

Source: *Euromonitor International from national sources*

Travel and Tourism

Travel and Tourism Statistics

Table 23.1

Average Tourist Nights in Accommodation Establishments 1990-2009
Nights

	1990	1995	2000	2004	2005	2006	2007	2008	2009
Western Europe									
Austria	4.90	4.80	4.00	3.58	3.55	3.46	3.41	3.40	3.37
Belgium									
Cyprus	12.80	11.02	6.70	6.73	6.79	6.32	6.19	6.27	6.15
Denmark									
Finland		1.84	1.90	1.83	1.84	1.82	1.82	1.80	1.79
France			1.88	1.82	1.81	1.82	2.18	1.84	1.85
Germany	2.20	2.39	2.32	2.25	2.22	2.19	2.18	2.17	2.16
Gibraltar									
Greece									
Iceland			1.86	1.80	1.80	1.80	1.80	1.80	1.80
Ireland									
Italy	3.53	3.55	3.50	3.31	3.33	3.27	3.26	3.26	3.25
Liechtenstein			2.12	2.10	2.20	2.10	2.20	2.20	2.20
Luxembourg		2.36	2.10	2.00	2.00	1.90	1.90	2.00	2.00
Malta			8.30	9.50	8.40	8.40	8.12	8.50	8.52
Monaco	2.96	2.84	2.87	2.78	2.81	2.92	2.88	3.00	3.05
Netherlands	2.39	1.93	1.90	1.80	1.80	1.80	1.78	1.76	1.75
Norway	1.73	1.61	1.67	1.66	1.65	1.62	1.63	1.65	1.65
Portugal	4.60	4.09	3.60	3.10	3.10	3.00	3.00	2.90	2.86
Spain	5.57	4.26	3.83	3.51	3.48	3.26	3.22	3.24	3.18
Sweden									
Switzerland	3.50	3.01	2.50	2.45	2.40	2.40	2.33	2.33	2.32
Turkey	3.43	4.00	4.20	3.29	3.20	2.90	2.94	3.12	3.10
United Kingdom									
Eastern Europe									
Albania		3.16	2.44	3.20	3.00	3.50	3.20	2.30	2.16
Belarus				2.77	2.93	3.00	3.04	2.99	3.00
Bosnia-Herzegovina			2.30						
Bulgaria		3.50	3.90	4.23	4.20	4.07	3.80	3.70	3.59
Croatia		5.29	5.49	5.08	4.48	4.33	4.17	4.07	3.95
Czech Republic	2.40	3.10	3.30	3.45	2.78	2.76	2.73	2.72	2.71
Estonia		1.81	1.53	1.95	1.98	2.01	2.00	1.94	1.93
Georgia									
Hungary	3.70	3.18	2.86	2.71	2.66	2.63	2.58	2.50	2.47
Latvia		2.85	2.90	2.32	2.23	2.23	2.11	2.15	2.13
Lithuania		2.15	2.22	2.10	2.15	2.06	1.94	1.87	1.82
Macedonia	3.20	3.60	3.90	4.00	3.90	3.80	3.80	3.70	3.67
Moldova				2.40	2.60	2.90	2.70	2.90	2.96
Montenegro									
Poland	1.37	1.43	2.00	1.91	1.93	1.93	1.95	1.96	1.97
Romania	2.96	3.40	3.20	3.25	3.20	3.18	2.94	2.89	2.83
Russia				5.00	4.81	5.30	5.30	5.37	5.48
Serbia				2.80	2.73	2.70	2.63	2.67	2.66
Slovakia	3.20	3.40	3.10	2.90	2.80	2.80	2.70	2.60	2.56
Slovenia		3.73	3.31	3.12	3.01	2.97	2.96	2.88	2.85
Ukraine			2.70	2.60	2.60	2.60	2.60	2.60	2.60

Source: *Euromonitor International from World Tourism Organisation*

Travel and Tourism Statistics | **Table 23.2**

Average Tourist Nights in the Country 1990-2009
Nights

	1990	1995	2000	2004	2005	2006	2007	2008	2009
Western Europe									
Austria			4.60	4.43	4.40	4.30	4.26	4.23	4.20
Belgium				2.32	2.31	2.29	2.31	2.28	2.28
Cyprus	10.28	7.99	7.52	7.86	7.94	7.52	7.39	7.50	7.40
Denmark					5.00	4.94	5.02	5.07	5.09
Finland			2.06	2.10	2.16	2.16	2.16	2.21	2.22
France	6.90	8.17	7.48	6.76	6.70	6.59	6.63	6.64	6.63
Germany				2.30	2.20	2.20	2.20	2.30	2.32
Gibraltar	3.00								
Greece				6.00	5.54	5.56	5.37	5.40	5.38
Iceland			1.80	1.80	1.80	1.80	1.80	1.80	1.80
Ireland	11.00	8.42	7.40	7.42	7.49	7.60	7.30	8.10	8.21
Italy				3.84	3.89	3.81	3.81	3.87	3.87
Liechtenstein	1.91	2.10	2.10	2.10	2.20	2.10	2.20	2.20	2.20
Luxembourg		3.00	2.80	2.90	2.70	2.70	2.60	2.60	2.58
Malta	9.26	9.80	8.40	9.70	9.50	9.50	8.90	8.50	8.30
Monaco									
Netherlands			2.70	2.60	2.50	2.50	2.54	2.50	2.50
Norway									
Portugal	7.40	7.00	6.70	4.35	4.40	3.85	4.20	4.00	3.91
Spain	4.83	5.20	5.50	5.76	5.60	5.20	5.11	5.12	5.01
Sweden				2.08	2.06	2.33	2.14	2.31	2.36
Switzerland				2.53	2.50	2.48	2.50	2.49	
Turkey	8.33	9.00	4.19	4.53	4.33	3.92	3.82	4.17	4.13
United Kingdom	10.90	9.40	8.08	8.20	8.30	8.40	7.70	7.70	7.70
Eastern Europe									
Albania			2.67	2.60	2.30	2.20	2.60	2.30	2.30
Belarus									
Bosnia-Herzegovina							2.30	2.20	2.15
Bulgaria	6.00	6.60	8.35	6.08	6.01	5.82	5.39	5.28	5.15
Croatia				5.39	5.43	5.43	5.33	5.38	5.37
Czech Republic	3.32	3.13	3.50	3.13	3.09	3.12	3.09	3.01	3.00
Estonia		1.90	1.90	2.00	2.05	2.12	2.11	2.05	2.05
Georgia			7.10						
Hungary	6.58	6.39	3.51	3.21	3.13	3.04	2.95	2.85	2.80
Latvia			2.60	2.20	2.21	2.29	2.29	2.24	2.25
Lithuania		3.50	3.20	2.59	2.59	2.52	2.41	2.26	2.21
Macedonia				2.20	2.30	2.20	2.30	2.30	2.30
Moldova				2.50	2.80	3.40	2.90	2.80	2.80
Montenegro							6.55	6.76	6.90
Poland		4.70	4.80	4.60	4.40	3.40	2.90	4.00	3.91
Romania			2.48	2.50	2.40	2.30	2.30	2.30	2.28
Russia				4.38	4.63	5.20	6.10	7.00	7.66
Serbia				2.17	2.19	2.16	2.12	2.16	2.15
Slovakia			3.90	3.30	3.20	3.20	3.10	3.00	2.96
Slovenia	3.10	3.12	3.12	2.91	2.80	2.78	2.78	2.73	2.71
Ukraine			5.30	4.00	3.80				

Source: *Euromonitor International from World Tourism Organisation*

Travel and Tourism Statistics

Table 23.3

Domestic Tourist Nights 1990-2009

'000 nights

	1990	1995	2000	2004	2005	2006	2007	2008	2009
Western Europe									
Austria	15,620	16,302	18,897	18,850	19,383	20,278	21,285	21,902	22,273
Belgium		3,054	4,045	4,090	4,313	4,737	5,220	5,422	5,639
Cyprus	178	374	597	1,069	1,040	1,114	1,169	1,159	1,181
Denmark		4,367	5,082	5,404	5,806	6,352	6,999	6,823	7,022
Finland		8,464	9,786	10,032	10,388	10,676	11,182	11,339	11,498
France	72,556	90,349	114,059	118,134	122,222	123,105	126,536	126,550	127,374
Germany		149,628	170,947	165,655	168,843	172,428	177,586	180,259	182,162
Gibraltar									
Greece	11,346	12,523	14,628	13,280	13,942	14,249	16,675	16,840	17,323
Iceland		246	296	323	361	387	437	429	440
Ireland		6,698	6,786	7,799	8,174	7,978	8,791	8,794	8,909
Italy	123,975	123,467	136,392	136,845	138,123	140,397	141,311	141,187	141,725
Liechtenstein		1	3	3	3	3	3	3	4
Luxembourg		81	68	85	85	77	78	78	78
Malta									
Monaco									
Netherlands	7,102	8,799	14,027	13,761	14,375	15,783	17,831	17,657	18,301
Norway	8,665	9,862	11,398	11,764	12,349	12,859	13,458	13,328	13,561
Portugal	7,295	7,580	9,693	11,139	11,648	12,350	12,968	13,024	13,330
Spain	50,869	58,281	83,382	100,044	106,875	115,088	116,597	113,188	114,591
Sweden	12,528	14,771	16,586	16,465	17,518	18,606	19,574	20,042	20,568
Switzerland	13,152	12,316	14,013	13,837	14,622	15,204	15,447	15,825	15,451
Turkey	6,878	9,624	16,351	18,341	18,807	21,476	22,223	20,809	21,254
United Kingdom		72,000	139,000	106,510	117,926	102,010	105,231	103,020	99,915
Eastern Europe									
Albania		76	143	153	214	323	375	360	389
Belarus				2,926	3,306	3,649	3,739	3,624	3,680
Bosnia-Herzegovina			522	476	497	543	598	625	664
Bulgaria		3,648	3,024	3,423	3,957	4,342	4,867	5,370	5,732
Croatia		4,370	2,949	2,900	2,862	2,886	2,951	3,024	3,066
Czech Republic	25,390	10,142	12,358	9,051	8,601	8,854	9,206	9,686	9,867
Estonia		293	459	691	751	989	1,175	1,120	1,182
Georgia			2,115						
Hungary		3,972	5,479	5,933	6,622	6,284	7,662	7,794	7,989
Latvia		735	669	717	796	855	979	941	976
Lithuania		326	293	511	728	934	1,082	1,057	1,112
Macedonia	738	464	443	289	275	267	283	277	277
Moldova			119	251	264	282	234	225	217
Montenegro		1,829	1,476	1,552	1,505	1,200	331	348	252
Poland	5,744	3,903	9,352	11,572	12,464	13,910	15,898	17,300	18,308
Romania		17,957	13,862	13,980	14,094	14,929	16,259	16,580	17,132
Russia				35,549	40,730	42,630	44,334	44,218	45,112
Serbia			6,968	3,362	3,198	3,120	3,187	3,230	3,236
Slovakia	8,320	2,179	3,768	4,148	3,978	3,936	4,082	4,620	4,773
Slovenia	1,986	2,066	1,860	1,707	1,653	1,746	1,839	1,943	2,003
Ukraine			7,986	8,486	8,554				

Source: *Euromonitor International from World Tourism Organisation*

| Travel and Tourism Statistics | | | | | | | | **Table 23.4** |

International Tourist Nights 1990-2009

'000 nights

	1990	1995	2000	2004	2005	2006	2007	2008	2009
Western Europe									
Austria	63,148	49,851	51,475	55,163	56,690	57,133	57,822	60,469	57,798
Belgium	7,032	7,895	10,184	10,315	10,297	10,634	10,976	11,120	11,257
Cyprus	9,426	14,222	16,790	13,554	13,899	13,227	13,129	13,151	13,012
Denmark		4,485	4,890	4,984	5,015	5,021	4,846	4,752	4,703
Finland	2,830	2,926	3,562	3,758	3,887	4,339	4,635	4,768	4,915
France	38,720	54,339	77,014	70,391	72,054	68,821	72,391	71,065	70,882
Germany		28,659	36,354	38,491	40,839	44,921	46,508	47,562	48,683
Gibraltar									
Greece	35,012	38,772	46,212	38,310	40,075	42,459	47,410	47,234	48,427
Iceland		598	890	1,146	1,208	1,341	1,480	1,517	1,569
Ireland	8,208	12,452	16,903	17,934	17,446	19,080	19,737	19,285	19,626
Italy	60,301	84,566	97,221	97,175	102,312	107,859	113,017	110,492	111,927
Liechtenstein		127	131	101	108	115	126	131	118
Luxembourg		1,051	1,169	1,195	1,275	1,284	1,360	1,297	1,301
Malta	9,604	7,632	6,978	7,725	7,603	7,377	7,976	7,977	8,039
Monaco		626	861	695	803	916	944	944	972
Netherlands	6,613	9,581	15,695	14,616	15,143	15,976	16,328	14,961	14,921
Norway	3,802	4,985	4,967	4,596	4,761	4,914	5,068	4,894	4,922
Portugal	19,349	20,357	24,102	23,002	23,873	25,216	26,769	26,204	26,722
Spain	68,630	101,182	143,762	134,654	138,762	151,940	155,093	155,364	159,053
Sweden	3,053	3,696	4,679	5,061	5,382	5,606	5,842	5,830	5,923
Switzerland	19,957	18,386	19,914	17,247	18,321	19,644	20,918	21,508	22,133
Turkey	13,271	18,438	28,377	49,614	55,996	46,588	56,491	56,873	57,068
United Kingdom	51,916	58,295	53,131	54,089	59,255	65,287	64,828	61,962	62,493
Eastern Europe									
Albania		89	98	90	130	137	173	131	131
Belarus				575	597	688	791	1,001	1,085
Bosnia-Herzegovina			254	444	469	574	672	697	725
Bulgaria		5,279	5,101	10,139	11,471	11,776	11,868	11,641	11,679
Croatia		4,574	15,125	17,072	18,415	17,807	17,988	17,675	17,499
Czech Republic	9,350	9,768	12,811	15,881	16,607	17,035	17,838	17,741	17,930
Estonia		615	1,253	2,602	2,791	2,772	2,668	2,727	2,718
Georgia			2,730						
Hungary		7,294	8,062	8,729	9,127	8,524	8,635	8,489	8,404
Latvia		668	691	1,158	1,507	1,745	1,780	1,913	2,003
Lithuania		415	570	1,131	1,334	1,451	1,509	1,544	1,579
Macedonia	474	243	439	329	391	392	457	475	490
Moldova		99	85	153	170	202	194	191	195
Montenegro		344	366	808	1,033	1,453	3,062	3,234	3,601
Poland	5,350	3,064	4,944	6,876	7,869	7,911	8,409	7,939	7,955
Romania	4,238	2,208	2,085	3,211	3,377	3,169	3,497	3,251	3,223
Russia				10,687	10,696	10,637	10,616	10,228	10,146
Serbia			376	798	933	949	1,240	1,195	1,253
Slovakia	1,936	2,340	3,138	3,820	4,055	4,362	4,406	4,443	4,535
Slovenia	1,573	2,059	2,758	3,258	3,322	3,401	3,707	3,659	3,729
Ukraine			948	1,380	1,395				

Source: *Euromonitor International from World Tourism Organisation*

Travel and Tourism Statistics

Table 23.5

Expenditure by Tourists 1985-2009
US$ million

	1985	1990	1995	2000	2004	2005	2006	2007	2008	2009
Western Europe										
Austria	2,723	7,723	11,657	8,463	9,237	9,316	9,626	10,561	11,432	11,902
Belgium	2,050	5,471	9,215	9,429	13,956	14,948	15,574	17,579	19,317	20,437
Cyprus	78	111	293	413	811	932	967	1,479	1,571	1,689
Denmark	1,410	3,676	4,280	4,669	7,269	6,850	7,428	8,791	9,678	10,233
Finland	777	2,740	2,319	1,852	2,821	3,057	3,424	3,983	4,501	4,902
France	4,557	12,424	16,328	17,906	28,703	30,458	31,239	36,743	43,346	47,251
Germany			52,194	52,824	71,187	74,189	74,123	83,156	91,692	94,933
Gibraltar										
Greece	368	1,090	1,322	4,558	2,872	3,039	2,997	3,423	3,930	4,178
Iceland	94	278	282	471	697	980	1,076	1,326	1,103	1,124
Ireland	429	1,159	2,030	2,600	5,177	6,074	6,862	8,656	10,425	11,439
Italy	1,880	14,045	12,420	15,685	20,460	22,370	23,152	27,329	30,839	32,855
Liechtenstein										
Luxembourg				1,318	2,911	2,977	3,138	3,480	3,842	4,064
Malta	50	134	200	200	255	268	320	376	431	473
Monaco										
Netherlands	3,416	7,376	11,455	12,191	16,348	16,140	17,087	19,110	21,825	23,404
Norway	1,722	3,679	4,221	4,558	8,489	10,111	11,586	14,043	15,932	17,145
Portugal	235	867	2,141	2,228	2,763	3,050	3,340	3,937	4,328	4,632
Spain	1,010	4,254	4,461	5,572	12,153	15,046	16,697	19,724	20,363	21,406
Sweden	1,967	6,134	5,621	8,048	10,165	10,771	11,529	13,975	15,432	16,403
Switzerland	2,399	5,817	7,346	6,335	8,104	8,782	9,252	10,116	10,973	11,403
Turkey	324	520	912	1,713	2,524	2,872	2,743	3,260	3,506	3,647
United Kingdom	6,369	19,063	24,268	38,262	56,444	59,532	63,319	71,519	68,792	70,721
Eastern Europe										
Albania			5	272	642	786	965	1,268	1,555	1,738
Belarus			87	243	450	448	586	606	668	707
Bosnia-Herzegovina				78	117	122	170	203	211	221
Bulgaria	74	257	195	538	1,363	1,309	1,478	1,826	2,380	2,635
Croatia			421	568	848	754	737	985	1,109	1,183
Czech Republic			1,633	1,276	2,280	2,405	2,765	3,647	4,587	5,146
Estonia			91	204	399	439	586	670	808	896
Georgia				110	147	169	167	176	204	212
Hungary	208	477	1,070	1,651	2,421	2,382	2,126	2,949	4,037	4,382
Latvia			24	247	377	584	704	927	1,142	1,297
Lithuania			108	253	636	744	909	1,144	1,497	1,725
Macedonia			27	34	55	62	71	102	136	155
Moldova			56	73	113	141	190	214	274	308
Montenegro								37	43	47
Poland	184	423	5,500	3,313	4,776	5,548	7,224	7,753	9,596	10,439
Romania		103	697	425	539	925	1,310	1,535	2,178	2,499
Russia			11,599	8,848	15,285	17,314	18,112	22,133	24,890	26,694
Serbia					208	260	322	1,194	1,251	1,345
Slovakia			330	296	745	844	1,060	1,533	2,165	2,504
Slovenia			524	511	868	950	974	1,144	1,314	1,415
Ukraine				576	2,463	2,805	2,834	3,569	4,023	4,313

Source: *Euromonitor International from World Tourism Organisation*

Table 23.6

Receipts from Tourism 1985-2009

US$ million

	1985	1990	1995	2000	2004	2005	2006	2007	2008	2009
Western Europe										
Austria	5,084	13,410	14,593	9,998	15,150	16,243	16,510	18,559	21,630	23,011
Belgium	1,663	3,718	5,719	6,592	9,208	9,845	10,311	10,996	11,810	12,314
Cyprus	380	1,258	1,783	1,941	2,241	2,318	2,381	2,686	2,770	2,854
Denmark	1,326	3,322	3,672	3,671	5,652	5,293	5,587	6,218	6,686	6,918
Finland	501	1,170	1,676	1,406	2,067	2,180	2,380	2,837	3,220	3,487
France	7,942	20,185	27,527	30,981	44,895	43,942	46,512	54,209	56,274	58,843
Germany			18,028	18,611	27,613	29,121	32,888	36,101	40,019	42,813
Gibraltar	15	112								
Greece	1,428	2,587	4,136	9,219	12,715	13,334	14,402	15,550	17,416	18,216
Iceland	41	139	167	227	370	408	478	601	624	653
Ireland	531	1,447	2,688	3,387	4,375	4,782	5,369	6,074	6,342	6,631
Italy	8,758	20,016	27,723	27,493	35,378	35,319	38,257	42,660	46,232	48,147
Liechtenstein	20									
Luxembourg				1,686	3,650	3,612	3,636	4,030	4,488	4,683
Malta	149	496	660	610	767	755	767	913	959	1,002
Monaco	300									
Netherlands	1,661	3,636	5,762	7,197	10,308	10,450	11,382	13,339	13,346	13,949
Norway	755	1,570	2,386	2,050	2,980	3,332	3,613	4,222	4,633	4,904
Portugal	1,137	3,555	4,339	5,243	7,672	7,676	8,416	10,175	10,980	11,714
Spain	8,151	18,593	25,388	31,454	45,067	47,789	51,297	57,734	61,978	65,131
Sweden	1,190	2,916	3,462	4,064	6,198	7,394	9,141	12,003	12,631	13,722
Switzerland	3,145	6,789	9,365	7,576	9,595	10,041	10,808	12,183	14,464	15,447
Turkey	1,482	3,308	4,957	7,636	15,888	18,152	16,853	18,487	21,951	22,795
United Kingdom	7,120	14,003	18,554	21,769	28,202	30,573	34,796	38,698	36,424	37,724
Eastern Europe										
Albania			7	398	735	854	1,012	1,378	1,714	1,919
Belarus			23	93	270	253	286	324	363	396
Bosnia-Herzegovina			7	233	481	519	607	729	826	883
Bulgaria	343	320	473	1,074	2,202	2,412	2,612	3,130	3,804	4,135
Croatia			1,351	2,758	6,727	7,370	7,990	9,233	11,267	12,079
Czech Republic	307	470	2,875	2,973	4,187	4,676	5,541	6,637	7,719	8,444
Estonia			353	505	887	971	1,024	1,036	1,212	1,257
Georgia				97	177	241	313	384	447	493
Hungary	512	1,000	1,723	3,733	3,914	4,120	4,254	4,739	6,033	6,352
Latvia			20	131	267	341	480	671	803	894
Lithuania			124	391	776	921	1,038	1,153	1,338	1,445
Macedonia		45	19	38	72	89	129	186	228	259
Moldova			57	39	91	103	115	167	212	238
Montenegro								629	755	829
Poland	118	358	6,600	5,677	5,833	6,274	7,239	10,599	11,771	12,993
Romania	182	106	590	359	503	1,052	1,308	1,606	1,992	2,216
Russia	163	410	4,312	3,430	5,530	5,870	7,628	9,607	11,944	13,501
Serbia					189	265	342	866	941	1,091
Slovakia			620	433	905	1,210	1,521	2,026	2,589	2,943
Slovenia			1,082	961	1,624	1,795	1,797	2,283	2,857	3,179
Ukraine				736	2,560	3,125	3,485	4,597	5,768	6,397

Source: *Euromonitor International from World Tourism Organisation*

Travel and Tourism Statistics

Table 23.7

Rooms in Tourist Accommodation 1990-2009
'000

	1990	1995	2000	2004	2005	2006	2007	2008	2009
Western Europe									
Austria	317.8	309.7	286.8	290.5	289.9	282.0	285.6	286.6	288.9
Belgium		59.7	61.9	64.0	66.6	67.8	67.7	67.9	68.3
Cyprus	24.5	35.0	43.4	45.5	45.2	44.4	43.8	42.9	42.5
Denmark	35.6	38.3	39.5	43.2	42.8	43.4	44.0	44.3	44.7
Finland	46.5	54.0	54.9	53.5	54.4	54.9	54.7	54.8	55.0
France	547.0	596.7	589.2	615.4	613.8	612.4	614.5	627.8	624.2
Germany		819.0	877.1	889.3	890.2	897.0	899.1	915.6	920.6
Gibraltar									
Greece	232.8	283.4	313.0	351.9	358.7	364.2	368.0	375.1	378.7
Iceland	3.3	4.9	6.0	7.5	8.0	8.0	8.5	9.1	9.3
Ireland	22.8	36.8	60.4	62.4	64.2	63.4	67.6	72.9	74.6
Italy	938.1	944.1	966.1	1,011.8	1,020.5	1,034.7	1,058.9	1,079.5	1,092.6
Liechtenstein			0.6	0.6	0.6	0.6	0.6	0.6	0.6
Luxembourg	7.9	8.2	7.7	7.4	7.5	7.5	7.6	7.6	7.6
Malta	34.2						17.5	18.3	18.7
Monaco			2.2	2.2	2.6	2.6	2.8	2.6	2.6
Netherlands	60.7	71.3	82.0	93.0	94.4	94.5	99.0	98.2	98.9
Norway	54.0	60.0	65.2	66.4	67.5	69.5	71.0	72.4	73.3
Portugal	79.4	90.0	97.7	112.7	116.1	117.6	118.0	121.0	122.1
Spain	603.0	564.6	677.1	767.0	797.4	810.6	821.1	838.5	847.7
Sweden	82.0	100.0	96.1	98.9	100.2	101.7	103.8	106.6	108.2
Switzerland	146.9	143.5	140.8	133.6	127.4	127.5	127.7	127.9	128.0
Turkey	82.1	133.2	155.4	217.1	230.6	241.3	251.5	266.9	274.4
United Kingdom		440.0	463.0	606.9	518.0	616.8	616.0	617.9	636.4
Eastern Europe									
Albania		3.0	3.0	3.0	3.5	4.0	4.3	4.1	4.2
Belarus			2.0	12.9	12.9	13.3	13.7	13.9	14.0
Bosnia-Herzegovina		1.1	4.4	8.4	8.7	9.0	10.8	11.1	11.5
Bulgaria		57.0		80.1	90.6	95.6	103.8	108.0	111.9
Croatia		85.4	81.3	79.2	80.7	76.0	76.1	77.2	76.6
Czech Republic	63.1	53.7	96.4	98.8	99.9	101.6	106.9	111.9	114.5
Estonia		4.4	7.6	15.0	16.6	17.8	19.3	20.5	21.4
Georgia			8.7	9.7	6.8	10.0	8.3	8.6	8.9
Hungary	34.0	47.8	57.9	64.3	66.1	66.9	65.6	65.8	65.8
Latvia		5.4	6.4	8.8	9.2	9.7	10.0	11.6	12.2
Lithuania		5.3	5.9	9.5	10.1	10.8	11.0	11.1	11.4
Macedonia	6.0	6.0	6.6	6.9	6.9	7.0	7.2	5.9	5.7
Moldova		2.6	3.0	2.6	2.5	2.5	2.3	2.4	2.3
Montenegro	16.0	16.0	15.8	16.7	17.5	17.4	18.0	18.1	18.2
Poland	43.4	48.2	60.9	83.0	84.9	88.4	93.9	103.7	107.6
Romania	87.1	95.5	95.4	101.6	105.8	111.8	112.2	116.9	121.2
Russia		214.1	183.4	178.6	199.0	208.3	219.4	247.9	258.0
Serbia			22.0	22.2	22.6	24.0	25.1	25.7
Slovakia	14.5	23.4	28.4	35.5	35.7	35.9	41.6	42.5	44.0
Slovenia		16.2	16.3	15.8	15.8	16.4	17.3	17.7	18.1
Ukraine			44.8	32.6	33.4				

Source: Euromonitor International from World Tourism Organisation

Table 23.8

Bed-places in Tourist Accommodation 1990-2009

'000

	1990	1995	2000	2004	2005	2006	2007	2008	2009
Western Europe									
Austria	587.8	583.8	580.7	570.8	571.4	572.5	573.7	579.8	587.9
Belgium		154.7	158.6	169.6	168.4	172.9	172.0	170.9	171.5
Cyprus	51.8	73.1	84.5	92.2	91.3	89.5	87.8	85.7	84.6
Denmark	88.5	99.0	102.1	109.1	108.1	108.9	110.3	112.3	113.2
Finland	97.4	113.0	117.3	120.1	117.6	119.0	118.9	119.2	119.5
France	1,082.1	1,193.3	1,178.3	1,230.8	1,227.6	1,224.8	1,229.1	1,255.7	1,248.4
Germany		1,490.9	1,649.2	1,667.9	1,678.3	1,690.9	1,703.3	1,737.9	1,751.1
Gibraltar									
Greece	438.4	535.8	594.0	668.3	682.1	693.3	700.9	715.9	723.4
Iceland	6.3	8.8	12.5	15.5	16.6	16.8	17.9	19.3	19.7
Ireland	45.2	79.8	140.2	145.3	149.6	148.8	157.4	168.7	173.5
Italy	1,703.5	1,738.0	1,854.1	1,999.7	2,028.5	2,087.0	2,142.8	2,201.8	2,238.0
Liechtenstein	1.2	1.2	1.2	1.2	1.2	1.3	1.3	1.2	1.1
Luxembourg			14.7	14.2	14.2	14.4	14.6	14.4	14.5
Malta	37.9	37.3	40.6	39.8	39.4	39.4	38.1	39.2	39.1
Monaco				3.7	5.3	5.3	4.2	5.9	6.1
Netherlands	111.3	142.5	173.0	189.8	192.2	192.1	200.3	198.6	200.0
Norway	112.7	131.2	140.6	141.1	143.6	151.3	154.3	157.3	160.1
Portugal	179.3	204.1	223.0	253.9	263.8	264.0	264.7	274.0	276.2
Spain	1,102.3	1,074.0	1,315.7	1,511.6	1,578.6	1,615.3	1,642.4	1,682.6	1,705.7
Sweden	125.9	173.1	188.3	190.0	197.5	201.3	207.4	218.2	222.8
Switzerland	269.8	265.0	259.7	251.3	239.2	240.4	241.0	241.3	241.8
Turkey	165.0	274.1	332.3	452.4	481.7	507.2	530.8	563.3	581.4
United Kingdom	993.5	879.7	1,111.0	1,223.0	1,062.3	1,255.7	1,250.5	1,256.6	1,292.6
Eastern Europe									
Albania		4.7	4.8	5.7	6.7	7.2	8.6	8.0	8.3
Belarus		1.0	14.4	23.6	23.5	24.1	24.6	24.4	24.6
Bosnia-Herzegovina		1.9	9.1	17.3	18.2	20.0	22.4	23.0	23.9
Bulgaria	114.3	114.2	120.2	171.0	221.1	252.3	273.3	276.6	285.8
Croatia		205.2	199.5	199.0	203.5	163.2	163.3	166.0	159.7
Czech Republic		131.2	236.5	229.7	232.2	236.1	248.0	258.1	260.7
Estonia		8.5	18.6	32.9	38.1	40.9	44.6	46.9	48.6
Georgia			17.2	18.1	14.0	20.5	16.7	17.6	18.3
Hungary	85.3	119.1	143.6	158.0	162.2	158.8	154.1	154.5	153.2
Latvia		14.0	11.9	17.9	19.2	19.7	20.7	23.5	24.5
Lithuania		10.5	11.1	18.6	19.9	21.5	21.9	22.0	22.5
Macedonia	15.1	15.0	16.1	16.5	16.4	16.8	17.1	13.2	12.8
Moldova		5.3	5.6	4.9	4.9	4.5	4.3	4.4	4.3
Montenegro	34.3	35.1	32.2	35.0	37.4	37.1	42.8	42.7	43.8
Poland	90.4	93.3	120.3	165.3	169.6	178.1	190.4	210.5	219.6
Romania	168.0	205.7	199.3	207.8	216.5	228.1	228.1	237.9	247.4
Russia		426.1	346.1	344.4	414.1	431.0	447.1	500.0	519.0
Serbia			48.0	48.4	49.1	52.5	55.1	56.6
Slovakia	33.6	53.9	73.0	90.0	90.1	91.0	105.7	108.8	112.9
Slovenia		33.9	33.5	32.7	33.2	34.4	36.2	37.9	39.0
Ukraine			102.9	84.3	86.8				

Source: *Euromonitor International from World Tourism Organisation*

Travel and Tourism Statistics

Table 23.9

Hotel Bed Occupancy Rates 1990-2009

% of beds occupied

	1990	1995	2000	2004	2005	2006	2007	2008	2009
Western Europe									
Austria	32.1	33.6	35.2	36.9	37.5	37.6	39.2	39.7	40.3
Belgium		31.3							
Cyprus	62.3	58.6	65.1	57.6	61.6	59.9	61.8	63.5	63.9
Denmark	34.7	35.5	37.4	35.6	36.2	38.0	39.0	37.0	37.2
Finland	48.6	45.0	47.8	46.3	47.8	49.9	51.6	51.9	52.6
France	52.4	49.5	60.3	58.6	59.1	60.4	62.0	61.4	61.8
Germany		33.9	35.0	34.2	35.0	35.9	36.7	36.5	36.8
Gibraltar	40.8								
Greece		56.6	65.0	55.6	58.6	59.8	57.0	56.7	56.3
Iceland	41.0	44.8	46.0	43.3	45.0	47.0	46.7	47.4	47.8
Ireland			65.0	60.0	62.0	64.0	64.0	58.0	57.3
Italy	41.5	40.0	42.7	39.8	40.1	40.8	41.4	40.2	40.2
Liechtenstein	33.4	28.4	30.9	24.2	25.6	25.6	27.9	30.9	32.5
Luxembourg		19.4	26.2	28.2	29.5	29.9	31.6	28.5	28.3
Malta	56.4	55.5	47.0	52.8	52.8	51.8	57.4	58.4	59.5
Monaco	55.7	49.5	71.5	58.0	58.4	58.8	63.6	61.1	61.7
Netherlands	38.5	35.3	48.5	42.1	42.1	45.3	46.7	46.0	46.8
Norway	35.4	36.7	37.5	37.0	38.1	38.9	39.5	37.8	37.7
Portugal	29.9	38.0	42.2	38.6	46.6	40.8	43.0	41.3	40.3
Spain	52.3	60.7	58.9	53.5	54.2	56.4	56.0	53.5	53.3
Sweden	31.0	32.0	35.0	34.3	35.0	36.1	37.2	36.0	36.2
Switzerland	44.0	38.5	42.3	39.2	39.7	41.7	43.6	44.5	45.6
Turkey	48.2	47.0	36.8	50.1	52.4	47.3	51.1	51.5	51.3
United Kingdom	57.0	44.0	43.0	45.0	44.0	47.0	48.0	44.0	44.0
Eastern Europe									
Albania		32.4	20.0	43.0	51.0	63.0	63.0	61.0	62.7
Belarus				40.5	45.5	49.3	50.4	51.7	52.8
Bosnia-Herzegovina			15.0						
Bulgaria		36.5	28.3	35.9	37.6	35.8	33.2	32.8	31.9
Croatia	16.6	11.1	24.8	27.5	28.7	34.8	35.2	34.2	35.1
Czech Republic	46.0	28.8	46.0	37.0	35.8	35.8	35.8	35.7	35.7
Estonia		35.0	48.0	47.0	48.0	47.0	44.0	41.1	40.0
Georgia			34.0						
Hungary	55.4	45.4	46.7	41.0	42.1	42.4	45.0	43.8	44.1
Latvia			32.0	31.5	36.4	35.6	36.5	33.2	32.5
Lithuania		23.0	28.4	36.7	40.8	42.1	46.3	44.9	45.8
Macedonia	10.9	10.6	15.0	10.3	11.1	10.8	11.8	18.9	20.9
Moldova		10.5	19.8	25.2	26.6	30.9	28.3	28.6	29.0
Montenegro							6.1	19.3	28.1
Poland	39.5	42.7	39.6	32.2	40.5	42.2	46.1	45.1	46.1
Romania		52.1	35.2	34.3	33.4	33.6	36.0	35.9	36.5
Russia		38.0	37.0	37.0	34.0	35.0	36.0	35.0	35.2
Serbia				23.7	23.4	22.7	23.1	21.9	21.6
Slovakia	48.7	31.9	29.2	34.7	35.0	35.7	33.7	31.9	31.4
Slovenia		33.4	39.4	48.0	47.6	47.6	47.4	45.6	45.2
Ukraine			24.0	31.0	33.0				

Source: Euromonitor International from World Tourism Organisation

Travel and Tourism Statistics

Table 23.10

International Tourist Arrivals 1990-2009

'000

	1990	1995	2000	2004	2005	2006	2007	2008	2009
Western Europe									
Austria		17,173	17,982	19,374	19,952	20,269	20,773	21,935	21,355
Belgium		5,560	6,457	6,710	6,747	6,995	7,045	7,165	6,814
Cyprus		2,100	2,686	2,349	2,470	2,401	2,416	2,404	2,141
Denmark		3,417	3,535	4,421	4,699	4,742	4,770	4,503	4,470
Finland			2,714	2,840	3,140	3,375	3,519	3,583	3,423
France		60,033	77,190	74,433	74,988	77,916	80,853	79,218	74,200
Germany		14,847	18,983	20,137	21,500	23,569	24,421	24,884	24,224
Gibraltar									
Greece		10,130	13,095	13,313	14,765	16,039	16,165	15,939	14,915
Iceland		474	634	836	871	971	1,054	1,106	1,235
Ireland		4,821	6,646	6,953	7,333	8,001	8,332	8,026	7,189
Italy		31,052	41,181	37,071	36,513	41,058	43,654	42,734	43,239
Liechtenstein		59	62	49	50	55	58	59	52
Luxembourg	694	768	852	878	913	908	917	879	849
Malta		1,116	1,216	1,156	1,171	1,124	1,244	1,291	1,183
Monaco		233	300	250	286	313	328	324	265
Netherlands		6,574	10,003	9,646	10,012	10,739	11,008	10,104	9,921
Norway		2,880	3,104	3,628	3,824	4,070	4,377	4,347	4,346
Portugal		9,511	12,097	10,639	10,612	11,282	12,321	12,616	12,968
Spain		38,803	47,898	52,430	55,914	58,004	58,666	57,192	52,231
Sweden		1,255	1,492	4,676	4,883	4,729	5,224	4,728	4,855
Switzerland		6,946	7,821	6,397	7,229	7,863	8,448	8,608	8,294
Turkey		7,083	9,586	16,826	20,273	18,916	22,248	24,994	25,506
United Kingdom		21,675	23,221	25,678	28,039	30,654	30,870	30,142	28,199
Eastern Europe									
Albania		1,997	1,304	1,304	1,956	2,445	2,515	2,592	2,698
Belarus		161	60	67	91	89	105	91	91
Bosnia-Herzegovina		37	171	190	217	256	306	322	311
Bulgaria		3,466	2,785	4,630	4,837	5,158	5,151	5,780	5,739
Croatia		1,324	5,831	7,912	8,467	8,659	9,307	9,415	9,335
Czech Republic			4,666	6,061	6,336	6,435	6,680	6,649	6,032
Estonia		530	1,220	1,750	1,917	1,940	1,900	1,970	1,979
Georgia		85	387	368	560	983	1,052	1,290	1,412
Hungary			11,207	12,212	9,979	9,259	8,638	8,814	9,058
Latvia			509	1,079	1,116	1,535	1,653	1,684	1,779
Lithuania		662	1,083	1,800	2,000	2,180	1,486	1,611	1,546
Macedonia		147	224	165	197	202	230	255	259
Moldova			19	24	23	13	13	7	5
Montenegro		68	69	188	272	378	984	1,031	1,044
Poland		19,215	17,400	14,290	15,200	15,670	14,975	12,960	11,890
Romania		2,963	3,274	4,436	3,925	4,059	5,193	5,960	6,384
Russia		9,250	19,072	19,892	19,940	20,168	20,527	21,566	19,420
Serbia			392	453	469	696	646	645	
Slovakia		903	1,053	1,401	1,515	1,612	1,685	1,767	1,298
Slovenia		732	1,090	1,499	1,555	1,617	1,751	1,771	1,668
Ukraine			6,431	15,629	17,631	18,936	23,122	25,392	20,741

Source: *Euromonitor International from World Tourism Organisation*

Travel and Tourism Statistics   **Table 23.11**

Tourist Arrivals by Method 2009
'000

	Air	Rail	Land	Sea
Western Europe				
Austria	1,101	2,343	17,379	116
Belgium	1,397	1,844	3,358	38
Cyprus	2,282			84
Denmark	4,987	1,734	3,388	1,808
Finland	1,640	210	572	902
France	31,320	11,824	26,563	4,443
Germany	8,951	1,470	12,935	50
Gibraltar	68		4	6
Greece	10,395	80	4,474	1,067
Iceland	932			7
Ireland	5,624	127	118	910
Italy	21,255	1,970	13,277	1,379
Liechtenstein			70	
Luxembourg	305	89	407	
Malta	1,238			19
Monaco	23	35	140	95
Netherlands	3,627	916	3,926	183
Norway	1,730	103	1,450	754
Portugal	7,520	106	4,590	53
Spain	39,174	221	10,827	1,486
Sweden	7,692	872	2,099	1,286
Switzerland	4,998	1,095	7,052	
Turkey	17,924	87	6,502	2,143
United Kingdom	21,746	2,739	340	3,584
Eastern Europe				
Albania	166	65	631	209
Belarus	442	2,557	876	
Bosnia-Herzegovina	86	22	197	
Bulgaria	2,375	79	2,962	49
Croatia	1,083	31	7,684	156
Czech Republic	2,859	128	3,181	
Estonia	111	57	435	987
Georgia	276	195	309	52
Hungary	3,089	3,072	2,192	43
Latvia	247	66	1,122	26
Lithuania	116	218	1,231	26
Macedonia	72	16	156	
Moldova	4	4	6	
Montenegro	182	62	691	76
Poland	4,117	1,241	6,016	236
Romania	1,462	206	6,440	156
Russia	3,436	10,105	7,391	516
Serbia	130	41	409	
Slovakia	362	54	870	2
Slovenia	319	162	1,123	28
Ukraine	1,042	12,588	5,593	316

Source: Euromonitor International from Trade Sources/National Statistics

Travel and Tourism Statistics

Table 23.12

Tourist Arrivals by Region 2009
'000

	Africa	Americas	East Asia /Pacific	Europe	Middle East	South Asia
Western Europe						
Austria	38	648	664	19,851	107	47
Belgium	61	385	251	6,026	22	70
Cyprus	7	25	16	2,044	45	4
Denmark		144	92	4,235		
Finland	10	150	301	2,913	11	37
France	1,728	5,793	3,403	62,589	686	
Germany	159	2,561	1,935	19,319	250	
Gibraltar						
Greece	46	859	189	13,780	41	1
Iceland	2	93	32	1,027		
Ireland	50	874	231	6,034		
Italy	305	3,366	1,260	37,850	237	222
Liechtenstein	2	2	1	47		
Luxembourg		31		780		
Malta		16		988	8	
Monaco	2	29	10	217	6	
Netherlands	79	1,012	637	8,193		
Norway		124	27	3,974		
Portugal		709	39	11,190		
Spain		2,252	231	49,748		
Sweden		259	242	4,354		
Switzerland	85	823	798	6,326	131	131
Turkey	212	587	591	21,796	1,086	1,235
United Kingdom	591	3,796	1,960	20,820	524	509
Eastern Europe						
Albania		63	17	1,398	1	
Belarus		1	1	89		
Bosnia-Herzegovina		8	5	297		
Bulgaria	2	108	55	5,535	22	18
Croatia	12	229	312	8,782		
Czech Republic	22	397	472	5,141		
Estonia	1	25	19	1,392		
Georgia	1	17	10	1,367	3	14
Hungary	9	253	103	3,194		
Latvia	3	41	24	1,704	2	4
Lithuania	1	24	18	834		
Macedonia		10	5	244		
Moldova		0	0	5		
Montenegro		8	3	1,033		
Poland	15	350	218	11,279	9	19
Romania	10	132	72	6,134	22	15
Russia	34	464	1,370	17,423	37	92
Serbia		13	8	624		
Slovakia	2	29	53	1,212	1	1
Slovenia	3	56	85	1,524		
Ukraine	8	135	37	20,532	16	13

Source: Euromonitor International from World Tourism Organisation